Time Out

New York

timeoutny.com

Published by Time Out Guides Ltd, a wholly owned subsidiary of Time Out Group Ltd.
Time Out and the Time Out logo are trademarks of Time Out Group Ltd.

© Time Out Group Ltd 2005
Previous editions 1990, 1992, 1994, 1996, 1997, 1998, 1999, 2000, 2001, 2002, 2003, 2004

10 9 8 7 6 5 4 3 2 1

This edition first published in Great Britain in 2005 by Ebury Press
Ebury is a division of the Random House Group Ltd
20 Vauxhall Bridge Road, London SW1V 2SA, England

Random House Australia Pty Ltd, 20 Alfred Street, Milsons Point, Sydney, New South Wales 2061, Australia
Random House New Zealand Ltd, 18 Poland Road, Glenfield, Auckland 10, New Zealand
Random House South Africa (Pty) Ltd, Endulini, 5A Jubilee Road, Parktown 2193, South Africa

Random House UK Ltd Reg. No. 954009

Distributed in USA by Publishers Group West
1700 Fourth Street, Berkeley, California 94710, USA

Distributed in Canada by Penguin Canada Ltd
10 Alcorn Avenue, Toronto, Ontario, Canada M4V 3B2

For further distribution details, see www.timeout.com.

ISBN 1-904978-34-7

A CIP catalog record for this book is available from the British Library.

Printed and bound in Germany by Appl
Papers used by Ebury Press are natural, recyclable products made from wood grown in sustainable forests.

Unflappable horses (and officers) of the NYPD's Mounted Unit patrol 42nd Street.

Contents

Edited and designed by Time Out New York Guides
475 Tenth Avenue, 12th floor
New York, NY 10018
Tel: 646-432-3000
E-mail: guides@timeoutny.com
www.timeoutny.com

Guides Director Killian Jordan
Senior Editors Melisa Coburn, Keith Mulvihill **Art Director** Noah Cornell **Photo Editors** Sarina Finkelstein, Jennifer Sutton
Project Editors Sarah Breckenridge, Stephanie Rosenbaum **Copy Chief** Ariana Donalds
Associate Editor Heather Tierney **Editorial Coordinator** Victoria Elmacioglu
Copy Editors Liz Gall, Ann Lien, Krissy Roleke **Researchers** Jessica Elkin, Barry Hirsch, Lauren Kay, Pei-Ru Keh, Katrin MacMillan, Michael Silverberg, Jill Thomas, Meghan Valerio
Publicity and Marketing Manager, U.S. Rosella Albanese

Time Out New York
E-mail: letters@timeoutny.com

President/Editorial Director Cyndi Stivers
Publisher Alison Tocci
Financial Director Daniel P. Reilly

Creative Director Ron de la Peña

Production Director Nestor Cervantes **Technology Manager** Jeffrey Vargas
Production Manager Audrey Calle **Associate Production Manager** Jim Schuessler
Advertising Production Manager Tom Oesau **Advertising Production Coordinator** Andrea Dunn
Advertising Designers Stephen de Francesco, Jamie Dunst, Mitchell Jordan **Digital Imaging Specialist** Chris Heins

Associate Publisher/Advertising Anne Perton **Advertising Manager** Tony Monteleone
Senior Account Managers Dan Kenefick, Melissa Keller **Account Managers** Sarah Bloomenthal, Joseph L. Katz, Lauren Newman, Paula Sarapin, Angela Van Hover, Robert Whiteside **Assistant to the Publisher** John Gregory

Associate Publisher/Marketing Marisa Guillen Fariña

Time Out Guides Ltd
Universal House
251 Tottenham Court Road
London W1T 7AB
Tel: +44 (0)20 7813 3000
Fax: +44 (0)20 7813 6001
E-mail: guides@timeout.com
www.timeout.com

Editorial/Managing Director Peter Fiennes **Series Editor** Ruth Jarvis **Business Manager** Gareth Garner
Deputy Series Editor Lesley McCave **Advertising Sales Director** Mark Phillips **Marketing Director** Mandy Martinez
Guides Production Director Mark Lamond **Guides Coordinator** Holly Pick

TIME OUT GROUP Chairman Tony Elliott **Managing Director** Mike Hardwick **Group Financial Director** Richard Waterlow
Group Commercial Director Lesley Gill **Group Art Director** John Oakey **Group Circulation Director** Jim Heineman

Contributors

History Kathleen Squires **Architecture** Eric P. Nash; *Building on greatness* Sam Clover **Cinema City** Keith Mulvihill, Melissa Anderson **New York Today** Billie Cohen **Where to Stay** Heather Tierney; *The (new) Harlem Renaissance* Andrea Duncan-Mao **Tour New York** Erin Clements **Downtown** Annie Bell; *Art of appreciation* Ayren Jackson **Midtown, Uptown** Mark Sinclair; *Steeple chase* Allison Hoffman; *Central Park, season by season* Stephanie Rosenbaum **Brooklyn** Beth Greenfield; *Freak like me* Reed Tucker **Queens** Karen Tina Harrison **The Bronx, Staten Island** Kathleen Squires; *VIP, RIP* Karen Tina Harrison **Museums** Ethan LaCroix, Andrea Scott; *Thoroughly Modern Manhattan* Julia Westerbeke; *Higher ground* Howard Halle **Restaurants** adapted from *Time Out New York Eating & Drinking 2005*; *History in the round* Charlotte Kaiser; *Grape nuts* Andrea Strong **Bars** adapted from *Time Out New York Nightlife 2005*; *And so to bed...* Victoria Elmacioglu **Shops & Services** Kelly McMasters; *On the record* Michael Silverberg; *A shop in the dark* Pei-Ru Keh **Festivals & Events** Ethan LaCroix **Art Galleries** Andrea Scott; *Two wrongs make a right* Barbara Pollack **Books & Poetry** Maureen Shelly **Cabaret & Comedy** Adam Feldman (cabaret), Jane Borden (comedy) **Children** Barbara Aria; *Here's to the babies who brunch* Katie Quirk **Clubs** Bruce Tantum **Film & TV** Joshua Rothkopf **Gay & Lesbian** Beth Greenfield **Music** Mike Wolf, K. Leander Williams, Jay Ruttenberg, Erin Meister (popular); Steve Smith (classical); *The house that jazz built* K. Leander Williams **Sports & Fitness** Reed Tucker **Theater & Dance** David Cote (theater), Gia Kourlas (dance) **Trips Out of Town** Erin Clements.

Maps J.S. Graphics (john@jsgraphics.co.uk); pages 411–414 reproduced by kind permission of the Metropolitan Transportation Authority.

Photography pages 3, 5, 63, 66, 77, 107, 130, 141, 301, 313, 361 Jeremy Balderson; pages 9, 169, 171, 181, 185, 190, 193, 195, 205, 207, 213 Philip Friedman; page 12 Collection of The New-York Historical Society 1858.28; pages 14, 249 Tara Germinsky; pages 15, 16, 19, 20, 103, 123 courtesy of the Library of Congress; page 18 courtesy of the '21' Club; page 21 *The New York Times*; page 24 Timothy Hursley; pages 27, 160 Peter Aaron/Esto; page 29 courtesy of Foster + Partners; page 30 Michael Moran; page 33 (top) courtesy of Photofest; page 35 Tom Rollo/Grace Photography Studio; page 36 Fred Askew; page 57 Alex Hayden; pages 65, 110 Sarina Finkelstein; page 69 Battman NYC; page 78 courtesy of the New York City Fire Department; pages 79, 83, 85, 126, 129, 136, 138, 299, 319, 395 Stefano Giovannini; page 80 Noah Kalina; page 86 Ryan Mesina; page 87 Thom Gilbert/Lower East Side Tenement Museum; page 90 Cheryl Hark; page 91 Miguel Cruz; page 92 Peter Peirce; page 95 Michael Ginsberg; pages 97, 240 Astrid Stawiarz; page 99 Bob Johnson; page 100 Kevin Poynter; pages 102, 256 Ethan Lercher/Bryant Park Restoration Corporation; pages 104, 175, 176, 178, 186, 189, 194, 197, 226, 243 David Leventi; page 111 Sheila Denvir; pages 113, 218 (bottom), 416 Todd Boebel; page 115 R. Mickens/American Museum of Natural History; page 116 courtesy of A'Lelia Bundles/Walker Family Collection; page 118 Cecilia Espinoza; page 121 Timothy Fadek; page 125 Laurie Macmillan Leddy; page 127 Tara Digiovanni; pages 131, 247, 250 June Deuell; page 132 courtesy of the Los Angeles Dodgers; page 135 D. DeMello/Wildlife Conservation Society; page 143 C. Chesek/American Museum of Natural History; page 149 Brooks Walker; page 152 Irving Solero; page 154 Elizabeth Felicella; page 157 Robert Polidori; page 159 courtesy of En Foco Inc.; pages 165, 170, 182 (bottom), 183 Bill Durgin; page 182 (top) Alexa Vachon; pages 184, 206, 209, 212, 253, 275, 287, 288, 293, 305, 316 Michael Scott Kenney; pages 198, 204, 210, 295, 297 Robert Granoff; page 201, 320, 324 Ian Gittler; page 218 (top), 230 Shaniqwa Jarvis; page 219 (top) Lee Powers; pages 219 (bottom), 229 Jordan Provost; page 225 Robert Bollinger; page 259 Chris Lee; page 263 Robert Mckeever; page 265 Jason Nocito; page 266 Ellen Page Wilson; page 268 Russell Williams; page 272 Keith Bedford; pages 283, 309 Lois Anshus; page 296 Katherine Oliver/Mayor's Office of Film, Theatre & Broadcasting; page 306 Alejandro Bulaevsky; page 314 (left) Anders Jones; page 314 (right) Marcelo Krasilicic; page 315 (left) Ben Colon; page 315 (right) Craig Wetherby; page 323 Julie Skarratt; page 327 Jay Blakesberg; pages 328–9, 352 Marty Sohl/Metropolitan Opera; page 338 Jason Klein; page 341 Brian Michael Thomas; page 349 Karl Giant; page 351 Anja Hitzenberger Photography; page 353 Bob Strovink; page 355 Nino Ruisi. The following images were provided by the featured establishments/artists: pages 11, 61, 73, 96, 146, 150, 153, 217, 225, 232, 239, 244, 255, 260, 271, 278, 281, 284, 298, 335, 360.

Introduction

Visitors to the Big Apple often say they want to have a "*real* New York experience." More often than not, this translates roughly into "What are the tourists *not* doing?" Blame it on the New York–based TV shows like *Sex and the City* (or anything on the E! network) that put a premium on keeping up with the latest fashions, dining at the newest restaurants and drinking Cosmopolitans at just-opened bars. The pressure to be hip in this town is palpable—that's just a fact of life. It's nearly impossible to keep up, even for New Yorkers. Luckily for you, the *Time Out New York Guide* is updated annually: We keep our finger on the pulse, so we can tell you where the action is, whether you're a foodie, an arty type or a shopaholic (see **Eat, Drink, Shop** *pp165–252*).

To all of you in search of uberhip, we say, "No problem"; check the **Clubs** chapter listings (*see pp287–293*) for the hottest DJs or the most unforgettable parties. Turn to **Museums** (*see pp143–163*) for the lowdown on the thrilling reopening of the Museum of Modern Art. And then...? Do what we do: Take in the often-underrated guilty pleasures of this spectacular, multifaceted place. Even the most hardened New Yorkers swoon during sunset on the observation deck of the Empire State Building; while paddling a rowboat in Central Park; or while riding on the Staten Island Ferry and glimpsing Lady Liberty standing tall in the harbor. Check out **Sightseeing** (*see pp69–163*), where we've assembled a mother lode of diverse activities, from the historical (Harlem Heritage Tours) and the deeply moving (a trip to Ellis Island) to the stomach-turning (the Cyclone roller coaster in Coney Island).

Whatever it is you crave, it's here. But be warned: Perhaps more than any other city in America, New York suffers from a severe case of multiple personality disorder—it's at once glamorous, annoying, dirty, exciting, tough, nutty and gorgeous. Such an array of character traits can leave newcomers feeling a bit disoriented. Our advice? After you've hit some of your must-see spots, take it down a notch. Stroll the streets of the West Village and peek in the windows of the graceful brownstones that line the quaint blocks, window-shop in Nolita, or just hang out at any sidewalk café and lazily watch the action pass you by.

Here's some more advice: Don't be shy; feel free to engage with locals. Sure, everyone appears to be in a rush to go somewhere, but New Yorkers are a pretty friendly lot, and we tend to have plenty to say about most any subject. Especially these days, which is why we included **New York Today** (*see pp35–37*), so you can bone up on what's on our minds. It's true that New Yorkers felt mentally isolated from America's heartland after the 2004 presidential election but, as it turns out, there is some common ground. Perhaps Woody Allen said it best in his 1977 film *Annie Hall:* "Don't you see? The rest of the country looks upon New York like we're left-wing, communist, Jewish, homosexual pornographers. I think of us that way sometimes, and I *live* here."

ABOUT THE TIME OUT CITY GUIDES

The *Time Out New York* guide is one of an expanding series of travel books produced by the people behind London's and New York's successful listings magazines. Our guides, now numbering about 50, are written and updated by resident experts who strive to provide you with the most up-to-date information you'll need to explore the city, whether you're a first-time visitor or a local.

The staff of *Time Out New York* magazine worked on this, the 13th edition, of the *Time Out New York Guide. TONY* has been "the obsessive guide to impulsive entertainment" for all city dwellers (and visitors just passing through) for ten years. Many chapters have been written from scratch; all have been thoroughly revised and offer new feature boxes.

THE LOWDOWN ON THE LISTINGS

Above all, we've tried to make this book as useful as possible. Websites, telephone numbers, transportation info, opening times, admission prices and credit-card details are included in our listings. And we've given details on facilities, services and events, all checked and correct at press time. However, owners and managers can change their policies with little notice. Before you go out of your way, we strongly advise you to call and check opening times, dates of exhibitions

> ▶ There is an online version of this book, along with guides to many more international cities, at **www.timeout.com**.

THE LAY OF THE LAND
We've included cross streets with every address, so you can easily find your way around. Fully indexed **color street maps**, as well as subway and bus maps, are at the back of the guide, starting on page 396.

TELEPHONE NUMBERS
All telephone numbers printed in this guide are written as dialed within the United States. Note that **you must always dial 1 and an area code**, even if the number you're calling is in the same area code as the one you're calling from. Manhattan area codes are 212 and 646; those in Brooklyn, Queens, the Bronx and Staten Island are 718 and 347; generally (but not always), 917 is reserved for cell phones and pagers.

Numbers preceded by 800, 877 and 888 can be called free of charge from within the U.S., and some of them can be dialed (though not necessarily for free) from the U.K.

To dial numbers given in this book from abroad, use your country's exit code (00 in the U.K.), followed by 1, the area code and the phone number.

When numbers are listed as letters for easy recall (e.g., 1-800-AIR-RIDE), dial the corresponding numbers on the telephone keypad. For more details on telephone usage, *see pp379–380*.

ESSENTIAL INFORMATION
For any practical information you might need for visiting the city—including visa and customs information, disabled access, emergency telephone numbers, a list of useful websites and the ins and outs of the local transportation network—see the **Directory** *(pp361–384)* at the back of this guide.

LET US KNOW WHAT YOU THINK
We hope you enjoy the *Time Out New York Guide,* and we'd like to know what you think of it. We welcome tips for places that you believe we should include in future editions and appreciate your feedback on our choices. Please e-mail us at guides@timeoutny.com.

and other particulars. While every effort has been made to ensure the accuracy of the information in this guide, the publishers cannot accept responsibility for any errors it may contain.

PRICES AND PAYMENT
We have noted whether venues accept credit cards and have listed the major ones— American Express (AmEx), Diners Club (DC), Discover (Disc), MasterCard (MC) and Visa (V). Many shops, restaurants and attractions will accept traveler's checks issued by a major financial institution (such as American Express).

The prices we've supplied should be treated as guidelines, not gospel. Fluctuating exchange rates and inflation can cause prices to change rapidly, especially in shops and restaurants. If costs vary wildly from those we've quoted, then ask whether there's a good reason—and please e-mail us to let us know. We aim to give the best and most up-to-date advice, so we always want to know if you've been badly treated or overcharged.

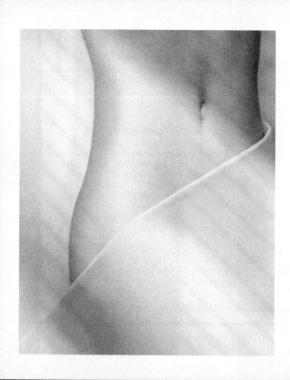

SOHO**GRAND**HOTEL

WWW.SOHOGRAND.COM
RESERVATIONS 800 965 3000
NEW YORK

TRIBECA
GRAND HOTEL

WWW.TRIBECAGRAND.COM
RESERVATIONS 877 519 6600
NEW YORK

In Context

Cranky Peg-leg Pete, a.k.a. **Peter Stuyvesant**, was NYC's first law-and-order mayor.

History

This is an incredible city—hey, I'm talking to *you*!

Q: How many polite, considerate New Yorkers does it take to screw in a lightbulb?
A: Both of them.

The greatest city in the world wasn't built with courtesy, all right? Call it attitude or chutzpah; cojones or street smarts: A pioneering amalgamation of inconsiderate characters has made this city what it is. A brief look back at New York's history shows just how its residents earned such a reputation, and explains why having what many would consider a rude 'tude has gotten them everywhere.

TRIBES AND TOURISTS
Members of the indigenous Lenape tribe were the original native New Yorkers. They lived among the meadows, forests and farms of the land they called Lenapehoking pretty much undisturbed by outsiders for thousands of years, until 1524, when their idyll was interrupted by tourists from

the Old World. The first European sightseer to cast his eyes upon this land was Giovanni da Verrazano, an Italian explorer commissioned by the French to find a shortcut to the Orient. Instead, he found Staten Island. Recognizing that he was on the wrong track, Verrazano pulled up anchor nearly as quickly as he had dropped it, never setting foot on land. Eighty-five years later, Englishman Henry Hudson was more favorably disposed. Commissioned by the Dutch, with the same goal of finding a shortcut to the Far East, Hudson sailed into Manhattan's natural deepwater harbor in September 1609, and was entranced by what lay before him. He lingered long enough to explore the entire length of the river that now bears his name, but it wasn't his fate to grow old in the place he admired and described in his logs as a "rich and pleasant land": On a return trip in 1611, Hudson's crew mutinied and cast him adrift. Still, his tales of the lush, river-crossed countryside had captured the Dutch imagination, and in 1624, the Dutch West India Company sent 110 settlers to establish a trading post here. They planted themselves at the southern tip of the island called Mannahata and christened the colony New Amsterdam. In bloody battles against the local Lenape, they did their best to drive the natives away from the little company town. But the Lenape were immovable.

In 1626, a man named Peter Minuit, New Amsterdam's first governor, thought he had solved the Lenape problem by pulling off the city's very first real-estate rip-off. The tribe had no concept of private land ownership, so Minuit made them an offer they couldn't refuse: He "bought" the island of Manhattan—all 14,000 acres of it—from the Lenape for 60 guilders' worth of goods. Legend famously values the purchase price at $24, but modern historians set the amount closer to $500. (These days, that wouldn't cover a month's rent for a closet-size studio apartment.) It was a slick trick, and a precedent for countless ungracious business transactions that would occur over the centuries.

The Dutch quickly made the port of New Amsterdam a center for fur trading. The population didn't grow as fast as the business, however, and the Dutch West India Company had a hard time finding recruits to move to an unknown island an ocean away. The company instead gathered servants, orphans and slaves, and other, more unsavory outcasts such as thieves, drunkards and prostitutes. The population grew to 400 within ten years, but given that one in every four structures was a tavern, drunkenness, crime and squalor prevailed. If the colony was to thrive, it needed a strong leader. Enter Dutch West India Company director Peter Stuyvesant.

THE FIRST TOUGH-GUY MAYOR

A one-legged, puritanical bully with a quick temper, Stuyvesant was less than popular: Rudeness was a way of life for Peg-leg Pete, as he was known. But he was the colony's first effective governor. He made peace with the Lenape, formed the first policing force (consisting of nine men), and cracked down on debauchery by shutting taverns and outlawing drinking on Sunday. He established the first school, post office, hospital, prison and poorhouse. Within a decade, the population quadrupled, and the settlement became an important trading port.

Lined with canals and windmills, and dotted with gabled farmhouses, New Amsterdam began to resemble its namesake city. Newcomers arrived to work in the fur and slave trades, or to farm. Soon, a dozen and a half languages could be heard in the streets—a fact that made the bigoted Stuyvesant nervous. In 1654, he attempted to quash immigration by turning away Sephardic Jews who were fleeing the Spanish Inquisition. But surprisingly for the time, the corporate honchos at the Dutch West India Company reprimanded him for his intolerance and overturned his decision, leading to the establishment of the earliest Jewish community in the New World. That was the first time the inflexible Stuyvesant was made to bend. The second time would put an end to the 40-year Dutch rule for good.

REVOLUTIONARY CITY

In late August 1664, English warships sailed into the harbor, set on taking over the now prosperous colony. To avoid bloodshed and destruction, Stuyvesant quickly surrendered. Soon after, New Amsterdam was renamed New York (after the Duke of York, brother of King Charles II), and Stuyvesant quietly retired to his farm. Unlike Stuyvesant, the English battled with the Lenape; by 1695, those members of the tribe who weren't killed off were sent packing upstate, and New York's European population shot up to 3,000. Over the next 35 years, Dutch-style farmhouses and windmills gave way to stately townhouses and monuments to English royals. By 1740, the slave trade had made New York the third-busiest port in the British Empire. The city, now home to more than 11,000 residents, was prosperous for a quarter-century more. But resentment was building in the colony, fueled by the ever-heavier burden of British taxation.

> **In 1825, the Erie Canal shortened the New York City–to–Buffalo journey from three weeks to one, and cut the shipping cost per ton from about $100 to $4.**

One angry young man was Alexander Hamilton, the illegitimate son of a Scottish nobleman; he arrived in New York from the West Indies in 1772. A fierce intellectual, Hamilton enrolled in King's College (now Columbia University) and became politically active, writing anti-British pamphlets, organizing an artillery company and serving as a lieutenant colonel in General George Washington's army. In these and other ways, he played a key role in a movement that would change the city—and the country—forever.

Fearing the brewing revolution, New York's citizenry fled in droves in 1775, causing the population to plummet from 25,000 to just 5,000. The following year, 100 British warships sailed into this virtual ghost town, carrying an intimidating army of 32,000—nearly four times the size of Washington's militia. Despite the British presence, Washington organized a reading of the Declaration of Independence, and patriots tore the statue of King George III from its pedestal in Bowling Green. Revolution was inevitable.

The battle for New York officially began on August 26, 1776, and Washington's army sustained heavy losses. Nearly a quarter of his men were slaughtered in a two-day period. As Washington retreated, a fire—thought to have been lit by patriots—destroyed 493 buildings, including Trinity Church, the tallest structure on the island. The British found a scorched city, and a populace living in tents.

The city continued to suffer for seven long years. Eventually, of course, Washington's luck turned. As the British left, he and his troops marched triumphantly down Broadway to reclaim the city as part of the newly established United States of America. A week and a half later, on December 4, 1783, the general bade farewell to his dispersing troops at Fraunces Tavern, which still stands on Pearl Street.

Alexander Hamilton, for his part, got busy in the rebuilding effort, laying the groundwork for New York institutions that remain vital to this day. He started by establishing the city's first bank, the Bank of New York, in 1784. When Washington was inaugurated as the nation's first president in 1789, at Federal Hall on Wall Street, he brought Hamilton on board as the first secretary of the treasury. Thanks to Hamilton's business savvy, trade in stocks and bonds flourished, leading to the establishment in 1792 of what would eventually be known

as the New York Stock Exchange. In 1801, Hamilton founded the *Evening Post* newspaper, still in circulation today as the *New York Post*. By 1804, he had helped make New York a world-leading financial center. The same year that his dream was realized, however, Hamilton was killed by political rival Aaron Burr in a duel in Weehawken, New Jersey.

BOOMTOWN

New York continued to grow and prosper for the next three decades. Maritime commerce soared, and Robert Fulton's innovative steamboat made its maiden voyage on the Hudson River in 1807. Eleven years later, a group of merchants introduced regularly scheduled shipping (a novel concept at the time) between New York and Liverpool on the Black Ball Line. Reflecting the city's status as America's shipping center, the urban landscape was ringed with sprawling piers, towering masts and billowing sails. A boom in the maritime trades lured hundreds of European laborers, and the city—still entirely crammed below Houston Street—grew more and more congested. Where Dutch farms and English estates once stood, taller, more efficient structures took hold, and Manhattan real estate became the most expensive in the world.

The first man to conquer the city's congestion problem was Mayor DeWitt Clinton, a brilliant politician and a protégé of Alexander Hamilton. Clinton's dream was to organize the entire island of Manhattan in such a way that it could cope with the eventual population creep northward. In 1807, he created a commission to map out the foreseeable sprawl. The commission presented its work four years later, and the destiny of this new city was made manifest: It would be a regular grid of

On the spot

Veni, vidi, Vento Before ultratrendy eatery Vento (*see p93*) moved into **28 Ninth Avenue**, the triangular-shaped building had a long, varied history, with two relative constants: nurse's uniforms and pain. During the Civil War, the building served as a hospital, where the Union Army's wounded were separated from their gangrenous limbs. Excruciation became more fun in the 1980s, when the legendary gay S&M club the Manhole moved in. Today, the only agony to be found is the sprained ankles suffered by trenditas negotiating the cobblestones in their Jimmy Choos.

crossing thoroughfares, 12 avenues wide and 155 streets long.

Then Clinton literally overstepped his boundaries to fulfill that destiny. In 1811, he presented a plan to build a 363-mile canal linking the Hudson River with Lake Erie. Many thought it impossible: At the time, the longest canal in the world ran a mere 27 miles. But he pressed on, and, with a silver tongue to rival a certain modern-day Clinton, raised a staggering $6 million for the project.

Work on the Erie Canal, begun in 1817, was completed in 1825—three years ahead of schedule. It shortened the journey between New York City and Buffalo from three weeks to one, and cut the shipping cost per ton from about $100 to $4. Goods, people and money poured into New York, fostering a merchant elite that moved northward to escape the urban crush. Estates multiplied above Houston Street even as 3,000 new buildings were erected below it—each grander and more imposing than its modest Colonial forerunners. Once slavery was officially abolished in New York in 1827, free blacks became an essential part of the workforce. In 1831, the first public transportation system began operation, pulling passengers in horse-drawn omnibuses to the city's far reaches.

BUMMERTOWN

As the population grew (swelling to 170,000 by 1830), so did New York City's problems. Tensions bubbled between immigrant newcomers and those who could trace their American lineage back a generation or two. Crime rose and lurid tales filled the "penny press," the city's proto-tabloids. While wealthy New Yorkers were moving as far "uptown" as Greenwich Village, the infamous Five Points neighborhood—the city's first slum—festered in the area now occupied by City Hall, the courthouses and Chinatown. Built on a fetid drained pond, Five Points became the ramshackle home of poor immigrants and blacks. Brutal gangs with colorful names like the Forty Thieves, Plug Uglies and Dead Rabbits often met in bloody clashes in the streets, but what finally sent a mass of 100,000 people scurrying from downtown was an outbreak of cholera in 1832. In just six weeks, 3,513 New Yorkers died.

In 1837, a financial panic left hundreds of Wall Street businesses crumbling. Commerce stagnated at the docks, the expanding real-estate market collapsed, and all but three city banks closed down. Fifty thousand New Yorkers lost their jobs, while 200,000 teetered on the edge of poverty. The panic also sparked an era of civil unrest and violence. In 1849, a xenophobic mob of 8,000, protesting the performance of an English actor at the Astor Place Opera House, was met by

Alexander Hamilton.

a militia that opened fire, killing 22 people. But the Draft Riots of 1863, which have been called "the bloodiest riots in American history," were much worse. After a law was passed exempting men from the draft for a $300 fee, the (mostly Irish) poor rose up, forming a mob 15,000 strong that rampaged through the city. They trashed police stations, draft boards, newspaper offices, expensive shops and wealthy homes before the chaos took a racial turn. Fueled by anger about the Civil War (for which they blamed blacks), and fearful that freed slaves would take away jobs, the rioters set fire to the Colored Orphan Asylum and vandalized black homes. Blacks were beaten in the streets, and some were lynched. A federal force of 6,000 men was sent to subdue the violence. After four days and at least 105 deaths, peace was finally restored.

PROGRESSIVE CITY

Amid the chaos of the mid-19th century, the pace of progress continued unabated. Compared with the major Southern cities, New York emerged nearly unscathed from the Civil War. The population ballooned to 2 million, and new technologies revolutionized daily life. The elevated railway, for example, helped extend the population into what is now the Upper East and Upper West Sides, while other trains connected the city with upstate New York, New England and the Midwest. By 1871, train traffic had grown so much that rail tycoon Cornelius Vanderbilt built the original Grand Central Depot, which could accommodate a then-considerable 15,000 passengers at a time. (It was replaced in 1913 by the current Grand Central Terminal.)

One ambitious project was inspired by the harsh winter of 1867. The East River froze over, halting water traffic between Brooklyn and Manhattan for weeks. Brooklyn, by then, had become the nation's third most populous city, and its politicians, businessmen and community leaders quickly realized that the boroughs had to be linked. Thus, the New York Bridge Company was incorporated. Its goal was to build the world's longest bridge, spanning the East River between downtown Manhattan and southwestern Brooklyn. Over 16 years (four times longer than projected), 14,000 miles of steel cable were stretched across the 1,595-foot span, while the towers rose a staggering 276 feet above the river. Disasters, worker deaths and corruption dogged the project, but the Brooklyn Bridge opened with triumphant fanfare on May 24, 1883. It remains one of the city's most beloved symbols.

CORRUPT CITY

As New York recovered from the turmoil of the mid-1800s, one extremely indecorous man—William M. "Boss" Tweed—was pulling the strings. Using his ample charm, the six-foot-tall, 300-pound bookkeeper, chair maker and volunteer firefighter became one of the city's most powerful politicians. He had been an alderman and district leader; he served in the U.S. House of Representatives, and as a state senator; and he was a chairman of the Democratic General Committee and leader of Tammany Hall, a political organization formed by craftsmen to keep the wealthy class's political clout in check. But even though Tweed opened orphanages, poorhouses and hospitals, his good deeds were overshadowed by his and his cohorts' gross embezzlement of city funds.

By 1870, members of the "Tweed Ring" had established a new city charter, granting themselves control of the city treasury. Using fake leases and wildly inflated bills for city supplies and services, Tweed and his cronies may ultimately have pocketed as much as $200 million, and caused the city's debt to triple. The work of cartoonist Thomas Nast, who lampooned Tweed in the pages of *Harper's Weekly,* helped to bring the Boss's transgressions to light. Tweed was eventually sued by the city for $6 million, and charged with forgery

Today's chic shops belie **Elizabeth Street**'s squalid past as a tenement row.

and larceny. In 1875, while being held in debtor's prison pending bail, he escaped. He was caught in Spain a year later and died in the slammer in 1878. But before his fall from power, Tweed's insatiable greed hurt many: As he was emptying the city's coffers, poverty spread. Then the bond market collapsed, the stock market took a nosedive, factories closed, and railroads went bankrupt. By 1874, New York estimated its homeless population at 90,000 souls. That winter, *Harper's Weekly* reported, 900 New Yorkers starved to death.

THE TWO HALVES

In September 1882, a new era dawned brightly when Thomas Alva Edison lit up half a square mile of lower Manhattan with 3,000 electric lamps. One of the newly illuminated offices belonged to a man known for brushing people aside when he strode down the sidewalks: financier J.P. Morgan, who was essential in bringing New York's—and America's— economy back to life. By bailing out a number of failing railroads, then merging and restructuring them, Morgan jump-started commerce in New York once again. Goods, jobs and businesses returned to the city, and soon, aggressive businessmen with names like Rockefeller, Carnegie and Frick wanted a piece of the action (none of them, by the way, were noted for *their* courtesy, either). They made New York the headquarters of Standard Oil and U.S. Steel, corporations that would go on to shape America's economic future and New York's reputation as the country's center of capitalism.

A shining symbol for less fortunate immigrants also made New York its home at that time: To commemorate America's freedom one hundred years after the Declaration of Independence, and to celebrate an international friendship, the French gave the Statue of Liberty to the United States. Sculptor Frédéric-Auguste Bartholdi had created the 151-foot-tall amazon using funds donated by French citizens, but their generosity could not cover the expense of building her base. Although the project was initially met with apathy by the U.S. government, Hungarian immigrant and publisher Joseph Pulitzer used his *World* newspaper to encourage Americans to pay for a pedestal. When she was finally unveiled in 1886, Lady Liberty measured 305 feet high—taller even than the towers of the Brooklyn Bridge.

Between 1892 and 1954, the statue welcomed more than 12 million immigrants into the harbor. Ellis Island, an immigration-processing center, opened in 1892, expecting to accommodate 500,000 people annually; it processed twice that number in its first year. In the 34-building complex, crowds of would-be Americans were herded through examinations, inspections and interrogations. Fewer than two percent were sent home, and others moved on, but 4 million stayed, turning New York into what British playwright Israel Zangwill called "the great melting pot where all the races of Europe are melting and reforming."

With little land left to develop in lower Manhattan, the city began a vertical race, building 66 skyscrapers by 1902.

Many of these new immigrants crowded into dark, squalid tenements on the Lower East Side, while millionaires like the Vanderbilts were building huge French-style mansions along Fifth Avenue. Jacob A. Riis, a Danish immigrant and police reporter for the *New York Tribune,* made it his business to expose this dichotomy, however impolite it may have seemed to the wealthy. Employing the relatively new technology of photography to accompany his written observations, Riis's 1890 book, *How the Other Half Lives* revealed, in graphic terms, the bitter conditions of the slums. The intrepid reporter scoured filthy alleys and overcrowded, unheated tenements, many of which lacked the barest minimum of light, ventilation and sanitation. Largely as a result of Riis's work, the state passed the Tenement House Act of 1901, which called for drastic housing reforms.

EXPANDING CITY

By the close of the 19th century, 40 fragmented governments had formed in and around Manhattan, creating political confusion on many levels. On January 1, 1898, the boroughs of Manhattan, Brooklyn, Queens, Staten Island and the Bronx consolidated to form New York City, America's largest city. More and more companies moved their headquarters to this new metropolis, increasing the demand for office space. With little land left to develop in lower Manhattan, New York embraced the steel revolution and grew skyward. Thus began an all-out race to build the tallest building in the world. By 1902, New York boasted 66 skyscrapers, including the 20-story Fuller Building (now known as the Flatiron Building) at Fifth Avenue and 23rd Street, and the 25-story *New York Times* tower in Longacre (now Times) Square. Within four years, they would be dwarfed by the 47-story Singer building on lower Broadway, which enjoyed the status of tallest building in the world for only 18 months. The 700-foot Metropolitan Life Tower on

Madison Square claimed the title in 1909, but the 792-foot Woolworth Building on Broadway and Park Place topped it in 1913—and held the distinction for nearly two decades.

If that wasn't enough to demonstrate New Yorkers' unending ambition, the city burrowed below the streets at the same time, starting work on the first underground transit system in 1900. The $35 million project took nearly four and a half years to complete. Less than a decade after opening, it was the most heavily traveled subway system in the world, carrying almost a billion passengers a year.

CITY OF MOVEMENT

By 1909, 30,000 factories were operating in the city, churning out everything from heavy machinery to artificial flowers. Brutal conditions worsened the situation for workers, who toiled long hours for meager pay. Young immigrant seamstresses worked 60-plus hours in the garment industry for just $5 a week. Mistrusted and abused, factory workers faced impossible quotas, had their pay docked for minor mistakes, and were often locked in the factories during working hours. In the end, it would take a tragedy for real changes to be made.

On March 25, 1911, a fire broke out at the Triangle Shirtwaist Company. Though it was a Saturday, some 500 workers—most of them teenage girls—were toiling in the Greenwich Village factory. Flames spread rapidly through the fabric-filled building. But as the girls rushed to escape, they found many of the exits locked. Roughly 350 made it out onto the adjoining rooftops before the inferno closed off all exits, but 146 young women perished. Many jumped to their deaths from windows on the eighth, ninth and tenth floors. Even in the face of such tragedy, justice was not served: The two factory

owners, tried for manslaughter, were acquitted. But the disaster did spur labor and union organizations, which pushed for—and won—sweeping reforms for factory workers.

Another sort of rights movement was taking hold during this time as well. Between 1910 and 1913, New York City was the site of the largest women's-suffrage rallies in the country. Harriet Stanton Blatch (daughter of famed suffragette Elizabeth Cady Stanton and founder of the Equality League of Self Supporting Women) and Carrie Chapman Catt (organizer of the New York City Women's Suffrage party) arranged attention-getting demonstrations intended to pressure the state into authorizing a referendum on a woman's right to vote. The measure's defeat in 1915 only steeled the suffragettes' resolve. Finally, with the support of Tammany Hall, the law passed in 1919, challenging the male stranglehold on voting throughout the country. (With New York leading the nation, the 19th Amendment was ratified in 1920.)

In 1919, as New York welcomed troops home from World War I with a parade along Fifth Avenue, the city also celebrated its emergence on the global stage. It had supplanted London as the investment capital of the world, and it was the center of publishing, thanks to two men: Pulitzer and Hearst. *The New York Times* had become the country's most respected newspaper; Broadway was the focal point of American theater; and Greenwich Village, once the home of an elite gentry, had become a world-class bohemia, where flamboyant artists, writers and political revolutionaries gathered in galleries and coffeehouses. John Reed, reporter on the Russian revolution and author of *Ten Days That Shook the World*, lived here, as did Edna

On the spot

'21' fun salute During the 13 years of national buzz-kill known as Prohibition, New York City was the tap through which the nation's bootlegged liquor flowed, and mob bosses like Al Capone were the barkeeps. Locals, too, had to have their hooch, so speakeasies flourished, and people imbibed more than ever. The most famous place to wet your whistle, Jack and Charlie's 21, took its name from its address, **21 West 52nd Street**; it lives on today as the somewhat more respectable '21' Club.

St. Vincent Millay, famous for her poetry and her public, unfettered love life.

The more personal side of the women's movement also found a home in New York City. A nurse and midwife who grew up in a family of 11 children, Margaret Sanger was a fierce advocate of birth control and family planning. She opened the first birth-control clinic in Brooklyn on October 16, 1916. Finding this unseemly, the police closed the clinic and imprisoned Sanger for 30 days. She pressed on and, in 1921, formed the American Birth Control League—the forerunner of Planned Parenthood—which researched birth control and provided gynecological services.

Forward-thinking women like Sanger set the tone for the Jazz Age, a time when women, now a voting political force, were moving beyond the moral conventions of the 19th century. The country ushered in the Jazz Age in 1919 by ratifying the 18th Amendment, which outlawed the distribution and sale of alcoholic beverages. Prohibition turned the city into the epicenter of bootlegging, speakeasies and organized crime. By the early 1920s, New York boasted 32,000 illegal watering holes—twice the number of legal bars before Prohibition.

In 1925, New Yorkers elected the magnetic James J. Walker as mayor. A charming ex-songwriter (as well as a speakeasy patron and skirt-chaser who would later leave his wife for a dancer), Walker matched his city's flashy style, hunger for publicity and consequences-be-damned attitude. Fame flowed in the city's veins: Home-run hero Babe Ruth drew a million fans each season to the New York Yankees' games, and sharp-tongued Walter Winchell filled his newspaper columns with celebrity tidbits and scandals. Alexander Woollcott, Dorothy Parker, Robert Benchley and other writers met daily to trade witticisms around a table at the Algonquin Hotel; the result, in 1925, was *The New Yorker*.

The Harlem Renaissance blossomed at the same time. Writers such as Langston Hughes, Zora Neale Hurston and James Weldon Johnson transformed the African-American experience into lyrical literary works, and white society flocked to the Cotton Club to see genre-defining musicians like Bessie Smith, Cab Calloway, Louis Armstrong and Duke Ellington. (Blacks were not welcome unless they were performing.) Downtown, Broadway houses were packed, thanks to brilliant composers and lyricists like George and Ira Gershwin, Irving Berlin, Cole Porter, Lorenz Hart, Richard Rodgers and Oscar Hammerstein II. Toward the end of the '20s, New York–born Al Jolson wowed audiences in *The Jazz Singer*, the first talking picture.

Duke Ellington dazzles **Harlem**, in 1943.

THE FALL AND RISE

The dizzying excitement ended on Tuesday, October 29, 1929, when the stock market crashed and widespread hard times began. Corruption eroded Mayor Walker's hold on the city: Despite a tenure that saw the opening of the Holland Tunnel, the completion of the George Washington Bridge and the construction of the Chrysler and Empire State Buildings, Walker's luster faded in the growing shadow of graft accusations. He resigned in 1932 as New York, in the depths of the Great Depression, had a staggering 1 million inhabitants out of work.

In 1934, an unstoppable force named Fiorello La Guardia took office as mayor, rolling up his sleeves to crack down on mobsters, gambling, smut and government corruption. La Guardia was the son of an Italian father and a Jewish mother. He was a tough-talking politician known for nearly coming to blows with other city officials, and he described himself as "inconsiderate, arbitrary, authoritative, difficult, complicated, intolerant and somewhat theatrical."

Ironworkers high on the **Empire State Building**'s girders.

La Guardia's act played well: He ushered New York into an era of unparalleled prosperity over the course of his three terms. During World War II, the city's ports and factories proved essential to the war effort. New Yorkers' sense of unity was never more visible than on August 14, 1945, when 2 million people spontaneously gathered in Times Square to celebrate the end of the war.

The "Little Flower" streamlined city government, paid down the debt and updated the transportation, hospital, reservoir and sewer systems. Additional highways made the city more accessible, and North Beach (now La Guardia) Airport became the city's first commercial landing field.

Helping La Guardia to modernize the city was urban planner Robert Moses, a hard-nosed visionary who would do much to shape—and in some cases, destroy—New York's landscape. Moses spent 44 years stepping on toes to build expressways, parks, beaches, public housing, bridges and tunnels, creating such landmarks as Shea Stadium, Lincoln Center, the United Nations complex and the Verrazano-Narrows Bridge.

THE MODERN CITY

Despite La Guardia's belt-tightening and Moses' renovations, New York began to fall apart financially. When WWII ended, 800,000 industrial jobs disappeared from the city. Factories in need of space moved to the suburbs, along with nearly 5 million residents. But more crowding occurred as rural African-Americans and Puerto Ricans flocked to the metropolis in the '50s and '60s, only to meet with ruthless discrimination and a dearth of jobs. Robert Moses' Slum Clearance Committee reduced many neighborhoods to rubble, forcing out residents in order to build huge, isolating housing projects that became magnets for crime. In 1963, the city also lost Pennsylvania Station—McKim, Mead & White's architectural masterpiece. Over the protests of picketers, the Pennsylvania Railroad Company demolished the site to make way for a modern station and Madison Square Garden. It was a giant wake-up call to New Yorkers: Architectural changes in the city were hurtling out of control.

But Moses and his wrecking ball couldn't knock over one steadfast West Village woman. An architectural writer and urban-planning critic named Jane Jacobs organized local residents when the city unveiled its plan to clear a 14-block tract of her neighborhood for more public housing. Her obstinacy was applauded by many, including an influential councilman named Ed Koch (who would become mayor in 1978). The group fought the plan and won, causing Mayor Robert F. Wagner to back down. As a result of Jacobs's efforts in the wake of Pennsylvania Station's demolition, the Landmarks Preservation Commission—the first such group in the U.S.—was established in 1965.

At the dawning of the age of Aquarius, the city harbored its share of innovative creators. Allen Ginsberg, Jack Kerouac and their fellow Beats gathered in Village coffeehouses to create a new voice for poetry. A folk-music scene brewed in tiny clubs around Bleecker Street, showcasing musicians such as Bob Dylan. A former advertising illustrator from Pittsburgh named Andy Warhol began turning the images of mass consumerism into deadpan, ironic art statements. Gay men and women, long a hidden part of the city's history, came out into the streets in 1969's Stonewall riots, sparked when patrons at the Stonewall Inn on Christopher Street resisted a police raid—and, in the process, gave birth to the modern gay-rights movement.

By the early 1970s, deficits had forced heavy cutbacks in city services. The streets were dirty, subway cars and buildings were scrawled with graffiti, crime skyrocketed, and the city's debt deepened to $6 billion. Despite the downturn, construction commenced on the World Trade Center; when completed, in 1973, its twin 110-story towers were the world's tallest buildings. Even as the Trade Center rose, the city became so desperately overdrawn that Mayor Abraham Beame appealed to the federal government for financial assistance in 1975. Yet President Gerald Ford refused to bail out the city, and New Yorkers faced his decision, summed up by the immortal *Daily News* headline, FORD TO CITY: DROP DEAD.

The President's callousness certainly didn't help matters. During the mid-'70s, Times Square degenerated into a sleazy morass of sex shops and porn palaces, drug use escalated, and subway ridership hit an all-time low. In 1977, serial killer Son of Sam terrorized the city. A blackout one hot August night that same year led to widespread looting and arson. The angst of the time fueled the angry punk culture that rose up around downtown clubs like CBGB, where the Ramones and other bands played fast and loud. At the same time, celebrities, designers and models converged on midtown to disco their nights away at Studio 54.

The Wall Street boom of the '80s and some adept fiscal petitioning by then-mayor Ed Koch brought money flooding back into New York. Gentrification glamorized neighborhoods like Soho, Tribeca and the East Village. But deeper ills persisted. In 1988, a demonstration against the city's efforts to impose a curfew and displace the homeless in Tompkins Square Park erupted into a violent clash with police. Crack use was epidemic in the ghettos, homelessness was rising, and AIDS became a new scourge. By 1989,

Local legends

citizens were restless for change. They turned to David N. Dinkins, electing him the city's first African-American mayor. A distinguished, soft-spoken man, Dinkins held office for only a single term—one marked by a record murder rate, flaring racial tensions in Washington Heights, Crown Heights and Flatbush, and the explosion of a terrorist bomb in the World Trade Center that killed 6, injured 1,000 and foreshadowed the catastrophic attacks of 2001.

Deeming the polite Dinkins ineffective, New Yorkers voted in former federal prosecutor Rudolph Giuliani. Like his predecessors Peter Stuyvesant and Fiorello La Guardia, Giuliani was an abrasive leader who used bully tactics to get things done. His "quality of life campaign" cracked down on everything from drug dealing and pornography to unsolicited windshield-washing. Even as multiple cases of severe police brutality grabbed the headlines,

crime plummeted, tourism soared, and New York became cleaner and safer than it had been in decades. Times Square was transformed into a family-friendly tourist destination, and the dot-com explosion brought a generation of young wanna-be millionaires to the Flatiron District's Silicon Alley. Giuliani's second term as mayor would close, however, on a devastating tragedy.

On September 11, 2001, terrorists flew two hijacked passenger jets into the Twin Towers of the World Trade Center, collapsing the entire complex and killing nearly 2,800 people. But the attack triggered a citywide sense of unity, and New Yorkers did what they could to help one another, from feeding emergency crews around the clock to cheering on workers en route to Ground Zero.

Two months later, billionaire Michael Bloomberg was elected mayor and took on

Key events in NYC history

1524 Giovanni da Verrazano sails into New York Harbor.
1624 First Dutch settlers establish New Amsterdam at the foot of Manhattan Island.
1626 Peter Minuit purchases Manhattan for goods worth 60 guilders.
1639 The Broncks settle north of Manhattan.
1646 Village of Breuckelen founded.
1647 Peter Stuyvesant becomes director general.
1664 Dutch rule ends; New Amsterdam renamed New York.
1754 King's College (now Columbia University) founded.
1776 Battle for New York begins; fire ravages the city.
1783 George Washington's troops march triumphantly down Broadway.
1784 Alexander Hamilton founds the Bank of New York.
1785 New York becomes the nation's capital.
1789 President Washington inaugurated at Federal Hall on Wall Street.
1792 New York Stock Exchange founded.
1804 New York becomes the country's most populous city, with 80,000 inhabitants; New-York Historical Society founded.
1811 Mayor DeWitt Clinton's grid plan for Manhattan introduced.
1825 New York Gas Light Company completes installation of first gas lamps on Broadway; Erie Canal completed.
1827 Slavery officially abolished in New York.

1833 *The New York Sun*'s lurid tales give birth to tabloid journalism.
1837 Financial panic nearly bankrupts the city.
1851 *The New York Daily Times* (now the *New York Times*) published.
1858 Work on Central Park begins; Macy's opens.
1863 Mobs take to the streets during bloody Draft Riots.
1870 Metropolitan Museum of Art founded.
1883 Brooklyn Bridge opens.
1886 Statue of Liberty unveiled.
1889 Barnard College opens; Stanford White designs an arch for Washington Square Park to commemorate the centennial of George Washington's inauguration.
1890 Jacob A. Riis publishes *How the Other Half Lives*.
1891 Carnegie Hall opens with a concert conducted by Tchaikovsky.
1892 Ellis Island opens.
1895 Oscar Hammerstein's Olympia Theater opens, creating Broadway theater.
1898 The city consolidates the five boroughs.
1902 The Fuller (Flatiron) Building becomes the world's first skyscraper.
1903 The New York Highlanders (later the New York Yankees) play their first game.
1904 New York's first subway line, the Interborough Rapid Transit Subway (IRT), opens; Longacre Square becomes Times Square.

the daunting task of repairing not only the city's skyline but also its battered economy and shattered psyche. He proved adept at steering the city back on the road to health as the stock market revived, downtown businesses reemerged and plans for rebuilding the Trade Center were drawn. True to form, however, New Yorkers debated the future of the site for more than a year until architect Daniel Libeskind was awarded the redevelopment job in 2003. His plan, called "Memory Foundations," aims to reconcile rebuilding and remembrance, with parks, plazas, a cultural center, a performing arts center, a memorial and a sleek new office tower. Nevertheless, conflict continues to plague every step of the project.

The summer of 2003 saw a blackout that shut down the city (and much of the Eastern seaboard). New Yorkers were sweaty but calm,

and again proved they possessed surprising reserves of civility as cafés set up candlelit tables and bodegas handed out free ice cream.

And yet, despite Bloomberg's efforts to make New York a more considerate and civil place—imposing a citywide smoking ban in bars and restaurants and a strict noise ordinance that would even silence the jingling of ice-cream trucks—New Yorkers continue to uphold their hard-edged reputation. Many are bellyaching about Bloomberg's plan to build a 75,000-seat arena on the West Side of Manhattan; they, too, are upholding the local tradition of crankiness. After all, if any of these rude, abrasive or inconsiderate people had their attitudes adjusted, New Yorkers wouldn't be where they are today, thriving in a city that is widely looked upon as the capital of the world. And no doubt they would offer a big, disrespectful Bronx cheer to those who disagree.

1908 First ball dropped to celebrate the new year in Times Square.
1910 McKim, Mead & White's Pennsylvania Station opens.
1911 The Triangle Shirtwaist Fire claims nearly 150 lives, spurring unionization.
1923 Yankee Stadium opens.
1924 First Macy's Christmas Parade, now the Thanksgiving Day Parade, held.
1929 The stock market crashes; Museum of Modern Art opens.
1931 George Washington Bridge completed; the Empire State Building opens; the Whitney Museum opens.
1934 Fiorello La Guardia takes office; Tavern on the Green opens.
1939 New York hosts a World's Fair.
1945 Two million gather in Times Square to celebrate the end of World War II.
1946 The New York Knickerbockers play their first game.
1950 United Nations complex completed.
1953 Robert Moses spearheads building of the Cross Bronx Expressway; 40,000 homes demolished in the process.
1957 The New York Giants baseball team moves to San Francisco; Brooklyn Dodgers move to Los Angeles.
1962 New York Mets debut at the Polo Grounds; Philharmonic Hall (later Avery Fisher Hall), the first building in Lincoln Center, opens; first Shakespeare in the Park performance.

1964 Verrazano-Narrows Bridge completed; World's Fair held in Flushing Meadows–Corona Park in Queens.
1969 The Stonewall riots in Greenwich Village give birth to the gay-rights movement.
1970 First New York City Marathon held.
1973 World Trade Center completed.
1974 First Greenwich Village Halloween Parade held.
1975 On the verge of bankruptcy, the city is snubbed by the federal government; *Saturday Night Live* debuts.
1977 Serial killer David "Son of Sam" Berkowitz arrested; Studio 54 opens; 4,000 arrested during citywide blackout.
1989 David N. Dinkins elected the city's first black mayor.
1993 A terrorist bomb explodes in the World Trade Center, killing 6 and injuring 1,000.
1997 Murder rate lowest in 30 years.
2001 Hijackers fly two jets into the Twin Towers, killing nearly 2,800 and demolishing the World Trade Center.
2002 Billionaire Michael Bloomberg becomes New York's 108th mayor.
2003 Smoking is banned in bars and restaurants; another blackout hits the city; a Staten Island Ferry crash claims 11 lives.
2004 The Statue of Liberty reopens for first time since September 11, 2001; the Time Warner Center opens; cornerstone laid for the Freedom Tower at Ground Zero.

The new **MoMA**.

Architecture

From skyline to streetscape, a city reinvents its landmarks.

Beneath the hard-bitten exterior of each New Yorker lies a romantic core where larger-than-life dreams take shape and are obsessively polished. Nowhere else in the city is this underlying dream machine more manifest than in our architecture. Decade after decade, no matter what calamity may befall the city, a pattern of hopeful reinvention remains constant. All over town, transformation is under way, and remarkable buildings of many sizes and styles are rising to reshape the skyline.

Cultural institutions remain in the vanguard of creative design, often vying with the art they contain. Foremost is Japanese architect Yoshio Taniguchi's glowing glass addition to the venerable **Museum of Modern Art** (*see*

p151), whose original design, by Philip L. Goodwin and Edward Durell Stone, was highly influential when MoMA opened in 1939. A skylighted, six-story, glass-sheathed atrium is part of the expansion, which has nearly doubled the size of the museum, to 630,000 square feet. The **Brooklyn Museum** (*see p147*) has a stunning refurbished entrance by James Stewart Polshek, who also designed the otherworldly crystalline cube at the **Rose Center for Earth and Space** at the **American Museum of Natural History** (*see p146*) and the subterranean performance space of **Zankel Hall** at **Carnegie Hall** (*see p325*). Polshek's tiara-shaped glass-and-steel entry to the Brooklyn institution replaces a blank space where a grand staircase once led to McKim, Mead & White's 1927 Beaux Arts court. The new entrance also gets a little touch of Las Vegas in the form of an impressively showy fountain.

The **Brooklyn Academy of Music** (*see p325*), once an isolated outpost of the arts near downtown Brooklyn, is on its way to becoming the epicenter of a major cultural complex. Charged with its design are cutting-edge architects Elizabeth Diller and Ricardo Scofidio and the cerebral Dutch architect Rem Koolhaas, whose most recent local project is the ubercool **Prada** store in Soho (575 Broadway at Prince St, 1-212-334-8888).

Ambitious plans for the BAM complex include an extraordinary eight-story, glass-walled boomerang by Mexican architect Enrique Norten that will house the **Brooklyn Public Library**'s **Visual and Performing Arts Library** (*see p124*) and a 299-seat theater designed by Frank Gehry and Hugh Hardy. Gehry (who put Bilbao, Spain, on the global culture map with his quilted-titanium-skinned Guggenheim) will also fashion a downtown performing-arts center at Ground Zero. New Yorkers can get a preview of his free-form designs by checking out the twisted titanium columns made by Gehry's studio for the **Tribeca Issey Miyake** boutique (119 Hudson at North Moore St, 1-212-226-0100).

Kevin Roche John Dinkeloo and Associates constructed another notable museum expansion: The curving granite wing of the **Museum of Jewish Heritage** (*see p161*), which includes the permanent outdoor installation *Garden of Stones* by environmental artist Andy Goldsworthy. The memorial garden is made up of 18 dwarf oak saplings planted in hollowed-out boulders. In Hebrew, the number *18* means "life" (it is the numerical value of the word *chai*), so the garden is a fitting tribute to the resilience of Jewish communities after the Holocaust. The new wing was also the first major downtown structure to begin construction after September 11, 2001.

In midtown, Austria native Raimund Abraham's **Austrian Cultural Forum** (11 E 52nd St between Fifth and Madison Aves, 1-212-319-5300) sports a louvered facade that glowers like a totemic mask, while the **American Folk Art Museum** (*see p152*), by Tod Williams Billie Tsien & Associates, is clad in panels of a delicately textured, weathered alloy that resembles stone more than metal. Interior walls that intersect at unexpected angles make the small museum appear surprisingly spacious.

As for Ground Zero itself, a basic outline under the stewardship of architect Daniel

Libeskind has been agreed to; specifics, including a projected completion date, remain up in the air, so to speak. Design of the **Freedom Tower**, whose spire will reach a height of 1,776 feet (symbolizing the year the U.S. was founded), was turned over to David Childs of Skidmore, Owings & Merrill, after lengthy political wrangling. The asymmetrical spire is meant to evoke both the Statue of Liberty's torch and the cable suspension of the Brooklyn Bridge.

To Libeskind, the challenge of rebuilding the World Trade Center is not only the structure itself but also the remapping of the neighborhood. The grid of streets through the superblock that the Twin Towers once occupied will be restored, integrating the new buildings into the landscape. Other defining features include the "Wedge of Light," a plaza where the sun will shine without shadow every September 11 between the times that the first tower was hit and the second one collapsed; and "Reflecting Absence," a meditative grotto 30 feet below street level, with two pools that will occupy the footprints of the original towers.

One of the truly spectacular downtown sights will be the new **World Trade Center PATH Station**, with a suspended ribbed-steel, wing-shaped canopy designed by Santiago Calatrava. The Spanish architect is known for innovative, nature-based solutions to construction challenges; his station alights like a dove of peace at the base of the complex. Its subterranean space, larger than the main concourse of Grand Central Terminal, is likely to be a nexus for the neighborhood.

Another great transportation annex will be David Childs's clamshell-shaped steel-and-glass addition to **Penn Station** (*see p364*), which will be built midblock behind the imposing Corinthian colonnade of McKim, Mead & White's 1913 **General Post Office** (421 Eighth Ave between 31st and 33rd Sts). The transparent multilevel station, still on the drawing board, aims to revive the awesome experience of arriving by rail in the majestic original Pennsylvania Station. As the critic Vincent Scully described the present experience below Madison Square Garden, "One scuttles in now like a rat."

Despite the tragic loss of life and property at the aggressively skyward-reaching World Trade Center, nothing can derail New York's powerful inclination to stretch for the clouds. A new set of twin towers, the **Time Warner**

▶ For more on New York's architectural highlights, see **Sightseeing** (*pp71–163*).

Center (10 Columbus Circle at Broadway), at the base of Central Park, has turned a once-anonymous section of the city into a destination. Filled with a mixture of popular high-end shops and haute restaurants, the building has quickly become an upper-midtown landmark.

Costas Kondylis's 72-story **Trump World Tower** (845 First Ave between 47th and 48th Sts) is the third-tallest residential building in the world. (The 863-foot black-glass monolith was surpassed in 2003 by the 883-foot 21st Century Tower apartment building in Dubai.) Denizens of Turtle Bay feared the freestanding tower would overshadow the iconic **U.N. Secretariat Building** to the south, but the World Tower's sleek-skinned design is remarkably reticent, reflecting rather than overpowering its environs. Skyscraper buffs will be interested in comparing it to the stately 41-story Beaux Arts **Ritz Tower** (109 E 57th St at Park Ave), which was the world's tallest residence when it was built, in 1925.

At 868 feet, the new **Bloomberg Tower** (731 Lexington Ave between 58th and 59th Sts), with its torqued central public space, is another sign that New York is not afraid to build tall. The edifice is the work of Cesar Pelli, who also designed the World Financial Center.

Other recent additions to the city include the splashy **Westin Hotel** (270 W 43rd St between Seventh and Eighth Aves); sheathed in purple, aqua and tangerine reflective glass and split vertically by a shooting-star beam of light, it is the first tall building in New York by the Miami-based firm Arquitectonica. The eccentrically angled glass facade of French architect Christian de Portzamparc's **LVMH Tower** (19 E 57th St between Fifth and Madison Aves) stands like a postmodernist miniglacier among more sober storefronts.

Building on greatness

If you look closely at the front windows of the **American Institute of Architects Center for Architecture** on La Guardia Place, you'll see a lot of nose prints. It's not that the windows aren't ever washed, it's that there's always something interesting going on inside—so sidewalk gawkers often push up against the glass to take a peek. Perhaps a model of a proposed skyscraper is on display in the street-level gallery; or a film is being screened in the auditorium two levels below, which can be glimpsed through a large cutaway in the floor. Or maybe it's a lecture on green architecture, a panel discussion on "picturesque" home design or a play lampooning contemporary architects. Whatever the lure is, it's meant to engage visitors in the complex but fascinating world of contemporary architecture, from design and debate to construction and preservation.

After five years of planning, the Center for Architecture opened to acclaim in the fall of 2003. While the timing was opportune in terms of the city's evolution—since September 11, 2001, public interest in urban planning has soared—the New York chapter of the AIA had long wanted to reach out to the community. Founded in 1867, the organization languished for years on the sixth floor of a Lexington Avenue edifice, far out of sight (and mind) of all but the most devoted architecture aficionados. In 1997, recognizing its isolation and perceived insularity, the AIA began searching Soho and the Village for new digs, finally opting for a vacant storefront in an early-20th-century industrial building. After a design competition, Andrew Berman Architect was chosen to transform the space into a fitting home for architectural debate.

The sweeping, light-filled design is a physical manifestation of AIA's goal of promoting transparency in its access and programming. Berman cut away large slabs of flooring at the street and basement levels, converting underground spaces into bright museum-quality galleries. He also installed a glass-enclosed library and conference room—open to the public—on the first floor, and a children's gallery and workshop on the mezzanine level. The building is New York's first public space to use an energy-efficient geothermal system. Fifty-five-degree water, drawn from two 1,260-foot wells, is piped through the building to help heat and cool it.

Green is good, but it's the Center's wide-ranging, politically neutral programming that makes the institution so precious to professionals and amateurs alike. "When choosing exhibitions," says Rick Bell, the Center's executive director, "we make a qualitative decision based on what's happening at the time. They're topical, timely and targeting issues that will affect a

Impressive skyscrapers fortify the southern entry to the electric carnival of Times Square: The **Condé Nast Building** (4 Times Sq at 42nd St) and the **Reuters Building** (3 Times Sq at 42nd St), both by Fox & Fowle, complement Kohn Pederson Fox's postmodern **5 Times Square** (Seventh Ave at 42nd St) and, most recently, David Childs's **Times Square Tower** (7 Times Sq between Broadway and Seventh Ave), which takes advantage of a zoning loophole to rise straight up for 47 stories. At the same time, the New York Times Company is laying the groundwork to extend Times Square's business district westward with a new headquarters lodged in a stunning 52-story, translucent-skinned tower by Italian architect Renzo Piano. Perhaps it will be more successful than Raymond Hood's green-tiled **McGraw-Hill Building** (330 W 42nd St between Eighth and Ninth Aves), which was intended to expand midtown in 1931 but still stands in relative isolation.

The slow concatenation of girders and glass in British architect Norman Foster's chrysalislike tower atop the 1928 Art Deco **Hearst Building** (959 Eighth Ave between 56th and 57th Sts) has been one of the most exciting architectural works-in-progress to watch in 2004.

The best place to keep tabs on these developments and others—from the proposals to remake the West Side's old **High Line** railway into a public space to Santiago Calatrava's striking model for a skyscraper resembling 12 glass cubes suspended between thin wires—is at the **AIA Center for Architecture** (*see p26* **Building on greatness**).

TALES OF OLD NEW YORK

Under New York's gleaming exoskeleton of steel and glass lies the heart of a 17th-century Dutch city. It began at the Battery and New

Pondering the shape of things to come at the **AIA Center for Architecture**.

neighborhood in the near future." Although programs can get a bit specialized sometimes—which window is best for daylight-friendly fenestration?—most are just plain cool, letting us glimpse what the city could or should look like. Planned shows for 2005 include a spring survey of work by graduates of the architecture schools of Columbia University, Pratt Institute, the Cooper Union and others, and an early-summer show exploring the legacy of the Urban Development Corporation, a state agency founded in 1968 to build housing for low- and middle-income families. October's Architecture Week is jam-packed with lectures, panel discussions, films and architectural tours. So whether you're interested in streetlights or skyscrapers, windows or walkways, don't just step up to the window—step inside. Chances are you'll never think about fenestration the same way again.

AIA Center for Architecture

536 La Guardia Pl between Bleecker and W 3rd Sts (1-212-683-0023/www.aiany.org). Subway: A, C, E, B, D, F, V to W 4th St.

York Harbor, one of the greatest naturally formed deepwater ports in the world. The former Alexander Hamilton Custom House of 1907, now the **National Museum of the American Indian** (*see p157*), was built by Cass Gilbert and is a symbol of the harbor's significance in Manhattan's growth. Before 1913, the city's chief source of revenue was customs duties. Gilbert's domed marble edifice is suitably monumental—its carved figures of the *Four Continents* are by Daniel Chester French, the sculptor of the Lincoln Memorial in Washington, D.C.

The Dutch influence is still traceable in the downtown web of narrow, winding lanes, like the streets in medieval European cities. Because the Cartesian grid that rules the city was laid out by the Commissioners' Plan in 1811, only a few samples of actual Dutch architecture remain, mostly off the beaten path. One of these is the 1785 **Dyckman Farmhouse Museum** (4881 Broadway at 204th St) in Inwood, Manhattan's northernmost neighborhood. Its gambrel roof and decorative brickwork reflect architectural fashion of the late 18th century. The oldest house still standing in the five boroughs is the **Pieter Claesen Wyckoff House Museum** (5816 Clarendon Rd at Ralph Ave, Flatbush, Brooklyn). Erected around 1652, it's a typical Dutch farmhouse with shingled walls and deep eaves. The **Lefferts Homestead** (Prospect Park, Flatbush Ave near Empire Blvd, Prospect Heights, Brooklyn), built between 1777 and 1783, combines a gambrel roof with column-supported porches, a hybrid style popular during the Federal period.

In Manhattan, the only building extant from pre-Revolutionary times is the stately columned and quoined **St. Paul's Chapel** (*see p80*), completed in 1766 (a spire was added in 1796). George Washington, a parishioner here, was officially received in the chapel after his 1789 presidential inauguration. The Enlightenment ideals upon which this nation was founded influenced the church's democratic, nonhierarchical layout. **Trinity Church** (*see p80*) of 1846, one of the first and finest Gothic Revival churches in the country, was designed by Richard Upjohn. It's difficult to imagine now that Trinity's crocketed, finialed 281-foot-tall spire held sway for decades as the tallest structure in Manhattan.

Holdouts remain from each epoch of the city's architectural history. An outstanding example of Greek Revival from the first half of the 19th century is the 1842 **Federal Hall National Memorial** (*see p80*), whose mighty marble colonnade was built to commemorate the site where George Washington took his oath of office. A larger-than-life statue of Washington

by the sculptor John Quincy Adams Ward stands in front. The city's most celebrated blocks of Greek Revival townhouses, built in the 1830s, are known simply as the **Row** (1–13 Washington Square North between Fifth Ave and Washington Square West); they're exemplars of the more genteel metropolis of Henry James and Edith Wharton.

Greek Revival gave way to Renaissance-inspired Beaux Arts architecture, which reflected the imperial ambitions of a wealthy young nation during the Gilded Age of the late 19th century. Like Emperor Augustus, who boasted that he had found Rome a city of brick and left it a city of marble, the firm of McKim, Mead & White built noble civic monuments and palazzi for the rich. The best-known buildings of the classicist Charles Follen McKim include the main campus of **Columbia University** (*see p115*), begun in the 1890s, and the austere 1906 **Morgan Library** (*see 150*). His partner, socialite and bon vivant Stanford White (scandalously murdered by his mistress's husband in 1906), designed more festive spaces, such as the **Metropolitan Club** (1 E 60th St at Fifth Ave) and the extraordinarily luxe Villard Houses of 1882, now incorporated into the **New York Palace** hotel (*see p55*).

Another Beaux Arts treasure from the city's grand metropolitan era is Carrère & Hastings's sumptuous white-marble **New York Public Library** of 1911 (*see p162*), built on a former Revolutionary War battleground; the site later hosted an Egyptian Revival water reservoir and, presently, the greensward of Bryant Park. The 1913 travertine-lined **Grand Central Terminal** (*see p364*) remains the elegant foyer of the city, thanks to preservationists (most prominently, Jacqueline Kennedy Onassis; *see p103* **Local legend**) who saved it from the wrecking ball.

MOVIN' ON UP

Cast-iron architecture peaked in the latter half of the 19th century, coinciding roughly with the Civil War era. Iron and steel components freed architects from the bulk, weight and cost of stone construction and allowed them to build higher. Cast-iron columns, cheap to mass-produce, could support a tremendous amount of weight. The facades of many Soho buildings, with their intricate details of Italianate columns, were manufactured on assembly lines and could be ordered in pieces from catalogs.

This led to an aesthetic of uniform building facades, which had a direct impact on the steel skyscrapers of the following generation. To enjoy one of the most telling vistas of skyscraper history, gaze northward from the 1859 **Cooper**

Union (*see p87*), the oldest existing steel-beam–framed building in America.

The most visible effect of cast-iron construction was the way it opened up solid-stone facades to expanses of glass. In fact, window-shopping came into vogue in the 1860s. Mrs. Lincoln bought the White House china at the **Haughwout Store** (488–492 Broadway at Broome St). The 1857 building's Palladian-style facade recalls Renaissance Venice, but its regular, open fenestration was also a portent of the future. (Look carefully: The cast-iron elevator sign is a relic of the world's first working SAFETY PASSENGER ELEVATOR, designed by Elisha Graves Otis.)

Once engineers perfected steel, which is stronger and lighter than iron, and created the interlocking steel-cage construction that distributed the weight of a building over its entire frame, the sky was the limit. New York is fortunate to have one building by the great skyscraper innovator Louis Sullivan, the 1898 **Bayard-Condict Building** (65–69 Bleecker St between Broadway and Lafayette St). Though only 13 stories tall, Sullivan's building, covered with richly decorative terra-cotta, was one of the earliest to apply a purely vertical design rather than imitate horizontal styles of the past. Sullivan wrote that a skyscraper "must be tall, every inch of it tall.… From bottom to top, it is a unit without a single dissenting line."

Chicago architect Daniel H. Burnham's 1902 **Flatiron Building** (*see p96*) is another standout; its breathtakingly modern design, combined with traditional masonry decoration, was made possible only by steel-cage construction.

The new century saw a frenzy of skyward manufacture, resulting in buildings of record-breaking height; the now modest-looking 30-story, 391-foot-tall **Park Row Building** (15 Park Row between Ann and Beekman Sts) was, when it was built in 1899, the tallest building in the world. That record was shattered by the 612-foot Singer Building in 1908 (demolished in the 1960s); the 700-foot **Metropolitan Life Tower** (1 Madison Ave at 24th St) of 1909, modeled after the Campanile in Venice's Piazza San Marco; and Cass Gilbert's Gothic masterpiece, the 792-foot **Woolworth Building** (*see p82*). The Woolworth reigned in solitary splendor until William Van Alen's metal-spired homage to the Automobile Age, the 1930 **Chrysler Building** (*see p105*), soared to 1,046 feet.

In a highly publicized race, the Chrysler was outstripped 13 months later, in 1931, by Shreve, Lamb & Harmon's 1,250-foot-tall **Empire State Building** (*see p103*). It has since lost its title to other giants: the 1,450-foot Sears Tower in Chicago (1974); the 1,483-foot Petronas Towers in Kuala Lumpur, Malaysia (1996); and the current record holder, the 1,671-foot Taipei 101 in Taiwan (2004). But the Empire State remains the quintessential skyscraper, one of the most recognizable buildings in the world, with its broad base, narrow shaft and distinctive needled crown. (The giant ape that scaled the side might have something to do with it, too.)

The Empire State's setbacks, retroactively labeled Art Deco (such buildings were then simply called "modern"), were actually a response to the zoning code of 1916 that required a building's upper stories to be tapered in order not to block sunlight and air circulation to the

In Context

The **Hearst Tower**'s Deco look. *See p27.*

See the light, at the new **Baruch College Academic Complex**. *See p31*.

streets. The code engendered some of the city's most fanciful designs, like the ziggurat-crowned **Paramount Building** (1501 Broadway between 43rd and 44th Sts) of 1926, and the romantically slender spire of the former **Cities Service Building** (70 Pine St at Pearl St), illuminated from within like a rare gem.

BRAVE NEW WORLD

The post–World War II period saw the ascendance of the International Style, pioneered by such giants as Le Corbusier and Ludwig Mies van der Rohe. The style's most visible symbol was the all-glass facade, like that found on the sleek slab of the **United Nations Headquarters** (*see p105*). The International Style relied on a new set of aesthetics: minimal decoration, clear expression of construction, an honest use of materials and a near-Platonic harmony of proportions. **Lever House** (390 Park Ave between 53rd and 54th Sts), designed by Gordon Bunshaft of Skidmore, Owings & Merrill, was the city's first all-steel-and-glass structure when it was built in 1952 (it recently received an award-winning brushup).

It's nearly impossible to imagine the radical vision this glass construction represented on the all-masonry corridor of Park Avenue, because nearly every building since has followed suit. Mies van der Rohe's celebrated bronze-skinned **Seagram Building** (375 Park Ave between 52nd and 53rd Sts), which reigns in imperious isolation on its own plaza, is the epitome of the architect's cryptic dicta "Less is more" and "God is in the details." The Seagram's detailing is exquisite—the custom-made bolts securing the miniature bronze piers that run the length of the facade must be polished by hand annually to keep them from oxidizing and turning green. It's truly the Rolls-Royce of skyscrapers.

High modernism began to show cracks in its facade during the mid-1960s. By then, New York had built too many such structures in midtown and below, and besides, the public had never fully warmed to the undecorated style (though for those with a little insight, the best glass boxes are fully rewarding aesthetic experiences). And the International Style's sheer arrogance in trying to supplant the traditional city structure didn't endear the movement to anyone, either.

The **MetLife Building** (200 Park Ave at 45th St), originally the Pan Am Building of 1963, was the prime culprit, not so much because of its design by Walter Gropius of the Bauhaus, but because of its presumptuous location, straddling Park Avenue and looming over Grand Central. There was even a plan at the time to raze Grand Central and build a twin Pan Am. The International Style had obviously reached its end when Philip Johnson, who was instrumental in defining the movement with his book *The International Style* (co-written with Henry-Russell Hitchcock), began disparaging the style as "glass-boxitis."

POSTMODERNISM AND BEYOND

Plainly, new blood was needed. A glimmer on the horizon was Boston architect Hugh Stubbins's silvery, triangle-topped **Citicorp Center** (Lexington Ave between 53rd and 54th Sts), which utilized daring contemporary engineering (the building cantilevers almost magically on high stilts above street level), while harking back to the decorative tops of yesteryear. The sly old master Philip Johnson turned the tables on everyone with the heretical "Chippendale" crown on his **Sony Building**, originally the AT&T Building (350 Madison Ave between 55th and 56th Sts), a bold throwback to decoration for its own sake.

Postmodernism provided a theoretical basis for a new wave of buildings that mixed past and present, often taking cues from the environs.

Some notable examples include Helmut Jahn's **425 Lexington Avenue** (between 43rd and 44th Sts) of 1988; David Childs's retro diamond-tipped **Worldwide Plaza** (825 Eighth Ave between 49th and 50th Sts) of 1989; and the honky-tonk agglomeration of Skidmore, Owings & Merrill's **Bertelsmann Building** (1540 Broadway between 45th and 46th Sts) of 1990. But even postmodernism became old hat. Too many architects relied on fussy fenestration and milquetoast commentary on other styles instead of creating vital new building facades.

The vast electronic spectacle of Times Square provides one possible direction. Upon seeing the myriad electric lights of Times Square in 1922, the British wit G.K. Chesterton remarked, "What a glorious garden of wonder this would be, to anyone who was lucky enough to be unable to read." This particular crossroads of the world continues to be at the cybernetic cutting edge: the 120-foot-tall, quarter-acre-in-area NASDAQ sign; the real-time stock tickers and jumbo TV screens everywhere; the news zipper on the original **New York Times Tower** (1 Times Sq between Broadway and Seventh Ave). The public's appetite for new images seems so insatiable that a building's fixed profile no longer suffices—only an ever-shifting electronic skin will do. The iconoclastic critic Robert Venturi, who taught us how to learn from Las Vegas, calls this trend "iconography and electronics upon a generic architecture."

Early-21st-century architecture is moving beyond applied symbolism to radical new forms facilitated by computer-based design methods. A stellar example is Kohn Pedersen Fox's stainless-steel-and-glass "vertical campus," the **Baruch College Academic Complex** (55 Lexington Ave between 24th and 25th Sts). The resulting phantasmic, fluid designs that curve and dart in sculptural space are so beyond the timid window-dressing of postmodernism that they really deserve a new label.

Known for designs that owe as much to conceptual art as to architecture, the firm of Diller & Scofidio is working on an eye-popping addition to staid Chelsea, the **Eyebeam** art and technology center, to be completed in 2007. The curvilinear walls of the planned museum are suggestive of film loops running through a projector.

Since the late 19th century, New York City has been the world's prime outdoor skyscraper museum. It may be founded on a very deliberate grid, but its growth has been organic. In the next decade, Manhattan may come to resemble a sculpture garden, as computer-aided designs bridge the gap between what is possible and what can be imagined.

Spider-Man 2.

Cinema City

New York's storied celluloid life is no urban legend.

New York, New York, it's a helluva town. / The Bronx is up but the Battery's down. / The people ride in a hole in the ground. / New York, New Yooooork…"

With these famous lyrics as accompaniment, three out-of-town sailors spend a breathless few minutes taking in a month's worth of dazzling sights: Wall Street, Chinatown, Little Italy, Central Park and, lastly, the Empire State Building. The opening montage of *On the Town* (1949) not only captures the giddy delirium of being in New York; it also takes its place in a long history of films that have been etched deep into the psyches of Americans, and helped to create the ever-evolving myth of the Big Apple.

At 24 frames a second, celluloid images have always projected the larger-than-life Gotham in all its glory (and infamy). Even hardened New Yorkers can get all goose-bumpy revisiting the filmic moments they think best capture their hometown. For some, it's King Kong's climb up the Empire State Building, clutching a screaming Fay Wray (*King Kong,* 1933); or Robert De Niro's cab cruising the darkened streets like a great white shark, in *Taxi Driver* (1976); or Meg Ryan and Billy Crystal's on-again, off-again romance (*When Harry Met Sally…*, 1989), which unfolds before a supporting cast of Manhattan landmarks like Washington Square Park, the Temple of Dendur in the Metropolitan Museum of Art and Katz's Delicatessen (where the simple words

"I'll have what she's having" were given new meaning in the American lexicon).

But who's kidding whom? It's not just New Yorkers who have succumbed to Gotham's movie persona. The city is a beacon that shines far and wide: All over the world, people's perceptions have been shaped by the film versions of life in our magnificent metropolis. "People talk about great cities like New York being fabled or legendary," says James Sanders, author of 2003's *Celluloid Skyline: New York and the Movies.* "Nowadays, the myth of the city travels around the world through films. Even people who have never visited Manhattan can visualize it. They feel like they know it," says Sanders.

Romance, adventure and excitement have always been the city's twinkling lure, its diamond-studded promise to all those consigned to the oblivion of tedious small towns and ho-hum hamlets. Of course, the foundation of New York's legend was laid in paintings, novels and radio shows in the decades before movies; however, with the advent of celluloid, the myth took on epic proportions, particularly in the 1930s, with films like *42nd Street* (1933), *Swing Time* (1936) and *Shall We Dance* (1937). These pictures, and dozens more like them, cemented the notion that NYC is a place where anything can—and will—happen. Ordinary, down-on-their-luck folks could come to New York and find fame and fortune simply by being plucky—and by having the leading lady break her ankle on the night of the big show.

As times and tastes changed, filmmakers of a new generation turned their backs on big sound-stage productions, opting instead for on-the-street shots that brought gritty authenticity to their flicks. Movies like *On the Waterfront* (1954), *The Man with the Golden Arm* (1955) and *Sweet Smell of Success* (1957) explored the darker, seamier side of our town. In place of the chorus girl with pie-in-the-sky dreams, these films featured longshoremen, junkies and petty gossip columnists eking out a living in the shadow of glittery skyscrapers. Such searing images only deepened the belief that, good or bad, *everything* happens in New York.

It turned out that the myth that is Manhattan had only just begun.

As the directors who were weaned on New York's most defining films came of age, they delved into their subconscious to create movies that would reshape our notion of why the city matters. In the 1970s, two films, shot on location within months of each other, depicted two wildly divergent views of the city. In most ways, Martin Scorsese's *Taxi Driver* and Woody Allen's *Annie Hall* couldn't be more different—Scorsese's lurid, neon-lit streets and

From top: *Manhattan, The Day After Tomorrow,* Al Pacino in *Serpico.*

hellish imagery stand in stark opposition to Allen's lush, gorgeous homage to the romance of the city—but they are complementary New York fantasies. Reality has no place in either one: The city becomes something it has been edging toward since its first depiction on the silver screen—less an actual place than a springboard for total creative reimagination.

Ultimately, it was Scorsese, Allen and, later, Spike Lee who would develop oeuvres that expanded the city's myth to incorporate a broader range of flavors and feature diverse ethnic groups and social classes. But even such heavyweights as these three don't stand alone: Each mines the past to imbue his films with New York's larger-than-life image. In *Manhattan* (1979), Allen employed classic black-and-white cinematography and Gershwin tunes to embellish the city with all the sparkle of *Footlight Parade* (1933). Lee's epic *Do the Right Thing* (1989) has overtones of *Dead End* (1937) and *Street Scene* (1931), each structured around a single day on a single nameless city block. Scorsese's *New York, New York* (1977) was perhaps most direct in its loving tribute to the big musical films of the 1930s and '40s.

In the months after September 11, 2001, many in the film industry began to wonder whether New York City's legendary splendor and magnificence could endure. What would people's perception of the city be after the deaths of nearly 2,800 people and the destruction of the

Set in the city

See NYC on the big screen in '05:

Dark Water
Dir. Walter Salles. With Jennifer Connelly and John C. Reilly.

Hide and Seek
Dir. John Polson. With Robert De Niro and Famke Janssen.

The Interpreter
Dir. Sydney Pollack. With Nicole Kidman and Sean Penn.

Romance & Cigarettes
Dir. John Turturro. With Susan Sarandon, Kate Winslet, James Gandolfini, Mandy Moore, Steve Buscemi and Aida Turturro.

Stay
Dir. Marc Forster. With Ewan McGregor and Naomi Watts.

World Trade Center—one of the central jewels in the city's gem-studded skyline? New Yorkers' collective grief was so great that they feared—at first—that the icon had been forever altered. Could portrayals of the city continue to achieve the gigantic fantastical proportions that audiences had come to know and love? The answer is yes, says Sanders. "People still want to see that New York." And not only see it but experience it, too, with the same mythical richness as before. Fantasy films like *Spider-Man* (2002) and *Men in Black II* (2002), action-adventure movies including *The Day After Tomorrow* (2004), and more heartwarming fare such as *Raising Victor Vargas* (2002) are undeniable proof.

"*Spider-Man* is very much a Hollywood film and very much a New York story. A kid from Queens finds fame and glory amid the skyscrapers of Manhattan," says Sanders. With the help of digital special effects, viewers were not just reveling in the streets of the city, they were able to fly high above them, swinging from one famed landmark to another—seemingly conquering a metropolis that, at times, has felt beyond reach. It was perhaps a new level of mythmaking, yet it proved once again that the celluloid image of New York is an enduring creation, forever changing, shifting and reinventing itself to meet the expectations of new generations.

Welcome to both New Yorks: the magical movie myth and the real thing. As you'll discover for yourself, it's exciting to be in a place that's at once real and unreal, where you can see familiar images glamorized on the big screen and pass by them the next day with a knowing smile. Note to film buffs: Check out the Upper West Side's Dakota, the site where an unsuspecting Mia Farrow conceives the spawn of Satan in *Rosemary's Baby* (1968); or 55 Central Park West, a few blocks south, where Sigourney Weaver falls prey to demonic possession in *Ghostbusters* (1984). If you're really feeling adventurous, trek out to Staten Island to see where the First Family of Mobdom, the Corleones (*The Godfather*, 1971), lived, at 110 Longfellow Road, in the swanky Emerson Hill neighborhood. The movie's outdoor festivities were filmed in the nearby garden of 120 Longfellow Road.

Most New Yorkers say they couldn't imagine living anywhere but here—they couldn't live without the excitement, the noise, the lights, the chaos or the endless possibilities. And who knows… Maybe while you're here, you'll get caught up in a bit of the cinematic yourself: In the middle of a crosswalk, you might stop dead in your tracks, pound your fist on the nearest taxi, and growl out your best *Midnight Cowboy*, "Hey, I'm *walkin'* here!" Just like in the movies.

The **Statue of Liberty** reopens.

New York Today

A resident's view of the capital of the world.

To understand the city, and to feel a part of it while you're here, you don't really need to know that the Indians supposedly sold the island of Manhattan to the Dutch for a few beads and some pocket lint. You do need to know about what's going on now, from a local's perspective. And how New Yorkers—never at a loss for an opinion—feel about it.

THE WAY WE ACT

A lot of people (mostly those pushing a political agenda) would have you believe that the New York you've just set foot on was created in a brief but harrowing period—from 8:45 to 10:30am on September 11, 2001, when two passenger planes toppled the city's tallest buildings. President George W. Bush certainly wanted people to think that, for the purposes of rallying the country around his War on Terror. To New Yorkers, however, the tragedy shaped the city, to be sure, but it hasn't defined it. The difference in perspective is not so surprising, really. We're our own breed, New Yorkers. And we've always seen ourselves as somewhat separate from the rest of the country. We look different, we live different, we have different opinions about the acceptable size of a living space and how much we're willing to pay for a good meal. Hell, we could secede tomorrow and probably be a lot happier; the rest of the country might not even notice. To some, we're the weirdos on the East Coast, the city with more homosexuals and fewer white people than anywhere else in the country. We confuse and scare certain folks.

Peace marchers protest during the 2004 Republican National Convention.

So welcome, ye bravehearts! If you've gotten this far, then you're clearly one of us.

Guess what else sets us apart? Yep, attitude. While the rest of the country hunkers down under Code Yellow terror alerts, we don't even blink about the Code Orange status we live with daily. We're a little ballsier here, a little more like the defiant Gloria Gaynor of that disco anthem: We will survive. We're tough and we take care of our own, but despite the attitude, we'll admit; We're better behaved than most movies would have you believe. The 2001 World Trade Center attack generated a citywide sense of brotherly love, and during the August 2003 blackout—the largest ever in North America—we remained cool, calm and collected.

Then came another huge test of character: the 2004 Republican National Convention. The ratio of Democrats to Republicans in this city of more than 4.5 million registered voters is about five to one. True, our current mayor and his predecessor both sign their loyalties to the GOP. But Rudy Giuliani came at a time when locals felt they needed a tough guy to clean up crime; and Michael Bloomberg has been more respected for his straight-talking business approach than for his party affiliation. So much for here at home. On the national scale, we skew way left of center. And we like it that way. There's certainly a part of us that wishes, deep down, that the rest of this country could be as diverse—in attitude, culture and

politics—and as tolerant and celebratory of these differences as we are. We can only imagine that's why you've chosen to visit NYC, as opposed to, for instance, Kansas.

So to say that most New Yorkers didn't exactly welcome the Republican National Convention is an understatement. Many felt that President Bush and his administration attached a disturbing nostalgia to 9/11, capitalizing on it in an attempt to unite the country behind an invasion agenda and solidify Bush's reelection prospects. In protest, upwards of half a million marchers (or thereabouts) took to the streets. Although most demonstrations were peaceful, more than 1,500 people were arrested, prompting charges that free speech was being quashed in the name of campaign strategy. Some protesters, and even random folks who were in the wrong place at the wrong time, were still fighting their arrests in court at press time.

These demonstrations were remarkable. People from all over the country flocked to this city in huge numbers to have their voices heard and their signs read (and, in some cases, their naked bodies seen) in a place known for its bluntly stated opinions. Fears of riots and violence proved unfounded. And even though all the anti-Republican hoopla didn't tip the election scales against George W. Bush, it galvanized a fed-up constituency and symbolized a city's— and a nation's—discontent. Dubya has the next four years to prove he can respond to those cries.

THE WAY WE LOOK

Whether you drive, fly, boat or bike into New York City, it's immediately obvious that this place is unlike any other. Even the city's physical makeup reflects its diversity. You've got historic buildings in lower Manhattan, modern skyscrapers in midtown, brownstones in Brooklyn, suburban homes in Queens, and everything from housing projects to mansions in the Bronx. Buildings are a serious business here, and we take all matters of real estate to heart, especially now that the price of a studio apartment in a Richard Meier–designed building has passed the $1 million mark.

One real-estate topic grabbing the headlines is the heated debate over whether to build a new football stadium on the West Side of Manhattan, near the Javits Center. The cons: Residents of the neighborhood don't want their homes razed and the region rezoned as a commercial parking-lot–cum–wasteland. Other New Yorkers aren't thrilled to foot the bill for a venue the Jets would use for a measly six games (that's roughly 24 hours!) each year. The pros: Mayor Bloomberg and his backers claim the stadium will bring loads of cash to a city that needs every penny. Oh, and then there's the real motive: A new stadium could help persuade the International Olympic Committee to select New York City as the site of the 2012 games.

The battle over Manhattan's West Side rages on, but the reopened Statue of Liberty is one piece of real estate everyone can agree on. Closed for security reasons after the World Trade Center attack, the national landmark remained conspicuously off-limits for years while the private foundation that runs it tried to raise money for the structural and safety work that would make it secure for visitors. Finally, in August 2004, the most visible symbol of American pride and the immigrant experience reopened her doors. You're still not allowed to hike all the way up to her crown, but her base is accessible once again.

In other big real-estate news, the huddled masses of Manhattan recently welcomed back one of the city's great art institutions. After two years of temporary relocation to a former stapler factory in Long Island City, Queens, the Museum of Modern Art (MoMA) returned in November to its newly improved and truly impressive home in midtown Manhattan.

MoMA's Queens sojourn, meanwhile, did wonders for the industrial-looking but culture-rich neighborhood of Long Island City, spurring art hounds to discover other venues such as the Noguchi Museum (also newly renovated), the Museum for African Art, the Socrates Sculpture Park and P.S. 1 Contemporary Art Center.

And despite the funding challenges they've faced since September 11, 2001, arts and nonprofit organizations have continued to showcase world-class works in both established and new spaces. During the past few years, we've welcomed new music venues (Zankel Hall), new theaters (the Dodger Stages) and new museums (the Rubin Museum of Art). One of this city's most valuable assets is its cache of creative people. And they're forward-thinking in the arts as well as in aggressively chasing down funding for them, so the rest of us can enjoy the city's vast riches.

THE WAY WE PLAY

Arts organizations may have to struggle to survive, but the city's restaurants just seem to keep raking it in. The spaces get bigger and bigger, and so do the tabs. This past year saw the opening of several supersize, high-end eateries, including Megu, Vento and the splashy new Jean-Georges Vongerichten affair, Spice Market. A few other high-profile newcomers are smaller in size, but they'll still take a gigantic chunk out of your wallet: At fancy-sushi joint Masa, you can easily drop $1,000 on dinner for two. Thomas Keller (of Napa Valley's French Laundry) recently unveiled a restaurant called Per Se: Spend nearly $150 per person on a prix-fixe dinner (that's without tax, tip or drinks) and you can see for yourself why the *New York Times* gave it four stars.

Since boring old everyday expenses like public transportation, taxi fares and property taxes have also risen, it's a wonder that New Yorkers can scrape together the cash for these over-the-top restaurants. But where there's a will, there's a way. We manage to find it; you can, too.

So bring some extra dough for at least one really good, really expensive meal (or better yet, hit a trendy spot for lunch and get the same great food for less). Just be sure to make your reservations way in advance—many of these chichi spots come with the It accessory of the year: a long wait.

Even if you skip the megameal, keep in mind that no matter where you eat, shop or stand in awe of the culture, what you need to fit in with the rest of us in this town is an attitude—just act like you belong, explore with an adventurous spirit, and take it all in.

And be prepared to share the details of your exploits when your trip ends. Unlike in Vegas, what happens here doesn't stay here. Whatever experiences you rack up, you'll want to brag about them loudly to your friends and family back home—and you should.

That's part of being a New Yorker.

Where to Stay

Where to Stay   **40**

Where to Stay

Midtown strikes back.

The perennial battle of downtown cool versus uptown chic rages on, but with a twist: The hotter-than-hot Meatpacking District may have to yield some coolness to—of all places—midtown. For years, developers lured in-the-know travelers below 14th Street, leaving midtown's many cookie-cutter business-traveler rooms vacant. But midtown wasn't going down without a fight, so this year, the area exults in a new crop of luxury hotels rife with sweet amenities like an in-room iPod, a flat-screen TV (complete with yoga channel) and even a recording studio. The three latest superstylish hostelries are the **Dream Hotel**, **70 Park Avenue** and the **Blakely New York**. And the appeal of these hotels doesn't end with jazzed-up room service; 70 Park houses the Silverleaf Tavern, a new-American restaurant, while the chill vibe at Dream Hotel's lounges, including the belowground Subconscious (accessible via a blue-glass elevator), gives similar downtown trend-havens a run for their money. At the same time, head-to-toe renovations have spruced up the **Metropolitan Hotel**, the **Hotel Roger Williams** and the **Habitat Hotel** (130 E 57th St at Lexington Ave, 1-212-753-8841, 1-800-497-6028, www.habitat-ny.com).

Other areas of the city continue to carve out niches. Chelsea offers stylish accommodations at budget prices; Soho is the king of designer chambers; and savvy uptown entrepreneurs are turning Harlem's beautiful brownstones into one-of-a-kind bed-and-breakfasts (see p60 **The (new) Harlem Renaissance**). New York has more small-chain and independent hotels than any other city in the country, and nearly half of its properties are unaffiliated with national or international chains. Tourism has picked up since the post–September 11 slump, so city hotels have responded by hiking rates (this year, prices went up $10 to $50 per room).

The best way to begin your hotel search is to choose the price range and neighborhood that interest you. The prices quoted in our listings are not guaranteed, but they should give you a

good idea of the hotel's average rack rates. And if you follow the tips below, you're likely to find slashed room prices, package deals and special promotions.

Weekend travelers, be warned: Many smaller hotels adhere to a strict three-night-minimum booking policy. Make sure to include New York's 13.625 percent room tax and a $2 to $6 per-night occupancy tax when planning your travel budget. Ask in advance about unadvertised costs—phone charges, minibars, faxes—so you're not surprised at checkout.

HOTEL-RESERVATION AGENCIES

Pre-booking blocks of rooms allows reservation companies to offer reduced rates. Discounts cover most price ranges, including economy; some agencies claim savings of up to 65 percent, though 20 percent is more likely. If you simply want the best deal, then mention the part of town you prefer and the rate you're willing to pay, and see what's available. The following agencies work with select New York hotels and are free of charge, though a few require payment for rooms at the time the reservation is made.

Hotel Reservations Network
10440 North Central Expwy, suite 400, Dallas, TX 75231 (1-214-369-1264/1-800-246-8357/ www.hotels.com).

Quikbook
381 Park Ave South, third floor, New York, NY 10016 (1-212-779-7666/1-800-789-9887/ www.quikbook.com).

timeoutny.com
The *Time Out New York* website offers online reservations at more than 300 hotels. You can search by arrival date or hotel name. (Full disclosure: *TONY* receives a commission from sales made through our partner hotel-reservation sites.)

BED-AND-BREAKFAST SERVICES/ SHORT-TERM APARTMENT RENTALS

Thousands of B&B rooms are available in New York, but in the absence of a central organization, some are hard to find. Many B&Bs are unhosted, and breakfast is usually Continental (if it's served at all), but the ambience is likely to be more personal than that of a hotel. A sales tax of 8.625 percent is added on hosted rooms—though not on unhosted apartments—if you stay more than seven days. For a longer visit, it can be cheaper and more

---

▶ For hotel listings with direct links to booking, visit **www.timeoutny.com**.
▶ For more on accommodations, see **Gay & Lesbian** (*pp299–309*).

Swimmers at **Hotel Gansevoort**'s pool can wave at bathers in Soho House's pool.

convenient to rent a place of your own; several of the agencies listed below specialize in short-term rentals of furnished apartments. One caveat: Last-minute changes can be costly; some agencies charge a fee or refuse to refund deposits for cancellations made less than ten days in advance. For gay-friendly B&Bs, *see p302*—straight guests are welcome, too.

CitySonnet
Village Station, P.O. Box 347, New York, NY 10014 (1-212-614-3034/www.citysonnet.com). **Rates** *$80–$165 B&B room; $80–$125 hosted artist's loft; $165–$375 unhosted artist's loft; $135–$375 private apartment.* **Credit** *AmEx, Disc, MC, V.*
This amiable artist-run agency specializes in downtown locations but has properties all over Manhattan. B&B rooms and short-term apartment rentals are priced according to room size, number of guests, and whether the bathroom is private or shared.

New York Habitat
307 Seventh Ave between 27th and 28th Sts, suite 306 (1-212-255-8018/www.nyhabitat.com). Subway 1, 9 to 28th St. **Rates** *$85–$165 unhosted studio; $135–$225 unhosted 1-bedroom apartment; $200–$375 unhosted 2-bedroom apartment.* **Credit** *AmEx, DC, Disc, MC, V.*
A variety of services are offered, from hosted B&Bs to short-term furnished apartment rentals, which can be charged by the day, week or month.

STANDARD HOTEL SERVICES
All hotels have air-conditioning—a relief in summer—unless otherwise noted. In the categories **Deluxe**, **Expensive** and **Moderate**, every hotel has the following amenities and services (unless otherwise stated): alarm clock, business center, cable TV, concierge, conference facility, currency exchange, dry cleaning, fax (in its business center or in the rooms), hairdryer, in-room safe, laundry, minibar, modem line, parking, radio, one or more restaurants, one or more bars, room service and voice mail. Additional services are noted at the end of each listing.

Most hotels in all categories have access for the disabled, nonsmoking rooms, and an iron with ironing board in the room or on request. Call to confirm. "Breakfast included" may mean either muesli and milk or a more generous spread of croissants, orange juice and café au lait. While many hotels claim a "multilingual" staff, that term may be used loosely.

Downtown below 23rd Street

Deluxe ($350 and up)

Hotel Gansevoort
18 Ninth Ave at 13th St (1-212-206-6700/1-877-726-7386/www.hotelgansevoort.com). Subway: A, C, E to 14th St; L to Eighth Ave. **Rates** *$395–$475 single/double; $625–$675 suite; from $5,000 duplex penthouse. 187 rooms.* **Credit** *AmEx, DC, Disc, MC, V.*

The lap of luxury is minimal-chic in the penthouse suite of the **Mercer**.

Opened in early 2004, this soaring contemporary structure stands out against the cobblestone streets and warehouses-turned-designer-shops of the Meat-packing District. Blueprinted by Stephen B. Jacobs, who also designed the Library Hotel (*see p54*), this 14-floor, full-service luxury hotel gets strong marks for style. Four 18-foot light boxes, which change color throughout the evening, frame the hotel's entrance, and eel-skin-wrapped pillars dot the lobby. Upstairs, the gray-on-gray color scheme may be a bit chilly, but the chambers are spacious and come with colored-glass doors, original photography from local artists and Molton Brown bath products. The private roof garden features a glassed-in heated pool with under-water music and 360-degree views of the city. Jeffrey Chodorow's glossy Japanese eatery Ono has a cov-ered terrace, private dining huts and a *robatayaki* bar—all behind a red velvet rope.
Hotel services *Dry cleaning (24hrs). Pet-friendly.*
Room services *CD player. Complimentary newspapers and magazines. Cordless phone. DVD player on request. High-speed wireless Internet. Plasma or LCD TV. Room service (24hrs).*

The Mercer

147 Mercer St at Prince St (1-212-966-6060/1-888-918-6060/www.mercerhotel.com). Subway: N, R, W to Prince St. **Rates** *$395–$620 single/double; $1,100–$2,100 suite. 75 rooms.* **Credit** *AmEx, DC, Disc, MC, V.*
Soho's first luxury boutique hotel has small touches that keep it a notch above nearby competitors. (Isaac Mizrahi designed the staff's sharp uniforms; the triple-threat lobby acts as a bar, library and lounge.) Rooms feature furniture by Christian Liagre, oversize

washrooms with tubs for two and Face Stockholm products. The restaurant, Mercer Kitchen (1-212-966-5454), serves Jean-Georges Vongerichten's stylish version of casual American cuisine.
Hotel services *Book and magazine library. CD/DVD library. Cell-phone and laptop-computer rental. Complimentary pass to nearby gym. Dry cleaning (24hrs). Pet-friendly. Ticket desk. Valet.* **Room services** *Cassette and CD players. Complimentary newspaper. DVD player and VCR on request. Fireplace in some rooms. Plasma TV. PlayStation.*

60 Thompson

60 Thompson St between Broome and Spring Sts (1-212-431-0400/1-877-431-0400/www.60thompson. com). Subway: C, E to Spring St. **Rates** *$370–$450 single/double; $520–$630 suite; $3,500 penthouse suite. 100 rooms.* **Credit** *AmEx, DC, Disc, MC, V.*
Still Soho's newest boutique hotel, 60 Thompson has been luring fashionable jet-setters since it opened four years ago. Designed by Thomas O'Brien of Aero Studios, the modern rooms offer pampering details like pure down duvets and pillows, Philosophy toi-letries and a "shag bag" filled with fun items to get you in the mood. The hotel is often used for fashion shoots—A60, the guests-only rooftop bar, which offers commanding city views, is particularly popu-lar. The highly acclaimed restaurant Kittichai (*see p176*) serves creative Thai cuisine beside a pool filled with floating orchids. In warmer months, request a table on the sidewalk terrace.
Hotel services *CD/DVD library. Cell-phone rental. Laptop computer on request. Valet.*
Room services *CD/DVD player. Complimentary newspaper. High-speed Internet. Microwave oven on request. Plasma TV.*

Soho House

29–35 Ninth Ave between 13th and 14th Sts (1-212-627-9800/www.sohohouse.com). Subway: A, C, E to 14th St; L to Eighth Ave. **Rates** *$350–$495 standard/deluxe; $650–$985 suite. 24 rooms.* **Credit** *AmEx, DC, Disc, MC, V.*

Become a celebrity (or at least live like one) by booking a room at the hotel inside this private club. The New York sibling of the original Soho House in London grants common folk access to 24 mod-château rooms, ranging from the moderate-size Playpen to the humongous Playground. All pack in a mother lode of style, thanks to Ilse Crawford's knack for mixing supermodern furniture (like huge, freestanding Boffi tubs) with antiques. A wall of drawers stands in for a minibar; inside, you'll find all things sexy—champagne, Ben & Jerry's ice cream, and a copy of the *Kama Sutra*. Hotel guests can also roam freely about the rest of the club's six floors, exploring the rooftop pool, the restaurant, multiple bars, the library and the spa.
Hotel services *Butler. CD/DVD library. Cell-phone rental. Dry cleaning (24hrs). Fitness center. Game room. Screening room. Spa. Swimming pool. Valet.* **Room services** *CD/DVD player. High-speed wireless Internet. Plasma or LCD TV. Refrigerator. Room service (24hrs).*

Expensive ($200 to $350)

Hotel on Rivington

107 Rivington St between Essex and Ludlow Sts (1-212-475-2600/www.hotelonrivington.com). Subway: F to Delancey St; J, M, Z to Delancey–Essex Sts. **Rates** *From $265 single/double; call or visit website for more rates. 110 rooms.* **Credit** *AmEx, Disc, MC, V.*

Hotel on Rivington has an awfully long history for a place that's not even open yet (at press time, it was scheduled to be fully operational in early 2005). Downtown developer Paul Stallings began construction on the 20-story, tiered glass structure five years ago, first dubbing it the Surface Hotel, then Downtown, before finally settling on the Hotel on Rivington. Every single one of the 110 glass-wrapped, India Mahdavi–designed rooms has an unobstructed city view. Guests are also promised 24-hour room service, a lobby-level gift shop stocked with high-design furniture and accessories, two invitation-only lounges (on the main and seventh floors), and a 5,000-square-foot bar-restaurant piloted by Wallsé chef Kurt Gutenbrunner. Minifridges hold single-serving cans of Sofia (as in Coppola) champagne, and wood-paneled drawers hide binoculars and an "intimacy kit" stocked with surprises from nearby Toys in Babeland (*see p251*).
Hotel services *Complimentary breakfast. Dry cleaning (24hrs). Fitness center. Gift shop. Valet.* **Room services** *CD player. DVD library. Flat-panel TV. High-speed wireless Internet. Room service (24hrs).*

The Inn at Irving Place

56 Irving Pl between 17th and 18th Sts (1-212-533-4600/1-800-685-1447/www.innatirving.com).

Subway: L, N, Q, R, W, 4, 5, 6 to 14th St–Union Sq. **Rates** *$325–$415 standard/deluxe; $475–$495 junior suite. 12 rooms.* **Credit** *AmEx, DC, Disc, MC, V.*

Edith Wharton would feel right at home in this 19th-century Victorian inn, housed in a pair of brownstones near Gramercy Park. The Inn is one of Manhattan's smallest hotels—and one of its most endearing. Fresh flowers are everywhere, and antique furnishings hark back to a bygone era. While some rooms are petite, each is decorated with turn-of-the-century elegance. But leave the little ones at home (children under 12 are not permitted). Bathrooms are stocked with Penhaligon's products (the same kind Prince Charles uses). At Lady Mendl's (1-212-533-4466, reservations required), the inn's pretty tearoom, damask love seats and a lavish tea-and-dessert menu create a perfect spot for brushing up on your manners. Ms. Wharton would approve.
Hotel services *Complimentary breakfast. Dry cleaning (24hrs). Ticket desk.* **Room services** *CD player. Digital cable. High-speed Internet. Room service (24hrs). VCR.*

The Maritime Hotel

363 W 16th St between Eighth and Ninth Aves (1-212-242-4300/www.themaritimehotel.com). Subway: A, C, E to 14th St; L to Eighth Ave. **Rates** *$265–$285 single/double; $650–$1,350 suite. 125 rooms.* **Credit** *AmEx, DC, Disc, MC, V.*

In 2002, architects of cool Eric Goode and Sean MacPherson (Bowery Bar, the Park) and developers Richard Born and Ira Drukier (the Mercer and Chambers hotels) created the high-gloss Maritime—part luxury yacht, part chic '60s airport lounge. The lobby is adorned with jellyfish-inspired chandeliers and murals of seaports. Modeled after ship cabins, quarters feature large porthole windows and glossy wood paneling. The hotel offers four food-and-drink spaces: Matsuri, a gorgeous Japanese restaurant; La Bottega (*see p187*), an Italian trattoria with a lantern-festooned patio; Cabana, an airy rooftop bar; and Hiro, a basement lounge that draws a buzzing crowd.
Hotel services *Complimentary pass to New York Sports Club. Discount parking and valet service. DVD library. Fitness center. Pet-friendly.* **Room services** *CD player. Complimentary in-room movies. DVD player. Flat-panel TV. High-speed wireless Internet. Room service (24hrs). Two-line telephone.*

The Ritz-Carlton New York, Battery Park

2 West St at Battery Pl (1-212-344-0800/www.ritzcarlton.com). Subway: 4, 5 to Bowling Green. **Rates** *$329–$560 single/double; $750–$4,500 suite. 298 rooms.* **Credit** *AmEx, DC, Disc, MC, V.*

For review, *see p64* **The Ritz-Carlton New York, Central Park**.

SoHo Grand Hotel

310 West Broadway between Canal and Grand Sts (1-212-965-3000/1-800-965-3000/www.soho grand.com). Subway: A, C, E, 1, 9 to Canal St.

Rates *$259–$499 single/double; $1,699–$3,500 suite. 366 rooms.* **Credit** *AmEx, DC, Disc, MC, V.*
The Grand makes good use of industrial materials like poured concrete, cast iron and bottle glass. The Bill Sofield–designed rooms, which include two spacious penthouses, use a restrained palette of grays and beiges, and photos from local galleries hang on the walls. Sip cocktails in the Grand Bar and Lounge, or dine on haute macaroni and cheese in the Gallery.
Hotel services *Beauty salon. Cell-phone rental. Dry cleaning (24hrs). Fitness center. Pet-friendly. Ticket desk. Valet. Video library.* **Room services** *CD player. High-speed Internet. Plasma TV. VCR.*
Other location *Tribeca Grand Hotel, 2 Sixth Ave between Walker and White Sts (1-877-519-6600).*

Wall Street District Hotel
15 Gold St at Platt St (1-212-232-7700/ www.wallstreetdistricthotel.com). Subway: A, C to Broadway–Nassau St; J, M, Z, 2, 3, 4, 5 to Fulton St. **Rates** *$199–$249 single/double; $299–$379 suite. 138 rooms.* **Credit** *AmEx, DC, Disc, MC, V.*
This small business-oriented hotel nicely fuses comfort with tech-savvy amenities like automated check-in kiosks and "cellular connectivity," or private phone lines that forward calls to a guest's cell phone. For just $25 more, you can upgrade to a deluxe room with higher-tech amenities (PCs with free Internet, white-noise machines); things to help prepare you for the big meeting (shoe shiner, trouser presser, complimentary breakfast); and a few low-tech mood lifters (gummy bears!). The hotel's restaurant and bar, San Marino Ristorante, serves casual Italian cuisine.
Hotel services *Business center. CD, periodical and video-game library. Dry cleaning (24hrs). Fitness center. Pet-friendly.* **Room services** *CD player. Complimentary newspaper. Laptop-computer rental. Room service (24hrs). VCR on request. Web TV.*

W New York–Union Square
201 Park Ave South at 17th St (1-212-253-9119/ www.whotels.com). Subway: L, N, Q, R, W, 4, 5, 6 to 14th St–Union Sq. **Rates** *$249–$549 single/double; $599–$1,800 suite. 270 rooms.* **Credit** *AmEx, DC, Disc, MC, V.*
For review, *see p56* **W New York–Times Square**.

Moderate ($100 to $200)

Abingdon Guest House
13 Eighth Ave between Jane and W 12th Sts (1-212-243-5384/www.abingdonhouse.com). Subway: A, C, E to 14th St; L to Eighth Ave. **Rates** *$149–$199 single/double; $229–$239 suite. 9 rooms.* **Credit** *AmEx, DC, Disc, MC, V.*
If you want to stay near the Meatpacking District but can't afford the Gansevoort, this charm-saturated inn is a good option. Named for nearby Abingdon Square park, the nine-room townhouse offers European ambience for a reasonable price. Each themed room is painted a different color and is appointed with plush fabrics; all have private

baths. The popular Brewbar Coffee doubles as a check-in desk and café, and you can sip your latte in the trellised garden out back.
Hotel services *Coffeebar.* **Room services** *Direct-dial phone numbers. Free local phone service. High-speed wireless Internet. VCR in some rooms.*

Chelsea Hotel
222 W 23rd St between Seventh and Eighth Aves (1-212-243-3700/www.hotelchelsea.com). Subway: C, E, 1, 9 to 23rd St. **Rates** *$110–$135 single/double with shared bath; $165–$185 single/double with private bath; $225 double studio; $325–$785 suite. 400 rooms.* **Credit** *AmEx, DC, Disc, MC, V.*
This funky hotel has a long (and infamous) past: Nancy Spungeon was murdered in Room 100 by Sex Pistol Sid Vicious. Built in 1884, the Chelsea has seen an endless parade of noteworthy guests: In 1912, *Titanic* survivors stayed here; other former residents include Mark Twain, Dee Dee Ramone, Thomas Wolfe and Madonna. Rooms are generally large with high ceilings, but certain amenities like flat-screen TVs, washer-dryers and marble fireplaces vary. The lobby doubles as an art gallery, and the basement cocktail lounge, Serena (1-212-255-4646), draws a stylin' crowd with nightly DJs.
Hotel services *Beauty salon. Concierge. Fitness center. Pet-friendly. Valet.* **Room services** *Fireplace, flat-panel TV, and kitchenette or refrigerator in some rooms. High-speed wireless Internet. Washer-dryer in some rooms.*

Cosmopolitan
95 West Broadway at Chambers St (1-212-566-1900/ 1-888-895-9400/www.cosmohotel.com). Subway: A, C, 1, 2, 3, 9 to Chambers St. **Rates** *$119–$169 single/ double. 115 rooms.* **Credit** *AmEx, DC, MC, V.*
Don't be fooled by the name of this small but well-maintained hotel—you won't find any trendy pink cocktails here, or even a bar to drink them in. The immaculate hotel is geared toward budget travelers with little need for luxury. Open continuously since the 1850s, it remains a tourist favorite for its Tribeca address and affordable rates. Minilofts—multilevel rooms with sleeping lofts—start at $119.
Hotel services *Discount parking.*
Room services *Smoking permitted in all rooms.*

The Wall Street Inn
9 South William St at Broad St (1-212-747-1500/ www.thewallstreetinn.com). Subway: 2, 3 to Wall St; 4, 5 to Bowling Green. **Rates** *$169–$450 single/double. Call for corporate and weekend rates. 46 rooms.* **Credit** *AmEx, DC, Disc, MC, V.*
In 1998, this boutique hotel started a trend by reincarnating an 1830s Lehman Brothers Bank building. Now the formerly sleepy landmark district is sprouting new patisseries, bars and restaurants along its cobblestone streets. Accommodations, all with marble baths, are tastefully appointed. To reach beyond financiers, the hotel offers hefty discounts on weekends. There's no restaurant or room service, but breakfast is included.

Hotel services *Cell-phone rental. Complimentary breakfast. Fitness center. Video library.*
Room services *Complimentary newspaper. Refrigerator. Two-line phone. High-speed wireless Internet. VCR.*

Washington Square Hotel

103 Waverly Pl between MacDougal St and Sixth Ave (1-212-777-9515/1-800-222-0418/www.washington squarehotel.com). Subway: A, C, E, B, D, F, V to W 4th St. **Rates** *$141–$194 single/double; $204–$210 quad. 165 rooms.* **Credit** *AmEx, MC, V.*
Bob Dylan and Joan Baez lived in this Greenwich Village hotel, back when they sang for change in nearby Washington Square Park. Today, the century-old hotel remains popular with travelers aiming to soak up Village life. Recent renovations include a refurbished lobby and the addition of a cozy bar-lounge that serves afternoon tea and light fare. The small rooms are currently being expanded into larger deluxe chambers with Art Deco furnishings and leather headboards. Rates include a complimentary Continental breakfast—or you can splurge on the Sunday jazz brunch at North Square (1-212-254-1200), the hotel's restaurant.
Hotel services *Complimentary breakfast. Fitness center. High-speed wireless Internet. Massage service.*
Room services *Complimentary newspaper. High-speed Internet in some rooms.*

Budget (less than $100)

Chelsea Lodge

318 W 20th St between Eighth and Ninth Aves (1-212-243-4499/www.chelsealodge.com). Subway: C, E to 23rd St. **Rates** *$90–$105 single/double with shared bath; $135–$150 deluxe with private bath; $195–$225 suite with private bath (each additional person $15; maximum 4 people). 26 rooms.* **Credit** *AmEx, DC, Disc, MC, V.*
Looking for style without paying the big bucks? This 22-room inn is housed in a landmark brownstone, but resembles a chic log cabin inside. All rooms (including four suites down the block at 334 West 20th Street) have new beds, televisions, showers and air-conditioners. Although most are fairly small, the rooms are so aggressively charming that reservations fill up quickly. (Psst! There's no sign outside, so be sure to write down the address.)
Room services *High-speed wireless Internet. VCR and kitchenette in suites.*

Chelsea Star Hotel

300 W 30th St at Eighth Ave (1-212-244-7827/1-877-827-6969/www.starhotelny.com). Subway: A, C, E to 34th St–Penn Station. **Rates** *$30 per person in dorms; $69–$105 single/double/triple/quad with shared bath; $129–$149 double with private bath; $159–$179 suite. 30 rooms.* **Credit** *AmEx, MC, V.*
Tired of sleeping in a boring beige box? Check in to this whimsical place, where your quarters might be decked out in floor-to-ceiling red rubber (the Belle du Jour) or Japanese paper screens (the Madame Butterfly). The 16 themed rooms are on the small side

though less pricey, and lavatories are shared. A recent renovation more than doubled the hotel's size; there are now 18 superior rooms and deluxe suites with custom mahogany furnishings, flat-panel TVs and private baths. Ultracheap, shared hostel-style dorm rooms are also available.
Hotel services *Bicycle and in-line-skate rental. Internet kiosk. Laundry. Safe-deposit boxes.*
Room services *DVD, flat-panel TV and high-speed Internet in some rooms.*

East Village Bed & Coffee

110 Ave C between 7th and 8th Sts (1-212-533-4175/ www.bedandcoffee.com). Subway: F, V to Lower East Side–Second Ave; L to First Ave. **Rates** *$75–$90 single; $85–$100 double. 12 rooms.* **Credit** *AmEx, MC, V.*
This unassuming East Village walk-up hides a quaint bed-and-breakfast—without the breakfast (morning caffeine is provided). Popular with European travelers, the 12 guest rooms come with eclectic furnishings and quirky themes, such as the Black and White Room and 110 Downing Street. Shared areas include two loftlike living rooms, bathrooms and a fully equipped kitchen. In nice weather, sip your java in the private garden.
Hotel services *Digital cable. Free bicycle rental and local phone service. Garden. High-speed Internet. Kitchen. Stereo. VCR. Video library.*
Other location *Second Home on Second Avenue, 221 Second Ave between 13th and 14th Sts (1-212-677-3161/www.secondhome.citysearch.com).*

Hotel 17

225 E 17th St between Second and Third Aves (1-212-475-2845/www.hotel17ny.com). Subway: L to Third Ave; N, Q, R, W, 4, 5, 6 to 14th St–Union Sq. **Rates** *$60–$120 single/double; $75–$150 triple. 120 rooms.* **Credit** *MC, V.*
The dank, divey Hotel 17 has been used for numerous magazine shoots—it has the perfect grungy cachet for modeling a $600 pair of Louis Vuitton stilettos. The hotel was partially renovated in 2003, which spruced up the lobby and covered exposed pipes. Labyrinthine corridors lead to tiny high-ceilinged rooms filled with discarded dressers and mismatched 1950s wallpaper. Expect to share the hallway bathroom with other guests. The affiliated Hotel 31 (*see p61*) has even less ambience, but it suffices as a Gramercy budget hotel.
Room services *VCR in some rooms.*

Larchmont Hotel

27 W 11th St between Fifth and Sixth Aves (1-212-989-9333/www.larchmonthotel.com). Subway: F, V to 14th St; L to Sixth Ave. **Rates** *$70–$95 single; $90–$115 double; $109–$125 queen. 60 rooms.* **Credit** *AmEx, DC, Disc, MC, V.*
Housed in a 1910 Beaux Arts building, the attractive, affordable Larchmont Hotel may be the best value in the heart of Greenwich Village. The decor (wicker furniture, floral bedspreads) recalls the set of *The Golden Girls*, but with prices this reasonable, you can accept low marks for style. All baths are shared, but your

room comes equipped with a washbasin, a robe and a pair of slippers.

Hotel services *Complimentary breakfast. Kitchenette on some floors.* **Room services** *Digital TV.*

Off-Soho Suites Hotel

11 Rivington St between Bowery and Chrystie St (1-212-979-9808/1-800-633-7646/www.offsoho.com). Subway: B, D to Grand St; F, V to Lower East Side– Second Ave; J, M, Z to Bowery. **Rates** *$79–$109 2-person suite with shared bath; $139–$209 4-person suite with private bath. 38 rooms.* **Credit** *AmEx, MC, V.*

These no-frill suites are a good value for the thriving Lower East Side (a couple of blocks from—not in— Soho). Rooms are bland but spacious, and have fully equipped kitchens. The reclusive-hipster destination restaurant Freemans (*see p171*) is hidden at the end of the alley across the street.

Hotel services *Café. Fitness room. High-speed wireless Internet. Pet-friendly.* **Room services** *Digital TV. Kitchen.*

Union Square Inn

209 E 14th St between Second and Third Aves (1-212-614-0500/www.nyinns.com). Subway: L to Third Ave; N, Q, R, W, 4, 5, 6 to 14th St–Union Sq. **Rates** *$89–$149 single/double. 45 rooms.* **Credit** *AmEx, MC, V.*

For review, *see p61* **Murray Hill Inn**.

Hostels

Bowery's Whitehouse Hotel of New York

340 Bowery between 2nd and 3rd Sts (1-212-477-5623/www.whitehousehotelofny.com). Subway: B, D, F, V to Broadway–Lafayette St; 6 to Bleecker St. **Rates** *$28–$57 single/double; $71–$81 triple. 220 rooms.* **Credit** *AmEx, Disc, MC, V.*

Even though the formerly seedy avenue known as the Bowery has seen pricey restaurants and flashy clubs pop up in recent years, the unapologetically second-rate Whitehouse Hotel is here to stay. Built in 1919 as housing for railroad workers, the renovated hotel offers semiprivate cubicles (ceilings are an open latticework, so snorers or sleep talkers may interrupt your slumber) at unbelievably low rates. Towels and linens are provided. A microwave and large-screen TV are available in the lounge at all times.

Hostel services *Concierge. DVD player, Internet and TV in lobby. DVD library. Fax. Luggage storage. Safe-deposit boxes. Self-serve laundry. TV in some rooms.*

Midtown

Deluxe ($350 and up)

The Alex

205 E 45th St between Second and Third Aves (1-212-867-5100/www.thealexhotel.com). Subway: 42nd St S, 4, 5, 6, 7 to 42nd St–Grand Central.

Rates *$375–$500 single/double; $400–$700 studio/ 1-bedroom; $1,000–$3,000 suite. 203 rooms.* **Credit** *AmEx, Disc, MC, V.*

This David Rockwell–designed hotel has a Zen theme: bamboo walls in the lobby, exotic Asian flowers scattered throughout the rooms, and built-in monitors displaying photos of rivers, rocks and leaves. The hotel keeps "preference profiles" on its guests, tracking everything from favorite ice-cream flavors to workout routines. Two thirds of the rooms are suites that feature full kitchens with Miele dishwashers and Sub-Zero refrigerators stocked with goodies from Dean & DeLuca. There's even an LCD TV in the bathroom, where you can lather up in a limestone tub with Frédéric Fekkai bath products. Riingo, Marcus Samuelsson's eclectic Japanese restaurant, provides room service ("breakfast" can mean pancakes with syrup, or miso soup and smoked salmon).

Hotel services *Cell-phone rental. Fitness center.* **Room services** *DVD player. Flat-screen TV. High-speed wireless Internet. Kitchen in some rooms. Room service (24hrs).*

The Benjamin

125 E 50th St at Lexington Ave (1-212-715-2500/ 1-888-423-6526/www.thebenjamin.com). Subway: E, V to Lexington Ave–53rd St; 6 to 51st St. **Rates** *$459–$529 single/double; $499–$659 suite. 209 rooms.* **Credit** *AmEx, DC, Disc, MC, V.*

You can get some serious shut-eye at this slumber-centric executive-suite hotel. A sleep concierge is on hand to help you choose from a customized "pillow menu" of 11 types, with fillings ranging from buckwheat hulls to water. Fido will sleep soundly too— the Benjamin is not only pet-friendly but completely pet-pampering. For an additional fee, four-legged friends can enjoy a selection of gourmet treats, a session with a pet psychic or an excursion in a pet taxi. The landmark building once housed the Hotel Beverly, which Georgia O'Keeffe painted from her apartment across the street.

Hotel services *Cell-phone rental. Fitness center. Pet-friendly. Spa.* **Room services** *Complimentary newspaper. Cordless phone. High-speed wireless Internet. Kitchenette.*

Four Seasons Hotel

57 E 57th St between Madison and Park Aves (1-212-758-5700/1-800-332-3442/www.fourseasons.com). Subway: N, R, W to Lexington Ave–59th St; 4, 5, 6 to 59th St. **Rates** *$455–$895 single/double; $1,550– $11,000 suite. 368 rooms.* **Credit** *AmEx, DC, Disc, MC, V.*

Everybody who's anybody—from music-industry executives to political figures—has stayed at this quintessentially New York luxury hotel. Renowned architect I.M. Pei's sharp geometric design (in neutral cream and honey tones) is sleek and modern, and rooms are among the largest in the city (the three-bedroom Royal Suite measures 2,000 square feet). From the higher floors, the views of the city are superb. In 2004, the hotel spa was renovated and now features high-tech

"spa-ology." The hotel is known for catering to a guest's every need; your 4am hot-fudge sundae is only a room-service call away.
Hotel services *Dry cleaning (24hrs). Fitness center. Gift shop. Spa.* **Room services** *CD/DVD library. Flat-panel TV. High-speed Internet. VCR in suites.*

The Muse

130 W 46th St between Sixth and Seventh Aves (1-212-485-2400/www.themusehotel.com). Subway: B, D, F, V to 47–50th Sts–Rockefeller Ctr. **Rates** *$379–$469 single/double; $509–$599 suite. 200 rooms.* **Credit** *AmEx, DC, Disc, MC, V.*
Pampering is the purpose at the Muse: Rooms are equipped with puffy feather beds, Modern Organic Products toiletries and in-room spa treatments. District (1-212-485-2999) is perfect for pretheater

The best Extras

These are the best hotels…

…for certified chocoholics
Indulge your sweet tooth at the lavish chocolate-themed Sunday brunch at Seppi's, in **Le Parker Meridien** (see p54).

…for relearning the Dewey decimal system
From erotic literature to astronomy and zoology, rooms at the **Library Hotel** (see p54) are organized and decorated according to the classic librarian's cataloging method.

…for time travel
Inside the **Inn at Irving Place** (see p43), elegant furnishings and antiques lend the feel of high society circa 1900—but with modern conveniences.

…for your own luxury pad in Soho
Designer Bill Sofield revamped the penthouse suites at the **SoHo Grand Hotel** (see p43) to lend the feel of a funky artist's loft—er, a *very successful* artist's loft.

…for a bit of Brit
Try the British Invasion package at the **Blakely New York** (see p51): English tea, biscuits, and CDs and DVDs from across the pond.

…for a touch of summer in winter
The rooftop bar at **Hotel Gansevoort** (see p41) is glassed in during the chilly months. Or soak up the warmth in one of the heated cabanas at the hotel's ground-floor restaurant, Ono.

eats, sending off diners with intermission goodie bags that includes candy and other treats.
Hotel services *Cell-phone rental. Fitness center. Valet.* **Room services** *CD player. High-speed wireless Internet. VCR on request.*

70 Park Avenue

70 Park Ave at 38th St (1-212-973-2400/www.70 parkavenuehotel.com). Subway: 42nd St S, 4, 5, 6, 7 to 42nd St–Grand Central. **Rates** *$375–$469 superior/deluxe; $465–$2,500 suite. 205 rooms.* **Credit** *AmEx, DC, Disc, MC, V.*
A $19 million renovation by designer Jeffrey Bilhuber has transformed the dingy Doral Park Avenue Hotel into an organic-modern oasis worthy of a spread in *Dwell.* Rooms, though small, are cleverly mirrored and accoutred in rich walnut and chocolate hues. High-tech amenities include 42-inch flat-screen TVs equipped with Nintendo 64 and a yoga channel (mats are available), and KioPhones from which guests can send e-mail, surf the Web or place room-service orders. Deep bathtubs and eucalyptus-scented Thymes Limited grooming products turn the lav into a minispa. The Silverleaf Tavern provides an around-the-clock room-service menu of creative American dishes, like duck rigatoni and short-rib knishes.
Hotel services *Complimentary wine every evening. Library. Pet-friendly. Valet.* **Room services** *CD/ DVD player. Complimentary newspaper. Flat-panel TV. High-speed wireless Internet. KioPhone. Nintendo. Room service (24hrs).*

St. Regis

2 E 55th St at Fifth Ave (1-212-753-4500/ www.stregis.com). Subway: E, V to Fifth Ave–53rd St. **Rates** *$695–$820 superior/deluxe; $1,150–$11,500 suite. 315 rooms.* **Credit** *AmEx, DC, Disc, MC, V.*
Fifth Avenue frippery at its best: In a 1904 Beaux Arts landmark building, the opulent St. Regis is adorned with ornate gold crown moldings, Louis XVI–style furniture, crystal chandeliers, marble baths, lavish rooms and silk wall coverings. Afternoon tea is served in the Astor Court, but if you need something stronger to make you merry, retire to the King Cole Bar, birthplace of the Red Snapper (a.k.a. the Bloody Mary).
Hotel services *Beauty salon. Car rental. Cell-phone rental. Fitness center. Florist. Gift shop. Spa. Ticket desk. Valet. Video library.* **Room services** *CD player. High-speed Internet. Nintendo and PlayStation on request. Room service (24hrs).*

Expensive ($200 to $350)

The Algonquin

59 W 44th St between Fifth and Sixth Aves (1-212-840-6800/1-800-555-8000/www.thealgonquin.net). Subway: B, D, F, V to 42nd St–Bryant Park; 7 to Fifth Ave. **Rates** *$200–$299 single/double; $299–$549 suite. 174 rooms.* **Credit** *AmEx, DC, Disc, MC, V.*
Literary greats like Alexander Woollcott and Dorothy Parker gathered in the lobby and the Round Table Room of this venerable hotel to gossip,

spar and change the world. Beautifully carved and upholstered chairs, old lamps, and large paintings of important figures of the 1920s and '30s uphold the hotel's Jazz Age splendor. The hallways are covered with *New Yorker*–cartoon wallpaper to commemorate Harold Ross, who secured funding for the magazine over long meetings at the Round Table. Quarters are on the small side and the decor is a bit dated, but the feel is still classic New York. Catch readings by local authors on some Mondays; cabaret performers take over in the Oak Room (*see p277*) Tuesday through Saturday.

Hotel services *Fitness center (24hrs). Ticket desk.*
Room services *CD player and VCR in suites. Complimentary magazines and newspapers. High-speed wireless Internet. Refrigerator in suites or on request.*

The Blakely New York

136 W 55th St between Sixth and Seventh Aves (1-212-245-1800/www.blakelynewyork.com). Subway: F, N, Q, R, W to 57th St. **Rates** *$245–$285 single/double; $325–$425 suite. 120 rooms.* **Credit** *AmEx, DC, Disc, MC, V.*

In the spring of 2004, the designers of superhip hotels the Maritime and the Mercer transformed the former Gorham Hotel into a slightly more traditional place, favoring comfort over style. Trimmed in oak and appointed with cherrywood furniture and paintings of fox hunts, the rooms recall an old English manor (or a Ralph Lauren catalog). Handsome marble bathrooms—some equipped with deep Jacuzzi tubs—are stocked with Frette robes and toiletries from Brit line Penhaligon's. There's no on-site spa, but massage therapists from chic mobile spa service Cortiva are on call 24/7 to provide in-room rubdowns. Abboccato, an Italian eatery from the owners of Molyvos, draws an upscale crowd.

Hotel services *Dry cleaning (24hrs). Mobile spa.*
Room services *CD/DVD player. Complimentary newspapers. Flat-panel TV. High-speed wireless Internet. Kitchenette. Video library.*

The Bryant Park Hotel

40 W 40th St between Fifth and Sixth Aves (1-212-642-2200/www.bryantparkhotel.com). Subway: B, D, F, V to 42nd St–Bryant Park; 7 to Fifth Ave. **Rates** *$265–$395 single/double; $395–$615 suite. 128 rooms.* **Credit** *AmEx, DC, MC, V.*

Former Ian Schrager partner Philip Pilevsky converted the 1924 American Radiator Building into his first New York property. And thanks to the hotel's close proximity to Bryant Park, a well-heeled clientele checks in each year during Fashion Week. The lobby, decked out with gorgeous red-tiled walls and mod white lamps, is the best part; the rather stark rooms look as if they were furnished from the West Elm catalog. At press time, a new Chinese restaurant was in the works (from Japanese chef Yuji Wakiya). Head downstairs for a cocktail in the vaulted Cellar Bar. Hidden beneath the lounge is a 70-seat screening room with red velour chairs and built-in desks.

Hotel services *Beauty salon. Fitness center. Screening room. Spa. Valet.* **Room services** *CD*

The Algonquin. *See p50.*

player. Digital movies on demand. High-speed Internet. Room service (24hrs). VCR.

Chambers

15 W 56th St between Fifth and Sixth Aves (1-212-974-5656/www.chambershotel.com). Subway: F to 57th St; N, R, W to Fifth Ave–59th St. **Rates** *$315–$400 single; $350–$400 double; $475–$500 studio; $650–$1,600 suite. 77 rooms.* **Credit** *AmEx, DC, Disc, MC, V.*

The style-saturated Chambers is as close as you're going to get to Soho in midtown. Developers Ira Drukier and Richard Born (of the Maritime and the Mercer) turned a parking garage into an industrial-chic hotel. David Rockwell–designed guest rooms resemble artists' lofts, with original artwork, brushed cement floors, oversize windows, stainless-steel track lighting, and funky glass desks with waxed paper and colored pencils for doodling. Area duvets, Japanese-style soaking tubs, Bumble and bumble bath products, Mario Badescu spa services and personal shopping by Henri Bendel complete the luxurious wallow. You'll find equally engaging creations of the culinary variety at the hotel's restaurant, Town (1-212-582-4445).

Sip cocktails and dream the impossible at the new **Dream Hotel**.

Hotel services *CD/DVD library. Complimentary pass to New York Sports Club. Computer rental. Personal shopping. Pet-friendly. Valet.* **Room services** *Cordless phone. High-speed Internet.*

Dream Hotel

210 W 55th St between Broadway and Seventh Ave (1-212-247-2000/1-866-437-3266/www.dreamny. com). Subway: N, Q, R, W to 57th St. **Rates** *$275–$575 single/double; $509–$5,000 suite. 228 rooms.* **Credit** *AmEx, Disc, MC, Visa.*

This year, hotelier Vikram Chatwal, who also brought us the Time Hotel, enlisted boldfaced names to turn the old Majestic Hotel into a luxury lodge with a trippy slumberland theme. David Rockwell dressed up the restaurant, an outpost of Serafina; spirituality maven Deepak Chopra conceived the ayurvedic spa; and Jed Leiber, who has produced albums for U2, owns the main-level recording studio. The lobby sums up the resulting aesthetic—walls are cloaked in Paul Smith–style stripes, a crystal boat dangles from the ceiling, and an enormous gold statue of Catherine the Great stands guard. Every room is lit by an ethereal blue glow and contains a feather-duvet-topped bed with a blue satin headboard; a washroom outfitted with Molton Brown products; a 37- or 42-inch Panasonic plasma TV with movies on demand; and an iPod, loaded with ambient music, connected to Bose speakers. Ava, the rooftop bar, offers panoramic views of the city.
Hotel services *Cell-phone rental. Complimentary breakfast. Dry cleaning (24 hrs). Fitness center. Flat-panel TV. Pet-friendly. Spa.* **Room services** *CD/DVD player on request. High-speed Internet. iPod. Movies on demand.*

Dylan

52 E 41st St between Madison and Park Aves (1-212-338-0500/1-800-553-9526/www.dylanhotel.com). Subway: 42nd St S, 4, 5, 6, 7 to 42nd St–Grand Central. **Rates** *$249–$549 single/double; $495–$1,200 suite. 107 rooms.* **Credit** *AmEx, DC, Disc, MC, V.*

If you ever fantasized about your eighth-grade chemistry teacher, then you'll love this breathtaking boutique hotel, fashioned out of the once crumbling 1903 landmark Chemist Club building. The lobby has a grand marble staircase, fluted columns and beautifully ornate moldings. Most rooms are flooded with natural light and have 11-foot ceilings and modern, dark-walnut furnishings. Washrooms sport basin-style bowl sinks, and beakers stand in for water glasses. The stunning Gothic Alchemy Suite, modeled after a medieval alchemist's lab, has soaring vaulted ceilings, leaded floor-to-ceiling windows and a spacious outdoor terrace.
Hotel services *Fitness center. Ticket desk. Valet.* **Room services** *CD player and VCR on request. Complimentary newspaper. High-speed Internet.*

Flatotel

135 W 52nd St between Sixth and Seventh Aves (1-212-887-9400/www.flatotel.com). Subway: N, R, W to 49th St; 1, 9 to 50th St. **Rates** *$249–$349 single/double; $499–$1,800 suite. 288 rooms.* **Credit** *AmEx, DC, MC, V.*

A slew of reality-TV shows, including *America's Next Top Model*, have been filmed at this contemporary hotel, which has suites large enough for an entire camera crew. Upon entrance, the Flatotel looks promising: Techno beats pump through the granite lobby, and dimly lit nooks and cowhide-and-leather couches are filled with cocktailers. But that's where the sleek stops—the rooms are far more basic, although still modern and roomy. A fitness center on the 46th floor offers striking city views. Moda (1-212-887-9880) serves Italian-inspired fare; in temperate weather, catch a breeze when you sip Bacardi in the restaurant's alfresco atrium. For private imbibing, just call the martini butler, who will mix the drink right in your room and present it on a silver tray. **Hotel services** *Cell-phone rental. Complimentary breakfast. Fitness center. Gift shop. Spa. Valet.* **Room services** *CD player. High-speed Internet. VCR.*

Hotel Elysée

60 E 54th St between Madison and Park Aves (1-212-753-1066/www.elyseehotel.com). Subway: E, V to Lexington Ave–53rd St; 6 to 51st St. **Rates** *$285–$395 single/double; $525 suite. 101 rooms.* **Credit** *AmEx, DC, Disc, MC, V.*
Built in the '20s, the Hotel Elysée is a well-preserved piece of New York's Jazz Age. Quarters are furnished with a touch of romance (period fabrics, antique furniture), and some rooms have colored-glass conservatories and terraces. Elysée is popular with publishers and literary types, who convene over complimentary wine and cheese in the evening. Downstairs is the Steakhouse at Monkey Bar (1-212-838-2600), where a well-coiffed clientele dines on fine cuts. For sister hotels, see Casablanca Hotel, the Library Hotel and the ultramod newcomer Hotel Gansevoort (*see p57, p54 and p41*).
Hotel services *Complimentary breakfast and pass to nearby gym. Valet. Video library.* **Room services** *CD player in suites. High-speed wireless Internet. VCR.*

Hotel Roger Williams

131 Madison Ave at 31st St (1-212-448-7000/1-888-448-7788/www.rogerwilliamshotel.com). Subway: 6 to 33rd St. **Rates** *$255–$340 single/double; $325–$450 suite. 191 rooms.* **Credit** *AmEx, DC, Disc, MC, V.*
This small, stylish hotel was recently acquired by the Oceana Hotel Group and then got a $5 million renovation that brought in a vibrant color palette of greens and bright tangerine. The soaring lobby has floor-to-ceiling windows, plenty of textured wood and a grand piano. Room amenities, such as bottled water, Aveda bath products and a modern office area, feel like home—if you're lucky enough to live like this. Each room on the penthouse level has access to a shared wraparound terrace. Lounge at the Roger, the hotel's new restaurant and bar, serves light fare and cocktails as well as around-the-clock room service.
Hotel services *CD library. Cell-phone rental. Complimentary newspapers and magazines. Fitness center. Valet.* **Room services** *High-speed wireless Internet. Plasma TV.*

The Iroquois

49 W 44th St between Fifth and Sixth Aves (1-212-840-3080/1-800-332-7220/www.iroquoisny.com). Subway: B, D, F, V to 42nd St–Bryant Park; 7 to Fifth Ave. **Rates** *$219–$425 single/double; $349–$849 suite. 114 rooms.* **Credit** *AmEx, DC, Disc, MC, V.*

The Iroquois is what you might find if you were to walk into a posh doorman building on the Upper East Side. A polished-stone lobby, a mahogany-paneled library, and rooms that are spacious and elegant (though a bit dingy) are the result of a massive renovation that morphed a former hostel into a full-service luxury hotel. Nine suites include additional treats like decorative fireplaces, Jacuzzis and Frette bathrobes. The James Dean Suite (No. 803), decorated with photographs of the rebel without a cause, commemorates the actor, who lived here in the 1950s. There's also a fitness center, a sauna and a library with computer access. Contemporary French fare is served in the hotel's restaurant, Triomphe (1-212-453-4233).
Hotel services *Cell-phone rental. Dry cleaning (24hrs). Fitness center. Sauna. Ticket desk. Video library.* **Room services** *CD player. High-speed Internet. Room service (24hrs). VCR.*

The Kitano

66 Park Ave at 38th St (1-212-885-7000/1-800-548-2666/www.kitano.com). Subway: 42nd St S, 4, 5, 6, 7 to 42nd St–Grand Central. **Rates** *$250–$650 single/double; $715–$2,100 suite. 149 rooms.* **Credit** *AmEx, DC, Disc, MC, V.*

The best Services

These are the top hotels for...

...your furry friends

The Benjamin (*see p49*) features more services for pets than any other NYC hotel, covering everything from pet transportation to pet psychics.

...the spy in you

Passersby—or those living in nearby apartments—can't see into the chambers at **Hotel on Rivington** (*see p43*), but you can see them, thanks to the binoculars stashed in every room.

...your yoga obsession

70 Park Avenue (*see p50*) offers in-room mats and flat-screen TVs with complimentary yoga channels.

...the iPod you left at home

At the new **Dream Hotel** (*see p52*), every room comes with an iPod juiced up with ambient tunes and cradled in a Bose SoundDock.

...your cheap-chic style

A night in one of the ten groovy rooms at **East Village Bed & Coffee** (*see p47*) will cost you less than $100—and that includes a morning cup of java in the garden.

The first Japanese-owned hotel in New York City is also the only hotel to offer heated commodes. Rooms feature silk-covered walls, smooth stone floors, Shiseido bath products and complimentary green tea. A one-of-a-kind tatami suite boasts painted shoji screens and a separate tea-ceremony room. Dine with chopsticks at the hotel's two casual Japanese restaurants, Nadaman Hakubai (1-212-885-7111) and Garden Cafe (1-212-885-7123).
Hotel services *Complimentary pass to nearby gym. Gift shop. Laundry drop-off. Ticket desk. Valet.*
Room services *CD player in some rooms. High-speed Internet.*

Le Marquis

12 E 31st St between Fifth and Madison Aves (1-212-889-6363/www.lemarquisny.com). Subway: 6 to 33rd St. **Rates** *$225–$355 single/double; $425–$650 suite. 120 rooms.* **Credit** *AmEx, DC, Disc, MC, V.*
Rooms at this delightful hotel are style-conscious, with black-and-white photographs of New York streetscapes on the walls, blue-and-tan-checkered carpeting, and Frette robes and Aveda products in the bathroom. The in-house 12:31 bar offers cocktails and light nibbles. And turndown service at Le Marquis means a chocolate on your pillow and a next-day weather forecast.
Hotel services *DVD library. Fitness center. Valet.*
Room services *CD/DVD player. High-speed Internet.*

Le Parker Meridien

118 W 57th St between Sixth and Seventh Aves (1-212-245-5000/1-800-543-4300/www.parker meridien.com). Subway: F, N, Q, R, W to 57th St. **Rates** *$325–400 single/double; $599–$3,000 suite. 731 rooms.* **Credit** *AmEx, DC, MC, V.*
This luxury hotel is sophisticated *and* kid-friendly. Its secret is the lavish breakfast-and-lunch restaurant Norma's (1-212-708-7460), which serves grown-ups gourmet dishes such as red-berry-risotto oatmeal and banana-macadamia-nut flapjacks and provides kids' cooking classes. Quarters are more corporate than cozy, but most come with commanding views of Central Park. There's also a rooftop pool, a pampering spa, and a 15,000-square-foot, state-of-the-art gym with a tournament racquetball court and more than 60 classes a week. The cute little hamburger joint in the lobby cooks up what some consider the city's best burger. Seppi's, the hotel's bistro, is known for its chocolate-themed Sunday brunch.
Hotel services *Cell-phone rental. Complimentary shuttle to Wall Street. Fitness center. Spa.* **Room services** *DVD player. High-speed Internet.*

The Library Hotel

299 Madison Ave at 41st St (1-212-983-4500/ www.libraryhotel.com). Subway: 42nd St S, 4, 5, 6, 7 to 42nd St–Grand Central; 7 to Fifth Ave. **Rates** *$325–$385 single/double; $425 suite. 60 rooms.* **Credit** *AmEx, DC, MC, V.*
Librarians are hot.... Or at least the staff is, at this literary-themed boutique hotel. More than 6,000 books were handpicked from indie-fave bookstore the Strand to match the themes of the rooms they adorn. Even before you enter, you'll see quotes from famous authors inscribed in the sidewalk. Lodgings are organized according to the Dewey decimal system and furnished by theme (Botany, Fairy Tales). The Love Room is strewn with rose petals; Casanova's autobiography sits on a bedside table in the Erotica Room. Rates include breakfast, evening wine-and-cheese gatherings in the second-floor Reading Room, and access to the mahogany-lined writer's den (which has a tiny terrace and a glowing fireplace). Hotel Giraffe, a sister hotel, embodies modern European style 15 blocks south.
Hotel services *Cell-phone rental. Complimentary breakfast, pass to nearby gym, and wine and cheese every evening. Ticket desk. Valet. Video library.*
Room services *CD player. High-speed Internet. VCR.*
Other location *Hotel Giraffe, 365 Park Ave South at 26th St (1-212-685-7700/1-877-296-0009/ www.hotelgiraffe.com).*

Metropolitan Hotel

569 Lexington Ave at 51st St (1-212-752-7000/ 1-800-836-6471). Subway: E, V to Lexington Ave–53rd St; 6 to 51st St. **Rates** *$250–$350 single/ double; $229–$699 suite. 722 rooms.* **Credit** *AmEx, DC, Disc, MC, V.*
Unveiled in 1961 as the Summit, this Art Deco hotel was the talk of the town. Two decades later, the look was toned down to match its new identity as the Loews New York Hotel. In 2000, architect Morris Lapidus—designer of many '50s-era hotels—returned the building to its original look. This year, hospitality-industry giant Doubletree acquired the place. Thanks to a $35 million renovation, rooms are now freshly outfitted with fluffy down comforters, flat-screen TVs and original artwork. The Met Grill offers casual American cuisine, and a lobby lounge draws hip guests and local imbibers. In keeping with Doubletree tradition, everyone receives a warm chocolate-chip cookie at check-in.
Hotel services *Barbershop. Fitness center (24hrs).*
Room services *Cordless phone. High-speed Internet. LCD TV.*

The Michelangelo

152 W 51st St between Sixth and Seventh Aves (1-212-765-1900/1-800-237-0990/www.michelangelo hotel.com). Subway: N, R, W to 49th St; 1, 9 to 50th St. **Rates** *$255–$495 single/double; $595–$1,735 suite. 178 rooms.* **Credit** *AmEx, DC, Disc, MC, V.*
This lavish, Renaissance-inspired hotel is the only U.S. location of a 19-branch Italian chain. So, it's not surprising that the lobby and chambers are appointed with plenty of Italian luxuries: peach marble, Venetian fabrics, oil paintings. The sizable rooms are accoutred in styles ranging from French country to Art Deco, and each contains two TVs and a large soaking tub. Complimentary breakfast includes Italian coffees and pastries. Fully equipped apartments are available for extended stays ($4,000 to $9,000 per month).

Get in a New York state of mind on the terrace of the **Hotel Roger Williams**. *See p53.*

Hotel services *Beauty salon. Cell-phone rental. Complimentary breakfast every day and limousine service to Wall Street (Mon–Fri). Dry cleaning (24hrs). Fitness center (24hrs). Valet.* **Room services** *CD player. Complimentary newspaper and shoe shine. DVD player, laptop computer and VCR on request. High-speed Internet.*

New York Palace

455 Madison Ave between 50th and 51st Sts (1-212-888-7000/1-800-697-2522/www.newyorkpalace.com). Subway: E, V to Fifth Ave–53rd St. **Rates** *$295–$720 single/double; $900–$12,000 suite. 896 rooms.* **Credit** *AmEx, DC, Disc, MC, V.*

It's hard to believe that the Palace, complete with red carpet, twinkling lights and fancy tea parties, was once owned by real-estate tycoon (and former jailbird) Leona Helmsley. Designed by McKim, Mead & White, the cluster of mansions now holds nearly 900 rooms ornamented in the Art Deco or neoclassic style. Tower suites have a top-tier terrace, solarium and private rooftop garden. Famous restaurant Le Cirque 2000 is now closed, but you

can still sip a Manhattan in the extravagant Louis XVI–style Villard Bar and Lounge.

Hotel services *Complimentary limousine service to Wall Street and shoe shine. Dry cleaning (24hrs). Fitness center. Video library.* **Room services** *Complimentary breakfast, dessert and newspaper in suites. Dual-line phone. Room service (24hrs).*

Park South Hotel

122 E 28th St between Park Ave South and Lexington Ave (1-212-448-0888/1-800-315-4642/www.parksouthhotel.com). Subway: 6 to 28th St. **Rates** *$209–$270 single/double; $330–$350 suite. 141 rooms.* **Credit** *AmEx, DC, Disc, MC, V.*

This quaint boutique hotel encourages its guests to brush up on local history—a mezzanine library is crammed with books on historic Gotham, and the walls are covered with images from the New-York Historical Society. Rooms are appointed in warm amber and brown tones, and some have dazzling views of the Chrysler Building. Bathrooms are stocked with Essential Oil products and thick terry-cloth

The library, from the **Library Hotel**. See p54.

bathrobes. The hotel's bar-restaurant, Black Duck (1-212-204-5240), serves live jazz with brunch.
Hotel services *Complimentary breakfast and newspaper. Fitness center. Valet. Video library.*
Room services *DVD player. High-speed Internet.*

The Roger Smith

501 Lexington Ave between 47th and 48th Sts (1-212-755-1400/1-800-445-0277/www.rogersmith. com). Subway: E, V to Lexington Ave–53rd St; 6 to 51st St. **Rates** *$265–$295 single/double; $330–$450 junior suite; $275–$400 suite. 130 rooms.*
Credit *AmEx, DC, Disc, MC, V.*
The spacious chambers at this arty spot make it a good option for families. Each room is decorated with unique furnishings and colorful wallpaper. Lily's restaurant serves contemporary American cuisine in a bright space with playful murals. The Roger Smith Gallery hosts rotating exhibits, and a few pieces by artist James Knowles (whose family owns the hotel) adorn the lobby.
Hotel services *Valet. Video library.*
Room services *CD player. Coffeemaker. Free local phone service. High-speed wireless Internet. Refrigerator. VCR.*

The Time

224 W 49th St between Broadway and Eighth Ave (1-212-320-2900/1-877-846-3692/www.thetimeny. com). Subway: C, E, 1, 9 to 50th St; N, R, W to 49th
St. **Rates** *$305–$410 single/double; $630–$730 suite; $2,500–$6,000 penthouse suite. 193 rooms.*
Credit *AmEx, DC, Disc, MC, V.*
Adam Tihany designed this boutique hotel to stimulate the senses with a single primary color (guest rooms are furnished entirely in either red, yellow or blue). Expect to find matching duvets, jelly beans and reading materials, as well as a chromatically inspired scent. Continental breakfast is included, and Océo, the hotel's restaurant, offers global cuisine in a setting that changes colors throughout the evening.
Hotel services *Cell-phone rental. Fitness center. Personal shopping. Ticket desk.* **Room services** *CD player and VCR on request. High-speed Internet.*

The Waldorf-Astoria

301 Park Ave at 50th St (1-212-355-3000/1-800-924-3673/www.waldorf.com). Subway: E, V to Lexington Ave–53rd St; 6 to 51st St. **Rates** *$275–$450 single; $300–$450 double; $400–$900 suite. 1,425 rooms.*
Credit *AmEx, DC, Disc, MC, V.*
Double-check your getup before entering this grand hotel—you won't be allowed in if you're wearing a baseball cap, T-shirt or even faded jeans. First built in 1893, the Waldorf-Astoria was the city's largest hotel and the birthplace of the Waldorf salad), but it was demolished to make way for the Empire State Building. This Art Deco Waldorf opened in 1931 and now has protected status as a historic hotel. It still caters to the high-and-mighty (guests have included Princess Grace, Sophia Loren and a long list of U.S. Presidents).
Hotel services *Beauty salon. Cell-phone rental. Fitness center. Spa. Valet.* **Room services** *Complimentary newspaper. Copier/printer. High-speed Internet. Kitchenette in some suites.*

The Warwick New York Hotel

65 W 54th St at Sixth Ave (1-212-247-2700/1-800-223-4099/www.warwickhotelny.com). Subway: E, V to Fifth Ave–53rd St; F to 57th St. **Rates** *$199–$395 single/double; $425–$1,250 suite. 426 rooms.*
Credit *AmEx, DC, MC, V.*
Built by William Randolph Hearst in 1927, the Warwick is listed by the National Trust for Historic Preservation. Guests have included Elvis and the Beatles. Although a bit faded, the rooms are exceptionally large by midtown standards. The top-floor Suite of the Stars, once the home of Cary Grant, has a wraparound balcony.
Hotel services *Cell-phone rental. Fitness center. Valet.* **Room services** *High-speed wireless Internet. VCR on request.*

W New York–Times Square

1567 Broadway at 47th St (1-212-930-7400/1-877-976-8357/www.whotels.com). Subway: N, R, W to 49th St; 1, 9 to 50th St. **Rates** *$259–$339 single/double; $499–$2,500 suite. 509 rooms.* **Credit** *AmEx, DC, Disc, MC, V.*
NYC's fifth and flashiest W location has a street-level vestibule with a waterfall (reception is on the seventh floor). To your right, the Living Room is a massive sprawl of white leather seating. Every

private room features a floating-glass desk and a sleek bathroom stocked with Aveda products, but it's the bed-to-ceiling headboard mirror and sexy room-service menu that get the mind racing. Steve Hanson's Blue Fin (1-212-918-1400) serves stellar sushi and cocktails.

Hotel services *Cell-phone rental. Fitness center. Gift shop. Pet-friendly. Spa. Valet.*
Room services *CD/DVD player. High-speed wireless Internet. VCR.*
Other locations *W New York, 541 Lexington Ave at 49th St (1-212-755-1200); W New York–The Court, 130 E 39th St between Park Ave South and Lexington Ave (1-212-685-1100); W New York–The Tuscany, 120 E 39th St between Park Ave South and Lexington Ave (1-212-686-1600); W New York–Union Square, 201 Park Ave South at 17th St (1-212-253-9119).*

Moderate ($100 to $200)

Broadway Inn
264 W 46th St at Eighth Ave (1-212-997-9200/1-800-826-6300/www.broadwayinn.com). Subway: A, C, E to 42nd St–Port Authority. **Rates** *$99–$199 single/double; $199–$275 suite. 41 rooms.* **Credit** *AmEx, DC, Disc, MC, V.*
This endearing little hotel can arrange a 35 to 40 per-cent discount on theater tickets; it also offers several Broadway dinner-and-show combinations. The warm lobby has exposed-brick walls, ceiling fans and shelves loaded with bedtime reading material. The fairly priced basic guest rooms and suites get lots of natural light. On the downside: There are no elevators, and the hotel is strict about its three-night-minimum policy on weekends.
Hotel services *Complimentary breakfast.*
Room services *High-speed wireless Internet. Kitchenette in suites.*

Casablanca Hotel
147 W 43rd St between Sixth Ave and Broadway (1-212-869-1212/1-800-922-7225/www.casablanca hotel.com). Subway: B, D, F, V to 42nd St–Bryant Park; N, Q, R, W, 42nd St S, 1, 2, 3, 9, 7 to 42nd St–Times Sq. **Rates** *$189–$305 single/double; $275–$395 suite. 48 rooms.* **Credit** *AmEx, DC, MC, V.*
This Moroccan-themed boutique hotel is run by the same people who own the Library Hotel (*see p54*). The lobby is an oasis in the middle of Times Square: Walls are adorned with blue and gold Mediterranean tiles, and giant bamboo shoots stand in tall vases. The theme is diluted in the basic rooms, but wicker furniture and wooden shutters warm up the accommodations. Rick's Café serves free wine and cheese to guests Monday through

Chain gang

Many of the familiar global chains have locations in New York, and although they don't offer oodles of cachet, they do have reasonable rates and reliable amenities.

The scruffy-trendy Lower East Side may be the last place you'd expect to find a HoJo's, but the **Howard Johnson's Express Inn** (135 E Houston St between First and Second Aves, 1-212-358-8844, www.hojo.com) is clean and affordable and provides a complimentary breakfast. High-end rooms have two double beds and a Jacuzzi.

It's hard to miss the assertive 45-story tower of the **Westin New York at Times Square** (270 W 43rd St at Eighth Ave, 1-888-627-7149, www.westinny.com). The lobby boasts a soaring seven-story atrium, while rooms have flat-panel TVs and, above the 15th floor, amazing views of Times Square.

Farther north, in Hell's Kitchen, the **Holiday Inn Midtown** (440 W 57th St between Ninth and Tenth Aves, 1-800-465-4329, www.hi57. com) offers a heated outdoor pool, a fitness center and two restaurants.

If it's romance you're after, hop over the East River to downtown Brooklyn's **New York Marriott at the Brooklyn Bridge**

New York Marriott at the Brooklyn Bridge.

(333 Adams St between Tillary and Willoughby Sts, Brooklyn Heights, 1-718-246-7000, www.brooklynmarriott.com), where for an extra $99, your room can be showered with white rose petals, dotted with scented candles and furnished with bubble-bath supplies. A bottle of Aria Estate champagne completes the package.

Big bed, bright colors at **Metropolitan Hotel** in midtown. *See p54.*

Saturday. Breakfast is complimentary, as is your copy of *Casablanca*.
Hotel services *Cell-phone rental. Complimentary breakfast and pass to nearby gym. Cybercafé. Dry cleaning (24hrs). Spa. Valet. Video library.*
Room services *CD player. High-speed wireless Internet. VCR.*

City Club Hotel

55 W 44th St between Fifth and Sixth Aves (1-212-921-5500/1-888-256-4100/www.cityclubhotel.com). Subway: B, D, F, V to 42nd St–Bryant Park; 7 to Fifth Ave. **Rates** *$195–$295 single/double; $225–$495 queen/king; $895–$1,200 suite. 65 rooms.* **Credit** *AmEx, DC, MC, V.*
The City Club Hotel is pure rock star: The lobby, which doubles as a tea salon, is hidden on the second floor; the staff is outfitted by Ted Baker; old vinyl records hang on the walls; and bedside tables are inlaid with mirrors. The stylish quarters are lavished with Hermès bath products, plush window-side daybeds, Jonathan Adler ceramics and works by other NYC artists. Some rooms have trompe l'oeil televisions (a remote-control-activated TV screen fades in through a mirror on the wall). Even a burger gets rock-star treatment: Daniel Boulud's DB Bistro Moderne (*see p191*) serves the city's priciest patty, a $99 hunk of ground sirloin liberally sprinkled with truffle shavings and stuffed with red-wine-braised short-rib meat and foie gras, on a Parmesan bun.
Hotel services *CD/DVD/video library. Cell-phone rental. Complimentary access to nearby gym. Discount parking. Pet-friendly. Ticket desk. Valet.*

Room services *CD/DVD player. Cordless phone. High-speed Internet. VCR.*

414 Hotel

414 W 46th St between Ninth and Tenth Aves (1-212-399-0006/www.414hotel.com). Subway: A, C, E to 42nd St– Port Authority. **Rates** *$99–$229 single/double. 22 rooms.* **Credit** *AmEx, MC, V.*
Tucked away on the Theater District's Restaurant Row, this small hotel feels like a secret you've been lucky to stumble upon. Immaculate rooms are tastefully appointed with suede headboards, vases full of colorful roses, and framed black-and-white photos of the city. There's a glowing fireplace in the lobby and a leafy courtyard outside.
Hotel services *Complimentary breakfast.*
Room services *Refrigerator in some rooms.*

Hotel Edison

228 W 47th St at Broadway (1-212-840-5000/ 1-800-637-7070/www.edisonhotelnyc.com). Subway: N, R, W to 49th St; 1, 9 to 50th St. **Rates** *$150 single; $160 double (each additional person $15, maximum 4 people); $180–$220 suite. 1,000 rooms.* **Credit** *AmEx, DC, Disc, MC, V.*
Theater lovers flock to this newly renovated Art Deco hotel for its affordable rates and convenient location. Rooms are of a standard size but are decidedly spruced up. Cafe Edison (1-212-840-5000), a classic diner just off the lobby, is a longtime favorite of Broadway actors and their fans—Neil Simon was so smitten with the place that he put it in one of his plays.

Hotel services *Fitness center. Gift shop. Ticket desk. Valet.* **Room services** *High-speed wireless Internet.*

Hotel 41

206 W 41st St between Seventh and Eighth Aves (1-877-847-4444/www.hotel41.com). Subway: N, Q, R, W, 42nd St S, 1, 2, 3, 9, 7 to 42nd St–Times Sq. **Rates** *$139–$239 single/double; $269–$489 suite. 47 rooms.* **Credit** *AmEx, Disc, MC, V.*

Although its looks are cool, this tiny boutique hotel feels comfy-warm: Reading lamps extend from dark-wood headboards, and triple-paned windows effectively filter out the cacophony from the streets below. The penthouse suite has a large private terrace with potted trees and views of Times Square. Bar 41 serves breakfast, light bites and drinks.

Hotel services *CD/DVD library. Complimentary breakfast. Espresso bar (24 hrs). Pet-friendly. Valet.* **Room services** *CD/DVD player. High-speed Internet.*

Hotel Metro

45 W 35th St between Fifth and Sixth Aves (1-212-947-2500/1-800-356-3870/www.hotelmetronyc.com). Subway: B, D, F, V, N, Q, R, W to 34th St–Herald Sq. **Rates** *$155–$325 single/double; $190–$400 suite. 179 rooms.* **Credit** *AmEx, DC, MC, V.*

It's not posh, but the Metro has good service and a charmingly retro vibe. Black-and-white portraits of Hollywood legends adorn the lobby, and the tiny rooms are neat and clean. Take in views of the Empire State Building from the rooftop bar of Metro Grill (1-212-947-2500).

Hotel services *Beauty salon. Complimentary breakfast. Fitness center. Library. Ticket desk.* **Room services** *High-speed wireless Internet. Refrigerator.*

Hotel Pennsylvania

401 Seventh Ave between 32nd and 33rd Sts (1-212-736-5000/1-800-223-8585/www.hotelpenn.com). Subway: A, C, E, 1, 2, 3, 9 to 34th St–Penn Station. **Rates** *$129–$200 single/double; $350–$1,000 suite. 1,700 rooms.* **Credit** *AmEx, DC, Disc, MC, V.*

Built in 1919 near the Pennsylvania Station and designed by McKim, Mead & White, Hotel Pennsylvania is one of the city's largest hotels. Its reasonable rates and convenient location (directly opposite Madison Square Garden and Penn Station, and one block south of Macy's) make it a popular tourist choice. Rooms are basic but have pleasant touches. The hotel's Cafe Rouge Ballroom once hosted such swing-era greats as Duke Ellington and the Glenn Miller Orchestra.

Hotel services *Gift shop. Pet-friendly. Ticket desk. Valet.* **Room services** *Internet.*

Hotel Thirty Thirty

30 E 30th St between Madison Ave and Park Ave South (1-212-689-1900/1-800-497-6028/www.thirtythirty-nyc.com). Subway: 6 to 28th St. **Rates** *$110–$215 single/double; $160–$305 suite. 250 rooms.* **Credit** *AmEx, DC, Disc, MC, V.*

Before it became a tony hotel, Thirty Thirty was a residence for single women, and 60 tenants still live here. Ambient music sets the tone in the spare, fash-

ionable, block-long lobby. Rooms are small but sleek and complemented by clean lines and textured fabrics. Executive-floor rooms are slightly larger, with nifty workspaces and slate bathrooms. The hotel's restaurant, Zanna, serves Mediterranean fare.

Hotel services *Complimentary pass to nearby gym. Florist. Ticket desk.* **Room services** *CD player. Internet.*

The Hudson

356 W 58th St between Eighth and Ninth Aves (1-212-554-6000/www.hudsonhotel.com). Subway: A, C, B, D, 1, 9 to 59th St–Columbus Circle. **Rates** *$175–$260 single/double; $330–$5,000 suite. 803 rooms.* **Credit** *AmEx, DC, Disc, MC, V.*

Sure, the rooms get points for looks, but just try turning around, or even finding a place to put down your suitcase. Outside of its teeny bedrooms, though, the Hudson has lots to offer. A lush courtyard is shaded with enormous potted trees, a rooftop terrace overlooks the Hudson River, and a glass-ceilinged lobby with imported English ivy is crawling with beautiful people. The Hudson Cafeteria and the three on-site bars lure the fabulous. This is the fourth New York palace in Ian Schrager's hip-hotel kingdom, which includes Morgans, the Paramount and the Royalton.

Hotel services *Cell-phone rental. Fitness center. Rooftop terrace.* **Room services** *CD player. High-speed Internet.*

Other locations *Morgans, 237 Madison Ave between 37th and 38th Sts (1-212-686-0300/1-800-334-3408); Royalton, 44 W 44th St between Fifth and Sixth Aves (1-212-869-4400/1-800-635-9013); Paramount, 235 W 46th St between Broadway and Eighth Ave (1-212-764-5500/1-800-225-7474).*

The Marcel

201 E 24th St at Third Ave (1-212-696-3800/www.nychotels.com). Subway: 6 to 23rd St. **Rates** *$185–$250 single/double. 97 rooms.* **Credit** *AmEx, DC, Disc, MC, V.*

Caffeine junkies will be in good hands at the sleek, chic Marcel—there's a complimentary espresso bar in the lobby that's always open. The hotel is frequented by fashion-industry types because of its easy access to downtown, midtown, and the Flatiron and Garment Districts. The compact rooms have nice touches like fresh flowers, modern wood furniture and multicolored, padded headboards. You'll find the same chic perks and low prices at four sister hotels, Ameritania Hotel, Amsterdam Court, the Moderne and the Bentley Hotel (*see p65*).

Hotel services *Espresso bar (24hrs). Ticket desk.* **Room services** *CD player. PlayStation. VCR on request.*

Other locations *Ameritania Hotel, 230 W 54th St at Broadway (1-888-664-6835); Amsterdam Court, 226 W 50th St between Broadway and Eighth Ave (1-888-664-6835); The Bentley, 500 E 62nd St at York Ave (1-888-664-6835); The Moderne, 243 W 55th St between Broadway and Eighth Ave (1-888-664-6835).*

The Roosevelt Hotel

45 E 45th St at Madison Ave (1-212-661-9600/1-888-833-3969/www.theroosevelthotel.com).

Subway: 42nd St S, 4, 5, 6, 7 to 42nd St–Grand Central. **Rates** $159–$419 single/double; $350–$750 suite. 1,013 rooms. **Credit** AmEx, DC, Disc, MC, V.
Several films have been shot here, including *Wall Street*, *The French Connection* and, more recently, *Maid in Manhattan*. Built in 1924, the enormous hotel was once a haven for celebs and socialites, and a certain nostalgic grandeur lives on in the lobby, which is decked with 27-foot fluted columns and acres of marble. Teddy's Table serves light bites, and the Madison Club Lounge (1-212-885-6192) dispenses cocktails in a gentleman's club–like setting.
Hotel services *Ballroom. Fitness center. Gift shop. Ticket desk. Valet.* **Room services** *High-speed wireless Internet. PlayStation. Room service (24hrs).*

Budget (less than $100)

Carlton Arms Hotel
160 E 25th St at Third Ave (1-212-679-0680/ www.carltonarms.com). Subway: 6 to 23rd St. **Rates** *$60–$75 single; $80–$95 double; $99–$112 triple. 54 rooms.* **Credit** *MC, V.*

The Carlton Arms Art Project started in the late '70s, when a small group of creative types brought new paint and fresh ideas to a run-down shelter. Today, the site is home to a cheerfully bohemian hotel with themed spaces (check out the English-cottage room). Discounts are offered for students, overseas guests and patrons on weekly stays. Most share baths; tack on an extra $15 for a private lavatory. Rooms are usually booked up a month ahead, so reserve in advance.
Hotel services *Safe. Telephone in lobby.*

The Gershwin Hotel
27 E 27th St between Fifth and Madison Aves (1-212-545-8000/www.gershwinhotel.com). Subway: N, R, W, 6 to 28th St. **Rates** *$33–$53 per person in 4- to 8-bed dorm; $99–$200 for 1–3 people in private room; $179–$289 suite. 58 beds in dorms; 133 private rooms.* **Credit** *AmEx, MC, V.*

This funky budget hotel has a Pop Art theme: Works by Lichtenstein line the hallways, and an original Warhol soup-can painting is hung in the lobby. Rates are extremely reasonable for a location just off Fifth Avenue. If you can afford a suite,

The (new) Harlem Renaissance

Just a quick subway ride from the crowds and tiresome hotel chains of central Manhattan lies a neighborhood rich in history, abounding in beautiful brownstones and brimming with enterprising energy. It's Harlem, and it's back in full swing. The latest—and best—way to get an authentic taste of uptown life is to unpack your bags at a freshly renovated, beautifully appointed bed-and-breakfast. For far less than the price of a beige-on-beige midtown room, you can tap into the heart of residential life in a vibrant urban neighborhood.

There's a lot going on uptown these days. New homesteaders and dedicated longtime inhabitants are restoring this once blighted 'hood to its historic grandeur. Harlem Week—originally the first week in August—has now extended informally to fill the entire month with free outdoor concerts, street fairs, walking tours, a film festival and the largest African-American book fair in the country, drawing upwards of 40,000 people. The Studio Museum in Harlem (*see p151*) anchors a burgeoning art scene; the famed Apollo Theater (*see p311*) jumps with performances by musical artists as diverse as Al Green and Morrissey; while black church services and gospel brunches draw visitors by the busload. You can bulk up on soul food at famous diners nearby like Amy Ruth's or Pan Pan (500 Malcom X Blvd [Lenox Ave] at 135th St), where Alicia Keys shot her "You Don't Know My Name" video.

The one thing Harlem *doesn't* have is a hotel, but a handful of enterprising locals have recently turned their historic brownstones into bed-and-breakfasts, providing personal service and, in some cases, superluxe amenities, all within walking distance of Harlem's best-known landmarks. Three B&Bs listed below are in Central Harlem, near 125th Street; the fourth, the **Harlem Landmark Guest House**, is farther north, on Sugar Hill (at 145th Street), Harlem's historic Gold Coast. Harlem Landmark is also the only one of the bunch to serve a breakfast that is included in the room rate. Both **102Brownstone** and **Efuru Guest House** refer guests to Settepani (1-917-492-4806), the café-patisserie across the street (102 provides a coupon for a free Continental breakfast there), while the **Harlem Flophouse** will whip up a hearty home-cooked breakfast for an additional charge. All four request deposits ranging from 20 to 50 percent and suggest booking at least a month in advance. (Word to the wise: Many deposits are nonrefundable after a certain time, so last-minute cancellations may cost you.)

Efuru Guest House
106 W 120th St at Malcolm X Blvd (Lenox Ave) (1-212-961-9855/www.efuru-nyc.com). Subway:

book the Lindfors (named after the building's designer), which has screen-printed walls and a sitting room. Gallery at the Gershwin, a new bar and lounge with glowing countertops and mod Lucite orbs, opened last year. At press time, Tang, an Asian restaurant serving small plates, was scheduled to open in spring 2005.
Hotel services *Internet kiosk. Transportation desk.*

Hotel 31

120 E 31st St between Park Ave South and Lexington Ave (1-212-685-3060/www.hotel31.com). Subway: 6 to 33rd St. Rates $85–$120 single/double; $125 triple. 70 rooms. **Credit** *MC, V.*
For review, *see p47* **Hotel 17**.

Murray Hill Inn

143 E 30th St between Lexington and Third Aves (1-212-683-6900/1-888-996-6376/www.nyinns.com). Subway: 6 to 28th St. **Rates** *$79–$95 double with shared bath; $95–$149 single/double with private bath. 50 rooms.* **Credit** *AmEx, MC, V.*
A recent renovation added hardwood floors and new bathrooms—most of which are private—to this affordable inn. Discounted weekly and monthly rates

are available. Book well in advance, or try the sister locations: Amsterdam Inn, Central Park Hostel and Union Square Inn (*see p67 and p49*).
Hotel services *Complimentary breakfast. Internet.*

Pickwick Arms

230 E 51st St between Second and Third Aves (1-212-355-0300/1-800-742-5945/www.pickwickarms.com). Subway: E, V to Lexington Ave–53rd St; 6 to 51st St. **Rates** *$79–$119 single; $139–$145 double. 370 rooms.* **Credit** *AmEx, DC, MC, V.*
The quarters at this no-frills hotel are simple, clean and bright, and many have private baths. (Some rooms share an adjoining facility; otherwise, guests share a lavatory down the hall.) There are two on-site restaurants as well as a rooftop garden.
Hotel services *Internet in lobby.*

Hostels

Chelsea Center

313 W 29th St between Eighth and Ninth Aves (1-212-643-0214/www.chelseacenterhostel.com). Subway: A, C, E to 34th St–Penn Station; 1, 9 to

More comforts than home, at the lavishly appointed **102Brownstone**.

2, 3 to 116th St. **Rates** *$75–$119 double with shared or private bath. 4 rooms.* **Credit** *MC, V.*
Efuru, a Nigerian word meaning "daughter of heaven," is the brainchild of owner Lydia Smith, who bought the once abandoned property through a lottery system in the late '90s and then endured a five-year renovation process. The result is a homey inn where guests can enjoy total privacy—each garden-level room has an entrance and patio—or mingle in a communal living room decorated with cozy antique couches and a working fireplace.

The four suites, painted in serene hues of green and blue, are basic but clean and comfy. All have queen beds, private baths and refrigerators; some have a kitchenette. The parlor floor is sometimes rented for parties or art exhibitions.
B&B services *Garden. High-speed Internet. Kitchenette in some rooms. TV in rooms.*
Nearby attractions *Apollo Theater. Bayou restaurant. Lenox Lounge jazz club. 125th Street shopping. Studio Museum in Harlem.* ▶

28th St. **Rates** *$28–$33 per person in dorm. 20 beds.* **Credit** *Cash only.*
Re-live your student days in a small, women-only hostel with shared rooms and a communal kitchen and living area. Bathrooms are clean, and a patio garden is out back. Rooms are nonsmoking, and lack air-conditioning, but the fees include breakfast. Visit the website for information on an East Village location. **Hostel services** *Fax. Garden. Internet. Kitchen. TV.*

Above 59th Street

Deluxe ($350 and up)

The Carlyle

35 E 76th St between Madison and Park Aves (1-212-744-1600/1-800-227-5737/www.thecarlyle.com). Subway: 6 to 77th St. **Rates** *$550–$825 single/double; $950–$3,200 suite. 179 rooms.* **Credit** *AmEx, DC, Disc, MC, V.*
An icon of New York glamour (and old money) for more than 70 years, the Carlyle has attracted generations of famous guests—especially those who value fresh flowers (the hotel spends more than $300,000 a year on orchids and other exotic blossoms). Artwork by Matisse and Picasso hangs in the lobby, and the famous Bemelmans Bar is lined with hand-painted murals by artist Ludwig Bemelmans, creator of the Madeline children's books. Accommodations are decorated with plush fabrics and stocked with Kiehl's products. Cafe Carlyle (*see p275*) has been the roost of cabaret singer Bobby Short for more than three decades. Children can explore the area with *Madeline's Guide to the Upper East Side*. **Hotel services** *Babysitting. Cell-phone rental. Complimentary breakfast. Dry cleaning (24hrs). Fitness center. Gift shop. Valet. Video library.* **Room services** *CD/DVD player. Complimentary newspaper. DVD library. High-speed wireless Internet. Room service (24hrs).*

Hôtel Plaza Athénée

37 E 64th St between Madison and Park Aves (1-212-734-9100/1-800-447-8800/www.plaza-athenee.com). Subway: F to Lexington Ave–63rd St. **Rates** *$495–$615 single/double; $1,200–$3,600 suite. 150 rooms.* **Credit** *AmEx, DC, Disc, MC, V.*

► ## The (new) Harlem Renaissance (continued)

The Harlem Flophouse

242 W 123rd St between Adam Clayton Powell Jr. Blvd (Seventh Ave) and Frederick Douglass Blvd (Eighth Ave) (1-212-662-0678/ www.harlemflophouse.com). Subway: A, C, B, D to 125th St. **Rates** *$65 single with shared bath; $90 double with shared bath. 4 Rooms.* **Credit** *MC, V.*
The dark-wood interior, moody lighting and lilting jazz make the Flophouse feel more like a 1930s speakeasy than a 21st-century bed-and-breakfast. Owner René Calvo, a globe-trotting thespian and former graphic designer, has created a sleepy hideaway out of an actual flophouse that had been in operation since 1917. After taking over in 2000, Calvo renovated room by room and filled the place with artifacts from his travels.
The airy suites have restored tin ceilings, glamorous chandeliers and working sinks in antique cabinets. For $15 a person ($25 per couple), you can eat a home-cooked breakfast in the communal dining room or garden. Want to stay in your pj's? A staff member will bring your meal to your room.
B&B services *Garden. High-speed wireless Internet. Laundry service. Private sink and dressing areas.*

Nearby attractions *Apollo Theater. Harlem USA Mall. Kitchenette Uptown restaurant. Studio Museum in Harlem.*

Harlem Landmark Guest House

437 W 147th St at Convent Ave (1-212-694-8800). Subway A, C, B, D to 145th St. **Rates** *$125–$175 double. 6 rooms.* **Credit** *AmEx, MC, V.*
In 2002, when the Duncan-White family—third-generation Harlemites—purchased this 1893 Romanesque-revival house on Sugar Hill, relatives from far and wide started visiting. The Duncan-Whites had so many guests, they decided to convert their single-family home—with 12-foot-high stamped-tin ceilings, mosaic-tiled fireplaces, elegantly carved banisters and original wood floors—into a six-room guesthouse, and move themselves down to the garden level. Each room is named for an icon of African-American music: The Ella Fitzgerald Egyptian suite features a private Jacuzzi set below a skylight; the Nat "King" Cole honeymoon suite is decked out with an antique four-poster bed and black-and-white wedding photos.
B&B services *Continental breakfast. In-room massage. Jacuzzi. Private on-site Pilates instruction (by appointment). Spray-on tanning.*

The first impression is of luxury: Italian marble floors, a butterfly motif and French antique furniture—and that's just the lobby. On a quiet, tree-lined residential block, the Hôtel Plaza Athénée impresses right from the start. In the luxurious rooms, you'll find fresh-cut flowers, plush robes and a basket of special jet-lag-fighting teas. Each European-style suite has a terrace and a solarium. Dine on creative American cuisine at the restaurant Arabelle (1-212-606-4647), or retreat to the private bar to spy on media-shy celebs. **Hotel services** *Fitness center.* **Room services** *CD player. Complimentary newspaper. Flat-panel TV. High-speed wireless Internet.*

The Lowell Hotel

*28 E 63rd St between Madison and Park Aves (1-212-838-1400/1-800-221-4444). Subway: F to 63rd St. **Rates** $465–$575 single/double; $775–$4,575 suite. 70 rooms.* **Credit** *AmEx, DC, Disc, MC, V.*
Renovated in 2003, this petite charmer is located on a posh street on the Upper East Side. Rooms in the landmark Art Deco building feature marble baths, Scandinavian down comforters and, in suites, wood-burning

fireplaces. The garden suite has two private terraces and a manicured flower bed. The Post House and Pembroke Room are the hotel's two white-tablecloth dining options. The Manhattan suite (where Madonna once lived) is an ode to the city, outfitted with NYC-themed books, photographs, CDs and DVDs. **Hotel services** *Babysitting. Cell-phone rental. Fitness center. Valet.* **Room services** *CD player. DVD player on request. Kitchenette. VCR.*

The Mandarin Oriental New York

*80 Columbus Circle at 60th St (1-212-805-8800/ www.mandarinoriental.com). Subway: A, C, B, D, 1, 9 to 59th St–Columbus Circle. **Rates** $625–$895 single/double; $1,600–$12,000 suite. 251 rooms.* **Credit** *AmEx, DC, Disc, MC, V.*
The Mandarin Oriental's New York location occupies 19 floors in the massive Time Warner shopping-dining-office-residential complex. Each superplush room comes with $27,000 worth of technology and priceless views of Central Park and the skyline. The hotel has an enormous full-service spa and fitness center (complete with a 75-foot pool). Dine on refined French-Japanese cuisine at Asiate, on the 35th floor,

Nearby attractions *Hamilton Grange (287 Convent Ave at 142nd St, 1-212-666-1640). Londel's Supper Club. Strivers' Row.*

102Brownstone

*102 W 118th St between Malcolm X Blvd (Lenox Ave) and Adam Clayton Powell Jr. Blvd (Seventh Ave) (1-212-662-4223/ www.102brownstone.com). Subway: 2, 3 to 116th St. **Rates** $99 double with shared bath; $140 double with private bath; $250 2-bedroom suite with private bath. 5 rooms.* **Credit** *AmEx, MC, V.*
Located near Marcus Garvey Park on a landmark, tree-lined street, 102 features five substantial suites, all newly renovated and individually themed by lively proprietor Lizette Agosto, who owns and lives in the 1892 Greek Revival row house with her husband. She says 102 is "not your typical B&B. We aren't up in your face. We want to give you the experience of what it would be like to live here in Harlem, in your own apartment."

The showpiece of 102 is the Metropolis, a two-bedroom apartment, with full kitchen, that occupies one entire floor of the brownstone. Individual rooms include the Zen Suite, which combines Japanese accents (a panel of shoji serves as a headboard) and antique Chinese

Harlem Flophouse.

furniture. The Luna Studio has deep burgundy walls, velvet curtains and leopard-print rugs, creating a boudoirlike (but not campy) feel. **B&B services** *DVD player. High-speed Internet. Jacuzzi. Kitchenette in some rooms.* **Nearby attractions** *Amy Ruth's restaurant. Harlemade boutique. Marcus Garvey Park. Native restaurant. St. Martin's Episcopal Church (230 Malcolm X Blvd [Lenox Ave] at 122nd St).*

Rise and shine in the garden suite at the **Lowell Hotel.** *See p63.*

or stop in for a cocktail at MObar. The Lobby Lounge offers breakfast, afternoon tea and late-night dessert. **Hotel services** *Cell-phone rental. Complimentary car service. Dry cleaning (24hrs). DVD library. Fitness center. Gift shop. Valet.* **Room services** *CD/DVD player. Flat-panel TV. High-speed wireless Internet. Room service (24hrs). Xbox.*

The Mark

25 E 77th St between Fifth and Madison Aves (1-212-744-4300/1-800-843-6275/www.themarkhotel.com). Subway: 6 to 77th St. **Rates** *$570–$600 single; $630–$660 double; $815–$2,500 suite. 176 rooms.* **Credit** *AmEx, DC, Disc, MC, V.*
Bono and other music-industry figures are said to be frequent guests of this toned-down sibling of the Mandarin Oriental. Potted palms and arched mirrors line the entryway, and the small marble lobby, appointed with 18th-century Piranesi prints and Veuve Clicquot magnums, is usually swarming with mature international guests and white-gloved bellmen. Especially popular are the clubby Mark's Bar and the elegant Mark's restaurant (1-212-879-1864). **Hotel services** *Cell-phone rental. Dry cleaning (24hrs). Fitness center. Free shuttle to Wall Street and Theater District. Valet. Video library.* **Room services** *CD player. Complimentary magazines and newspapers. High-speed Internet. Kitchenette. Printer. VCR.*

The Pierre

2 E 61st St at Fifth Ave (1-212-838-8000/1-800-743-7734/www.fourseasons.com/pierre). Subway: N, R, W to Fifth Ave–59th St. **Rates** *$425–$950 single; $475–$995 double; $625–$3,800 suite. 201 rooms.* **Credit** *AmEx, DC, Disc, MC, V.*
This glamorous New York classic marks its 75th birthday in 2005. A black-and-white-checkered sidewalk leads up to the gleaming gold lobby. Front rooms overlook Central Park, and wares from fancy neighboring stores are on display in the lobby. In addition to dry cleaning, the hotel offers hand-laundering for precious garments. There are three restaurants, including the opulent Café Pierre. **Hotel services** *Beauty salon. Cell-phone rental. Dry cleaning (24hrs). Fitness center. Free shuttle to Theater District. Ticket desk. Valet.* **Room services** *CD player. Exercise equipment. High-speed wireless Internet. PlayStation and VCR on request.*

The Ritz-Carlton New York, Central Park

50 Central Park South between Fifth and Sixth Aves (1-212-308-9100/www.ritzcarlton.com). Subway: F to 57th St; N, R, W to Fifth Ave–59th St. **Rates** *$650–$1,075 single/double; $1,395–$12,500 suite. 277 rooms.* **Credit** *AmEx, DC, Disc, MC, V.*
Frill seekers will adore the fresh orchids and original art sprinkled throughout the hotel. Rooms with park views come with telescopes and bird-watching tips. The swank, on-site La Prairie at the Ritz-Carlton Spa offers treatments like a firming facial with champagne and caviar, and jet-lag therapy. The elegant dining option, Atelier (1-212-521-6125), boasts sycamore walls and a former Le Cirque 2000 chef. The coolest amenity is human: A "technology butler" is on call 24/7, should you need help downloading those new MP3s. For the Battery Park location, *see p43.* **Hotel services** *Cell-phone rental. Fitness center with personal trainers. Free overnight shoe shine and shuttle within midtown. Valet.* **Room services** *CD/DVD player. Complimentary newspapers. DVD library. High-speed Internet.*

Trump International Hotel & Tower

1 Central Park West at Columbus Circle (1-212-299-1000/1-888-448-7867/www.trumpintl.com). Subway: A, C, B, D, 1, 9 to 59th St–Columbus Circle. **Rates** *$425–$625 single/double; $845–$1,895 suite. 167 rooms.* **Credit** *AmEx, DC, Disc, MC, V.*
After the first phase of a $10 million renovation, Donald Trump's glass-and-steel skyscraper is more sparkling than the display cases at Tiffany's. Remodeled suites in green, sand and cinnamon tones feature 42-inch plasma TVs and breathtaking views of Central Park. Each guest is assigned a personal assistant and in-room chef. Better yet, head downstairs to Jean Georges (1-212-299-3900), the restaurant named for four-star maestro Jean-Georges Vongerichten. **Hotel services** *Beauty salon. Cell-phone rental. DVD library. Fitness center. Personal attaché service.* **Room services** *CD/DVD player. Computer. Flat-panel TV. High-speed wireless Internet. Kitchenette.*

Expensive ($200 to $350)

The Melrose Hotel

*140 E 63rd St between Lexington and Third Aves
(1-212-838-5700/www.melrosehotel.com). Subway:
F to Lexington Ave–63rd St; N, R, W to Lexington
Ave–59th St; 4, 5, 6 to 59th St.* **Rates** *$219–$319
single/double; $349–$1,200 suite. 306 rooms.*
Credit *AmEx, DC, Disc, MC, V.*
From 1927 to 1981, this building was the Barbizon
Hotel, an exclusive women-only hotel and host to the
likes of Grace Kelly and Liza Minnelli. In 2002, it
reopened as the Melrose, spiffed up with cherrywood
furniture, gilded mirrors and the original marble
floor restored. Tower suites boast landscaped balconies with Corinthian pillars and fab views of the
city lights. The Library Bar features smart cocktails
and a full menu.
Hotel services *CD/video library. Fitness center. Spa.
Ticket desk. Valet.* **Room services** *CD player. High-
speed Internet. PlayStation. VCR.*

On the Ave Hotel

*2178 Broadway at 77th St (1-212-362-1100/1-800-
509-7598/www.ontheave-nyc.com). Subway: 1, 9 to
79th St.* **Rates** *$225–$365 single/double; $275–
$395 suite; $425–$795 penthouse. 266 rooms.*
Credit *AmEx, DC, Disc, MC, V.*
On the Ave brings some sorely needed style to the
Upper West Side's stodgy hotel scene. Winning
attractions include industrial-style bathroom sinks
and penthouse suites with fantastic balcony views
of Central Park. (All guests have access to a balcony on the 16th floor.) On the Ave's Citylife Hotel
Group sibling is Thirty Thirty (*see p59*).
Hotel services *Dry cleaning (24hrs). Video library.*
Room services *CD player. Complimentary
newspaper. High-speed Internet. Plasma TV. VCR.*

The Plaza Hotel

*768 Fifth Ave at Central Park South (1-212-759-3000/
1-800-759-3000/www.fairmont.com). Subway: N, R, W
to Fifth Ave–59th St.* **Rates** *$289–$795 single/double;
$525–$2,200 suite. 805 rooms.* **Credit** *AmEx, DC,
Disc, MC, V.*
Built in 1907 and renowned for its baroque splendor, the Plaza Hotel is convenient to Fifth Avenue's
most exclusive stores. More than half of the luxurious
rooms and suites still have their original marble
fireplaces (alas, no longer working). After a rigor-
ous day of ritzy shopping, unwind at the 8,000-
square-foot spa or with a spot of tea in the Palm
Court (1-212-546-5200). The Plaza is among the kid-
friendliest hotels in the city and offers the Eloise
Program, which is named for the Plaza-dwelling
heroine of Kay Thompson's children's books, and
includes everything from etiquette classes to tours
of the city's toy stores.
Hotel services *Beauty salon. Fitness center.
Florist. Gift shop. Men's clothing store.
Pet-friendly. Spa. Ticket desk.*
Room services *Complimentary newspaper.
Computer. DVD/VCR on request. High-
speed Internet.*

Moderate ($100 to $200)

The Bentley Hotel

*500 E 62nd St at York Ave (1-212-644-6000/1-888-
664-6835/www.nychotels.com). Subway: F to Lexington
Ave–63rd St; 4, 5, 6 to 59th St.* **Rates** *$150–$250
single/double; $200–$275 suite. 200 rooms.*
Credit *AmEx, DC, Disc, MC, V.*
Once inside the Bentley's sleek rooms, it's hard to
notice anything other than the sweeping vistas from
the floor-to-ceiling windows. Converted from an office
building in 1998, this slender 21-story hotel is an ideal
getaway for weary execs, thanks to solid sound-
proofing and blackout shades. Sip cappuccino in the
mahogany-paneled library or take in even more views
from the glittering rooftop restaurant.
Hotel services *Complimentary pass to nearby gym.*
Room services *CD player. Complimentary
newspaper. High-speed wireless Internet.*
Other locations *Ameritania Hotel, 230 W 54th St at
Broadway (1-888-664-6835); Amsterdam Court,*

Local legend

Eloise defines New York the way Madeline
defines Paris." So wrote the *New York
Times* in 1955, when Kay Thompson
introduced the world to her mischievous,
bandy-legged heroine, in the first of five
beloved children's books. A garrulous
six-year-old with a blithe disregard for
authority and a fondness for pranks,
Eloise lives in the swanky Plaza Hotel,
ordering room service, "skibbling" up and
down the stairs and wreaking delightful
havoc. Fans still arrange to meet under
illustrator Hillary Knight's portrait of
Eloise, which hangs opposite the entrance
to the Plaza's Palm Court.

Dawdle in the shady courtyard at uptown's **Hostelling International New York**. *See p67.*

226 W 50th St between Broadway and Eighth Ave (1-888-664-6835); The Marcel, 201 E 24th St at Third Ave (1-212-696-3800); The Moderne, 243 W 55th St between Broadway and Eighth Ave (1-888-664-6835).

Country Inn the City

270 W 77th St between Broadway and West End Ave (1-212-580-4183/1-800-572-4969/www. countryinnthecity.com). Subway: 1, 9 to 79th St. **Rates** *$150–$210 single/double. 4 rooms.* **Credit** *Cash only.*

You can escape to the country without leaving the city at this charming bed-and-breakfast on the West Side. Four-poster beds, flagons of brandy, and moose heads in the hallways make this intimate inn a special retreat.
Room services *Free local phone service. Kitchenette.*

Hotel Beacon

2130 Broadway between 74th and 75th Sts (1-212-787-1100/1-800-572-4969/www.beaconhotel.com). Subway: 1, 2, 3, 9 to 72nd St. **Rates** *$180–$235 single/double; $250–$500 suite. 245 rooms.* **Credit** *AmEx, DC, Disc, MC, V.*

The Beacon offers good value in a desirable residential neighborhood that's only a short walk from Central and Riverside Parks. Rooms are clean and spacious and include marble baths. For $5, guests can purchase a pass to the nearby Synergy gym. Quell your post-workout hunger at the classic diner Viand Cafe.
Hotel services *Babysitting. Internet.*
Room services *Kitchenette.*

Hotel Belleclaire

250 W 77th St at Broadway (1-212-362-7700/ www.hotelbelleclaire.com). Subway: 1, 9 to 79th St. **Rates** *$100–$119 single with shared bath; $189–$219 single/double with private bath; $289–$229 suite. 200 rooms.* **Credit** *AmEx, DC, Disc, MC, V.*

Housed in a landmark building near Lincoln Center and Central Park, the Belleclaire is a steal for savvy budget travelers. Rooms feature goose-down comforters, sleek padded headboards and mod lighting fixtures. Every room comes with a refrigerator—perfect for chilling your protein shake while you're hitting the new state-of-the-art fitness center.
Hotel services *Cell-phone rental. Fitness center. Gift shop. Massage service.* **Room services** *CD player. Direct-dial phone numbers. Internet. Nintendo.*

The Lucerne

201 W 79th St at Amsterdam Ave (1-212-875-1000/ 1-800-492-8122/www.thelucernehotel.com). Subway: 1, 9 to 79th St. **Rates** *$180–$280 single/double; $220–$400 suite. 187 rooms.* **Credit** *AmEx, DC, Disc, MC, V.*

The historic Lucerne has an elaborate prewar facade and ornate columns. A rooftop patio offers views of Central Park and the Hudson River. The rooms, though, are far from fabulous. Instead, seek style in the hotel's breezy ground-floor French bistro, Nice Matin (1-212-873-6423).
Hotel services *Fitness center.* **Room services** *High-speed Internet. Plasma TV.*

Wyman House

36 Riverside Dr at 76th St (1-212-799-8281/ www.wymanhouse.com). Subway: 1, 2, 3, 9 to 72nd St. **Rates** *$175–$250 single/double. 6 rooms.* **Credit** *Cash only.*

Since 1986, Pamela and Ron Wyman have hosted many happy travelers at their 1888 home. Each of the six apartment-style suites has a unique shabby-chic decor. The Conservatory is the largest, with sunny yellow walls and a Moroccan-themed bathroom. Note: All rooms are walk-ups, the minimum booking is three nights, and children under 12 are not allowed.

Hotel services *Complimentary breakfast first day of stay. Free local phone service.* **Room services** *High-speed wireless Internet. Kitchenette. VCR.*

Budget ($100 or less)

Amsterdam Inn

340 Amsterdam Ave at 76th St (1-212-579-7500/ www.amsterdaminn.com). Subway: 1, 9 to 79th St. Rates $69–$89 single/double with shared bath; $79–$149 with private bath. 30 rooms. **Credit** *AmEx, MC, V.*

For review, *see p61* **Murray Hill Inn.**

Hostels

Central Park Hostel

19 W 103rd St at Central Park West (1-212-678-0491/www.centralparkhostel.com). Subway: B, C to 103rd St. Rates $26–$35 for a bed in shared room; $99–$129 private room with shared bath. 250 beds. **Credit** *MC, V.*

This tidy hostel, housed in a recently renovated brownstone, offers dorm-style rooms that sleep four, six or eight people; private chambers with two beds are also available. All baths are shared.
Hostel services *Lockers. Travel desk.*

Hostelling International New York

891 Amsterdam Ave at 103rd St (1-212-932-2300/ www.hinewyork.org). Subway: 1, 9 to 103rd St. Rates $29–$40 dorm rooms; $120 family rooms; $135 private room with bath. 624 beds. **Credit** *AmEx, DC, MC, V.*

The city's only *real* hostel (i.e., a nonprofit accommodation that belongs to the International Youth Hostel Federation) is a gabled, Gothic-inspired brick-and-stone building the length of an entire city block. The immaculate rooms are spare but air-conditioned. There is a shared kitchen and a large backyard.
Hostel services *Café. Conference facility. Courtyard. Fax. Game room. Gift shop. Internet kiosk. Library. Lockers. Self-serve laundry. Shuttles. Travel desk. TV lounge.* **Room services** *Air-conditioning.*

International House

500 Riverside Dr at Tiemann Pl (1-212-316-8436/ www.ihouse-nyc.org). Subway: 1, 9 to 125th St. Rates $120–$130 single; $135–$145 double/suite. 11 rooms. **Credit** *MC, V.*

Located on a peaceful block overlooking Grant's Tomb and the small but well-tended Sakura Park, this hostel has rooms with private bathrooms and refrigerators. Summer, when foreign graduate students check out, is the best time to book.
Hostel services *Bar. Cafeteria. Self-serve laundry.* **Room services** *Air-conditioning. Cable TV.*

Jazz on the Park Hostel

36 W 106th St between Central Park West and Manhattan Ave (1-212-932-1600/www.jazzhostel.com). Subway: B, C to 103rd St. Rates $25–$38, 4- to 12-bed dorm; $50–$85 2-bed dorm (maximum 2 people); $110 private room with bath. 310 beds. **Credit** *MC, V.*

Jazz on the Park is the trendiest hostel in the city. The lounge, outfitted like a space-age techno club, sports a piano and pool table, while karaoke swings in the basement. In summer, the back patio hosts a barbecue weekly. Linens and lockers are provided.
Hostel services *Air-conditioning. Café. Complimentary breakfast. Fax. Internet. Private lockers. Self-serve laundry. TV room.*
Other location *Jazz on the Town Hostel, 307 E 14th St between First and Second Aves (1-212-228-2780).*

Brooklyn

Akwaaba Mansion

347 MacDonough St between Lewis and Stuyvesant Aves, Bedford-Stuyvesant, Brooklyn (1-718-455-5958/ www.akwaaba.com). Subway: A, C to Utica Ave. Rates $150 single/double weekdays; $165 single/ double weekends (each additional person $30, maximum 4 people). 4 rooms. **Credit** *MC, V.*

This gorgeous, restored 1860s mansion with a wide screened-in porch and flower gardens is worth the trek to eastern Brooklyn. The individually themed rooms at Akwaaba ("welcome," in Ghanaian) are decorated with African artifacts and textiles. A hearty Southern-style breakfast and complimentary afternoon tea are served in the dining room or on the porch.

Awesome Bed & Breakfast

136 Lawrence St between Fulton and Willoughby Sts, Fort Greene, Brooklyn (1-718-858-4859/ www.awesome-bed-and-breakfast.com). Subway: A, C, F to Jay St–Borough Hall; M, R to Lawrence St; 2, 3 to Hoyt St. Rates $72–$150 single/double; $150–$200 triple/quad. 7 rooms. **Credit** *AmEx, MC, V.*

This bi-level guesthouse could be a setting for MTV's *The Real World:* Themed rooms have goofy details like giant daisies and purple drapes, and the snazzy bathrooms are communal. Complimentary breakfast is included, delivered to your door promptly at 8am. Plans to double the B&B's capacity are in the works.

Bed & Breakfast on the Park

113 Prospect Park West between 6th and 7th Sts, Park Slope, Brooklyn (1-718-499-6115/www.bbnyc.com). Subway: F to Seventh Ave. Rates $155–$225 single/ double; $250–$325 suite. 7 rooms. **Credit** *AmEx, MC, V (checks preferred).*

Staying at this 1895 parkside brownstone is like taking up residence on the set of *The Age of Innocence.* The parlor floor is crammed with elaborately carved antique furniture, and guest rooms are outfitted with love seats and canopy beds swathed in French linens.

Union Street Bed & Breakfast

405 Union St between Hoyt and Smith Sts, Carroll Gardens, Brooklyn (1-718-852-8406). Subway: F, G to Carroll St. Rates $100 single; $165 double. 7 rooms. **Credit** *AmEx, MC, V.*

Formerly known as Angelique Bed & Breakfast, this quasi-Victorian-style inn is housed in an 1898 brownstone with a pleasant back garden. Room prices decrease with each additional night's stay.

AT HISTORIC GRAND CENTRAL IT'S TIME FOR...

... Free Tours
Wednesdays & Fridays, 12:30 pm
Scheduled group tour (nominal
charge). Call (212) 340-2347
for information.

... Free Souvenir
Grand Central postcards. Mention
this ad in the Time Out New York
Guide Book to the "I Love NY"
booth on Main Concourse.
Limited to supply on hand, one set per person
with this ad. Valid through April 30, 2006.

... Food Galore
5 restaurants and lounges, 18 eateries,
and The Grand Central Market.

... Fabulous Shopping
Shop 50 specialty stores.

Open Seven Days a Week
Go to GrandCentralTerminal.com
for complete information and events

IT'S TIME FOR SOMETHING GRAND.

TONY

Sightseeing

Features

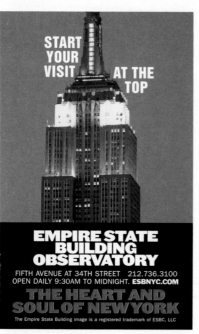

Introduction

It's a helluva town with a helluva lot to do.

Whoever thinks sightseeing is a vacation probably hasn't taken in many sights. The truth is, trying to cram a ton of rewarding activity into a short amount of time can be downright exhausting, especially in a city as action-packed as New York. So brace yourself; the stimulation is constant and the pace is demanding, but the energy is thrilling, and the payoff for exploring the wonders of America's greatest city is *huge*.

What you need is focus—and we're here to help. In the pages that follow, we've done the heavy lifting so you don't have to. Whether you're into art, jazz, food, shoes, or just good ol' window-shopping and people-watching, we'll keep you busy.

Now for a few tips on what to do (New Yorkers are hardwired to give advice):

No trip to the Big Apple would be complete without visiting a skyscraper, so why not go to the one that kicked off the race to the top? The **Woolworth Building** (*see p82*), once the world's tallest, has a neo-Gothic lobby that'll take your breath away. For tourists of a more contemporary bent, the newly renovated **Museum of Modern Art** (*see p151*) is sure to dazzle. Stop in at the **MoMA Design Store** (*see p245*), where you can actually handle the goods: a multitude of sleek items for your abode and more than 2,000 book titles. When you're hungry, nothing satisfies like a New York deli. At **Katz's** (*see p171*), pastrami sandwiches are piled so high that just one could feed a family. And to feel a deep emotional connection to the city's storied past and richly textured present, visit the **Statue of Liberty & Ellis Island Immigration Museum** (*see p77*).

During your stay, Mother Nature will surely call. Relieve yourself in the posh facilities of **Trump Tower** (*see p214*), which are beneath a waterfall at the end of a pink-marble hallway. Why shouldn't that be fun, too?

The best Sights & attractions...

...for feeling like an archaeologist
The subterranean metro stop at Central Park West and West 81st Street, below the **American Museum of Natural History**, is lined with fossils waiting to be discovered. *See p146.*

...for watching the sunset
A beer, a burger and the sun slowly dropping behind the Hudson River at the **79th Street Boat Basin** add up to the perfect way to relax before a night on the town. *See p114.*

...for getting a bird's-eye view without leaving the ground
Check out the panoramic scale model of NYC at the **Queens Museum of Art**. *See p154.*

...for getting queer-eyed
Hang out on Eighth Avenue in **Chelsea**. *See p94.*

...for celebrating George W.
Drink up at **Fraunces Tavern**, where George W. (George Washington, that is) raised a glass with the troops after kicking some redcoat butt. *See p155.*

...for flirting with a genius
You can't help going gaga for the smarty-pants behind the Genius Bar at the **Apple Store**. *See p251.*

...for seeing the writing on the wall
Hunts Point, in the South Bronx, is the best place to find kickin' graffiti. *See p135.*

...for going online for free!
Send your e-mail from Wi-Fi oasis **Bryant Park**. *See p102.*

...for checking out the hottest chicks
The birders' journal at the **Loeb Boathouse** in Central Park will keep you abreast of our local feathered friends. *See p108.*

...for pretending it's 1883
Walk to Brooklyn—across the **Brooklyn Bridge**. *See p120.*

Tour New York

Take a hike. Or a bike. Or a boat. Or a rickshaw.

There are as many different ways to see New York as there are thrilling city sights. Whether you prefer traditional (ye olde red double-decker bus) or off-beat (a pilgrimage to the East Village haunts frequented by your punk-rock heroes), there's a tour badge with your name on it. For additional inspiration, refer to the Around Town section of *Time Out New York* magazine, a weekly listing of urban treks to suit all tastes.

By bicycle

For more city biking, *see p334* **Active sports**.

Bike the Big Apple

1-201-837-1133/www.bikethebigapple.com.
Tours *Call or visit website for schedule.*
Fees *$59–$79 (includes bicycle and helmet rental).*
Credit *AmEx, DC, Disc, MC, V.*
Licensed guides take cyclists through both historic and newly hip neighborhoods. Half- and full-day rides are family-friendly, gently paced, and can be customized to your interests and riding level. Check the website for seasonal events and deals.

Central Park Bike Tours

Bite of the Apple Tours (1-212-541-8759/ www.centralparkbiketour.com). **Tours** *Apr–Oct 10am, 1, 4pm. Nov–Mar by reservation only.*
Fees *$35, children under 15 $20 (includes bicycle rental).* **Credit** *AmEx, Disc, MC, V.*
Bite of the Apple focuses on Central Park. The main tour visits such park attractions as the John Lennon memorial at Strawberry Fields, Belvedere Castle and the Shakespeare Garden. Film buffs will enjoy the Central Park Movie Scenes Bike Tour (Sat, Sun 10am, 1pm), which takes you past sites for movies like *When Harry Met Sally…* and *Wall Street*. Most tours run a leisurely two hours; hard-core bikers might consider the three-hour Manhattan Island Bicycle Tour ($45, by appointment only). Spanish-language tours are available.

By boat

The Adirondack

Chelsea Piers, Pier 62, 22nd St at the Hudson River (1-800-701-7245/1-646-336-5270/www.sail-nyc.com).

▶ If you plan on visiting several museums and taking a boat tour, *see p147* **Package deals** for reduced-fare passes.

Subway: C, E to 23rd St. **Tours** *May–Oct 15 Mon–Sat 1, 3:30, 6, 8:30pm; Sun 10:30am.*
Fees *$35 for day sails, $45 for evening and Sunday-brunch sails.* **Credit** *AmEx, MC, V.*
Built in 1994, the *Adirondack* is a beautiful three-masted replica of a classic 19th-century schooner. Sip from your complimentary glass of wine (beer and soft drinks are also offered) as the ship sails from Chelsea Piers to Battery Park, past Ellis Island, out to the Statue of Liberty, and around to Governors Island and the Brooklyn Bridge.

Circle Line Cruises

Pier 83, 42nd St at the Hudson River (1-212-563-3200/www.circleline.com). Subway: A, C, E to 42nd St–Port Authority. **Tours** *Call or visit website for schedule.* **Fees** *$26, seniors $20, children $13.* **Credit** *AmEx, DC, Disc, MC, V.*
Circle Line's famous three-hour, guided circumnavigation of Manhattan is one of the best ways to take in the city's sights. You can also join themed tours, such as the New Year's Eve cruise, the DJ dance party or the fall foliage ride to Bear Mountain, in the Hudson Valley. For a quick adventure (April to October), there's a roaringly fun 30-minute ride on a speedboat called the *Beast*.
Other location *South Street Seaport, Pier 16, South St between Burling Slip and Fulton St (1-212-630-8888).*

NY Waterway

Pier 78, 38th St at the Hudson River (1-800-533-3779/www.nywaterway.com). Subway: A, C, E to 42nd St–Port Authority. **Tours** *Call or visit website for schedule.* **Fees** *two-hour Manhattan cruise $25, seniors $20, children $12.* **Credit** *AmEx, Disc, MC, V.*
The scenic two-hour ride makes a complete circuit around Manhattan's landmarks. A 60-minute tour focuses on the skyline of lower Manhattan.
Other location *South Street Seaport, Pier 17, South St at Fulton St.*

Pioneer

South Street Seaport Museum, 207 Front St between Beekman and Fulton Sts (1-212-748-8786/www.southstreetseaportmuseum.org). Subway: A, C to Broadway–Nassau St; J, M, Z, 2, 3, 4, 5 to Fulton St. **Tours** *Call for schedule.* **Fees** *$25, children under 12 $15.*
Credit *AmEx, MC, V.*
Built in 1885, the 102-foot *Pioneer* is the only iron-hulled merchant sailing ship still in existence. Sails billow overhead as you cruise down the East River and around New York Harbor. The *Pioneer* also offers educational children's programs.

Shearwater **Sailing**

North Cove, Hudson River between Liberty and Vesey Sts (1-212-619-0885/1-800-544-1224/ www.shearwatersailing.com). **Tours** *Apr 15– Oct 15 Mon–Thu 10am–4:30pm, 5:30–7pm; Fri, Sat 10am–4:30pm, 10–11:30pm; Sun noon–2pm.* **Fees** *$45, children $25.* **Credit** *AmEx, DC, Disc, MC, V.*
Set sail on the *Shearwater,* an 82-foot luxury yacht built in 1929. Certain rides, such as the champagne brunch or full-moon sail, are lovely ways to take in the skyline.

Staten Island Ferry

Battery Park, South St at Whitehall St (1-718-727-2508/www.siferry.com). Subway: 1, 9 to South Ferry; 4, 5 to Bowling Green. **Open** *24hrs daily.* **Fee** *free.*
During this commuter barge's 25-minute crossing, you'll get stunning panoramas of lower Manhattan and the Statue of Liberty. Boats depart South Ferry at Battery Park. Call or visit the website for current schedules.

By bus

D3 Busline

1-212-533-1664/1-866-336-4837/www.d3 busline.com. **Tours** *Fri, Sat 8pm–2am.* **Fee** *$60.* **Credit** *AmEx, MC, V.*
A night out on the leather-seated "trans-lounge limo bus" includes an open bar and a DJ, as well as VIP entrance into select Manhattan hot spots. The Brooklyn tour carries you to area bars and nightclubs. The fee includes everything but drinks at the venues.

Gray Line

777 Eighth Ave between 47th and 48th Sts (1-212-445-0848/1-800-669-0051, ext 3/www.grayline newyork.com). Subway: A, C, E to 42nd St–Port Authority. **Tours** *Call or visit website for schedule.* **Fees** *$35–$99.* **Credit** *AmEx, Disc, MC, V.*
This *is* your grandma's classic red double-decker (the line runs other buses too), but with something to interest everyone. Gray Line offers more than 20 bus tours, from a basic two-hour ride (with more than 40 hop-on, hop-off stops) to the guided Manhattan Comprehensive, which lasts eight and a half hours and includes lunch, admission to the United Nations tour, and a boat ride to Ellis Island and the Statue of Liberty.

By copter, carriage or rickshaw

Liberty Helicopter Tours

Downtown Manhattan Heliport, Pier 6, East River between Broad St and Old Slip (1-212-967-6464/ 1-800-542-9933/www.libertyhelicopters.com). Subway: R, W to Whitehall St; 1, 9 to South Ferry. **Tours** *Jan, Feb 9am–7pm daily. Mar–Dec 9am–9pm daily.* **Fees** *$56–$275.* **Credit** *AmEx, MC, V.*

The Lady herself, from a **Circle Line** tour. *See p72.*

There won't be any daredevil swooping and diving—Liberty's helicopters provide a fairly smooth flight—but the views are excitement enough. Even a five-minute ride (durations vary) is long enough to give you a thrilling look at the Empire State Building and Central Park.
Other location *VIP Heliport, Twelfth Ave at 30th St.*

Manhattan Carriage Company

200 Central Park South at Seventh Ave (1-212-664-1149/www.ajnfineart.com/mcc.html). Subway: N, Q, R, W to 57th St. **Tours** *Mon–Fri 10am–2am; Sat, Sun 8am–2am.* **Fees** *$40 per 20-minute ride (extended rides by reservation only). Hours and prices vary during holidays.* **Credit** *AmEx, MC, V (reserved tours only).*
The beauty of Central Park seems even more romantic from the seat of a horse-drawn carriage. Choose your coach from those lined up on the streets along the southern end of the park, or book in advance.

Manhattan Rickshaw Company

1-212-604-4729/www.manhattanrickshaw.com. **Tours** *Tue–Sun noon–midnight and by appointment.* **Fees** *$10–$50, depending on duration and number of passengers.* **Credit** *Cash only.*
Manhattan Rickshaw's pedicabs operate in Greenwich Village, Soho, Times Square and the Theater District. If you see one that's available, hail the driver. (Fares should be determined before you jump in.) For a prearranged pickup, make reservations 24 hours in advance.

The ultimate traveling companion.

MetroCard can take you to all the famous places in the entire city. And, with an Unlimited Ride Card, you can hop on and off New York City Transit subways and local buses as many times as you like, all day long. It's the fastest, least expensive way to see it all.

You can choose from several Unlimited Ride MetroCards, including our 1-Day Fun Pass and our 7-Day Unlimited Ride MetroCard.

You can buy MetroCard at many hotels, the New York Convention & Visitors Bureau (810 7th Avenue at 53rd Street), and the New York Transit Museum in Brooklyn Heights and the Museum's Gallery & Store at Grand Central Terminal. You can also buy it at subway station vending machines with your debit or credit card, or cash.

For more information, call 800-METROCARD (800-638-7622); in NYC, call 212-METROCARD.

New York City Transit *Going your way*

www.mta.info

George E. Pataki
Governor, State of New York

Peter S. Kalikow
Chairman, MTA

By foot

Adventure on a Shoestring
1-212-265-2663. **Tours** *Sat, Sun. Call for schedule and to make reservations.* **Fee** *$5.* **Credit** *Cash only.*
The motto of this organization, which celebrates its 42nd anniversary this year, is "Exploring the world within our reach…within our means," and founder Howard Goldberg is dedicated to revealing the "real" New York. The walks take you from one charming neighborhood to another, and topics can include Millionaire's Row and Haunted Greenwich Village. Special theme tours, including tributes to Jackie O, Katharine Hepburn and Marilyn Monroe, are also available.

Big Onion Walking Tours
1-212-439-1090/www.bigonion.com. **Tours** *Sept–May Fri–Sun and major holidays 1–3pm. Jun–Aug Wed–Sun 1–3pm.* **Fees** *$12, seniors and students $10.* **Credit** *Cash only.*
New York was known as the Big Onion before it became the Big Apple. The tour guides will explain why, and they should know—all guides hold advanced degrees in history (or a related field), resulting in astoundingly informative tours of the city's historic districts and ethnic neighborhoods. Check the website for meeting locations. Private tours are also available.

Bronx Tours
1-646-685-7725/www.bronxtours.net. **Tours** *Call for schedule and to make reservations.* **Fee** *$35.* **Credit** *AmEx, Disc, MC, V.*
On these van tours, Bronx native Maurice Valentine shows that there's more to his borough than Yankee Stadium and the Bronx Zoo. Hip-hop music provides a funky aural backdrop as passengers are guided through unsung neighborhoods like Fordham, Hunts Point and Mott Haven.

Greenwich Village Literary Pub Crawl
New Ensemble Theatre Company (1-212-613-5796/ www.geocities.com/newensemble). Tour meets at the White Horse Tavern, 567 Hudson St at 11th St. Subway: 1, 9 to Christopher St–Sheridan Sq. **Tours** *Sat 2pm (reservations requested).* **Fees** *$15, seniors and students $12 (drinks not included).* **Credit** *Cash only.*
Local actors from the New Ensemble Theatre Company take you to the past haunts of famous writers. Watering stops include Chumley's (a former speakeasy) and Cedar Tavern, where Jack Kerouac and a generation of Abstract Expressionist painters, including Jackson Pollock, drank with their peers.

Harlem Heritage Tours
1-212-280-7888/www.harlemheritage.com. **Tours** *Call or visit website for schedule and meeting locations.* **Fees** *$20–$100 (reservations required).* **Credit** *AmEx, MC, V.*
Now operating more than 15 bus and walking tours, Harlem Heritage shows visitors the soul of Harlem.

Harlem Song, Harlem Nights takes you to landmarks such as the Apollo Theater. The Renaissance tour walks you through Prohibition-era speakeasies, nightclubs and onetime residences of artists, writers and musicians.

Municipal Art Society Tours
1-212-935-3960/recorded information 1-212-439-1049/www.mas.org. **Tours** *Call or visit website for schedule and meeting locations.* **Fees** *$12–$15 (reservations may be required for some tours).* **Credit** *Cash only.*
The society organizes bus and walking tours in New York and even New Jersey. Many, like Art Deco Midtown, have an architectural bent. There's also a free guided walk through Grand Central Terminal on Wednesdays at 12:30pm (suggested donation $10). Private tours are available by appointment.

NYC Discovery Walking Tours
1-212-465-3331/nycdiscovery@hotmail.com. **Tours** *Sat, Sun. Call for schedule and meeting locations.* **Fees** *$12, food tours $17–$18 (food included).* **Credit** *Cash only.*
These walking tours cover six different themes: American history (American Revolution to Civil War), biography (George Washington to John Lennon), culture (art to baseball), neighborhood (Brooklyn Bridge area to Central Park), indoor winter (like the Secrets of Grand Central), and tasting-and-tavern (food-and-drink landmarks; drinks not included). The company has 80 year-round selections; private tours are available by appointment.

Radical Walking Tours of New York
1-718-492-0069/www.radicalwalkingtours.com. **Tours** *Call or visit website for schedule and meeting locations.* **Fee** *$10 (no reservations required).* **Credit** *Cash only.*
Historian and author Bruce Kayton guides these walks through Greenwich Village, the Lower East Side and other bastions of the counterculture.

Rock & Roll Walking Tour
Rock Junket NYC (1-212-696-6578/www. rockjunket.com). **Tours** *Mon–Fri by appointment; Sat 1pm.* **Fee** *$20.* **Credit** *Cash only.*
Rocker guides Bobby Pinn and Ginger Ail lead this East Village walk to legendary rock, punk and glam sites (famous album-cover locations; where the Ramones called home), from the 1960s to the present.

Soundwalks
www.soundwalk.com. **Tour** *CDs and MP3s are available for purchase on website and in various stores.* **Fees** *vary.*
These self-guided audio tours provide insight into life in Chinatown, Times Square, Little Italy, Dumbo and other nabes. The cinematic soundtracks layer the voices of narrators, selected for their connection to the 'hood, with various sound clips and street noises. Celebrated writer Paul Auster recently narrated the Ground Zero Sonic Memorial Soundwalk.

Sightseeing

Downtown

Things aren't the way they used to be—and that's okay.

The wheels of change are always in motion, however slowly, in downtown New York. Everything you experience today—even changes that seem to have happened overnight—is the product of years of evolution. The Latino-heavy **Lower East Side** was once predominantly Jewish; posh **Soho** was previously seedy; and the **Meatpacking District**, at one time teeming with butchers, is now a prime destination for chic shoppers and trend-seeking diners. Downtown has not only been changing, it's been improving. Thanks to an extensively renovated waterfront and a $24 million program to create and restore parks below 14th Street, more and more New Yorkers are happily heading to the southern stretch of the island to relax and play. Downtown is also the site of the 2001 attack on the **World Trade Center**, where, after a massive cleanup effort, the cornerstone of the planned Freedom Tower was laid on July 4, 2004. It serves as a reminder of what New Yorkers do best—move forward.

Battery Park

The fact that you're on an island is most obvious when you explore the southern tip of Manhattan. The Atlantic Ocean breezes are a vivid natural reminder of the route taken by millions who traveled here by ship. Trace their journey past the golden torch of the **Statue of Liberty** (open once again to tourists), through the immigration and quarantine centers of **Ellis Island** and, finally, to the statue-dotted promenade of **Battery Park**. Today the harbor is filled during summer with sailboats and Jet Ski riders who jump the wakes left by motorboats. One of the most peaceful experiences in the city is sitting on a bench in Battery Park and looking toward the Statue of Liberty, Ellis Island and Staten Island.

The promenade is also a stage for applause- (and money-) hungry performers, who entertain crowds waiting to be ferried to the Statue of Liberty and Ellis Island. The park itself often plays host to events such as the **River to River Festival** (*see p256*), a celebration of downtown, featuring a variety of arty goings-on, including free outdoor music on summer evenings. **Castle Clinton**, inside the park, is an intimate, open-air setting for concerts. Built

in 1812 to defend the city against possible attacks by the British, the castle (really a former fort) has been a theater and an aquarium; it now also serves as a visitors' center and ticket booth for Statue of Liberty and Ellis Island tours.

As you join the throngs making their way to Lady Liberty, you can head east along the shore, from which several ferry terminals jut into the harbor. The **Whitehall Ferry Terminal**, built in 1907 and renovated in 1954, is the boarding point for the famous **Staten Island Ferry** (*see p73*). The free 25-minute ride to Staten Island offers an unparalleled view of the downtown Manhattan skyline and, of course, a closer look at the iconic statue. The terminal, which was damaged by fire in 1991, remains open as it undergoes reconstruction.

In the years before the Brooklyn Bridge was built, the beautiful **Battery Maritime Building** (11 South St between Broad and Whitehall Sts) served as a terminal for many ferry services between Manhattan and Brooklyn. Get a better view, with a cocktail in hand, from the terrace of the **Rise Bar**, located on the 14th floor of the luxe **Ritz-Carlton New York** hotel (*see p43*). Another patch of grass lies north of Battery Park: the triangle of **Bowling Green**, the city's oldest park, which received an expensive makeover that was completed in 2004. It's the front lawn of the beautiful 1907 Beaux Arts **Alexander Hamilton Custom House**, now home to the **National Museum of the American Indian** (*see p157*). On the north side of the triangle, sculptor Arturo DiModica's muscular bronze bull represents the potent capitalism of the **Financial District**. At the new permanent headquarters of the **Skyscraper Museum** (*see p156* **Higher ground**), explore the history of the high-rise buildings that have made the city's skyline a world-renowned iconic image.

Other historical sites are close by: the rectory of the **Shrine of St. Elizabeth Ann Seton**, a 1790 Federal building dedicated to the first American-born saint; and **New York Unearthed**, a tiny offshoot of the **South Street Seaport Museum** (*see p158*), whose collection documents 6,000 years of New York's archaeological past. The **Fraunces Tavern Museum** (*see p155*) is a restoration

Your ship has come in at the **South Street Seaport**. *See p81.*

of the alehouse where George Washington celebrated his victory over the British. After a bite, you can examine the Revolution-era relics displayed in the tavern's period rooms. The **New York Vietnam Veterans Memorial** (55 Water St between Coenties Slip and Hanover Sq, www.nyvietnamveteransmemorial.org) stands one block to the east. Erected in 1985 and given a newly designed plaza in 2001, it features the Walk of Honor—a pathway inscribed with the names of the 1,741 New Yorkers who lost their lives in Southeast Asia—and a touching memorial etched with excerpts from letters, diary entries and poems written by Americans during the conflict.

Nearby, the **Stone Street Historic District** includes one of Manhattan's oldest roads. The once derelict bit of Stone Street between Coenties Alley and Hanover Square was recently spiffed up, and office workers and visitors now frequent its restaurants, bars and shops, including **Ulysses** (95 Pearl St at Stone St, 1-212-482-0400), a popular watering hole, and **Financier Patisserie** (62 Stone St between Hanover Sq and Mill Ln, 1-212-344-5600), a French bakery and café.

Battery Park

Between Battery Pl, State and Whitehall Sts. Subway: R, W to Whitehall St; 1, 9 to South Ferry; 4, 5 to Bowling Green.

New York Unearthed

17 State St between Pearl and Whitehall Sts, behind the Shrine of St. Elizabeth Ann Seton (1-212-748-8628). Subway: R, W, to Whitehall St. **Open** *Mon–Fri by appointment only.* **Admission** *free.*

Shrine of St. Elizabeth Ann Seton

7 State St between Pearl and Whitehall Sts (1-212-269-6865/www.setonshrine-ny.org). Subway: R, W to Whitehall St. **Open** *Mon–Fri 6:30am–5pm; Saturdays by appointment only; Sundays before and after 11am Mass.* **Admission** *free.*

The Statue of Liberty & Ellis Island Immigration Museum

1-212-363-3200/www.ellisisland.org/ www.nps.gov/stli. Travel: R, W to Whitehall St or 1, 9 to South Ferry, then take the Statue of Liberty Ferry, departing every 25 minutes from gangway 4 or 5 in southernmost Battery Park. **Open** *Ferry runs Mon–Fri 8:30am–3:30pm; Sat, Sun 8:30am–4:30pm. Purchase tickets at Castle Clinton in Battery Park. Call 1-212-269-5755 for departure times.* **Admission** *$10, seniors $8, children 4–12 $4; children under 4 free.* **Credit** *Cash only.*
Frédéric-Auguste Bartholdi's *Liberty Enlightening the World*, a gift from the people of France, was unveiled in 1886. Tourists are welcome to explore a portion of the statue and all of the exterior grounds. There's ample room to absorb the 1883 Emma Lazarus poem that includes the renowned lines "Give me your tired, your poor / Your huddled mass-

es yearning to breathe free." The inside of the statue (Miss Liberty's framework was designed by Gustave Eiffel) was closed to the public for security reasons after September 11, 2001, but reopened in August 2004. Continue your tour by hopping aboard another boat to the Ellis Island Museum, which carefully documents the deeply moving history of the approximately 12 million immigrants who passed through Ellis Island between 1892 and 1954.

Battery Park City & Ground Zero

The streets are bustling around Ground Zero, the site of the 2001 attack on the World Trade Center, and reconstruction is under way. The area is surrounded by a large fence on which historical pictures of downtown's development

Local legend

Brooklyn firefighter **Stephen Siller** had just finished his shift on the morning of September 11, 2001, and was on his way to play golf with his brothers when the first plane hit the World Trade Center. Siller turned around and drove straight for the site, but was stopped short at the Brooklyn Battery Tunnel, already closed to vehicular traffic. So the 34-year-old strapped on his 40-pound gear and continued on foot through the tunnel to the place now known as Ground Zero. After phoning his wife from the Brooklyn side, he was not heard from again. Since 2002, an annual 5K run in late September traces Siller's route, commemorating his effort. He was one of 343 firefighters who died in the attack.

and September 11th devastation are hung. Tourists still come in droves to pay their respects to the nearly 2,800 people who lost their lives that day. After a worldwide design competition for the rebuilding of the WTC area, the plan created by Studio Daniel Libeskind was selected in early 2003. A refined version of the plan was released in fall 2003, and the first cornerstone of the **Freedom Tower**, an elegant spiraling skyscraper featured in the winning design, was laid in summer 2004.

Immediately to the west of Ground Zero, the city-within-a-city **World Financial Center** is fully recovered from September 11. Completed in 1988, architect Cesar Pelli's four glass-and-granite, postmodern office towers—each crowned with a different geometric form—surround an upscale retail area, a series of plazas with terraced restaurants, and a marina where private yachts and water taxis to New Jersey are docked. The **Grill Room** (2 World Financial Center between South End Ave and West St, 1-212-945-9400), serves superb seafood with a view of the Hudson River to match. The glass-roofed **Winter Garden**, a popular venue for concerts and other forms of entertainment, resumed its performance schedule in September 2002, after being badly damaged on 9/11. Restaurants and shops in the area, such as **SouthWestNY** (2 World Financial Center between Liberty and Vesey Sts, 1-212-945-0528), and **Century 21** (22 Cortlandt St between Broadway and Church St, 1-212-227-9092) started reopening as early as February 2002. Just south of the World Financial Center lies **Battery Park City**, devised by Nelson A. Rockefeller (the governor of New York from 1959 to 1973) as the site of apartment housing and schools. Home to roughly 9,000 people, the self-contained neighborhood includes restaurants, cafés, shops, a marina and—best of all—92 glorious riverside acres. Sweeping views of the Hudson River and close proximity to the downtown financial scene have also made this an ideal spot for office space. Still, the most impressive aspects of Battery Park City are its esplanade and strolling park (officially called **Nelson A. Rockefeller Park**), which run along the Hudson River north of the Financial Center and connect to Battery Park at the south. Close by the marina is the 1997 **Police Memorial** (Liberty St at South End Ave), a granite pool and fountain that symbolically trace the life span of a police officer through the use of moving water. The names of the fallen are etched in the wall. In addition to providing inspiring sunset views, the esplanade is a paradise for bikers, skaters and joggers. Here, too, the **Irish Hunger Memorial** (Vesey St at

There's lots of liberty (and plenty of photo ops) in **Battery Park**. *See p76.*

North End Ave) pays tribute to those who suffered the hardships of the Irish Famine.

The northern end of the park features the large **North Lawn,** which becomes a surrogate beach in summer. Sunbathers, kite fliers and soccer players vie for a bit of the turf. Basketball and handball courts, concrete tables inlaid with chess and backgammon boards, and playgrounds with swings are some of the built-in recreation options. The park ends at Chambers Street but allows access to the piers beyond, which are being claimed for public use. In fact, some sections have already become part of the western waterfront's **Hudson River Park,** where you'll find jogging and biking trails and, on the piers below Canal Street, all kinds of activities, from kayaking to swinging on a trapeze.

Situated between Battery Park City and Battery Park are the inventively designed **South Cove,** the **Robert F. Wagner Jr. Park** (an observation deck offers fabulous views of the harbor and the Verrazano-Narrows Bridge) and New York City's Holocaust-

remembrance archive, the **Museum of Jewish Heritage** (*see p161*). The entire park area is dotted with sculptures, including Tom Otterness's whimsical *The Real World.* The park hosts outdoor cultural events during the warmer months.

Battery Park City Authority
1-212-417-2000/www.batteryparkcity.org.
The neighborhood's official website lists events and has a great map of the area.

Lower Manhattan Cultural Council
1-212-219-9401/www.lmcc.net.
An information service for artists and the public, the LMCC offers details on cultural events in and around lower Manhattan.

World Financial Center & Winter Garden
From Albany to Vesey Sts, between the Hudson River and West St (1-212-945-2600/www.worldfinancial center.com). Subway: A, C, to Broadway–Nassau St; E to World Trade Ctr; J, M, Z, 2, 3, 4, 5 to Fulton St.
Call for information about free events ranging from concerts to food tastings.

Money-honeys do their thing at the **New York Stock Exchange**. See p81.

Wall Street

Since the city's earliest days as a fur-trading post, wheeling and dealing has been New York's favorite pastime, and commerce, the backbone of its prosperity. Wall Street (or merely "the Street" if you want to sound like a trader) is the thoroughfare synonymous with the world's greatest den of capitalism.

Wall Street is actually less than a mile long; it took its name from a defensive wooden wall that the Dutch built in 1653 to mark what was then the northern limit of New Amsterdam. The southern tip of Manhattan is generally known as the Financial District. In the days before telecommunications, financial institutions established their headquarters in the area to be near the city's active port. Here, corporate America made its first audacious architectural statements.

Notable structures include the former **Merchants' Exchange** at 55 Wall Street (between Hanover and William Sts), with its stacked rows of Ionic and Corinthian columns, giant doors and remarkable 12,000-square-foot ballroom; the **Equitable Building** (120 Broadway between Cedar and Pine Sts), whose greedy use of vertical space helped to instigate the zoning laws now governing skyscrapers (stand across the street from the building to get the optimal view); and **40 Wall Street** (between Nassau and William Sts), which went head-to-head with the Chrysler Building in 1929 battling for the title of "world's tallest building." (The Empire State Building trounced them both a year later.)

The Gothic Revival spire of the Episcopalian **Trinity Church** rises at the western end of Wall Street. It was the island's tallest structure when completed in 1846 (the original burned down in 1776; a second was demolished in 1839). Stop in and see brokers praying for a bull market, or stroll through the adjacent cemetery, where cracked and faded tombstones mark the final resting places of dozens of past city dwellers, including signers of the Declaration of Independence and the Constitution. **St. Paul's Chapel**, a satellite of Trinity Church, is an oasis of peace in the midst of frantic business activity. The chapel is New York City's only extant pre-Revolutionary building (it dates from 1766), and one of the finest Georgian structures in the country. Miraculously, both landmark churches survived the World Trade Center attack; although mortar fell from their facades, the steeples remained intact.

A block east of Trinity Church, the **Federal Hall National Memorial** is a Greek Revival shrine to American inaugural history (sort of—the original building was demolished in 1812). On this spot, General Washington was sworn in as the country's first President on April 30, 1789.

The nerve center of the U.S. economy is the **New York Stock Exchange** (11 Wall St between Broad and New Sts). Unfortunately, for security reasons, the Exchange is no longer open to the public. Not to worry: The busy street outside the NYSE is an endless pageant, as brokers, traders and their minions march up and down Broad Street. For a lesson on Wall Street's influence through the years, check out the **Museum of American Financial History**, on the ground floor of what was once John D. Rockefeller's Standard Oil Building.

The **Federal Reserve Bank**, a block north on Liberty Street, is an imposing structure built in the Florentine style. It holds the nation's largest store of gold—just over 9,000 tons—in a vault five stories below street level.

Federal Hall National Memorial

26 Wall St at Nassau St (1-212-825-6888). Subway: 2, 3, 4, 5 to Wall St. **Open** *Mon–Fri 9am–5pm.* **Admission** *free.*

Federal Reserve Bank

33 Liberty St between Nassau and William Sts (1-212-720-6130/www.newyorkfed.org). Subway: 2, 3, 4, 5 to Wall St. **Open** *Mon–Fri 9:30–11:30am, 1:30–2:30pm; tours every hour on the half hour. Tours must be arranged at least one week in advance; tickets are sent by mail.* **Admission** *free.*

Museum of American Financial History

See p156 for listing.

St. Paul's Chapel

209 Broadway between Fulton and Vesey Sts (1-212-233-4164/www.saintpaulschapel.org). Subway: A, C to Broadway–Nassau St; J, M, Z, 2, 3, 4, 5 to Fulton St. **Open** *Mon–Sat 10am–6pm; Sun 9am–4pm.*

Trinity Church Museum

Broadway at Wall St (1-212-602-0872/www.trinitywallstreet.org). Subway: R, W to Rector St; 2, 3, 4, 5 to Wall St. **Open** *Mon–Fri 9am–11:45am, 1–3:45pm; Sat 10am–3:45pm; Sun 1–3:45pm. Closed during concerts.* **Admission** *free.*

South Street Seaport

New York's importance as a port has diminished, but its initial fortune rolled in on the swells that crash around its deepwater harbor. The city was perfectly situated for trade with Europe; after 1825, goods from the Western Territories arrived via the Erie Canal and Hudson River. And because New York was the point of entry for millions of immigrants by 1892, its character was shaped by the waves of humanity that arrived at its docks. The **South Street Seaport** is the best place to appreciate this seafaring heritage.

Redeveloped in the mid-1980s, the Seaport includes reclaimed and renovated buildings converted to shops, restaurants, bars and a museum. It's not an area that New Yorkers often visit, despite its rich history. The Seaport's public spaces are a favorite of street performers, and the shopping area of **Pier 17** is little more than a picturesque tourist-trap of a mall by day and an after-work watering hole by night (outdoor concerts in the summer do manage to attract locals). Antique vessels are docked at neighboring piers. The **South Street Seaport Museum** (*see p158*) details New York's maritime history and is located within the restored 19th-century buildings of **Schermerhorn Row** (2–18 Fulton St, 91–92 South St and 189–195 Front St), which were constructed on landfill in 1812. At **11 Fulton Street**, the **Fulton Market**, with its gourmet food stalls and seafood restaurants, is a great place for people-watching and oyster-slurping. Familiar national-chain stores such as J. Crew and Abercrombie & Fitch line the surrounding streets.

If you enter the Seaport area from Water Street, the first thing you'll notice is the

Don't miss NYC firsts

As the oldest part of the city, downtown was the stage for many New York firsts. Be sure to check out the first...

...millionaire

John Jacob Astor's vast uptown (at the time) holdings are marked by **Astor Place**. *See p90.*

...drag festival

Wigstock first kicked up its heels in Tompkins Square in 1985, thanks to drag star Lady Bunny and friends. *See p91.*

...Jewish settlement

Spanish Jews fleeing the Inquisition in 1654 made lower Manhattan their new home. Visit their **First Shearith Israel Graveyard**. *See p89.*

...American-born saint

The **Shrine of St. Elizabeth Ann Seton** is just north of Battery Park. *See p77.*

whitewashed **Titanic Memorial Lighthouse**, originally erected on top of the **Seaman's Church Institute** (Coenties Slip and South St) the year after the great ship sank. The monument was moved to its current location in 1976. The area offers fine views of the **Brooklyn Bridge** (*see p120*).

South Street Seaport

*From John St to Peck Slip, between Water St and East River (1-212-732-7678/www.southstreet seaport.com). Subway: A, C to Broadway–Nassau St; J, M, Z, 2, 3, 4, 5 to Fulton St. **Open** Mon–Fri 10am–9pm; Sat, Sun 10am–7pm.*

Civic Center & City Hall

Sightseeing

The business of running New York takes place in the many grand buildings of the Civic Center, an area that formed the budding city's northern boundary in the 1700s. **City Hall Park**, where you'll find a granite "time wheel" that displays the park's history, was treated to an extensive renovation in 1999. The pretty landscaping and abundant benches make it a popular lunchtime spot for area office workers. Like the steps of City Hall, the park has been the site of press conferences and political protests for years. (Under former Mayor Rudy Giuliani, the steps were closed to such activity, though civil libertarians successfully defied the ban in April 2000.) **City Hall**, at the northern end of the park, houses the mayor's office and the legislative chambers of the City Council, and is therefore usually buzzing with preparations for Hizzoner's comings and goings. When City Hall was completed in 1812, its architects were so confident the city would grow no farther north that they didn't bother to put any marble on its northern side.

The building, a beautiful blend of Federalist form and French Renaissance detail, is unfortunately closed to the public (except for scheduled group tours). Facing City Hall, the much larger, golden-statue-topped **Municipal Building** contains other civic offices, including the marriage bureau (note the nervous, happy brides- and grooms-to-be awaiting their ceremonies, particularly in the early morning).

Park Row, east of City Hall Park and now lined with cafés, electronics shops and the campus of **Pace University**, once held the offices of 19 daily papers and was known as Newspaper Row. It was also the site of Phineas T. Barnum's sensationalist American Museum, which burned down in 1865.

Facing the park from the west is Cass Gilbert's famous **Woolworth Building**

(233 Broadway between Barclay St and Park Pl), a vertically elongated Gothic-cathedral-style office building called the Mozart of skyscrapers (and, alternatively, the Cathedral of Commerce). Be sure to look skyward, both at the striking facade and in the stunning lobby.

The houses of crime and punishment are also located in the Civic Center, near **Foley Square**, which was once a pond and later the site of the city's most notorious 19th-century slum, Five Points. These days, you'll find the **State Supreme Court** in the **New York County Courthouse** (60 Centre St at Pearl St), a hexagonal Roman revival building whose beautiful rotunda is decorated with the mural *Law Through the Ages*. The **United States Courthouse** (40 Centre St between Duane and Pearl Sts) is a Corinthian temple crowned with a golden pyramid. Next to City Hall, on Chambers Street, is the 1872 **Old New York County Courthouse**, more popularly known as the Tweed Courthouse, a symbol of the runaway corruption of mid-19th-century municipal government. Boss Tweed, leader of the political machine Tammany Hall, pocketed $10 million of the building's huge $14 million cost. The remainder was still enough to buy a beautiful edifice; the Italianate detailing is exquisite. The **Criminal Courts Building and Bernard Kerik Detention Complex** (100 Centre St between Leonard and White Sts), is the district's most intimidating pile. The hall's architecture—great granite slabs and looming towers guarding the entrance—is downright Kafkaesque.

All of these courts are open to the public, weekdays from 9am to 5pm. Your best bets for legal drama are the Criminal Courts: If you can't slip into a trial, then you can at least observe legal eagles and their clients. Or, for a grim twist on dinner theater, you can sit and witness the pleas at Arraignment Court, which last until 1am, in the same building.

A major archaeological discovery, the **African Burial Ground** (Duane St between Broadway and Centre St) is the small remnant of a five-and-a-half-acre cemetery where between 10,000 and 20,000 African men, women and children were buried. The cemetery, which closed in 1794, was unearthed during construction of a federal office building in 1991 and designated a National Historic Landmark.

City Hall

City Hall Park, from Vesey to Chambers Sts, between Broadway and Park Row (1-212-788-3000/ www.nyc.gov). Subway: J, M, Z to Chambers St; 2, 3 to Park Pl; 4, 5, 6 to Brooklyn Bridge–City Hall. For group tours only; call two weeks in advance.

Soho street vendors' wares are guaranteed to go straight to your head.

Tribeca & Soho

Tribeca (the <u>Tri</u>angle <u>Be</u>low <u>Ca</u>nal Street) is a textbook example of the gentrification process in lower Manhattan. Much of the neighborhood throbs with energy, but a few pockets appear abandoned—the cobblestones crumbling and dirty, the cast-iron buildings chipped and unpainted. Don't let your eyes fool you; even these derelict areas are targeted for deluxe makeovers.

The rich and famous weren't really here first, but visible gentrification has led some to think of them as pioneers: Many big-name entertainers (Robert De Niro, Edward Burns and Christy Turlington among them) and established, successful artists such as Richard Serra live in the area. There's a host of haute restaurants, including **Chanterelle** (2 Harrison at Hudson St, 1-212-966-6960) and **Nobu** (*see p168*); celeb-sighting bistros, such as the long-running **Odeon** (145 West Broadway at Duane St, 1-212-233-0507); and posh bars, especially in the section of Tribeca that borders Soho. Relative newcomer **Landmarc** (*see p167*) is popular with baby-toting residents who come for the very good French, Italian and American food and, more to the point, the low-markup wine list. Clubs and performance spaces, like the **Knitting Factory** (*see p316*), contribute to the area's cultural scene.

Buildings in Tribeca are generally larger than those in Soho, particularly near the river; many warehouses are rapidly being converted into condos. Fine small-scale cast-iron architecture stands along White Street and the parallel thoroughfares. As in Soho, you'll find galleries, salons, furniture stores, spas and other businesses that cater to the neighborhood's stylish residents. Frank Gehry's multimillion-dollar interior for the **Tribeca Issey Miyake** boutique (119 Hudson St at North Moore St, 1-212-226-0100) is a stunning recent addition.

Tribeca is also the unofficial headquarters of New York's film industry. De Niro's **Tribeca Film Center** (375 Greenwich St at Franklin St) houses screening rooms and production offices in the old Martinson Coffee Building. His restaurant, **Tribeca Grill**, is on the ground floor. In addition, De Niro hosts the **Tribeca Film Festival** (*see p254*), which draws a crowd to the neighborhood each April.

► For more on Soho's art scene, see **Art Galleries** and **Museums** (*pp262–271* and *pp143–163*).
► For more on area shops, see **Shops & Services** (*pp214–252*).

Soho, New York's glamorous downtown shopping destination, was once an industrial zone known as Hell's Hundred Acres. In the 1960s, the neighborhood was earmarked for destruction, but its signature cast-iron warehouses were saved by the many artists who inhabited them. (Urban-planning theorist Chester A. Rapkin coined the name *Soho*, for South of Houston Street, in a 1962 study of the neighborhood.) The **King and Queen of Greene Street** (respectively, 72–76 Greene St between Broome and Spring Sts, and 28–30 Greene St between Canal and Grand Sts) are prime examples of the area's cast-iron-architecture landmarks. As loft living became fashionable and buildings were renovated for residential use, landlords were quick to sniff the potential for profits. Soho morphed into a playground for the young, the beautiful and the rich. While it's still a pleasure to stroll around the cobblestone streets, large chain stores are rapidly moving in among the boutiques and bistros, causing a number of hip shops to head east. Most of the galleries that made Soho an art hot spot in the 1970s and '80s have decamped to cheaper (and now trendier) neighborhoods like West Chelsea and Brooklyn's Dumbo. Surprisingly, some garment-factory sweatshops remain in Soho, especially near Canal Street, though the same elegant buildings may also house graphic-design studios, magazine publishers and record labels.

Upscale hotels like the **Mercer, 60 Thompson** and **SoHo Grand** (*see p42 and p43*) keep the fashionable coming to the area; shop names run from Banana Republic and Old Navy to Marc Jacobs and Prada. Soho is also the place to go for high-end home furnishings at design stores such as **Moss** (*see p245*).

West Broadway, Soho's main thoroughfare, is a magnet for way-out-of-towners. On the weekend, you're as likely to hear French, German and Italian as you are to catch a blast of Brooklynese.

The **New Museum of Contemporary Art** (*see p151*) just left the neighborhood to inhabit a temporary space in Chelsea while construction continues on its new home on the Bowery, scheduled to open in 2006. But you can still find the small, increasingly popular **New York**

Built to last

Tribeca's high concentration of distinguished late-19th-century structures makes the neighborhood an architecture buff's dream. About three quarters of these buildings occupy a designated historical district, which protects not just the edifices but also the stone-paved streets and metal awnings left over from the days when the Washington Market's wholesale food vendors dominated Tribeca's west side. Thanks to the activism of a group of preservationists in the '80s, these impressive sites will be around for a long time to come. Here are a few favorites.

6 Harrison Street

between Greenwich and Hudson Sts
The red-brick and granite Mercantile Exchange was built between 1872 and 1884 to regulate the trade of butter and cheese and, in the late 1980s, was made into an office building. An ornate cupolaed clock tower caps the edifice's five stories. The American Institute of Architects (and we always agree with the AIA) declares it a "hearty pile and a must-see work."

135 Hudson Street

at Beach St
Once a Pony Express office, this 1886 masonry warehouse was one of the earliest commercial buildings to be converted to artists' studios. Its street-level arches are supported by massive cylindrical brick columns.

451 Washington Street

between Desbrosses and Watts Sts
Completed in 1871, the original Fleming Smith warehouse is a golden-hued, late-Victorian stunner, with steep gables, dormer windows and contrasting brick trim. Copper cornice detailing gilds the lily even further. The bistro Capsouto Frères has occupied the first floor since 1980.

85 Leonard Street

between Broadway and Church St
The marvel of cast-iron technology changed the face of Soho and Tribeca in the mid-19th century. Slender, mass-produced columns allowed for much larger windows, brightening dim interiors (and giving rise to a retail trend with legs: window shopping). Cast iron's premier architect, James Bogardus, had his own warehouse here. Note to those in line at the Knitting Factory next door: This building is the only one in the city known for certain to be the work of Bogardus.

City Fire Museum (*see p163*), a former fire station that houses a collection of antique engines dating from the 1700s.

To the west of West Broadway, tenement- and townhouse-lined streets contain remnants of the Italian community that once dominated the area. Elderly men and women walk along **Sullivan Street** to the **St. Anthony of Padua Roman Catholic Church** (No. 155 at W Houston St), which was dedicated in 1888. You'll find old-school neighborhood flavor in businesses such as **Joe's Dairy** (No. 156 between Houston and Prince Sts, 1-212-677-8780), **Pino's Prime Meat Market** (No. 149 between Houston and Prince Sts, 1-212-475-8134) and, on Prince Street, the **Vesuvio Bakery** (160 Prince St between Thompson St and West Broadway, 1-212-925-8248), whose old-fashioned facade has appeared in dozens of commercials.

Little Italy & Nolita

Little Italy, which once ran from Canal to Houston Streets between Lafayette Street and the Bowery, hardly resembles the insular community famously portrayed in Martin Scorsese's *Mean Streets*. Italian families have fled Mott Street and gone to the suburbs, Chinatown has crept north, and rising rents have forced mom-and-pop businesses to surrender to the stylish boutiques of **Nolita**—North of Little Italy (a misnomer, since it actually lies within Little Italy). Another telling change in the 'hood: **St. Patrick's Old Cathedral** (260–264 Mulberry St between Houston and Prince Sts) now holds services in English and Spanish, *not* Italian. Completed in 1809 and restored after a fire in 1868, this was New York's premier Catholic church until it was demoted, upon consecration of the Fifth Avenue cathedral of the same name. But ethnic pride remains. Italian-Americans flood in from the outer boroughs to show their love for the old neighborhood during the **Feast of San Gennaro** (*see p258*) every September. Aside from the tourist-oriented Italian cafés and restaurants on Mulberry Street between Canal and Houston Streets, pockets of the past linger. Elderly locals (and in-the-know young ones) buy olive oil and fresh pasta from venerable shops such as **DiPalo's Fine Foods** (200 Grand St at Mott St, 1-212-226-1033) and sandwiches packed with *salume* and cheeses at the **Italian Food Center** (186 Grand St at Mulberry St, 1-212-925-2954).

Of course, Little Italy is the site of several notorious Mafia landmarks. The brick-fronted store occupied by the accessories boutique **Amy Chan** (247 Mulberry St between Prince and Spring Sts) was once the Ravenite Social Club—Mafia kingpin John Gotti's headquarters

Mulberry Street's **Feast of San Gennaro**.

from the mid-1980s until his arrest (and imprisonment) in 1990. Mobster Joey Gallo was shot to death in 1972 while celebrating a birthday with his family at **Umberto's Clam House** (1-212-431-7545), which has since moved around the corner to 178 Mulberry Street at Broome Street. The restaurants in the area are mostly undistinguished, overpriced grill-and-pasta houses, but two reliable choices are **Il Cortile** (125 Mulberry St between Canal and Hester Sts, 1-212-226-6060) and **La Mela** (167 Mulberry St between Broome and Grand Sts, 1-212-431-9493). Drop in for dessert and espresso at one of the many small cafés, such as **Caffè Roma** (385 Broome St at Mulberry St, 1-212-226-8413), which opened in 1891.

Chichi restaurants and boutiques have, it seems, popped up daily in Nolita over the past few years. Elizabeth, Mott and Mulberry Streets, between Houston and Spring Streets in particular, are now the source of everything from perfectly cut jeans to handblown glass. The young, the insouciant and the vaguely European still congregate outside eateries like **Bread** (*see p167* **Bread Tribeca**) and **Cafe Habana** (*see p169*). Even before the Nolita boom, the grand **Police Headquarters Building** (240 Centre St between Broome and Grand Sts) was converted into pricey co-op apartments.

Taste a bit of the Far East in **Chinatown**, where the chow is fun (and cheap).

Chinatown

Take a few steps south of Broome Street and west of Broadway, and you will feel as though you've entered a completely different country. You won't hear much English spoken along these crowded streets lined by stands stocked with fish, fruit and vegetables. Manhattan's Chinatown is the largest Chinese community outside Asia. Even though some residents eventually decamp to one of the four other Chinatowns in the city (two each in Queens and Brooklyn), a steady flow of new arrivals keeps this original hub full-to-bursting, with thousands of legal and illegal residents packed into the area surrounding East Canal Street. Many work and live here and never leave the neighborhood. Chinatown's busy streets get even wilder during the **Chinese New Year** festivities, in February (*see p261*), and around the Fourth of July, when the area is the city's best source of (illegal) fireworks.

Food is everywhere. The markets on Canal Street sell some of the best, most affordable seafood and fresh produce in the city—you'll see buckets of live eels and crabs, neatly stacked greens, and piles of hairy rambutans (cousins of the lychee). Street vendors sell satisfying snacks such as pork buns and sweet egg pancakes by the bagful. Mott Street, from Kenmare to Worth Streets, is lined with restaurants representing the cuisine of virtually every province of mainland China and Hong Kong; the Bowery, East Broadway and Division Street are just as diverse. Adding to the mix are increasing numbers of Indonesian, Malaysian, Thai and Vietnamese eateries and stores.

Canal Street, a bargain hunter's paradise, is infamous as a source of knockoff designer handbags, perfumes and other goods. The area's many gift shops are stocked with fun, inexpensive Chinese products, from good-luck charms to kitschy pop-culture paraphernalia.

Sites of historical interest include the antiques shop **Chu Shing** (12 Mott St between Chatham Sq and Mosco St, 1-212-227-0279); it was once the New York office of the Chinese revolutionary Dr. Sun Yat-sen, known as the father of modern China. **Wing Fat Shopping** is a strange little subterranean mall with its entrance at

Chatham Square (No. 8, to the right of the OTB parlor), rumored to have been a stop on the Underground Railroad 25 years before the Chinese began populating this area in the 1880s.

A statue of the philosopher marks **Confucius Plaza**, at the corner of the Bowery and Division Street. In **Columbus Park**, at Bayard and Mulberry Streets, elderly men and women gather around card tables to play mahjongg and dominoes (you can hear the clacking tiles from across the street) while younger folks practice martial arts. The **Museum of Chinese in the Americas** (*see p160*) hosts exhibitions and events that explore the Chinese immigrant experience in the Western Hemisphere. In the **Eastern States Buddhist Temple of America**, you'll be dazzled by the glitter of hundreds of Buddhas and the aroma of wafting incense. Donate $1, and you'll receive a fortune slip.

For a different perspective on the area's culture, visit the noisy, dingy **Chinatown Fair** (at the southern end of Mott Street), an amusement arcade where some of the East Coast's best *Street Fighter* players congregate. Older kids hit Chinatown to eat and drink: **Joe's Shanghai** (9 Pell St between Bowery and Mott St, 1-212-233-8888) is famous for its soup dumplings, boiled pillows of dough filled with pork and broth; and **Happy Ending** (302 Broome St between Eldridge and Forsyth Sts, 1-212-334-9676), a popular nightspot for downtown denizens of every ethnic group, occupies a former massage parlor (the name of the bar is a nod to its roots).

Chinatown
Subway: B, D to Grand St; J, M, Z, N, Q, R, W, 6 to Canal St.

Eastern States Buddhist Temple of America
64 Mott St between Bayard and Canal Sts (1-212-966-6229). Subway: J, M, Z, N, Q, R, W, 6 to Canal St. **Open** *9am–6pm daily.*

Lower East Side

The **Lower East Side** was shaped by New York's immigrants, millions upon millions of whom poured into the city from the late 19th century onward. The resulting patchwork of dense communities is great for dining and exploration. Today, Lower East Side residents are largely Asian and Latino families, with an increasing number of hipsters sharing small apartments. Early inhabitants were mostly Eastern European Jews. Mass tenement housing was built to accommodate the 19th-century influx of immigrants, which included many German, Hungarian, Irish and Polish families. Their unsanitary, airless and overcrowded living conditions were documented near the end of that century by photographer and writer Jacob A. Riis in *How the Other Half Lives;* the book's publication fueled reformers, who prompted the introduction of building codes. To better understand how these immigrants lived, take a tour conducted by the **Lower East Side Tenement Museum** (*see p155*).

Between 1870 and 1920, hundreds of synagogues and religious schools were established. Yiddish newspapers and associations for social reform and cultural studies flourished, as did vaudeville and classic Yiddish theater. (The Marx Brothers, Jimmy Durante, Eddie Cantor, and George and Ira Gershwin were just a few of the entertainers who once lived in the district.) Currently, only about 10 percent of the LES population is Jewish; the **Eldridge Street Synagogue** often has a hard time rounding up the ten adult males required to conduct a service. Still, the synagogue has not missed a Sabbath or holiday service in more than 115 years. **First Shearith Israel Graveyard** (on the southern edge of Chinatown) is the burial ground of the country's first Jewish community. It has gravestones that date from 1683, including those of Spanish and Portuguese Jews who fled the Inquisition.

Puerto Ricans and Dominicans began to move to the Lower East Side after World War II. Colorful awnings mark the area's bodegas, and

The **Lower East Side Tenement Museum**.

many restaurants serve such Caribbean standards as *mofongo* and *cuchifritos*. In the summer, the streets throb with the sounds of salsa and merengue as residents hang out, savor freshly shaved ices with fruit syrup, drink beer and play dominoes.

In the 1980s, a new breed of immigrant began moving in: young artists and musicians attracted by low rents. Bars, boutiques and music venues sprang up on and around Ludlow Street, creating an annex to the East Village. This scene is still thriving, though rents have risen sharply. For live music, check who's playing at **Arlene's Grocery**, the **Bowery Ballroom**, and **Tonic** (*see p312, and p319*). The sign at **Pianos** (*see p318*), a popular bi-level bar, is a holdover from the piano store that had been in that spot for decades. A burgeoning art scene is also springing up; **Rivington Arms** and **Participant Inc.** (*see p262*) are storefront galleries that showcase young artists.

The Lower East Side's reputation as a haven for political radicals lives on at **ABC No Rio** (*see p274* **Our Unorganicized Reading**), which was established in 1980 after squatters took over an abandoned ground-floor space; it now houses a gallery and performance space. Meanwhile, a few luxe apartment complexes have moved in, and **Hotel on Rivington** (*see p43*), a new high-rise building in this low-rise 'hood, is difficult to miss.

Despite the trendy shops that have cropped up along the block, Orchard Street below Stanton Street remains the heart of the **Orchard Street Bargain District**, a row of stores selling utilitarian goods. This is the place for cheap hats, luggage, sportswear and T-shirts. In the 1930s, Mayor Fiorello La Guardia forced pushcart vendors off the streets and into large indoor marketplaces. Although many of these bazaars are now a thing of the past, **Essex Street Markets** (120 Essex St between Delancey and Rivington Sts) is still going strong as a purveyor of all things Latino, from groceries to religious icons.

Vestiges of the neighborhood's Jewish roots remain. **Katz's Delicatessen** (*see p171*) sells some of the best pastrami in New York (FYI, Meg Ryan's famous faux-orgasm scene in *When Harry Met Sally…* was filmed here). People come from all over for the crunchy dills at **Guss' Pickles** (*see p242*), another Lower East Side favorite and film star (it's in *Crossing Delancey*).

The Lower East Side is a nosher's paradise. Pay tribute to the neighborhood's Eastern European origins with a freshly baked bialy from **Kossar's Bialystoker Kuchen Bakery** (367 Grand St between Essex and Norfolk Sts, 1-212-473-4810). If you're in need of a sweeter hunk of dough, head a few doors over to the **Doughnut Plant** (379 Grand St between

Art of appreciation

Native New Yorkers are famous for their hometown pride. But David Niles, founder of **Tribute**, downtown's New York–centric arts and culture center, is poised to take his place beside Woody Allen and the Notorious B.I.G. in the gaga-for-Gotham Hall of Fame.

"New York has survived so much," says Niles, a born-and-bred Manhattanite who runs a high-definition-television production company by day. "It's not easy here. Sometimes, it's not fun. But there's just something about it."

That "something" led him to conceive, design and personally fund Tribute's ethereal, minimalist 12,000-square-foot gallery—containing exhibits, interactive installations, several projection screens and two cinemas—on the first and second floors of the Standard Oil Building.

Niles's goal for Tribute—to portray the strength of New York and its inhabitants while celebrating facets of city life so often taken for granted—is most affectingly exemplified by the installation *Last Call*, by resident artist

Jack Dowd. Part homage to NYC bars, part reference to Leonardo's *The Last Supper*, the life-size re-creation of a pub at closing time includes such characters as a cheating husband, a rose-peddling woman and a municipal worker whose sagging pants reveal an eyeful of ass-crack.

"You can't talk about this city without mentioning September 11," says Niles, though he insists his brainchild is not a memorial. Even so, Tribute's 15-minute centerpiece film, "Remember"—which intersperses classic overhead shots of NYC landmarks with candid and staged shots of irate cabbies, rush-hour traffic and subway performers—devotes three minutes to the World Trade Center attack.

Also recalling September 11 are *Memorial Hall*, a nine-foot-high panoramic photo of Ground Zero; and "Brothers," an eight-minute documentary featuring firefighters' personal accounts of the infamous day. "Living Timeline," meanwhile, compresses the 350-

Essex and Norfolk Sts, 1-212-503-3700), where high-quality organic doughnuts are available in flavors such as coconut and white peach. Nostalgic goodies like taffy and PEZ fill the shelves of **Economy Candy** (108 Rivington St between Essex and Ludlow Sts, 1-212-254-1832).

Eldridge Street Synagogue

12 Eldridge St between Canal and Division Sts (1-212-219-0888/www.eldridgestreet.org). Subway: F to East Broadway. **Tours** *Tue, Thu 11:30am, 2:30pm and by appointment; Sun 11am–3pm on the hour.* **Admission** *$5, seniors and students $3; self-guided tours $1.*

First Shearith Israel Graveyard

55–57 St. James Pl between James and Oliver Sts. Subway: J, M, Z to Bowery.

East Village

Scruffier than its genteel western counterpart, the **East Village** has a long history as a countercultural hotbed. Originally considered part of the Lower East Side, the neighborhood boomed in the 1960s when writers, artists and musicians moved in, transforming it into the hub for the period's social revolution.

Clubs and coffeehouses thrived, including the **Fillmore East,** on Second Avenue between 6th and 7th Streets (the theater has been demolished), and the **Dom** (23 St. Marks Pl between Second and Third Aves), where the Velvet Underground often headlined (now a condo). In the '70s, the neighborhood took a dive as drugs and crime prevailed— but that didn't stop the influx of artists and punk rockers. In the early '80s, East Village galleries were among the first to display the work of groundbreaking artists Jean-Michel Basquiat and Keith Haring. The nabe's past as an alt-scene nexus of arts and politics gets a nod with **Howl!** (*see p258*)—a late-summer festival organized by the Federation of East Village Artists. Poetry, jazz and film events celebrate the community's vibrant heritage.

Today, the area east of Broadway between Houston and 14th Streets is no longer quite so edgy, though remnants of its spirited past endure. A generally amiable population of ravers, punks, yuppies, hippies, homeboys, vagrants and trustafarians (those wanna-be bohos funded by family money) has crowded into the neighborhood's tenements, alongside a few elderly holdouts from previous waves of immigration. Check out the indie record shops, bargain restaurants, grungy bars, punky clubs and funky, cheap clothing stores. At 10th Street and Second Avenue, on the eastern end of historic Stuyvesant Street, sits the East Village's unofficial cultural center: **St. Mark's Church in-the-Bowery** (*see p352*)

year history of New York City into a ten-minute film looped on a rear-projection screen.

"People have left here saying things like, 'I'm so proud to be a New Yorker,' and 'I really get New York now,'" says Niles. "That's exactly the response I was going for."

Tribute

24 Broadway at Bowling Green (1-212-952-1000/www.tribute-nyc.com). Subway: 4, 5 to Bowling Green. **Open** *Mon–Sat 10am–6pm; Sun 1–6pm.* **Admission** *$7.* **Credit** *AmEx, Disc, MC, V.*

Danspace Project). St. Mark's was built in 1799, on the site of Peter Stuyvesant's farm. Stuyvesant, one of New York's first governors, is buried in the adjacent cemetery. The church is rented by arts groups, such as the experimental theater troupe **Ontological at St. Mark's** (1-212-533-4650).

St. Marks Place (8th St between Lafayette St and Ave A) is the East Village's main drag. The Bolshevik Leon Trotsky ran a printing press at 77 St. Marks Place in 1917, and poet W.H. Auden lived there from 1953 to 1972 (between First and Second Aves). Number 77 currently houses the regional Mexican restaurant **La Palapa** (1-212-777-2537). The street is less highbrow now, but also less gritty—it's a sanitized, gentrified version of its former selves. Lined with stores, bars and street vendors, St. Marks stays packed until the wee hours with crowds browsing for bargain T-shirts, records and books. The more interesting places are to the east; you'll find cafés and shops on and around Avenue A between 6th and 10th Streets. Since tattooing became legal again in New York City in 1997 (it had been banned in 1961), a number of parlors have opened up, including the famous **Fun City** (94 St. Marks Pl between First Ave and Ave A, 1-212-353-8282), whose awning advertises CAPPUCCINO & TATTOO.

Astor Place, with its 1970s balanced-cube sculpture, is always swarming with young skateboarders and other modern-day street urchins. It is also the site of Peter Cooper's recently refurbished **Cooper Union**, the city's first—and only—free private college. In the 19th century, Astor Place marked the boundary between the slums to the east and some of the city's most fashionable homes. **Colonnade Row** (428–434 Lafayette St between Astor Pl and E 4th St) faces the distinguished Astor Public Library building, which theater legend Joseph Papp rescued from demolition in the 1960s. Today, it's the **Public Theater** (*see p347*)—a haven for first-run American plays, the headquarters of the **Shakespeare in Central Park** festival (*see p347*) and the trendy **Joe's Pub** (*see p316*).

On the Bowery, east of Lafayette Street, are several missionary organizations that cater to the down-and-out—reminders of the street's famous past as a center for legions of bums, winos and flophouses. In recent years, a few restaurants have also set up shop. Hallowed **CBGB** (*see p313*), the birthplace of American punk, still packs in guitar bands, both new and used. Many other local bars and clubs successfully apply the cheap-beer-and-loud-music formula, including **Continental** and the **Mercury Lounge** (*see p314 and p317*).

East 7th Street is a Ukrainian stronghold; the focal point is the Byzantine **St. George's Ukrainian Catholic Church** at Number 30. Across the street, there's often a long line of beefy fraternity types waiting to enter **McSorley's Old Ale House** (*see p206*), which touts itself as the city's oldest pub in a single location (1854); it still serves just one kind of beer—its own brew, available in light or dark versions. For those who would rather shop than sip, the eclectic boutiques of young designers and vintage-clothing dealers dot 7th, 8th and 9th Streets.

Curry Row, on 6th Street between First and Second Avenues, is one of several Little Indias in New York. Roughly two dozen Indian restaurants sit side by side (contrary to a oft-told joke, they do not share a single kitchen),

On the spot

Fire flight At the turn of the 20th century, the East Village was known as Little Germany, and the heart of the community was **St. Mark's Lutheran Church**, at 323–327 East 6th Street. But today, it's easier to find *biryani* than bratwurst here. Why? On June 15, 1904, 1,300 people boarded the *General Slocum* steamship for the congregation's annual outing. A fire broke out on board, and 1,021 people—more than 800 of them St. Mark's parishioners—were killed. Hoping to escape the memories of the tragedy, many survivors decamped to the Upper East Side's burgeoning German community in Yorkville.

and they remain popular with diners on an extremely tight budget. The line of shiny Harleys on 3rd Street between First and Second Avenues tells you that the New York chapter of the **Hells Angels** is based here.

Alphabet City, occupying Avenues A through D, stretches toward the East River. The largely working-class Latino population has been overtaken by professionals willing to pay higher rents. Avenue C is known as Loisaida Avenue, an approximation of "Lower East Side" when pronounced with a Spanish accent. The neighborhood's long, rocky romance with the drug trade is mostly a thing of the past.

For those who appreciate funky charm, Alphabet City has its attractions. Two churches on 4th Street are built in the Spanish-colonial style: **San Isidro y San Leandro** (345 E 4th St between Aves C and D) and **Iglesia Pentecostal Camino Damasco** (289 E 4th St between Aves B and C). The **Nuyorican Poets Cafe** (*see p274*), a 30-year-old clubhouse for espresso-drinking beatniks, is famous for its slams, in which performance poets do lyric battle before a score-keeping audience. **Tompkins Square Park** (from 7th to 10th Sts, between Aves A and B) has been a frequent site for demonstrations and rioting. The last major uprising was about 15 years ago, when the city decided to evict squatters from the park and renovate it to suit the area's increasingly affluent residents. The Square also hosted the city's first (now annual) drag celebration, **Wigstock**. These days, it's still the community park of the East Village. Latino bongo beaters, longhairs with acoustic guitars, punky squatters, mangy dogs, yuppie stroller-pushers and the homeless mingle in the park.

North of Tompkins Square, around First Avenue and 11th Street, are remnants of earlier communities: discount fabric dealers, Italian cheese shops, Polish butchers and two great Italian coffeehouses: **De Robertis** (176 First Ave between 10th and 11th Sts, 1-212-674-7137) and **Veniero's Pasticceria and Caffe** (342 E 11th St at First Ave, 1-212-674-7264) are still wonderful for pastries and old-world ambience.

Greenwich Village

Stretching from Houston Street to 14th Street, between Broadway and Sixth Avenue, **Greenwich Village**'s leafy streets have inspired bohemians for almost a century. It's a place for idle wandering, for candlelit dining in out-of-the-way restaurants, and for hopping between bars and cabaret venues. The Village gets mobbed in mild weather and has lost some of its quaintness, but much of what has always attracted painters and poets to New

Power play at **Washington Square Park**.

York still exists. Sip a fresh roast in honor of the Beats—Jack Kerouac, Allen Ginsberg and their buddies—as you sit in their former haunts. Kerouac's favorite was **Le Figaro Café** (184 Bleecker St at MacDougal St, 1-212-677-1100). The **Cedar Tavern** (82 University Pl between 11th and 12th Sts, 1-212-929-9089), which was originally at the corner of 8th Street, is where the leading figures of Abstract Expressionism's boys' club discussed how best to apply paint: Franz Kline, Jackson Pollock, Larry Rivers, and Willem de Kooning drank under this banner in the 1950s.

The hippies who tuned out in **Washington Square Park**, once a potter's field, are still there in spirit, and often in person: The park hums with musicians and street artists (though the once ubiquitous pot dealers have become victims of hidden surveillance cameras). In warmer months, this is one of the best people-watching spots in the city. Chess hustlers and students from New York University join in, along with today's new generation of idlers: hip-hop kids who drive down to West 4th Street in their booming Jeeps, and Generation-Y skateboarders who clatter around the fountain and near the base

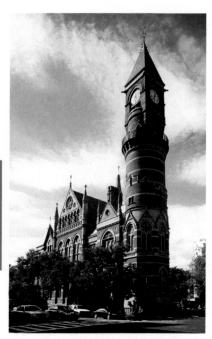

Gothic-fabulous **Jefferson Market Library**.

Fifth Avenue. The landmark building hosts exhibitions, lectures and art auctions.

Greenwich Village continues to change with the times, for better and for worse. **Eighth Street** is currently a long procession of piercing parlors, punky boutiques and shoe stores; in the 1960s, it was the closest New York got to San Francisco's Haight Street. (Jimi Hendrix's **Electric Lady Studios** is still at 52 W 8th Street between Fifth and Sixth Avenues.)

Once the dingy but colorful stomping ground of Beat poets and folk and jazz musicians, **Bleecker Street** between La Guardia Place and Sixth Avenue is now simply an overcrowded stretch of poster shops, cheap restaurants and music venues for the college crowd. Bob Dylan lived at and owned **94 MacDougal Street** (on a row of historic brownstones near Bleecker Street) through much of the '60s, performing in Washington Square Park and at clubs such as **Cafe Wha?** on MacDougal Street, between Bleecker and West 3rd Streets. The famed **Village Gate** jazz club once stood at the corner of Bleecker and Thompson Streets; it's been carved up into a CVS pharmacy and a small theater, though the Gate's sign is still in evidence. The new **AIA Center for Architecture** (*see p26* **Building on greatness**), a comprehensive resource for building and planning in New York, is just up the road, on La Guardia Place.

In the triangle formed by Sixth Avenue, Greenwich Avenue and 10th Street, you'll see the Gothic-style **Jefferson Market Library** (a branch of the New York Public Library); the lovely flower-filled garden facing Greenwich Avenue once held the Art Deco **Women's House of Detention** (Mae West did a little time there in 1926, on obscenity charges stemming from her Broadway show *Sex*), torn down in 1974. On Sixth Avenue at West 4th Street, stop by "the Cage," outdoor basketball courts where outstanding schoolyard players showcase their shake-and-bake moves.

of the **Washington Arch**. A modest-size replica of Paris's Arc de Triomphe, the arch was built in 1895 to honor George Washington, and was recently refurbished.

The Village has been fashionable since the 1830s, when the wealthy built handsome townhouses around **Washington Square**. A few of these properties are still privately owned and occupied; many others have become part of the ever-expanding **New York University** campus. NYU also owns the **Washington Mews**, a row of charming 19th-century buildings that were once stables; they line a tiny cobblestone cul-de-sac just north of the park between Fifth Avenue and University Place. Several literary figures, including Henry James, Herman Melville and Mark Twain, lived on or near the square. In 1871, the local creative community founded the **Salmagundi Club**, America's oldest artists' club, which is now situated north of Washington Square on

Jefferson Market Library
425 Sixth Ave at 10th St (1-212-243-4334).
Subway: A, C, E, B, D, F, V to W 4th St.
Open *Mon, Wed noon–8pm; Tue 10am–6pm; Thu noon–6pm; Fri 1–6pm; Sat 10am–5pm.*

Salmagundi Club
47 Fifth Ave at 12th St (1-212-255-7740/ www.salmagundi.org). Subway: L, N, Q, R, W, 4, 5, 6 to 14th St–Union Sq. **Open** *For exhibitions only; phone for details.* **Admission** *free.*

Washington Square Park
From W 4th St to Waverly Pl, between MacDougal St and University Pl. Subway: A, C, E, B, D, F, V to W 4th St.

▶ For more on downtown dining and nightlife, see **Restaurants**, **Bars** and **Music** (*pp167–201, pp203–213* and *pp311–330*).

West Village & Meatpacking District

While the **West Village** now harbors a wide range of celebrities (Sarah Jessica Parker and hubby Matthew Broderick, former mayor Ed Koch), it has managed to retain a low-key, everyone-knows-one-another feel. The area west of Sixth Avenue to the Hudson River, below 14th Street to Houston Street, still possesses the features that molded the Village's character. Only in this neighborhood could West 10th Street cross West 4th Street, and Waverly Place cross…Waverly Place. (The West Village follows not the later grid but the original horse paths that ran through it.) Locals fill the bistros along Hudson Street and patronize the shops lining Bleecker Street—you won't risk getting stuck in too many tourist traps this far west.

The northwest corner of this area is known as the **Meatpacking District**. Since the 1930s, it was primarily a wholesale meat market; until the 1990s, it was also a choice haunt for prostitutes, many of them transsexual. In recent years, however, the atmospheric cobblestone streets have seen the arrival of a new type of tenant: The once lonely **Florent** (69 Gansevoort St between Greenwich and Washington Sts, 1-212-989-5779), a 24-hour French diner that opened in 1985, is now part of a chic scene that includes swinging watering hole **APT** (*see p292*) and the restaurants **Pastis** (9 Ninth Ave at Little W 12th St, 1-212-929-4844), **Vento** (675 Hudson St at Ninth Ave, 1-212-699-2400; *see also p14* **Veni, vidi, Vento**) and **5 Ninth** (5 Ninth Ave at Little W 12th St, 1-212-929-9460), among many others. Restaurants, bars and clubs now dramatically outnumber meatpacking plants, and on the weekends, the neighborhood is overrun with party-hearty crowds.

The district also lures the fashion faithful with hot destinations such as **Jeffrey New York, Alexander McQueen, Catherine Malandrino, Stella McCartney** (*see p215, p216 and p220*) and rockin' **Le Dernier Cri**. As rents rose, meat dealers and artists' studios were forced out to make space for boutique hotels and clubs. Neighborhood residents started the Save Gansevoort Market campaign, and won landmark status for the area in September 2003.

The neighborhood's bohemians may be diminishing, but several historic nightlife spots soldier on to the south: **The White Horse Tavern** (567 Hudson St at 11th St, 1-212-989-3956) is supposedly where poet Dylan Thomas went on his last drinking binge before his death, in 1953. Earlier in the century, John Steinbeck and John Dos Passos passed time at **Chumley's** (*see p206*), a still-unmarked Prohibition-era speakeasy at 86 Bedford Street. Writer Edna St. Vincent Millay lived at **75½ Bedford Street**, built in 1873, and later inhabitants include Cary Grant and John Barrymore. Only nine feet wide, it's one of the narrowest residential buildings in the entire city. On and just off Seventh Avenue South are jazz and cabaret clubs, including **Village Vanguard** (*see p322*).

The West Village is also renowned as a gay neighborhood, though much of the scene has moved north to Chelsea (*see p94*). **The Stonewall** (*see p305*), on Christopher Street, is next to the original Stonewall Inn, the site of the 1969 rebellion that marked the birth of the modern gay-liberation movement. Same-sex couples stroll along **Christopher Street** (from Sheridan Square to the Hudson River), and plenty of shops, bars and restaurants are out and proud. The Hudson Riverfront features grass-covered piers, food vendors and picnic tables—ideal for warm-weather dawdling by folks of any sexual persuasion.

The best Places…

…for a quick fling
Trapeze School New York. *See p338.*

…for a law-and-order fix
Criminal Courts Building. *See p82.*

…for a juicy soup dumpling
Joe's Shanghai. *See p87.*

…for a peek at the pre-urban city
New York Unearthed. *See p76.*

…for a romantic (free) sunset cruise
Staten Island Ferry. *See p73.*

…for remembering the Ramones
CBGB. *See p313.*

…for seeing how the other half lived
Lower East Side Tenement Museum. *See p155.*

…for the freshest mozzarella
DiPalo's Fine Foods. *See p85.*

…for a moment of quiet reflection
St. Paul's Chapel. *See p80.*

…for shoe nirvana
Jeffrey New York. *See p215.*

Sightseeing

Midtown

The middle of the island can feel like the center of the universe.

Every day, the area known as midtown (roughly from 14th St to 59th St, between the East and Hudson Rivers) earns its reputation as one of the most hectic, breathtaking urban landscapes on the planet. During the day, people jostle their way along the sidewalks as yellow cabs and delivery trucks dart up, down and across the streets. The frenetic action continues above- and belowground: Each skyscraper is a monument to the buzz of commercial activity, while hordes of commuters ride an around-the-clock network of underground trains and subways. The area is home to the city's most famous landmarks: the **Empire State Building**, the **Chrysler Building**, **Rockefeller Center**, **Times Square** and **Grand Central Terminal**. Haute fashion is conceived around Seventh Avenue, publicized on Madison and sold along Fifth. But there's more to midtown than glistening towers and high-octane commerce. Cultural heavyweights such as the **Museum of Modern Art**, **Broadway** and the **Theater District**, **Carnegie Hall** and the **New York Public Library** draw their own crowds. Midtown is also where you'll find the folksy **Union Square Greenmarket** and the quaint, tree-lined streets of **Chelsea**, **Tudor City** and **Gramercy Park**. Everywhere you look, you'll see shopping galore, from street peddlers pushing designer knockoffs to soigné boutiques and world-class department stores. Although it may sound like a corny line from a Broadway musical, midtown's got it all.

Chelsea

Not so long ago, Chelsea was a mostly working-class and industrial neighborhood. Now it's the epicenter of the city's gay life (see pp299–309), but residents of all types inhabit the blocks between 14th and 29th Streets west of Fifth Avenue. There's a generous assortment of bars and restaurants, most of which are clustered along Eighth Avenue. Pioneers such as **Dia:Chelsea** (see p148) have led the art

▶ For information on multimuseum discount packages, see p147 **Package deals**.
▶ For more on area museums, see pp143–163.

crowd northward from Soho, and the whole western edge of Chelsea is now the city's hottest gallery zone. The far-west warehouse district, a nesting ground for fashionable lounges and nightclubs, is also seeing more residential use.

The **Annex Antiques Fair & Flea Market** (see p242) operates year-round on weekends, in a couple of empty parking lots and a garage. Ornate wrought-iron balconies distinguish the **Chelsea Hotel** (see p46), which has been a magnet for international bohemians since the 1950s. In the '60s and '70s, Andy Warhol's superstars (the Chelsea Girls) made the place infamous; punk rock conferred its notoriety in the '80s, when Nancy Spungen was stabbed to death by boyfriend Sid Vicious in room 100. Stop by for a peek at the lobby artwork and the grunge-glamorous guests, and linger over a drink in the luxe basement lounge, **Serena**. Occupying the long stretch of 23rd Street between Ninth and Tenth Avenues, **London Terrace** is a distinctive 1920s Tudor-style apartment complex that's home to a number of celebrities, including Debbie Harry.

Chelsea has its fair share of cultural offerings. The **Joyce Theater** (see p350) is a brilliantly renovated Art Deco cinema that presents better-known contemporary dance troupes. The **Dance Theater Workshop** (see p351) performs at the **Bessie Schönberg Theater** (219 W 19th St between Seventh and Eighth Aves, 1-212-691-6500), and toward the river on 19th Street sits the **Kitchen** (see p352), a pioneering experimental-arts center.

Cushman Row (406–418 W 20th St between Ninth and Tenth Aves), in the **Chelsea Historic District**, is an example of how the area looked when it was developed in the mid-1800s (although its grandeur was later affected by the intrusion of noisy elevated railways). Just north is the block-long **General Theological Seminary of the Episcopal Church**, whose gardens offer a pleasant respite for reflection. The seminary's land was part of the estate known as Chelsea, owned by poet Clement Clarke Moore (of "'Twas the night before Christmas" fame).

The former Nabisco plant on Ninth Avenue—where the first Oreo cookie was made, in 1912—has been renovated and now is home

Foodies flock to **Chelsea Market** for fresh fish, organic produce and...Emeril.

to the **Chelsea Market**. (The former factory site is a conglomeration of 18 structures built between the 1890s and the 1930s.) The ground-floor food arcade offers artisanal bread, fresh lobster, wine, hand-decorated cookies and imported Italian foods, among other treats. Upper floors house several media companies, including the Oxygen Network and the Food Network studios, where shows such as *Emeril Live* and *Molto Mario* are taped.

Chelsea's art galleries, occupying former warehouses in the 20s west of Tenth Avenue, draw an international audience of aesthetes, especially on weekends. Many of the major galleries that had been priced out of Soho (retail shops replaced them) found new homes here; bars and restaurants on the prowl for cheaper space followed suit. Evolving much like Soho did, this area has become just as expensive.

If you work up an appetite with all that galleryhopping, then you can pick from the 1929 Art Deco **Empire Diner** (210 Tenth Ave at 22nd St, 1-212-243-2736), French hangout **La Lunchonette** (130 Tenth Ave at 18th St, 1-212-675-0342) or creative American bistro the **Red Cat** (*see p187*). These pioneers have been joined by a host of upstarts, including beautiful-people hot spot **La Bottega** (*see p187*), whose huge outdoor terrace is the place to be in summer months. Or try the Bollywood-themed **Bombay Talkie** (189 Ninth Ave at 21st St, 1-212-242-1900) for Indian *dosas* and *kati* rolls; the sliver-of-Barcelona tapas bar **Tía Pol**

(205 Tenth Ave between 22nd and 23rd Sts, 1-212-675-8805); or the popular **Half King** (*see p273*), a pub co-owned by Sebastian Junger, author of *The Perfect Storm*.

You can watch the sunset from one of the Hudson River piers, once terminals for the world's grand ocean liners. While many city piers remain in a state of ruin, the four between 17th and 23rd Streets have been transformed into the mega sports center and TV- and film-studio complex **Chelsea Piers** (*see p334*). When you're down by the river, the **Starrett-Lehigh Building** (601 W 26th St at Eleventh Ave) comes into view. The stunning 1929 structure was left in disrepair until the dot-com boom of the late '90s, when media companies, photographers and fashion designers snatched up the loftlike spaces.

Chelsea Historic District
From 20th to 22nd Sts, between Ninth and Tenth Aves. Subway: C, E to 23rd St.

Chelsea Market
75 Ninth Ave between 15th and 16th Sts (www.chelseamarket.com). Subway: A, C, E to 14th St; L to Eighth Ave. **Open** *Mon–Fri 8am–8pm; Sat, Sun 10am–8pm.*

General Theological Seminary of the Episcopal Church
175 Ninth Ave between 20th and 21st Sts (1-212-243-5150/www.gts.edu). Subway: C, E to 23rd St. **Open** *Mon–Thu noon–3pm; Fri 11am–3pm weather permitting.* **Admission** *free.*

Down on the farm (without leaving the city!) at the **Union Square Greenmarket**. *See p97.*

Flatiron District & Union Square

The **Flatiron District**, which extends from 14th to 29th Streets between Fifth and Park Avenues, gives downtown a run for its money in terms of cachet—and cool. This chic enclave is full of retail stores that are often less expensive but just as stylish as those below 14th Street. The area is compact enough that tourists can hit all the sights on foot and then relax with a cocktail at a local watering hole.

Two public commons lie within the district: Madison and Union Squares. **Madison Square** (from 23rd to 26th Sts, between Fifth and Madison Aves) was the site of P.T. Barnum's Hippodrome and the original Madison Square Garden—the scene of the scandalous murder of its architect, Stanford White (recounted in E.L. Doctorow's novel *Ragtime,* also adapted as a film). After years of neglect, the statue-filled Madison Square Park finally got a face-lift in 2001. For ages, the vicinity bordering the park's east side was notable only for the presence of the monolithic **New York Life Insurance Company** building (51 Madison Ave between 25th and 26th Sts) and the **Appellate Division Courthouse** (35 E 25th St at Madison Ave). Now, numerous swank dining options have

injected some café-society liveliness into this once dull district, especially the Indian-inspired **Tamarind** (41 E 22nd St at Broadway, 1-212-674-7400) and **Dévi** (*see p189*), along with Tom Colicchio's glorious side-by-side-by-side trifecta on 19th Street: **'wichcraft, Craft** and **Craftbar** and (*see p188*). During the warmer months, stop by Danny Meyer's **Shake Shack** (south side of Madison Square Park, near 23rd St at Madison Ave, 1-212-889-6600), a hot-dog, hamburger and ice-cream stand where you can dine alfresco, surrounded by lush foliage.

Just south of Madison Square is a famously triangular Renaissance palazzo, the **Flatiron Building**. The neighborhood was christened in honor of the structure, which was the world's first steel-frame skyscraper.

In the 19th century, the neighborhood went by the moniker of Ladies' Mile, thanks to the ritzy department stores that lined Broadway and Sixth Avenue to the west. These huge retail palaces attracted the carriage trade, wealthy women who bought the latest imported fashions and household goods. By 1914, most of the department stores had moved north, leaving their proud cast-iron buildings behind. Today, the nabe is peppered with bookshops and photo studios and labs (it was known as New York's photo district well into the 1990s), and supermodels. The area has also reclaimed its history and is once again a prime shopping destination. Broadway between 14th and 23rd Streets is a tasteful home-furnishings strip; be sure to take a spin through the eclectic, expensive six-story home-design store **ABC Carpet & Home** (see p244). Fifth Avenue below 23rd Street is a clothing mecca: Many upscale shops, including the exclusive **Paul Smith** (see p228), showcase the latest designs. In the mid-'90s, big Internet companies began colonizing the lofts on Fifth Avenue and Broadway, and the district was dubbed Silicon Alley. Even though many dot-coms went bust and others have decamped to surrounding areas, the label remains in use.

Union Square (from 14th to 17th Sts, between Union Sq East and Union Sq West) is named after neither the Union of the Civil War nor the lively labor rallies that once took place here, but simply for the union of Broadway and Bowery Lane (now Fourth Avenue). From the 1920s until the early 1960s, Union Square gained a reputation as the favorite location for rabble-rousing political oratory, from AFL-CIO rallies to anti–Vietnam War protests. Following September 11, 2001, the park became a focal point for the city's outpouring of grief. It's now best known as the home of the **Union Square Greenmarket**, an excellent farmers' market, and the buildings flanking the square are used for a variety of commercial purposes. They include the **W New York–Union Square** hotel (see p45), the giant **Zeckendorf Towers** residential complex (1 Irving Pl between 14th and 15th Sts), a **Virgin Megastore** (see p248), and a **Barnes & Noble** bookstore (see p273). Several fine restaurants are also in close proximity, most notably the elegant **Union Square Cafe** (21 E 16th St between Fifth Ave and Union Sq West, 1-212-243-4020). In summer,

the outdoor **Luna Park** bar (Union Square Park, 17th St between Broadway and Park Ave South, 1-212-475-8464) beckons the cocktail crowd, while skateboarders commandeer the Greenmarket space during the evenings. Just off the square to the east is the **Vineyard Theatre** (see p347), an Off Broadway venue featuring the works of such well-respected playwrights as Craig Lucas and Paula Vogel.

Flatiron Building

175 Fifth Ave between 22nd and 23rd Sts. Subway: N, R, W to 23rd St.

Union Square Greenmarket

From 16th to 17th Sts, between Union Sq East and Union Sq West (1-212-788-7476). Subway: L, N, Q, R, W, 4, 5, 6 to 14th St–Union Sq. **Open** *Mon, Wed, Fri, Sat 8am–6pm.*

Gramercy Park & Murray Hill

You need a key to enter Gramercy Park, a tranquil, gated green square at the bottom of Lexington Avenue (between 20th and 21st Sts). Who gets a key? Only the lucky people who live in the beautiful townhouses and apartment buildings that ring the park. Anyone, however, can enjoy the charms of the surrounding district. Gramercy Park was developed in the 1830s to resemble a London square. **The Players** (16 Gramercy Park South between Park Ave South and Irving Pl), a private club and residence, is housed in an 1845 brownstone formerly owned by actor Edwin Booth; the 19th-century superstar was the brother of Abraham Lincoln's assassin, John Wilkes Booth. Edwin had the interior revamped as a club for theater professionals. Next door is the Gothic-Revival **National Arts Club**, at

Sightseeing

On the spot

Beat street In a famously transient life, King of the Beats Jack Kerouac stopped at this West Chelsea building just long enough to make history. After halfhearted stints at Columbia University, as a merchant marine and in the U.S. Navy, Kerouac drove west in 1949 with boho cowboy Neal Cassady. He then made his way back east, landing with his mother, Gabrielle, who was living at **454 West 20th Street**. Inspired by his travels, Kerouac wrote what would become *On the Road* during three weeks in the spring of 1951, on a single roll of typing paper.

number 15, whose members often donate their work in lieu of annual dues.

Irving Place, a strip leading south from the park to 14th Street, is named after author Washington Irving. Near the corner of 15th Street, **Irving Plaza** (*see p316*), a medium-size live-music venue that has been around since the early 1990s (when the Dave Matthews Band played here as an opening act), hosts everyone from old-timers like Van Morrison to newer acts like the Hives. At the corner of Park Avenue South and 17th Street stands the final headquarters of the once omnipotent **Tammany Hall** political machine. Built in 1929, the building now houses the **New York Film Academy** and the **Union Square Theater**.

A few blocks away, the **Theodore Roosevelt Birthplace**, a national historic site, holds a small museum. The President's actual birthplace was demolished in 1916, but it has since been fully reconstructed, complete with period furniture and a trophy room. The low, fortresslike **69th Regiment Armory** (68 Lexington Ave between 25th and 26th Sts), currently used by the New York National Guard, hosted the sensational 1913 Armory Show, which introduced Americans to Cubism, Fauvism and Dadaism. The tradition continues at the annual **Armory Show** (*see p254*).

The largely residential area bordered by 23rd and 30th Streets, and Park Avenue and the East River is known as **Kips Bay**, named for Jacobus Henderson Kip, whose farm covered the area in the 17th century. Third Avenue is the neighborhood's main thoroughfare, and a locus of ethnic eateries representing a variety of Eastern cuisines, including Afghan, Tibetan and Turkish, along with nightspots such as the **Rodeo Bar & Grill** (*see p323*), a Texas-style roadhouse that offers food and live roots music. Lexington Avenue between 27th and 30th Streets has been dubbed **Curry Hill** because of its many Indian restaurants and grocery stores.

Murray Hill spans 30th to 40th Streets between Third and Fifth Avenues. Townhouses of the rich and powerful were once clustered around Madison and Park Avenues. While it's still a fashionable neighborhood, only a few streets retain the elegance that made Murray Hill so distinctive. **Sniffen Court** (150–158 E 36th St between Lexington and Third Aves) is an unspoiled row of 1864 carriage houses located within earshot of the Queens Midtown Tunnel's ceaseless traffic. One of the area's most impressive attractions, the **Morgan Library** (*see p150*), also on 36th Street, is closed for renovation until 2006. The charming exhibition space occupies two buildings (one of which was J. Pierpont Morgan's personal

Steeple chase

Nestled between high-rises and skyscraping cathedrals of commerce, midtown's churches offer spiritual and physical refuge—and a pleasing architectural counterpoint to the surrounding towers of glass and steel. Visit them while strolling the area's dense streets; each building is worth a closer look.

Up Park Avenue from Grand Central sits **St. Bartholomew's Church** (Park Ave between 50th and 51st Sts; Mon–Wed, Fri 8am–6pm; Thu 8am–7:30pm; Sun 8am–8:30pm). Built in 1918 on the site of a brewery, this grand Episcopal cathedral—now a designated landmark—has Byzantine-style gold mosaics in the foyer and behind the high altar. It also houses New York's largest pipe organ, with 12,438 pipes. Classical-music concerts are presented throughout the year. In the summertime, local office workers eat lunch on St. Bart's wide front steps, but the church's terrace café offers a comfortable alternative.

St. Patrick's Cathedral (*see p105*), two blocks west on 50th Street, adds Gothic

grace to Fifth Avenue. The diocese of New York bought the land for an orphanage in 1810, but then in 1858, it switched gears and began construction on what would become the country's largest Catholic church. Today, the white marble spires are dwarfed by Rockefeller Center but, inside, visitors are treated to a still-stunning array of vaulted ceilings, stained-glass windows from Chartres and altars designed by Tiffany & Co.

Two blocks up Fifth Avenue, the Anglican **St. Thomas Church** (Fifth Ave at 53rd St; 7am–6pm daily) shares a crowded block of 53rd Street with the Museum of Modern Art. The interior of the squat, French-Gothic structure, finished in 1913, is decorated in heavy oak and cool, dark limestone. Behind the altar is an enormous floor-to-ceiling altarpiece, or reredos, depicting an intricate panorama of biblical scenes carved out of white stone. St. Thomas has one of America's best boys' choirs, which sings five weekly services in addition to an annual concert series.

library), and holds manuscripts, books, prints, and silver and copper collections owned by the famously acquisitive banker.

National Arts Club
15 Gramercy Park South between Park Ave South and Irving Pl (1-212-475-3424/www.nationalartsclub.org). Subway: 6 to 23rd St. **Open** *For exhibitions only. Call or visit website for information.*

Theodore Roosevelt Birthplace
28 E 20th St between Broadway and Park Ave South (1-212-260-1616/www.nps.gov/thrb). Subway: 6 to 23rd St. **Open** *Tue–Sat 9am–5pm.* **Tours** *Tue–Sat 10am–4pm; tours depart on the hour.* **Admission** *$3, children under 18 free.* **Credit** *Cash only.*

Herald Square & Garment District

The heart of America's multibillion-dollar clothing industry is New York's **Garment District** (roughly from 34th to 40th Sts, between Broadway and Eighth Ave), where platoons of designers—and thousands of workers—create the clothes we'll be wearing next season. The main drag, **Seventh Avenue**, has a fitting (but rarely used) moniker, Fashion Avenue. Although most garment-manufacturing has left Manhattan, the area is still gridlocked by delivery trucks and workers pushing racks of clothes up and down the streets. Trimming, button and fabric shops line the sidewalks, especially on 38th and 39th Streets.

A once thriving fur market is in retreat, now occupying only 28th to 30th Streets between Seventh and Eighth Avenues. On Seventh Avenue at 27th Street is the **Fashion Institute of Technology** (www.fitnyc.edu), a state college where those who aspire to vie with alumni Jhane Barnes and Calvin Klein in making their mark on fashion. The school's museum mounts stellar free exhibitions.

Beginning on 34th Street at Broadway and stretching all the way to Seventh Avenue, **Macy's** (*see p215*) is still the biggest—and busiest—department store in the world. Across the street is the younger, trendier chain store **H&M**, located at 2 Herald Square. **Herald Square**, named for a long-gone newspaper, is surrounded by this retail wonderland. The area's lower section is known as **Greeley Square**, after Horace Greeley, owner of the *Herald*'s rival, the *Tribune* (which previously employed Karl Marx as a columnist); the previously grungy square now offers bistro chairs and rest areas for weary pedestrians. To the east, the many restaurants and shops of

Past Gucci and Ungaro, the **Fifth Avenue Presbyterian Church** (Fifth Ave at 55th St; Mon–Fri 9am–5pm; Sat, Sun 9am–4pm) occupies a corner of 55th Street, and is right next to the Henri Bendel department store. The brown-sandstone steeple was the tallest in New York when the building was completed, in 1876, and the plain New England–Gothic facade conceals a two-level sanctuary that was built without right angles.

Farther west and south, off Times Square on 46th Street, the diminutive Episcopal **Church of Saint Mary the Virgin** (46th St between Sixth and Seventh Aves; Mon–Fri 7am–7pm; Sat 10:30am–5:30pm; Sun 8am–6pm) is wedged between Rosie O'Grady's pub and a Comfort Inn. Finished in 1895 just off what was then called Longacre Square, the church was fondly referred to as Smokey Mary's (a nod to the thick incense clouds that filled the interior) by the Broadway performers who visited between shows. The vaulted Gothic ceiling is painted with twinkling golden stars.

St. Bartholomew's Church.

The guitar-playing Naked Cowboy (thankfully, clad in briefs) is a **Times Square** fixture.

Koreatown line 32nd Street between Broadway and Madison Avenue.

The giant circular building on Seventh Avenue between 31st and 33rd Streets is the sports-and-entertainment arena **Madison Square Garden** (*see p331*). It occupies the site of the old Pennsylvania Station, a McKim, Mead & White architectural masterpiece that was razed in the 1960s—an act so soulless, it spurred the creation of the Landmarks Preservation Commission. (For more on the city's architecture, *see pp24–31*.) The railroad terminal, now known as **Penn Station**, lies beneath the Garden and serves approximately 600,000 people daily, more than any other station in the country. Fortunately, the aesthetic tide has turned. In 2001, the city approved a $788 million restoration-and-development project to move Penn Station across the street, into the **General Post Office** (formally known as the James A. Farley Post Office Building; 421 Eighth Ave between 31st and 33rd Sts, 1-800-275-8777), another McKim, Mead & White design. The project will connect the post office's two buildings with a soaring glass-and-nickel-trussed ticketing hall and concourse. When the new Penn Station is finally realized (no earlier than 2006), Amtrak service will roll in (along with rail links to Newark, La Guardia and JFK airports), while the current Penn Station will remain a hub for New Jersey Transit and the Long Island Rail Road.

Herald Square

Junction of Broadway and Sixth Ave at 34th St. Subway: B, D, F, V, N, Q, R, W to 34th St–Herald Sq.

Broadway & Times Square

Around 42nd Street and Broadway, an area sometimes called "the crossroads of the world," the night is illuminated not by the moon and the stars but by acres of glaring neon and sweeping arc lamps. Even native New Yorkers are electrified by this larger-than-life light show of corporate logos. No area better represents the city's glitter than Times Square, where zoning laws actually require businesses to include a certain level of illuminated signage on their facades.

Originally called Longacre Square, **Times Square** was renamed after the *New York Times* moved to the site in the early 1900s and announced its arrival with a spectacular New Year's Eve fireworks display. At the present 1 Times Square building (formerly the Times Tower), the *Times* erected the world's first ticker sign, and the circling messages—the stock-market crash of 1929, JFK's assassination, the 2001 World Trade Center attack—have been known to stop the midtown masses in their tracks. The Gray Lady is now located on 43rd Street between Seventh and Eighth Avenues but will move soon to a new $84 million tower on Eighth Avenue between 40th and 41st Streets. However, the sign remains at the original locale and marks the spot where New Year's Eve is traditionally celebrated.

Times Square is really just the elongated intersection of Broadway and Seventh Avenue, but it's also the heart of the **Theater District**. More than 40 stages showcasing extravagant dramatic productions are situated on the streets that cross Broadway. Times Square's once-famous sex trade is now relegated to short stretches of Seventh and Eighth Avenues.

The Theater District's transformation began in 1984, when the city condemned many properties along 42nd Street ("the Deuce") between Seventh and Eighth Avenues. A few years later, the city changed its zoning laws, making it harder for adult-entertainment establishments to operate. The results include places like **Show World** (669 Eighth Ave between 42nd and 43rd Sts), formerly a noted sleaze palace that now gets by with X-rated video sessions instead of live "dance" productions.

The streets west of Eighth Avenue are filled with eateries catering to theatergoers, especially along **Restaurant Row** (46th St between Eighth and Ninth Aves). This stretch is also popular *after* the theaters let out, when the street's bars host stand-up comedy and campy drag cabaret.

The area's office buildings are filled with entertainment companies: recording studios, record labels, theatrical agencies and screening rooms. The **Brill Building** (1619 Broadway at 49th St) has long been the headquarters of music publishers and producers, and such luminaries as Jerry Lieber, Mike Stoller, Phil Spector and Carole King wrote and auditioned their hits here. Visiting rock royalty and aspiring musicians drool over the selection of new and vintage guitars (and other instruments) for sale along **Music Row** (48th St between Sixth and Seventh Aves). Eager teens congregate under the windows at **MTV's** home base (1515 Broadway at 45th St), hoping for a wave from a guest celebrity like Beyoncé from the second-floor studio above. The glittering glass case that serves as headquarters to magazine-publishing giant **Condé Nast** (Broadway at 43rd St) gleams at 4 Times Square. The **NASDAQ** electronic stock market is housed in the same building, and its **MarketSite Tower**, a cylindrical eight-story video screen, dominates Times Square.

Glitzy attractions strive to outdo one another in ensnaring the endless throngs of tourists. **Madame Tussaud's New York**, a Gothamized version of the London-based wax-museum chain, showcases local legends such as Woody Allen and Jennifer Lopez. On Broadway, the noisy **ESPN Zone** (1472 Broadway at 42nd St, 1-212-921-3776) offers hundreds of video games and enormous TVs showing all manner of sporting events, and the 110,000-square-foot **Toys "R" Us** flagship store (*see p242*) boasts a 60-foot-tall indoor Ferris wheel.

Make a brief detour uptown on Seventh Avenue for a glimpse of the great classical-music landmark **Carnegie Hall** (*see p325*), on 57th Street, two blocks south of Central Park. Nearby is the famous **Carnegie Deli**

(854 Seventh Ave at 55th St, 1-212-757-2245), maestro of the Reuben sandwich.

West of Times Square, in the vicinity of the **Port Authority Bus Terminal** (on Eighth Ave) and the Lincoln Tunnel's traffic-knotted entrance, is an area historically known as **Hell's Kitchen**, where a gang- and crime-ridden Irish community scraped by during the 19th century. Italians, Greeks, Puerto Ricans, Dominicans and other ethnic groups followed. The neighborhood maintained its tough reputation through the 1970s, when, in an effort to invite gentrification, local activists renamed it Clinton, after onetime mayor (and governor) DeWitt Clinton. Crime has indeed abated, and in-the-know theatergoers fill the ethnic eateries along Ninth Avenue, which cost less and serve more interesting food than the traditional pretheater spots.

The extreme West Side is rather desolate, but the **Jacob K. Javits Convention Center** (Eleventh Ave between 34th and 39th Sts) draws crowds to its various trade shows. Maritime enthusiasts will appreciate the area along the Hudson River between 46th and 52nd Streets. The **USS *Intrepid*** (*see p162*), a decommissioned naval aircraft carrier, houses a sea, air and space museum (and a Concorde jet), and big crowds flock to the river when cruise ships, especially the world's largest ocean liner, the *Queen Mary 2,* dock at the terminal near 50th Street. During **Fleet Week** (*see p255*) every summer, the West Side fills with white-uniformed sailors on shore leave. You'll find the **Circle Line** terminal (*see p72*) on 42nd Street at Pier 83.

Madame Tussaud's New York

234 W 42nd St between Seventh and Eighth Aves (1-800-246-8872/www.nycwax.com). Subway: A, C, E to 42nd St–Port Authority; N, Q, R, W, 42nd St S, 1, 2, 3, 9, 7 to 42nd St–Times Sq. **Open** *10am–8pm daily.* **Admission** *$25, seniors $22, children 4–12 $19, children under 3 free.*

Times Square Visitors' Center

1560 Broadway between 46th and 47th Sts, entrance on Seventh Ave (1-212-869-1890/www.timessquare bid.org). Subway: N, R, W to 49th St; 1, 9 to 50th St. **Open** *8am–8pm daily.*

Fifth Avenue

Synonymous with *chic* and *moneyed,* Fifth Avenue caters to the elite; it's also the main route for the city's many ethnic (and inclusive) parades: National Puerto Rican Day, Gay and Lesbian Pride, and many more. Even without a parade, the street hums with activity as the sidewalks fill with all types, from gawking tourists to smartly dressed society matrons.

Sightseeing

Green peace in **Bryant Park**.

The **Empire State Building**, located smack-dab in the center of midtown, is visible from most parts of the city and beyond (at night, it's lit in showy colors to celebrate the holiday or special event in progress). Craning your neck at the corner of 34th Street to see story after story extend into the sky gives a breathtaking perspective of the gargantuan structure. The building's 86th-floor observation deck offers brilliant views in every direction; go at sunset to glimpse the longest shadow you'll ever see, cast from Manhattan all the way across the river to Queens. For a weekday break from sightseeing, catch a few winks in a cozy **MetroNaps** pod (1-212-239-3344), located in the famous skyscraper. This new company welcomes midtown executives and others looking to recharge with a quick snooze.

Impassive stone lions, dubbed Patience and Fortitude by Mayor Fiorello La Guardia, guard the steps of the **New York Public Library** (*see p162*), a beautiful Beaux Arts building at 41st Street. (A lovely library gift shop is just across Fifth Avenue.) The Rose Main Reading Room, on the library's top floor, is a hushed sanctuary of 23-foot-long tables and matching oak chairs, where bibliophiles can read, write and do research. Situated behind the library is **Bryant Park**, a well-cultivated green space that hosts a dizzying schedule of free entertainment

during the summer (*see p256*). The luxe **Bryant Park Hotel** (*see p51*) occupies the former American Radiator Building on 40th Street. Designed by architect Raymond Hood in the mid-1920s and recently renovated, the structure is faced with near-black brick and trimmed in gold leaf. Alexander Woollcott, Dorothy Parker and friends held court and traded barbs at the **Algonquin** (*see p50*); the lobby is still a great place to meet for a drink.

Veer off Fifth Avenue into the 19 buildings of **Rockefeller Center** and you'll see why this interlacing of public and private space is so lavishly praised. After plans for an expansion of the Metropolitan Opera on the site fell through in 1929, John D. Rockefeller Jr., who had leased the land on behalf of the Met, set about creating a complex to house radio and television corporations. Designed by Raymond Hood and many other prominent architects, the "city within a city" grew over the course of more than 40 years, with each new building conforming to the original master plan and Art Deco design. As you stroll down the Channel Gardens from Fifth Avenue, the stately **General Electric Building** gradually appears above you. The sunken plaza in the complex is the winter home of an oft-packed ice-skating rink (*see p335*); a giant Christmas tree looms above it each holiday season (*see p261*). The plaza is the most visible entrance to the restaurants and shops in the underground passages that link the buildings.

The center is filled with murals, sculptures, mosaics and other artwork. Perhaps the most famous pieces are the rink-side *Prometheus* sculpture, by Paul Manship, and José María Sert's murals in the GE Building. But wander around, and you'll be treated to many more masterworks. On weekday mornings, a crowd of (mainly) tourists gathers at the **NBC** television network's glass-walled, ground-level studio (where the *Today* show is shot), at the southwest corner of Rockefeller Plaza and 49th Street. When the show's free concert series in the plaza hosts big-name guests like Norah Jones, Sting and Queen Latifah, the throng swells mightily.

Radio City Music Hall, on Sixth Avenue at 50th Street, was the world's largest cinema when it was built, in 1932. This Art Deco jewel (the backstage tour is one of the best in town) was treated to a $70 million restoration in 1999; it's now used for music concerts and for traditional Christmas and Easter shows featuring the renowned Rockettes.

Facing Rockefeller Center is the beautiful **St. Patrick's Cathedral** (*see p98* **Steeple chase**), the largest Catholic cathedral in the United States. A few blocks north, a cluster of museums—the **American Folk Art Museum**, the **Museum of Arts & Design**

and the **Museum of Television & Radio** (*see
p152 and p161*) is anchored by the recently
renovated **Museum of Modern Art** (*see
p150*). **Swing Street**, or 52nd Street between
Fifth and Sixth Avenues, is a row of former
1920s speakeasies; the only venue
still open from that period is the **'21' Club**
(21 W 52nd St between Fifth and Madison Aves,
1-212-582-7200; *see p18* **'21' fun salute**).
The bar downstairs buzzes at night; upstairs,
the restaurant is a popular power-lunch spot.

The blocks off Fifth Avenue between
Rockefeller Center and Central Park South
showcase expensive retail palaces bearing
names that were famous long before the concept
of branding was developed. Along the stretch
between **Saks Fifth Avenue** (49th to 50th Sts;
see p215) and **Bergdorf Goodman** (at 58th St;
see p214), the rents are the highest in the world;
tenants include Cartier, Versace, **Tiffany & Co.**,
and **Gucci** (*see p233 and p220*). These chic
retailers have been joined in recent years by
the first U.S. outpost of Swedish clothing
giant H&M and the **National Basketball
Association** (666 Fifth Avenue at 52nd St,
1-212-515-6221). Fifth Avenue is crowned by
Grand Army Plaza at 59th Street. A gilded
statue of General William Tecumseh Sherman
presides over this public space; to the west stands
the elegant **Plaza Hotel** (*see p65*); to the north,
the luxe **Pierre** hotel (*see p64*). From here, you
can enter Central Park, where the din of city
streets gives way to relative serenity.

Empire State Building

*350 Fifth Ave between 33rd and 34th Sts (1-212-736-
3100/www.esbnyc.com). Subway: B, D, F, V, N, Q, R,
W to 34th St–Herald Sq.* **Open** *Observatories
9:30am–midnight daily (closed during extreme
weather). Last elevator up 11:15pm.* **Admission** *$12,
seniors and children 12–17 $11, children 6–11 $7,
children under 5 free.* **Credit** *Cash only.*
To say they don't build 'em like they used to is an
understatement. Financed as a speculative venture
by General Motors executive John J. Raskob, builders
broke ground for the Empire State Building in 1930.
It sprang up in 14 months with amazing speed, completed more than a month ahead of schedule and
$5 million under budget. The 1,250-foot tower
snatched the title of world's tallest building from
under the nose of the months-old, 1,046-foot Chrysler
Building, conveniently showing up Raskob's Detroit
rival Walter P. Chrysler.

NBC

*30 Rockefeller Plaza, 49th St between Fifth and Sixth
Aves (1-212-664-3700/www.nbc.com). Subway: B, D,
F, V to 47–50th Sts–Rockefeller Ctr.* **Tours** *Mon–
Sat 8:30am–5:30pm; Sun 9:30am–4:30pm; tours
depart every 15 minutes.* **Admission** *$17.95;
seniors, students and children 6–16 $15.50; children
under 6 not admitted.*

Peer through the *Today* show's studio window with
a horde of fellow onlookers, or pay admission (at the
NBC Experience Store, www.shopnbc.com) for
a guided tour of the studios. The tours are led by
pages, many of whom—Ted Koppel, Kate Jackson,
Michael Eisner, Marcy Carsey, and others—have
gone on to bigger and better things in show biz. (For
information on NBC tapings, *see p298*.)

Radio City Music Hall

See p318 for listing. **Tours** *11am–3pm daily.*
Admission *$17, seniors $14, children under 12 $10.*

Rockefeller Center

*From 48th to 51st Sts, between Fifth and Sixth
Aves (1-212-632-3975/tickets 1-212-664-7174/www.
rockefellercenter.com). Subway: B, D, F, V to 47–
50th Sts–Rockefeller Ctr. Mon–Sat 10am–
5pm; Sun 10am–4pm; tours depart on the hour.*
Admission *$12, seniors and children 6–16 $10.*
Exploring the center is free. For guided tours in and
around the historic buildings, however, advance
tickets are necessary and available by phone, online
or at the NBC Experience Store (*see above*).

Local legend

It took more than ten years of unflagging—
and very public—effort for the notoriously
private **Jacqueline Kennedy Onassis** to
save Grand Central Terminal, America's
most famous train station. After the
glorious (original) Pennsylvania Station
was demolished in 1964, developers
unveiled plans for an office tower over the
crumbling Grand Central. But Jackie O
would have none of it. She drafted civic
leaders, architects and celebrities for her
Committee to Save Grand Central, which
in 1978 finally won a Supreme Court
decision affirming landmark status for the
beloved Beaux Arts building.

The holiday light show at **Grand Central Terminal**. *See p105.*

St. Patrick's Cathedral

Fifth Ave between 50th and 51st Sts (1-212-753-2261). Subway: B, D, F to 47–50th Sts–Rockefeller Ctr; E, V to Fifth Ave–53rd St. **Open** *6:30am–8:45pm daily.* **Tours** *Call for tour dates and times.* **Admission** *free.*

Midtown East

The area east of Fifth Avenue may seem less appealing to tourists than Times Square or Rockefeller Center. Although the neighborhood is home to some of the city's most recognizable landmarks—the United Nations, Grand Central Terminal and the Chrysler Building—the grid of busy streets is lined with large, imposing buildings, and the bustling sidewalks are all business. The area is a little thin on plazas and street-level attractions, but it compensates with a dizzying array of world-class architecture.

Grand Central Terminal, a 1913 Beaux Arts train station, is the city's most spectacular point of arrival (unlike Penn Station, Grand Central is used only for commuter trains). The station stands at the junction of 42nd Street and Park Avenue, the latter rising on a viaduct that curves around the terminal. Since its renovation, completed in 1998, the terminal itself has become a destination, with classy restaurants and bars, such as the **Campbell Apartment** cocktail lounge (off the West Balcony, 1-212-953-0409), the grottolike **Grand Central Oyster Bar & Restaurant** (Lower Concourse, 1-212-490-6650), and star chef Charlie Palmer's **Métrazur** (East Balcony, 1-212-687-4600). The Lower Concourse food court spans the globe with its fairly priced lunch options. One notable oddity: The constellations on the Main Concourse ceiling are drawn in reverse, as if seen from outer space.

Rising like a phoenix behind Grand Central, the **MetLife Building** (*see p31*), formerly the Pan Am Building, was once the world's largest office tower. Now, its most celebrated tenants are the peregrine falcons that nest on the roof and feed on pigeons snatched midair. On Park Avenue is the famed **Waldorf-Astoria** (*see p56*), formerly located on Fifth Avenue but rebuilt here in 1931 after the original was demolished to make way for the Empire State Building. Other must-see buildings in the area include **Lever House** (390 Park Ave between 53rd and 54th Sts), the **Seagram Building** (375 Park Ave between 52nd and 53rd Sts), **Citicorp Center** (from 53rd St to 54th St, between Lexington and Third Aves), and the stunning Art Deco skyscraper on the corner of Lexington Avenue and 51st Street, formerly the General Electric Building (and before that, the RCA Victor Building). A Chippendale crown tops Philip Johnson's postmodern icon, the **Sony Building** (550 Madison Ave between 55th and 56th Sts), formerly the AT&T Building. Inside, the **Sony Wonder Technology Lab** (*see p284*) is a hands-on thrill zone of science in action.

Along the river to the east lies **Tudor City**, a pioneering 1925 residential development and a high-rise version of England's Hampton Court. The neighborhood is dominated by the **United Nations Headquarters** (U.N. Plaza, First Ave between 42nd and 48th Sts) and its famous glass-walled **Secretariat** building. Although you don't need a passport, you will be leaving U.S. soil when you enter the U.N. complex—it's an international zone, and the vast buffet at the **Delegates Dining Room** (fourth floor, 1-212-963-7626) puts cultural diversity on the table. The grounds and the Peace Garden along the East River are off-limits for security reasons. Unless you pay for a guided tour, the only accessible attractions are the exhibitions in the lobby and the bookstore and gift shop on the lower level. But right across First Avenue is **Dag Hammarskjöld Plaza** (47th St between First and Second Aves), named for the former U.N. Secretary General. Here, you can stroll through a lovely garden honoring actress Katharine Hepburn (who used to live nearby).

East 42nd Street holds still more architectural distinction, including the Romanesque-revival hall of the former **Bowery Savings Bank** (No. 110) and the Art Deco details of the **Chanin Building** (No. 122). Completed in 1930, the gleaming **Chrysler Building** (at Lexington Ave) pays homage to the automobile. Architect William Van Alen outfitted the main tower with colossal radiator-cap eagle "cargoyles" and a brickwork relief sculpture of racing cars complete with chrome hubcaps. A needle-sharp stainless-steel spire was added to the blueprint so the finished product would be taller than 40 Wall Street, which was under construction at the same time. The **Daily News Building** (No. 220), another Art Deco gem designed by Raymond Hood, was immortalized in the Superman films; although the namesake tabloid no longer has offices here, the lobby still houses the paper's giant globe.

Grand Central Terminal

From 42nd to 44th Sts, between Vanderbilt and Lexington Aves. Subway: 42nd St S, 4, 5, 6, 7 to 42nd St–Grand Central. **Tours** *Call 1-212-697-1245 for information.*

United Nations Headquarters

First Ave at 46th St (1-212-963-7710/tours 1-212-963-8687/www.un.org). Subway: 42nd St S, 4, 5, 6, 7 to 42nd St–Grand Central. **Tours** *Mar–Dec Mon–Fri 9:30am–4:45pm; Sat, Sun 10am–4:30pm. Jan, Feb Mon–Fri 9:30am–4:45pm.* **Admission** *$10.50, seniors $8, students $7, children 5–14 $6, children under 5 not admitted.*

Sightseeing

Uptown

City scenery, gorgeous greenery, the elite and the street. All together now...

The word *uptown* evokes both stately Fifth Avenue mansions and still-swinging former speakeasies in Harlem. Uptown is where you'll find famous outposts of high culture, such as the West Side's **Lincoln Center** and the East Side's **Museum Mile**, as well as the colorful street culture of **El Barrio** and **Washington Heights**. The hustle and bustle of the Financial District and midtown subside as you head farther north in Manhattan—the neighborhoods above 59th Street are relatively calm—but you won't miss it. At the narrow tip of the island, where the East and Hudson Rivers meet, the city can seem seductively tranquil. Uptown is graced with lush foliage and resplendent views, and not much tops a beautiful day in magnificent **Central Park**.

Central Park

This 843-acre patch of the great outdoors was the first man-made public park in the U.S. In 1853, the newly formed Central Park Commission chose landscape designer Frederick Law Olmsted and architect Calvert Vaux to turn this vast tract of rocky swampland into a rambling oasis of greenery. The parks commission, inspired by the great parks of London and Paris, imagined a place that would provide city dwellers respite from the crowded streets. A noble thought, but one that required the eviction of 1,600 mostly poor or immigrant inhabitants, including residents of Seneca Village, the city's oldest African-American settlement. But clear the area, the city did, and the rest is history.

In 2003, the park celebrated its 150th anniversary, and it has never looked better, thanks to the Central Park Conservancy, a private nonprofit civic group formed in 1980 that has been instrumental in restoration and maintenance. A horse-drawn carriage is still the sightseeing vehicle of choice for many tourists (and even a few romantic locals, though they'd never admit to it); plan on paying $34 for a 20-minute tour. (Carriages line up along Central Park South between Fifth Avenue and Columbus Circle.)

▶ For more on uptown's museums, *see pp143–163.*
▶ For nearby art galleries, *see pp262–271.*

The park is dotted with landmarks. **Strawberry Fields**, near the West 72nd Street entrance, memorializes John Lennon, who lived in the nearby **Dakota** (*see p114*). Also called the International Garden of Peace, this sanctuary features a mosaic of the word IMAGINE, donated by the Italian city of Naples. More than 160 species of flowers and plants from all over the world bloom here (including strawberries, of course). The statue of Balto, a heroic Siberian husky (East Dr at 67th St), is a favorite sight for tots. Slightly older children appreciate the statue of Alice in Wonderland, just north of the **Conservatory Water** at the East 74th Street park entrance.

In winter, ice-skaters lace up at **Wollman Rink** (midpark at 62nd St; *see also p336*), where the skating comes with a picture-postcard view of the fancy hotels surrounding the park. A short stroll to about 64th Street brings you to the **Friedsam Memorial Carousel**, still a bargain at a dollar a ride. (For more park activities for children, *see p284*.)

Come summer, kites, Frisbees and soccer balls fly every which way across **Sheep Meadow**, the designated quiet zone that begins at 66th Street. The sheep are gone (they grazed here until 1934), replaced by sunbathers improving their tans and scoping out the thonged throngs. The hungry (and affluent) can repair to glitzy **Tavern on the Green** (Central Park West at 67th St, 1-212-873-3200), which sets up a grand outdoor café in the summer, complete with a 40-foot-long bar made with trees from city parks. However, picnicking alfresco (or snacking on a hot dog from one of the park's food vendors) is the most popular option. East of Sheep Meadow, between 66th and 72nd Streets, is the **Mall**, where you'll find volleyball courts and plenty of in-line skaters. East of the Mall's **Naumburg Bandshell** is **Rumsey Playfield**—site of the annual **Central Park SummerStage** series (*see p256*), an eclectic roster of free and benefit concerts held from Memorial Day weekend to Labor Day weekend. One of the most popular meeting places in the park is the grand **Bethesda Fountain and Terrace**, near the midpoint of the 72nd Street Transverse Road. *Angel of the Waters,* the sculpture in the center of the fountain, was created by Emma Stebbins, the first woman to be granted a major public-

The green acres of Central Park's **Great Lawn** are pastoral perfect.

art commission in New York. North of it is the **Loeb Boathouse** (midpark at 75th St), where you can rent a rowboat or gondola to take out on the lake, which is crossed by the elegant **Bow Bridge**. The bucolic park views enjoyed by diners at the nearby **Central Park Boathouse Restaurant** (midpark at 75th St, 1-212-517-2233) make it a lovely place for brunch or drinks. The thickly forested **Ramble**, between 73rd and 79th Streets, is a favorite spot for bird-watching, offering glimpses of more than 70 species.

Farther north is the popular **Belvedere Castle**, a recently restored Victorian building that sits atop the park's second-highest peak. It offers excellent views and also houses the **Henry Luce Nature Observatory**. The open-air **Delacorte Theater** hosts **Shakespeare in Central Park** (*see p256*), a summer tradition of free performances of plays by the Bard and others. The **Great Lawn** (midpark between 79th and 85th Sts) is a sprawling stretch of grass that doubles frequently as a concert spot for just about any act that can rally a six-figure audience, from the New York Philharmonic to the Dave Matthews Band. (At other times, it's the favored spot of seriously competitive soccer teams and much less cutthroat teams of Hacky Sackers and their dogs.) Several years ago, the **Reservoir** (midpark between 85th and 96th Sts) was renamed in honor of the late Jacqueline Kennedy Onassis (*see p103* **Local legend**), who used to jog around it.

Central Park Zoo

830 Fifth Ave between 63rd and 66th Sts (1-212-439-6500/www.centralparkzoo.org). Subway: N, R, W to Fifth Ave–59th St. **Open** *Apr–Oct Mon–Fri 10am–5pm; Sat, Sun 10am–5:30pm. Nov–Mar 10am–4:30pm daily.* **Admission** *$6, seniors $1.25, children 3–12 $1.* **Credit** *Cash only.*

This is the only place in New York City where you can see polar bears swimming underwater. The Tisch Children's Zoo was recently spiffed up, and the George Delacorte Musical Clock delights kids every half hour.

Central Park, season by season

Even without Christo's recent *Gates* project—a spectacular art installation of 7,500 archways hung with sheets of saffron-hued fabric—a stroll through Manhattan's grandest park is worth a visit in any season. In summer, thousands of visitors flood the famous green spot to take advantage of a slew of mostly free operas, concerts and plays, but the park is a boon to locals and tourists throughout the year. Here are a few of our favorite activities, from alfresco tango lessons in June to cozy carriage rides in December. For a list of day-by-day happenings, visit the Central Park Conservancy at www.centralparknyc.org.

Spring

Scope chicks From green herons to snowy egrets and red-tailed hawks, more than 70 species of birds reside in the park, and hundreds more drop in during the spring and fall migrations. The densely wooded Ramble is a birders' paradise, as is the north end of the park above 103rd Street. To see what's been spotted lately, scan the birders' journal on display in the Loeb Boathouse.

Board silly At the Chess and Checkers House, just west of the Dairy at 65th Street, get your butt kicked by an old guy at one of 24 outdoor playing tables. Chess and checker sets can be borrowed from the Dairy with a valid photo ID.

Flower power Celebrate the return of spring with a stroll through the Conservatory Garden at the northeast end of the park. In March and April, flower beds are filled with daffodils, crocuses and tulips, and magnolia, quince and crab-apple trees are in bloom.

Summer

Get reel The fishing is strictly catch-and-release, but the Charles A. Dana Discovery Center provides free rods and bait to help you land largemouth black bass, catfish and bluegills in the Harlem Meer. Take advantage Tuesdays through Sundays, mid-April through mid-October.

Be ballsy Informal pickup games happen all over the park during the summer. Basketball: The most popular games are at the Great Lawn playground, Saturdays 9am till dusk, and Sundays 1pm till dusk. Ultimate Frisbee: From Memorial Day through Labor Day, join the Central Park Nomads at the "Dustbowl," at 97th Street on the east side of the park (Tue, Thu 6pm–dusk; Sat 3–6pm). Soccer: An international crowd convenes next to SummerStage, south of 72nd Street near Fifth Avenue, on Wednesdays at 6pm and Saturdays from 11am to 1pm.

Take two June through September, tango aficionados dance outside at the south end of the Mall near the Shakespeare Statue, from 6 to 9pm every Saturday. Live music is provided twice monthly, and there's a free lesson at 7pm.

Fall

Cheer-a-thon Applaud the sweaty throngs as they cross the finish line of the world-famous New York City Marathon in early November. Runners enter the Park at Engineers' Gate (Fifth Ave at 90th St), head south to exit the park at 59th Street and then reenter the Park at Columbus Circle to end their five-borough trek near Tavern on the Green. Participants begin the course at 10am; front-runners finish between noon and 1pm. By midafternoon, the south end of the park is mobbed with limping, water-guzzling marathoners wrapped in the day's most coveted accessory—the Mylar sheets handed out at the finish line. For more information, go to www.nyrrc.org.

Splash of color Watch the brilliant changing leaves of maple and oak trees reflected in the water as you row a rental boat around Central Park Lake, or go the romantic route and ride in an authentic Venetian gondola.

On a string Catch the puppets in action at the Swedish Cottage Marionette Theater (*see p286*). This newly refurbished 1876 building is the headquarters of the Citywide Puppets in the Parks program as well as the home base for one of the country's few remaining marionette companies. Original productions based on classic fairy tales are presented throughout the year.

Winter

Slip and slide Beat the crowd at Wollman Rink by hitting the ice just as the rink opens at 10am. Or come down for a moonlit after-dinner spin before closing time: 10pm on Wednesdays and Thursdays; 11pm, Fridays and Saturdays; 9pm, Sundays.

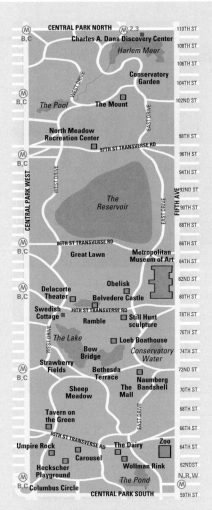

Charles A. Dana Discovery Center

Park entrance on Malcolm X Blvd (Lenox Ave) at 110th St (1-212-860-1370/www.centralparknyc.org). Subway: 2, 3 to 110th St–Central Park North. **Open** *Tue–Sun 10am–5pm.* **Admission** *free.*

Stop by for weekend family workshops, cultural exhibits and outdoor performances on the plaza next to the Harlem Meer. From April to October, the center lends out fishing rods and bait, and on select Thursday mornings, park rangers lead bird-watching walks. Call ahead for the schedule.

The Dairy

Park entrance on Fifth Ave at 66th St (1-212-794-6564/www.centralparknyc.org). Subway: N, R, W to Fifth Ave–59th St. **Open** *Summer 11am–5pm daily. Winter 10am–5pm daily.* **Admission** *free.*

Built in 1872 to show city kids where milk comes from (cows, in this case), the Dairy is now the Central Park Conservancy's information center, complete with interactive exhibits, videos explaining the park's history, and a gift shop.

Henry Luce Nature Observatory

Belvedere Castle, midpark off the 79th St Transverse Rd (1-212-772-0210). Subway: B, C to 81st St–Museum of Natural History. **Open** *Tue–Sun 10am–5pm.* **Admission** *free.*

During the spring and fall hawk migrations, park rangers discuss the various birds of prey found in the park and help visitors spot raptors from the castle roof. You can also borrow a naturalist kit that includes binoculars, maps and bird-identification guides.

Upper East Side

Gorgeous prewar apartments owned by blue-blooded socialites, soigné restaurants filled with the Botoxed ladies-who-lunch set… This is the picture most New Yorkers have of the **Upper East Side**, and you'll certainly see plenty of supporting evidence on Fifth, Madison and Park Avenues. There's a history to this reputation: Encouraged by the opening of Central Park in the late 19th century, the city's more affluent residents began building mansions along Fifth Avenue. By the beginning of the 20th century, even the superwealthy had warmed to the idea of giving up their large homes for closer quarters—provided they were near the park. As a result, apartments and hotels began springing up in 1881, continuing until 1932. (A few years later, working-class folks settled around Second and Third Avenues, following construction of an elevated East Side train line.) Architecturally, the overall look of the neighborhood, especially from Fifth to Park Avenues, is remarkably homogeneous. Along the expanse known as the **Gold Coast**—Fifth, Madison and Park Avenues from 61st to 81st Streets—you'll see the great old mansions, many of which are now foreign consulates. The structure at 820 Fifth Avenue

Snuggle up Get cozy in a horse-drawn carriage and enjoy the park in winter as you clip-clop under snow-dusted trees. Then warm up with a hot toddy at the historic Oak Bar (*see p210*) in the Plaza Hotel.
Downhill racer Cedar Hill (east side between 76th and 79th Sts) and Pilgrim Hill (just past the Conservatory Water) have been snow-day sledding destinations for generations of city youngsters. Feel like a kid again as you watch them zoom by.

These mansions at Fifth Avenue and 84th Street are now a girls' school.

(at 64th St) was one of the earliest luxury-apartment buildings on the avenue. New York's ultimate gingerbread house is 45 East 66th Street (between Madison and Park Aves). Architect Stanford White designed 998 Fifth Avenue (at 81st St) in the image of an Italian Renaissance palazzo. Some wonderful old carriage houses adorn 63rd and 64th Streets.

Philanthropic gestures made by the moneyed class over the past 130 years have helped to create a cluster of art collections, museums and cultural institutions. In fact, Fifth Avenue from 82nd to 104th Streets is known as **Museum Mile** because it is flanked by the **Metropolitan Museum of Art**; the Frank Lloyd Wright–designed **Guggenheim Museum**; the **Cooper-Hewitt, National Design Museum** (in Andrew Carnegie's former mansion); the **Jewish Museum**; the **Museum of the City of New York**; and El Museo del Barrio. (For complete listings, see pp143–163.)

Madison Avenue from 57th to 86th Streets is New York's world-class ultraluxe shopping strip. The snazzy department store **Barneys New York** (see p214) offers chic designer fashions and witty, often audacious window displays. For a postspree pick-me-up, order a cup of divinely rich hot chocolate and a Paris-perfect pastry at **La Maison du Chocolat** (see p240). While bars and restaurants dominate most of the north-south avenues, hungry sightseers can pick up a snack (or picnic supplies) at the well-stocked **Grace's**

Market Place (1237 Third Ave between 71st and 72nd Sts, 1-212-737-0600) or at the Italian gourmet-food shop **Agata & Valentina** (1505 First Ave at 79th St, 1-212-452-0690). Savor your meal on a park bench along the East River promenade leading to **Carl Schurz Park** (see p111).

Yorkville

Not much remains of the old German and Hungarian immigrant communities that filled **Yorkville** with delicatessens, beer halls and restaurants. Two flashbacks are the 71-year-old **Elk Candy Company** (1628 Second Ave between 84th and 85th Sts, 1-212-585-2303), which is famous for its chocolates and handmade marzipan, and the nearly 50-year-old **Heidelberg** (see p197), where dirndl-wearing waitresses serve steins of Spaten and platters piled with sausages from the wurstmeisters at nearby butcher shop **Schaller & Weber** (1654 Second Ave at 86th St). Worthy newcomers include **Beyoglu** (see p197), a stylish spot for Mediterranean mezes, and **Jackson Hole** (232 E 64th St between Second and Third Aves, 1-212-371-7187), a casual diner beloved by locals for its big, juicy burgers with deliciously messy toppings. Relax over a cocktail at the candlelit **Stir** (163 First Ave between 73rd and 74th Sts, 1-212-744-7190), which offers an elegantly loungey atmosphere and a cool specialty-drinks menu.

Gracie Mansion, at the eastern end of 88th Street, is the only Federal-style mansion in Manhattan, and it's been New York's official mayoral residence since 1942. The green-shuttered yellow edifice, built in 1799 by Scottish merchant Archibald Gracie, is the focal point of tranquil **Carl Schurz Park**, named in honor of the German immigrant who became a newspaper editor and U.S. senator. In 2002, Gracie Mansion's living quarters were opened to the public for the first time in 60 years; the current mayor, billionaire Michael Bloomberg, eschews the mayor's traditional address in favor of his own Beaux Arts mansion at 17 East 79th Street (between Fifth and Madison Aves). The tour also winds through the formerly private living room, guest suite and smaller bedrooms. Reservations are a must. The **Henderson Place Historic District** (at East End Ave between 86th and 87th Sts), one block from Gracie Mansion, consists of two dozen handsome Queen Anne row houses, which were commissioned by furrier and real-estate developer John C. Henderson. Twenty-four of the original 32 houses remain, but the cul-de-sac looks much as it did in 1882; the original turrets, double stoops and slate roofs remain intact.

Although the city is home to approximately 400,000 Muslims, the dramatic **Islamic Cultural Center** (1711 Third Ave at 96th St, 1-212-722-5234), built in 1990, is New York's first major mosque.

Gracie Mansion Conservancy

Carl Schurz Park, 88th St at East End Ave (1-212-570-4751). Subway: 4, 5, 6 to 86th St. **Tours** *Mar–mid-Nov Wed 10, 11am, 1, 2pm.* **Admission** *$7, seniors $4, students and children under 12 free. Reservations required; same-day reservations not permitted.* **Credit** *Cash only.*

Roosevelt Island

Walk along East 59th Street to the East River, and you'll see **Roosevelt Island**, a submarine-shaped isle about 300 yards away from Manhattan. A major destination for both locals and savvy tourists on the night of July 4, it affords prime views of the city's fireworks. The enclave, a state-planned residential community created in 1975, is home to roughly 10,000 people, including a large contingent of U.N. employees.

Until 1921, Roosevelt was known as Blackwell's Island, after Englishman Robert Blackwell, who bought it from the Dutch (who "bought" it from Native Americans) and moved there in 1676. The family's rebuilt clapboard farmhouse is in Blackwell Park, adjacent to Main Street (the island's only commercial strip). In the 1800s, a lunatic asylum, a smallpox hospital, prisons and workhouses were also built here.

The best way to get to Roosevelt Island is to take the **Tramway**, which crosses the East River from 59th Street in Manhattan. (The F train also stops on the island.) When you're near the Manhattan tram station, stop by the **Bridgemarket** complex (First Ave at 59th St), opened in 1999 in a former farmers' market under the Queensboro Bridge. The space now houses the **Terence Conran Shop** (*see p221* **Conceptually yours**) and **Guastavino's** restaurant (409 E 59th St between First and York Aves, 1-212-980-2455), named for the maker of the tiles that line its high, curved ceilings. The Spanish builder's legacy can also be seen in the Grand Central Oyster Bar, on Ellis Island (*see p77*) and in various subway stations.

On the spot

Sleazy Street Back in the '80s, the tony Upper West Side townhouse at **307 West 74th Street** was the home of Sidney Biddle Barrows, a blue-blooded blond who ran a high-class call-girl ring. When police raided her apartment one October day in 1984, details of the high-society scandal were the talk of the town. Dubbed "the Mayflower Madam" by the tabloids, Barrows pleaded guilty to the misdemeanor charge of promoting prostitution and was fined $5,000. She now makes a nice (legal) living as an author (she's written two books) and on the lecture circuit.

Once on Roosevelt Island, take in the panoramas of the Manhattan skyline from the riverfront promenades. Wander down the **Meditation Steps** (located just north of the tram stop) or take one of the river-hugging paths down to **Southpoint**, a new public space at the island's southern tip.

Roosevelt Island Operating Corporation

591 Main St (1-212-832-4540/www.rioc.com). Open Mon–Fri 9am–5pm. Call for event details and maps of the island.

Roosevelt Island Tramway

Board tram on Second Ave at 59th St in Manhattan. **Fee** *one way $2.*

Upper West Side

Housing a population that's older than downtown's, but looser than the Upper East Side's, this four-mile-long stretch west of Central Park is culturally rich and cosmopolitan. As on the UES, New Yorkers were drawn here during the late 19th century after the completion of Central Park, the opening of local subway lines and Columbia University's relocation to Morningside Heights. In the 20th century, many Central Europeans found refuge here; in the '60s, Puerto Ricans settled along Amsterdam and Columbus Avenues. These days, new real-estate development is reducing eye-level evidence of old immigrant life, and the neighborhood's long-standing intellectual, politically liberal spirit has waned (a bit) as apartment prices have risen. Still, sections of Riverside Drive, West End Avenue and Central Park West continue to rival the grandeur of the East Side's Fifth and Park Avenues.

The gateway to the UWS is **Columbus Circle**, where Broadway meets 59th Street, Eighth Avenue, Central Park South and Central Park West—a rare rotary in a city of right angles. The architecture around it could make anyone's head spin. A 700-ton statue of Christopher Columbus, positioned at the entrance to Central Park, goes almost unnoticed in the shadow of the new **Time Warner Center** across the street, which houses the offices of the media conglomerate, along with luxury apartments, **Jazz at Lincoln Center**'s stunning new **Frederick P. Rose Hall** (*see p323*) and the **Mandarin Oriental Hotel** (*see p63*). The first seven levels of the enormous glass complex are filled with high-end retailers and gourmet restaurants, including **Per Se** (*see p191*), the four-star venture of celebrated chef Thomas Keller. On the south side of the circle

is a windowless white-granite structure, built as a modern-art gallery by Huntington Hartford in 1964. **The Museum of Arts & Design** (*see p152*) has bought the building and, after renovation, will move into its new home in 2007. The circle also bears Donald Trump's signature: He stuck his name on the former Gulf & Western Building when he converted it into the predictably glitzy **Trump International Hotel & Tower** (*see p64*).

The Upper West Side's seat of highbrow culture is **Lincoln Center** (*see p326*), a complex of concert halls and auditoriums built in the 1960s. It is home to the New York Philharmonic, the New York City Ballet and the Metropolitan Opera, along with a host of other arts organizations. The big circular fountain in the central plaza is a popular gathering spot, especially in summer, when amateur dancers converge on it to dance alfresco at **Midsummer Night Swing** (*see p257*). Lincoln Center has begun a billion-dollar overhaul that includes a redesign of public spaces, refurbishment of the various aging halls and construction of new buildings. The other, less formal cultural venues on the UWS include the **Makor/Steinhardt Center** (35 W 67th St between Central Park West and Columbus Ave, 1-212-601-1000, www.makor.org), where you can attend lectures, films, readings and live music performances, often with a folky or Jewish flavor; **Symphony Space** (*see p329*), where the World Music Institute books music and dance programs and acclaimed actors read short stories aloud as part of the Selected Shorts program; and **El Taller Latino Americano** (2710 Broadway at 104th St, 1-212-665-9460, www.tallerlatino.org), which offers a full range of cultural events.

Around Sherman and Verdi Squares (from 70th to 73rd Sts, where Broadway and Amsterdam Ave intersect) classic early-20th-century buildings stand cheek-by-jowl with newer, often mundane high-rises. The jewel is the 1904 **Ansonia Hotel** (2109 Broadway between 73rd and 74th Sts). Over the years, Enrico Caruso, Babe Ruth and Igor Stravinsky have lived in this Beaux Arts masterpiece, which was also the site of the Continental Baths (the gay bathhouse and cabaret where Bette Midler got her start) and Plato's Retreat (a swinging '70s sex club). On Broadway, the crowded 72nd Street subway station, which opened in 1904, is notable for its Beaux Arts entrance (a modern glass-topped entrance is across the street). The **Beacon Theatre** (*see p312*), formerly Manhattan's only rococo-style 1920s movie palace, is now the city's premier midsize concert venue, presenting an eclectic

Jazz at Lincoln Center's Allen Room. *See p322.*

menu of music, African-American regional theater and headliner comedy events.

Once Central Park was completed, magnificently tall residential buildings rose up to take advantage of the views along Central Park West. The first of these great buildings was the **Dakota** (at 72nd Street). The fortresslike 1884 luxury apartment building is known as the setting for *Rosemary's Baby* and as the site of John Lennon's murder, in 1980 (Yoko Ono still lives here). You might recognize **55 Central Park West** (at 66th St) from the movie *Ghostbusters*. Built in 1930, it was the first Art Deco building on the block. Heading north on Central Park West, you'll spy the massive twin-towered **San Remo Apartments** (at 74th Street), which also date from 1930. A few blocks north, the **New-York Historical Society** (*see p157*) is the city's oldest museum, built in 1804. Across the street, the glorious **American Museum of Natural History** (*see p146*) has been given an impressive face-lift, making even the fossils look fresh again. Dinosaur skeletons, a permanent rain-forest exhibit and an IMAX theater (which shows Oscar-winning nature documentaries) lure adults and school groups. Perhaps most popular is the museum's newest wing, the amazing, glass-enclosed **Rose Center for Earth and Space**, which includes the retooled Hayden Planetarium.

The cluster of classic groceries and restaurants and lining the avenues of the neighborhood's northern end is where the Upper West Side shops, drinks and eats. **H&H Bagels** (*see p177* **History in the round**) is the city's largest bagel purveyor. To see West

The best Places to…

…walk in circles
Spiral around (and around) the ramps inside the **Guggenheim** museum. *See p148.*

…get high
Get a bird's-eye view of the Hudson River from the tower of **Riverside Church**. *See p114.*

…clap and cheer
Catch a rising star at the **Apollo**'s famed Amateur Night. *See p117.*

…keep it real
Commune with your inner Holden Caulfield at the **American Museum of Natural History**. *See p146.*

Siders in their natural habitat, get in line at the perpetually jammed smoked-fish counter at **Zabar's** (*see p241*). This upscale gourmet market also stocks 250 cheeses, fancy prepared foods and kitchen equipment.

On Amsterdam Avenue, the legendary (though scruffy) **Barney Greengrass—The Sturgeon King** (*see p195*) is an old-fashioned deli and restaurant that specializes in smoked fish, along with what may be the city's best chopped liver. Prefer your seafood uncooked? Slurp down some oysters or nibble on a well-composed raw-fish plate at the "bait bar" of the yacht-styled **Neptune Restaurant** (*see p195*). Cheerful, pretty **Sarabeth's** (423 Amsterdam Ave between 80th and 81st Sts, 1-212-496-6280) is a favorite local brunchtime destination, thanks to its delicious pancakes, waffles and egg dishes. **A** (947 Columbus Ave between 106th and 107th Sts, 1-212-531-1643), named for the A train, has an island vibe and an affordable Pan-Caribbean menu. On Sundays, locals browse the Greenflea outdoor flea market and indoor farmers' market at **IHS 44** (Columbus Ave between 76th and 77th Sts), a public middle school. Before, during or after your stroll, stop for a snack or a sandwich at the popular **Columbus Bakery** (474 Columbus Ave between 82nd and 83rd Sts, 1-212-724-6880), or sate your sweet tooth at **Café Lalo** (201 W 83rd St between Amsterdam Ave and Broadway, 1-212-496-6031), a lively, frequently packed spot famous for its lavish desserts and a cameo in the gooey Tom Hanks–Meg Ryan romance *You've Got Mail*.

Designed by Central Park's Frederick Law Olmsted, **Riverside Park** is a sinuous stretch of riverbank that starts at 72nd Street and ends at 158th Street, between Riverside Drive and the Hudson River. You'll probably see yachts, along with several houseboats, berthed at the **79th Street Boat Basin**; in the summertime, there's an open-air café in the adjacent park. Several sites provide havens for reflection. The **Soldiers' and Sailors' Monument** (89th St at Riverside Dr), built in 1902 by French sculptor Paul E.M. DuBoy, honors Union soldiers who died in the Civil War, and a 1908 memorial (100th St at Riverside Dr) pays tribute to fallen firemen. **Grant's Tomb**, the mausoleum of former President Ulysses S. Grant, is also located in the park. Across the street stands the towering Gothic-style **Riverside Church** (Riverside Dr at 120th St, 1-212-870-6700, www.theriversidechurchny.org), built in 1930. The tower contains the world's largest carillon (74 bells, played every Sunday at 10:30am), as well as a pair of nesting peregrine falcons.

Five-year-old **Rose Center for Earth and Space** is out of this world. *See p114.*

General Grant National Memorial
Riverside Dr at 122nd St (1-212-666-1640).
Subway: 1, 9 to 125th St. **Open** *9am–5pm daily.*
Admission *free.*
Who's buried in Grant's Tomb? Technically, no one—the crypts of Civil War hero and 18th President Ulysses S. Grant and his wife, Julia, are in full aboveground view. Note: The memorial is closed on Thanksgiving, Christmas and New Year's Day.

Morningside Heights

Morningside Heights runs from 110th Street (also known west of Central Park as Cathedral Parkway) to 125th Street, between Morningside Park and the Hudson River.
The Cathedral Church of St. John the Divine and the campus of **Columbia University** exert considerable influence over the surrounding neighborhood.

One of the oldest universities in the U.S., Columbia was chartered in 1754 as King's College (the name changed after the Revolutionary War). It moved to its present location in 1897. Thanks to the large student population of Columbia and its sister school, Barnard College, the area has an academic feel, with bookshops, inexpensive restaurants and coffeehouses lining Broadway between 110th and 116th Streets. **Le Monde**

(2885 Broadway between 112th and 113th Sts, 1-212-531-3939), a quiet brasserie-bar, attracts young locals with its generous beer selection.
Mondel Chocolates (2913 Broadway at 114th St, 1-212-864-2111) has been fulfilling students' candy cravings since 1943, but it's perhaps best known as the chocolatier of choice for the late Katharine Hepburn; her standing monthly order is still tacked on the wall behind the counter. **Kitchenette Uptown** (*see p198*) is a popular brunch spot with a sweet, all-American feel; the mac and cheese and meat loaf draw locals at lunch and dinner, too. For a taste of the South, try an order of thick-cut pork chops smothered in creamy gravy or the flaky cornmeal-crusted catfish at the down-home **Miss Mamie's Spoonbread Too** (366 W 110th St between Manhattan and Columbus Aves, 1-212-865-6744).

The Cathedral Church of St. John the Divine is the seat of the Episcopal Diocese of New York. Known affectionately by locals as St. John the Unfinished, the enormous cathedral (already larger than Notre Dame in Paris!) will undergo hammering and chiseling well into this century. Construction began in 1892 in Romanesque style, was put on hold for a Gothic Revival redesign in 1911, then ground to a halt in 1941, when the U.S. entered World War II. Work resumed in earnest in 1979, but a fire in 2001 destroyed the church's gift shop and badly damaged two 17th-century Italian tapestries, further delaying completion. In addition to Sunday services, the cathedral hosts concerts and tours. In the fall, its renowned **Blessing of the Animals**, during the Feast of St. Francis, draws pets and their people from all over the city. Just behind the cathedral is the green expanse of **Morningside Park** (from 110th to 123rd Sts, between Morningside Ave and Morningside Dr).

The Cathedral Church of St. John the Divine

1047 Amsterdam Ave at 112th St (1-212-316-7540/www.stjohndivine.org). Subway: B, C, 1, 9 to 110th St–Cathedral Pkwy. **Open** *8am–6pm daily.* **Fees** *$5, seniors and students $4.* **Credit** *MC, V.*

Local legend

In 1916, **Madame C.J. Walker**, the first African-American millionaire in the United States, bought a townhouse at 104 West 136th Street in Harlem. A master marketer and tireless promoter, Walker began her business empire with a homemade hair conditioner and later expanded the enterprise into an extensive line of hair-care and beauty products formulated for African-Americans. After her death in 1919, her daughter, A'Lelia, turned the house into a literary salon, which was frequented by the stars of the Harlem Renaissance. The Countee Cullen Regional Branch Library now stands on the site of the Walker home.

Harlem

Harlem is not just a destination on Manhattan island—it's the cultural capital of black America. More than any other New York City address, Harlem is a state of mind as well as a place in the world. Harlem today is no longer the neglected "raisin in the sun," as it is described in Langston Hughes's famous poem "Harlem: A Dream Deferred," and it's not the powder keg of the '60s that his words presaged, either. The Harlem Renaissance of the 1920s and '30s—the cultural explosion that gave us the likes of Hughes, Zora Neale Hurston and Duke Ellington—continues to live on in memory. But these days, there's a new Harlem renaissance, in large part due to private real-estate investment and government support for local entrepreneurs and business development.

Harlem began as a suburb for well-to-do whites in the 19th century, after the West Side railroad was built. The area is blessed with stately brownstones in varying stages of renovation, often right next to blocks of towering public housing. Thanks to a thriving black middle class, Harlem's cultural and religious institutions are seeing renewed interest and funding, and new commercial enterprise abounds. Still, the neighborhood's history remains visible. Some of the fabled locations of the original Harlem Renaissance have been restored, if not enshrined. And while many stages in Harlem's celebrated jazz clubs, theaters and ballrooms have been replaced by pulpits, the buildings still stand.

Despite the retail infusion and influx of development money, a social and psychological divide persists between Harlem and the rest of Manhattan. Visitors might sense an edginess due to real-estate speculation by downtowners and the infiltration of superstores. Still, violence and street crime are at a modern-era low, and the nabe is more welcoming to tourists than in recent memory.

West Harlem, from Fifth to St. Nicholas Avenues, is the Harlem of popular imagination, and 125th Street ("the one-two-five") is its lifeline. Start at the crossroads: the 274,000-square-foot **Harlem USA Mall** (300 W 125th St between Adam Clayton Powell Jr. Blvd [Seventh Ave] and Frederick Douglass Blvd [Eighth Ave], www.harlem-usa.com). The mall features a **Magic Johnson multiplex movie theater** (Frederick Douglass Blvd [Eighth Ave] at 124th St, 1-212-665-6923) and the **Hue-Man Bookstore** (*see p273*), the country's third-largest shop specializing in African-American titles. The building also houses retail megastores such as Old Navy, Modell's, Starbucks and a Disney store. Across the street is the 91-year-old **Apollo Theater** (*see p311*), which still hosts live concerts, a syndicated television program and the classic Amateur Night every Wednesday. A few blocks west, other touches of old Harlem linger: **Showman's Bar** (375 W 125th St at Frederick Douglass Blvd [Eighth Ave], 1-212-864-8941), a mecca for jazz lovers, and the reconstituted **Cotton Club** (666 W 125th St at Riverside Dr, 1-212-663-7980), which hosts gospel brunches and evening jazz and blues sessions. To the east of the mall is the **Lenox Lounge** (*see p212*), still cooking with old-school jazz. A well-regarded fine-arts center, the **Studio Museum in Harlem** (*see p151*) exhibits work by many local artists. The offices of former President Bill Clinton are at 55 W 125th Street (between Fifth Ave and Malcolm X Blvd [Lenox Ave]). Harlem's rich history is preserved in the archives of the **Schomburg Center for Research in Black Culture** (*see p163*). This branch of the New York Public Library contains more than 5 million documents, artifacts, films and prints relating to the cultures of peoples of African descent, with an emphasis on the African-American experience. The **Abyssinian Baptist Church**, where Harlem's controversial 1960s congressman Adam Clayton Powell Jr. once preached, is celebrated for its history, political activism and rousing gospel choir. The church harbors a small museum dedicated to Powell, who was the first black member of New York's City Council.

Harlem is also a destination for stylish plus-size fashions. Check out the **Soul Brothers Boutique** (115 W 128th St between Malcolm X Blvd [Lenox Ave] and Adam Clayton Powell Jr. Blvd [Seventh Ave], 1-212-749-9005), where you can find T-shirts that celebrate the neighborhood, black political figures and '70s blaxploitation films. (You may also want to visit **Freedom Hall**, an active radical-politics lecture facility and bookstore next door.) That generously sized clothing will come in handy if you sample the smothered pork chops and collard greens with fatback at **Sylvia's** (328 Malcolm X Blvd [Lenox Ave] between 126th and 127th Sts, 1-212-996-0660), Harlem's tourist-packed soul-food restaurant. **Bayou** (308 Malcolm X Blvd [Lenox Ave] between 125th and 126th Sts, 1-212-426-3800), the handsome Cajun eatery down the street is a more attractive alternative. Walk off some of your meal with a stroll around **Marcus Garvey Park** (a.k.a. Mount Morris Park, from 120th to 124th Sts, between Madison Ave and Mount Morris Park West), where the brownstone revival is in full swing.

Harlem's historic districts continue to gentrify. The **Mount Morris Historic District** (from

Apollo Theater.

119th to 124th Sts, between Malcolm X Blvd [Lenox Ave] and Mount Morris Park West) boasts charming brownstones and a collection of religious buildings in a variety of architectural styles. These days, new boutiques, restaurants and sidewalk cafés dot the walk down the double-wide **Malcolm X Boulevard (Lenox Ave)**. **Harlemade** (No. 174 between 118th and 119th Sts, 1-212-987-2500, www.harlemade.com) sells tees with Afro- and Harlem-centric messages and images, along with postcards, books and other neighborhood-related memorabilia. **Xukuma** (No. 183 at 119th St, 1-212-222-0490), a delightful home-design shop that carries its own line of body products, would seem right at home in Soho. Just a few years ago, finding bistro food or a cup of espresso was a tough task up here; now restaurant and bar **Native** (*see p198*) serves a global "all world" menu, while the **Settepani Bakery** (No. 196 at 120th St, 1-917-492-4806) offers cappuccino, tempting pastries and Italian-style sandwiches.

Another area with a historic past is **Strivers' Row**, also known as the St. Nicholas Historic District. Running from 138th to 139th Streets, between Adam Clayton Powell Jr. Boulevard (Seventh Ave) and Frederick Douglass Boulevard (Eighth Ave), these blocks of majestic houses were developed in 1891 by David H. King Jr. and designed by three different architects, including Stanford White. In the

A courtyard at the **Cloisters**. *See p119.*

1920s, prominent members of the black community, the legendary Eubie Blake and W.C. Handy among them, lived in this area. Now, more upwardly mobile strivers are moving in, and so have stylish boutiques such as **Grandview** (2531 Frederick Douglass Blvd [Eighth Ave] between 135th and 136th Sts, 1-212-694-7324). Owner Veronica Jones hawks eclectic contemporary clothing and accessories, mostly by African-American designers. Along the way, there's plenty of good eating: **Londel's Supper Club** (*see p198*), owned by former police officer Londel Davis, serves some of the best blackened catfish in town; **Home Sweet Harlem Café** (270 W 135th St at Frederick Douglass Blvd [Eighth Ave], 1-212-926-9616) is the place for smoothies, soy burgers and hearty soups.

The 'hood comes alive after dark, especially at the not-to-be-missed **St. Nick's Pub** (773 St. Nicholas Ave at 149th St, 1-212-283-9728), where you can hear live jazz every night (except Tuesday) for a small cover charge. **Sugar Shack Gift and Café Shop** (2611 Frederick Douglass Blvd [Eighth Ave] at 139th St, 1-212-491-4422) is also a local favorite.

Heading east on West 116th Street, you'll pass through a dizzying smorgasbord of cultures. There's a West African flavor between Malcolm X and Adam Clayton Powell Jr. Boulevards, especially at the Senegalese restaurant **Le Baobab** (No. 120, 1-212-864-4700). On the north side of the street is one of the Reverend Al Sharpton's favorite restaurants, **Amy Ruth's** (No. 113, 1-212-280-8779), where Southern-style ribs and fried or smothered chicken and waffles

are de rigueur. Continue east, past the silver-domed **Masjid Malcolm Shabazz** (No. 102, 1-212-662-2200), the mosque of Malcolm X's ministry, to the **Malcolm Shabazz Harlem Market** (No. 52, 1-212-987-8131), an outdoor bazaar where vendors sell T-shirts, toiletries and (purportedly) African souvenirs. (Don't miss Harley the Buckle Man, custom-belt-buckle maker for rap stars.)

East of Fifth Avenue is **East Harlem**, sometimes called **Spanish Harlem** but better known to its primarily Puerto Rican residents as **El Barrio**. North of 96th Street and east of Madison Avenue, El Barrio moves to a different beat. Its main east-west cross street, East 116th Street, shows signs of a recent influx of Mexican immigrants, but between Fifth and Park Avenues, the thoroughfare's main attraction is actually the unusually high concentration of botanicas, or shops that supply candles, charms, oils, potions, orisha-priestess readings and other elements of the Catholic-tinged Santeria religion. **Rendon Otto Chicas** (60 E 116th St at Madison Ave, 1-212-289-0378), a.k.a. La Casa de las Velas or the House of Candles, is particularly kid- and tourist-friendly. **Patsy's Pizzeria** (2287 First Ave between 117th and 118th Sts, 1-212-534-9783), which serves pizzas with wafer-thin crusts from one of the handful of coal-fired ovens left in Manhattan, is a reminder of the neighborhood's Italian past. From 96th to 106th Streets, a little touch of East Village–style bohemia can be detected in such places as **Carlito's Café y Galería** (1701 Lexington Ave between 106th and 107th Sts, 1-212-348-7044), which presents music, art and poetry performances. Nearby is the **Graffiti Hall of Fame** (106th St between Madison and Park Aves), a schoolyard that celebrates great old- and new-school "writers." Be sure to check out **El Museo del Barrio** (*see p159*), Spanish Harlem's community museum.

Hamilton Heights (named for Alexander Hamilton, who owned a farm and estate here in 1802) extends from 125th Street to the Trinity Cemetery at 155th Street, between Riverside Drive and St. Nicholas Avenue. The former factory neighborhood developed after the West Side elevated train was built in the early 20th century. Today, it's notable for the elegant turn-of-the-century row houses in the **Hamilton Heights Historic District**, which extends from 140th to 145th Streets, between Amsterdam and Edgecomb Avenues—just beyond the Gothic Revival–style campus of the **City College of New York** (Convent Ave at 138th St).

The Abyssinian Baptist Church
132 W 138th St between Malcolm X Blvd (Lenox Ave) and Adam Clayton Powell Jr. Blvd (Seventh Ave) (1-212-862-7474/www.abyssinian.org). Subway: 2, 3 to 135th St. Open Mon–Fri 9am–5pm.

Washington Heights & Inwood

The area from West 155th Street to Dyckman (200th) Street is called **Washington Heights**; venture north of that and you're in **Inwood**, Manhattan's northernmost neighborhood, where the Harlem and Hudson Rivers converge. A growing number of artists and young families are relocating to these parts, attracted by the Art Deco buildings, big parks, hilly streets and (comparatively) low rents.

Since the 1920s, waves of immigrants have settled in Washington Heights. In the post–World War II era, many German-Jewish refugees (including Henry Kissinger, Dr. Ruth Westheimer and Max Frankel, a former executive editor of the *New York Times*) moved to the western edge of the neighborhood. Broadway once housed a sizable Greek population—opera singer Maria Callas lived here in her youth. But in the last few decades, the southern and eastern parts of the 'hood have become predominantly Spanish-speaking due to the large Dominican population that has settled here.

A trek along Fort Washington Avenue from about 173rd Street to Fort Tryon Park puts you in the heart of what is now being called **Hudson Heights**—the Gold Coast of Washington Heights. Start at the **George Washington Bridge**, the city's only bridge across the Hudson River. A pedestrian walkway (also a popular route for cyclists) allows for dazzling Manhattan views. Under the bridge on the New York side is a diminutive lighthouse—those who know the children's book *The Little Red Lighthouse and the Great Gray Bridge* will recognize it immediately. Stop along the way at restaurant **Bleu Evolution** (808 W 187th St between Fort Washington and Pinehurst Aves, 1-212-928-6006) for a touch of downtown-style hipness, or hold out for the lovely **New Leaf Café** (1 Margaret Corbin Dr near Park Dr, 1-212-568-5323) within the Frederick Law Olmsted–designed **Fort Tryon Park**.

At the northern edge of the park are the **Cloisters** (*see p147*), a museum built in 1938 using segments of five medieval cloisters shipped from Europe by the Rockefeller clan. It currently houses the Metropolitan Museum of Art's permanent medieval-art collection, including the exquisite Unicorn Tapestries, woven circa 1500 A.D.

Inwood stretches from Dyckman Street up to 218th Street, the last residential block in Manhattan. Dyckman buzzes with street life and nightclubs from river to river, but north of that, the island narrows considerably and the parks along the western shoreline culminate in the wilderness of **Inwood Hill Park**. Some believe that this is the location of the legendary 1626 transaction between Peter Minuit and the Native American Lenapes for the purchase of a strip of land called Manahatta—a plaque at the southwest corner of the ballpark near 214th Street marks the purported spot. The 196-acre refuge contains the island's last swath of virgin forest and salt marsh and offers a view of New Jersey's Palisades. Frederick Law Olmsted, best known for his work as one of the designers of Central Park, also laid out the design for this park. Massive glacier-deposited boulders (called erratics) are scattered over the hilly terrain. Today, with a bit of imagination, you can hike in this mossy forest and picture Manhattan as it was before development.

Morris-Jumel Mansion
65 Jumel Terr between 160th and 162nd Sts (1-212-923-8008/www.morrisjumel.org). Subway: C to 163rd St–Amsterdam Ave. Open Wed–Sun 10am–4pm. Admission $3, seniors and students $2, children under 12 free.
Built in 1765, Manhattan's only surviving pre-Revolutionary manse was originally the heart of a 130-acre estate that stretched from river to river (on the grounds, a stone marker points south with the legend NEW YORK, 11 MILES). George Washington planned the battle of Harlem Heights here in 1776, after the British colonel Roger Morris moved out. The handsome 18th-century Palladian-style villa offers fantastic views. Its former driveway is now Sylvan Terrace, which boasts the largest continuous stretch (one block) of old wooden houses in Manhattan.

Brooklyn

This borough's got bridges, beaches, brews and a lively scene of its own.

Brooklyn, land of brownstones, tree-lined streets and a full seven miles of beaches, has a fiercely independent spirit. It was, after all, a city unto itself for nearly half a century before becoming a borough in 1898. Also known as Kings County, Brooklyn isn't just a bedroom community for priced-out Manhattanites; it's a metropolis with its own pace, styles, cultures and ambience. In the past decade, scores of new restaurants, bars, galleries and boutiques have sprung up, and artists seeking affordable space have moved in among the lifelong residents of close-knit ethnic enclaves, including Caribbean, Chinese, Italian and Russian neighborhoods.

Sometimes, the blending of the old and the new is complicated. Hipster bars catering to scruffy artists in Williamsburg have rankled a few longtime residents of the Hasidic community there, for example, just as some established Italian-American and Puerto Rican families are still not quite used to the new cool factor (chic shops, swanky dining) in Carroll Gardens. Nowhere are these culture clashes more obvious than in Red Hook, Dumbo and Downtown Brooklyn, still largely ungentrified 'hoods that have been attracting the attention of giant brands such as Ikea, Target and even the New Jersey Nets. Last year, developers and investors unveiled a controversial plan to raze a number of establishments, including residences, to build an 800,000-square-foot urban complex with a basketball arena, offices, and residential and retail spaces at the bustling intersection of Flatbush and Atlantic Avenues. The project has the blessing of the mayor and a slew of local officials, but many area residents are rallying against it.

Either way, this much is certain: Everyone wants a piece of Brooklyn these days, and once you get a taste of the place for yourself, you'll quickly see why. For more details on the borough's offerings, contact **Brooklyn Information and Culture** (1-718-855-7882, www.brooklynx.org) or **Heart of Brooklyn: A Cultural Partnership** (1-718-638-7700, www.heartofbrooklyn.org).

The best Places to…

…get in the groove

Dancers and steel drums fill the streets at the **West Indian–American Day Carnival** in Crown Heights. See p258.

…go on a bistro binge

Mussels, red wine and steak frites are plentiful along **Smith Street**'s popular Restaurant Row. See p122.

…listen to the waves (and the violins)

Mozart adds to the lovely riverside views at **Bargemusic**. See p328.

…catch a pop fly

The **Brooklyn Cyclones** circle the bases while you load up on wieners and beer at Coney Island's KeySpan Park. See p332.

…scope out the scenesters

Northsix, in Williamsburg, showcases the hottest bands and coolest kids. See p317.

Brooklyn Heights & Dumbo

Brooklyn Heights has been the borough's toniest address since the end of World War II. The neighborhood was born when entrepreneur Robert Fulton's first steam-powered ferry linked Manhattan to the quiet fishing village on the western edge of Long Island in 1814. The streets of Brooklyn Heights—particularly Cranberry, Hicks, Pierrepont and Willow—are lined with beautifully maintained Greek Revival and Italianate row houses dating from the 1820s. In 1965, 30 blocks of the area were designated Brooklyn's first historic district. Today, Henry and Montague Streets, the main drags, are packed with shops, restaurants and bars. The **Brooklyn Heights Promenade**, which offers spectacular vistas of Manhattan, is just a quick walk from the end of the magnificent **Brooklyn Bridge**. The vision of German-born civil engineer John Augustus Roebling (who did not live to see its completion), the structure was the first to use steel cables. It connects Downtown Brooklyn with Manhattan and provides glorious views of the Statue of Liberty and New York Harbor. As you walk, bike or blade along its promenade, look for plaques detailing the story of the bridge's construction.

The **Brooklyn Bridge** (and Walt Whitman's poetry) gets into lots of wedding shots.

More remnants of bygone Breuckelen abound at the **Brooklyn Historical Society** building, which, when completed in 1881, was the first in New York to use locally produced terra-cotta on its facade (it reopened in late 2003, following an extensive restoration). The grand **Borough Hall** (209 Joralemon St at Court St, Brooklyn Heights, www.brooklyn-usa.org) stands as a monument to Brooklyn's past as an independent municipality. Completed in 1851, the Greek Revival edifice—later crowned with a Victorian cupola—was renovated in the late 1980s. The building is linked to the **New York State Supreme Court** (360 Adams St between Joralemon St and Tech Pl) by **Cadman Plaza** (from Prospect St to Tech Pl, between Cadman Plaza East and Cadman Plaza West). Nearby, at the junction of Court and Remsen Streets, farmers peddle fresh produce on Tuesday, Thursday and Saturday mornings during most seasons.

If the Heights is too staid for your taste, you might prefer the still-evolving waterside neighborhood of **Dumbo** (<u>D</u>own <u>U</u>nder the <u>M</u>anhattan <u>B</u>ridge <u>O</u>verpass), which also provides impressive sight lines to Manhattan. A fine viewing perch is below the Brooklyn Bridge at the **Fulton Ferry Landing**, which juts out over the East River at Old Fulton and Water Streets, and is close to two newly refurbished green spots—**Empire-Fulton Ferry State Park** and **Brooklyn Bridge Park** (riverside between the Manhattan and Brooklyn Bridges). Also at the water's edge is the posh and pricey **River Café** (*see p199*); breathtaking views of the Manhattan skyline have made the adjacent pier a favorite photo site for Chinese wedding parties. You'll enjoy the view even more with a cone from the **Brooklyn Ice Cream Factory** (Fulton Ferry Landing between Old Fulton and Water Sts, 1-718-246-3963).

Drawn by the cobblestone streets and loft spaces in red-brick warehouses, artists flocked to Dumbo in the 1970s and '80s, and kept on coming through the go-go '90s. The arrival of several chic boutiques as well as home stores like **ABC Carpet & Home** (*see p244*) and **West Elm** (75 Front St at Main St, Dumbo, 1-718-875-7757) has some people saying that the area has lost its rough-hewn charm. Don't believe it. You can still get lost among the quiet side streets, and the **d.u.m.b.o. arts center** (30 Washington St between Plymouth and Water Sts, 1-718-694-0831, www.dumboartscenter.org) continues to promote the work of community artists through its gallery and sponsorship of the annual **d.u.m.b.o. art under the bridge** festival (*see p260*), held in mid-October. **St. Ann's**

> ► For a map of **Brooklyn**, *see pp408–409.*

Warehouse (38 Water St between Dock and Main Sts, 1-718-254-8779) hosts offbeat concerts, readings and theater productions that often feature high-profile artists. The well-loved Halcyon (*see p248* On the record) is a DJ haunt and record shop that relocated here from Cobble Hill.

Dumbo dining also boasts its share of attractions. Pizza lovers can sample a coal-fired pie at the venerable Grimaldi's (*see p199*), which claims the title of America's first (and some say best) pizzeria. For a real sit-down meal—accompanied by a couple of good stiff drinks and the occasional live band—try Superfine (126 Front St between Jay and Pearl Sts, 1-718-243-9005), which offers Mediterranean-style cuisine (and a jammin' Sunday bluegrass brunch); Rice (81 Washington St between Front and York Sts, 1-718-222-9880), an outpost of an ultrapopular Soho Asian eatery; or the elegant Five Front (5 Front St between Dock and Old Fulton Sts, 1-718-625-5559), serving New American cuisine. To linger over a latte, make a beeline for the airy café and bar at the Dumbo General Store (111 Front St between Adams and Washington Sts, 1-718-855-5288), which also hawks art supplies. And to quell your candy cravings, don't miss the always-packed Jacques Torres Chocolate shop (*see p238 for listing*), where French confectionery artist Torres whips up cocoa-butter masterpieces and spectacular hot chocolate. Almondine (85 Water St between Main and Dock Sts, 1-718-797-5026), across the street, sells his artisanal breads and pastries.

Brooklyn Bridge
Subway: A, C to High St; J, M, Z to Chambers St; 4, 5, 6 to Brooklyn Bridge–City Hall.

The Brooklyn Historical Society
128 Pierrepont St at Clinton St, Brooklyn Heights (1-718-222-4111/www.brooklynhistory.org). Subway: M, R to Court St; 2, 3, 4, 5 to Borough Hall. **Open** *Wed, Thu, Sat 10am–5pm; Fri 10am–8pm; Sun noon–5pm.* **Admission** *$6; seniors, students and children 12–18 $4; children under 12 free.* **Credit** *AmEx, MC, V.*

Boerum Hill, Carroll Gardens, Cobble Hill & Red Hook

One of Brooklyn's most striking examples of rapid gentrification can be found on Smith Street, which stretches from Boerum Hill to Carroll Gardens and has come to be known as the borough's Restaurant Row. This strip was targeted for urban renewal in the 1990s and given a face-lift that included wrought-iron streetlamps and new sidewalks. Now good, affordable restaurants and cafés pack in

discerning diners. Hot eateries along Smith Street include classic bistro Bar Tabac (No. 128 at Dean St, Boerum Hill, 1-718-923-0918); French-Chinese Chance (No. 223 at Butler St, Carroll Gardens, 1-718-242-1515) and New American Chestnut (No. 271 between DeGraw and Sackett Sts, Carroll Gardens, 1-718-243-0049). Many of the area's shops are run by artists and designers selling their own wares; these stand shoulder to shoulder with a swiftly shrinking number of Latino restaurants, bodegas and social clubs that have (barely) survived the transition. Playful, pretty women's clothing is for sale at Frida's Closet (No. 296 between Sackett and Union Sts, Carroll Gardens, 1-718-855-0311) and Flirt (No. 252 between DeGraw and Douglass Sts, 1-718-858-7931), where many of the pieces are hand-crafted by local designers. Interior-design fanatics will appreciate Swallow (No. 361 between Carroll and 1st Sts, 1-718-222-8201), which showcases an impressive collection of delicate, decorative handblown-glass objects, and Zipper (No. 333 between Carroll and President Sts, 1-718-596-0333), a sharp-looking outpost of a Los Angeles–based shop.

Along nearby Atlantic Avenue are haute home furnisher City Foundry (No. 365 between Bond and Hoyt Sts, Boerum Hill, 1-718-923-1786); Rico (No. 384 between Bond and Hoyt Sts, 1-718-797-2077), which sells art, lighting and furnishings; and stylish women's clothier Butter (No. 389 between Bond and Hoyt Sts, 1-718-260-9033).

The mile-long stretch of Atlantic Avenue between Henry and Nevins Streets, known by locals as the Fertile Crescent, is crowded with Middle Eastern restaurants and retail food markets. The granddaddy of them all is Sahadi Importing Company (No. 187 between Clinton and Court Sts, Cobble Hill, 1-718-624-4550), a 57-year-old neighborhood institution that sells olives, spices, cheeses, nuts and other gourmet treats. Atlantic Avenue is also considered the northern border of Cobble Hill, a quaint neighborhood with a small-town feel. Less restaurant-heavy than nearby Smith Street, shady Court Street is dotted with boutiques and shops such as Book Court (No. 163 at Dean St, Cobble Hill, 1-718-875-3677), which carries Brooklyn guidebooks and histories; and the charming Sweet Melissa (No. 276 between Butler and Douglass Sts, 1-718-855-3410) which serves brunch, lunch and afternoon tea in a pretty back garden. Farther south, you'll cross into the still predominantly Italian-American Carroll Gardens. Pick up a prosciutto loaf from the Caputo Bakery (No. 329 between Sackett and Union Sts, Carroll Gardens, 1-718-875-6871);

some freshly made mozzarella at **Caputo's Fine Foods** (No. 460 between 3rd and 4th Pls, 1-718-855-8852); and an aged *soppressata* salami from **Esposito and Sons** (No. 357 between President and Union Sts, 1-718-875-6863); then, relax in **Carroll Park** (from President to Carroll Sts, between Court and Smith Sts) and watch the old-timers play bocce. Take a walk over the Brooklyn-Queens Expressway to the industrial waterfront of Cobble Hill to find the corner building housing the cool bar **B61** and, upstairs, the hip Mexican bistro **Alma** (*see p199*), whose open-air rooftop dining area has a great view of the East River and lower Manhattan.

Southwest of Cobble Hill and Carroll Gardens lies rough-and-tumble **Red Hook**, offering a mix of industrial-waterfront surrealism, local-artist studios, and a fast-growing crop of bars and eateries. There's the roadhouse-style **Moonshine** (317 Columbia St between Hamilton and Woodhull Sts, Red Hook, 1-718-422-0563); contemporary French restaurant **360** (360 Van Brunt St between Sullivan and Wolcott Sts, 1-718-246-0360), which offers a $25 three-course prix fixe; and **Hope & Anchor** (347 Van Brunt St at Wolcott St, 1-718-237-0276), a diner with occasional drag shows and karaoke nights. Getting to the 'hood is a challenge—from the F and G subway station at Smith–9th Street, it's either a long walk or a connecting B77 bus ride. But it's worth it for a glimpse of the tough, pregentrified life of old New York. Decaying piers are an appropriately moody backdrop for massive cranes, empty warehouses and trucks clattering over cobblestoned streets. But this slice of gritty Brooklyn of yore may not be around for long: In addition to the many restaurants and artists' lofts that have crept into the region (for art-show schedules, check with the **Brooklyn Waterfront Artists Coalition**, 1-718-596-2507, www.bwac.org), plans are afoot to turn one of the biggest waterfront warehouses into condos and to construct a massive Ikea furniture shop on a disused old pier. A new pickup spot for the **New York Water Taxi** (1-212-742-1969, www.nywatertaxi.com) is sure to bring in a fresh crop of curious Manhattanites.

Park Slope & Prospect Heights

Welcome to Brooklyn's suburbs. **Park Slope** has a relaxed, upscale feel, owing to its charming Victorian brownstones, leafy streets and proximity to Prospect Park. Seventh Avenue is the main commercial drag. Fifth Avenue is the hot strip for unique boutiques and good restaurants, including the Venetian-accented

al di là (*see p199*); the eclectic favorite **Blue Ribbon Brooklyn** (*see p174 for listing*); and the New American **Stone Park Cafe** (324 Fifth Ave at 3rd St, 1-718-369-0082). Park Slope's lesbian community is very visible: At the **Lesbian Herstory Archives** (*see p300*), you can peruse books and memorabilia; at **Ginger's Bar** (*see p307*) or either location of the popular **Tea Lounge** (350 Seventh Ave at 10th St, 1-718-768-4966; 837 Union St between Sixth and Seventh Aves, 1-718-789-2762), you can peruse the readers.

Central Park may be bigger and more famous, but **Prospect Park** has a more rustic quality than its rectangular sibling to the west, and Brooklynites adore it. This masterpiece, also designed by Frederick Law Olmsted and Calvert Vaux, is a stellar spot for bird-watching, especially with a little guidance from the **Prospect Park Audubon Center at the Boathouse** (park entrance on Ocean Ave at Lincoln Rd, Prospect Heights, 1-718-287-3400). Or pretend you've left the city altogether by boating or hiking amid the waterfalls, reflecting pools and wildlife habitats of the recently

Local legend

Lyman Beecher was a firebrand Presbyterian minister whose controversial abolitionist views led him from Boston to Cincinnati to Brooklyn, where he joined his son, minister Henry Ward Beecher, in preaching against the immorality of slavery at the Plymouth Church, at 75 Hicks Street in Brooklyn Heights. Lyman's daughter, Harriet Beecher Stowe, took up the cause as well, publishing her classic novel *Uncle Tom's Cabin* in 1852.

restored 150-acre **Ravine District** (park entrances on Prospect Park West at 3rd, 9th and 15th Sts, Park Slope). The 526-acre rolling green park was created with equestrians in mind; you can saddle a horse at the nearby **Kensington Stables** (*see p336*) or hop on a bike and pedal alongside bladers and runners. Children enjoy riding the hand-carved horses at the park's antique **Carousel** (Flatbush Ave at Empire Blvd) and playing with animals in the **Prospect Park Zoo** (park entrance on Flatbush Ave near Ocean Ave, Prospect Heights, 1-718-399-7339).

The verdant expanse of **Green-Wood Cemetery** is about a 15-minute walk from Prospect Park. A century ago, this 478-acre site vied with Niagara Falls as New York State's greatest tourist attraction. Filled with Victorian mausoleums, cherubs and gargoyles, Green-Wood is the resting place of some half-million New Yorkers, including Jean-Michel Basquiat, Leonard Bernstein and Mae West.

The central branch of the **Brooklyn Public Library** (Grand Army Plaza, Prospect Heights, 1-718-230-2100) sits near Prospect Park's main entrance and the massive Civil War memorial arch at **Grand Army Plaza** (intersection of Flatbush Ave, Eastern Pkwy and Prospect Park West). The library's Brooklyn Collection includes thousands of artifacts and photos that trace the borough's history. Just around the corner are the tranquil **Brooklyn Botanic Garden** and recently spruced-up **Brooklyn Museum** (*see p147*), which has a renowned Egyptology collection and a new glass facade and mesmerizing fountain display.

Brooklyn Botanic Garden

From Eastern Pkwy to Empire Blvd, between Flatbush and Washington Aves, Prospect Heights (1-718-623-7200/www.bbg.org). Subway: B, Q, Franklin Ave S to Prospect Park; 2, 3 to Eastern Pkwy–Brooklyn Museum. **Open** *Apr–Sept Tue–Fri 8am–6pm; Sat, Sun 10am–6pm. Oct–Mar Tue–Fri 8am–4:30pm; Sat, Sun 10am–4:30pm.* **Admission** *$5, seniors and students $3, children free. Free Tuesday; late-Nov–Feb Tue–Fri.*

Green-Wood Cemetery

Fifth Ave at 25th St, Green-Wood Heights (1-718-768-7300/www.green-wood.com). Subway: M, R to 25th St. **Open** *8am–5pm daily.* **Admission** *free.*

Prospect Park

Main entrance on Flatbush Ave at Grand Army Plaza, Prospect Heights (1-718-965-8999/www.prospectpark.org). Subway: B, Q, Franklin Ave S to Prospect Park; F to 15th St–Prospect Park; 2, 3 to Grand Army Plaza.

Fort Greene, Greenpoint & Williamsburg

Fort Greene, with its stately Victorian brownstones and other grand buildings, has undergone a major revival over the past decade.

Freak like me

It's just not summer without Eak the Geek and his freaky pals at Sideshows by the Seashore (*see p127*). The extravaganza's veteran MC, the **Amazing Blazing Tyler Fyre**, introduces such colleagues as contortionist Ravi the Bendable Boy from Bombay, snake charmer Princess Ananka and the aforementioned, heavily tattooed Eak. Fyre, 28, has talents of his own, including sword swallowing and playing the Human Blockhead.

Time Out: **What hurts most—swallowing a sword or pounding a nail into your face?**
Tyler Fyre: Right now, it's pounding the nail. I just moved up in nail size. I can definitely feel it when the spike goes into my nose.
TONY: **That doesn't sound like a trick you can ease into.**
TF: That trick came really easy to me. Some kids will laugh at the dinner table and squirt milk out of their nose; I'd laugh and shoot spaghetti and meatballs out of my nose.
TONY: **And sword swallowing?**
TF: It took years of grueling training to learn that. People don't want to teach it for a couple of reasons. For one, you don't want to teach someone a skill that could kill them. And also, part of what makes the show great is that it's novel. You don't want there to be 100 other sword swallowers living in your community—though we have in New York City the highest concentration of sword swallowers in the world.
TONY: **What's that, two?**
TF: No, *six*. There are 68 working sword swallowers in the world; six of us are here.
TONY: **How do you all find work?**
TF: New York is a great town, so there's enough variety-arts work for all of us.

It has long been a center of African-American life and business—Spike Lee, Branford Marsalis and Chris Rock have all lived here. **Fort Greene Park** (from Myrtle to DeKalb Aves, between St. Edwards St and Washington Park) was conceived in 1846 at the behest of poet Walt Whitman (then editor of the *Brooklyn Daily Eagle*); its master plan was fully realized by the omnipresent Olmsted and Vaux in 1867. At the center of the park stands the Prison Ship Martyrs Monument, erected in 1909 in memory of more than 11,000 American prisoners who died on British ships that were anchored nearby during the Revolutionary War.

The **Lafayette Avenue Presbyterian Church** (85 South Oxford St at Lafayette Ave, Fort Greene, 1-718-625-7515) was founded by a group of abolitionists; Abraham Lincoln's oldest son, Robert Todd Lincoln, broke ground for the church in 1860. Its subterranean tunnel once served as a stop on the Underground Railroad. The celebrated stained-glass windows created by Louis Comfort Tiffany are being restored.

A year after the church was established, the **Brooklyn Academy of Music** (BAM, *see p325*) was founded in Brooklyn Heights, and was later moved to its current site on Fort Greene's southern border. BAM is America's oldest operating performing-arts center. It once presented the likes of Edwin Booth and Sarah Bernhardt; now it's known for ambitious cultural performances of all kinds. In recent

years, it has added several venues that show cutting-edge dance, theater, music and film programs and draw audiences from throughout the metropolitan area. From October through December, BAM hosts the **Next Wave Festival** (*see p260*). For a bite before the show, try French eatery **À Table** (*see p199*).

Also world-famous—though perhaps to a different audience—is the cheesecake at **Junior's Restaurant** (386 Flatbush Ave at DeKalb Ave, Fort Greene, 1-718-852-5257), just three blocks away. A slew of popular hangouts can be found nearby along **DeKalb Avenue**, including the funky South African **i-Shebeen Madiba** (No. 195 between Adelphi St and Carlton Ave, 1-718-855-9190); lively bistro **Chez Oskar** (No. 211 at Adelphi St, 1-718-852-6250); and groovy bar and restaurant **Liquors** (No. 219 between Adelphi and Clermont Sts, 1-718-488-7700), known for its killer mojitos.

Williamsburg is further along in hipness than Fort Greene, especially if you're 22, in a band and well tattooed. Just one subway stop from the East Village (on the L line), **Bedford Avenue** is the neighborhood's main drag, though you'll also find plenty of restaurants and nightspots along North 6th Street and Grand Avenue. During the day, **Verb Cafe** (218 Bedford Ave between North 4th and 5th Sts, Williamsburg, 1-718-599-0977) is the nabe's prime slacker hangout; at night, the scene moves to eateries like the Thai palace

TONY: Do you and the other sideshow performers ever step out together on a lunch break?

TF: A couple of years ago, we'd all go cash our paychecks at the bank together on payday. It'd be me; the tattooed man; the snake charmer, who was a tall Amazon girl with blue hair; and Koko the Killer Clown, who's a little dwarf. We'd all just be waiting in line at the bank like everyone else.

TONY: Have you ever been injured?

TF: Last year, the moment I'd always wondered about happened: The neon sword broke inside of me. I just sat there and thought, Well, I always wondered what this would be like. So I pulled the sword out. We were able to design it with an internal core that would allow me to pull all the broken glass out—but that is, of course, pulling broken glass up your throat. I was cut on both sides of my throat. I took a week off from solid foods.

Hot dog! It's **Coney Island**. See p127.

SEA (*see p200*), funky Japanese **Bozu** (296 Grand St between Havemeyer and Roebling Sts, 1-718-384-7770) and the laid-back but cool **Diner** (85 Broadway at Berry St, 1-718-486-3077). You'll also find the distinctly untrendy neighborhood fixture and gustatory treasure **Peter Luger** (*see p200*), which grills what may be the best steak (porterhouse only) in the entire city.

The area also has dozens of art galleries, such as the local fave **Pierogi 2000** (*see p270*). But the core of the art scene is the **Williamsburg Art & Historical Center** (135 Broadway at Bedford Ave, 1-718-486-7372, www.wahcenter.org), in a landmark 1929 bank building. The performance and live-music scenes thrive, too; worth-a-trip spaces include **Galapagos**, **Northsix**, **Pete's Candy Store**, as well as **Warsaw at the Polish National Home** (*see p315, p317, p318 and p319*) in nearby **Greenpoint**.

Long before the hipster invasion, Billyburg's waterfront location made it ideal for industry; after the Erie Canal linked the Atlantic Ocean to the Great Lakes, in 1825, the area became an even more bustling port. Companies such as Pfizer and Domino Sugar started here. But by the late 20th century, businesses began to abandon the enormous industrial spaces—the landmark Domino refinery finally closed last year. Meanwhile, the beloved **Brooklyn Brewery** (79 North 11th St between Berry St and Wythe Ave, 1-718-486-7422, www.brooklyn brewery.com) is located in a former ironworks. Visit during happy hour on Friday evenings or take a tour on Saturday.

Williamsburg is also one of New York's many curious multiethnic amalgams. To the south, Broadway divides a Latino neighborhood from a lively community of Hasidic Jews, while the northern half extending into Greenpoint contains Polish and Italian settlements (with old-time delis and restaurants to match).

Bedford-Stuyvesant, Crown Heights & Flatbush

Although Harlem gets props for being the cultural capital of black America, it's rivaled in size and architectural splendor by **Bed-Stuy**. Join the annual **Brownstoners of Bedford-Stuyvesant Inc. House Tour** (1-718-574-1979), held the third Saturday in October, rain or shine. The **Concord Baptist Church of Christ** (833 Gardner Blvd between Madison St and Putnam Ave, Bedford-Stuyvesant, 1-718-622-1818) offers gospel music from one of the largest African-American congregations in the United States.

There's plenty to do south of Bed-Stuy, in the largely West Indian neighborhoods of **Crown Heights** and **Flatbush** (both also have sizable Jewish populations). Calypso and soca music blare from open windows—especially on Labor Day, when the annual **West Indian–American Day Carnival** (*see p258*) is held in all its raucous glory. In Flatbush, try the sublime oxtail soup at Caribbean eatery **Sybil's** (2210 Church Ave at Flatbush Ave, 1-718-469-9049).

Bay Ridge & Bensonhurst

Bay Ridge and **Bensonhurst**, the settings for *Saturday Night Fever*, are mostly residential, but they're still hopping. Eating options abound on the main drags of Third, Fourth and Fifth Avenues between Bay Ridge Parkway and 88th Street. For Lebanese cuisine, try **Karam** (8519 Fourth Ave between 85th and 86th Sts, Bay Ridge, 1-718-745-5227). Ninety-year-old

Hinsch's Confectionery (8518 Fifth Ave between 85th and 86th Sts, 1-718-748-2854) froths a mean egg cream, a fizzy New York specialty made of chocolate syrup, milk and seltzer. The disco in which John Travolta strutted is now a gay club called **Spectrum** (802 64th St at Eighth Ave, 1-718-238-8213).

You can see the **Verrazano-Narrows Bridge** from just about anywhere in Bay Ridge. Completed in 1964, it connects Brooklyn to Staten Island. A Dutch settlement in the 19th century, Bay Ridge later became a summer retreat for moneyed Manhattanites. You can still see grand old homes—including the arts-and-crafts **Jones House** (8220 Narrows Ave at 83rd St), known locally as the Gingerbread House.

If you find Manhattan's Little Italy too touristy, check out Bensonhurst's version: a stretch of 18th Avenue between 68th and 77th Streets known as Cristoforo Colombo Boulevard. There are old-fashioned Italian men's social clubs, delis stocked with fresh pasta and shops selling Italian music. At **Villabate Pasticceria & Bakery** (7117 18th Ave between 71st and 72nd Sts, 1-718-331-8430), Italian-speaking customers shout out their orders for cannoli and cookies.

Brighton Beach & Coney Island

Brighton Beach is also known as Little Odessa because of its large Russian immigrant population. Wander the aisles of **M&I International Foods** (249 Brighton Beach Ave between Brighton 1st and 2nd Sts, Brighton Beach, 1-718-615-1011), a huge Russian deli and grocery. Or make a reservation at a local nightclub, such as the **National Restaurant** (273 Brighton Beach Ave between Brighton 2nd and 3rd Sts, 1-718-646-1225), where the

dress is flashy, the food and vodka are plentiful, and the over-the-top burlesque shows are downright trippy.

Coney Island, on the peninsula just west of Brighton Beach, is a summertime destination. After decades of decay, the weirdly wonderful community—known for its amusement park, beach and boardwalk—has made a comeback. The biggest improvement is seaside **KeySpan Park**, home to the **Brooklyn Cyclones** (*see p332*), a minor-league baseball affiliate of the New York Mets. If you're a thrill-seeker, take a spin on the Cyclone at **Astroland Amusement Park** (*see p280*): A ride on the 78-year-old wooden roller coaster lasts less than two minutes, but the first drop is nearly vertical, and the cars clatter along the 2,640 feet of track at speeds of up to 60 miles per hour.

A stroll along the boardwalk will take you to the **New York Aquarium** (*see p286*), where a family of beluga whales is in residence. The oddball **Sideshows by the Seashore** (*see p124* **Freak like me**) is put on by **Coney Island USA**, an organization that keeps the torch burning for early-20th-century Coney life. The **Mermaid Parade** (*see p257*) and **Nathan's Famous Fourth of July Hot Dog Eating Contest** (Takeru Kobayashi, last year's winner, stuffed down 53½ dogs—with buns—in 12 minutes) are two popular, quirky annual Coney Island events. And on Friday evenings throughout the summer, a fireworks display (9:30pm) is the perfect nightcap to a day of sandy adventures.

Coney Island USA

1208 Surf Ave at W 12th St, Coney Island (1-718-372-5159/www.coneyislandusa.com). Subway: D, F, Q to Coney Island–Stillwell Ave. **Open** *Call or visit website for schedule.* **Admission** *$5, children under 12 $3.*

On the spot

Writer's block Harlem-born playwright Arthur Miller lived in many an NYC zip code, but his best-known character—the down-on-his-luck Willy Loman of the play *Death of a Salesman*—lived deep in the heart of Brooklyn, surrounded by encroaching tenements. Perhaps if Willy had lived in better digs, as Miller did, life wouldn't have looked so bleak. When the writer created his 1949 masterpiece, which won a Pulitzer Prize and two Tony Awards, he was living at **31 Grace Court**, which still stands in posh Brooklyn Heights.

Queens

The city's biggest borough finally gets its due.

Sightseeing

New York's change-or-die ethos is visible all over the borough of Queens. For decades, most Manhattanites thought of this borough across the East River only as a place to catch a plane, cheer on the Mets or take in a U.S. Open tennis match. That's old-hat now.

An explosion of art venues, a vibrant new-immigrant street culture, and big jumps in Manhattan and Brooklyn real-estate prices have caused even die-hard New Yorkers to stop viewing Queens as terra incognita. Thanks to the Museum of Modern Art's two-year relocation (as MoMA QNS) to Long Island City, Manhattan's culturati were lured across the water. Once there, they stayed to check out the museums, galleries and studio spaces that had sprouted in abandoned factories, warehouses and waterfront lots. MoMA is now back at its midtown headquarters, but the Queens art scene—and the communities that have sprung up around it—continues to thrive.

The creative commotion is drawing attention to the fact that Queens is an affordable, interesting place to live. Converted lofts, row houses and 1920s-era apartment buildings in Long Island City, Astoria, Sunnyside, Woodside and Jackson Heights are being snapped up. Even Hollywood is onto this trend; Astoria was cast as the predictably too-cute home base of Kate Hudson's single-girl character in the 2004 film *Raising Helen.*

Queens owns the distinction of being the world's most ethnically diverse urban area: More than one third of its 2-million-plus residents are foreign-born. As a result of this off-the-charts demographic mix, Queens boasts strong neighborhood identities and a global array of authentic, inexpensive ethnic restaurants and shops.

To start your Queens tour, take the 7 train—a designated National Millennium Trail (like the historic Appalachian Trail) that earns its nickname International Express for around-the-world districts it passes through. From the first stop, Vernon Blvd–Jackson Ave in **Long Island City**, it's only a few blocks' walk to the historic waterfront. There, the **Gantry Plaza**

► For a map of **Queens**, see p410.
► For more on area museums, *see* pp143–163.

State Park (48th Ave at Center Blvd), named for its hulking 19th-century railroad gantries, features postcardworthy views of the city skyline and is an excellent vantage point for the July 4 fireworks.

You can get a sense of Long Island City's scrappy dockside origins in the boxing-themed **Waterfront Crabhouse** (2-03 Borden Ave at 2nd St, Long Island City, 1-718-729-4862), an old-time saloon and oyster bar in an 1880s brick edifice. Back near the subway stop are some other fine places to grab a bite: the French bistro **Tournesol** (50-12 Vernon Blvd between 50th and 51st Aves, 1-718-472-4355) and the Italian **Manetta's** (1076 Jackson Ave at 49th Ave, 1-718-786-6171).

If you stroll a few blocks east on Jackson Avenue, you'll pass **P.S. 1 Contemporary Art Center**, a progressive museum that sponsors the hot **Warm Up** series of summer art parties (*see p258*). Stop for a look at the 1904 baroque Beaux Arts excesses of the **Long Island City Courthouse** (25-10 Court Sq at Thomson Ave, Long Island City). Nearby, a well-preserved row of 1890s Italianate brownstones constitutes the **Hunters Point Historic District** (45th Ave between 21st and 23rd Sts).

Riding on the 7 train is especially thrilling as it emerges above ground, just past the second stop, Hunters Point Ave: Look out the left windows to catch the marvelous graffiti-covered walls of the 5 Pointz (formerly called the Phun Phactory; www.5ptz.com), an outdoor graf-art gallery; seconds later, you'll see the Manhattan skyline through the spans of the **59th Street Bridge** (a.k.a. Queensboro Bridge), opened in 1909. It signifies glamorous New York in Woody Allen's film *Manhattan* and is celebrated in the Simon and Garfunkel hit "The 59th Street Bridge Song (Feelin' Groovy)." The SILVERCUP sign, visible from the Queensboro Plaza platform, announces Silvercup Studios, once a bread bakery and now a TV and film studio (*Sex and the City* and *The Sopranos* have shot interiors here).

Back when Los Angeles was still a sleepy orange grove, western Queens was filled with busy film studios. W.C. Fields and the Marx Brothers clowned at Famous Players/Lasky Studios. Now called Kaufman Astoria Studios—where *The Cosby Show* was filmed and *Sesame Street*'s Big Bird still roosts—this 14-acre facility also houses the **American Museum of the**

It's cool to be hot at **P.S. 1**'s summertime Warm Up party. *See p128.*

See p128.

Moving Image, which entices cinephiles with interactive exhibitions and screenings.

At Queensboro Plaza, transfer to an N or W train and head north to Astoria. You can get off at Broadway for a visit to the recently renovated **Noguchi Museum**, where you'll find works by the visionary Japanese sculptor as well as seasonal exhibitions. Nearby is **Socrates Sculpture Park**, a four-and-a-half-acre public space given to large-scale outdoor works, as well as films and concerts during the summer. At the end of the subway line (Astoria–Ditmars Blvd), walk west to **Astoria Park** (from Astoria Park South to Ditmars Blvd, between Shore Blvd and 19th St), which features dramatic views of two bridges: the **Triborough Bridge**, a Robert Moses–conceived automotive labyrinth that connects Queens, the Bronx and Manhattan; and the 1916 **Hell Gate Bridge**, a single-arch steel masterpiece that was the template for the Sydney Harbour Bridge in Australia.

Astoria, New York's Greek-American stronghold, bursts with Hellenic eateries known for impeccably grilled seafood. **Taverna Kyclades** (33-07 Ditmars Blvd between 33rd and 35th Sts, Astoria, 1-718-545-8666) has a breezy Aegean atmosphere and a smoker-friendly patio. Dirt-cheap **Uncle George's** (33-19 Broadway at 34th St, 1-718-626-0593) is beloved by locals. One of the city's very few Central European beer gardens, **Bohemian Hall** (29-19 24th Ave at 29th St, 1-718-274-0043), hosts Czech-style indoor and outdoor dining and drinking. **Le Sans Souci** (44-09 Broadway at 44th St, 1-718-728-2733) is a charming new French café and restaurant. South of Astoria Boulevard, enjoy a (legal) hookah pipe with your coffee at one of the Egyptian cafés along **Steinway Street**.

Find your way back to the 7 train and ride to the 74th St–Broadway stop. This is the crossroads of **Jackson Heights**, a dizzyingly multiculti neighborhood, even by Queens standards, and a cheap-eats paradise. **Bombay Harbour** (72-32 Broadway between 72nd and 73rd Sts, Jackson Heights, 1-718-898-5500) has an exceptional, inexpensive lunch buffet. Shops selling saris, spices, videos and gold jewelry line the block of 74th Street between Roosevelt and 37th Avenues. **Delhi Palace** (37-33 74th St, 1-718-507-0666) is a good eating alternative to the always crowded **Jackson Diner** (37-47 74th St between Roosevelt and 37th Aves, 1-718-672-1232), which, despite its name, offers Indian cuisine.

Main Street in **Flushing**

The neighborhoods surrounding Jackson Heights are also distinct ethnic enclaves. Argentines gather at **La Fusta** (80-32 Baxter Ave between Broadway and Layton St, Elmhurst, 1-718-429-8222), a welcoming, wood-beamed steakhouse. Mexicans congregate at Roosevelt Avenue's innumerable taco and *torta* stands. Beneath Latin American soccer-team banners, Peruvians dine on sprightly ceviche and greaseless fried seafood at **La Pollada de Laura** (102-03 Northern Blvd at 102nd St, Corona, 1-718-426-7818). And everyone seems to convene at **Green Field** (108-01 Northern Blvd at 108th St, Corona, 1-718-672-5202), a cavernous, boisterous Brazilian *rodizio* serving an all-you-can-eat cornucopia of South American appetizers and grilled meats.

At the end of the 7 train lies **Flushing**. It was settled as "Vlissingen" by egalitarian Dutch, who were joined by pacifist Friends (Quakers) seeking their own freedom in the New World. These settlers authored the Flushing Remonstrance, a 1657 edict that boldly extended "the law of love, peace and liberty" to Jews and Muslims; the groundbreaking document is now regarded as a precursor to the U.S. Constitution's First Amendment. Today, Flushing is full of churches, synagogues, mosques, and Buddhist and Hindu temples. The weathered, wooden **Friends Meeting House** (137-16 Northern Blvd between Main and Union Sts, Flushing, 1-718-358-9636), built in 1694 and recently renovated, remains.

Next door is **Kingsland Homestead**, a 1785 farmhouse that overlooks a cluster of trees in adjoining Weeping Beech Park (which dates to the mid-19th century). Kingsland is home to the **Queens Historical Society** and hosts regular exhibitions on local life; 2005's major show is "40 Years of Chinese Immigrants in Queens." You can take another step back in time at the **Voelker Orth Museum**, a lovingly restored 1880s Victorian gingerbread house and herb garden that sponsors walking tours, concerts, art and gardening workshops, and popular period-costume dances and tea parties. **Flushing Town Hall**, a fanciful Romanesque-revival edifice built during the Civil War, harbors local arts groups and hosts jazz concerts, chamber music and multimedia exhibits. Here, you can catch the **Queens Jazz Trail**, a monthly trolley tour of the homes of jazz greats who have resided in the borough, including Louis Armstrong, Count Basie, John Coltrane, Ella Fitzgerald, Dizzy Gillespie, Billie Holiday and Lena Horne. The centerpiece of the tour is the **Louis Armstrong House** museum.

If exploring Flushing has jump-started your appetite, you're in luck: The mile-and-a-half stretch of **Main Street** south of Northern Boulevard is one of the world's most vibrant and fastest-growing Chinatowns. The Pan-Asian restaurant row centered around Main Street includes **Sichuan Dynasty** (135-32 40th Rd between Main and Prince Sts, Flushing, 1-718-961-7500), where $16.95 buys you *three* zesty central-Chinese entrées, such as chicken with three peppers and garlicky *ma-la* shrimp. For dim sum, try **Gum Fung** (136-28 39th Ave between Main and 138th Sts, 1-718-762-8821), where well-stocked carts make the rounds of the vast dining room from 9am to 4pm every day. The appropriately named **Spicy & Tasty** (39-07 Prince St between Roosevelt and 39th Aves, 1-718-359-1601) tempts diners with a made-to-order appetizer bar and stir-your-own shabu-shabu soup. Two doors down (but with the same address) is **Sentosa** (1-718-886-6331), which plies avid Chinatowners with curry- and coconut-spiked Malaysian cuisine, a fusion of Chinese and Indonesian tastes. Scores of Korean eateries cater to the area's now prosperous first wave of Asian immigrants; the blond-wood-furnished **Cho Sun Oak** (137-40 Northern Blvd between Main and Union Sts, 1-718-461-6464) asks $19.95 for a buffet of marinated meat and seafood that you grill at your table.

Many Flushing dining pilgrims don't realize that the area is also the borough's repository of major cultural institutions. The massive **Flushing Meadows–Corona Park**, where the 1939 and 1964 World's Fairs were held, houses several

Rockaway pipeline

Waimea Bay, Waikiki Beach, Santa Cruz... and Queens? That's right; if you have a surfboard and a MetroCard, you can catch a wave in New York City. As JFK-departing jets roar overhead, a stalwart community of urban surfers takes to the water year-round at **Rockaway Beach**, Queens, on the Atlantic coastline. When the surf's up—especially August through October, which is hurricane season—surfers from all around the city hop the A train, angling their boards into the last, emptiest car and getting to the beach just as the sun comes up.

Fanatics have been hanging ten here since the '60s explosion of surf culture, which went hand in hand with the music of the Beach Boys, cult movies like *The Endless Summer,* and the glorification of a laid-back sand-and-surf lifestyle. The sport got a more recent boost with the popularity of the surfer-chick flick *Blue Crush* and two powerhouse documentaries, *Riding Giants* and *Step into Liquid,* about big-wave riding.

Now the scene is an all-ages mix of weekday diehards (who squeeze in an hour or two before heading off to day jobs), weekend summer-share buddies and visiting day-trippers (dubbed by locals as downies or DFDs, short for "down for the day"). Some board-toting DFDs come from as far away as Hawaii, Brazil, Japan and Australia to earn their New York City bragging rights; men outnumber women by about five to one.

So how are the waves? One top local surfer explains why the waters are a challenge: "Strong currents come off the offshore jetties, and waves break cleanly in an unbroken line." After the late-summer hurricanes have passed, the most dramatic waves come in the wake of the potent nor'easter storms in February and March.

Water temps vary from the mid-30s (around zero Celsius) in January (when there's often a thin blanket of snow on the beach) to the mid-70s (mid-20s Celsius) in August.

From the 1890s through the 1950s, pint-size bungalows served as hot-weather retreats for working-class Italian, Jewish and Irish families. In the 1960s, demographics shifted as the city moved to tear down many of the original porched cottages to make room for charm-free high-rise housing projects. These days, cheaply built bungalows near the water are rented out by groups of surfers for the summer. Beach 88th Street alone houses 15 to 20 group-rental houses; in the evening, the sand-dusted strip becomes one big, barefoot barbecue.

The surfing scene is at its liveliest during summer dawns and dusks, and the crowds can cause problems. The eight gregarious members who stay in a cottage on Beach 90th Street call themselves the "Sand Flea Surf Club," and they have posted a prominent do's-and-don'ts sign on the boardwalk for visitors, to encourage respect for the rules of the wave.

Surfers also congregate under the umbrella of Surfrider NYC, which lobbies for cleaner, more accessible beaches, and sponsors surf tournaments and beach cleanups. But—just as in Maui or Malibu—the real action is in the water, where the next wild ride is waiting.

Rockaway Beach

Most surfers hang out between Beach 88th and 90th Sts. Surfing is permitted year-round, but prohibited from 9am to 5pm, from Memorial Day to Labor Day. Subway: A to Beach 89th St. For wave conditions and other information, visit www.surfrider.org/nyc and www.newyorksurf.com.

museums. The destination includes the **Queens Zoo**, whose natural environments include a lush parrot habitat; the Philip Johnson–designed **Queens Theatre in the Park**, an indoor amphitheater; the **New York Hall of Science**, an acclaimed interactive museum with a new exhibition wing; the **Queens Botanical Garden**, a 39-acre cavalcade of greenery; and the **Queens Museum of Art**, whose fascinating pièce de résistance is the *Panorama of the City of New York*, a 9,335-square-foot, 895,000-building scale model (1 inch equals 100 feet) of all five boroughs. The World Trade Center, however, has been replaced by a miniature version of *Tribute in Light*, the city's first memorial of September 11, 2001.

The park also encompasses **Shea Stadium** (*see p332* **New York Mets**), home base of the Mets; the **USTA (United States Tennis Association) National Tennis Center**, where the **U.S. Open** (*see p334*) raises a racket at the end of each summer; and the **Unisphere**, a mammoth steel globe that became famous as the symbol of the 1964 World's Fair. (A few years back, borough native Donald Trump installed a scaled-down copy of this Queens icon in front of his hotel on Manhattan's Columbus Circle.)

The **Queens Cultural Trolley** (1-718-592-9700, ext 306) takes tourists on a 70-minute loop through the park and nearby neighborhoods, including Jackson Heights and Corona—for free. Stops include the Louis Armstrong House, Jackson Heights' Baby Bollywood and the Pan-Latin bazaar that is Roosevelt Avenue. The trolley runs on weekends at noon, 1, 2:30 and 4:30pm.

Busy **Jamaica**, in the southern part of the borough, is the center of African-American commerce, hip-hop culture and—true to its name—Caribbean immigration. From the Jamaica Center–Parsons/Archer station of the E, J and Z trains, walk to bustling **Jamaica Avenue**. The **Tabernacle of Prayer** is an Evangelical church set in a splendid former movie palace, the Loews Valencia. Bishop Ronny Davis's high-energy Sunday gospel service is far less overrun with tourists than its Harlem counterparts. Down Jamaica Avenue, within King Park, is **King Manor Museum**, the early-19th-century residence of Rufus King, a three-term New York senator and early opponent of slavery.

Jamaica's down-home flavor is best sampled at **Carmichael's** (117-08 Guy R. Brewer Blvd at Foch Blvd, Jamaica, 1-718-723-6908), a pristine 1950s diner slinging all-day breakfasts of salmon croquettes and grits 'n' gravy. On Wednesday nights, Carmichael's resounds with a lively jazz jam and is accessible, in speakeasy fashion, through a basement door.

The borough is also blessed with two alternating-season Thoroughbred tracks: **Aqueduct** (*see p334*), near JFK Airport, and the prettier **Belmont Park** (*see p334*), just over the borough's eastern border. At these legendary ovals, even the horses have New York attitude, dispensing with their work in a New York minute or two.

American Museum of the Moving Image
35th Ave at 36th St, Astoria (1-718-784-0077/ www.movingimage.us). Subway: G, R, V to Steinway St. **Open** *Wed, Thu noon–5pm; Fri noon–8pm; Sat, Sun 11am–6:30pm.* **Admission** *$10, students $7.50, children 5–18 $5, children under 5 free. No strollers. Free Fri 4–8pm.* **Credit** *AmEx, MC, V.* For review, *see p161*.

Discover Queens
www.discoverqueens.info. This website offers current cultural and entertainment information (including details about museums and attractions not covered in this chapter), as well as discount coupons.

Local legend

During **Jackie Robinson**'s glory days at Ebbets Field in Brooklyn, his real home base was in Queens. The first African-American to play major league baseball, in 1947, Robinson often took the Interboro Parkway from the Dodgers' stadium in Flatbush to his home at 112-40 177th St, in the Addisleigh Park area of Saint Albans, an enclave that was also home to Lena Horne, Count Basie and Ella Fitzgerald. To honor the Hall of Fame second baseman, his former commuting route was renamed the Jackie Robinson Parkway in 1998.

Flushing Meadows–Corona Park

From 111th St to Van Wyck Expwy, between Flushing Bay and Grand Central Pkwy (1-718-760-6565). Subway: 7 to Willets Point–Shea Stadium.

Flushing Town Hall/Flushing Council on Culture and the Arts/ Queens Jazz Trail

137-35 Northern Blvd between Leavitt St and Linden Pl, Flushing (1-718-463-7700/www.flushingtownhall. com/www.queensjazztrail.com). Subway: 7 to Flushing– Main St. **Open** *Mon–Fri 9am–5pm; Sat, Sun noon– 5pm.* **Tours** *Jazz Trail first Saturday of the month at 10am; reservations required.* **Admission** *free. Jazz Trail $26.* **Credit** *AmEx, MC, V.*

King Manor Museum

King Park, Jamaica Ave at 153rd St, Jamaica (1-718-206-0545/www.queensnewyork.com/ cultural/rufus/king.html). Subway: E, J, Z to Jamaica Center–Parsons/Archer; F to Parsons Blvd. **Open** *Sat, Sun, and second and last Tuesday of the month 12:15–2pm.* **Admission** *suggested donation $2, children $1.* **Credit** *Cash only.*

Kingsland Homestead/ Queens Historical Society

143-35 37th Ave between Bowne St and Parsons Blvd, Flushing (1-718-939-0647, ext 17/www.queens historicalsociety.org). Subway: 7 to Flushing–Main St. **Tours** *Tue, Sat, Sun 2:30–4:30pm, and by appointment.* **Admission** *$3, seniors and students $2.* **Credit** *Cash only.*

Louis Armstrong House

34-56 107th St between 34th and 37th Aves, Corona (1-718-478-8274/www.satchmo.net). Subway: 7 to 103rd St–Corona Plaza. **Open** *Tue–Fri 10am–5pm; Sat, Sun noon–5pm.* **Tours** *Mon–Fri noon–4pm, on the hour; Sat, Sun 10am–4pm, on the hour.* **Admission** *$8, seniors and children $6.* **Credit** *MC, V ($15 minimum).*

New York Hall of Science

47-01 111th St at 47th Ave, Corona (1-718-699-0005/www.nyhallsci.org). Subway: 7 to 111th St. **Open** *Jul, Aug Mon 9:30am–2pm; Tue–Fri 9:30am–5pm; Sat, Sun 10:30am–6pm. Sept–Jun Tue–Thu 9:30am–2pm; Fri 9:30am–5pm; Sat, Sun noon–5pm. Lab Thu, Fri 2–4:45pm; Sat, Sun noon–5:45pm.* **Admission** *$9; seniors, students and children 5–17 $6; children 2–4 $2.50. Free Sept–Jun Fri 2–5pm.* **Credit** *AmEx, DC, Disc, MC, V.* For review, *see p163.*

The Noguchi Museum

9-01 33rd Rd between Vernon Blvd and 10th St, Long Island City (1-718-204-7088/www.noguchi. org). Travel: N, W to Broadway, then take the Q104 bus to 11th St; or 7 to Vernon Blvd–Jackson Ave, then take the Q103 bus to 10th St. **Open** *Wed–Fri 10am–5pm; Sat, Sun 11am–6pm.* **Admission** *$5, seniors and students $2.50.* **Credit** *AmEx, DC, MC, V.* For review, *see p154.*

P.S. 1 Contemporary Art Center

22-25 Jackson Ave at 46th Ave, Long Island City (1-718-784-2084/www.ps1.org). Subway: E, V to 23rd St–Ely Ave; G to 21st St–Jackson Ave; 7 to 45th Rd– Court House Sq. **Open** *Mon, Thu–Sun noon–6pm.* **Admission** *suggested donation $5, seniors and students $2. Warm Up Jul–early Sept, Sat 2–9pm $8.* **Credit** *AmEx, MC, V.* For review, *see p151.*

Queens Botanical Garden

43-50 Main St between Dahlia and Elder Aves, Flushing (1-718-886-3800/www.queensbotanical. org). Subway: 7 to Flushing–Main St. **Open** *Apr–Oct Tue–Fri 8am–6pm; Sat, Sun 8am–7pm. Nov–Mar Tue–Sun 8am–4:30pm. Open on Monday holidays.* **Admission** *free.*

Queens Museum of Art

New York City Building, park entrance on 49th Ave at 111th St, Flushing Meadows–Corona Park, Queens (1-718-592-9700/www.queensmuseum.org). Subway: 7 to 111th St. Walk south on 111th, then turn left onto 49th Ave. Continue into the park and over the Grand Central Parkway bridge. Museum is on the right, beside the Unisphere. **Open** *Jul–Sept Wed–Sun 1–8pm. Sept–Jun Wed–Fri 10am–5pm.* **Admission** *$5, seniors and children $2.50, children under 5 free.* For review, *see p154.*

Queens Theatre in the Park

Flushing Meadows–Corona Park (1-718-760-0064/ www.queenstheatre.org). Travel: 7 to Willets Point– Shea Stadium, then take the Shea Stadium exit to meet shuttle, which starts picking up passengers from the subway station one hour before curtain; the shuttle makes return trips until one hour after show ends. Call or visit website for show times and ticket prices.

Queens Zoo

Flushing Meadows–Corona Park, 53-51 111th St between 53rd and 54th Aves (1-718-271-1500/ www.queenszoo.com). Subway: 7 to 111th St. **Open** *Mon–Fri 10am–5pm; Sat, Sun, holidays 10am–5:30pm. Call for summer hours.* **Admission** *$5, seniors $1.25, children 3–12 $1, children under 3 free.* **Credit** *Cash only.*

Socrates Sculpture Park

Broadway at Vernon Blvd, Long Island City (1-718-956-1819/www.socratessculpturepark.org). Travel: N, W to Broadway, then take the Q104 bus to Vernon Blvd. **Open** *10am–sunset, except on movie nights.* **Admission** *free.*

Tabernacle of Prayer

165-11 Jamaica Ave between Merrick Blvd and 165th St, Jamaica (1-718-657-4210/www.forministry.com/ 11432top1). Subway: E, J, Z to Jamaica Center–Parsons/ Archer; F to Parsons Blvd. **Tours** *Call for information.*

Voelker Orth Museum

149-19 38th Ave between 149th Pl and 149th St, Flushing (1-718-359-6227/www.voelkerorth museum.org). Subway: 7 to Flushing–Main St. **Open** *Wed, Sat, Sun 1–4pm, and by appointment.* **Admission** *suggested donation $2.*

The Bronx

Poet Ogden Nash once wrote, "The Bronx? No thonx!" We beg to differ.

The northernmost borough is rich in parks, educational institutions and lively ethnic neighborhoods; it also boasts a burgeoning art scene, a world-famous baseball stadium and numerous historical museums. And for trivia fans: It's the only piece of the city attached to the U.S. mainland, and it's the only borough graced with an article. The area once belonged to the family of Jonas Bronck, a Dutch farmer who owned a 500-acre homestead in what is now the southeastern Morrisania section. Back in the 1630s, people would say they were going to visit "the Broncks," and the name stuck.

Throughout the early decades of the 20th century, the Bronx, like Queens and Brooklyn, drew much of its population from the ever-expanding pool of Irish, German, Italian and Eastern European Jewish immigrants. These new Americans, many of whom had rarely ventured beyond their home villages before setting out for the New World, flocked to the Bronx for its cheap rents and open spaces. After WWII, as the borough grew more urbanized, descendants of the old European immigrants moved farther out, to the suburbs of Long Island and nearby Westchester. Fresh waves of newcomers, hailing from Central America, Puerto Rico, Albania and Russia, as well as Hispaniola and other points in the West Indies, took their places.

Along with the population shifts, the Bronx has probably witnessed more upheaval than the rest of the city combined. Robert Moses, the city planner who was both revered and reviled for his remaking of the five boroughs, linked them with expressways and bridges. Moses used brute force to address the challenge of building grand public works in a densely populated urban area, and the Bronx felt the brunt of it. From the late 1940s until the early '70s, thousands of Bronx residents saw their apartment buildings razed to make room for the Whitestone and Throgs Neck Bridges, the east-to-west Cross Bronx Expressway, and the north-to-south Bruckner Boulevard extension of the New England Thruway. Cut off from their surrounding communities, many neighborhoods fell into neglect, a condition exacerbated by the economic and social downturns that plagued the entire city in the '60s and '70s.

These days, the borough is finding its feet again. Some spots around the South, East and Central Bronx are still in slow and painful transition, and they don't invite tourism. Yet arts communities have sprouted in Mott Haven and Hunts Point; the zoo and botanical garden are more attractive than ever; and numerous areas—the Grand Concourse, Arthur Avenue, Riverdale, City Island and Pelham Bay Park—are safe and welcoming to visitors. These varied locales hold promise for sightseers of all interests.

You don't have to be a sports fanatic to recognize one of the borough's best-known landmarks. Located at 161st Street and River Avenue, **Yankee Stadium** has seen baseball's most famous legends come and go, from Babe Ruth and Joe DiMaggio to A-Rod. When there isn't a day game, the Yankees organization gives tours of the clubhouse, the dugout and the famous center-field Monument Park. The coolest way to get to the game is by boat: the **NY Waterway** (*see p72*) will ferry you to and from the stadium (from Manhattan or New Jersey), aboard the *Yankee Clipper* (natch).

Architecture buffs can start their Bronx tour with a stroll along the six-and-a-half mile **Grand Concourse**, in the West Bronx. Engineer Louis Risse designed the boulevard, which stretches from 138th Street to Mosholu Parkway, in 1892, six years before the Bronx officially became one of the five boroughs of New York City. Buildings here date mostly from the '20s through the early '40s and display a trove of Art Deco–inspired styles. Erected in 1937 at the corner of 161st Street, **888 Grand Concourse** has a concave entrance of gilded mosaic and is topped by a curvy metallic marquee. Inside, the mirrored lobby's central fountain and sunburst-patterned floor could rival those of any hotel on Miami's Ocean Drive. But the landmark **Andrew Freedman Home**, a 1924 French-inspired limestone palazzo between McClennan and 166th Streets, is the grandest building on the Grand Concourse. Freedman, a millionaire subway contractor, set aside the bulk of his $7 million estate to build a retirement home for wealthy people who had fallen on hard times. Today, the building still houses the elderly, but a dramatic reversal of fortune is no longer a residency requirement.

There's plenty along the Concourse to appease culture cravings. The **Bronx Museum of the Arts**, established in 1971 and housed in a former synagogue, exhibits high-quality contemporary and historical works by Bronx-

Stripes are always in fashion at the **Bronx Zoo**'s Tiger Mountain exhibit. *See p136.*

based artists, including many of African-American, Asian and Latino heritage. Lovers of literature will enjoy the **Edgar Allan Poe Cottage**, a small wooden farmhouse where the writer lived from 1846 to 1849 and penned the poem "Annabel Lee." Moved to the Grand Concourse from its original spot on Fordham Road in 1913, the museum has period furniture and information about Poe and his work.

Those wanting a closer look at the up-and-coming arts scene in **Mott Haven** and the South Bronx should hop on the **Bronx Culture Trolley**, a free shuttle that visits the area's hottest galleries, performance spaces and museums. The Bronx Museum of the Arts, the **Hostos Art Gallery** (part of the **Center for the Arts & Culture** at Hostos Community College), the **Pregones Theater** (571–575 Walton Ave between 149th and 150th Sts, 1-718-585-1202, www.pregones.org) and the **Blue Ox Bar** (Third Ave at E 139th St, 1-718-402-1045)—are a few of the participating institutions that schedule screenings and performances along the trolley's route. One of the borough's newest draws is the **Studio Art Gallery** (642 Rosedale Ave between Randall and Seward Aves, 1-718-589-0455). Call for an appointment to view works by the most talented locals (admission $2).

Tucked in the southeastern corner of the Bronx, **Hunts Point** looks like an industrial wasteland, but over the past decade, it has become increasingly popular as a live-work destination for pioneering artists. In 1994, a group of artists and community leaders converted a 12,000-square-foot industrial building into the **Point Community Development Corporation** (940 Garrison Ave at Manida St, 1-718-542-4139, www.thepoint.org), a performance space, gallery and business incubator. The Point holds Breakbeats, a break-dance performance, on Tuesdays from 7 to 9pm, and leads lively walking tours (call for reservations) like Mambo to Hip-Hop, which covers the history of locally born music genres. Creative types stage performances at the nearby **Bronx Academy of Arts and Dance (BAAD!)**, and more than a dozen painters and sculptors work in the academy's studios. Annually, the organization presents BAAD! Ass Women, a celebration of works by female artists; the springtime Boogie Down Dance Series; and Out Like That, a gay-and-lesbian arts festival. Hunts Point is also home to the city's largest wholesale markets for produce, meat and fish, which turn the predawn hours into a chaotic bazaar. (The markets are open to the public, but sales are in bulk only, and browsing is discouraged.)

Education enthusiasts know that the Bronx High School of Science counts six Nobel Prize winners among its alumni—the most of any high school in the world—and that the borough boasts many other respected schools. Fordham Road, which runs east to west, from the Harlem River to the Hutchinson River, will lead you to **Fordham University** (441 E Fordham Rd between Third and Washington Aves), a Jesuit institution founded in 1841. The grounds hold several

A tsunami of salami awaits you at **Arthur Avenue**'s Italian delis. *See p137.*

remarkable buildings, including the grand neo-Gothic **Keating Hall** and the handsome Greek Revival **Rose Hill Administration Building**, once a manor house. To visit, call security ahead of time (1-718-817-2222).

Naturally, the Bronx has green space aplenty. Spread out over 250 acres and bisected by the Bronx River, the **New York Botanical Garden** is a magical respite from cars and concrete, comprising 48 gardens and plant collections, including the Rockefeller Rose Garden, the Everett Children's Adventure Garden and the last 50 original acres of a forest that once covered all of New York City. In springtime, the gardens are frothy with pastel blossoms as clusters of lilac, cherry, magnolia and crab-apple trees burst into bloom, followed in fall by vivid foliage in the oak and maple groves. On a rainy day, you can stay warm and dry inside the **Enid A. Haupt Conservatory**, a striking glass-walled greenhouse built in 1902. It offers seasonal exhibits as well as the World of Plants, a series of environmental galleries that will send you on an ecotour through tropical rain forests, deserts and palm-tree oases. The new high-tech **Nolan Greenhouses**, which are made up of 24 connected glass sheds, will be used for public displays, botanical research and conservation projects.

The borough's most famous attraction, the **Bronx Zoo**, opened in 1899; at 265 acres, it's the largest urban zoo in the U.S. The zoo shuns cages in favor of indoor and outdoor environments that mimic the natural habitats of more than 4,000 mammals, birds, reptiles and other animals.

Nearly a hundred species, including monkeys, leopards and tapirs, live inside the lush, steamy **Jungle World**, a re-creation of an Asian rain forest inside a 37,000-square-foot building. Opened in 1999, the superpopular **Congo Gorilla Forest** has turned six and a half acres into a dramatic Central African rain-forest habitat. A glass-enclosed tunnel winds through the forest, allowing visitors to get close to the dozens of primate families in residence, including 26 majestic western lowland gorillas. One "celebrity" is native daughter Pattycake, the first gorilla born in New York City. For those who prefer cats, the newly opened **Tiger Mountain** has six adult Siberian tigers, who look particularly regal on snowy days. If you take the Bengali Express Monorail (which travels through the Wild Asia Encampment), try to grab a seat up front for prime viewing of antelope, Indian rhinos and Asian elephants.

Pelham Bay Park, in the borough's northeastern corner, is the city's biggest bucolic playground. You're best off with a car or a bike if you want to explore the park's 2,765 acres, once home to the Siwonay Indians. Pick up a map at the Ranger Nature Center, near the entrance on Bruckner Boulevard at Wilkinson Avenue. The **Bartow-Pell Mansion Museum**, in the park's southeastern quarter, overlooks Long Island Sound. Completed in the 1842, the elegantly furnished Greek Revival building faces a reflecting pool surrounded by gardens. The park's 13 miles of coastline border the Hutchinson River to the west and the Long Island Sound and Eastchester Bay to the east.

In summer, locals crowd **Orchard Beach**; created in the 1930s, it's one of the few Robert Moses projects welcomed by all.

Perhaps the leafiest neighborhood is **Riverdale**, along the northwest coast of the Bronx. Huge homes perch on narrow, winding streets in this storybook town atop a hill overlooking the Hudson River. Theodore Roosevelt, Mark Twain and Arturo Toscanini have all lived in **Wave Hill House**, an 1843 stone mansion located on a former private estate that is now a cultural and environmental center. Wave Hill's 28 acres of cultivated gardens and woodlands provide lovely views of the river. The art gallery shows nature-themed exhibits, and the organization presents concerts and performances year-round. If you crave a day outdoors on foot or on bike, then try the quiet pathways of the Hudson River–hugging **Riverdale Park**. Enter this swath of forest preserve along Palisade Avenue between 232nd and 254th Streets. You can continue your hiking (or biking) down Spaulding Lane (off 248th St), which offers a gurgling stream and waterfall, or on Ladd Road (north of 255th St), where three modernist houses sit like serene Buddhas in the woods.

Down the slope from Riverdale, you'll find **Gaelic Park**, a longtime gathering place for the area's Irish-American community. Located just west of Broadway and on the north side of 240th Street, near **Manhattan College**, this is where Irish hurling and football teams compete regularly on weekends. The 1,146-acre **Van Cortlandt Park** (entrance on Broadway at 244th St) is nearby; cricket teams made up mostly of West Indian immigrants are a common sight here. You can also hike through a 100-year-old forest, play golf on a municipal course or rent horses at stables in the park. **Van Cortlandt House Museum**, a fine example of pre-Revolutionary Georgian architecture, was built by Frederick Van Cortlandt in 1748; it later served as a headquarters for George Washington during the Revolutionary War. Donated to the city by the Van Cortlandt family, it's the oldest building in the borough.

Once you've exhausted yourself in the great outdoors, kick back at the **Riverdale Garden** (4576 Manhattan College Pkwy near 242nd St, 1-718-884-5232), which provides a pleasant backyard patio and a creative American menu. Or take home a rich, velvety cheesecake from the **S&S Cheesecake Factory** (222 W 238th St between Broadway and Review Pl, 1-718-549-3888). Local pub **An Béal Bocht** (445 W 238th St between Greystone and Waldo Aves, 1-718-884-7127) has Guinness, live Irish bands and ceilidh dancing.

Belmont, home of the Bronx's **Little Italy**, is the real culinary mecca. You'll hear plenty of Italian spoken on lively **Arthur Avenue** (www.arthuravenuebronx.com), the neighborhood's main drag, which is lined with Italian delis, restaurants, markets and cafés. Stop for a chicken Parmesan hero at **Roma Luncheonette** (636 E 187th St at Belmont Ave, 1-718-367-9189). Browse and graze at the **Arthur Avenue Retail Market** (Crescent Ave at 186th St), an indoor bazaar built in the 1940s when former Mayor Fiorello La Guardia campaigned to get pushcarts off the street. (The market is closed on Sundays.) Inside is **Mike's Deli** (2344 Arthur Ave between Crescent Ave and E 186th St, 1-718-295-5033), where you can try the trademark *schiacciata* (Italian for "squashed") sandwich of grilled vegetables, or Big Mike's Combo, a roll loaded with Provolone cheese and Italian cold cuts like mortadella, prosciutto and salami. Can't see a red, white and green flag without jonesing for pizza? Stop in for a pie at the popular **Full Moon Pizzeria** (600 E 187th St at Arthur Ave, 1-718-584-3451), where soccer fans gorge on crackling thin-crust pizza while watching a match on TV. If you're in the mood for a full meal, we recommend old-style red-sauce joints **Mario's** (2342 Arthur Ave between Crescent Ave and E 186th St, 1-718-584-1188), **Dominick's** (2335 Arthur Ave between Crescent Ave and E 187th St, 1-718-733-2807) and **Roberto's** (603 Crescent Ave at Hughes Ave, 1-718-733-9503)—regulars love to argue about which place is the best.

Old salts—and seafood fans—should stop at **City Island**. Located just east of Pelham Bay Park and surrounded by the waters of Eastchester Bay and the Long Island Sound,

Sightseeing

The best Places to...

...get some green
Take a stroll among the graceful trees of the **New York Botanical Garden** (see p136).

...stuff yourself silly
Never say *basta* when you're cruising the many Italian delis and trattorias along **Arthur Avenue** (see p137).

...talk to the animals
See what the Siberian tigers are up to at the Bronx Zoo's **Tiger Mountain** (see p136).

...hear the sounds of summer
Dream along with a concert in the gardens of **Wave Hill House** (see p137) or scream along with the fans at **Yankee Stadium** (see p134).

City Island could pass for a sleepy New England village, except that it's accessible by a crosstown city bus. Settled in 1685, the island was once a prosperous shipbuilding center with a busy fishing industry, a history reflected in the streets lined with Victorian captains' houses. Nautical activity still abounds, especially in the summer, but recreational boating is the main industry now. Seafood restaurants, marine-themed bars, six yacht clubs and a couple of sail makers crowd the docks. Join the warm-weather hordes at **Johnny's Famous Reef Restaurant** (2 City Island Ave at Belden St,

1-718-885-2086) for steamed clams, cold beer and great views, or relax with teatime treats at **Alice's City Island** (296 City Island Ave between Fordham and Hawkins Sts, 1-718-885-0808). For a romantic getaway, book a room at **Le Refuge Inn** (*see p201*), a restored 19th-century sea captain's house where you can enjoy a sophisticated French menu in elegant surroundings. Few commercial fishermen remain, but you'd hardly know it at **Rosenberg's Boat Livery** (663 City Island Ave at Bridge St, 1-718-885-1843), a bait-and-tackle shop that rents motorboats by the day.

VIP, RIP

New Yorkers spend their lives in pursuit of the right address, and more than 300,000 of them have made Woodlawn Cemetery in the North Bronx their oh-so-fashionable (permanent) place of residence. For many, it's the nicest place they've ever rested their bones. Although Brooklyn's Green-Wood Cemetery gets all the good press, stately, well-manicured Woodlawn is well worth a stop on the way to Wave Hill or Van Cortlandt Park. As you meander along graceful paths shaded by massive oak trees, the cemetery's 400 gently sloping acres, interspersed with flowering shrubs and emerald lawns, can feel a lot like Central Park—only quieter. Eloquent headstones pay homage, and money talks through elaborate mausoleums designed in neoclassical, Gothic, Art Deco and Egyptian styles by the reigning architects of the day.

A stroll through Woodlawn is a crash course in New York history. Opened during the Civil War, it welcomed fallen Union soldiers. Later, it became the resting place for such Gilded Age moguls as Joseph Pulitzer, F.W. Woolworth, R.H. Macy and Jay Gould. Five New York City mayors, including Fiorello La Guardia, made their final public appearance at Woodlawn. In 1912, Woodlawn took in seven unfortunates from the *Titanic;* nine victims of the World Trade Center attack were laid to rest here in 2001.

The extension of the subway into the Bronx in 1916 made nonsectarian Woodlawn the preferred destination of African-Americans prominent in the Harlem Renaissance. Madame C.J. Walker (*see p116* **Local legend**), America's first black millionaire (thanks to her self-made hairdressing empire), arrived in 1919, and poet Countee Cullen capped his inkwell in 1946. Among jazz greats, Duke Ellington, Miles Davis, Coleman Hawkins,

Milt Jackson, Illinois Jacquet and Lionel Hampton all came here after they'd played their last licks.

Aside from these musicians, Woodlawn's most visited graves belong to *Moby Dick* author Herman Melville, who died in obscurity in 1891; suffragist Elizabeth Cady Stanton; music maestro Irving Berlin; and Wild West icon Bat Masterson, whose gunslinging exploits were depicted in a top-rated TV series in the late 1950s.

To those who fall in love with the place, take note: The cemetery has enough burial space for the next 50 years. And you don't have to be a New Yorker to get in. At Woodlawn, you become one.

Woodlawn Cemetery
Entrance at Webster Ave and E 233rd St (1-718-920-0500). Subway: 4 to Woodlawn. **Open** *8:30am–5pm daily.* **Admission** *free. Maps and photo permits available at the visitors' entrance.*

The Livery also doubles as a bustling bar (locals call it the Worm Hole).

As revitalization spreads across its landscape, the Bronx is becoming known as New York City's renaissance borough. Each year brings more to do, see and explore here, and the borough's citizens are more concerned than ever with preserving—and appreciating—their home.

Bartow-Pell Mansion Museum

895 Shore Rd North at Pelham Bay Park (1-718-885-1461). Travel: 6 to Pelham Bay Park, then take the Bee-Line bus 45 (ask driver to stop at the Bartow-Pell Mansion; bus does not run on Sunday), or take a cab from the subway station. **Open** *Wed, Sat, Sun noon–4pm.* **Admission** *$2.50, seniors and students $1.25, children under 12 free.* **Credit** *Cash only.*

Bronx Academy of Arts and Dance (BAAD!)

841 Barretto St between Garrison and Lafayette Aves, second floor (1-718-842-5223/www.bronx academyofartsanddance.org). Subway: 6 to Hunts Point Ave. **Open** *Check website for hours and prices.*

Bronx Culture Trolley

The Bronx Council on the Arts (1-718-931-9500, ext 33/www.bronxarts.org). Subway: 2, 4, 5 to 149th St–Grand Concourse. **Open** *Feb–Jun, Oct–Dec first Wednesday of the month. Trolley picks up passengers starting at 5:30pm at Hostos Center for the Arts & Culture (see right); leaves at 6pm.* **Admission** *free.*

The nonprofit Bronx Council on the Arts sponsors a monthly free trolley tour that stops at art galleries, performance spaces and museums in Mott Haven South and other areas in the South Bronx.

Bronx Museum of the Arts

1040 Grand Concourse at 165th St (1-718-681-6000/www.bxma.org). Subway: B, D, 4 to 161st St–Yankee Stadium. **Open** *Wed noon–9pm; Thu–Sun noon–6pm.* **Admission** *$5, seniors and students $3, children under 12 free. Free Wednesday.*

Bronx Zoo/ Wildlife Conservation Society

Bronx River Pkwy at Fordham Rd (1-718-367-1010/www.bronxzoo.org). Subway: 2, 5 to West Farms Sq–East Tremont Ave. **Open** *Apr–Oct Mon–Fri 10am–5pm; Sat, Sun, holidays 10am–5:30pm. Nov–Mar 10am–4:30pm.* **Admission** *$8, seniors and children $6, children under 2 free. Voluntary donation Wednesday. (Some rides and exhibitions are extra.)* **Credit** *Cash only.*

City Island

Travel: 6 to Pelham Bay Park, then take the Bx29 bus to City Island. Call or visit the website of the City Island Chamber of Commerce (1-718-885-9100/www.cityisland.com) for information on events and activities.

Edgar Allan Poe Cottage

2640 Grand Concourse at Kingsbridge Rd (1-718-881-8900). Subway: B, D, 4 to Kingsbridge Rd.

Open *Sat 10am–4pm; Sun 1–5pm.* **Admission** *$3, seniors and students $2.*

Grand Concourse

From Mosholu Pkwy to 138th St. Subway: 4 to 149th St–Grand Concourse or 161st St–Yankee Stadium.

Hostos Center for the Arts & Culture

450 Grand Concourse at 149th St (1-718-518-4455/www.hostos.cuny.edu). Subway: 2, 4, 5 to 149th St–Grand Concourse. **Open** *Gallery Mon–Sat 10am–6pm.*

Museum of Bronx History

Valentine-Varian House, 3266 Bainbridge Ave between Van Cortlandt Ave and E 208th St (1-718-881-8900/www.bronxhistoricalsociety.org). Subway: D to Norwood–205th St. **Open** *Sat 10am–4pm; Sun 1–5pm.* **Admission** *$3; seniors, students and children $2.*

Operated by the Bronx County Historical Society, the Museum of Bronx History is located in the Valentine-Varian House, a Federal-style fieldstone residence built in 1758. The Society offers tours that explore various neighborhoods and historic periods.

New York Botanical Garden

Bronx River Pkwy at Fordham Rd (1-718-817-8700/www.nybg.org). Travel: B, D, 4 to Bedford Park Blvd, then take the Bx26 bus to Garden gate; or Metro-North (Harlem Line local) from Grand Central Terminal to Botanical Garden. **Open** *Apr–Oct Tue–Sun, Mon holidays 10am–6pm. Nov–Mar Tue–Sun 10am–5pm.* **Admission** *$6, seniors $3, students $2, children $1, children under 2 free. Free Wednesday all day, Sat 10am–noon.* **Credit** *Cash only.*

The basic $6 fee is for the grounds only; a $13 Garden Passport includes admission to the Adventure Garden, the Haupt Conservatory and tram tours. If you're traveling from Manhattan, a $15.50 Getaway ticket (available at Grand Central Terminal) buys you round-trip travel on Metro-North's Harlem train line and a Garden Passport.

Pelham Bay Park

1-718-430-1890. Subway: 6 to Pelham Bay Park.

Van Cortlandt House Museum

Van Cortlandt Park, entrance on Broadway at 244th St (1-718-543-3344/www.vancortlandthouse.org). Subway: 1, 9 to 242nd St–Van Cortlandt Park. **Open** *Tue–Fri 10am–3pm; Sat, Sun 11am–4pm.* **Admission** *$5, seniors and students $3, children under 12 free. Free Wednesday.* **Credit** *Cash only.*

Wave Hill House

249th St at Independence Ave (1-718-549-3200/www.wavehill.org). Travel: Metro-North (Hudson Line local) from Grand Central Terminal to Riverdale. **Open** *Apr 15–Oct 14 Tue–Sun 9am–5:30pm (Jun–Jul Wed 9am–9pm). Oct 15–Apr 14 Tue–Sun 9am–4:30pm.* **Admission** *$4, seniors and students $2, children under 6 free. Free Tuesday all day, Sat 9am–noon and Dec–Feb all times.* **Credit** *Cash only.*

Sightseeing

Staten Island

It's part of the city, but a world unto itself.

Staten Island has always been regarded as a stepsister of the other four boroughs. In fact, in 1993, tenuous relations with the city government caused 65 percent of the island's residents to vote to secede from the City of New York. The state refused to acknowledge the referendum, and the case was closed. Fortunately, the near-divorce spurred an era of renewed appreciation for what many consider to be the forgotten borough. And with a small but active artistic community and a mellow selection of historic attractions, the island and its great views certainly merit exploration, especially in fine weather.

Giovanni da Verrazano was the first European to discover this hilly chunk of land (1524), but it was actually named by Henry Hudson, who dubbed it *Staaten Eylandt* (Dutch for "State's Island") in 1609. Early settlements were repeatedly wiped out by Native American resistance, but the Dutch eventually took hold in 1661. The isle became a peaceful plot of land, with shipping and manufacturing emerging on the northern shore, and farms and small hamlets sprouting up to the south. In 1898, the island was incorporated as one of the five boroughs. Still, the predominantly rural area didn't have much of a connection to the rest of the city until 1964, when the **Verrazano-Narrows Bridge** connected the island to Brooklyn's Bay Ridge neighborhood.

The best-known link to the city, however, is the famous (and free) **Staten Island Ferry**, which passes the Statue of Liberty before sliding into the St. George terminal (currently undergoing an $81 million renovation). Many of the island's sights are just steps away. On the Esplanade, next to the terminal, is *Postcards,* by Japanese architect Masayuki Sono. Dedicated in September 2004, the $2.7 million sculpture is a memorial to the 253 Staten Islanders lost on September 11, 2001. Another addition to the Esplanade will be the **National Lighthouse Center and Museum** (1-718-556-1681, www.lighthousemuseum.org), scheduled to open in the summer of 2005. The complex will include a restored lighthouse, a lightship, piers and exhibits. Baseball fans will love the harborside **Richmond County Savings Bank Ballpark**, home of the minor-league Staten Island Yankees. Those up for a stroll can wander along the waterfront and enjoy the view of Manhattan's

downtown skyline, then head south a few blocks for a burger and beer at the **Cargo Cafe** (120 Bay St between Slossen Terr and Victory Blvd, 1-718-876-0539). The popular bar and grill displays a rotating collection of paintings by local artists. Walking north and then west along Richmond Terrace to Westervelt Avenue, then uphill two blocks to St. Marks Place, you'll come upon the **St. George–New Brighton Historic District**, a landmark neighborhood full of Queen Anne and Colonial Revival buildings that date back to the early 1830s.

While the waterfront is easy to get to and has stunning views, inland areas provide ample opportunities for exploration, too. Buses and the single-line Staten Island Railroad depart from St. George for destinations along the eastern half of the island. Visitors with an interest in architecture and the arts should see the stately Greek Revival structures that form the nucleus of the 83-acre **Snug Harbor Cultural Center**. Opened in 1833 as a maritime hospital and sailors' home, the center was converted into a visual and performing arts complex in 1976. The **Jacques Marchais Museum of Tibetan Art** (*see p159*), a reproduction of a small Himalayan temple with a tranquil meditation garden, showcases a compact collection of Tibetan and Buddhist artifacts, artworks and religious items. Nearby, guides in period garb give tours of the 27 restored buildings of **Historic Richmond Town**, the island's onetime county seat. Take a look at **Voorlezer's House**, the nation's oldest former schoolhouse (circa 1695); there's also a general store, a blacksmith, a basket weaver and a working farm.

Staten Island is a dining destination as well, especially around Port Richmond. Islanders swear that the bubbling thin-crust pie at **Denino's Tavern** (524 Port Richmond Ave between Hooker Pl and Walker St, 1-718-442-9401), in business since 1937, is the best pizza in NYC. For dessert, stroll across the street for one of **Ralph's Famous Italian Ices** (501 Port Richmond Ave at Catherine St, 1-718-273-3675). You can also dine by candlelight at the **Parsonage** (74 Arthur Kill Rd at Clarke Ave, 1-718-351-7879), located in a pre–Civil War home in the middle of Historic Richmond Town.

Outdoorsy types can travel by bus from the ferry to **High Rock Park** at the heart of the

Showcasing the work of local artists, **Snug Harbor Cultural Center** is no mere safe haven. *See p142.*

island; this is the main access point for more than 30 miles of hiking trails. On a summer day, a 40-minute ride on the S78 bus will take you to the island's southeastern coast, where you can swim, picnic and even fish at **Wolfe's Pond Park** (Cornelia Ave at Hylan Blvd, 1-718-984-8266). A little farther south, tour the historic **Conference House**, a museum of Colonial life. Just a short walk away, you can admire the passing sailboats from Tottenville Beach, at the very tip of the island.

If wildlife and nature are more your scene, the **Staten Island Zoo**, adjacent to Clove Lakes Park, boasts one of the East Coast's largest reptile collections. The compact zoo isn't as grand as its Bronx cousin, but the farm animals and re-creation of a South American rain forest make it an appealing family destination.

After a day spent exploring, you'll head back to Manhattan with a better sense of the New York that's not often seen by tourists. It's a working-class haven, with charms all its own. And Staten Islanders are just fine with that, thank you very much.

Alice Austen House

2 Hylan Blvd between Bay and Edgewater Sts (1-718-816-4506/www.aliceausten.org). Travel: From the Staten Island Ferry, take the S51 bus to Hylan Blvd. **Open** *Mar–Dec Thu–Sun noon–5pm (closed major holidays).* **Admission** *suggested donation $2.* **Credit** *Cash only.*
The family home of pioneering photographer Alice Austen is a lovely Victorian Gothic cottage with a scenic view of New York Bay. It contains more than 3,000 of her glass-negative photos, which document life in the Gilded Age. The house also hosts rotating photographic exhibits.

Conference House (Billopp House)

*7455 Hylan Blvd at Craig Ave (1-718-984-2086/
www.theconferencehouse.org). Travel: From the
Staten Island Ferry, take the S78 bus to Craig Ave.*
Open *Apr 1–Dec 15 Fri–Sun 1–4pm.* **Admission** *$3,
seniors and children $2.* **Credit** *Cash only.*
New York's oldest surviving manor house was
already nearly 100 years old when Britain's Lord
Howe parleyed with John Adams and Benjamin
Franklin here in 1776, in an attempt to put the
brakes on the American Revolution. Today, the fully
restored house still commands a striking view overlooking Raritan Bay and serves as a museum of
Staten Island life during Colonial times.

Garibaldi-Meucci Museum

*420 Tompkins Ave at Chestnut Ave (1-718-
442-1608/www.garibaldimeuccimuseum.org).
Travel: From the Staten Island Ferry, take the S78
bus to Chestnut Ave.* **Open** *Tue–Sun 1–5pm.*
Admission *suggested donation $3.* **Credit** *Cash only.*
In 2002, a Congressional resolution declared Italian-
American Antonio Meucci, not Alexander Graham
Bell, the true inventor of the telephone. The house
where Meucci lived for most of his life is a museum.

High Rock Park

*200 Nevada Ave at Rockland Ave (1-718-667-2165/
www.sigreenbelt.org). Travel: From the Staten Island
Ferry, take the S62 bus to Manor Rd, then the S54
bus to Nevada Ave.* **Open** *dawn–dusk daily. Visitors'
Center Mon–Fri 8:30am–5pm.* **Admission** *free.*
This 90-acre park is part of the Greenbelt, Staten
Island's whopping 2,800 acres of parkland. Hike the
mile-long Swamp Trail, climb Todt Hill, or explore
trails through forests, meadows and wetlands.

Historic Richmond Town

*441 Clarke Ave between Richmond Rd and St.
Patricks Pl (1-718-351-1611/www.historicrichmond
town.org). Travel: From the Staten Island Ferry, take
the S74 bus to St. Patricks Pl.* **Open** *Sept–May
Wed–Sun 1–5pm. Jun–Aug Wed–Sat 10am–5pm;
Sun 1–5pm.* **Admission** *$5, seniors $4, children
5–17 $3.50, children under 5 free.* **Credit** *Cash only.*

Richmond County Savings Bank Ballpark

*75 Richmond Terr at Wall St (1-718-720-9265/
tickets 1-718-720-9200/www.siyanks.com). Travel:
From the Staten Island Ferry, follow signs to
ballpark.* **Open** *Jun–Aug.* **Admission** *reserve $9,
box seats $11.* **Credit** *AmEx, Disc, MC, V.*
This stadium (known for its impressive waterside
views) is the home turf of the Staten Island Yankees,
a minor-league affiliate of the famed New York
Yankees organization.

Staten Island Zoo

*614 Broadway between Glenwood Pl and
West Raleigh Ave (1-718-442-3100/www.
statenislandzoo.org). Travel: From the Staten
Island Ferry, take the S48 bus to Broadway.*
Open *10am–4:45pm daily (closed major holidays).*
Admission *$5, seniors $4, children 3–14 $3,*
*children under 3 free. Free Wed 2–4:45pm
(suggested donation $2).* **Credit** *Cash only.*

Snug Harbor Cultural Center

The colonnaded main buildings of the cultural
center are stunning examples of Greek Revival
architecture. An arts complex since 1976,
Snug Harbor now includes the Newhouse
Center for Contemporary Art and the 400-seat
Music Hall, the city's second-oldest concert
venue (Carnegie Hall opened one year earlier,
in 1891). Also sharing the parklike grounds
are the Noble Maritime Collection, the
Botanical Garden and the Children's Museum.

Snug Harbor Cultural Center

*1000 Richmond Terr between Snug Harbor Rd and
Tysen St (1-718-448-2500/tickets 1-718-815-
7684/www.snug-harbor.org). Travel: From the
Staten Island Ferry, take the S40 bus to the north
gate (tell the bus driver).* **Open** *Galleries Tue–Sun
10am–5pm.* **Admission** *$3, seniors and children
under 12 $2.* **Credit** *AmEx, MC, V.*

Art Lab

*Building H, Visitors' Center (1-718-447-8667/
www.artlab.info).* **Open** *Mon 4–8pm; Tue–Thu
10am–8pm; Fri–Sun 10am–5pm.* **Admission** *free*
This nonprofit space offers classes in fine arts, crafts
and photography for children and adults. The Art
Lab Gallery exhibits the work of a different local
artist each month.

The Noble Maritime Collection

*Building D (1-718-447-6490/www.noblemaritime.
org).* **Open** *Thu–Sun 1–5pm.* **Admission** *$3,
seniors and students $2, children under 10 free.*
Credit *AmEx, MC, V.*
The collection of works by noted maritime artist
John A. Noble also includes his houseboat studio,
built with parts from larger boats.

Staten Island Botanical Garden

*Building L, Visitors' Center (1-718-273-8200/
www.sibg.org).* **Open** *dawn–dusk daily.*
Admission *Chinese Scholar's Garden $5; seniors,
students and children $4. Grounds and other gardens
free.* **Credit** *AmEx, MC, V.*
Stroll through more than 20 themed gardens and
plantings, from the White Garden (based on Vita
Sackville-West's creation at Sissinghurst Castle)
and the tranquil, pavilion-lined Chinese Scholar's
Garden to the delightful Secret Garden, complete
with a child-size castle, a maze and a secluded
walled garden.

Staten Island Children's Museum

Building M (1-718-273-2060). **Open** *Sept 2–Jul 4
Tue–Sun noon–5pm. Jul 5–Sept 1 Tue–Sun 11am–
5pm.* **Admission** *$5, children under 1 free.*
Credit *AmEx, Disc, MC, V.*
Interactive exhibits include a playground, a chil-
dren's theater and family workshops.

Museums

MoMA is back in Manhattan, but every borough has its treasures.

New York's trove of cultural institutions offers everything from old masters at the **Frick Collection** to mummies at the **Metropolitan Museum of Art** (which locals simply call the Met). Whether your passion is fine art or fashion, science or sex, the city has a museum to match it. The big news this year is that the **Museum of Modern Art** (a.k.a. MoMA) has returned to midtown Manhattan, after two years spent in Queens while a $425 million renovation nearly doubled the building's size to 630,000 square feet (*see p153* **Thoroughly Modern Manhattan**). The striking new glass-and-granite structure holds a must-see collection for contemporary art fans.

Manhattan is not the only borough to boast great museums. The **Brooklyn Museum**, the city's second-largest arts institution, got a face-lift of its own in 2004. Showy outdoor fountains and a broad plaza flank the entrance, and the Beaux Arts facade now sports a crown a bit like the Statue of Liberty's. The useum's varied programming allows it to present from exhibits of up-and-coming artists while maintaining one of the world's leading collections of Egyptian artifacts.

Contemporary-art lovers won't want to miss Long Island City, in Queens, home of MoMA affiliate **P.S. 1 Contemporary Art Center**; in the summertime, schedule your visit on a

Boning up on T. rex is a tall order at the **American Museum of Natural History**. *See p146.*

Manhattan is Modern Again

**The Museum of Modern Art
Now Open at 11 W. 53 St.**

MoMA
(212) 708-9400 MoMA.org

Installation view, featuring Barnett Newman. *Broken Obelisk.* 1963–69. Cor-Ten steel, in two parts.
The Museum of Modern Art. Given anonymously. Photo: © 2004 Timothy Hursley

Saturday, when the museum hosts an outdoor party in its courtyard (*see p293* **P.S. 1 Warm Up**). Deeper into the borough, the **Queens Museum of Art** displays a stunning attraction: a remarkably detailed, 9,000-plus-square-foot diorama of New York City in miniature, complete with a tiny plane taking off from La Guardia Airport every 15 minutes.

Easy-to-reach options extend beyond the city limits. Across the Hudson River, New Jersey's **Liberty Science Center** is an unexpected pleasure, with lively interactive exhibits for all ages and rooftop views of Manhattan and the **Statue of Liberty**. And one of the country's leading Minimalist art collections is housed at **Dia:Beacon**, in the Hudson River Valley, just an 80-minute train ride away.

Whereas Dia:Beacon occupies an old Nabisco factory, several of New York City's museums were once the palatial mansions of some of New York's wealthiest citizens. These former residences include the exceptional Frick Collection (essential for serious art lovers) and the **Cooper-Hewitt, National Design Museum**. By contrast, the **Lower East Side Tenement Museum** has lovingly re-created the far more modest domiciles (and detailed the habits) of its original tenants.

Many of New York's museums are in structures as impressive as their collections. At 2 million square feet, the Met is the city's largest. Slightly farther uptown, the elegant, iconic white spiral of Frank Lloyd Wright's **Solomon R. Guggenheim Museum** is a favorite of tourists and natives alike. And all the way downtown, the Smithsonian Institution's **National Museum of the American Indian** sits in a 1907 Beaux Arts masterpiece—the Alexander Hamilton Custom House, designed by Cass Gilbert.

In a city as eclectic as this, it is only natural that in addition to such grand offerings, there are a few unusual ones. You may not have gone on vacation to watch TV, but a visit to the **Museum of Television & Radio** could change your mind. One block south of MoMA, visitors can watch episodes of their favorite program, be it *Star Trek* or *The Muppet Show*.

Visiting several venues in a single day can be exhausting. Similarly, it's self-defeating to attempt to hit all the major collections during one visit to an institution as large as the Met or the **American Museum of Natural History**. So plan, pace yourself, and don't forget to eat: A host of excellent museum cafés and restaurants afford convenient breaks. Delicious spots for refueling include Sarabeth's at the **Whitney Museum of American Art**; the elegant Café Sabarsky at the **Neue Galerie**; the **Jewish Museum**'s Café Weissman; and a

more formal option, the Modern, at MoMA. It may be tempting to save museums for a rainy day, but remember that most sites offer cool, air-conditioned relief on sticky summer days and cozy warmth, come winter.

If the weather is too gorgeous to stay indoors, bear in mind that gardens are the hidden gems of several New York museums. The Brooklyn Museum abuts the **Brooklyn Botanic Garden** (*see p124*), where enticements include a Japanese garden complete with pavilion, wooden bridges and a Shinto shrine. **The Cloisters**, in northern Manhattan's Fort Tryon Park, was John D. Rockefeller's gift to New York. The reconstructed monastery houses the Met's stellar collection of medieval art. In summer, bring a picnic lunch and relax on lush grounds that provide spectacular views of the Hudson River and the rocky cliffs of the Palisades, in New Jersey.

Brace yourself for local admission prices; they can be steep (tickets to the newly renovated MoMA cost $20 per adult). This is because most of the city's museums are privately funded and receive little or no government support. Even so, a majority of them, including MoMA, the Whitney and the Guggenheim offer at least one evening a week when admission fees are either waived or switched to a voluntary donation. Most museums also offer discounts to students and senior citizens with valid IDs. And although the Met suggests a $12 donation for adults, you can pay what you wish any time you visit.

Nothing is more exciting than discovering the secrets of a new museum on your own, but many institutions offer tours that are both entertaining and educational. For example, the audio tour at the **Ellis Island Immigration Museum** and the (mandatory) guided tours at the Lower East Side Tenement Museum and the **Museum of Jewish Heritage** provide visitors with fascinating insight into NYC's immigrant roots.

Most New York museums are closed on major U.S. holidays (*see p372* **Holidays**). Nevertheless, some institutions are open on certain Monday holidays, such as Columbus Day and Presidents' Day. A few places, like Dia:Beacon and the Queens Museum of Art, change their hours seasonally; it's wise to call before setting out.

▶ See *Time Out New York* for reviews and listings of current exhibitions.
▶ For dining options near museums, see **Restaurants** (*pp167–201*).

Sightseeing

The **Brooklyn Museum** shows off its shimmering new face-lift. *See p147.*

Security has been tightened at most museums. Guards at all public institutions will ask you to open your purse or backpack for inspection; umbrellas and large bags must be checked (free of charge) at a coatroom.

Most museums are accessible to people with disabilities, and furnish free wheelchairs.

Major institutions

American Museum of Natural History/Rose Center for Earth and Space

Central Park West at 79th St (1-212-769-5100/ www.amnh.org). Subway: B, C to 81st St–Museum of Natural History. **Open** *10am–5:45pm daily.* **Admission** *suggested donation $12, seniors and students $9, children 2–12 $7.* **Credit** *AmEx, MC, V.* The thrills begin when you cross the threshold of the Theodore Roosevelt Rotunda, where you're confronted with a towering barosaurus that's rearing high on its hind legs to protect its young from an attacking allosaurus. This impressive welcome to the world's largest museum of its kind acts as a reminder to visit the dinosaur halls, on the fourth floor. During the museum's mid-1990s renovation, several specimens were remodeled to incorporate discoveries made during that time. The T. rex, for instance, was once

believed to have walked upright, Godzilla-style; it now stalks prey with its head lowered and tail raised parallel to the ground.

The rest of the museum is equally dramatic. The Hall of Biodiversity examines world ecosystems and environmental preservation, and a life-size model of a blue whale hangs from the cavernous ceiling of the Hall of Ocean Life. The impressive Hall of Meteorites was brushed up and reorganized in 2003. The space's focal point is Anighito, the largest iron meteor on display anywhere in the world, weighing in at 34 tons (more than 30,000 kilos).

The spectacular $210 million Rose Center for Earth and Space—dazzling to come upon at night—is a giant silvery globe where you can discover the universe via 3-D shows in the Hayden Planetarium and light shows in the Big Bang Theater. An IMAX theater screens larger-than-life nature programs, and you can always learn something new from the innovative temporary exhibitions, an easily accessible research library (with vast photo and print archives), several cool gift shops and a friendly, helpful staff. Every year since 1998, the museum has constructed a tropical-butterfly conservatory in the Hall of Oceanic Birds, where visitors can mingle with 500 live specimens from October to May. Starting May 14, T. rex gets some company in the form of the exhibition "Dinosaurs Alive: Ancient Fossils, New Ideas," which will remain on view through January 18, 2006.

Brooklyn Museum

200 Eastern Pkwy at Washington Ave, Prospect Heights, Brooklyn (1-718-638-5000/www.brooklyn museum.org). Subway: 2, 3 to Eastern Pkwy–Brooklyn Museum. **Open** *Wed–Fri 10am–5pm; Sat, Sun 11am–6pm. First Saturday of the month (except September) 11am–11pm.* **Admission** *$8, seniors and students $4, children under 12 free (must be accompanied by an adult). Free first Saturday of the month (except September) 5–11pm.* **Credit** *AmEx, MC, V.*

Brooklyn's premier institution is a tranquil alternative to Manhattan's big-name spaces; it's rarely crowded. Among the museum's many assets is a rich, 4,000-piece Egyptian collection, which includes a gilded-ebony statue of Amenhotep III and, on a ceiling, a large-scale rendering of an ancient map of the cosmos. You can even view a mummy preserved in its original coffin.

Masterworks by Cézanne, Courbet and Degas, part of an impressive European painting and sculpture collection, are displayed in the museum's skylighted Beaux Arts Court. On the fifth floor, American paintings and sculptures include native son Thomas Cole's *The Picnic* and Louis Rémy Mignot's *Niagara*, a stunning vista of the falls. Don't miss the renowned Pacific Island and African galleries (this was the first American museum to display African objects as art).

Planned 2005 exhibitions From late May through early September, a selection of Monet's paintings of London will be on display, followed by the first show ever to explore slide projection as a contemporary art form, and a retrospective of the contemporary landscape photographs of Edward Burtynsky (both Oct 2005 through Jan 2006).

The Cloisters

Fort Tryon Park, Fort Washington Ave at Margaret Corbin Plaza (1-212-923-3700/ www.metmuseum.org). Travel: A to 190th St, then take the M4 bus or follow Margaret Corbin Dr north, for about the length of five city blocks, to the museum. **Open** *Mar–Oct Tue–Sun 9:30am–5:15pm. Nov–Feb Tue–Sun 9:30am–4:45pm.* **Admission** *suggested donation (includes admission to the Metropolitan Museum of Art on the same day) $12, seniors and students $7, children under 12 free (must be accompanied by an adult).* **Credit** *AmEx, DC, Disc, MC, V.*

Set in a lovely park overlooking the Hudson River, the Cloisters houses the Met's medieval art and architecture collections. A path winds through the peaceful grounds to a castle that seems to have survived from the Middle Ages. (It was built a mere 60 years ago, using pieces of five medieval French cloisters.) Be sure to check out the famous Unicorn Tapestries, the 12th-century Fuentidueña Chapel and *The Annunciation Triptych* by Robert Campin.

Cooper-Hewitt, National Design Museum

2 E 91st St at Fifth Ave (1-212-849-8400/ www.cooperhewitt.org). Subway: 6 to 96th St. **Open** *Tue–Thu 10am–5pm; Fri 10am–9pm; Sat 10am–6pm; Sun noon–6pm.* **Admission** *$10, seniors and students $7, children under 12 free.* **Credit** *AmEx, Disc, MC, V.*

The Smithsonian's National Design Museum was once the home of industrialist Andrew Carnegie (there is still a lovely lawn behind the building). Now it's the only museum in the U.S. dedicated to domestic and industrial design, and it boasts a fascinating roster of temporary exhibitions. On view through January 15, 2006, is "Extreme Textiles: Designing for High Performance." Starting in March 2006, check out a roundup of 500 years' worth of eating utensils titled "Feeding Desire: The Tools of the Table, 1500–2005," on view through August 13. American Sign Language interpretation is available on request.

Dia:Beacon

3 Beekman St, Beacon, NY 12508 (1-845-440-0100/ www.diabeacon.org). Travel: Take Metro-North (Hudson line) to Beacon. Exit the train station at the rear of the platform on the river side (the west side). Turn left on Red Flynn Dr, follow it over the railroad tracks to Beekman St, and turn right. Dia:Beacon is the next driveway on the right. **Open** *Mid-Apr–mid-Oct Mon, Thu–Sun 11am–6pm. Mid-Oct–mid-Apr Mon, Fri–Sun 11am–4pm. (Days and times vary with the availability of natural light. Best to call first.)* **Admission** *$10, seniors and students $7.* **Credit** *AmEx, MC, V.*

Dia Art Foundation's latest outpost, housed in a former factory, is nothing short of amazing. Redesigned by artist Robert Irwin and architectural team OpenOffice, the building contains 240,000 square feet of exhibition space, lit exclusively by natural light. It's the perfect context for viewing the monumental Minimalist and Conceptual gems permanently on view, including Michael Heizer's plunging steel-lined shafts *North, East, South, West* and three of Richard Serra's massive steel *Torqued Ellipses.*

Package deals

If you're planning to take in multiple museums—and you're likely to add a Circle Line tour or a visit to the Empire State Building—consider buying a nine-day **CityPass** for $53 (children 6–17 $41). Similarly, the **New York Pass** covers admission to more than 40 of the city's top attractions and cultural institutions, and provides discounts on shopping, restaurants and other activities. The card costs $49 for the day (children 2–12 $39) and $135 for the week (children $95). Compare benefits and purchase cards at www.citypass.com and www.newyorkpass.com.

Sightseeing

Dia:Chelsea

*548 W 22nd St between Tenth and Eleventh Aves
(1-212-989-5566/www.diachelsea.org).*
Closed until late 2006.
The Chelsea branch of this New York stalwart, usually given to single-artist projects, is undergoing renovation and will reopen sometime in 2006.

The Frick Collection

1 E 70th St between Fifth and Madison Aves (1-212-288-0700/www.frick.org). Subway: 6 to 68th St–Hunter College. **Open** *Tue–Sat 10am–6pm; Sun 1–6pm.* **Admission** *$12, seniors $8, students $5, children 10–18 $5 (children under 16 must be accompanied by an adult; children under 10 not admitted).* **Credit** *AmEx, Disc, MC, V.*
The opulent residence that houses this private collection of great masters (from the 14th through the 19th centuries) was originally built for industrialist Henry Clay Frick. The firm of Carrère &

Top ten Must-sees

Amenhotep III
Brooklyn Museum. *See p147.*

Composition 8, Wassily Kandinsky
Solomon R. Guggenheim Museum. *See p148.*

Les Demoiselles d'Avignon, Pablo Picasso
The Museum of Modern Art. *See p151.*

North, East, South, West, Michael Heizer
Dia:Beacon. *See p147.*

Panorama of the City of New York
Queens Museum of Art. *See p154.*

The Dancer, Gustav Klimt
Neue Galerie. *See p152.*

Stettheimer Dollhouse
Museum of the City of New York. *See p156.*

St. Francis in the Desert, Giovanni Bellini
The Frick Collection. *See p148.*

Tyrannosaurus rex
American Museum of Natural History. *See p146.*

Young Woman with a Water Pitcher, Johannes Vermeer
Metropolitan Museum of Art. *See p148.*

Hastings (which also did the New York Public Library) designed the 1914 structure in an 18th-century European style, with a beautiful interior court and reflecting pool. The permanent collection boasts world-class paintings, sculpture and furniture by the likes of Rembrandt, Vermeer, Renoir and French cabinetmaker Jean-Henri Riesener. Upcoming exhibits include the only U.S. stop on a traveling survey of portraits by Flemish master Hans Memling (Oct 6–Dec 31).

Solomon R. Guggenheim Museum

1071 Fifth Ave at 89th St (1-212-423-3500/www.guggenheim.org). Subway: 4, 5, 6 to 86th St. **Open** *Mon–Wed, Sat, Sun 10am–5:45pm; Fri 10am–8pm.* **Admission** *$15, seniors and students with a valid ID $10, children under 12 free (must be accompanied by an adult). Half-price Fri 5–8pm.* **Credit** *AmEx, MC, V.*
Even if your hectic museumhopping schedule doesn't allow time to view the collections, you must get a glimpse (if only from the outside) of this dramatic spiral building, designed by Frank Lloyd Wright. In addition to works by Manet, Kandinsky, Picasso, Chagall and Louise Bourgeois, the museum owns Peggy Guggenheim's trove of Cubist, Surrealist and Abstract Expressionist works, along with the Panza di Biumo Collection of American Minimalist and Conceptual art from the 1960s and '70s. In 1992, the addition of a ten-story tower provided space for a sculpture gallery (with views of Central Park), an auditorium and a café.
Planned 2005 exhibitions A site-specific installation by French Conceptualist Daniel Buren will grace the main rotunda (through May 15). The museum will also do a little navel-gazing, with the first-ever exhibition dedicated to the career of artist, curator and educator Hilla Rebay (1890–1967), whose Museum of Non-Objective Painting was the forerunner of the Guggenheim (May 19–Aug 7).

Metropolitan Museum of Art

1000 Fifth Ave at 82nd St (1-212-535-7710/www.metmuseum.org). Subway: 4, 5, 6 to 86th St. **Open** *Tue–Thu, Sun 9:30am–5:30pm; Fri, Sat 9:30am–9pm. No strollers on Sundays.* **Admission** *suggested donation (includes admission to the Cloisters on the same day) $12, seniors and students $7, children under 12 free.* **Credit** *AmEx, DC, Disc, MC, V.*
It could take days, even weeks, to cover the Met's 2 million square feet of gallery space, so it's best to be selective. Besides the enthralling temporary exhibitions, there are excellent collections of African, Oceanic and Islamic art, along with more than 3,000 European paintings from the Middle Ages up through the fin de siècle period, including major works by Titian, Brueghel, Rembrandt, Vermeer, Goya and Degas. Egyptology fans should head straight for the glass-walled atrium housing the Temple of Dendur. The Greek and Roman halls have received a graceful makeover, and the incomparable medieval armor collection—

European sculpture at the **Metropolitan Museum of Art**. *See p148.*

Can't keep our eyes from the circling skies of Van Gogh's *Starry Night* at **MoMA**. *See p151.*

a huge favorite with adults and children—was recently enriched by gifts of European, North American, Japanese and Islamic armaments.

The Met has also made significant additions to its modern-art galleries, including major works by American artist Eric Fischl and Chilean Surrealist Roberto Matta. Contemporary sculptures are displayed each year in the Iris and B. Gerald Cantor Roof Garden (May through late fall, weather permitting). If you're in town for a long holiday weekend, don't despair. The Met opens its doors on Monday holidays, including Martin Luther King Day, Presidents' Day, Memorial Day and the Monday between Christmas and New Year's Day.

A large, round desk in the Great Hall (staffed by volunteers who speak multiple languages) is the hub of the museum's excellent visitors' resources. (Foreign-language tours are also available; 1-212-570-3711.) Once you're in the thick of the type of art that interests you most—from Greek kouroi to colorful Kandinskys—we recommend seeking out a spot of relative privacy and calm. The Met is dotted with plenty of them; you just have to know where to look. The Engelhard Court, which borders Central Park, has benches, a trickling fountain, trees, ivy and stunning examples of Tiffany stained glass, to further encourage restful contemplation. (If you'd like to grab a drink or a snack in less-than-hectic surroundings, try the recently opened American Wing Café.) The

Astor Court, on the second floor, is a garden modeled on a Ming-dynasty scholar's courtyard. Wooden paths border a naturally lit, gravel-paved atrium . The nearby Asian galleries, full of superb bronzes, ceramics and rare wooden Buddhist images, seldom get heavy foot traffic. At the western end of the museum, rest on a bench in the Robert Lehman Wing, then commune with Botticelli's *Annunciation*.

Planned 2005 exhibitions "Diane Arbus Revelations," a major retrospective of the photographer, includes never-before-seen prints and contact sheets (through May 30). The Marquesas Islands, northeast of Tahiti—immortalized in Gauguin's paintings—was home to accomplished traditions of sculpture and decorative arts, as seen in "Adorning the World: Art of the Marquesas Islands" (May 10–Jan 16). In the spring and summer, a major exhibition of the Surrealist painter Max Ernst will be on loan to the Met (Apr 7–Jul 10).

The Morgan Library
29 E 36th St between Madison and Park Aves (1-212-685-0008/www.morganlibrary.org).
Closed until early 2006.
Undergoing a dramatic expansion, the Morgan has temporarily closed its doors. Plans have been made to display some of the archive's rare manuscripts and books in alternative locations. Call or visit the website for details.

The Museum of Modern Art

11 W 53rd St between Fifth and Sixth Aves (1-212-708-9400/www.moma.org). Subway: E, V to Fifth Ave–53rd St. **Open** *Mon, Wed, Thu, Sat, Sun 10:30am–5:30pm; Fri 10:30am–8pm.* **Admission** *(includes admittance to MoMA galleries and film programs) $20; seniors 65 and over $16 with current ID; full-time students $12 with current ID; children 16 and under free (must be accompanied by an adult). Free Fri 4–8pm.* **Credit** *AmEx, MC, V.*

The Museum of Modern Art contains the world's finest and most comprehensive holdings of 20th-century art, including an unsurpassed photography collection. In November 2004, the museum opened its revamped West 53rd Street home (*see p153* **Thoroughly Modern Manhattan**). Highlights of the permanent collection include the best of Matisse, Picasso, Van Gogh, Giacometti, Lawrence, Pollock, Rothko and Warhol, among many others. The outstanding Film and Media department archives more than 25,000 films.

Planned 2005 exhibitions The summer will bring a major survey of more than 500 works, most in luminous tones of black and white, by contemporary American photographer Lee Friedlander (Jun 10–Aug 29). MoMA returns to its roots in "Pioneering Modern Painting: Cézanne and Pissarro 1865–1885," which considers the work of two masters in light of their 20-year friendship (Jun 24–Sept 12). A selection of the paintings of Elizabeth Murray, whose shaped canvases combine elements of Cubism and Pop Art, is planned for the fall.

New Museum of Contemporary Art

Interim location *556 W 22nd St at Eleventh Ave (1-212-219-1222/www.newmuseum.org). Subway: C, E to 23rd St.* **Open** *Tue, Wed, Fri, Sat noon–6pm; Thu noon–8pm.* **Admission** *$6, seniors and students $3, children under 18 free. Half-price Thu 6–8pm.* **Credit** *AmEx, Disc, MC, V.*

While its new digs on the Bowery are under construction (the opening is slated for 2006), the New Museum will occupy 7,000 square feet of ground-floor space in the Chelsea Art Museum. Its retrospectives of midcareer artists—South Africa's William Kentridge, Los Angeles' Paul McCarthy, New York's Carroll Dunham—attract serious crowds, though not every group show is strong.

P.S. 1 Contemporary Art Center

22-25 Jackson Ave at 46th Ave, Long Island City, Queens (1-718-784-2084/www.ps1.org). Subway: E, V to 23rd St–Ely Ave; G to 21st St–Jackson Ave; 7 to 45th Rd–Court House Sq. **Open** *Mon, Thu–Sun noon–6pm.* **Admission** *suggested donation $5, seniors and students $2.* **Credit** *AmEx, MC, V.*

Cutting-edge shows and an international studio program make each visit to this freewheeling contemporary-art space a treasure hunt, with artwork turning up in every corner, from the stairwells to the basement. In a distinctive Romanesque-revival building that still bears some resemblance to the public school it once was,

P.S. 1 mounts shows that appeal to adults and children. P.S. 1 became an affiliate of MoMA in 1999, but it has a wholly independent schedule of temporary exhibitions, along with a decidedly global outlook.

The Studio Museum in Harlem

144 W 125th St between Malcolm X Blvd (Lenox Ave) and Adam Clayton Powell Jr. Blvd (Seventh Ave) (1-212-864-4500/www.studiomuseum.org). Subway: 2, 3 to 125th St. **Open** *Wed–Fri, Sun noon–6pm; Sat 10am–6pm. Guided tours by appointment.* **Admission** *suggested donation $7, seniors and students $3, children under 12 free.* **Credit** *Cash only.*

When the Studio Museum opened in 1968, it was the first black fine-arts museum in the country, and it remains the place to go for historical insight into African-American art and that of the African diaspora. Under the leadership of director Lowery Stokes Sims (formerly of the Met) and chief curator Thelma Golden (formerly of the Whitney), this favorite has evolved into the city's most exciting showcase for contemporary African-American artists.

Whitney Museum of American Art

945 Madison Ave at 75th St (1-800-944-8639/1-212-570-3676/www.whitney.org). Subway: 6 to 77th St. **Open** *Wed, Thu, Sat, Sun 11am–6pm; Fri 1–9pm.* **Admission** *$12, seniors and students $9.50, children under 12 free. Voluntary donation Fri 6–9pm.* **Credit** *AmEx, MC, V.*

Like the Guggenheim, the Whitney is set apart by its unique architecture: It's a Marcel Breuer–designed gray granite cube with an all-seeing upper-story "eye" window. When Gertrude Vanderbilt Whitney, a sculptor and art patron, opened the museum in 1931, she dedicated it to living American artists. Today, the Whitney holds about 15,000 pieces by nearly 2,000 artists, including Alexander Calder, Willem de Kooning, Edward Hopper (the museum holds his entire estate), Jasper Johns, Louise Nevelson, Georgia O'Keeffe and Claes Oldenburg. Still, the museum's reputation rests mainly on its temporary shows, particularly the exhibition everyone loves to hate, the Whitney Biennial. Held in even-numbered years, the Biennial remains the most prestigious (and controversial) assessment of contemporary art in America. The Whitney's small midtown Altria branch, located in a corporate atrium space across the street from Grand Central Terminal, mounts solo commissioned projects. At the main building, there are free guided tours daily and live performances on select Friday nights. Sarabeth's, the museum's café, is open daily till 4:30pm, offering sandwiches and such.

Planned 2005 exhibitions An examination of the enigmatic abstract drawings of Cy Twombly and a midcareer survey of the mind-boggling installations of Tim Hawkinson are scheduled. Packing all four floors of the museum with edgy works, the 2006 Whitney Biennial (early spring) may well be *the* show of the year; it's definitely the one you'll want to say you've seen.

Other location *Whitney Museum of American Art at Altria, 120 Park Ave at 42nd St (1-917-663-2453).*

Art & design

American Folk Art Museum

45 W 53rd St between Fifth and Sixth Aves (1-212-265-1040/www.folkartmuseum.org). Subway: E, V to Fifth Ave–53rd St. **Open** *Tue–Thu, Sat, Sun 10:30am–5:30pm; Fri 10:30am–7:30pm.* **Admission** *$9, seniors and students $7, children under 12 free. Free Fri 5:30–7:30pm.* **Credit** *AmEx, Disc, MC, V.*

Art is everywhere in the American Folk Art Museum (formerly the Museum of American Folk Art). Designed by architects Billie Tsien and Tod Williams, the architecturally stunning eight-floor building is four times larger than the original Lincoln Center location (now a branch of the museum) and includes a café. The range of decorative, practical and ceremonial folk art encompasses pottery, trade signs, delicately stitched log-cabin quilts and windup toys. **Other location** *2 Lincoln Sq, Columbus Ave between 65th and 66th Sts (1-212-595-9533).*

Dahesh Museum of Art

580 Madison Ave between 56th and 57th Sts (1-212-759-0606/www.daheshmuseum.org). Subway: E, V to Fifth Ave–53rd St; F to 57th St. **Open** *Tue–Sun 11am–6pm. First Thursday of the month 11am–9pm.* **Admission** *$9, seniors and students $4, children under 12 free. Free first Thursday of the month 6–9pm.* **Credit** *AmEx, MC, V.*

This major repository of 19th- and 20th-century academic art has recently expanded its exhibition space tenfold, with a new three-story Madison Avenue site and a new entrance fee (the museum used to be free). Take a break here from the hubbub of nearby Niketown and other megastores to revel in the romantic work on display in the permanent collection, which includes exotic landscapes and lustrous marble nymphs.

The Museum at FIT

Seventh Ave at 27th St (1-212-217-5800/www.fitnyc.edu). Subway: 1, 9 to 28th St. **Open** *Tue–Fri noon–8pm; Sat 10am–5pm.* **Admission** *free.*

The Fashion Institute of Technology houses one of the world's most important collections of clothing and textiles, curated by the influential fashion historian Valerie Steele. Incorporating everything from extravagant costumes to sturdy denim work clothes, the exhibitions touch on the role fashion has played in society since the beginning of the 20th century.

The Museum of Arts & Design

40 W 53rd St between Fifth and Sixth Aves (1-212-956-3535/www.americancraftmuseum.org). Subway: E, V to Fifth Ave–53rd St. **Open** *Mon–Wed, Fri–Sun 10am–6pm; Thu 10am–8pm.* **Admission** *$9, seniors and students $6, children under 12 free. Voluntary donation Thu 6–8pm.* **Credit** *AmEx, Disc, MC, V.*

Formerly the American Crafts Museum, this is the country's leading museum for contemporary crafts in clay, cloth, glass, metal and wood. It changed its name to emphasize the correspondences among art, design and craft. The museum plans to move to a new home in the former Huntington Hartford building at Columbus Circle in 2007, but for now, visitors can peruse the jewelry, ceramics and other *objets* displayed on four floors.

National Academy Museum

1083 Fifth Ave at 89th St (1-212-369-4880/www.nationalacademy.org). Subway: 4, 5, 6 to 86th St. **Open** *Wed, Thu noon–5pm; Fri–Sun 11am–6pm.* **Admission** *$10, seniors and students $5, children under 12 free.* **Credit** *Cash only.*

Housed in an elegant Fifth Avenue townhouse, the Academy's museum has more than 5,000 works of 19th- and 20th-century American art. The permanent collection includes pieces by Frank Gehry, Robert Rauschenberg, Jasper Johns, Louise Bourgeois, and John Singer Sargent.

Neue Galerie

1048 Fifth Ave at 86th St (1-212-628-6200/www.neuegalerie.org). Subway: 4, 5, 6 to 86th St. **Open** *Mon, Sat, Sun 11am–6pm; Fri 11am–9pm.* **Admission** *$10, seniors and students $7 (children 12–16 must be accompanied by an adult; children under 12 not admitted).* **Credit** *AmEx, MC, V.*

This elegant museum is devoted entirely to late-19th- and early-20th-century German and Austrian fine and decorative arts. The brainchild of the late art dealer Serge Sabarsky and cosmetics mogul Ronald S. Lauder, it has the largest concentration of works by Gustav Klimt and Egon Schiele outside Vienna. You'll

The Museum at FIT.

Thoroughly Modern Manhattan

After a two-and-a-half-year sojourn, during which one of the world's great modern-art museums camped out in a refurbished stapler factory in Queens, the **Museum of Modern Art** (*see p151*) made a triumphant return to Manhattan last November—just in time for its 75th anniversary. With its soaring, six-story atrium, huge lobby and spacious galleries, architect Yoshio Taniguchi's $425 million redesign has doubled the size of the museum, which now covers a grandiose 630,000 square feet.

Taniguchi, who won the commission in 1997 in a surprise triumph over high-profile architects like Rem Koolhaus and Bernard Tschumi, has removed visual clutter (escalators in the lobby, columns in the galleries) to create serene settings for the museum's vast and varied collections. The new space certainly has showstopping elements—that dramatic atrium, for example, rising 110 feet above the ground floor—but the emphasis remains squarely on the art.

For starters, there's a lot more room in which to display it. The gallery space now totals 125,000 square feet (40,000 more than before). The second floor, which is dedicated to contemporary art, now covers 16,000 square feet, with a permanent gallery for new-media and video installations. The third-floor photography galleries have also been expanded to accommodate the dramatically scaled work of such artists as Andreas Gursky. Subtle tweaks in the galleries include smaller light fixtures, hidden air-conditioning ducts, and walls that seem almost to float, thanks to neat half-inch recesses where the walls meet the ceilings. Two auditoriums on the lower level now have upgraded digital-sound and projection systems.

Thankfully, the museum is far from being a sealed-off temple to high culture. The glass-fronted north facade and the windows installed throughout the exhibition spaces frame views of the surrounding neighborhoods, reminding visitors that MoMA, along with much of the art it houses, owes a debt to the dynamism of New York. MoMA director Glenn D. Lowry says, "We wanted the museum to seem like a laboratory, open to the city—to be an urban center without distracting from the art."

In that vein, a new high-end restaurant, the Modern, opened in January, adjoining the

museum; it's being run by Midas-touch restaurateur Danny Meyer, with chef Gabriel Kreuther (of the well-regarded Atelier) in the kitchen. Cafe 2 and Terrace 5, more casual options, serve lunch and snacks.

Not everything is new at MoMA, however. Its original 1939 facade along West 53rd Street has been restored and its Bauhaus staircase preserved. The sculpture garden, backed by a matte-black-granite–and–glass wall that has the sleek, muted power of a Minimalist sculpture, has been returned to Philip Johnson's original, larger plan from 1953. Even the sky-high Cesar Pelli Museum Tower, built in 1984, seems less obtrusive, its base now exposed to the garden and dressed with the thematic black granite and glass. As Lowry explains, "Yoshio wanted to create a building that was integrated into the preexisting architecture, to weave them together so that you would not be able to tell whether you were in a new or old part of the building." It's a guessing game, all right—one that, by turns, makes the art lover's experience fresh and familiar, and that much more exciting.

Rock fans won't want to miss the **Noguchi Museum** in Long Island City, Queens.

also find a bookstore, a chic (and expensive) design shop and Café Sabarsky (*see p196*), serving updated Austrian cuisine and ravishing Viennese pastries.

The Noguchi Museum

9-01 33rd Rd between Vernon Blvd and 10th St, Long Island City, Queens (1-718-204-7088/www.noguchi.org). Travel: N, W to Broadway, then take the Q104 bus to 11th St; or 7 to Vernon Blvd–Jackson Ave, then take the Q103 bus to 10th St. **Open** *Wed–Fri 10am–5pm; Sat, Sun 11am–6pm.* **Admission** *$5, seniors and students $2.50. No strollers.* **Credit** *Cash only.*

In addition to his famous lamps, artist Isamu Noguchi (1904–1988) designed stage sets for Martha Graham and George Balanchine, as well as large-scale sculptures of supreme simplicity and beauty. The museum is located in a 1920s-era factory in Queens; galleries surround a serene sculpture garden that was designed by Noguchi himself. The building, recently renovated (to the tune of $13.5 million), now stays open year-round. Look for new second-floor galleries devoted to Noguchi's interior design, a new café and a shop. Shuttle service from Manhattan is available on weekends (call the museum for more information).

Queens Museum of Art

New York City Building, park entrance on 49th Ave at 111th St, Flushing Meadows–Corona Park, Queens (1-718-592-9700/www.queensmuseum.org). Subway: 7 to 111th St. Walk south on 111th St, then turn left onto 49th Ave. Continue into the park and over the Grand Central Parkway bridge. Museum is on the right, beside the Unisphere. **Open** *Jul–Sept Wed–Sun 1–8pm. Sept–Jun Wed–Fri 10am–5pm; Sat, Sun noon–5pm.* **Admission** *$5, seniors and students $2.50, children under 5 free.* **Credit** *Cash only.*

Located on the grounds of the 1939 and 1964 World's Fairs, the QMA holds one of the area's most amazing sights: a 9,335-square-foot scale model of New York City that is accurate down to the square inch. The model, first a popular exhibit at the 1964 World's Fair, was last updated and carefully cleaned by its original builders in 1994, so some recent changes are not reflected. The World Trade Center, however, has been replaced by a miniature version of *Tribute in Light*, the city's first memorial of September 11, 2001.

Planned 2005 exhibitions A pair of complementary shows look at art and India; one is devoted to contemporary art from the subcontinent, the other to work by Indian-born artists working in the U.S. (through Jun 12). During the summer, the museum becomes a showcase for artists' gardens, with five site-specific outdoor projects installed throughout Flushing Meadows (Jun 26–Oct 9).

Auction houses

You don't have to be a millionaire to peruse most of the high-end items that go on the block at NYC's esteemed auction houses. Indeed, exhibitions of the art and artifacts slated for sale precede auctions, and while these showings are designed to drum up interest from potential buyers, the general public is often welcome. Shows at these sites can be a great alternative to packed museums, especially when juicy celebrity estates are on the block. So stop by: You might see something you'd like to take home.

Christie's
20 Rockefeller Plaza, 49th St between Fifth and Sixth Aves (1-212-636-2000/www.christies.com). Subway: B, D, F, V to 47–50th Sts–Rockefeller Ctr. **Open** *Mon–Fri 9:30am–5:30pm.* **Admission** *free.*
Dating from 1766, Christie's joins Sotheby's (*see below*) as one of New York's premier auction houses. Architecturally, the building alone is worth a visit, particularly for its cavernous three-floor lobby featuring a specially commissioned mural by artist Sol LeWitt. Most auctions are open to the public, with viewing hours scheduled in the days leading up to the sale. Hours vary with each exhibition, so call or visit the website for details.

Phillips, de Pury & Co.
450 W 15th St at Tenth Ave, third floor (1-212-940-1200/www.phillipsdepury.com). Subway: A, C, E to 14th St; L to Eighth Ave. **Open** *Mon–Sat 10am–5pm; Sun 1–5pm.* **Admission** *free.*
Held in the spring and fall, Phillips's auctions are organized into four categories: contemporary art, photography, jewelry, and 20th- and 21st-century design. Adhering to the quality-over-quantity ethos, this auction house specializes in small, meticulously curated lots. The art is usually on public view for one to two weeks leading up to the sale. Call ahead for hours and sale info.

Sotheby's
1334 York Ave at 72nd St (1-212-606-7000/www. sothebys.com). Subway: 6 to 68th St–Hunter College. **Open** *Mon–Sat 10am–5pm; Sun 1–5pm (weekend hours change seasonally).* **Admission** *free.*
Sotheby's, with offices from London to Singapore, is the world's most famous auction house. The New York branch regularly holds public sales of antique furniture and jewelry in one lot, and pop-culture memorabilia in another. Spring and fall see the big sales of modern and contemporary art. Public exhibitions are usually short—four or five days—and held just prior to the auction. Schedules and hours vary with each show, so call or visit Sotheby's website for details.

Swann Auction Galleries
104 E 25th St between Park and Lexington Aves, sixth floor (1-212-254-4710/www.swanngalleries.com). Subway: 6 to 23rd St. **Open** *Mon–Thu 10am–6pm; Fri 10am–5pm; Sat 10am–4pm (closed Saturdays in the summer).* **Admission** *free.*
Although Swann originally specialized in books, it has grown to include auctions of a variety of art forms. Things slow down in the summer, but during the rest of the year, Swann holds sales almost every week. Works are usually exhibited beginning the Saturday before a Thursday sale. Hours are subject to change, so call in advance to confirm.

Arts & culture

Historical

American Museum of Natural History
See p146 for listing.

Fraunces Tavern Museum
54 Pearl St at Broad St (1-212-425-1778/www. frauncestavernmuseum.org). Subway: J, M, Z to Broad St; 4, 5 to Bowling Green. **Open** *Tue, Wed, Fri 10am–5pm; Thu 10am–7pm; Sat 11am–5pm.* **Admission** *$3, seniors and children 6–18 $2, children under 6 free.* **Credit** *Cash only.*
This 18th-century tavern was George Washington's watering hole and the site of his famous farewell to the troops at the Revolution's close. During the mid- to late 1780s, the building housed the fledgling nation's departments of war, foreign affairs and treasury. In 1904, Fraunces became a repository for artifacts collected by the Sons of the Revolution in the State of New York. Ongoing exhibits include "George Washington: Down the Stream of Life," which examines America's first President. The tavern and restaurant (1-212-968-1776) serve hearty fare at lunch and dinner, Monday through Saturday.

Lower East Side Tenement Museum
90 Orchard St at Broome St (1-212-431-0233/ www.tenement.org). Subway: F to Delancey St; J, M, Z to Delancey–Essex Sts. **Open** *Visitors' center Mon–Fri 11am–5:30pm; Sat, Sun 10:45am–5:30pm.* **Admission** *$12, seniors and students $10.* **Credit** *AmEx, MC, V.*
Housed in an 1863 tenement building along with a gallery, shop and video room, this fascinating museum is accessible only by guided tour. The tours, which regularly sell out (definitely book ahead), explain the daily life of typical tenement-dwelling immigrant families. (See the website for 360-degree views of the museum's interior.) From April to December, the museum also leads walking tours of the Lower East Side.

Merchant's House Museum
29 E 4th St between Lafayette St and Bowery (1-212-777-1089/www.merchantshouse.com). Subway: B, D, F, V to Broadway–Lafayette St; 6 to Bleecker St. **Open** *Mon, Sat, Sun noon–5pm; Thu, Fri 1–5pm.* **Admission** *$6, seniors and students $4.* **Credit** *Cash only.*
New York City's only preserved 19th-century family home is an elegant, late Federal–Greek Revival house stocked with the same furnishings and decorations that filled its rooms when it was inhabited from 1835 to 1933 by hardware tycoon Seabury Treadwell and his descendants.

Mount Vernon Hotel Museum and Garden
421 E 61st St between First and York Aves (1-212-838-6878/www.mvhm.org). Subway: N, R, W to Lexington Ave–59th St; 4, 5, 6 to 59th St.

Open *Sept–Jul Tue–Sun 11am–4pm; last tour departs at approximately 3:15pm.*
Admission *$5, seniors and students $4, children under 12 free.* **Credit** *AmEx, Disc, MC, V.*
This historic landmark was built in 1799 as a carriage house for Abigail Adams Smith (daughter of John Adams, second President of the United States) and her husband, Colonel William Stevens Smith. It functioned as a hotel from 1826 to 1833, serving as a bucolic getaway from the overcrowding of lower Manhattan, and is now a quaint museum filled with period articles and furniture.

Museum of American Financial History

28 Broadway between Beaver St and Exchange Pl (1-212-908-4110/www.financialhistory.org). Subway: 1, 9 to Rector St. **Open** *Tue–Sat 10am–4pm.* **Admission** *$2.* **Credit** *AmEx, MC, V.*
The permanent collection, which traces the development of Wall Street and America's financial markets, includes ticker tape from the morning of the big crash of October 29, 1929, an 1867 stock ticker and the earliest known photograph of Wall Street.

Museum of the City of New York

1220 Fifth Ave between 103rd and 104th Sts (1-212-534-1672/www.mcny.org). Subway: 6 to 103rd St. **Open** *Tue–Sun 10am–5pm.* **Admission** *suggested donation $7; seniors, students and children $5; families $15.* **Credit** *AmEx, MC, V.*
Located at the northern end of Museum Mile, this institution contains a wealth of city history and includes paintings, sculptures, photographs, military and naval uniforms, theater memorabilia, manuscripts, ship models and rare books. The extensive toy collection, full of New Yorkers' playthings dating from the colonial era to the present, is especially well loved. Toy trains, lead soldiers and battered teddy bears share shelf space with exquisite bisque dolls (decked out in extravagant Paris fashions) and lavishly appointed dollhouses. Don't miss the amazing Stettheimer Dollhouse, created during the 1920s by Carrie Stettheimer, whose artist friends re-created their masterpieces in miniature to hang on the dollhouse's walls. Look closely and you'll even spy a tiny version of Marcel Duchamp's famous *Nude Descending a Staircase.*

Higher ground

Good things come in small packages, but the last place you'd expect to learn that lesson is at the **Skyscraper Museum**. Still, after six years of mounting exhibitions in various lower-Manhattan spaces, the once peripatetic institution has settled into a small but exhilarating new home on the ground floor of the 38-story Ritz-Carlton tower in Battery Park City. In just 5,000 square feet—very modest by institutional standards—the space manages to evoke the scale and aspirations of the Skyscraper Museum's subject matter.

To achieve this, architects Skidmore, Owings & Merrill paneled the ceilings and floors in reflective stainless steel. "The ceilings are actually only about 12 feet at their highest," says Carol Willis, the museum's founder and director, "but the material creates a much greater sense of space." Strolling through the place is both thrilling and unnerving. "An electrician described it best," Willis says. "It reminded him of being up in a building under construction. The architects loved hearing that, because it was exactly what they were after." A ramp running along the glassed-in front of the building rises from the main entrance to a pair of second-floor galleries, which are dominated by tall

rolling vitrines that seem to go on forever, thanks to the mirrorlike ceilings.

Besides creating the illusion of walking the steel high above Manhattan, the new space allows the museum to operate like any other. "Our function is to collect, preserve and interpret history," Willis says. But collecting was difficult during the institution's itinerant years. Now acquisitions of photographs, architectural renderings, blueprints and assorted ephemera occur more frequently. A group of artifacts relating to the Woolworth Building, for example, includes not only period photos and drawings but also an item straight out of the old five-and-dime: a cardboard packet of sewing needles adorned with an image of Cass Gilbert's architectural masterpiece.

Education is the word that Willis, an architectural historian, uses most often to describe the museum's main function. Two photomurals, for instance, depict the tip of Manhattan. The first, from 1955, shows a scene basically unchanged from the 1920s; the next picture, taken in 1975, looks completely different, thanks in large part to the addition of the World Trade Center. The murals are textbook illustrations of the degree to which construction in New York depends on the boom-and-bust cycles of real

Museum of Sex

233 Fifth Ave at 27th St (1-212-689-6337/
www.museumofsex.com). Subway: N, R, W, 6 to
28th St. **Open** *Sun–Fri 11am–6:30pm; Sat*
11am–8pm. **Admission** *$14.50, students $13.50.*
Children under 18 not admitted.
Despite the subject matter, don't expect too much tit-
illation at this museum, which opened in 2002 to
mixed reviews. Instead, you'll find presentations of
historical documents and items—many of which were
too risqué to be made public in their own time—that
explore prostitution, burlesque, birth control, obscenity and fetishism. In 2002, the museum acquired an
extensive collection of pornography from a retired
Library of Congress curator (apparently, he applied
his professional skills to recreational pursuits as well).
Thus, the Ralph Whittington Collection features thousands of items, including 8mm films, videos, blow-up
dolls and other erotic paraphernalia.

National Museum of the American Indian

George Gustav Heye Center, Alexander Hamilton
Custom House, 1 Bowling Green between State and
Whitehall Sts (1-212-514-3700/1-212-514-3888/
www.americanindian.si.edu). Subway: R, W to
Whitehall St; 1, 9 to South Ferry; 4, 5 to Bowling
Green. **Open** *Sun–Wed, Fri 10am–5pm; Thu*
10am–8pm. **Admission** *free.*
This branch of the Smithsonian Institution displays
its collection around the grand rotunda of the 1907
Custom House, at the very bottom of Broadway
(which began as an Indian trail). The life and culture
of Native Americans is presented in rotating exhibitions—from intricately woven fiber Pomo baskets
to beaded buckskin shirts and moccasins—along
with contemporary artwork. The exhibition "First
American Art: The Charles and Valerie Diker
Collection of American Indian Art," open through
April 2006, features fine crafts and decorative objects.

The New-York Historical Society

170 Central Park West between 76th and 77th Sts
(1-212-873-3400/www.nyhistory.org). Subway: B, C
to 81st St–Museum of Natural History. **Open** *Tue–*
Sun 10am–6pm. **Admission** *$10, seniors and*
students $5, children under 12 free when accompanied
by an adult. **Credit** *Cash only.*
New York's oldest museum, founded in 1804, was
one of America's first cultural and educational

estate, Willis explains, adding that the
Skyscraper Museum itself was the beneficiary
of a market lull that prodded the building's
owners, Millennium Partners, to donate
vacant space to the museum.
    The whole enterprise is clearly a personal
passion for Willis, and she evinces the
single-minded intensity of someone who had
a dream and saw it through. In her office, she
pulls out an album of 500 photographs of
the Empire State Building under construction,
compiled by the original contractors. The
pictures aren't terribly beautiful, but they
illustrate the techniques that enabled the
edifice to rise skyward at a breathtaking
pace—in little more than a year, from start to
finish. Willis's eyes light up as she peruses
the images. "Everyone knows the Lewis
Hines photos," she says, referring to the
iconic images of ironworkers laboring on the
then tallest building in the world, "but these
show you *how it got done.*" At the Skyscraper
Museum, that story is just as important as
the Empire State Building itself.

The Skyscraper Museum

39 Battery Pl between Little West St and 1st
Pl (1-212-968-1961/www.skyscraper.org).
Subway: 4, 5 to Bowling Green. **Open** *Wed–*
Sun noon–6pm. **Admission** *$5, seniors and*
students $2.50.

institutions. Highlights in the vast Henry Luce III Center for the Study of American Culture include George Washington's Valley Forge camp cot, a complete series of the extant watercolors from Audubon's *The Birds of America* and the world's largest collection of Tiffany lamps. In 2004, the Society celebrated its bicentennial with the fascinating "Alexander Hamilton: The Man Who Made Modern America." The show explored the life of one of the nation's most underrated founders. In 2005, a Smithsonian traveling show, "First Ladies: Political Role and Public Image" (through Jun 5), examines the evolution of the presidential wife's role over the last two centuries.

South Street Seaport Museum

Visitors' center, 12 Fulton St at South St (1-212-748-8600/www.southstseaport.org). Subway: A, C to Broadway–Nassau St; J, M, Z, 2, 3, 4, 5 to Fulton St. **Open** *Apr–Oct 10am–5pm daily. Nov–Mar Fri–Sun 10am–5pm.* **Admission** *$8, students $6, children 5–12 $4, children under 5 free.* **Credit** *AmEx, MC, V.*
Occupying 11 blocks along the East River, the museum is an amalgam of galleries, historic ships, 19th-century buildings and a visitors' center. Wander around the rebuilt streets and pop in to see an exhibition on marine life and history before climbing aboard the four-masted 1911 *Peking.* The seaport is generally thick with tourists, but it's still a lively place to spend an afternoon, especially for families with children who are likely to enjoy the

---

The best Rest stops

Need to catch your breath? These tranquil spots are hidden in NYC museums.

The Noguchi Museum garden

The galleries circle a stunning garden that sets the sculptor's works amid cherry and birch trees and Japanese pines. *See p154.*

The Fuentidueña Chapel

The contemplative air of the **Cloisters**, the Met's medieval branch in Fort Tryon Park, is even more calming in this spare 12th-century Spanish chapel. *See p147.*

Garden of Stones

Andy Goldsworthy's outdoor installation at the **Museum of Jewish Heritage** invites remembrance. *See p161.*

Japan Society's courtyard

Prior to a film or an art exhibit, get into an appropriately Zen frame of mind in the waterfall-cooled bamboo garden. *See p159.*

---

atmosphere and intriguing seafaring memorabilia. Exhibitions in 2005 include "Child's Play at the Seaport," a collection of 19th- and early 20th-century games and toys (Feb–Dec), and "Walt Whitman and the Promise of Democracy," devoted to the 150th anniversary of the poet's masterwork *Leaves of Grass* (Jul–Dec).

The Statue of Liberty & Ellis Island Immigration Museum

See p77 for listing.
After security concerns placed the statue off-limits for nearly three years, its pedestal finally reopened for guided tours in summer 2004 (though you still can't climb up to the crown). On the way back to Manhattan, the Statue of Liberty ferry will stop at the popular Immigration Museum, on Ellis Island, through which more than 12 million entered the country. The exhibitions are a moving tribute to the people from so many different countries who made the journey to America, dreaming of a better life. The $6 audio tour, narrated by Tom Brokaw, is highly informative.

International

Asia Society and Museum

725 Park Ave at 70th St (1-212-288-6400/www.asia society.org). Subway: 6 to 68th St–Hunter College. **Open** *Tue–Thu, Sat, Sun 11am–6pm; Fri 11am–9pm.* **Admission** *$10, seniors $7, students $5, children under 16 free. Free Fri 6–9pm.* **Credit** *Cash only.*
The Asia Society sponsors study missions and conferences while promoting public programs in the U.S. and abroad. The headquarters' striking galleries host major exhibitions of art culled from dozens of countries and time periods—from ancient India and medieval Persia to contemporary Japan—and assembled from public and private collections, including the permanent Mr. and Mrs. John D. Rockefeller III collection of Asian art. A spacious, atriumlike café, with a Pan-Asian menu, and a beautifully stocked gift shop make the society a one-stop destination for anyone who has an interest in Asian art and culture.

China Institute

125 E 65th St between Park and Lexington Aves (1-212-744-8181/www.chinainstitute.org). Subway: F to Lexington Ave–63rd St; 6 to 68th St–Hunter College. **Open** *Mon, Wed, Fri, Sat 10am–5pm; Tue, Thu 10am–8pm.* **Admission** *$5, seniors and students $3, children under 12 free. Free Tue, Thu 6–8pm.* **Credit** *AmEx, MC, V.*
Consisting of just two small galleries, the China Institute is somewhat overshadowed by the nearby Asia Society. But its rotating exhibitions, including works by female Chinese artists and selections from the Beijing Palace Museum, are compelling. The institute also offers lectures and courses on myriad subjects such as calligraphy, Confucius and cooking.

El Museo del Barrio captures the face (and frocks) of Spanish Harlem.

El Museo del Barrio

*1230 Fifth Ave between 104th and 105th Sts
(1-212-831-7272/www.elmuseo.org). Subway:
6 to 103rd St.* **Open** *Wed–Sun 11am–5pm.*
Admission *$6, seniors and students $4, children
under 12 free when accompanied by an adult. Seniors
free Thursday.* **Credit** *AmEx, MC, V.*
Located in Spanish Harlem (a.k.a. *el barrio*), El Museo
del Barrio is dedicated to the work of Latino artists
who reside in the U. S. as well as Latin American masters. The 8,000-piece collection ranges from pre-
Columbian artifacts to contemporary installations. In
2005, the museum's programs will include "The
Revolution and Beyond: Casasola 1900–1940," featuring more than 100 photographs from Archivo
Casasola that document Mexico's transition to the
industrial era (Apr 12–Sept 11), and El Museo's Bienal
"The (S) Files 2005" (Sept 29, 2005–Jan 29, 2006), showing work by young artists who live in the NYC area.

Goethe-Institut New York/ German Cultural Center

*1014 Fifth Ave at 82nd St (1-212-439-8700/www.
goethe.de/ins/us/ney). Subway: 4, 5, 6 to 86th St.*
Open *Gallery Mon–Fri 10am–5pm. Library Tue, Thu
noon–7pm; Wed, Fri, Sat noon–5pm.* **Admission** *free.*
Goethe-Institut New York is a branch of the international German cultural organization founded in
1951. Housed in a landmark Fifth Avenue mansion
across from the Metropolitan Museum of Art, the
institute mounts shows featuring German-born contemporary artists and presents concerts, lectures
and film screenings. German-language books,
videos and periodicals are available in the library.

The Hispanic Society of America

*Audubon Terrace, Broadway between 155th and
156th Sts (1-212-926-2234/www.hispanicsociety.org).
Subway: 1 to 157th St.* **Open** *Tue–Sat 10am–4:30pm;
Sun 1–4pm.* **Admission** *free.*
The Hispanic Society has the largest assemblage of
Spanish art and manuscripts outside Spain. Look for
two portraits by Goya and the lobby's bas-relief of
Don Quixote. The collection is dominated by religious
artifacts, including 16th-century tombs from the
monastery of San Francisco in Cuéllar, Spain. You'll
also find decorative-art objects and thousands of
black-and-white photographs that document life in
Spain and Latin America from the mid-19th century
to the present. The Society's library is closed Sundays.

Jacques Marchais Museum of Tibetan Art

*338 Lighthouse Ave off Richmond Rd (1-718-
987-3500/www.tibetanmuseum.com). Travel: From
the Staten Island Ferry, take the S74 bus to Lighthouse
Ave.* **Open** *Wed–Sun 1–5pm.* **Admission** *$5,
seniors and students $3, children under 12 $2.*
Credit *AmEx, MC, V.*
This tiny hillside museum contains a formidable
Buddhist altar, lovely gardens and a large collection
of Tibetan art that includes religious objects,
bronzes and paintings. Every October, the museum hosts a Tibetan festival.

Japan Society

*333 E 47th St between First and Second Aves (1-212-
752-3015/www.japansociety.org). Subway: E, V to
Lexington Ave–53rd St; 6 to 51st St.* **Open** *Tue–Fri*

11am–6pm; Sat, Sun 11am–5pm. **Admission** *$5, seniors and students $3.* **Credit** *AmEx, Disc, MC, V.*
In a serene space complete with waterfall and bamboo garden, the Japan Society presents performing arts, lectures, exchange programs and special events. The gallery shows traditional and contemporary Japanese art. In April 2005, the Society will present the Takashi Murakami–curated "Little Boy: The Arts of Japan's Exploding Subcultures," which examines Japanese youth culture's worldwide influence. A language center and library are open to members and students.

Jewish Museum

1109 Fifth Ave at 92nd St (1-212-423-3200/ www.thejewishmuseum.org). Subway: 4, 5 to 86th St; 6 to 96th St. **Open** *Sun–Wed 11am–5:45pm; Thu 11am–8pm; Fri 11am–3pm. Closed on Jewish holidays.* **Admission** *$10, seniors and students $7.50, children under 12 free when accompanied by an adult. Voluntary donation Thu 5–8pm.* **Credit** *AmEx, MC, V.*
The Jewish Museum, in the 1908 Warburg Mansion, contains a fascinating collection of more than 28,000 works of art, artifacts and media installations. A two-floor permanent exhibit, "Culture and Continuity: The Jewish Journey," examines Judaism's survival and the essence of Jewish identity. Temporary exhibitions in 2005 include "The Power of Conversation: Jewish Women and Their Salons" (through Jul 10);

"Maurice Sendak," which will focus on the artist's work and his Jewish identity (Apr 15–Aug 14); and "Common Ground," an exploration of modern American-Jewish life (Sept 22, 2005–Jan 22, 2006). The museum's Café Weissman serves contemporary kosher fare.

Museum for African Art

36-01 43rd Ave at 36th St, third floor, Long Island City, Queens (1-718-784-7700/www.africanart.org). Subway: 7 to 33rd St. **Open** *Mon, Thu, Fri 10am–5pm; Sat, Sun 11am–6pm.* **Admission** *$6; seniors, students and children $3; children under 6 free.* **Credit** *Cash only.*
This institution, located in the now trendy art mecca of Long Island City, features exhibitions of African art that change about twice a year. The quality of the work—often on loan from private collections—is exceptional. Recent shows include "Personal Affects: Power and Poetics in Contemporary South African Art" and "Glimpses from the South: A Selection of African Art from the Johannesburg Art Gallery." The remarkable gift shop is filled with African art objects and crafts.

Museum of Chinese in the Americas

70 Mulberry St at Bayard St, second floor (1-212-619-4785/www.moca-nyc.org). Subway: J, M, Z, N,

The château-style Warburg Mansion, on Fifth Avenue, now houses the **Jewish Museum**.

Q, R, W, 6 to Canal St. **Open** *Tue–Thu, Sat, Sun noon–6pm; Fri noon–7pm.* **Admission** *suggested donation $3, seniors and students $1, children under 12 free. Free Friday.*
In the heart of downtown Manhattan's Chinatown, a century-old former schoolhouse holds a two-room museum focused on Chinese-American history and the Chinese immigrant experience. Call for details about walking tours of the neighborhood.

Museum of Jewish Heritage– A Living Memorial to the Holocaust

Robert F. Wagner Jr. Park, 36 Battery Pl at First Pl (1-646-437-4200/www.mjhnyc.org). Subway: 1, 9 to South Ferry; 4, 5 to Bowling Green. **Open** *Sun–Tue, Thu 10am–5.45pm; Wed 10am–8pm; Fri, eve of Jewish holidays 10am–3pm (until 5pm in the summer).* **Admission** *$10, seniors $7, students $5, children under 12 free. Free Wed 4–8pm.*
Credit *AmEx, MC, V.*
Opened in 1997 and expanded in 2003, this museum offers one of the most moving cultural experiences in the city. Detailing both the horrific attacks on and the inherent joys of Jewish life during the past century, the collection consists of 24 documentary films, 2,000 photographs and 800 cultural artifacts, many donated by Holocaust survivors and their families. The Memorial Garden features English artist Andy Goldsworthy's permanent installation *Garden of Stones,* 18 fire-hollowed boulders, each planted with a dwarf oak sapling.

Rubin Museum of Art

150 W 17th St at Seventh Ave (1-212-620-5000/ www.rmanyc.org). Subway: 1, 9 to 18th St.
Open *Tue, Sat 11am–7pm; Wed, Sun 11am–5pm; Thu, Fri 11am–9pm. $7, seniors and students $5, children under 12 free.* **Credit** *AmEx, Disc, MC, V.*
Possibly inspired by the benevolence of the deities portrayed in the 900 Himalayan paintings, prints, sculptures and textiles they own, Donald and Shelley Rubin decided to share the wealth. In the fall of 2004, they opened the Rubin Museum of Art in a 70,000-square-foot Chelsea building a few blocks east of the gallery district (formerly occupied by a Barneys department store). The holdings, which span the 2nd to the 19th centuries, are displayed on six floors of exhibition space. In addition to the impressive permanent collection, check out related traveling exhibitions by contemporary artists, and the talks, films and family programs. Or sit down to some East-West fusion cuisine in the café.

Scandinavia House: The Nordic Center in America

58 Park Ave between 37th and 38th Sts (1-212-879-9779/www.scandinaviahouse.org). Subway: 42nd St S, 4, 5, 6, 7 to 42nd St–Grand Central. **Open** *Tue–Sat noon–6pm.* **Admission** *suggested donation $3, seniors and students $2.* **Credit** *AmEx, MC, V.*
You'll find all things Nordic, from Ikea designs to the latest Finnish film, at this modern center, the leading cultural link between the United States and the five Nordic countries (Denmark, Finland,

Iceland, Norway and Sweden). Often incorporating works on loan from museums in those countries, the sleek glass-and-wood Scandinavia House features exhibitions, films, concerts, lectures, symposia and readings, as well as kid-friendly programming at the Heimbold Family Children's Learning Center. The AQ Café is a bustling lunch spot with a menu overseen by NYC's most famous Swedish chef, Marcus Samuelsson.

Yeshiva University Museum

Center for Jewish History, 15 W 16th St between Fifth and Sixth Aves (1-212-294-8330/www.yumuseum.org). Subway: F, V to 14th St; L to Sixth Ave. **Open** *Tue–Thu, Sun 11am–5pm.* **Admission** *$6; seniors, students and children 5–16 $4; children under 5 free.* **Credit** *AmEx, Disc, MC, V.*
The museum usually hosts one major exhibition and several smaller shows each year, mainly centered on Jewish themes. It's located in the Center for Jewish History, a separate organization that also offers exhibits and educational programs.

Media

American Museum of the Moving Image

35th Ave at 36th St, Astoria, Queens (1-718-784-0077/www.movingimage.us). Subway: G, R, V to Steinway St. **Open** *Wed, Thu noon–5pm; Fri noon–8pm; Sat, Sun 11am–6:30pm.* **Admission** *$10, seniors and students $7.50, children 5–18 $5, children under 5 free. Free Fri 4–8pm. No strollers.*
Credit *AmEx, MC, V.*
Only a 15-minute subway ride from midtown Manhattan, Moving Image is one of the city's most dynamic institutions. Located in the restored complex that once housed the original Kaufman Astoria Studios (*see p128*), AMMI offers daily film and video programming. The museum also displays famous movie props and costumes, including the chariot driven by Charlton Heston in *Ben-Hur* and the Yoda puppet used in *Star Wars: Episode V–The Empire Strikes Back.*

The Museum of Television & Radio

25 W 52nd St between Fifth and Sixth Aves (1-212-621-6800/www.mtr.org). Subway: B, D, F to 47–50th Sts–Rockefeller Ctr; E, V to Fifth Ave–53rd St. **Open** *Tue–Sun noon–6pm; Thu noon–8pm.* **Admission** *$10, seniors and students $8, children under 14 $5.* **Credit** *Cash only.*
This nirvana for boob-tube addicts and pop-culture junkies contains an archive of more than 100,000 radio and TV programs. Head to the fourth-floor library to search the computerized system for your favorite *Star Trek* or *I Love Lucy* episodes, then walk down one flight to take a seat at your assigned console. (The radio listening room operates the same way.) Screenings of modern cartoons, public seminars and special presentations are offered. Recent programs were devoted to television superheroes, American political ads, and the history of gay and lesbian characters on TV.

Intrepid Sea-Air-Space Museum.

Military

Intrepid Sea-Air-Space Museum

USS Intrepid, *Pier 86, 46th St at the Hudson River (1-212-245-0072/www.intrepidmuseum.org). Travel: A, C, E to 42nd St–Port Authority, then take the M42 bus to Twelfth Ave.* **Open** *Apr–Sept Mon–Fri 10am–5pm; Sat, Sun 10am–6pm. Oct–Mar Tue–Sun 10am–5pm. Last admittance one hour before closing.* **Admission** *$14.50; seniors, veterans and students $10.50; children 6–17 $9.50; children 2–5 $2.50; children under 2 and servicepeople on active duty free.* **Credit** *AmEx, MC, V.*

Climb inside a model of a wooden Revolutionary-era submarine, try out a supersonic-flight simulator, and explore dozens of military helicopters, fighter planes and more aboard this retired aircraft carrier. A barge next to the *Intrepid* displays a British Airways Concorde and holds exhibits on the history of supersonic flight. Additional artifacts in the collection include a Cobra attack copter and a Tomcat fighter jet. During Fleet Week (*see p255*), the *Intrepid* hosts contests and other fun events for sailors (for more information, go to www.fleetweek.navy.mil).

New York Public Library

The vast New York Public Library (NYPL) is the largest, most comprehensive library system in the world. Unless you're interested in a specific subject, your best bet is to visit the system's flagship, officially known as the Humanities and Social Sciences Library. Information on the entire system can be found at www.nypl.org.

Donnell Library Center

20 W 53rd St between Fifth and Sixth Aves (1-212-621-0618). Subway: E, V to Fifth Ave–53rd St. **Open** *Mon, Wed, Fri 10am–6pm; Tue, Thu 10am–8pm; Sat 10am–5pm; Sun 1–5pm.* **Admission** *free.*

This branch of the NYPL has an extensive collection of records, films, videotapes and DVDs, along with screening facilities. The Donnell specializes in foreign-language books (in more than 80 languages); there's also a children's section containing roughly 100,000 books, films, records and cassettes.

Humanities and Social Sciences Library

455 Fifth Ave at 42nd St (1-212-930-0830). Subway: B, D, F, V to 42nd St–Bryant Park; 7 to Fifth Ave. **Open** *Tue, Wed 11am–7:30pm; Thu–Sat 10am–6pm.* **Admission** *free.*

When people mention "the New York Public Library," most are referring to this imposing Beaux Arts building. Two massive stone lions, dubbed Patience and Fortitude by former mayor Fiorello La Guardia, flank the main portal. Free guided tours (at 11am and 2pm) stop at the beautifully renovated Rose Main Reading Room and the Bill Blass Public Catalog Room, which offers free Internet access. Lectures, author readings and special exhibitions are definitely worth checking out.

The New York Public Library for the Performing Arts

40 Lincoln Center Plaza at 65th St (1-212-870-1630). Subway: 1, 9 to 66th St–Lincoln Ctr. **Open** *Tue, Wed, Fri, Sat noon–6pm; Thu noon–8pm.* **Admission** *free.*

One of the world's great performing-arts research centers, this facility houses an endless collection of films, letters, manuscripts, videotapes—and half a million sound recordings. Visitors can browse through books, scores and recordings, or attend a concert or lecture.

Schomburg Center for Research in Black Culture

515 Malcolm X Blvd (Lenox Ave) at 135th St (1-212-491-2200). Subway: 2, 3 to 135th St. **Open** *Tue, Wed noon–8pm; Thu, Fri noon–6pm; Sat 10am–6pm.* **Admission** *free.*
An extraordinary trove of vintage literature and historical memorabilia relating to black culture and the African diaspora is housed in an institution founded in 1926 by its first curator, bibliophile Arturo Alfonso Schomburg. The Center hosts jazz concerts, films, lectures and tours.

Science, Industry and Business Library

188 Madison Ave at 34th St (1-212-592-7000). Subway: 6 to 33rd St. **Open** *Tue–Thu 10am–8pm; Fri, Sat 10am–6pm.* **Admission** *free.*
Opened in 1996, this Gwathmey Siegel–designed branch of the NYPL is dedicated to science, technology, business and economics. It has a circulating collection of 50,000 books and an open-shelf reference collection of 60,000 volumes, and it provides access (at no charge) to 100 electronic databases. Free tours are given at 2pm on Tuesdays and Thursdays.

Science & technology

Liberty Science Center

251 Phillip St, Jersey City, NJ 07305 (1-201-200-1000/www.lsc.org). Travel: PATH to Pavonia/ Newport, then take the NJ Transit Hudson-Bergen Light Rail to Liberty State Park. **Open** *Tue–Sun 9:30am–5:30pm (also open Mondays in the summer).* **Admission** *$10, seniors and children 2–18 $8, children under 2 free. Combined entry to center, IMAX and Hi-Def movies $16.50, seniors and children 2–18 $14.50, children under 2 $10.* **Credit** *AmEx, Disc, MC, V.*
This terrific science museum for kids has three floors of innovative, hands-on exhibits, including a 100-foot-long, pitch-dark "touch tunnel," a bug zoo and a scale model of the Hudson River estuary, plus daily demonstrations explaining the hows and whys of science in everyday life. The center also boasts the country's largest IMAX cinema, which screens short documentaries such as "Forces of Nature" and "Bugs!" From the observation tower, you get great views of Manhattan and an unusual sideways look at the Statue of Liberty. On weekends, take the NY Waterway ferry (*see p72*) here. In late 2005, the center will begin construction on a major expansion, slated for completion in 2007.

New York Hall of Science

47-01 111th St at 47th Ave, Flushing Meadows–Corona Park, Queens (1-718-699-0005/www.nyhallsci.org). Subway: 7 to 111th St. **Open** *Jul, Aug Mon 9:30am–2pm; Tue–Fri 9:30am–5pm; Sat, Sun 10:30am–6pm. Sept–Jun Tue–Thu 9:30am–2pm; Fri 9:30am–5pm; Sat, Sun noon–5pm.* **Admission** *$9, seniors and students $6, children 2–4 $2.50. Free Sept–Jun Fri 2–5pm. Science playground $3 plus general admission (open Mar–Dec, weather permitting).* **Credit** *AmEx, DC, Disc, MC, V.*
The fun-for-all-ages New York Hall of Science, built for the 1964 World's Fair and recently expanded, demystifies its subject through colorful hands-on exhibits about biology, chemistry and physics, with topics such as "The Realm of the Atom" and "Marvelous Molecules." Kids can burn off surplus energy—and perhaps learn a thing or two—in the 30,000-square-foot outdoor science playground.

Urban services

New York City Fire Museum

278 Spring St between Hudson and Varick Sts (1-212-691-1303/www.nycfiremuseum.org). Subway: C, E to Spring St; 1, 9 to Houston St. **Open** *Tue–Sat 10am–5pm; Sun 10am–4pm.* **Admission** *suggested donation $5, seniors and students $2, children under 12 $1.* **Credit** *AmEx, DC, Disc, MC, V.*
An active firehouse from 1904 to 1959, this museum is filled with gadgetry and pageantry, from late-18th-century hand-pumped fire engines to present-day equipment. The museum also houses a permanent exhibit commemorating firefighters' heroism after the attack on the World Trade Center.

New York City Police Museum

100 Old Slip between South and Water Sts (1-212-480-3100/www.nycpolicemuseum.org). Subway: 2, 3 to Wall St; 4, 5 to Bowling Green. **Open** *Tue–Sat 10am–5pm; Sun 11am–5pm.* **Admission** *suggested donation $5, seniors $3, children 6–18 $2.* **Credit** *Cash only.*
The New York Police Department's tribute to itself features exhibits on its history and the tools and transportation of the trade. You can also pick up officially licensed NYPD paraphernalia.

New York Transit Museum

Corner of Boerum Pl and Schermerhorn St, Brooklyn Heights, Brooklyn (1-718-694-1600/www.mta.info/mta/museum). Subway: A, C, G to Hoyt–Schermerhorn. **Open** *Tue–Fri 10am–4pm; Sat, Sun noon–5pm.* **Admission** *$5, seniors and children 3–17 $3.* **Credit** *Cash only.*
The Transit Museum continues its commemoration of the subway's 100th birthday through spring 2005. "Centennial Celebration" features subway-related artifacts on loan from the extensive collections at the Museum of the City of New York and the New-York Historical Society (*see p156 and p157*), as well as items from the Transit Museum's own collection. In its permanent "Moving the Millions: New York City's Subways from Its Origins to the Present" exhibit, visitors can check out—and even board—vintage subway and el cars. The museum also has a great gallery and gift shop in Grand Central Terminal.
Other location *New York Transit Museum Gallery Annex & Store, Grand Central Terminal, Main Concourse, 42nd St at Park Ave, adjacent to stationmaster's office (1-212-878-0106).*

Eat, Drink, Shop

Minado
JAPANESE SEAFOOD BUFFET
6 e. 32nd st. new york, ny 10016 | 212. 725. 1333
we also offer catering services

LUNCH | mon - fri : 11:30am - 2:30 pm | sat - sun : 11:30am- 3:00pm
DINNER | mon - thurs : 6:00pm - 10:00pm
| fri - sat : 5:30pm - 10:00pm | sun : 5:00pm - 9:00pm

WWW.MINADO.COM
LITTLE FERRY, NJ • CARLE PLACE, NY • NATICK, MA • PARSIPPANY, NJ

Restaurants

Eat, drink and be merry. Repeat.

New York is the pinnacle of the food lovers' world because it truly has something for everyone. Just look at the intersection of 17th Street and Irving Place, near Union Square, where the restaurant **Pure Food and Wine** (*see p185* **Vegetative state**) serves upscale raw-food and vegan dinners around the corner from celebrity chef Mario Batali's Spanish-accented houses of ham, **Casa Mono** and **Bar Jamón** (*see p189*). It's a sign of the times: While New Yorkers still love their pastrami (and their porterhouses), even nonvegetarians are enjoying high-end meatless cuisine. Still hooked on carbs? We've got plenty of those, too, in the form of good old-fashioned bagels (*see p177* **History in the round**). If wine's your thing, there's no reason to settle for the same old glass of red. In **Grape nuts** (*see p192*), we tell you about an Italian wine bar that refuses to serve Chianti, a new restaurant with 100 wines by the glass and several restaurants that offer superlow markups on their bottles. Of course, we realize that some of you are game for anything; for you, we recommend a new batch of flashy, fabulous venues (*see p174* **Dinner theater**). No matter where you go, you're bound to run into something tasty along the way.

Tribeca & south

American

Bubby's
120 Hudson St at North Moore St (1-212-219-0666). Subway: 1, 9 to Franklin St. **Open** *Mon–Thu 8am–11pm; Fri 8am–midnight; Sat 9am–4pm, 6pm–midnight; Sun 9am–10pm.* **Average main course** *$13.* **Credit** *AmEx, DC, Disc, MC, V.*
Hordes descend on weekend mornings, when a "we love kids!" attitude and no-brunch-reservations policy add up to barely controlled chaos. (Naturally, if you've got energetic toddlers in tow, this can be a good thing.) For something calmer, try a weekday dinner of alphabet soup, homemade potato chips with blue-cheese sauce, mac and cheese, or slow-cooked barbecue. Mountainous wedges of pie are the best dessert option. **Other location** *1 Main St at Plymouth St, Dumbo, Brooklyn (1-718-222-0666).*

French

Bouley
120 West Broadway at Duane St (1-212-964-2525). Subway: A, C, 1, 2, 3, 9 to Chambers St.

Open *11:30am–3pm, 5–11pm daily.* **Average main course** *$34.* **Credit** *AmEx, DC, Disc, MC, V.*
In the elegant, vaulted space that used to house Bouley Bakery, culinary superstar David Bouley has returned to his haute-cuisine standard. This doesn't mean everything's swimming in butter and cream; the kitchen is big on *sous-vide* cooking (a more sophisticated version of boil-in-a-bag). Wild salmon is sealed in plastic and lightly poached, then served, with its natural juices intact, alongside a gloss of deeply fragrant white-truffle sauce. Lobster and bouillabaisse are shining examples of seafood cooked just to the trembling point of pearly perfection. If the $75 tasting menu makes you blanch, there are prix-fixe lunch deals for $35 and $45. But if money's no object, spend it here.

Landmarc
179 West Broadway between Leonard and Worth Sts (1-212-343-3883). Subway: 1, 9 to Franklin St. **Open** *Mon–Fri noon–3:30pm, 5:30pm–2am; Sat 5:30pm–2am.* **Average main course** *$23.* **Credit** *AmEx, DC, Disc, MC, V.*
Chef Marc Murphy has wooed the neighborhood with a well-executed menu of reliable bistro and trattoria favorites—*boudin noir,* frisée *aux lardons,* mussels, pastas, and excellent grilled steaks and chops. An extremely enticing bottles-only wine list (priced just a tad above retail) is also served in half-bottle portions. The exposed metal and brick add a pleasingly rough edge to the elegant dark wood in the bi-level space.

Italian

Bread Tribeca
301 Church St between Walker and White Sts (1-212-343-8282). Subway: A, C, E to Canal St. **Open** *Mon–Thu 11am–11pm; Fri 11am–midnight; Sat, Sun 10:30am–midnight.* **Average main course** *$20.* **Credit** *AmEx, DC, Disc, MC, V.*
This spin-off of Nolita's popular panino shop has moved far beyond its original sandwich premise, serving rustic Italian pastas like tagliatelle laced with braised lamb, as well as fresh-from-the-fryer

---

▶ For the newest restaurants, pick up the current issue of ***Time Out New York***.
▶ For thousands of restaurant reviews, consult the ***Time Out New York Eating & Drinking*** guide, available on newsstands and at **eatdrink.timeoutny.com**.

---

fritto misto and wood-fired steaks. The crowd is sexy; the loft-size room, trendy but relaxed; and the strawberry soup with vanilla gelato, simply perfect. **Other location** *Bread, 20 Spring St between Elizabeth and Mott Sts (1-212-334-1015).*

Dominic
349 Greenwich St between Harrison and Jay Sts (1-212-343-0700). **Open** *Mon–Thu noon–2:30pm, 5:30–10:30pm; Fri noon–2:30pm, 5:30–11pm; Sat 5:30–11pm.* **Average main course** *$24.* **Credit** *AmEx, DC, MC, V.*

Chef John Villa, who makes his own pasta, loves experimenting with spices and herbs, especially mint, which pops up in appetizers of yellowtail, octopus and cockles, as well as in his *strozzapreti*. Portions are generous, and deft servers work tableside when preparing the classic Caesar salad or filleting the fish of the day. Pork fans will appreciate the mix of sweet, salty and bitter flavors in the honey-accented *porchetta* and its wonderfully crunchy rind. Even by Tribeca standards, the space is large, with high ceilings, exposed-brick walls, sidewalk tables, a few luxurious booths and a window into the kitchen.

Pace
121 Hudson St at North Moore St (1-212-965-9500). **Subway:** *1, 9 to Franklin St.* **Open** *Mon–Sat 5:30–10:30pm.* **Average main course** *$24.* **Credit** *AmEx, DC, Disc, MC, V.*

The new Italian eatery from Jimmy Bradley and Danny Abrams (the Harrison, Mermaid Inn, Red Cat) achieves a been-there-forever look with murals on distressed walls and a rough-hewn bar. Executive chef Joey Campanaro has built a menu of simple plates: lots of vegetables; *crudo* like raw local bass or bluefin tuna; straightforward pastas; and big-flavored main courses such as *cacciucco* (a Tuscan seafood stew), and a bone-in rib-eye steak for two.

Japanese

Nobu
105 Hudson St at Franklin St (1-212-219-0500). **Subway:** *1, 9 to Franklin St.* **Open** *Mon–Fri 11:45am–2:15pm, 5:45–10:15pm; Sat, Sun 5:45–10:15pm.* **Average hot dish** *$16.* **Average sushi roll** *$8.* **Credit** *AmEx, DC, Disc, MC, V.*

Nobu is now past its tenth year, and it's still impossible to get a table. Celebrity sightings remain as commonplace as orders of chef Nobu Matsuhisa's signature black cod in miso. Matsuhisa is still masterful, and the restaurant continues to add to its stockpile of awards. The sushi is impeccable, but the cooked dishes are downright sexy, from seared slices of fish glossed with a hint of *yuzu* and sesame and olive oils to rock-shrimp tempura with chili aioli. The salmon-skin roll is as succulent as ever, with slices of cucumber enfolding salty salmon skin, avocado, carrots and *shiso* leaves. If you're not one of the celebrity regulars, you can always try your luck at Next Door Nobu, the no-reservations sibling. **Other location** *Next Door Nobu, 105 Hudson St at Franklin St (1-212-334-4445).*

Seafood

Coast
110 Liberty St between Greenwich St and Trinity Pl (1-212-962-0136). **Subway:** *R, W to Cortlandt St.* **Open** *7am–midnight daily.* **Average main course** *$20.* **Credit** *AmEx, Disc, MC, V.*

Overlooking the World Trade Center site, Coast serves superbly fresh seafood in a comfortable, casual setting. A bar, lounge and dining room are on the main floor, a private dining room is upstairs, and there's even a fish market stocked with catches from owner Eric Tevrow's supplier, Early Morning Seafood. Wall Streeters and Ground Zero visitors can get three meals a day, starting with a scrambled-egg-and-lobster sandwich. For lunch and dinner: crab rolls to go, or eat-in entrées such as grilled swordfish or pot-roasted salmon.

Citizens, lend us your ears! **Cafe Habana**'s grilled corn is heaven on a stick.

Chinatown, Little Italy & Nolita

Chinese

Golden Unicorn

18 East Broadway between Catherine and Market Sts (1-212-941-0911). Subway: F to East Broadway. **Open** *9am–10pm daily.* **Average main course** *$15.* **Credit** *AmEx, DC, Disc, MC, V.*
Thankfully, the carts at this hectic, bi-level dim sum parlor have English labels, which make ordering easy for novices. Spring rolls, *shumai,* pork buns and shrimp dumplings are familiar and satisfying. If the movable feast doesn't whet your appetite, the regular menu is also available during dim sum hours; try the clams in black-bean sauce. Arrive before 10am on weekends to beat the crowds.

Peking Duck House

28 Mott St between Mosco and Pell Sts (1-212-227-1810). Subway: J, M, Z, N, Q, R, W, 6 to Canal St. **Open** *Sun–Thu 11:30am–10:30pm; Fri, Sat 11:30am–11:30pm.* **Average main course** *$15.* **Credit** *AmEx, MC, V.*
Order the three-way Peking duck, dispatched by savvy chefs brandishing their knives with aplomb, and you'll feast on everything but the quack. The succulent, aromatic bird yields a main course (sliced meat rolled up in thin pancakes with sweet plum sauce), a stir-fry made with vegetables and leftover bits of meat, and a cabbage soup made with the bones. Peking duck isn't the only thing served here, but it's definitely the best.

Cuban

Cafe Habana

117 Prince St at Elizabeth St (1-212-625-2001). Subway: N, R, W to Prince St; 6 to Spring St. **Open** *9am–midnight daily.* **Average main course** *$10.* **Credit** *AmEx, DC, MC, V.*
The fashionistas milling around Nolita don't look like they eat, but they do—here. They storm this chrome corner fixture for the addictive grilled corn doused in butter and rolled in grated cheese and chili powder. Staples include a gooey pressed Cuban sandwich of roast pork, ham, melted Swiss and pickles; crisp beer-battered catfish tortas with spicy mayo; and juicy marinated skirt steak with yellow rice and black beans. Locals love the take-out annex next door: You can get that corn on a stick to go. **Other location** *Cafe Habana to Go, 229 Elizabeth St between Houston and Prince Sts (1-212-625-2001).*

Eclectic

Public

210 Elizabeth St between Prince and Spring Sts (1-212-343-7011). Subway: N, R, W to Prince St;

Out-of-this-world cuisine is prepared with surgical precision at **wd-50**. *See p171.*

See p171.

6 to Spring St. **Open** *Sun–Wed 10am–midnight; Thu–Sat 10am–4am.* **Average main course** *$20.* **Credit** *AmEx, MC, V.*
Designed by Adam Farmerie and his team at AvroKo, this venture is high on concept, using machine-age glass lamps and prewar office doors to create "a utopian vision of civilized society." Farmerie's brother Brad, who worked at London's acclaimed Providores, has created the menu in tandem with Providores' chefs, New Zealanders Anna Hansen and Peter Gordon. Look for a global Kiwi influence in dishes like grilled kangaroo on coriander falafel, scallops with plantain crisps, or New Zealand venison with pomegranates and truffles.

Italian

Da Nico

164 Mulberry St between Broome and Grand Sts (1-212-343-3177). Subway: J, M, Z to Bowery; 6 to Spring St. **Open** *Sun–Thu noon–11pm; Fri, Sat noon–midnight.* **Average main course** *$15.* **Credit** *AmEx, DC, MC, V.*
If Little Italy is on your must-see list, steer past the red-sauce tourist traps and into the serene back garden at Da Nico. Attentive waiters serve coal-oven-baked pizzas, saucy pastas and generously portioned (if underseasoned) main dishes like veal saltimbocca. The pizza is your best bet: crisp yet tender crust, bright tomato sauce and fresh toppings. For dessert, try the softball-size *tartufo*, a globe of ice cream coated in crunchy chocolate and filled with candied cherries and walnuts. Or just share the free plate of piping-hot *zeppole*.

L'Asso

192 Mott St at Kenmare St (1-212-219-2353). Subway: J, M, Z to Bowery; 6 to Spring St. **Open** *Sun–Thu noon–midnight; Fri, Sat noon–1am.* **Average main course** *$13.* **Credit** *Cash only.*
It's tempting to gorge yourself on antipasti, stuffed calamari or bruschetta at this cheerful spot, but to pass up a perfect Margherita, to not take a chance on the Pizza Patata (with potatoes, walnuts and rosemary), to not delight your tongue with the truffled portobellos of the *tartufo…che tragedia!* Owner Robert Benevenga has perfected the art of the wood-oven pizza. Like the name says, the pizza is ace.

Peasant

194 Elizabeth St between Prince and Spring Sts (1-212-965-9511). Subway: J, M, Z to Bowery; 6 to Spring St. **Open** *Tue–Sat 6–11pm; Sun 6–10pm.* **Average main course** *$22.* **Credit** *AmEx, MC, V.*
The open kitchen is a magical little brick-on-brick workshop where chef-owner Frank DeCarlo pulls sizzling hen, shimmery sardines and deep pans of rabbit lasagna from a crackling fire. Reading the Italian-only menu in the dim, candlelit room can be a challenge. Then again, you could just close your eyes and point, since nearly all of DeCarlo's rustic dishes are masterful: spicy charred octopus, crisp-crusted pizzas, luscious skate. And as soon as you place your order (whether here or in Cantina 194, the charming subterranean wine bar next door), the local holy trinity arrives: fresh ricotta, a bottle of olive oil from nearby Italian grocery DiPalo's and a basket of bread from Sullivan Street Bakery.

Seafood

Bar Tonno

17 Cleveland Pl at Spring St (1-212-966-7334).
Subway: 6 to Spring St. **Open** *5pm–3am daily.*
Average small plate *$13.* **Credit** *AmEx, MC, V.*
Think all raw fish is sushi? Think again: Although
these small plates of *crudo* are almost Japanese in
presentation, the flavors are vividly Italian. True to
its name, the narrow restaurant has no tables, just
a long 28-seat bar facing a nifty display of horizontal
wine bottles. The pairings are sexy, surprising and
smart, from sleek yellowtail dribbled with ginger
oil to a rich, meaty bite of tuna matched with an
almost aggressively oceanic sea-urchin sauce and a
sprinkle of sea salt.

Vietnamese

Doyers Vietnamese Restaurant

*11 Doyers St between Bowery and Pell St (1-212-
513-1521). Subway: J, M, Z, N, Q, R, W, 6 to
Canal St.* **Open** *Sun–Thu 11am–10pm; Fri, Sat
11am–11pm.* **Average main course** *$8.*
Credit *AmEx.*
Prepare to get lost on your way to this nearly hidden restaurant, tucked in a basement on a zigzag-
ging Chinatown alley. But the tasty food and low
prices are worth the search. The 33 appetizers
include balls of grilled minced shrimp wrapped
around sugarcane sticks (a combination of sweet
and smoky tastes with soft, chewy textures) and a
delicious Vietnamese crêpe filled with shrimp and
pork. Hot-pot soups, served on a tabletop stove,
have an exceptional fish-broth base and brim with
vegetables. For maximum enjoyment, come with a
crowd and sample everything you can.

Lower East Side

American Creative

wd-50

*50 Clinton St between Rivington and Stanton Sts
(1-212-477-2900). Subway: F to Delancey St; J, M,
Z to Delancey–Essex Sts.* **Open** *Mon–Sat 6–11pm;
Sun 6–10pm.* **Average main course** *$24.*
Credit *AmEx, DC, MC, V.*
The creations of wildly talented chef Wylie
Dufresne and his partners are utterly new—either
totally fascinating or really freaky, depending on
your point of view. Imagine pickled calf's tongue
with onion streusel and balls of fried mayonnaise;
venison tartare with edamame ice cream; and halibut with bizarre but satisfying smoked mashed
potatoes. Pastry chef Sam Mason does his part by
pairing fresh strawberries with olive caramel and
Parmesan ice cream; chocolate panna cotta gets a
slick of corn coulis and a dainty cluster of salted
caramel popcorn—Cracker Jacks for the too-cool-
for-school set.

Delis

Katz's Delicatessen

205 E Houston St at Ludlow St (1-212-254-2246).
Subway: F, V to Lower East Side–Second Ave.
Open *Sun–Tue 8am–10pm; Wed, Thu 8am–11pm;
Fri, Sat 8am–3am.* **Average sandwich** *$11.*
Credit *AmEx, MC, V ($20 minimum).*
This cavernous old dining hall is a repository of
living history. Arrive at 11am on a Sunday, and the
line may be out the door. Grab a ticket and approach
the long counter. First, a hot dog. The crisp-skinned,
all-beef wieners here are without peer. Then shuffle
down, stuff a dollar in the tip jar and order your
stacked sandwich (half portions are now available).
Roast beef goes quickly (steer clear of the evening
remains). The brisket rates, but don't forget the
horseradish. And the hot pastrami? It's simply the
best. Everything tastes better with one of the 16 draft
beers; but if you're on the wagon, grab a bottle of
Dr. Brown's Cel-Ray Tonic.

Eclectic

Freemans

*2 Freeman Alley off Rivington St between
Bowery and Chrystie St (1-212-420-0012).*
*Subway: F, V to Lower East Side–Second Ave;
J, M, Z to Bowery.* **Open** *Mon–Fri 6pm–
midnight; Sat, Sun 11am–4pm, 6pm–midnight.*
Average main course *$22.* **Credit** *AmEx, DC,
Disc, MC, V.*
This nifty little place hidden at the end of Freeman
Alley was a secret for about a day—until a bunch

Hot pastrami on rye at **Katz's Delicatessen**.

of scenesters decided it would be the hot spot of the moment. Those in the know feast on affordable dishes like juicy whole trout, warm artichoke dip, rich wild-boar terrine, and perfect batches of mac and cheese, plus a few retro oddities like "devils on horseback" (prunes stuffed with blue cheese and wrapped in bacon), all served under the gaze of a dozen mounted animal heads.

Schiller's Liquor Bar

131 Rivington St at Norfolk St (1-212-260-4555). Subway: F to Delancey St; J, M, Z to Delancey–Essex Sts. **Open** *Tue–Thu 8am–1:30am; Fri 8am–2am; Sat 10am–2am; Sun 10am–1:30am.* **Average main course** *$12.* **Credit** *AmEx, MC, V.*
Keith McNally, owner of Balthazar, Lucky Strike and Pastis, has yet another red-hot restaurant in a trendy neighborhood, decorated once again with old mirrors and antique subway tiles. But McNally says Schiller's Liquor Bar is "a bohemian alternative" to his style-conscious bistros; no dish except steak costs more than $15. The 95-seat eatery serves fancy-free brunch, lunch and dinner, with a menu of Franco-Brit comfort-food staples like Welsh rarebit, steak frites and lamb curry. Don't know much about wine, but know what you like? Try one of the six bottles labeled simply "cheap," "decent," or "good."

French

Pink Pony

175 Ludlow St between Houston and Stanton Sts (1-212-253-1922). Subway: F, V to Lower East Side–Second Ave. **Open** *10am–2am daily.* **Average main course** *$12.* **Credit** *Cash only.*
High ceilings, romantic messages on the wall, slow but congenial service, and moody lighting all add to the Pony's boho Parisian charm. The dependable kitchen offers sweet and savory delectables till late at night. Books are piled on the shelves, an old-fashioned jukebox plays Nina Simone and Coltrane, and poetry readings are a regular fixture.

Italian

Grotto

100 Forsyth St between Broome and Grand Sts (1-212-625-3444). Subway: B, D to Grand St. **Open** *Mon–Wed 6–11pm; Thu–Sat 6pm–midnight.* **Average main course** *$17.* **Credit** *AmEx, DC, Disc, MC, V.*
Look for the below-street-level neon sign, then watch your step down the steep stairs into this charming red-walled restaurant. The romantically lit back garden is perfect for sipping wine and enjoying creative Italian dishes such as juicy fennel-dusted pork over creamy polenta, or a salad of frisée and arugula with *bresaola*, pine nuts and lime vinaigrette. Even cannoli gets a twist: Grotto's version is a tower of flaky pastry disks sandwiching dreamy chocolate-chip-flecked ricotta.

Japanese

Cube 63

63 Clinton St between Rivington and Stanton Sts (1-212-228-6751). Subway: F to Delancey St; J, M, Z to Delancey–Essex Sts. **Open** *Mon–Thu noon–3pm, 5pm–midnight; Fri, Sat noon–3pm, 5pm–1am; Sun 2pm–midnight.* **Average sushi meal** *$19.* **Credit** *DC, Disc, MC, V.*
The chic dining room is just a sliver, but the inventive flavors created by Ben and Ken Lau know no bounds. Jumbo specialty rolls crowd nearly every table: Shrimp tempura hooks up with eel, avocado, cream cheese and caviar in the Tahiti roll; the Volcano is crab and shrimp topped with a pile of spicy lobster salad, and the entire dish is set aflame with a blowtorch. Pull yourself away from the delicious raw fish for a bite of Tuna Nuta, miniature chunks of lightly seared tuna atop honey-mustard-glazed spears of asparagus.

Sachi's on Clinton

25 Clinton St between Houston and Stanton Sts (1-212-253-2900). Subway: F to Delancey St; J, M, Z to Delancey–Essex Sts. **Open** *Mon–Thu 6pm–midnight; Fri–Sun 6pm–1am.* **Average sushi meal** *$25.* **Credit** *AmEx, DC, MC, V.*
Unimpressed with simply great sushi offerings, New Yorkers expect something more. No wonder Sachi's on Clinton feels the need to up the stakes:

Eat, Drink, Shop

The best Eateries…

…for surefire aphrodisiacs
Babbo (*see p180*), **BLT Steak** (*see p194*), **Pearl Oyster Bar** (*see p185*).

…for scoring with a local
Alma (*see p199*), **Bao 111** (*see p179*), **The Elephant** (*see p179*).

…for wooing on a budget
al di là (*see p199*), **Grotto** (*see p173*), **In Vino** (*see p176*).

…for a cozy morning after
Bubby's (*see p167*), **Kitchenette Uptown** (*see p198*), **Pink Pony** (*see p173*).

…for popping the question
JoJo (*see p196*), **Le Refuge Inn** (*see p201*), **River Café** (*see p199*).

…for remembering why you proposed in the first place
Blue Hill (*see p179*), **Gramercy Tavern** (*see p188*) **Dévi** (*see p189*).

…for impressing the in-laws
'Cesca (*see p195*), **Pace** (*see p168*).

It offers rare sake imported from the 850-year-old Japanese producer Sudo Honke and features a design-conscious dining room with tangerine walls, a sleek concrete-and-bamboo garden, sliding wood screens for intimate dining areas, and tantalizing glass display cases for the oh-so-fresh fish at the sushi bar. Sachi's also specializes in appetizing soba dishes and *kushiage,* skewers of deep-fried fish and vegetables. Yum.

Spanish

Suba

109 Ludlow St between Delancey and Rivington Sts (1-212-982-5714). Subway: F to Delancey St; J, M, Z to Delancey–Essex Sts. **Open** *Mon–Thu 6–10:30pm; Fri–Sun 6–11:30pm.* **Average main course** *$20.* **Credit** *AmEx, MC, V.*

The clamor at the street-level tapas bar might be obnoxious, but down the suspended steel staircase is another scene entirely. A moat surrounds the small dining room, and Suba's new chef, Alex Ureña, fuses traditional Spanish dishes with modern techniques. Duck breast with white-peach coulis and cinnamon sauce is an undeniably sexy offering, especially when followed by the sultry dark-chocolate almond cake or a lime-pie cocktail.

Soho

American

Blue Ribbon

97 Sullivan St between Prince and Spring Sts (1-212-274-0404). Subway: C, E to Spring St. **Open** *Tue–Sun 4pm–4am.* **Average main course** *$22.* **Credit** *AmEx, DC, MC, V.*

This comfortably welcoming dining room, with red-painted brick walls and gently tilted mirrors, is packed until the wee hours, thanks to a sprawling, something-for-everyone menu; friendly, well-informed service; and a killer raw bar. Prices can be a bit high for what you get: Fried chicken is fabulously crisp and greaseless, but $21? Still, the raw

Dinner theater

This year, tiny boîtes are out, and big, splashy venues with Asian-inspired high style are in. The thrill is in the grand scale and over-the-top details; it's the difference between being courtside at a Knicks game in Madison Square Garden and watching it on TV in some dive bar.

Of all the new megarestaurants, the most theatrical is **Megu** (62 Thomas St between Church St and West Broadway, 1-212-964-7777). Sprawling over 13,000 square feet, the $8 million Japanese temple serves up to 300 diners a night. As you descend the wraparound staircase into the dining room, eventually coming face to face with an enormous Buddha (carved out of ice nightly), it's easy to imagine yourself in a scene from *Kill Bill*—though the only weapons around are the skewers from the melt-in-your-mouth kebabs of kobe beef. The food is equally dramatic: oysters marinated in bonito essence and then grilled tableside on a hot stone; sashimi salad assembled at your table by two servers—one tossing vegetables and nuts, the other drizzling hot sesame oil over slivers of raw snapper. Think of it as dinner and a show in one, since that's pretty much what a meal here will cost you.

Snug and cozy may be the usual style in the West Village, but **En Japanese Brasserie** (435 Hudson St between Leroy and Morton Sts, 1-212-647-9196) breaks the mold. The Hudson Street restaurant, with a soaring ceiling and a vast wall of windows, is spread out over several levels. Warm tofu, made fresh throughout the day, is a particular draw, along with Japanese-inspired dishes like Berkshire pork belly braised in house-made miso, foie gras and poached daikon with white miso vinegar, and seared *chutoro* marinated in garlic and soy.

Nearby in the trend-happy Meatpacking District, slick restaurants are still drawing crowds. Superstar chef-entrepreneur Jean-Georges Vongerichten—who gave us Jean Georges, JoJo (*see p196*), Vong, V Steakhouse and more—packs hundreds of scene-seekers into **Spice Market** (403 W 13th St at Ninth Ave, 1-212-675-2322) for fruity cocktails and pricey snack-and-share plates. In the dining areas and subterranean lounge, the ambience is that of a giant opium den, where you're pampered by a phalanx of sultry servers in free-flowing backless pajamas. The most successful dishes are the gussied-up versions of street-cart grub, like chicken samosas and mushroom egg rolls. But then again, everything tastes a little spicier when your table is wedged between Karl Lagerfeld's and Scarlett Johansson's.

oysters are pristine; the fried ones, even better; and chunks of juicy hanger steak, served with flaky battered onion rings and sautéed wild mushrooms, will happily sate late-night cravings.

Other location *Blue Ribbon Brooklyn, 280 Fifth Ave between Garfield Pl and 1st St, Park Slope, Brooklyn (1-718-840-0404).*

Fanelli's Cafe

94 Prince St at Mercer St (1-212-226-9412). Subway: N, R, W to Prince St. **Open** *Mon–Thu 10am–2:30am; Fri, Sat 10am–3am; Sun 11am–12:30am.* **Average main course** *$10.* **Credit** *AmEx, MC, V.*
Fanelli's has stood at this cobblestoned intersection since 1847, and local artists and worldly tourists pour into the lively landmark for perfectly charred beef patties on toasted onion rolls. The long bar, prints of boxing legends and checkered tablecloths add to the effortless charm. Chalkboard specials, such as pumpkin ravioli or grilled mahimahi with lime and coriander, are surprisingly good offerings in a sea of pub grub. There's no music loop; just the low thrum of a contented crowd.

French

Balthazar

80 Spring St between Broadway and Crosby St (1-212-965-1414). Subway: N, R, W to Prince St; 6 to Spring St. **Open** *Mon–Wed 7:30–11:30am, noon–5pm, 6pm–1am; Thu 7:30–11:30am, noon–5pm, 6pm–1:30am; Fri 7:30–11:30am, noon–5pm, 6pm–2am; Sat 10am–4pm, 6pm–2am; Sun 10am–4pm, 5:30pm–midnight.* **Average main course** *$21.* **Credit** *AmEx, MC, V.*
Drop in at 10pm on a Saturday night, and this still-cool bistro will be packed with rail-thin lookers in head-to-toe Prada and equally trendy boys in chic hoodies and groovy sneakers. But the bread is great, the food is good, and the service is surprisingly friendly. The three-tiered Balthazar seafood platter casts the most impressive shadow of any appetizer in town. Frisée *aux lardons* is exemplary, as is roasted chicken on mashed potatoes for two, or skate with brown butter and capers. These days, the only not-so-Gallic detail is the lack of cigarette smoke.

Over-the-top **Megu** in Tribeca doesn't stint on the bells and whistles.

Named for the abandoned elevated railroad tracks nearby, the three-level **Highline** (835 Washington St between Little W 12th and 13th Sts, 1-212-243-3339) takes diners on a mod trip to Thailand. In the Pool Lounge, a glistening fountain is surrounded by disco balls and groovy, retro egg-shaped chairs; on the cruise-ship-style upper deck, patrons can lounge on beds as they munch on chef Peter Pitakwong's fusion appetizers, including foie gras dumplings and spring rolls stuffed with pad thai noodles. Innovative main dishes include steamed striped bass in seaweed broth with sautéed lotus root, and spicy grilled squid and asparagus bundled and tied in a single giant broad noodle.

At **Ono** (18 Ninth Ave at 13th St, 1-212-206-6700)—an 11,200-square-foot, Jeffrey Beers–designed theme park in the achingly hip Hotel Gansevoort—executive chef Scott Ubert and sushi chef Kazuhiko "Kazu" Hashimoto prepare breakfast, lunch and dinner in an open kitchen. Grab a seat at the 50-foot sushi bar and watch Kazu work his raw magic while other chefs fire up *robato* grills and baste lobster with sizzling soy butter. In the garden, heat lamps keep guests warm while they relax in cabanas or snuggle on a wicker-frame bed.

Kittichai.

Pan-Latin

Besito

357 West Broadway between Broome and Grand Sts (1-212-966-2030). Subway: C, E to Spring St; 1, 9 to Canal St. **Open** *5:30pm–midnight daily.* **Average main course** *$15.* **Credit** *AmEx, MC, V.*
Mexican-born chef Arturo Tellez riffed on one of his mother's shrimp dishes to create Besito's signature appetizer, a mix of shrimp, calamari and avocado tossed with tomato-citrus dressing. It's just one highlight on a menu packed with lively Nuevo Latino combinations like mango-chipotle-glazed pork chops and grilled T-bone steak with chimichurri sauce. You can pair such specialties with wines from Mexico, Spain or Argentina, then linger over a Cuban coffee and ponder what fun it would be to climb the stone wall behind the bar.

Thai

Kittichai

60 Thompson Hotel, 60 Thompson St between Broome and Spring St. **Open** *6–11:30pm daily.* **Average main course** *$22.* **Credit** *AmEx, DC, Disc, MC, V.*
As a kid, Ian Chalermkittichai would drag a cart through the streets of Bangkok, hawking his mother's curries. Now he's presiding over the kitchen at Kittichai, a Thai restaurant with somewhat more ambitious plans: Owner Robin Leigh (Bond St,

Town) hired the prolific Rockwell Group to design the space (formerly Thom) and a feng shui master to bless it. The dark, alluring dining room features patio gazebos enclosed in black bamboo, swaths of Thai silk and an aquarium resembling a birdcage. Chalermkittichai does his part with family-style entreés such as *pad phed* lamb (pesto-marinated lamb loin with foie gras and eggplant) and desserts like champagne mangoes with black sticky rice.

East Village

American Creative

Hearth

403 E 12th St at First Ave (1-646-602-1300). Subway: L to First Ave. **Open** *Tue, Thu, Sun 6–10pm; Fri, Sat 6pm–midnight.* **Average main course** *$24.* **Credit** *AmEx, DC, MC, V.*
True to its name, there is a hearth here, but the real warmth comes from the staff, which seems to be genuinely interested in helping you pick the right dish, and equally interested in finding out afterward what you thought of it. At this upscale but not too pricey place, the fare is rich, hearty and seasonal—look for dishes like braised lamb shoulder and ribs served with lamb tongue, or monkfish osso buco surrounded by saffron risotto and calamari, which turns out to be a great adaptation of the classic veal shank dish.

Indian

Brick Lane Curry House

306–308 E 6th St between First and Second Aves (1-212-979-2900). Subway: F, V to Lower East Side–Second Ave; 6 to Astor Pl. **Open** *Sun–Thu 1–11pm; Fri, Sat 1pm–1am.* **Average main course** *$12.* **Credit** *AmEx, DC, Disc, MC, V.*
Specializing in *phal*, a habanero-fired curry that's popular along London's Brick Lane restaurant row, Curry House issues a how-hot-can-you-go challenge to every diner. Its 11 types of curry are rated according to spiciness. The menu warns that *phal*, the hottest, is "more pain and sweat than flavor," so sensitive palates should go with mild-but-lively *jalfrazi* sauce, which is excellent over lamb.

Italian

In Vino

215 E 4th St between Aves A and B (1-212-212-539-1011). Subway: F, V to Lower East Side–Second Ave. **Open** *Sun–Thu 5–11pm; Fri, Sat 5pm–midnight.* **Average small plate** *$10.* **Credit** *MC, V.*
The warning is on the first page of the extensive wine list: There's no Chianti or Barolo in the house, so don't even ask. Why? "Because Chianti sucks," says the bartender. If you enjoy wines from Southern Italy, however, take a seat: This wine-and-appetizer bar carries hundreds that you can pair

with crostini, cheese-layered *gratinatos,* divine meat and cheese platters, and other rustic snacks. The cavelike room is cozy as all get-out; bring a date and settle in for the night.

Supper

156 E 2nd St between Aves A and B (1-212-477-7600). Subway: F, V to Lower East Side–Second Ave. **Open** *Mon–Thu 5pm–midnight; Fri 5pm–1am; Sat 11am–1am; Sun 11am–midnight.* **Average main course** *$13.* **Credit** *Cash only.* This addition to Frank Prisinzano's pair of well-priced eateries (Frank, Lil' Frankie's) proves that a good dinner can be an uncomplicated affair. A big chalkboard menu hangs over the crammed-together wooden tables, which are lit with antique chandeliers (there's also a cool private dining room in the basement wine vault). Simplicity rules the menu, as in a salad of coaster-size beet slices and silky goat cheese—or in pastas like linguine glossed with butter and fresh mint, gnocchi with tomato, and spaghetti with lemon and Parmesan. A small wine bar next door (offering the same menu) handles the overflow.

Japanese

Jewel Bako

239 E 5th St between Second and Third Aves (1-212-979-1012). Subway: F, V to Lower East Side–Second Ave. **Open** *Mon–Sat 6:30–10:30pm.* **Omakase** *$50, $85.* **Credit** *AmEx, Disc, MC, V.*

History in the round

Like many New Yorkers, bagels traveled from afar to make this metropolis their home. When Jewish Eastern European immigrants began arriving in New York City in the late 19th century, they brought with them a taste for dense, chewy breads, including a ring-shaped roll known by the Yiddish word *beygl,* derived from the German word *beugel,* meaning "bracelet" or "ring."

Peddlers walked the crowded, tenement-lined streets of the Lower East Side (a common destination for Jewish newcomers), brandishing long sticks stacked with fresh bagels. Competition was fierce, and in 1907, a very exclusive bagel bakers' union formed in New York City. (One of its rules stipulated that only the sons of members could become apprentices.) The union knew the real secret of making a fine bagel—give it a quick bath in boiling water before baking. This brief dunk is responsible for the bagel's signature shiny crust and chewy interior.

As Jews in New York began moving out of the Lower East Side, they took their culinary traditions with them. Bagels, which became a standard offering in delicatessens throughout the city, were typically flavored with onions or poppy seeds and topped with a thick "schmear" of cream cheese and a piece of the salty smoked salmon known as lox. As Jewish humor and traditions became part of the city's cultural fabric, so did bagels. For Jews and gentiles alike, weekend brunch just isn't complete without bagels, coffee and the plump Sunday edition of the *New York Times.*

Although bagels can be found everywhere from Starbucks to McDonald's these days, tracking down the traditional boiled-and-baked version can be tough. Most bakeries use mechanized ovens that steam-mist the dough instead of boiling it, which results in soft, puffy rolls without the classic chewy crust.

If you want a taste of the real, old-fashioned thing, pick up a fresh-from-the-oven example at the legendary **H&H Bagels**, from either in the Upper West Side shop (2239 Broadway at 80th St, 1-212-595-8003) or the big factory in Hell's Kitchen (639 W 46th St between Eleventh and Twelfth Aves, 1-212-595-8000), across from the *Intrepid* Sea-Air-Space Museum. Both locations are open 24/7. H&H also ships its bagels worldwide.

While H&H's creations are the perfect snack, just one roll from **Ess-a-Bagel** (359 First Ave at 21st St, 1-212-980-1010; 831 Third Ave at 51st St, 1-212-980-4315) could easily be a meal for two or three. Since 1976, this family-run operation has been making monstrously big bagels with exceptional texture and flavor. Just be sure to come early on weekends, or you risk waiting in a line that snakes out the door.

Eat, Drink, Shop

You say garbanzo bean, I say **Chickpea**—but we both get killer falafel.

Jack and Grace Lamb were redefining the sushi experience for New Yorkers long before the recent explosion of high-profile Japanese restaurants. Supremely fresh fish (often flown in from far, far away) is sliced with surgical precision and delivered on stylish plates and trays. Aficionados are so seduced by the excellent sushi and sashimi that they forgive the restaurant's quirks. A meal for two can easily run to $150, and you probably won't be stuffed when you leave. But compared to the sky-high prices at places like Masa and Megu (*see p174* **Dinner theater**), everything at this East Village charmer seems like a steal. For a more casual (and less expensive) experience, try the low-key Jewel Bako Makimono.
Other location *Jewel Bako Makimono, 101 Second Ave between 5th and 6th Sts (1-212-253-7848).*

Middle Eastern

Chez Es Saada
42 E 1st St between First and Second Aves (1-212-777-5617). Subway: F, V to Lower East Side–Second Ave. **Open** *Mon–Thu 6–10:30pm; Fri, Sat 6–11:30pm.* **Average main course** *$25.* **Credit** *AmEx, MC, V.*

After eight years of serving sexy cocktails and tasty meze to a fashionable downtown crowd, Chez Es Saada is still a cool spot for a hot date. Flickering candles abound, and rose petals are sprinkled nightly around the sultry first-floor bar and throughout the underground dining room. The menu now encompasses delights like Armenian *manti* (lamb-stuffed dumplings served with tangy yogurt) and ravishing, fall-off-the-bone beef short ribs simmered with dried fruit and spices. Even traditional items like chicken shawarma get a twist, arriving on a platform of house-made pita topped with hummus and tomato confit. Linger late on weekends and your dessert may come with a glitzy belly dance.

Chickpea
23 Third Ave at St. Marks Pl (1-212-254-9500). Subway: N, R, W to 8th St–NYU; 6 to Astor Pl. **Open** *Mon–Wed 8am–3am; Thu–Sat 10am–4am; Sun 10am–1am.* **Average sandwich** *$3.* **Credit** *AmEx, MC, V.*

Desperate for a crowd-pleasing name, this snappy little restaurant held a much publicized contest for its moniker. The pita is a bit chewy, but the bright-green falafel—packed with cilantro and parsley—is wonderful, as is the hybrid "shawafel" (a combo of spit-grilled lamb shawarma and falafel patties).

Pan-Asian

Bao 111

111 Ave C between 7th and 8th Sts (1-212-254-7773). Subway: F, V to Lower East Side–Second Ave. **Open** *Mon–Sat 6pm–2am; Sun 6pm–midnight.* **Average main course** *$18.* **Credit** *AmEx, MC, V.*

Judging by its live jazz, crowded bar and Vietnamese-fusion menu, Bao 111 could easily be mistaken for an expat hangout in Hong Kong. Start with the dreamy house cocktail (banana rum, mango and lime) or lemongrass-infused sake, followed by coconut-tempura shrimp, ginger-infused braised chicken, or crispy frog legs with basil mayonnaise, all presented with gracious flair. The famed grilled short ribs on lemongrass skewers are reason enough to wander into the depths of Alphabet City.

Other location *Bao Noodles, 391 Second Ave between 22nd and 23rd Sts (1-212-725-7770).*

Seafood

The Mermaid Inn

96 Second Ave between 5th and 6th Sts (1-212-624-5870). Subway: F, V to Lower East Side–Second Ave. **Open** *Sun–Thu 5–11pm; Fri, Sat 5pm–midnight.* **Average main course** *$16.* **Credit** *AmEx, DC, Disc, MC, V.*

The menu changes seasonally, but locals come back for the fabulous, well-stuffed lobster roll, which eschews the usual hot-dog bun for a wrapping of toasted brioche. Spaghetti with shrimp, scallops and calamari in a spicy marinara sauce topped with arugula is another must-have. Everything's even better in the summer, when you can idle in the pleasant back garden.

Thai

The Elephant

58 E 1st St between First and Second Aves (1-212-505-7739). Subway: F, V to Lower East Side–Second Ave. **Open** *Sun–Thu noon–3:45pm, 5:30pm–midnight; Fri, Sat noon–3:45pm, 5:30pm–1am.* **Average main course** *$15.* **Credit** *AmEx.*

Red walls, leopard-print banquettes and Asian-themed artwork lend a Bangkok-meets-Paris feel to this popular East Village spot, which serves mild, user-friendly Thai with an occasional French twist. Crab cakes, lively with cilantro, come with a sizable green-papaya salad. Seafood dishes—steamed sea bass with grilled eggplant and sautéed baby spinach, barbecued fillet of salmon, steamed mussels—are exceedingly good. Fans of key lime pie will like the lighter-than-air lemongrass tart.

Vegetarian & Organic

Angelica Kitchen

300 E 12th St between First and Second Aves (1-212-228-2909). Subway: L to First Ave; N, Q, R, W, 4, 5, *6 to 14th St–Union Sq.* **Open** *11:30am–10:30pm daily.* **Average main course** *$10.* **Credit** *Cash only.*

This vegetarian mecca has been around since hippie was hip, and the neither the vibe nor the quality of the clever dishes has changed much. A 34-term cheat sheet on the back of the menu explains what *umeboshi* and kombu are and why they're good for you. The Pantry Plate is a sampler of starters like walnut-lentil pâté, pickled seasonal vegetables, or couscous-and-vegetable salad tossed in cilantro vinaigrette. You might think you're chowing on a Reuben sandwich when you bite into the fresh sourdough baguette layered with thick slices of marinated, baked tempeh and homemade mushroom gravy; it's served with raw spinach, ruby kraut and mashed potatoes.

Greenwich Village

American

Peanut Butter & Co.

240 Sullivan St between Bleecker and W 3rd Sts (1-212-677-3995). Subway: A, C, E, B, D, F, V to W 4th St. **Open** *Sun–Thu 11am–9pm; Fri, Sat 11am–10pm.* **Average sandwich** *$6.* **Credit** *AmEx, DC, Disc, MC, V.*

Nutella-bred Europeans may recoil in horror, but to Americans, nothing says "happy childhood" like a peanut-butter sandwich. Every day, the staff grinds a fresh batch of peanut butter, which is used to create gooey mood-pacifiers like the popular Elvis—the King's infamous grilled favorite of peanut butter, banana and honey. Owner Lee Zalben confesses to a weakness for the warm sandwich of cinnamon-raisin peanut butter, vanilla cream cheese and tart apple slices. Goober-free menu items, like tuna melts and bologna sandwiches, continue the brown-bag theme. For dessert, Death by Peanut Butter is a landslide of ice cream, Peanut Butter Cap'n Crunch, peanut-butter chips and peanut-butter sauce.

American Creative

Blue Hill

75 Washington Pl between Washington Sq West and Sixth Ave (1-212-539-1776). Subway: A, C, E, B, D, F, V to W 4th St. **Open** *Mon–Sat 5:30–11pm; Sun 5:30–10pm.* **Average main course** *$25.* **Credit** *AmEx, DC, MC, V.*

Chefs Dan Barber and Michael Anthony succeed so consistently because of their solid foundation in classical French cooking and a knack for scoring the best local produce year-round. When in season, Blue Hill's strawberries have more berry flavor, and its heirloom tomatoes are juicier, than anywhere else. The poached foie gras, duck breast in beurre blanc, tender roasted chicken and mango sorbet could inspire poetry. Blue Hill is a restaurateur's restaurant with a simple, handsome dining room and knowledgeable, unintimidating service.

Eat, Drink, Shop

Italian

Babbo

110 Waverly Pl between MacDougal St and Sixth Ave (1-212-777-0303). Subway: A, C, E, B, D, F, V to W 4th St. **Open** *Mon–Sat 5:30–11:30pm; Sun 5–11pm.* **Average main course** *$27.* **Credit** *AmEx, Disc, MC, V.*

Regulars know that ordering gets more frustrating with each visit. Once you taste a Babbo dish, you have to order it again. So you're either "stuck" with lamb's-tongue salad painted with the thick yolk of a poached egg, or saucy parcels of beef-cheek ravioli—or you'll have to spring for more than you could possibly eat at one sitting. Who can blame you? Mario Batali's fluffy gnocchi are blanketed with tender shreds of oxtail; Two-Minute Calamari—a red soup exploding with caper berries and rings of white squid—is a bowlful of fireworks. Have it all, then throw in the *frittelle di* ricotta with caramelized banana, gelato and chocolate sauce.

Korean

Mandoo Bar

71 University Pl between 10th and 11th Sts (1-212-358-0400). Subway: L, N, Q, R, W, 4, 5, 6 to 14th St–Union Sq. **Open** *Mon–Thu 11:30am–11pm; Fri, Sat 11:30am–midnight; Sun noon–11pm.* **Average main course** *$10.* **Credit** *AmEx, MC, V.*

In its brighter, hipper new location in the Village, the popular Mandoo Bar can now justify the second part of its name. The amply equipped slate bar on the ground floor is flanked by flat-screen televisions that loop the DVD du jour. Well-prepared *mandoo,* or Korean dumplings, remain the centerpiece at both branches. (Try one of the $8 lunch-box specials.) Follow them with mouthwatering *bulgogi* or exceptional *jap chae,* made with sweet-potato (instead of the typical glass) noodles. The unusually delicious cheesecake comes in soy and almond varieties. **Other location** *2 W 32nd St between Fifth Ave and Broadway (1-212-279-3075).*

Pizza

John's Pizzeria

278 Bleecker St between Sixth and Seventh Aves (1-212-243-1680). Subway: A, C, E, B, D, F, V to W 4th St. **Open** *Mon–Sat 11:30am–11:30pm; Sun noon–11:30pm.* **Average large pizza** *$14.* **Credit** *Cash only.*

This is NYC pizza at its best: It's made in an old coal-fired oven, and it has a chewy, thin crust that's properly charred in spots and layered with just enough sauce and cheese. If you need some meat to go with your 'za, the pepperoni is fantastic, as are the killer meatballs in tomato sauce. The setting is classic pizza-parlor—well-worn wooden booths, old newspaper clippings extolling the virtues of John's pie, and the requisite misty murals of the old country.

Other locations *260 W 44th St between Broadway and Eighth Ave (1-212-391-7560); 408 E 64th St between First and York Aves (1-212-935-2895).*

Seafood

Cru

24 Fifth Ave at Ninth St (1-212-529-1700). Subway: A, C, E, B, D, F, V to W 4th St; N, R, W to 8th St–NYU. **Open** *Tue–Sat 5:30–11pm.* **Average main course** *$34.* **Credit** *AmEx, MC, V.*

When Washington Park, cheffed by hotshot Jonathan Waxman, closed abruptly at the end of 2003, owner Roy Welland suddenly had an empty lot and an incredible stash of wine in the cellar. Now the 62-seat space has been completely transformed into a quieter, more elegant restaurant. Of the 3,000 or so bottles on the 200-page wine list, a third are Burgundies—a versatile match for modern European dishes like *tagliarini* with squid, and assorted *crudo* like fluke and arctic char. A front lounge doubles as a wine bar and tasting room; walk-ins and solo diners can mingle at the communal counter.

West Village & Meatpacking District

American

Corner Bistro

331 W 4th St at Jane St (1-212-242-9502). Subway: A, C, E to 14th St; L to Eighth Ave. **Open** *11:30am–4am daily.* **Average burger** *$5.* **Credit** *Cash only.*

A Corner Bistro burger is cheap, delish and no-frills, and served on a flimsy paper plate tossed on a scuffed-up bar table. To get your hands on one (and you *will* need both hands), you may have to wait in line for a good hour, especially on weekend nights. Fortunately, several two-dollar drafts are offered, the game is on the tube, and a jukebox covers everything from Calexico to Coltrane. The cheeseburger is just $4.75, but you might as well go for the legendary Bistro Burger, a fat patty of gloriously broiled beef topped with cheese and several strips of supersmoky bacon for $5.50. Skip the watery chili and so-so fries; it's all about the beef.

Cafés

A Salt & Battery

112 Greenwich Ave between 12th and 13th Sts (1-212-691-2713). Subway: A, C, E to 14th St; L to Eighth Ave. **Open** *noon–10pm daily.* **Average main course** *$10.* **Credit** *AmEx, MC, V.*

The name is one of the most painful restaurant puns ever. But A Salt & Battery is about as authentic as any non-U.K. fish-and-chips joint could be. The batter is light and crisp, the cod is tender, and the chips are Brit-style soggy, even before you douse them with malt vinegar. Stick with the basic cod or try the

Technicolor dream dumplings are ripe for the picking at **Mandoo Bar**. *See p180.*

more intensely flavored chunks of batter-fried cod roe—wrapped in a London newspaper. At the larger East Village location, you can bite into savory pies or slog happily through an all-day fried breakfast. **Other location** *80 Second Ave between 4th and 5th Sts (1-212-254-6610).*

Tea & Sympathy
108–110 Greenwich Ave between 12th and 13th Sts (1-212-989-9735). Subway: A, C, E to 14th St; L to Eighth Ave. **Open** *Mon–Fri 11:30am–10:30pm; Sat 9:30am–10:30pm; Sun 9:30am–10pm.* **Average main course** *$11.* **Credit** *MC, V.*
You'll get excellent tea at this tiny, tightly packed British emporium, but the waitresses are usually saucy rather than sympathetic. The food is manna for homesick Brits: shepherd's pie, bangers and mash, Heinz canned spaghetti on toast, buttery Cornish pasties, and a Sunday dinner of roast beef and Yorkshire pudding. The Stilton-and-walnut salad is commendable, as are moreish nursery desserts like sticky toffee pudding and apple crumble. But the local favorite is the classic afternoon tea, a $20 spread that includes a wide selection of teas

(brewed properly, in a pot), finger sandwiches, cakes, and scones with clotted cream and jam.

Eclectic

August
359 Bleecker St between Charles and W 10th Sts (1-212-929-4774). Subway: 1, 9 to Christopher St. **Open** *Mon–Thu 5:30pm–midnight; Fri 5:30pm–1am; Sat 11am–4pm, 5:30pm–1am; Sun 11am–4pm, 5:30pm–midnight.* **Average main course** *$15.* **Credit** *AmEx, MC, V.*
This narrow little restaurant gets the urban-rustic thing just right. A glowing wood-burning oven at the back of the cozy dining room is the source of many of the best dishes here: Alsatian *tarte flambée* (a puffy flatbread slathered with caramelized onions, bacon and crème fraîche); pillowy little gnocchi baked with sausage, broccoli rabe and walnuts; and succulent rabbit with bread stuffing. But the downstairs kitchen deserves kudos, too: Spaghetti carbonara is pure bacony bliss, and little crunchy-creamy ham croquettes are irresistible. For dessert, try the chocolate-drenched profiteroles or a

Chefs' secrets revealed!

Sure they can can cook, but where do they eat?

What's your favorite after-work spot?

"Blue Ribbon, because they're open really late, and usually, that's when I'm eating."
Sue Torres, chef-owner, Sueños. *See p187.*

Where do you go when you're in the mood for classic New York?

"Katz's Deli. I can't get that anywhere but New York."
Luigi Comandatore, owner, Bread and Bread Tribeca. *See p167.*

Where do you go when you have company in town?

"The Red Cat. The food is dressed up enough so it feels like an occasion, but simple enough so it still feels like you're eating real food."
Lee Zalben, founder, Peanut Butter & Co. *See p179.*

Where do you like to go for a date?

"The Four Seasons. If I were on a date with my wife, that's where I'd go. It's the ultimate New York experience. I think it's a perfect place."
Jonathan Waxman, chef, Barbuto. *See p184.*

Spotted Pig.

Can't deal with the line at nearby Pastis? Duck into sweet little Paradou and you'll soon be surrounded by hydrangea and ivy in the back garden, sharing creations like the *tartine* sampler (tiny toasts topped with delightful homemade spreads) or savory buckwheat crêpes. Dessert crêpes are lavished with chestnut cream or chocolate. Good news for folks who club at neighboring Cielo: Paradou now offers a scaled-down menu on Friday and Saturday after 1:30am (the spicy merguez sandwich should get you back on your feet again).

Italian

Barbuto

775 Washington St between Jane and W 12th Sts (1-212-924-9700). Subway: A, C, E to 14th St; L to Eighth Ave. **Open** *Mon–Fri 8am–3pm, 5:45pm–midnight; Sat 5:45pm–midnight; Sun 2–9:30pm.* **Average main course** *$18.* **Credit** *AmEx, Disc, MC, V.*
Owner Fabrizio Ferri (who runs the Industria Superstudio complex) teamed with chef Jonathan Waxman to create a season-driven kitchen anchored by both a brick and a wood oven. Most entrées are priced under $20, and the earthy cooking is top-notch. Marvelously light calamari comes in lemon-garlic sauce; *chitarra all'aia* mixes pasta with crushed walnuts, garlic, olive oil and Parmesan; Vermont veal is perfectly fried. In summer, the garage doors go up and a crowd of stylists, assistants, yuppies and West Village whatevers mob the corner from breakfast until last call.

dish of gelato from the Lower East Side's famed Laboratorio del Gelato. A glassed-in back patio eases the crush.

Spotted Pig

314 W 11th St at Greenwich St (1-212-242-9502). Subway: A, C, E to 14th St; L to Eighth Ave. **Open** *Mon–Fri noon–2am; Sat, Sun 11am–2am.* **Average main course** *$15.* **Credit** *AmEx, MC, V.*
Brick archways, a pressed-tin ceiling and retro farm-animal pictures make this perpetually jammed two-room pub feel like London. Most of the beer is brewed in Brooklyn, and the menu, well, it's actually quite Italian, thanks to consultant Mario Batali and chef April Bloomfield, a bona fide British import from London's highly regarded, Italian-inspired River Café. The small menu changes daily but always includes Bloomfield's melt-in-your-mouth ricotta *gnudi* and rich smoked-haddock chowder, as well as a handful of heartier dishes like pork sausages resting on polenta—a sly spin on bangers and mash.

Japanese

Kirara

33 Carmine St between Bedford and Bleecker Sts (1-212-741-2123). Subway: A, C, E, B, D, F, V to W 4th St. **Open** *Mon–Sat noon–11pm; Sun 2–11pm.* **Average main course** *$18.* **Credit** *AmEx, MC, V.*
The sushi here is quite a hit: slender slices of gleaming fresh fish atop just-the-right-size mounds of vinegar-seasoned rice. Better still, the kitchen sends out its tasty signature corn tea with every meal. Made by boiling dried, roasted corn in water, the slightly sweet tea cleanses the palate and aids digestion. And unlike sake, it won't go to your head.

Sumile

154 W 13th St between Sixth and Seventh Aves (1-212-989-7699). Subway: F, V, 1, 2, 3, 9 to 14th St; L to Sixth Ave. **Open** *Mon–Thu 5:30–10:30pm; Fri, Sat 5:30–11pm.* **Average main course** *$28.* **Credit** *AmEx, MC, V.*
Cool aqua-and-gray tones and Japanese-inspired chairs and hanging lamps set the stage for chef Josh DeChellis, formerly of Bouley. His meticulously executed and brilliantly conceived Asian-influenced small plates ($14 each) include tea-smoked *unagi* on boiled daikon, and poached *hamachi* with pickled melon and nori-spiked salt.

French

Paradou

8 Little W 12th St between Ninth Ave and Washington St (1-212-463-8345). Subway: A, C, E to 14th St; L to Eighth Ave. **Open** *Mon–Wed 4pm–midnight; Thu 4pm–1am; Fri, Sat noon–5:30am; Sun noon–10pm.* **Average main course** *$19.* **Credit** *Disc, MC, V.*

Eat, Drink, Shop

Korean

Do Hwa
55 Carmine St at Bedford St (1-212-414-2815).
Subway: 1, 9 to Houston St. **Open** *Sun, Mon*
5–11pm; Tue–Sat 5pm–midnight. **Average main**
course *$18.* **Credit** *AmEx, Disc, MC, V.*
Classic dishes continue to please at this downtown
destination, whether or not you've cooked them yourself (some tables have built-in barbecues). Newer
items include *duk boki*, sticky-rice cakes sautéed with
vegetables in a red-pepper sauce. Movie-poster menu
covers are a shout-out to Quentin Tarantino, one of
the eatery's co-owners.

Seafood

Pearl Oyster Bar
18 Cornelia St between Bleecker and W 4th Sts (1-212-
691-8211). Subway: A, C, E, B, D, F, V to W 4th St.

Open *Mon–Fri noon–2:30pm, 6–11pm; Sat 6–11pm.*
Average main course *$22.* **Credit** *MC, V.*
Now twice its original size (thanks to a recently
added dining room), Pearl still draws crowds for
chef Rebecca Charles's straightforward New
England–style seafood. The gussied-up lobster
roll—with chunky lobster salad spilling out of a
toasted, butter-drenched hot-dog bun—is her signature dish. Other fishy favorites include fresh
steamers, clam chowder accented with smoky
bacon, pan-roasted oysters and boiled or grilled
whole lobster. Follow these up with a hot-fudge
sundae or a slice of blueberry pie.

Chelsea

American

Cafeteria
119 Seventh Ave at 17th St (1-212-414-1717).
Subway: 1, 9 to 18th St. **Open** *24hrs daily.*

Vegetative state

Whether you're a vegetarian, a vegan or
just a food-lovin' omnivore looking to cool
your jets after a few too many late nights
hoovering diner food, you're in luck—this
tough-talking, hot-dog-chomping city has
become increasingly veg-friendly in the last
few years. And instead of a blissed-out,
ponytailed dude slopping hummus behind
a counter, many of the newly stylish
destinations come with pedigreed celeb
chefs and organic-wine lists.

At **Pure Food and Wine** (54 Irving Pl
between 17th and 18th Sts, 1-212-477-
1010), the city's first upscale raw eatery,
chefs Matthew Kenny and Sarma Melngailis
create standout uncooked dishes like
ginger-spiked avocado rolls and lasagna
layered with marinated vegetables and
fresh basil-pistachio pesto. On Tuesday
nights, the East Village's chic little **Counter**
(105 First Ave between 6th and 7th Sts,
1-212-982-5870) goes raw, with chef
Michele Thorne whipping up special tasting
menus. On other evenings, the kitchen
turns out a delectable mix of raw and
cooked items, including green-curry
tempura, barbecued seitan sandwiches,
curried plantain dumplings and herbed wild-
rice risotto cakes. Much of the produce
used is grown in the owners' rooftop
garden, and the wine list is strictly organic.

Unlike many of the interchangeable
Indian restaurants in what locals have

Black-eyed-pea fritters at **Counter**.

dubbed Curry Hill, **Saravanaas**
(81 Lexington Ave at 26th St, 1-212-
679-0204) is no typical steam-table-buffet
joint. Instead, at this first American
outpost of a popular South Indian chain,
six chefs make everything to order,
including two-foot-long *dosas,* spicy rice
dishes and house-made breads.

A posh spin-off of the more casual
Candle Café a few blocks away,
Candle 79 (154 E 79th St at Lexington
Ave, 1-212-537-7179) dishes up its
elegant, globally inspired vegetarian fare
in an earth-toned duplex with cushy
mocha-toned banquettes. The menu offers
spiced edamame, squash risotto drizzled
with sherry-pumpkin sauce, porcini
stroganoff, and dark chocolate cake with
peanut-butter mousse.

Eat, Drink, Shop

La Bottega.

Average main course *$17.* Credit *AmEx, DC, Disc, MC, V.*

Artists, celebs and wanna-bes converge on the oh-so-white dining room to give everyone who passes by the once-over. Needless to say, food is not the first thing on their minds. Still, everyone's gotta eat, and Cafeteria sates the design-savvy herds with pricey down-home favorites. Mac and cheese is nearly perfect, with a crumbly crust and a gooey fontina-cheddar interior. Other classics—like gravy-heavy meat loaf served with a tomato-and-red-pepper relish, and a charred, juicy burger with blue cheese—are equally satisfying. If you're on a strictly liquid diet, nourish yourself in the tiny basement bar.

The Red Cat

227 Tenth Ave between 23rd and 24th Sts (1-212-242-1122). Subway: C, E to 23rd St. Open *Mon–Thu 5:30–11pm; Fri, Sat 5:30pm–midnight; Sun 5–10pm.* Average main course *$21.* Credit *AmEx, DC, MC, V.*

Art-world luminaries and London Terrace residents descend on this comfortable, reliable, handsome eatery, which has red walls and crisp white tablecloths. Although the kitchen gives almost every dish an intriguing twist, do not attempt to eat lightly here. The Red Cat specializes in all that's hearty: gargantuan pork chops, Parmesan-covered french fries, extra-juicy shell steak and big-time sweets like banana splits and apple tarts.

American Creative

Amuse

108 W 18th St between Sixth and Seventh Aves (1-212-929-9755). Subway: 1, 9 to 18th St. Open *Mon–Sat noon–midnight.* Average main course *$15.* Credit *AmEx, DC, MC, V.*

Under the direction of chef-owner Gerry Hayden (Aureole, Tribeca Grill), this place has become a sleek dining hall where you order by price ($5, $10, $15, $20). Portions get larger, techniques more refined and ingredients dearer with each increase. Five-dollar fries come with a luscious, eggless béarnaise, and the $10 cumin-spiced pork tortilla is like a barbecue-sauced sloppy joe with bite. On the higher end, juicy, peppered Long Island duck breast is bathed in a deep, dark fig reduction.

Cafés

City Bakery

3 W 18th St between Fifth and Sixth Aves (1-212-366-1414). Subway: L, N, Q, R, W, 4, 5, 6 to 14th St–Union Sq. Open *Mon–Fri 7:30am–7pm; Sat 7:30am–6pm; Sun 9am–6pm.* Salad bar *$12 per pound.* Credit *AmEx, MC, V.*

Although the bakery side is still going strong, most locals come to hit the gorgeously stocked salad bar or sip fresh fruit-spiked lemonade (in summer) or superrich hot chocolate with house-

made marshmallows (in winter). In the morning, don't miss the ravishing croissants (plain and—a City Bakery twist—pretzel) and *pains au chocolat.* And don't even think of leaving without trying the heavenly "melted chocolate" cookie.

Indian

Dimple

11 W 30th St between Fifth Ave and Broadway (1-212-643-9464). Subway: N, R, W to 28th St. Open *Mon–Fri 10:30am–8pm; Sat, Sun 11am–8pm.* Average main course *$5.* Credit *AmEx, Disc, MC, V.*

Dimple's not just Indian, it's kosher and vegetarian, too. All the veggie classics are here, along with superspicy, delicious street food. The crowning glory is the full menu of *chat,* or snacks, such as the sweet-sour, hot-cold mixture of samosa, fried potatoes, chickpeas and yogurt topped with tamarind and mint chutneys.

Italian

La Bottega

Maritime Hotel, 88 Ninth Ave at 17th St (1-212-243-8400). Subway: A, C, E to 14th St; L to Eighth Ave. Open *Mon, Tue 7–11:30am, 5pm–1am; Wed, Thu 7–11:30am, 5pm–2am; Fri 7–11:30am, 5pm–3am; Sat 11am–4pm, 5pm–3am; Sun 11am–4pm, 5pm–1am.* Average main course *$18.* Credit *AmEx, DC, Disc, MC, V.*

Given how popular this place is—especially during summer, when the vast lantern-lit terrace is jammed with a fashionable Euro crowd—the reasonably priced chow is much better than it needs to be. La Bottega has the classic trattoria mix: pasta, meat, fish and pizzas. Truffle oil is liberally sprinkled on starters, from a wet, tangy version of beef carpaccio to a tower of shredded artichoke. Pastas can be uninspired, but entrées such as a spice-dusted *branzino* roasted on a cedar plank match quality with style.

Mexican

Sueños

311 W 17th St at Eighth Ave (1-212-243-1333). Subway: A, C, E to 14th St; L to Eighth Ave; 1, 9 to 18th St. Open *Mon–Sat 6pm–midnight; Sun 11:30am–3:30pm, 6pm–midnight.* Average main course *$18.* Credit *AmEx, MC, V.*

Sue Torres (formerly of Rocking Horse Cafe and Hell's Kitchen) combines fiestalike hot-pink and pumpkin-orange decor, glammed-up margaritas and a $50 daredevil chili-tasting menu with authentic Mexican food (a woman stands on a platform in the dining room mashing avocados for guacamole and cranking out handmade tortillas to order). Lively dishes include goat-cheese empanadas in smoky jalapeño coulis, chorizo quesadillas and red snapper wrapped in a banana leaf.

Eat, Drink, Shop

Pan-Asian

Biltmore Room

290 Eighth Ave between 24th and 25th Sts (1-212-807-0111). Subway: C, E to 23rd St. **Open** *Mon–Thu noon–2:30pm, 6–10:30pm; Fri noon–2:30pm, 6–11:30pm; Sat 6–11:30pm; Sun 6–10:30pm.* **Average main course** *$28.* **Credit** *AmEx, DC, MC, V.*
Named after a legendary hotel, the Biltmore Room lives up to the swanky promise implicit in its name. The dining room shimmers with crystal chandeliers, mirrors, brass doors, and marble floors and columns. On the Asian-inspired menu: Goan-spiced rack of lamb, giant prawns wrapped in crispy noodles and Indian-spiced Alaskan salmon. Making hot post-dessert plans? Retire to the designated cell-phone booth, a soundproof brass vestibule with a beige leather interior.

Sapa

43 W 24th St between Broadway and Sixth Ave (1-212-929-1800). Subway F, V, N, R, W to 23rd St. **Open** *Mon–Thu 5:30–11:30pm; Fri, Sat 5:30pm–12:30am; Sun 5:30–10:30pm.* **Average main course** *$24.* **Credit** *AmEx, Disc, MC, V.*
The savvy AvroKo design team, fresh from its success with Public in Nolita, has designed another gorgeous, immaculate dining room—a perfect setting for inventive cocktails, a sexy crowd and a French-Vietnamese menu by chef Patricia Yeo. Sapa's "roll bar" serves variations on spring and summer rolls, including ones with raw wild salmon and cucumber, or foie gras and duck. Among the adventurous main dishes are cider-braised monkfish, and scallops marinated in cane sugar.

Gramercy & Flatiron

American Creative

Craftbar

47 E 19th St between Broadway and Park Ave South (1-212-780-0880). Subway: N, R, W, 6 to 23rd St. **Open** *Sun–Thu noon–11pm; Fri, Sat noon–midnight.* **Average main course** *$25.* **Credit** *AmEx, DC, Disc, MC, V.*
Tucked between Tom Colicchio's superachieving oldest child (Craft) and happy-go-lucky baby (sandwich shop 'wichcraft), middle kid Craftbar matches the top-notch ingredients of the former with the snack-and-munch cheer of the latter. The long, narrow dining room is positively raucous, the busy bar is jammed with chatty drinkers, and the chunky wooden tables are filled with wine-swigging groups. Appetizers rate highest, especially a lavish platter of Italian, Spanish and house-cured meats and the addictive pork-stuffed sage leaves. Desserts like chocolate *pot de crème* and steamed lemon pudding are sheer heaven.
Other locations *Craft, 43 E 19th St between Broadway and Park Ave South (1-212-780-0880); 'wichcraft, 49 E 19th St between Broadway and Park Ave South (1-212-780-0577).*

Gramercy Tavern

42 E 20th St between Broadway and Park Ave South (1-212-477-0777). Subway: N, R, W, 6 to 23rd St. **Open** *Mon–Thu noon–2pm, 5:30–10pm; Fri noon–2pm, 5:30–11pm; Sat 5:30–11pm; Sun 5:30–10pm.* **Three-course prix fixe** *$72.* **Credit** *AmEx, DC, Disc, MC, V.*
Fronted by exec chef John Schaefer, this longtime favorite continues to produce top-notch food, served in a lively setting geared for big-city pampering. The ever-changing menu delights with dishes like sea-urchin-and-crabmeat ragout, braised lamb and ricotta *raviolini* over roasted shallots, and salt-baked salmon with sweet corn. As always, the servers are able to answer any question and intuit any need. Pastry star Claudia Fleming has moved on, but current dessert chef Michelle Antonishek upholds the restaurant's standard for superb sweets. If money (and time) is no object, splurge on one of the lavish seven-course tasting menus.

American Regional

Blue Smoke

116 E 27th St between Park Ave South and Lexington Ave (1-212-243-4020). Subway: 6 to 28th St. **Open** *Mon–Wed 11:30am–11pm; Thu–Sat noon–1am.* **Average main course** *$16.* **Credit** *AmEx, DC, Disc, MC, V.*
Barbecue is a hot topic in Manhattan these days, and Danny Meyer's sophisticated joint is a top contender. Chef Kenny Callaghan knows his wet sauces and dry rubs: The menu highlights the best of regional barbecue styles, from St. Louis spareribs to Memphis baby backs. You'll also find plenty of surprises like hush puppies with jalapeño marmalade, and barbecued mussels with tomatoes and smoked pork. Devil's food cupcakes are down-home sweet.

French

Les Halles

411 Park Ave South between 28th and 29th Sts (1-212-679-4111). Subway: 6 to 28th St. **Open** *noon–midnight daily.* **Average main course** *$19.* **Credit** *AmEx, DC, Disc, MC, V.*
Is Anthony Bourdain in the kitchen? Fans of the hedonistic celebrity chef's books and TV shows want to know. It's certainly a packed house—loud, cramped and underlit. First clue on what to order: a meat case filled with entrecôte, *filet de boeuf* and *côte d'agneau*. Clue number two: the steak knife at every place setting. The usual suspects fill out the rest of the menu: onion soup, frisée salad with *lardons*, duck confit and *boudin noir*. So, *is* Bourdain at the stove? As the French hostess told us, " 'Ee eez not 'ere. 'Ee eez too famoos." No matter—the flavorful steaks still show his flair. The restaurant recently added a gourmet market next door.
Other location *15 John St between Broadway and Nassau St (1-212-285-8585).*

Ixta.

Indian

Dévi

8 E 18th St at Fifth Ave (1-212-691-1300).
Subway: N, R, W, 6 to 23rd St. **Open** *Mon–Thu*
noon–2:30pm, 5:30–10:30pm; Fri, Sat noon–
2:30pm, 5:30–11pm; Sun 5:30–10:30pm. **Average**
main course *$21.* **Credit** *AmEx, Disc, MC, V.*
Dangling from the ceiling like clusters of shiny hard
candies, ornate multicolored lanterns cast a warm
glow over diners, who are surrounded by gauzy saffron draperies in the bi-level dining room. Start with
a citrusy Dévi Fizz cocktail, nibble some crisp
samosas, then pamper yourself with inspired Indian
dishes like velvety yam dumplings in an aromatic
spiced tomato gravy; stuffed baby eggplant bathed
in spicy peanut sauce; or moist chunks of chicken
with pistachios, cilantro and green chilies.

Mexican

Ixta

48 E 29th St between Madison Ave and Park Ave
South (1-212-683-4833). Subway: 6 to 28th St.
Open *Mon–Fri noon–3pm, 5–11pm; Sat, Sun*
5–11pm. **Average main course** *$19.*
Credit *AmEx, Disc, MC, V.*
A modern bistro with a popular tequila bar and front
patio, Ixta combines the best of casual cantinas and
high-end *nuevo mexicano* kitchens. From the former,
it gets its convivial buzz and killer guacamole; from
the latter, its sleek, tropical look and adventurous
recipes. A succulent ceviche duo swims in lime-
brightened broth so good, you'll drink it up like gaz-
pacho. Tender duck is encrusted with pumpkin seeds;
sushi-grade tuna is swathed in earthy tortillas; and a
lighthearted salad marries tender calamari with
banana and sugared walnuts.

Spanish

Casa Mono/Bar Jamón

Casa Mono, 52 Irving Pl at 17th St; Bar Jamón,
125 E 17th St at Irving Pl (1-212-253-2773).
Subway: L to Third Ave; N, Q, R, W, 4, 5, 6 to 14th
St–Union Sq. **Open** *Casa Mono noon–midnight*
daily; Bar Jamón 2pm–2am daily. **Average small**
plate *$9.* **Credit** *AmEx, MC, V.*
Part of Mario Batali's ever-expanding restaurant
spread, this busy (and tiny) tapas restaurant (Bar
Jamón is the equally teeny wine bar around the corner) specializes in making dreaded foods irresistible.
Fried sweetbreads in a nutty batter, oxtail-stuffed
piquillo peppers, baby squid with plump white
beans, tripe with sausage: It's all good, especially
with a glass of wine or sherry from the extensive
Iberian-focused list.

Yes, you get fries with that $29 burger at **DB Bistro Moderne**. *See p191.*

Steakhouse

Wolfgang's Steakhouse

4 Park Ave at 33rd St (1-212-889-3369). Subway: 6 to 33rd St. Open Mon–Fri noon–10pm; Sat 5–10pm. **Average main course** *$35.* **Credit** *AmEx, DC, Disc, MC, V.*

Call it *déjà-jus*: Owner and Peter Luger alum Wolfgang Zweiner (he of the sirloin-thick German accent and moustache) spent 40 years as a waiter at Brooklyn's landmark meatery, and he does things the Luger way. Sliced slabs of deeply satisfying, aged-on-site porterhouse arrive on sizzling platters, and every dessert, be it crème brûlée or key lime pie, comes with a mound of sweetened whipped cream. But Wolfgang's also has much that Luger's lacks: a stunning space in the former Vanderbilt hotel, which is outfitted with a Guastavino-tiled, vaulted ceiling; a choice of cuts (including filet mignon and rib eye); fish for noncarnivores; superior service…and it takes credit cards.

Midtown West

Ethiopian

Meskerem

468 W 47th St between Ninth and Tenth Aves (1-212-664-0520). Subway: C, E to 50th St. Open 11:30am–11pm daily. **Average main course** *$12.* **Credit** *AmEx, Disc, MC, V.*

If you don't mind trekking west across a drab stretch of 47th Street, you'll be rewarded with massive portions of tasty, authentic Ethiopian grub, including *wots* (stews). Go meaty with *tibs wot* (garlicky prime-beef chunks), or meat-free with staples like *misir alecha* (lentils in ginger and garlic), *misir wot* (spicy lentils) and *shiro wot* (spicy chickpeas). The ground-red-pepper mixture *berbere* is the fire in those *wots*—and it's not for the faint of hot, though there's plenty of *injera* bread to soak up the spices. **Other location** *124 MacDougal St between Bleecker and W 3rd Sts (1-212-777-8111).*

French

DB Bistro Moderne

55 W 44th St between Fifth and Sixth Aves (1-212-391-2400). Subway: B, D, F, V to 42nd St–Bryant Park; 7 to Fifth Ave. **Open** *Mon–Sat noon–2:30pm; Sun 5–10pm.* **Average main course** *$27.* **Credit** *AmEx, DC, MC, V.*

Master of haute cuisine Daniel Boulud dresses down at this still-suave two-room spot, where you can order a beer with dinner and you don't have to speak in reverent whispers. Savor buttery, tender little bits of escargot and wild mushrooms, then proceed to the $29 DB Burger (freshly ground sirloin filled with braised, shredded short ribs and foie gras), the famous first salvo of the city's haute-burger wars. It has been one-upped in its own home by a $99 DB Burger Royale, which is topped with freshly shaved black truffle. These aren't exactly bistro prices, but considering Boulud sells $160 tasting menus at Daniel, we'll give him credit for trying. **Other locations** *Café Boulud, 20 E 76th St between Fifth and Madison Aves (1-212-772-2600); Daniel, 60 E 65th St between Madison and Park Aves (1-212-288-0033).*

Per Se

Time Warner Center, 10 Columbus Circle at Broadway, fourth floor (1-212-823-9335). Subway: A, C, B, D, 1, 9 to 59th St–Columbus Circle. **Open** *Mon–Thu 5:30–10pm; Fri, Sat 11:30am–1:30pm, 5:30–10:30pm; Sun 11:30am–1:30pm, 5:30–10pm.* **Prix fixe** *$125–$150.* **Credit** *AmEx, MC, V.*

Thomas Keller, the legendary perfectionist behind California's famed French Laundry, is now working his tasting-menu magic in New York. Even though getting one of the 74 seats in his luxurious restaurant in the Time Warner Center can take hours of speed-dialing (reservations are taken two months in advance), you're very likely to have one of the greatest (and longest) meals of your life. Each dish in the lengthy procession of plates is a jewel of just a few bites, from the initial "salmon cone" (a crisp sesame *tuile* filled with crème fraîche and salmon tartare) through delights like caviar-topped cauliflower panna cotta and butter-poached lobster, followed by whimsical desserts like "coffee and doughnuts," a warm, sugar-coated beignet served with coffee *semifreddo.* A meal with Keller is over-the-top in every way, and the equally over-the-top bill is worth every penny.

Mexican

Hell's Kitchen

679 Ninth Ave between 46th and 47th Sts (1-212-977-1588). Subway: C, E to 50th St. **Open** *Sun, Mon 5–11pm; Tue–Fri 11:30am–3:30pm, 5pm–midnight; Sat 5pm–midnight.* **Average main course** *$18.* **Credit** *AmEx, MC, V.*

This eatery's loose but sophisticated interpretation of Mexican food starts with a complimentary crock of black beans, corn and cilantro drizzled with a creamy poblano sauce—perfect for dipping the thin triangles of sweet corn bread. Plantain empanadas filled with goat cheese swim in pools of tomato coulis, and fig *mole* graces a duck confit. Entrées are sauced-up, too: A potato pancake is piled with mushrooms and goat cheese, and it gets both sweetness and spark from a grape-chipotle sauce.

Middle Eastern

Taboon

773 Tenth Ave at 52nd St (1-212-713-0271). Subway: C, E to 50th St. **Open** *Mon–Thu 6–11pm; Fri 6–11:30pm; Sat noon–3pm, 6–11:30pm; Sun noon–3pm.* **Average main course** *$24.* **Credit** *AmEx, MC, V.*

A *taboon* is a wood-burning clay oven, and the best seats in this restaurant are those overlooking the hearth, where sweet, smoky aromas rise from the baking rosemary bread and the sizzling porterhouse steaks. The cold meze are lovely as well. Try plump grape leaves stuffed with rice, mint and pignoli, or fluffy zucchini cakes with feta, Parmesan, scallions, mint and yogurt. *Malabi,* rose-infused cream scattered with fresh berries and taboon-baked baklava, is a deliciously fruity, creamy and crunchy dessert.

Steakhouse

Keens Steakhouse

72 W 36th St between Fifth and Sixth Aves (1-212-947-3636). Subway: B, D, F, V, N, Q, R, W to 34th St–Herald Sq. **Open** *Mon–Fri 11:45am–3pm, 5:30–10:30pm; Sat 5–10:30pm; Sun 4–8pm.* **Average main course** *$32.* **Credit** *AmEx, DC, Disc, MC, V.*

At 140-year-old Keens, once a private men's club, you get the allure of a New York that is no more. Beveled-glass doors, a working fireplace and a forest's worth of dark wood suggest the days when the legendary "Diamond Jim" Brady piled his table with bushels of oysters, slabs of beef and tankards of ale. Sirloin and porterhouse (for two) hold their own against any steak in the city. Lunch is a bargain in the tavern: A crisp disk of prime-rib hash topped with a fried egg is only $10.

Midtown East

American

P.J. Clarke's

915 Third Ave at 55th St (1-212-317-1616). Subway: E, V to Lexington Ave–53rd St; 6 to 51st St. **Open** *11:30am–3am daily.* **Average main course** *$15.* **Credit** *AmEx, DC, MC, V.*

The celebrated saloon is long in the tooth (120 years old), but a recent face-lift (augmented menu, nightly specials) has revitalized the old boy. The bar up front attracts a pin-striped after-work crowd, while the dining room in back pulls in a slightly more mature,

Eat, Drink, Shop

blazer-wearing set. P.J.'s burger is still honest and juicy; go ahead, customize it with cheese, bacon, chili or béarnaise sauce. Cobb salad, with bright greens and lots of blue cheese, is a meal in itself. As long as your stomach is partying like it's 1959, stick to the classics: Sink your teeth into a slab of cheesecake.

French

Artisanal

2 Park Ave at 32nd St (1-212-725-8585). Subway: 6 to 33rd St. **Open** *Mon–Thu noon–11pm; Fri, Sat noon–midnight; Sun 11am–3pm, 5–10pm.* **Average main course** *$23.* **Credit** *AmEx, MC, V.*
At Artisanal, 250 varieties of cheese—chèvres and cheddars, Gorgonzolas and Gruyères, robiolas and Reblochons—are displayed as if they were prize orchids. Chef-owner Terrance Brennan nods to Alsace with his *boudin blanc,* rillettes and rabbit in riesling with shredded-rutabaga "sauerkraut." Crisp

skate takes to its blood-orange sauce like a party girl to a Cosmopolitan. Still, this is the place to discover just how much cheese you can really handle. An appetizer of raclette? A basket of puffy *gougères*? How about a cheese plate for dessert? About 160 wines in the cellar are available by the glass, all the better to pair with your favorite…cheese.

Indian

Dawat

210 E 58th St between Second and Third Aves (1-212-355-7555). Subway: N, R, W to Lexington Ave–59th St; 4, 5, 6 to 59th St. **Open** *Mon–Sat noon–3pm, 5:30–11pm; Sun 5–10:30pm.* **Average main course** *$19.* **Credit** *AmEx, DC, Disc, MC, V.*
Dawat is perfect for both power lunches and romantic dinners. Indian-food maven Madhur Jaffrey's menu is surprisingly light. Fried appetizers such as *aloo tikkyas* (potato-and-curry-leaf patties with corian-

Grape nuts

Want to get out of that same old cabernet-and-chardonnay rut? New York City's restaurants are on a mission to liven up your drink order, offering innovative, attractively priced wine lists that showcase everything from New York State gems to little-known Italian varietals.

At the West Village's sweet, welcoming **Home Restaurant** (20 Cornelia St between Bleecker and W 4th Sts, 1-212-243-9579), owners David Page and Barbara Shinn don't offer a single French, Italian or even Californian bottle. Instead, their East Coast list focuses on New York State wines, including a merlot from their own vineyard on Long Island. The wines match well with locally inspired dishes like clam chowder, juicy burgers with homemade ketchup, and cider-cured pork roast. A similar passion for local vines can be found at the **Tasting Room** (72 E 1st St between First and Second Aves, 1-212-358-7831), a snug East Village spot whose wine-friendly, shareable dishes are meant to complement an all-American wine list highlighting some of New York's best.

Organic, biodynamic or sustainably grown wines are the focus at several new places, including Matthew Kenney's **Pure Food and Wine** (*see p185* **Vegetative state**) near Union Square; the East Village's sleek little **Counter** (*see p185* **Vegetative state**); and the pint-size but robustly Italian **Quartino Bottega Organica** (11 Bleecker St between Bowery and Broadway, 1-212-529-5133).

To increase your Italian-wine knowledge one glass at a time, start at Tribeca's new **Della Rovere** (250 West Broadway at Beach St, 1-212-334-3470), where owner Billy Doyle's by-the-glass list contains 100 choices that represent all 20 Italian wine regions. At the East Village's **In Vino** (*see p176*), you won't find a Barolo or a Chianti in the place. Instead, Luigi Iasilli has filled his cellar with intriguing Southern Italian choices, including bottles from Sardinia, Sicily, Calabria, Basilicata and Abruzzi.

Making wine more affordable is a surefire way to get bottles on the table. It's definitely working at the casual seafood eatery **Mermaid Inn** (*see p179*), where owners Jimmy Bradley and Danny Abrams have bucked the standard restaurant markup (200 to 300 percent) in favor of a simple $15 on every bottle. At Tribeca's popular **Landmarc** (*see p167*), the 300 bottles on the list are priced barely above retail. None are offered by the glass, but at these prices, you can order a half bottle for what a glass would cost elsewhere.

Brown-bagging your own special bottle is also gaining in popularity. Both **Django** (*see p193*) and **Montrachet** (239 West Broadway between Walker and White Sts, 1-212-219-2777) waive their corkage fees once a week, Django on Saturdays and Montrachet on Mondays. As a result, elegant Montrachet has become a weekly wine-lovers' party, with oenophile patrons bringing in their favorite Burgundies to accompany

der and chili chutneys) are not at all oily; entrées are flavorful without being overseasoned. Don't neglect the seafood: Sweet, moist Parsi-style salmon is smothered with fresh coriander, steamed in a banana leaf, then unwrapped and presented like a gift.

Kosher

Solo

550 Madison Ave between 55th and 56th Sts (1-212-833-7800). Subway: E, V to Fifth Ave–53rd St; 6 to 51st St. **Open** *Mon–Thu noon–2:30pm, 5–11pm; Fri noon–2:30pm; Sat one hour after sundown–midnight; Sun 10am–2pm, 4–10pm.* **Average main course $36. Credit** *AmEx, DC, Disc, MC, V.* Hidden away in the climate-controlled deadness of the Sony Atrium is a new haute-cuisine kosher kitchen, replete with its very own team of eagle-eyed rabbis. Executive chef Hok Chin's Asian-Mediterranean menu sounds beautiful and tastes

better. Duck breast is baked in puff pastry and served on a bed of lightly sautéed pea shoots. Chilean sea bass is perfectly prepared—flaky but not dry under an earthy drizzle of truffle oil. Finish with the warm chocolate cake doused in chocolate sauce. P.S. Men not wearing sports jackets risk being banished to an out-of-the-way corner.

Mediterranean

Django

480 Lexington Ave at 46th St (1-212-871-6600). Subway: 42nd St S, 4, 5, 6, 7 to 42nd St–Grand Central. **Open** *Mon–Fri 11:30am–2pm, 5:30–10:30pm; Sat 6–10:30pm.* **Average main course $26. Credit** *AmEx, DC, Disc, MC, V.* Restaurant-design whiz David Rockwell has created a ground-floor lounge—decorated with lipstick-red walls, cushy low chairs and cascading strings of crystal beads—that's worthy of Scheherazade.

Antipasti at **In Vino**.

contemporary French dishes like roasted whole squab stuffed with truffles. If you really know your grapes, you can take the What's My Wine challenge presented by Montrachet sommelier Bernie Sun. For this blind tasting game, Sun pours a wine in a chosen price range, then asks the taster six

questions (country, region, appellation or village, year, grape and producer). You'll get a discount (around 10 percent off) for every question you answer correctly, and the bottle is free if you get all six right. So far, reports Sun, only one person has completely nailed the quiz.

Eat, Drink, Shop

The chefs at **Taboon** keep the (oven) fires burning in Hell's Kitchen. *See p191.*

Upstairs in the dining room, Cedric Tovar, formerly of Town, brings his mastery of Mediterranean ingredients to fresh sweet-pea soup with *serrano* ham, smoky grilled quail with bruschetta, and a beautifully spiced beef tagine. For a true midnight-at-the-oasis experience, ask for a table under the fabulous draped-fabric tent.

Mexican

Maracas

317 E 53rd St between First and Second Aves (1-212-593-6600). Subway: 6 to 51st St.
Open *Mon–Thu 5–11pm; Fri, Sat 5pm–midnight.*
Average main course *$14.* **Credit** *AmEx, DC, Disc, MC, V.*
This recently opened restaurant is loud, colorful and ready to party. The speakers explode with Spanish rock, the staff serenades diners with maracas, and campy drinks like prickly-pear margaritas come with cactus-shaped stirrers. Native Mexican chef Abraham Flores crafts lively Nuevo Latino dishes: chalupas with black beans, chorizo and cotija cheese; jicama-watercress salad with citrus vinaigrette; and grilled tuna rubbed with ancho-chili powder.

Pan-Asian

Tao

42 E 58th St between Madison and Park Aves (1-212-888-2288). Subway: N, R, W to Fifth Ave–59th St. **Open** *Mon, Tue 11:30am–midnight; Wed–Fri 11:30am–1am; Sat 5pm–1am; Sun 5pm–midnight.* **Average main course** *$22.* **Credit** *AmEx, DC, MC, V.*

A magnificent, scenic palace, Tao is packed to the glowing Chinese lanterns with wealthy businesspeople, trendy Manhattanites and intrepid suburbanites. The bar is eternally thronged, and the stunning dining room has an over-the-top Far Eastern vibe, thanks to curly bamboo, Asian art and a 16-foot, 4,000-pound stone Buddha. The menu—yes, there's food—offers generic small plates (dumplings, satay) and decent entrées. Tao is one of New York's first restaurants to serve kobe beef, and it's worth ponying up for the buttery pleasure of a few ounces, which you cook at your table on a hot stone.

Steakhouse

BLT Steak

106 E 57th St between Park and Lexington Aves (1-212-752-7470). Subway: N, R, W to Lexington Ave–59th St; 4, 5, 6 to 59th St. **Open** *Mon–Thu 11:45am–2:30pm, 5:30–11pm; Fri 11:45am–2:30pm, 5:30–11:30pm; Sat 5:30–11:30pm.*
Average main course *$32.* **Credit** *AmEx, DC, Disc, MC, V.*
Chef Laurent Tourondel mastered fish at Cello; now he's moved on to the meat course. BLT (Bistro Laurent Tourondel) Steak is his interpretation of an American steakhouse, in an elegant room with ebony tables and walnut floors. Traditionalists can get Caesar salad or shrimp cocktail to start, or trust Tourondel's whims and try the beef carpaccio with lemon and arugula, or tuna tartare with soy-lime dressing. The meats are marvelous, if modest—only the 40-ounce porterhouse for two was really humongous—but no one can complain about the selection of sides: eight takes on potato; ten additional vegetables and starches (don't miss

the huge, heavenly onion rings); plus six sauces, including béarnaise and caper-brown butter. True to the chef's lofty pedigree is a foie gras BLT with apple-smoked bacon. It's so good, he named it after himself.

Upper West Side

Delis

Barney Greengrass—
The Sturgeon King
541 Amsterdam Ave between 86th and 87th Sts (1-212-724-4707). Subway: 1, 9 to 86th St. **Open** *Tue–Fri 8:30am–4pm; Sat, Sun 8:30am–5pm.* **Average main course** *$13.* **Credit** *Cash only.*
Although the decor is pretty shabby, this legendary deli and restaurant is always packed for weekend brunch. Egg platters with succulent sturgeon or silky Nova Scotia salmon are a relative bargain at $12, since you won't be hungry again for weeks. The same goes for the sandwiches, such as satiny smoked sablefish on pumpernickel. For tasty sipping, try the cold, creamy pink borscht, served straight up in a glass.

Italian

'Cesca
164 W 75th St between Columbus and Amsterdam Aves (1-212-787-6300). Subway: 1, 2, 3, 9 to 72nd St. **Open** *Restaurant Tue–Thu, Sun 5–11pm; Fri, Sat 5–11:30pm. Wine bar Tue–Thu 5pm–midnight; Fri, Sat 5pm–1am; Sun 5–11pm.* **Average main course** *$27.* **Credit** *AmEx, DC, Disc, MC, V.*
Tom Valenti has done it again: The savvy Italian-American chef has opened another Upper West Side clubhouse for his well-heeled pasta-loving patrons. Start with irresistible Parmesan fritters, marinated baby artichokes with creamy fresh ricotta, or wild-mushroom-studded *arancini* (fried rice balls), then move on to lusty Southern Italian–inspired pastas, followed by great *secondi* like caponata-crusted swordfish or a hunky lamb shank. A more casual menu is offered in the busy wine bar up front.

Lisca
660 Amsterdam Ave at 92nd St (1-212-799-3987). Subway: 1, 2, 3, 9 to 96th St. **Open** *Mon–Sat noon–3pm, 5pm–midnight; Sun noon–3pm, 5–11pm.* **Average main course** *$16.* **Credit** *Cash only.*
The name of this recently opened Tuscan restaurant sounds much more enticing in Italian than it does in English: *Lisca* means "fish skeleton." At Hadi Alavian's 50-seat eatery, the focus is seafood (for example, octopus served with black chickpeas, onions and lemon dressing). Homemade pastas stick to the rustic seafood theme—squid-ink ravioli filled with shrimp, scallops and lobster—as do main courses like whole *branzino,* snapper or halibut roasted in terra-cotta pots. A few meaty items, such as osso bucco and grilled sirloin steak, should keep carnivores from carping.

Mexican

Rosa Mexicano
61 Columbus Ave at 62nd St (1-212-977-7700). Subway: 1, 9 to 66th St–Lincoln Ctr. **Open** *Sun, Mon noon–3pm, 5–10:30pm; Tue–Sat noon–3pm, 5pm–midnight.* **Average main course** *$23.* **Credit** *AmEx, DC, Disc, MC, V.*
The jazzy Technicolor journey up vivid terrazzo steps to the cavernous dining room at Rosa II is a far cry from Rosa's original, comfortably worn-in location on First Avenue. But the famous guacamole is still loaded with fresh cilantro, and zingy mahimahi ceviche is a teetering tower. As the waiter unwraps a parchment package of braised lamb shank, the rich aroma of chili, cumin and clove envelopes the table. Veracruz-style red snapper is stuffed with crab and brightened with a punchy sauce of tomatoes, olives and capers.
Other location *1063 First Ave at 58th St (1-212-753-7407).*

Seafood

Neptune Restaurant &
Bait Bar
511 Amsterdam Ave at 84th St (1-212-496-4100). Subway: 1, 9 to 86th St. **Open** *Mon 5:30–10pm; Tue–Thu 5:30–11pm; Fri 5:30–11:30pm; Sat 11:30am–3pm, 5:30–11:30pm; Sun 11:30am–3pm,*

Onion rings at **BLT Steak**. See p194.

5:30–10pm. **Average main course** $21.
Credit *AmEx, MC, V.*
The owners of downtown's Jane offer inventive seafood amid appealing yachtlike decor. Belly up to the Bait Bar, which serves imaginative $6 *crudo* plates: tender raw yellowtail drizzled with honey; whole dill-and-Dijon-laced wild salmon with blueberries. The blue-crab panna cotta is an ultrarich disk of crab-flecked cream sprinkled with toasted almonds and smoked paprika. A main-course cioppino features lobster-size *langoustines* in a garlicky tomato broth. Cool off with an ice-cream float that's made with locally brewed Boylan's soda and vanilla gelato.

Turkish

Zeytin
519 Columbus Ave at 85th St (1-212-579-1145). Subway: B, C to 86th St. **Open** *Sun–Thu noon–10:30pm; Fri, Sat noon–11:30pm.* **Average main course** $15. **Credit** *AmEx, MC, V.*
Kemal Binici, who formerly ran French and Italian restaurants in this Upper West Side corner space, is finally serving food from his native Turkey. Offerings include a traditional shepherd's salad of roughly chopped ripe tomatoes, cucumbers, red onions and peppers tossed in olive oil and vinegar, plus *patlican salata* (charcoal-grilled eggplant) and assorted kebabs. Draw out the evening with one of the creative house martinis before the meal and a tiny cup of sludgy Turkish coffee after.

Vietnamese

Monsoon
435 Amsterdam Ave at 81st St (1-212-580-8686). Subway: B, C to 81st St–Museum of Natural History; 1, 9 to 79th St. **Open** *Sun–Thu 11:30am–11:30pm; Fri, Sat 11:30am–midnight.* **Average main course** $15. **Credit** *AmEx, MC, V.*
Ceiling fans, bamboo shades and a lush garden mural create a pleasant space for locals to satisfy their cravings for lemongrass, ginger, gingko and aromatic fresh herbs. The seemingly endless selections start with a long list of dim sum and unusual summer rolls. Chicken-mango rolls with wasabi-jalapeño sauce are delicious, as is the more typical beef bun with bean sprouts, scallions and *nuoc cham*. Ginger sneaks in everywhere but is best at dessert, when big, pungent chunks are buried in ice cream.

Upper East Side

American Creative

davidburke & donatella
133 E 61st St between Park and Lexington Aves (1-212-813-2121). Subway: N, R, W to Lexington Ave–59th St; 4, 5, 6 to 59th St. **Open** *Mon–Fri noon–2:30pm, 5–10pm; Sat 5–10:30pm; Sun*

11am–2:30pm, 4:30–9pm. **Average main course** $30. **Credit** *AmEx, DC, Disc, MC, V.*
Don't let the play-with-your-food gimmicks of culinary merry prankster David Burke fool you: This guy knows how to cook. His food runs the gamut from just fine (handmade *garganelli* with seafood) and fantastic (the "Bronx-style" filet mignon of veal) to fabulously silly (a cheesecake-lollipop "tree" with bubble-gum whipped cream). Donatella's surname is not Versace but rather Arpaia; she's a lawyer-turned-restaurateur who manages the vibrant and occasionally overwhelming social scene in the front of the house.

Austrian

Café Sabarsky
Neue Galerie, 1048 Fifth Ave at 86th St (1-212-288-0665). Subway: 4, 5, 6 to 86th St. **Open** *Mon, Wed 9am–6pm; Thu–Sun 9am–9pm.* **Average main course** $14. **Credit** *AmEx, MC, V.*
Come for the culture, stay for the *schlag*? Well, actually, it's the other way around: More of the well-heeled, gray-haired patrons come to the elegant Neue Galerie to visit the Viennese restaurant and pastry palace than to see the collection of German and Austrian art upstairs. Smoked trout and goulash with spaetzle are just preludes to the real works of art—apple strudel swaddled in crackling golden pastry, feather-light quark cheesecake, luscious Sacher torte, and magnificent cream-topped (*mit schlag*) coffee. Breakfast is a particularly serene moment for appreciating the beautifully carved dark-wood walls and the leafy park views.

French

JoJo
160 E 64th St between Lexington and Third Aves (1-212-223-5656). Subway: F to Lexington Ave–63rd St. **Open** *Sun–Thu noon–2:30pm, 5:30–10pm; Fri, Sat noon–2:30pm, 5:30pm–11pm.* **Average main course** $25. **Credit** *AmEx, MC, V.*
At Jean-Georges Vongerichten's most intimate and lovable venue, you'll feel as if you were dining in the celebrity chef's private townhouse. Dishes are crowd-pleasers, but with surprising twists: Nuggets of red and yellow beets are paired fondue-style with a crock of melted goat cheese; foie gras brûlée arrives with a glassy, brittle top. Deep-red chunks of venison are tossed with tangy wild greens and pomegranate seeds, as though the chef had turned his head for a second and the meat threw itself into a salad. Food historians may never agree on the precise origin of the molten chocolate cake, but it might as well have been invented here: It's a divinely gloppy ending.

La Goulue
746 Madison Ave between 64th and 65th Sts (1-212-988-8169). Subway: 6 to 68th St–Hunter College. **Open** *noon–11:30pm daily.* **Average main course** $29. **Credit** *AmEx, DC, MC, V.*

Have a seat, and a view of the Manhattan skyline, at Brooklyn's **Alma**. *See p199.*

One of the best hangouts around is packed with moneyed, well-brushed Upper East Siders. The grand mahogany-paneled bistro has prices to match the neighborhood, but the menu comes with flourishes that lift it above the usual steak-frites territory. Escargots are nestled in creamy custard topped with red-wine sauce; frisée *aux lardons* (a salad that's more bacon and eggs than greens) is properly unctuous. Green-peppercorn sauce swathes a gorgeous slab of beef, while plump, juicy scallops loll on a mound of lobster risotto. For dessert, a lavish puffy chocolate soufflé with ice cream is so indulgent, it seems immoral not to clean your plate.

German

Heidelberg
1648 Second Ave between 85th and 86th Sts (1-212-628-2332). Subway: 4, 5, 6 to 86th St. **Open** *Mon–Sat 11:30am–10:30pm; Sun noon–10pm.* **Average main course** *$15.* **Credit** *AmEx, DC, Disc, MC, V.*
For nearly 50 years, this Yorkville holdover has clung to its roots: dirndl-clad waitresses, men in lederhosen and steins of Spaten. Schaller & Weber, the neighboring butcher, supplies much of the meat; sausage platters are weighted down with *bauernwurst, weisswurst* and bratwurst. Cheese fondue is a perpetual favorite, but there are more adventurous choices, too (pig's knuckles, anyone?). Most dishes

come with spaetzle, sauerkraut or potato salad, but don't fill up—you'll want to try the homemade apple strudel or chocolate fondue.

Japanese

Sushi of Gari
402 E 78th St between First and York Aves (1-212-517-5340). Subway: 6 to 77th St. **Open** *Tue–Sat 5–10:45pm; Sun 5–9:45pm.* **Average sushi meal** *(8 pieces, 1 roll) $20.* **Credit** *AmEx, DC, MC, V.*
Adventurous eaters brave long lines so they can cram into this small place for *omakase* sushi-tasting menus (called Gari's Choice) that run between $70 and $80 a person. Chef Masatoshi Sugio may pair seared foie gras with daikon radish; salmon with tomato and onion; or spicy tuna with mayo, Tabasco and sesame oil. If you want sashimi, pay the extra $13 for the "special" version, which swaps exotic fishes for the usual tuna and yellowtail.
Other location *370 Columbus Ave between 77th and 78th Sts (1-212-362-4816).*

Turkish

Beyoglu
1431 Third Ave at 81st St (1-212-288-0033). Subway: 6 to 77th St. **Open** *noon–11:30pm daily.* **Average main course** *$14.* **Credit** *AmEx, MC, V.*

Nothing says "That's amore!" like a pizza pie at **Grimaldi's**. *See p199.*

The stylish decor is offbeat and whimsical: flower-painted orange and lime-green walls, and tasseled curtains draped across floor-to-ceiling windows. Light *kofta*, made with lentils, red pepper and cracked wheat, are perfect with a squeeze of lemon, and a grilled whole *branzino* is nicely charred but still moist. Finish with squares of buttery baklava.

Above 116th Street

American

Kitchenette Uptown

1272 Amsterdam Ave between 122nd and 123rd Sts (1-212-531-7600). Subway: 1, 9 to 125th St. **Open** *8am–11pm daily.* **Average main course** *$16.* **Credit** *AmEx, DC, MC, V.*
Riding the wave of South Harlem gentrification, Kitchenette Uptown brings Tribeca-style country dining to a sunlit space in Morningside Heights. At brunch, order the BLT on challah—it does cartwheels around the egg dishes. Hearty cheese grits with homemade turkey sausage and biscuits also make a great meal, followed by a down-home slice of cherry pie. All-day breakfast and weekend brunch attract a lively group of university types, as does the BYOB dinner with chicken potpie and four-cheese macaroni.
Other location *Kitchenette, 80 West Broadway at Warren St (1-212-267-6740).*

American Regional

Londel's Supper Club

2620 Frederick Douglass Blvd (Eighth Ave) between 139th and 140th Sts (1-212-234-6114). Subway: B, C to 135th St. **Open** *Tue–Sat 11:30am–4pm, 5–11pm; Sun noon–5pm.* **Average main course** *$20.* **Credit** *AmEx, DC, Disc, MC, V.*
For a Yankee town, New York sure has a lot of soul-food options, and Londel's is one of the choicest. Tuxedoed waiters serve fried chicken that's molar-rattlingly crunchy. The secret: It's fried, then baked. Other standards prove just as tasty, including the cornmeal-crusted whiting fingers, blackened catfish fillet, and mac and cheese topped by ribbons of crisped cheddar. Live jazz on Fridays and Saturdays adds to the good-time vibe.

Caribbean

Native

1161 Malcolm X Blvd (Lenox Ave) at 118th St (1-212-665-2525). Subway: 2, 3 to 116th St. **Open** *Mon–Thu 11am–11pm; Fri, Sat 11am–midnight; Sun 11am–10pm.* **Average main course** *$12.* **Credit** *AmEx, MC, V.*
This loungey, brick-walled restaurant and bar draws a hip Harlem crowd. The small dining room is lined with velvet banquettes and lit with funky wall sconces. The food from chef Brian Washington-Palmer (Bleu Evolution) is just as cool,

and it includes an all-in-one bowl of red rice, black beans, garlicky spinach and fried plantains; spicy blackened snapper; and a seafood cobbler of scallops and crab swimming in coconut-curry broth. Washington-Palmer's take on fried chicken—a panfried cutlet over mashed potatoes and collards in cumin cream sauce—is a successful original.

Brooklyn

American Creative

River Café
1 Water St at Old Fulton St, Dumbo, Brooklyn (1-718-522-5200). Subway: A, C to High St; F to York St. **Open** *Mon–Sat noon–3pm, 5:30–11pm; Sun 11:30am–3pm, 5:30–11pm.* **Prix fixe** *$70.* **Credit** *AmEx, DC, Disc, MC, V.*
From your table aboard a genteel barge anchored at the foot of the Brooklyn Bridge, you can gaze at the twinkling Financial District. The menu adds global elements that make classic American dishes sparkle. Wake up your taste buds with a kicky Taylor Bay scallop ceviche; move on to a pancetta-wrapped black sea bass with fondant potatoes and a briny vinaigrette. The wine list is pricey, but a few affordable offerings and a thoughtful selection of half bottles keep it sober—so you don't have to.

French

À Table
171 Lafayette Ave at Adelphi St, Fort Greene, Brooklyn (1-718-935-9121). Subway: C to Lafayette Ave; G to Fulton St. **Open** *Tue–Thu 11:30am–3:30pm, 5–10:30pm; Fri 11:30am–3:30pm, 5–11:30pm; Sat 10:30am–3:30pm, 5–11:30pm; Sun 10:30am–3:30pm, 5–10:30pm.* **Average main course** *$18.* **Credit** *AmEx, MC, V.*
Lively French banter erupts frequently between patrons and proprietor Jean-Baptiste Caillet in this genial bistro, which is conveniently close to the Brooklyn Academy of Music. A lofty ceiling and wooden tables draped with red-and-white-checked tablecloths make a comfortable setting for pre-concert dinners. Beets, mâche and Roquefort are tossed in a happy threesome; spinach salad with avocado gets a zesty lemon vinaigrette; monkfish is topped by a tangy Provençale sauce of tomatoes and olives. The restaurant's name roughly translates as "dinner's ready," so come and get it!

Italian

al di là
248 Fifth Ave at Carroll St, Park Slope, Brooklyn (1-718-783-4565). Subway: M, R to Union St. **Open** *Mon, Wed, Thu 6–10:30pm; Fri, Sat 6–11pm; Sun 6–10pm.* **Average main course** *$16.* **Credit** *MC, V.*
Superb food, a small storefront dining room and a

no-reservations policy add up to a wait no matter when you arrive. But it's worth hanging around; husband-and-wife team Emiliano Coppa and Anna Klinger (the chef) prepare serious Northern Italian fare and serve it with uncommon grace and good nature. Entrées include diaphanous ravioli stuffed with beets and ricotta, and braised rabbit with black olives and polenta. The *gianduiotto*—a log of chocolate ice cream, chopped hazelnuts and whipped cream—is unbeatable.

Miss Williamsburg Diner
206 Kent Ave between Metropolitan Ave and North 3rd St, Williamsburg, Brooklyn (1-718-963-0802). Subway: L to Bedford Ave. **Open** *Tue–Sun 6–11pm.* **Average main course** *$14.* **Credit** *Cash only.*
The look is pure Americana—the restaurant is located in a classic 1940s diner—but the flavors are richly Italian. The *affettati*, an appetizer sampler of cured meats, includes paper-thin *speck*, prosciutto and mortadella. Bubbling-hot lasagna is drenched in creamy béchamel sauce, and red snapper is matched with a surprising variety of stewed vegetables. Cloudlike gnocchi "soufflé" is worth the trip across the bridge. A fenced-in flower garden welcomes alfresco dining. **Other location** *Miss Williamsburg Porta Via, 228 E 10th St between First and Second Aves (1-212-228-5355).*

Mexican

Alma
187 Columbia St at DeGraw St, Cobble Hill, Brooklyn (1-718-643-5400). Subway: F, G to Carroll St. **Open** *Mon, Wed, Thu 6–10:30pm; Fri, Sat 6–11pm; Sun 6–10pm.* **Average main course** *$15.* **Credit** *MC, V.*
From the subway, it's a long walk west (when you get to the far side of the Brooklyn-Queens Expressway overpass, you're almost there), but if you want to chill with local margarita-lovin' arty types, skip Smith Street's bistros-by-the-dozen and head over to this sexy Mexi spot. Have a drink (or shoot a game of pool) at ground-floor bar, B61, then head upstairs to Alma's colorful dining room. In good weather, snag a table on the rooftop deck, which offers great industrial-chic views of the Brooklyn waterfront and the downtown Manhattan skyline. Citrusy ceviche of shrimp, scallop and bass has a hint of jalapeño; a side of black beans with sticky, luscious sautéed plantains is pure South-of-the-Border comfort. You can get traditional favorites (enchiladas, fajitas) along with *nuevo* creations like grilled duck breast with tomatoes and roasted peanuts.

Pizza

Grimaldi's
19 Old Fulton St between Front and Water Sts, Dumbo, Brooklyn (1-718-858-4300). Subway: A, C to High St; F to York St. **Open** *Mon–Thu 11:30am–11pm; Fri 11:30am–midnight; Sat*

noon–midnight; Sun noon–11pm. **Large plain pizza** *$14.* **Credit** *Cash only.*

Long before the area was called Dumbo, Patsy Grimaldi was rotating pies in the 800-degree brick-walled coal oven. (He learned his trade from *the* Patsy, his uncle Patsy Lancieri.) The area's influx of professionals (and their pizza-loving offspring) can make it hard to get a table on weekends. Still, the excellent pizzas are worth the wait.

Steakhouse

Peter Luger

178 Broadway at Driggs Ave, Williamsburg, Brooklyn (1-718-387-7400). Subway: J, M, Z to Marcy Ave. **Open** *Sun–Thu 11:30am–10pm; Fri, Sat 11:30am–11pm.* **Steak for two** *$65.* **Credit** *Debit cards or cash only.*

Does this Williamsburg landmark deserve its rep as one of the best steakhouses in America? A four-star experience this isn't, but the quality of the beef may make you forgive any shortcomings. Established as a German beer hall in 1887, the restaurant serves only one cut: a porterhouse that's charbroiled black on the outside, tender and pink on the inside. Service is slow, provided by crusty waiters who would rather give out wisecracks than water. Remember to stuff your wallet before you stuff your face; Luger's doesn't take credit cards (although it will accept debit cards).

Thai

SEA Thai Restaurant and Bar

114 North 6th St at Berry St, Williamsburg, Brooklyn (1-718-384-8850). Subway: L to Bedford Ave. **Open** *Mon–Thu 11:30am–1am; Fri, Sat 11:30am–2am.* **Average main course** *$9.* **Credit** *AmEx, MC, V.*

You may mistake SEA for a nightclub, given the reverberating dance music and a mod lounge com-

Tax and tipping

Most New York restaurants don't add a service charge to the bill unless there are six or more people in your party. So it's customary to give 15 to 20 percent of the total bill as a tip. The easiest way to figure out the amount is to double the 8.625 percent sales tax. Complain—preferably to a manager—if you feel the service is under par, but only in the most extreme cases should you completely withhold a tip. Remember that servers are paid far below minimum wage and rely on tips to pay the rent. Bartenders get tipped, too; $1 a drink should ensure friendly pours until last call.

plete with bubble-chair swing. Get a table by the reflecting pool, which is presided over by Buddha, and flip through the campy postcard menu—surprise! For a place so stylin', prices are cheap and the food is remarkably good. Stuffed with shrimp and real crab, Jade Seafood Dumplings come with a nutty Massaman sauce, while the Queen of Siam beef with basil and red chili is best when you ask the kitchen to fire it up.

Other location *SEA, 75 Second Ave between 4th and 5th Sts (1-212-228-5505).*

American Creative

LIC Café

5-48 49th Ave between Vernon Blvd and 5th St, Long Island City, Queens (1-718-752-0282). Subway: 7 to Vernon Blvd–Jackson Ave. **Open** *Mon, Tue noon–4pm; Wed–Sat noon–4pm, 6–10pm.* **Average main course** *$14.* **Credit** *AmEx, MC, V.*

LIC Café's owner, French-trained caterer Peter Yurasits, serves his inventive yet inexpensive cuisine to an avid audience. At this comfortably modern, clubby little eatery, tablehopping, BYOB-sharing and CD requests are the norm, as are flavorful takes on familiar dishes like pesto pasta, crab cakes and teriyaki salmon.

Greek

Cávo

42-18 31st Ave between 42nd and 43rd Sts, Astoria, Queens (1-718-721-1001). Subway: G, R, V to Steinway St. **Open** *Mon–Sat 5pm–2am; Sun noon–4am.* **Average main course** *$18.* **Credit** *AmEx, MC, V.*

Cávo's sprawling outdoor patio is enclosed by tall mosaics of limestone and polished blue pebbles, and water cascades down one of the walls. It makes the ideal setting for sampling a few meze (like the perfectly fried seafood in a light chickpea batter) and a glass of fruit-packed sangria. Every generous plate—seafood pasta, veal chop—is super delicious. After 11pm, Cávo morphs into a nightclub that's packed with young Astorians.

Indian

Ashoka

74-14 37th Ave between 74th and 75th Sts, Jackson Heights, Queens (1-718-898-5088). Subway: E, F, V, G, R to Jackson Hts–Roosevelt Ave; 7 to 74th St–Broadway. **Open** *11:30am–10:15pm daily.* **Average main course** *$8.* **Credit** *AmEx, MC, V.*

Local Indian diners flock here, as do adventurous gourmands tired of the crowds at the nearby (and some say overhyped) Jackson Diner. Ashoka's lunch and dinner buffets present the standard dishes; the à la carte menu offers a variety of regional main-

Dive into the tasty offerings at **SEA Thai Restaurant and Bar** in Williamsburg. *See p200.*

stays. Full-flavored meat and vegetable dishes complement breads such as *gobi* (cauliflower-filled) nan.

Latin American

Fatty's Cafe

25-01 Ditmars Blvd at Crescent St, Astoria, Queens (1-718-762-7071). Subway: N, W to Astoria–Ditmars Blvd. **Open** *Mon–Thu 2–11pm; Fri 2pm–midnight; Sat 11am–midnight; Sun 11am–10pm.* **Average main course** *$9.* **Credit** *Cash only.*

Thanks to the ministrations of Dominican owner-bartender Fernando Peña and his partner Suzanne Furboter, displaced Manhattanites and borough-trekking visitors in Astoria now have a hip watering hole. Fatty's Cafe serves jalapeño turkey burgers, grilled cheese sandwiches, creative takes on Cuban pressed sandwiches and some of the best mojitos around. On weekends, the kitchen whips up a stellar brunch.

Bronx

French

Le Refuge Inn

620 City Island Ave at Sutherland St, City Island, Bronx (1-718-885-2478). Travel: 6 to Pelham Bay Park, then take the Bx29 bus to Sutherland St. **Open** *Tue–Sat 6–9pm; Sun noon–3pm, 6–9pm.* **Prix fixe** *$45.* **Credit** *AmEx.*

A French country inn on an island...in the Bronx? Bask in the Gallic charm of this sweet bed-and-breakfast inn and restaurant on City Island. Dine fireside or overlooking the harbor. As the name implies, you'll feel far, far away from the city as you choose between French classics like truffled duck-liver mousse or snails in puff pastry, followed by pan-seared striped bass, bouillabaisse or filet mignon. Profiteroles, crème brûlée, and chocolate mousse torte ensure a sweet ending.

Bars

In a city of 5,000 pubs, taverns and more, there are mixed blessings galore.

Need to wet your whistle? You've come to the right town: Almost 5,000 watering holes keep the booze, whether flutes of French champagne or steins of Belgian brew, flowing till dawn.

Downtown

Tribeca & south

Bridge Cafe
279 Water St at Dover St (1-212-227-3344). Subway: A, C to Broadway–Nassau St; J, M, Z, 2, 3, 4, 5 to Fulton St. Open Sun, Mon 11:45am–10pm; Tue–Thu 11:45am–11pm; Fri 11:45am–midnight; Sat 5pm–midnight. Average drink $8. Credit AmEx, DC, Disc, MC, V.
New York's oldest restaurant and bar (1794) is tucked in the shadow of the Brooklyn Bridge. History resounds in the original pressed-tin ceiling and grand oak bar. Monday through Wednesday, the entire 90-bottle, all-American wine list is slashed 30 percent, and each selection is available by the glass at any time. A full menu (American creative) is featured at the bar.

Dekk
134 Reade St between Greenwich and Hudson Sts (1-212-941-9401). Subway: 1, 2, 3, 9 to Chambers St. Open Mon–Fri 11am–4am; Sat, Sun 10am–4am. Average drink $8. Credit AmEx, MC, V.
Decorated with antique Parisian subway seats and French doors, Dekk has a screening room in the back that shows depraved films like Cecil B. Demented and Tromeo and Juliet.

Megu Kimono Lounge
For listing, see p174 Dinner theater.
Megu's 13,000-square-foot space is showstopping: White columns are fashioned from porcelain rice bowls and sake bottles; the lounge is decorated with kimono fabrics. Cocktails are just as fancy: The Autumn Rain is a refreshing blend of citrus vodka, elderflower syrup, Asian-pear puree and ginger. There's even sparkling sake, in case plain sake seems too understated.

66
241 Church St between Leonard and Worth Sts (1-212-925-0202). Subway: 1, 9 to Franklin St. Open Mon–Thu 6pm–1am; Fri, Sat 6pm–2am; Sun 6–11:30pm. Average drink $10. Credit AmEx, MC, V.
The decor (white on white; Meier, Eames and Knoll) is uncommonly sleek, with drinks to match, at the bar of Asiaphile Jean-Georges Vongerichten's Chinese restaurant.

Chinatown, Little Italy & Nolita

Cantina
194 Elizabeth St between Prince and Spring Sts (1-212-965-9511). Subway: J, M, Z to Bowery; N, R, W to Prince St; 6 to Spring St. Open Tue–Sun 7pm–2:30am. Average glass of wine $8. Credit AmEx, MC, V.
Peasant's downstairs sister (also called Peasant Wine Bar), is a candlelit, brick-walled enoteca that pours a great selection of Italian wine. The vinos pair well with tasty bites like crunchy cheese-accented grissini, olives and roasted red peppers.

Double Happiness
173 Mott St between Broome and Grand Sts (1-212-941-1282). Subway: B, D to Grand St; J, M, Z to Bowery. Open Sun–Wed 6pm–2am; Thu 6pm–3am; Fri, Sat 6pm–4am. Average drink $9. Credit AmEx, MC, V.
Through the door at the bottom of the steep stairs, you'll encounter the first happiness: an underground stone-walled haunt perfect for trysts. Other joys include clubby music (deejayed rock, funk and soul), lots of eye candy (best viewed Thursdays through Saturdays) and an Asian-themed cocktail list that one-ups the usual cloyingly sweet choices (try a soothing green-tea martini).

Odea
389 Broome St at Mulberry St (1-212-941-9222). Subway: J, M, Z to Bowery; 6 to Spring St. Open Sun–Wed 6pm–2am; Thu–Sat 6pm–4am. Average drink $10. Credit AmEx, DC, Disc, MC, V.
This lounge nails the industrial-chic look—high ceilings, wood beams and brick walls painted black—but includes some old-fashioned touches that soften the room. Stay long enough and you'll find yourself nibbling on tasty tapas such as eggplant mousse or figs wrapped in prosciutto.

Lower East Side

The Delancey
168 Delancey St at Clinton St (1-212-254-9920). Subway: F to Delancey St; J, M, Z to Delancey–Essex Sts. Open 5pm–4am daily. Average drink $6. Credit MC, V.
The rooftop is what keeps the crowds coming back—a wood deck lined with potted palms and equipped with a fishpond, a bar and a margarita machine. When the alfresco party ends at midnight, you can head down to the main floor for deejayed music or into the basement to catch a live show.

The scenery's swell at **Thom Bar** in Soho's 60 Thompson Hotel. *See p205.*

The Lotus Lounge

35 Clinton St at Stanton St (1-212-253-1144). Subway: F to Delancey St; J, M, Z to Delancey–Essex Sts. **Open** *8am–4am daily.* **Average drink** *$5.* **Credit** *AmEx, DC, Disc, MC, V.*
At this longtime-favorite neighborhood lounge, you can linger for ages over coffee or beer while reading old books or contemplating the meaning of life. By day, the Lotus Lounge serves good, cheap sandwiches and salads. Come dusk, laid-back characters chat over low-priced drinks.

Nautilus

100C Forsyth St between Broome and Grand Sts (1-212-625-3444). Subway: B, D to Grand St. **Open** *Mon–Sat 6pm–2am.* **Average drink** *$8.* **Credit** *AmEx, Disc, MC, V.*
Inspired by *20,000 Leagues Under the Sea,* Nautilus is decorated with portholes and diving-helmet lamps. Come summertime, take your mojito and cruise out to the Mediterranean-style garden.

Punch and Judy

26 Clinton St between Houston and Stanton Sts (1-212-982-1116). Subway: F to Delancey St; J, M, Z to Delancey–Essex Sts. **Open** *Sun–Wed 6pm–2am; Thu–Sat 6pm–4am.* **Average glass of wine** *$10.* **Credit** *AmEx, MC, V.*
This stylish, modern wine bar and lounge, furnished

> ▶ For a comprehensive guide to notable New York bars, pick up a copy of the *Time Out New York Nightlife* guide, or subscribe to the online version at **eatdrink.timeoutny.com.**

with 1930s theater seats and red couches, offers 150 wines that pair beautifully with nibbles like a lobster club sandwich, cheese plates, or a *caprese* salad in which the ingredients are rolled up sushi-style.

Schiller's Liquor Bar

See p173 for listing.
Keith McNally's downtown bar attracts the hepcats with decidedly unsnobbish wine-list categories ("cheap," "decent" and "good").

Soho

The Ear Inn

326 Spring St between Greenwich and Washington Sts (1-212-226-9060). Subway: C, E to Spring St; 1, 9 to Canal St. **Open** *noon–4am daily.* **Average drink** *$6.* **Credit** *AmEx, Disc, MC, V.*
The Ear Inn has been popular with those haunting the docks of the Lower West Side, from stevedores to artists, since its establishment in 1816. The decor is basic (dark wood, rickety tables and chairs) but its simplicity and its mellow staff enhance the relaxed vibe. Visit Monday to Wednesday nights for live music; Saturdays from 3 to 5pm for poetry readings. Free snacks (fried chicken, mussels or sausage) and cheap drinks are served weekdays between 4 and 7pm.

Fanelli's Cafe

94 Prince St at Mercer St (1-212-226-9412). Subway: N, R, W to Prince St. **Open** *Sun–Thu 10am–1:30am; Fri, Sat 10am–3:30am.* **Average drink** *$5.* **Credit** *AmEx, MC, V.*
On a lovely cobblestoned corner, this 1847 joint claims to be the second-oldest continuously operat-

ing bar and restaurant in the city. Prints of boxing legends and one of the city's best burgers add to the easy feel. The banter of locals and the merry clinking of pint glasses sound just like the old days.

Pfiff

35 Grand St at Thompson St (1-212-334-6841). Subway: A, C, E, 1, 9 to Canal St. **Open** *Mon–Thu noon–1am; Fri, Sat noon–4am; Sun 12:30pm–midnight.* **Average drink** *$8.* **Credit** *AmEx, Disc, MC, V.*

For such a svelte little restaurant, Pfiff's bar sure can hold its liquor. Besides fancy cocktails, there's an impressive selection of single malts and ports. The seven seats go fast on weekdays from 5 to 7pm, when happy shoppers review their purchases. Later, locals sip sangria and chat over soft house beats. Order a basket of fries, voted "best new spuds in town" by *TONY* readers; it will vanish in a *pfiff.*

Thom Bar

60 Thompson Hotel, 60 Thompson St between Broome and Spring Sts (1-212-219-3200). Subway: C, E to Spring St. **Open** *5pm–2am daily.* **Average drink** *$11.* **Credit** *AmEx, DC, Disc, MC, V.*

Everybody knows that downtown is simply the coolest, and it doesn't get any cooler than this. Good-looking media types gather to celebrate their wonderfulness in a sleek, shimmering lounge. A-60, the rooftop bar, is for hotel guests only, but if you're looking gorgeous and it's slightly off-hours, then you might be able to sneak up for drinks and a killer view.

East Village

Arshile Night Lounge

166 First Ave between 10th and 11th Sts (1-212-228-0444). Subway: L to First Ave; 6 to Astor Pl. **Open** *Mon, Wed–Sun 6pm–4am.* **Cover** *Sat, Sun $5–$10.* **Average drink** *$10.* **Credit** *AmEx, MC, V.*

Models and celebs have been known to visit this bi-level, multimood lounge. Downstairs has more of a VIP feel (i.e., private tables surrounded by potted trees). Upstairs has a bar and banquettes with tables, as well as a DJ who pumps rock & roll, hip-hop and even some '80s pop.

Decibel

240 E 9th St between Second and Third Aves (1-212-979-2733). Subway: N, R, W to 8th St–NYU; 6 to Astor Pl. **Open** *Mon–Sat 8pm–3am; Sun 8pm–1am.* **Average drink** *$10.* **Credit** *AmEx, MC, V ($15 minimum).*

Decibel is Japanese through and through, and it's got a helluva sake bar. Most of the staff speaks little to no English, so be prepared to get lost in translation occasionally, especially when it comes to snacks, which can be as mundane as rice crackers or as outré as shark fins and jellyfish. The drinks are a bit more straightforward: Sex on the Beach in Japan is the same as Sex on the Beach anywhere else.

In Vino

215 E 4th St between Aves A and B (1-212-539-1011). Subway: F, V to Lower East Side–Second Ave. **Open** *Sun–Thu 5:30pm–midnight; Fri, Sat 5:30pm–1am.* **Average glass of wine** *$8.* **Credit** *MC, V.*

Come to savor Southern Italian vinos: The small cavelike space offers hundreds of regional wines that can accommodate such tasty, rustic appetizers as tomato-and-truffle crostini.

Kasadela

647 E 11th St at Ave C (1-212-777-1582). Subway: L to First Ave. **Open** *Tue–Thu, Sun 5:30pm–12:30am; Fri, Sat 5:30pm–1:30am.* **Average drink** *$7.* **Credit** *MC, V.*

Owners Yujen Pan and Keika Kan have re-created a traditional *izakaya* (Japanese pub), and it's a cheery little spot outfitted with floor-to-ceiling windows, strings of ruby lights and snug seating arrangements. Patrons can sip one of 30 sakes at bargain prices, and four ultrafresh versions of the fermented brew are available on tap. Sautéed smelts and fried oysters may be acquired tastes for you, but they're authentic Japanese pub grub.

Lit Lounge

93 Second Ave between 5th and 6th Sts (1-212-777-7987). Subway: F, V to Lower East Side–Second Ave; 6 to Astor Pl. **Open** *5pm–4am daily.* **Average drink** *$5.* **Credit** *AmEx, Disc, MC, V ($20 minimum).*

Rheingold and rock & roll reign at this divey hot spot where Motherfucker hostess Justine D. holds a Friday night party, and Carlos D. (Interpol) occasionally stops by to DJ. Most nights, garage bands play in the

Eat, Drink, Shop

The beauty of fruity rules at **Odea**. *See p203.*

basement; on the weekends, students swarm the main floor for Red Bull–and–vodka specials. The attached Fuse Gallery exhibits art by musicians— Mark Mothersbaugh of Devo had a recent show— and other iconoclasts, such as H.R. Giger.

McSorley's Old Ale House
15 E 7th St between Second and Third Aves (1-212-473-9148). Subway: N, R, W to 8th St–NYU; 6 to Astor Pl. **Open** *Mon–Sat 11am–midnight.* **Average beer** *$2.* **Credit** *Cash only.*
It would take days to read the appreciative newspaper clips on the walls of this 1854 drinking landmark. Order a house beer—Dark Ale (sweet and smooth) or Light Ale (smooth with a bite)—and the veteran Irish waiters will bring you double mugs of suds. The sawdusted floor and never-dusted chandelier add to the old-time feel. Look up bartender-poet Geoffrey Bartholomew's book, *The McSorley Poems*, before stopping by.

Nublu
62 Ave C between 4th and 5th Sts (1-212-979-9925). Subway: F, V to Lower East Side–Second Ave. **Open** *7pm–4am daily.* **Average drink** *$6.* **Credit** *Cash only.*
First-timers at this remote Alphabet City outpost will have to ask the smokers outside if they've come to the right place: It's marked only by a blue light. Inside, a trendy crowd settles in for the European beer selection and the offbeat jazz and avant-garde acts. Live Brazilian music and dancing are the draw on

Three amigas at **Lit Lounge**. *See p205.*

Wednesday nights. In summer, a pleasant backyard garden eases the pressure on the small space.

Greenwich Village & Noho

Five Points
31 Great Jones St between Bowery and Lafayette St (1-212-253-5700). Subway: B, D, F, V to Broadway–Lafayette St; 6 to Bleecker St. **Open** *5pm–midnight daily.* **Average drink** *$8.* **Credit** *AmEx, DC, MC, V.*
A happy hour has to stretch to please difficult New Yorkers, so Five Points gives us $5 martinis and $1 oysters every day from 5 to 7pm. We sip, slurp and take in the gentle design: fresh seasonal flowers, a mahogany harvest table for a bar, a trickling water fountain made from a white-oak log. Even the crankiest among us emerges a little happier.

Marion's Continental Restaurant & Lounge
354 Bowery between Great Jones and E 4th Sts (1-212-475-7621). Subway: B, D, F, V to Broadway–Lafayette St; 6 to Bleecker St. **Open** *5:30pm–2am daily.* **Average drink** *$7.* **Credit** *AmEx, DC, Disc, MC, V.*
Marion's hasn't been serving old-fashioned cocktails forever, but it sure feels that way. Decorated with thrift-shop paintings and bric-a-brac, this retro shrine to '50s New York nightlife has the air of a festive but down-to-earth supper club, with fabulous music that varies from lounge and Latin to lovely soul.

Table 50
See p291 for listing.
It's always cool in this basement bar, and it would feel Zen-like if the techno weren't so loud. Grab a candlelit nook and sink into a leather banquette, but stay away from the seemingly guileless Painkiller (a concoction of coconut, rum and orange juice). One too many of those, and the hall of mirrors leading to the blood-red bathroom might look more like a terrifying carnival maze than a playful remnant of the space's smutty heyday as an S&M bar.

West Village & Meatpacking District

APT
See p292 for listing.
By shifting its focus from door attitude to DJs, APT lives up to the polish of India Mahdavi's sleek design.

Chumley's
86 Bedford St between Barrow and Grove Sts (1-212-675-4449). Subway: 1, 9 to Christopher St–Sheridan Sq. **Open** *Mon–Thu 4pm–midnight; Fri 4pm–2am; Sat, Sun noon–2am.* **Average drink** *$6.* **Credit** *Cash only.*
The two unmarked entrances to Chumley's reflect its speakeasy roots. Since its opening, in 1922, the place has poured pints for its share of famous authors; notice the countless book covers displayed

So many sakes, so little time, at **Kasadela** in the East Village. *See p205.*

on the walls. A working fireplace, free-roaming Labradors and sawdusted floors maintain the scruffy yet genteel sensibility.

Cielo
See p288 for listing.
Dig the soulful house music and sip from a $9 flute of champagne at this cool, attitude-free Village spot.

Level V
675 Hudson St at 14th St (1-212-699-2410). Subway: A, C, E to 14th St; L to Eighth Ave. **Open** *Tue, Wed 8pm–3am; Thu–Sat 8pm–4am.* **Average drink** *$10.* **Credit** *AmEx, DC, Disc, MC, V.*
The door policy is strict, the clientele is more Upper East Side than downtown, the music is hip-hop, and the decor is contemporary cool (electric-blue lighting washes over black leather couches and elegant glass tables). If you get past the velvet rope, order a Level V (fresh lime, Vox raspberry and green-apple foam) and enjoy the eye candy orbiting the room.

The Other Room
143 Perry St between Greenwich and Washington Sts (1-212-645-9758). Subway: 1, 9 to Christopher St–Sheridan Sq. **Open** *Sun, Mon 5pm–2am; Tue–Sat 5pm–4am.* **Average drink** *$7.* **Credit** *Cash only.*
Doubling as an art gallery for up-and-coming photographers, the Other Room is sleek and civilized. You won't find any hard liquor (keeps out the louts), but the selection of fine beer and wine is varied and vast. The cool minimalist design allows patrons to focus on conversation. And the people who come here—gay, straight, fashionistas, 9-to-5 execs—are likely to have something interesting to say.

Other locations *Anotheroom, 249 West Broadway between Beach and North Moore Sts (1-212-226-1418); The Room, 144 Sullivan St between Houston and Prince Sts (1-212-477-2102).*

Spice Market
403 W 13th St at Ninth Ave (1-212-675-2322). Subway: A, C, E to 14th St; L to Eighth Ave. **Open** *6pm–2am daily.* **Average drink** *$12.* **Credit** *AmEx, DC, MC, V.*
Glide down the dramatic staircase and enter a glamorous world where votives flicker over a fashionable crowd that comes for the scene, the fruity cocktails and the street-market-inspired dishes. (*See also p174* **Dinner theater***.*)

Ye Waverly Inn
16 Bank St at Waverly Pl (1-212-929-4377). Subway: 1, 2, 3, 9 to 14th St. **Open** *5pm–4am daily.* **Average drink** *$8.* **Credit** *AmEx, DC, Disc, MC, V.*
Not many places are more typical of old Greenwich Village than this former tavern, nestled in a 160-year-old brownstone. The tiny bar seats a handful of patrons and offers wines by the glass, a stellar selection of single-malts and Charles Mingus on the speakers, all of which combine to make it a fine place to round out a date. Grab a seat near the same flickering fireplace Robert Frost once wrote beside, and wax poetic.

> ▶ For more on nightlife, see **Clubs**, **Gay & Lesbian** and **Music** (*pp287–293, pp299–309* and *pp311–330*).

Chelsea

Flatiron Lounge
37 W 19th St between Fifth and Sixth Aves (1-212-727-7741). Subway: F, V, N, R, W to 23rd St; 1, 9 to 18th St. **Open** *Sun–Wed 5pm–2am; Thu–Sat 5pm–4am.* **Average drink** *$10.* **Credit** *AmEx, MC, V.*
To get to the 30-foot mahogany bar (built in 1927), follow an arched hallway warmed by the soft glow of candles. You'll find an Art Deco space with red leather booths, round glass tables, flying-saucer-shaped lamps and an imaginative cocktail menu. Co-owner Julie Reiner is the mistress of mixology: The Persephone, for instance, is a subtle pomegranate martini named for the queen of Hades.

Glass
287 Tenth Ave between 26th and 27th Sts (1-212-904-1580). Subway: 1, 9 to 28th St. **Open** *Tue–Sat 8pm–4am.* **Average drink** *$9.* **Credit** *AmEx, DC, Disc, MC, V.*

German-born architect Thomas Seeser designed Glass, a stunning bar with Jacobsen egg chairs and custom-made cocktail tables. The washroom's one-way mirror allows pedestrians to witness plenty of nose powdering. In the all-season bamboo garden (open for smokers), artistic young things while away the night stargazing. A mix of Latin and house music plays, and bar nibbles (panini and bruschetta) help to soak up the cheap wine from nearby art openings.

Hiro
Maritime Hotel, 366 W 17th St at Ninth Ave (1-212-727-0212). Subway: A, C, E to 14th St; L to Eighth Ave. **Open** *10pm–4am daily.* **Average drink** *$10.* **Credit** *AmEx, MC, V.*
Past the guard at the speakeasy window is a vast, vaulted room lined with backlit paper screens. The place is often filled with girls in tube tops and banker types who love them, as well as an occasional Rolling Stones heiress (Elizabeth Jagger, Theodora Richards). Signature cocktails, such as the Sakenade (sake, fresh ginger and lemon juice), are the kinds of

And so to bed...

You've shopped all over Soho, explored the newly expanded MoMA and indulged in a multiple-course meal at Jean Georges. Now how about a nightcap before you turn in—or a stiff drink to rev up your engine? Whatever your mood, whether it's a glass of port or a snifter of cognac, cocktail diva Audrey Saunders, beverage director of the swank **Bemelmans Bar at the Carlyle** (35 E 76th St at Madison Ave, 1-212-744-1600), will devise the right concoction for your palate. Her menu features a nice array of ports, but the Madeira—a buttery Leacock's Bual Vintage 1934 reminiscent of homespun maple syrup—is what the bar's banquette-based imbibers are ordering more often of late. You can also choose from a slew of cognacs and Armagnacs or, for a more creative variation, try Saunders's Garden of Eden (cognac and passion-fruit-flavored cognac). The highbrow beverages complement the elegant clientele, the white-jacketed service and Ludwig Bemelmans' whimsical murals, which exude the same magic as his Madeline books.

If you're fortunate enough to be visiting during the warmer months (May through October), stop by **Rare View** (303 Lexington Ave at 37th St, 16th floor, 1-212-481-1999), which provides an ideal setting for sipping an after-dinner drink. Unparalleled views

of the Chrysler and Empire State Buildings make this bar on the rooftop of the Shelburne Hotel a revelation to boarders and visitors alike. To optimize the prime perspective, kick back on one of the lounge beds, under strings of lights that jack up the twinkle and ambience factors. Although Rare View has a decent selection of ports and sherries, its strength is in the list of creative cocktails. In the summertime, you can chill with a Strawberry Cooler (Bacardi and fresh strawberry puree); come winter, the restaurant bar downstairs serves up a heartwarming view of Lexington Avenue as well as an espresso martini that pairs perfectly with such desserts as chocolate-chip bread pudding.

For a more intimate experience, head to the West Village and tuck yourself into a booth at **Bar Next Door** (129 MacDougal St between 3rd and 4th Sts, 1-212-529-5945). Hidden in the basement of a beautifully restored townhouse, Next Door feels like a secret you're lucky to know. The romantic nook evokes old New York as well as Lerici, owner Vittorio Antonini's hometown, on the Italian Riviera. It's no coincidence, then, that in addition to the long wine list there are 25 types of grappa and 7 types of *limoncello* (both are traditional Italian digestifs). Of course, several special spirits are available,

Eat, Drink, Shop

delicious drinks that taste benign but quickly kick
your ass—as they should, for $12.

Open

559 W 22nd St at Eleventh Ave (1-212-243-1851).
Subway: C, E to 23rd St. **Open** *5pm–2am daily.*
Average drink *$7.* **Credit** *AmEx, MC, V.*
Note the industrial-cool concrete floor, apple-red
banquettes, gentle pink light and white-tiled walls.
This spot could easily stand in for one of the shiny
white art galleries that line the block. The monitor
above the polished wood bar even plays video art
instead of sports. During the week, the early shift
consists of gallerygoers and artists sipping wine and
eating tapas. On weekends, a live DJ transforms the
space into a slick, buzzing lounge.

Passerby

436 W 15th St between Ninth and Tenth Aves
(1-212-206-7321). Subway: A, C, E to 14th St;
L to Eighth Ave. **Open** *Mon–Sat 6pm–2am.*
Average drink *$8.* **Credit** *AmEx, MC, V.*
The unmarked Passerby is a sort of clubhouse for
arty types. Flashing colored floor panels, created by

artist Piotr Uklansky, almost synchronize with the
DJ's beats and lend an ambient glow. Early evening,
this is a civilized place for a drink; later, things get
deliciously raucous.

Peter McManus Café

152 Seventh Ave at 19th St (1-212-929-9691).
Subway: 1, 9 to 18th St. **Open** *Mon–Sat 11am–*
4am; Sun noon–4am. **Average drink** *$6.*
Credit *Cash only.*
This family-owned saloon, at its present address
since 1936, has been used as a location to boost the
street cred of shows like *Seinfeld* and *Law & Order.*
Have a few shots backed with McManus Ale and
stare at the goldfish tank; or slip into one of the two
old-school telephone booths to call your lifeline.

Ruby Falls

609 W 29th St between Eleventh and Twelfth Aves
(1-212-643-6464). Subway: A, C, E, 1, 2, 3, 9 to
34th St–Penn Station. **Open** *Gallery Wed–Sat*
11am–7pm. Lounge Thu–Sat 11pm–4am. **Cover** *$20.*
Average drink *$10.* **Credit** *AmEx, DC, Disc, MC, V.*
By day, paintings are on display under a magnifi-

such as Navan, a Madagascar vanilla
liqueur, and high-end cognacs like Belle
de Brillet (made with pear essence). Low
ceilings and exposed-brick and stone walls
provide superb acoustics for the regularly
scheduled live jazz performances. If your
postdinner drinks by music and candlelight
evolve into a late-night philosophical
discussion, then you may find yourself
hungry again: A full menu is offered until
2am (3am on weekends) from adjacent
trattoria La Lanterna di Vittorio.

One of the most recent additions to the
Lower East Side's heated-up nightlife scene
is **East Side Company Bar** (49 Essex St
between Broome and Delancey Sts, 1-212-
614-7408). If you can't get into Milk &
Honey, the elusive reservations-only bar
owned by famed mixologist Sasha Petraske,
then you'll fare much better at his other
downtown spot, where you can confidently
stroll in off the street. The debonair space
has a '40s-era vibe and features reasonable
drink prices and a tasty raw bar. Its snug
proportions, pressed-tin ceilings and
intimate leather booths—not to mention its
devotion to the art of the cocktail—make it
the perfect spot for a postprandial beverage,
especially after a meal at one of the excellent
restaurants that have blossomed along
Clinton Street.

Light up the night at **Rare View**.

Red, hot and bothered, downstairs in **Kemia Bar**'s Bedouin oasis.

cent skylight. At night, the space becomes a lounge with a $20 cover. To corral the crowds, the owners divided the 7,500-square-foot warehouse into three sections: a ground-level bar, an elevated champagne lounge and a VIP area high above the action and next to the DJ booth. Female servers wear J. Lo's line of lingerie; boy servers don Hilfiger House. As for you: no jeans, no sneakers and, please, no trucker hats.

Midtown West

Ava Lounge
Majestic Hotel, 210 W 55th St between Seventh Ave and Broadway (1-212-956-7020). Subway: N, Q, R, W to 57th St. **Open** *Mon, Tue 5pm–3am; Wed–Fri 5pm–4am; Sat 6pm–4am; Sun 6pm–3am.* **Average drink** *$9.* **Credit** *AmEx, Disc, MC, V.*
The top of the Majestic Hotel has been transformed into a penthouse lounge and rooftop deck with views of both the twinkling cityscape and the blonds in black who serve key lime martinis and Flirtinis. Modern, chic and slick without being oppressively overdesigned, the space is often used for private parties, and the outdoor patio is a lure for smokers.

Hudson Bar
The Hudson, 356 W 58th St between Eighth and Ninth Aves (1-212-554-6343). Subway: A, C, B, D, 1, 9 to 59th St–Columbus Circle. **Open** *Mon–Sat 4pm–2am; Sun 4pm–1am. Library bar Mon–Sat noon–2am; Sun noon–1am.* **Average drink** *$10.* **Credit** *AmEx, DC, Disc, MC, V.*
Like a lime-green stairway to heaven, an escalator leads to the lobby of Ian Schrager's Hudson hotel, where you'll find three separate bars. Most dazzling

is the postmodern Hudson Bar, with a backlit glass floor and a ceiling fresco by Francesco Clemente. The Library bar marries class (leather sofas) and kitsch (photos of cows in pillbox hats). If that's too cute, then get some air in the seasonal Private Park (April to November), the leafy, cigarette-friendly outdoor bar lit by candle chandeliers.

Kemia Bar
630 Ninth Ave at 44th St (1-212-582-3200). Subway: A, C, E to 42nd St–Port Authority. **Open** *Tue–Fri 6pm–1am; Sat 8pm–2am.* **Average drink** *$8.* **Credit** *AmEx, MC, V.*
Descending into this lush Middle Eastern oasis is like penetrating the fourth wall of a brilliant stage set. Gossamer fabric billows from the ceiling, ottomans are clustered around low tables, and dark-wood floors are strewn with rose petals. A soulful DJ helps, as do the luscious libations.

Oak Bar
The Plaza Hotel, 768 Fifth Ave at Central Park South (1-212-546-5320). Subway: N, R, W to Fifth Ave–59th St. **Open** *Mon–Sat 11:30am–1:30am; Sun 11:30am–midnight.* **Average drink** *$10.* **Credit** *AmEx, DC, Disc, MC, V.*
Small wonder Gloria Steinem once refused to leave this stunning classic, formerly open to men only, even after the manager removed her table. Study the Ashcan School murals by Everett Shinn while sipping a single malt ($13 to $24 per glass), and bend an elbow where Diamond Jim Brady and George M. Cohan once tippled.

Single Room Occupancy
360 W 53rd St between Eighth and Ninth Aves (1-212-765-6299). Subway: B, D to Seventh Ave; C, E

to 50th St. **Open** Mon, Tue 7:30pm–2am; Wed–Sat 7:30pm–4am. **Average drink** $8. **Credit** AmEx.
It's hard to overstate the importance of feeling like a New York insider. At this wine and beer speakeasy, where you must ring the doorbell to enter, you'll be deliciously in the know. SRO comfortably fits 20 or so, but more have been known to squeeze into the cavelike medieval-modern space. Locals think of owner Markos as the host of their favorite nightly party, and on one random evening per month, he rewards them by bringing in go-go dancers.

Town
Chambers, 15 W 56th St between Fifth and Sixth Aves (1-212-582-4445). Subway: F to 57th St; N, R, W to Fifth Ave–59th St. **Open** noon–1am daily. **Average drink** $12. **Credit** AmEx, DC, Disc, MC, V.
Monied drinkers in their middle years pick from four designated drinking areas: the narrow bar at the head of the passageway that leads to the restaurant; the spacious back balcony bar; the hotel's lofty lobby bar; and the mezzanine bar. There's a pricey wine list, but you might prefer a sassy house cocktail like the Town Plum, made with plum nectar and the premium French grape vodka, Cîroc.

Midtown East

Brasserie
100 E 53rd St between Park and Lexington Aves (1-212-751-4840). Subway: E, V to Lexington Ave–53rd St; 6 to 51st St. **Open** Mon–Thu 11am–midnight; Fri, Sat 11am–1am; Sun 11am–10pm. **Average drink** $9. **Credit** AmEx, DC, Disc, MC, V.
Take an architectural tour: This striking spot, located in the basement of Mies van der Rohe's Seagram Building, was outfitted by Diller + Scofidio. It features backlit bottles stored horizontally behind opaque glass, a long granite bar and curved walls made of pear wood. Spy on new arrivals via stop-motion images displayed on screens mounted above the bar.

Opia
See p277 for listing.
This sexy, spacious lounge serves unusual, fancy cocktails; the full menu includes sushi and desserts.

P.J. Clarke's
915 Third Ave at 55th St (1-212-317-1616). Subway: E, V to Lexington Ave–53rd St; 6 to 51st St. **Open** 11am–4am daily. **Average drink** $7. **Credit** AmEx, DC, Disc, MC, V.
P.J. Clarke's has been a beloved saloon since 1884, but the storied, hard-drinking hacks, pols, molls and palookas of yore have been supplanted by briefcase-toting execs, cashmere-clad couples and baseball-capped buddies. Recently restored to vintage perfection, Clarke's draws the likes of Johnny Depp and Bill Murray. Bartenders are polite and pours are generous. Must-peeks: the Tiffany stained glass in the men's room and the

cozy dining alcove where Renée Zellweger and Salma Hayek order steak to amp up their real-girl cred.

Sakagura
211 E 43rd St between Second and Third Aves (1-212-953-7253). Subway: 42nd St S, 4, 5, 6, 7 to 42nd St–Grand Central. **Open** Mon–Thu noon–2:30pm, 6pm–midnight; Fri noon–2:30pm, 6pm–2am; Sat 6pm–2:30am; Sun 6pm– midnight. **Average drink** $7. **Credit** AmEx, DC, Disc, MC, V.
At Sakagura, you'll have to do a little work: Walk through the unmarked lobby of an office building, down a few stairs and along a basement corridor. Finally, enter a quiet room of bamboo and blond wood and prepare to learn about sake. The 200 kinds available here, categorized by region, are served in delicate handblown-glass vessels. If you can't decide, try a Sakagura Tasting Set, which teams an appetizer, entrée and dessert with three corresponding sakes. Check out the candlelit restrooms, cleverly fashioned from giant sake casks.

Tao
See p194 for listing.
This sceney palace is forever packed to the Chinese lanterns; a 16-foot stone Buddha towers over the dining room.

The best Bars to...

...drink yourself under the picnic table
Astoria is home to more than just great Greek food: The **Bohemian Hall and Beer Garden** (see p213) serves $4 quaffs indoors and out—perfect with huge platters of Czech sausage.

...whet your artistic appetite
The theme hits you the moment you enter **Galapagos** (see p213), where an enormous reflecting pool doubles as an art installation.

...spoil your dinner
Fill up on $1 oysters and $5 fruity martinis at the **Five Points** (see p206) happy hour, from 5 to 7pm every day.

...keep it real all year round
In summer, the **Delancey** (see p203) treats you to Sunday BBQ on its roof deck; in winter, the fireplace sparks no-frills fun.

...take your breath away
Head up to the **Metropolitan Museum of Art Balcony Bar and Roof Garden** (see p212) for spectacular views of Central Park and the skyline on either side of it.

Eat, Drink, Shop

Uptown

Upper West Side

Mod

505 Columbus Ave between 84th and 85th Sts (1-212-989-3600). Subway: B, C to 86th St. **Open** *Mon–Fri 6pm–4am; Sat, Sun 8pm–4am.* **Average drink** *$6.* **Credit** *AmEx, Disc, MC, V.*
At Mod, kitsch is king: Tunes from the '70s, '80s and '90s blare as revelers gulp frozen drinks and munch flashback food—PB&J, Rice Krispies Treats, Chex party mix—in a room decked out in Andy Warhol prints, primary colors and Lava lamps. During the week, bingo and karaoke theme nights rule. For a blast to the past, this is your ticket.

Upper East Side

Barbalùc Wine Bar

135 E 65th St between Park and Lexington Aves (1-212-774-1999). Subway: F to Lexington Ave–63rd St; 6 to 68th St–Hunter College. **Open** *Mon–Sat 6pm–midnight.* **Average glass of wine** *$11.* **Credit** *AmEx, DC, MC, V.*
The kitchen emphasizes food from the northeastern Italian district of Friuli, and the upstairs bar follows through by offering what is perhaps the city's most extensive list of Friulian wine, including two dozen by the glass. The mood is quite civil, and on Fridays, a pleasant jazz trio softens the stark white-on-white decor.

I'm **Superfine**; thanks for asking. *See p213.*

Metropolitan Museum of Art Balcony Bar and Roof Garden

1000 Fifth Ave at 82nd St (1-212-535-7710). Subway: 4, 5, 6 to 86th St. **Open** *Balcony Bar Fri, Sat 4–8pm. Roof Garden May–Oct Tue–Thu, Sun 9:30am–5:15pm; Fri, Sat 9:30am–8pm.* **Average drink** *$7.* **Credit** *AmEx, MC, V.*
Among the Met's countless treasures is the Balcony Bar, which springs to life on weekends. Thirty café tables, a few makeshift bars and a string quartet are all it takes. If you'd rather survey the magnificent skyscrapers rising above Central Park, then visit the Iris and B. Gerald Cantor Roof Garden for piña coladas and breathtaking views.

212 Restaurant & Bar

133 E 65th St between Park and Lexington Aves (1-212-249-6565). Subway: F to Lexington Ave–63rd St; 6 to 68th St–Hunter College. **Open** *Sun–Wed noon–midnight; Thu–Sat noon–1am.* **Average drink** *$9.* **Credit** *AmEx, MC, V.*
The drink list is longer than the dinner menu, and the vodka list (75 varieties) is longer than either the red- or the white-wine list. For a disco-bar meet market, that seems right, and so do the many specialty martinis and vodka cocktails. Girls sip Pink Bunnies; the boys, Blue Bunnies. Both concoctions are touted as having Viagra-like properties.

Above 116th Street

The Den

2150 Fifth Ave between 131st and 132nd Sts (1-212-234-3045). Subway: 2, 3 to 135th St. **Open** *Mon–Thu 6pm–1am; Fri, Sun 6pm–4am.* **Average drink** *$9.* **Credit** *AmEx, Disc, MC, V.*
Under the glow of a classic old streetlamp, a dapper doorman tips his derby and welcomes visitors to a subterranean lounge set in a Harlem brownstone. Designer Carlos Jimenez, whose résumé includes industry (food) and Flow, has cast a lush red haze over the '20s-era room, which is lined with exposed brick and accented by a copper-topped bar.

Lenox Lounge

288 Malcolm X Blvd (Lenox Ave) between 124th and 125th Sts (1-212-427-0253). Subway: 2, 3 to 125th St. **Open** *noon–4am daily.* **Cover** *varies.* **Average drink** *$5.* **Credit** *AmEx, DC, MC, V.*
This is where a street hustler named Malcolm worked before he got religion and added an X to his name. Now the famous Harlem bar, lounge and jazz club welcomes a mix of old-school cats and unobtrusive booze hounds. Settle into the refurbished Art Deco area in front or take a table in the zebra-papered back room, then tune in to the haunting presence of Billie Holiday and Miles Davis.

Brooklyn

Bembe

81 South 6th St at Berry St, Williamsburg (1-718-387-5389). Subway: J, M, Z to Marcy Ave;

You're in the right area code at hookup-happy **212 Restaurant & Bar**. *See p212.*

L to Bedford Ave. **Open** *Mon–Thu 7:30pm–4am; Fri–Sun 7pm–4am.* **Average drink** *$5.* **Credit** *Cash only.*

At an unmarked hideaway under the Williamsburg Bridge, the swinging clientele dances by candlelight to Latin beats laid down by sexy DJs. Take a breather from the samba or salsa and refuel with tequila shots at the sleek wooden bar. Regulars swear by the unusual postshot practice of sucking the lime slice after dipping one side in fresh-ground coffee and the other in sugar. You'll have to try it for yourself.

Galapagos

See p315 for listing.

This perennial Williamsburg fave doubles as a performance space for all kinds of art.

Moto

394 Broadway at Hooper St, Williamsburg (1-718-599-6895). Subway: J, M to Hewes St. **Open** *Sun–Thu 6pm–2am; Fri, Sat 6pm–3am.* **Average drink** *$6.* **Credit** *Cash only.*

Owners Billy Phelps and John McCormick have somehow created a café-bar evocative of 1930s Paris, in a former check-cashing store beneath the J-M elevated tracks. (The film *Eat This New York* captured Moto's rocky transformation on celluloid.) However, the menu is Italian, the wines are handpicked, and the beers include Belgian Corsendonk. The Pan-Euro attitude, easy subway access, and good food and drink in an intimate triangular room make Moto a must-go.

SEA Thai Restaurant and Bar

See p200 for listing.

The Asian-mod design, poolside Buddha and electronica soundtrack set the mood for specialty cocktails like the mango margarita or the Kluay Mai (rum, pineapple juice and ginger).

Superfine

126 Front St at Pearl St, Dumbo (1-718-243-9005). Subway: A, C, to High St; F to York St. **Open** *Tue–Thu 11:30am–3pm, 6pm–1am; Fri 11:30am–3pm, 6pm–4am; Sat 2pm–4am; Sun 11am–3pm, 6pm–1am.* **Average drink** *$6.* **Credit** *AmEx, MC, V.*

Praised for its weekend Southwestern Chili Brunch, this eatery is also a fine place for drinks any evening of the week (and there's a tiny art gallery and scruffy types in smart-guy glasses). The worn-in mix-and-match furniture is usually occupied by young, suited professionals downing Cosmos, or arty locals who hang at the pool table. You might even see regulars from the Federation of Black Cowboys, who hitch their horses at the door before they take their usual seats at the bar.

Queens

Bohemian Hall and Beer Garden

29-19 24th Ave between 29th and 30th Sts, Astoria (1-718-274-0043). Subway: N, W to Astoria Blvd. **Open** *Mon–Thu 5pm–2am; Fri 5pm–4am; Sat, Sun noon–4am.* **Average drink** *$4.* **Credit** *MC, V ($10 minimum).*

Echt *Mitteleuropa* in the Greek precinct of Astoria? Czech! This authentic (circa 1910) beer hall is a throwback to the time when hundreds of such places dotted the town; the vibe manages to combine the ambience of that era with the youthful spirit of a junior year in Prague. Go for the cheap, robust platters of Czech sausage, $4 Stolis, Spaten Oktoberfests and the rockin' juke. Roughly from Memorial Day to October, the hall's huge, tree-canopied, picnic-table-lined beer garden (smoking allowed) beckons with thrilling unpretentiousness.

Shops & Services

Want it, need it, have to have it? We've got you covered.

Shopping in New York City can be more overwhelming than trying to hail a rush-hour taxi in the middle of a downpour. You can locate just about anything you'd ever want here—the problem is narrowing down your many options (oh, and paying for your fabulous finds). We'll help you navigate the complicated world of New York shopping like a pro, whether your taste leans toward Fifth Avenue glam or thrift-store grunge. You might even end up with a few bucks left for that taxi.

SHOP AROUND

Shopping events such as Barneys' ever-popular semiannual warehouse sales and designers' frequent sample sales are excellent sources for reduced-price clothing by fashion's biggest names. To find out who's selling where during any given week, consult the Check Out section of *Time Out New York*. The **S&B Report** ($15; 1-877-579-0222, www.lazarshopping.com) and the **SSS Sample Sales** hotline (1-212-947-8748, www.clothingline.com) are also great discount resources. Sales are usually held in the designers' shops or in rented loft spaces. Typically, you may find that the loft sales are not equipped with changing rooms, so bring a courageous spirit (and plenty of cold, hard cash!) and remember to wear appropriate undergarments.

The cutting edge of fashion has spread beyond the Lower East Side and Nolita. In the past few years, trendy designers have ventured farther afield: Harlem, the Meatpacking District and Brooklyn's Williamsburg are now on the fashion-forward radar. To find out who's making waves in New York's design scene, visit the *TONY* website (www.timeoutny.com), click on Check Out, and scan the archives.

Pressed for time? Head to one of New York's shopping malls…Yes, we said *shopping mall*. You won't get the best deal or the uniqueness of a boutique, but the **Manhattan Mall** (Sixth Ave at 33rd St), the **Shops at Columbus Circle** (Time Warner Center, 10 Columbus Circle at 59th St), and the myriad stores in **Trump Tower** (Fifth Ave at 56th St), **Grand Central Terminal** (42nd Street at Park Ave) and South Street Seaport's cobblestoned **Pier 17** (Fulton St at the East River) are convenient options.

Thursday is the universal—though unofficial—shop-after-work night; most stores remain open until at least 7pm. Stores downtown generally stay open an hour or so later than those uptown, but for places that truly burn the midnight oil, *see p241* **A shop in the dark**. Certain businesses have multiple locations. If a shop has more than two branches, then check the business pages in the phone book for additional addresses.

One-stop Shopping

Department stores

Barneys New York

660 Madison Ave at 61st St (1-212-826-8900/ www.barneys.com). Subway: N, R, W to Fifth Ave–59th St; 4, 5, 6 to 59th St. **Open** *Mon–Fri 10am–8pm; Sat 10am–7pm; Sun 11am–6pm.* **Credit** *AmEx, MC, V.*
The top designers are represented at this bastion of New York style. At Christmastime, Barneys has the most provocative windows in town. Its Co-op branches carry young designers as well as secondary lines from heavies like Marc Jacobs and Theory. Every February and August, the Chelsea Co-op hosts the Barneys Warehouse Sale, where prices are reduced 50 to 80 percent.
Other locations *throughout the city.*

Bergdorf Goodman

754 Fifth Ave at 57th St (1-212-753-7300/www. bergdorfgoodman.com). Subway: E, V to Fifth Ave–53rd St; N, R, W to Fifth Ave–59th St. **Open** *Mon–Wed, Fri, Sat 10am–7pm; Thu 10am–8pm; Sun noon–6pm.* **Credit** *AmEx, DC, MC, V.*
Barneys aims for a young, trendy crowd; Bergdorf's is dedicated to an elegant, understated clientele that has plenty of disposable income. Luxury clothes, accessories and even stationery are found here, along with an over-the-top Beauty Level. The famed men's store is across the street (745 Fifth Ave).

Bloomingdale's

1000 Third Ave at 59th St (1-212-705-2000/www. bloomingdales.com). Subway: N, R, W to Lexington Ave–59th St; 4, 5, 6 to 59th St. **Open** *Mon–Fri 10am–8:30pm; Sat 10am–7pm; Sun 11am–7pm.* **Credit** *AmEx, MC, V.*
Bloomies is a gigantic, glitzy department store offering everything from handbags and cosmetics to furniture and designer duds. Brace yourself for the crowds—this store ranks among the city's most popular tourist attractions, right up there with the Empire State Building. Check out the cool, new

Find Belle—Sigerson Morrison's lower-priced shoe line—at **Bloomingdale's**. *See p214.*

little-sister branch in Soho. You'll find a side-by-side comparison of the two stores on page 217.
Other location *504 Broadway between Broome and Spring Sts (1-212-279-5900).*

Henri Bendel
712 Fifth Ave at 56th St (1-212-247-1100/www. henribendel.com). Subway: E, V to Fifth Ave–53rd St; N, R, W to Fifth Ave–59th St. **Open** *Mon–Wed, Fri, Sat 10am–7pm; Thu 10am–8pm; Sun noon–6pm.* **Credit** *AmEx, DC, Disc, MC, V.*
Bendel's lavish quarters resemble an opulently appointed townhouse. There are elevators, but it's nicer to saunter up the elegant, winding staircase. Prices are comparable to those of other upscale stores, but the merchandise seems more desirable here—must be those darling brown-striped shopping bags.

Jeffrey New York
449 W 14th St between Ninth and Tenth Aves (1-212-206-1272). Subway: A, C, E to 14th St; L to Eighth Ave. **Open** *Mon–Wed, Fri 10am–8pm; Thu 10am–9pm; Sat 10am–7pm; Sun 12:30–6pm.* **Credit** *AmEx, MC, V.*
Jeffrey Kalinsky, a former Barneys shoe buyer, was a Meatpacking District pioneer with his namesake shop, a branch of the Atlanta original. Designer clothing abounds—Helmut Lang, Versace and Yves Saint Laurent. But the centerpiece is the shoe salon, which features Manolo Blahnik, Prada and Robert Clergerie.

Lord & Taylor
424 Fifth Ave between 38th and 39th Sts (1-212-391-3344). Subway: B, D, F, V to 42nd St–Bryant Park; *7 to Fifth Ave.* **Open** *Mon, Wed–Fri 10am–8:30pm; Tue 9am–8:30pm; Sat 10am–7pm; Sun 11am–7pm.* **Credit** *AmEx, Disc, MC, V.*
Classic goes far at Lord & Taylor, in clothing and presentation; this is where the tradition of dramatic Christmas window displays began. Check out two recent dining additions: An American Place and the Signature Café, both run by celebrity chef Larry Forgione.

Macy's
151 W 34th St between Broadway and Seventh Ave (1-212-695-4400/www.macys.com). Subway: B, D, F, V, N, Q, R, W to 34th St–Herald Sq; 1, 2, 3, 9 to 34th St–Penn Station. **Open** *Mon–Sat 10am–8:30pm; Sun 11am–7pm.* **Credit** *AmEx, MC, V.*
Behold the real miracle on 34th Street. Macy's has everything: designer labels and lower-priced knock-offs, a pet-supply shop, a restaurant in the Cellar (the housewares section), a Metropolitan Museum of Art gift shop and—gulp—a McDonald's on the kids' floor. The store also offers Macy's by Appointment, a free service that allows shoppers to order goods or clothing over the phone and have those purchases shipped anywhere in the world (1-800-343-0121).

Saks Fifth Avenue
611 Fifth Ave at 50th St (1-212-753-4000). Subway: E, V to Fifth Ave–53rd St. **Open** *Mon–Wed, Fri, Sat 10am–7pm; Thu 10am–8pm; Sun noon–6pm.* **Credit** *AmEx, DC, Disc, MC, V.*
Although Saks maintains a presence in 24 states, this location is the original, started in 1924 by New York retailers Horace Saks and Bernard Gimbel.

Eat, Drink, Shop

The store features all the big names in women's fashion, an excellent menswear department, fine household linens and attentive customer service. New management is discussing a major overhaul for 2005, and at press time, Frank Gehry's name had made the rumor mill.

Takashimaya

693 Fifth Ave between 54th and 55th Sts (1-212-350-0100). Subway: E, V to Fifth Ave–53rd St. **Open** *Mon–Sat 10am–7pm; Sun noon–5pm.* **Credit** *AmEx, DC, MC, V.*
Step out of the Fifth Avenue hustle-bustle and into Takashimaya to behold the Zen garden of the retail world. Explore floor by floor, indulging your senses as you pass beauty essentials, furniture, and the men's and women's signature clothing collections. A cup of tea in the basement Tea Box makes the perfect end to a trip to consumer nirvana.

National chains

Many New Yorkers regard chain stores as unimaginative places to shop, but that doesn't mean you won't have to stand behind a long line of locals while waiting at the register. Stores such as **Anthropologie**, **Banana Republic**, **Express**, **H&M**, **Old Navy** and **Urban Outfitters** abound. **Target** finally succumbed to the NYC rat race, opening a store in Brooklyn in 2004 and planning two more—one in the Bronx and another in Manhattan—at press time. To find the nearest location of your favorite chain, refer to the phone book.

Critics' picks Give it

These stores are not gift shops, strictly speaking, but they've got terrific giveables.

Kiehl's
To both the men and the women on your list, give the gift of beauty...or free samples. *See p234.*

MoMA Design Store
Dig through plastic cubes full of low-priced, high-design doodads. *See p245.*

Takashimaya
The first floor harbors a foolproof collection of unique objects. *See p216.*

Tiffany & Co.
Not all baubles here are priceless: Key rings, money clips and even some jewelry pieces are under $100, *and* they come in the coveted blue box. *See p233.*

Fashion

Flagships

These big-name designers have clotheshorses chomping at the bit for new designs and seasonal collections.

Alexander McQueen

417 W 14th St between Ninth and Tenth Aves (1-212-645-1797/www.alexandermcqueen.com). Subway: A, C, E to 14th St; L to Eighth Ave. **Open** *Mon–Sat 11am–7pm; Sun 12:30–6pm.* **Credit** *AmEx, DC, Disc, MC, V.*
A barrel-vaulted ceiling and serene lighting make the rebellious Brit's Meatpacking District store feel like a religious retreat. But the topstitched denim skirts and leather jeans are far from monastic.

Bottega Veneta

699 Fifth Ave between 54th and 55th Sts (1-212-371-5511/www.bottegaveneta.com). Subway: E, V to Fifth Ave–53rd St; N, R, W to Fifth Ave–59th St. **Open** *Mon–Wed, Fri, Sat 10am–6:30pm; Thu 10am–7pm; Sun noon–5pm.* **Credit** *AmEx, DC, Disc, MC, V.*
At this luxe Italian label's largest store worldwide, a dramatic leather-and-steel staircase links the ground floor with a mezzanine. The gargantuan emporium stocks the complete line of shoes and handbags, along with men's and women's apparel available only here.

Burberry

9 E 57th St between Fifth and Madison Aves (1-212-407-7100/www.burberry.com). Subway: E, V to Fifth Ave–53rd St; N, R, W to Fifth Ave–59th St. **Open** *Mon–Fri 9:30am–7pm; Sat 9:30am–6pm; Sun noon–6pm.* **Credit** *AmEx, DC, Disc, MC, V.*
Now that Burberry has ballooned to 24,000 square feet in this six-story tower, it can peddle more of its trademark tartan-plaid wares, as well as its baby and home-accessories lines.
Other location *131 Spring St between Greene and Wooster Sts (1-212-925-9300).*

Catherine Malandrino

652 Hudson St at Little W 12th St (1-212-929-8710/www.catherinemalandrino.com). Subway: A, C, E to 14th St; L to Eighth Ave. **Open** *Mon–Sat 11am–7pm; Sun noon–6pm.* **Credit** *AmEx, MC, V.*
Parisian clothier Catherine Malandrino recently unveiled her 3,000-square-foot shop in the fashion fest that is the Meatpacking District, showcasing her exquisitely crafted ensembles as well as furniture, artwork and an in-store coffee bar.
Other location *468 Broome St at Greene St (1-212-925-6765).*

Chanel

15 E 57th St between Fifth and Madison Aves (1-212-355-5050/www.chanel.com). Subway: E, V to Fifth Ave–53rd St; N, R, W to Fifth Ave–59th St. **Open** *Mon–Wed, Fri 10am–6:30pm; Thu*

10am–7pm; Sat 10am–6pm; Sun noon–5pm.
Credit *AmEx, DC, MC, V.*
With a facade that resembles the iconic Chanel No. 5 perfume bottle, the brand's flagship conjures the spirit of Madame Coco herself. Fashion architect Peter Marino recently redesigned the space, multiplying the area to 9,750 square feet of divine Frenchness (up from a mere 6,500). Drop in at Chanel Fine Jewelry (733 Madison Ave at 64th St, 1-212-535-5828) for correspondingly elegant baubles and beads.
Other locations *139 Spring St at Wooster St (1-212-334-0055); 737 Madison Ave at 64th St (1-212-535-5505).*

Diane von Furstenberg, the Shop
385 W 12th St between Washington St and Eleventh Ave (1-646-486-4800/www.dvf.com). Subway: A, C, E to 14th St; L to Eighth Ave. **Open** *Mon–Wed, Fri 11am–7pm; Thu 11am–8pm; Sat 11am–6pm; Sun noon–5pm.* **Credit** *AmEx, Disc, MC, V.*
Although she's known for her classic wrap dress (she sold 5 million of them in the 1970s), indefatigable socialite Diane von Furstenberg has installed much more at this soigné space, which resembles the inside of a glittery jewel box. Whether you go for ultrafeminine dresses or sporty knits, you'll emerge from the changing room feeling like a princess.

Baby Bloom

Uptown institution Bloomingdale's goes *mano a mano* against its new downtown sister.

Bloomingdale's
See p214.
Age: 133 years
Square footage: 924,000 (ten levels)
Building's claim to fame: The shopping mecca's Art Deco edifice, completed in 1931, still turns heads.
Nickname: Bloomies
Crowd: Runs the demographic gamut from excitable teenagers to little old ladies.
Cinematic cameos: The films *Serendipity* and *The Family Man* were shot inside the store (and Rachel of *Friends* worked here).
Eateries: Shoppers can feast on bistro fare at Le Train Bleu (sixth floor), salads at Forty Carrots (metro level), and sandwiches at the 59th and Lex Grill (on the men's mezzanine).
Available only here: Home furnishings, bedding, glassware and furs, plus wedding-registry favorites like Wedgwood and Cuisinart. The department store also has three personal shoppers: one for men, one for women and—perhaps not as well known—one for beauty products.

Bloomingdale's Soho
See p214 for listing.
Age: One year
Square footage: 124,000 (six levels)
Building's claim to fame: The circa 1862 factory building had housed the beloved Canal Jeans Company, which subsequently reopened a few blocks up Broadway.
Nickname: TBD. We're rooting for Li'l Bloomies, Bloomies Lite or B.S.
Crowd: Teenyboppers, moneyed locals and everyone else clogging Soho's sidewalks.
Cinematic cameos: None yet; stay tuned.
Eateries: Bloom (fifth floor) serves light salads, while Café 504 (second floor) sells MarieBelle hot chocolate, Zaro's pastries and the store's signature frozen yogurt.
Available only here: The focus is on hot young designers such as Viktor & Rolf and celeb darling Zac Posen, who has created pencil skirts exclusively for this outpost. A gift section sells Canon Elph cameras and iPods, while haute products from Jo Malone and Pout fill the cosmetics department.

Eat, Drink, Shop

Top of the heap

Slaves to fashion, meet your makers.

Daniel Silver and
Steven Cox, of
menswear line Duckie
Brown, sold at
Barneys New York.
See p214.

ISA owners Holly
Harnsongkram and Isa
Saalabi. *See p223.*

Joe Corre and
Serena Rees of
Agent Provocateur.
See p226.

Colin and Latisha
Daring of **Pieces**.
See p223.

Eat, Drink, Shop

Dolce & Gabbana

*825 Madison Ave between 68th and 69th Sts
(1-212-249-4100/www.dolcegabbana.it). Subway: 6
to 68th St–Hunter College.* **Open** *Mon–Wed, Fri,
Sat 10am–6pm; Thu 10am–7pm; Sun noon–5pm.*
Credit *AmEx, DC, MC, V.*
The Italian design team of Domenico Dolce and
Stefano Gabbana gives love to uptowners and down-
towners alike. Visit the tonier Madison Avenue locale
(and see for yourself how close the Canal Street
knockoffs come to the real thing), or shop the West
Broadway store for the D&G line.
Other location *D&G, 434 West Broadway between
Prince and Spring Sts (1-212-965-8000).*

Donna Karan New York

*819 Madison Ave between 68th and 69th Sts (1-212-
861-1001/www.donnakaran.com). Subway: 6 to 68th
St–Hunter College.* **Open** *Mon–Wed, Fri, Sat
10am–6pm; Thu 10am–7pm; Sun noon–6pm.*
Credit *AmEx, DC, MC, V.*
Created around a central garden with a bamboo forest, Donna Karan's upscale flagship caters to men,
women and the home. Check out the organic café at
the nearby DKNY store, as well as Donna-approved
reads, clothing, shoes and vintage furniture.
Other location *DKNY, 655 Madison Ave at 60th
St (1-212-223-3569).*

Gucci

*685 Fifth Ave at 54th St (1-212-826-2600/www.
gucci.com). Subway: E, V to Fifth Ave–53rd St.*
Open *Mon–Wed, Fri 10am–6:30pm; Thu, Sat 10am–
7pm; Sun noon–6pm.* **Credit** *AmEx, DC, Disc, MC, V.*
The abstract decadent vibe pulsing through this five-
story temple of fashion hasn't faded with the departure of Tom Ford, who designed the store. Men's and
women's shoe departments are spread out on their
own floors, and even if you're not in the market, the
jewels on the ground level are worth a gander.
Other location *840 Madison Ave between 69th and
70th Sts (1-212-717-2619).*

Jill Stuart

*100 Greene St between Prince and Spring Sts (1-212-
343-2300/www.jillstuart.com). Subway: N, R, W to
Prince St; 6 to Spring St.* **Open** *Mon–Sat 11am–7pm;
Sun noon–6pm.* **Credit** *AmEx, MC, V.*
Vintage mixes with vixen at Stuart's cavernous boutique. Womenswear and accessories (including shoes,
handbags, casual and cocktail clothes) for the young
and modern make their home upstairs, but head
downstairs to find a boudoirlike setting—complete
with antique armoire and Victorian garment rack—
devoted to a vintage collection handpicked by Stuart.

Louis Vuitton

*1 E 57th St at Fifth Ave (1-212-758-8877/www.
vuitton.com). Subway: F to 57th St; N, R, W to Fifth
Ave–59th St.* **Open** *Mon–Wed, Fri, Sat 10am–7pm;
Thu 10am–8pm; Sun noon–6pm.* **Credit** *AmEx, DC,
Disc, MC, V.*
Vuitton's flagship was recently relocated and
revamped to celebrate the company's 150th anniver-

sary. The four-story, glass-encased, 20,000-square-
foot retail cathedral certainly gives cause for jubila-
tion: Crane your neck to view the three-floor-high
LED wall screen and antique LV trunks suspended
from the ceiling. The much-coveted bags and ready-
to-wear collection are here as well.
Other location *116 Greene St between Prince and
Spring Sts (1-212-274-9090).*

Marc Jacobs

*163 Mercer St between Houston and Prince Sts
(1-212-343-1490/www.marcjacobs.com). Subway: B,
D, F, V to Broadway–Lafayette St; N, R, W to Prince
St; 6 to Bleecker St.* **Open** *Mon–Sat 11am–7pm; Sun
noon–6pm.* **Credit** *AmEx, DC, Disc, MC, V.*
Men and women get fashion parity at Jacobs's Soho
boutique. A separate-but-equal policy rules on the
designer's Bleecker Street strip, where a trio of
stores—men's, women's and accessories—keeps the
West Village well outfitted.
Other locations *Marc by Marc Jacobs, 403–405
Bleecker St at 11th St (1-212-924-0026); Marc
Jacobs Accessories, 385 Bleecker St at Perry St
(1-212-924-6126).*

Prada

*575 Broadway at Prince St (1-212-334-
8888/www.prada.com). Subway: N, R, W to Prince St.*
Open *Mon–Sat 11am–7pm; Sun noon–6pm.*
Credit *AmEx, Disc, MC, V.*
The Rem Koolhaas–designed Soho flagship cemented
Prada's status as the label of choice for New York's
fashion fleet (yes, you still have to put your name on
a waiting list to buy the latest shoe styles). The giant
wood *Wave* structure is the store's focal point. If
you're interested only in accessories, then skip the
crowds at the two larger shops and stop by the small
Fifth Avenue location.
Other locations *724 Fifth Ave at 57th St (1-212-
664-0010); 841 Madison Ave at 70th St (1-212-
327-4200).*

Ralph Lauren

*867 Madison Ave at 72nd St (1-212-606-2100/
www.polo.com). Subway: 6 to 68th St–Hunter College.*
Open *Mon–Wed, Fri, Sat 10am–7pm; Thu 10am–8pm;
Sun noon–5pm.* **Credit** *AmEx, DC, Disc, MC, V.*
Ralph Lauren spent $14 million turning the old
Rhinelander mansion into an Ivy League dream
of a superstore: It's filled with oriental rugs, English
paintings, riding whips, leather club chairs, old
mahogany and fresh flowers. The young homeboys,
skaters and bladers who've adopted Ralphie's togs
head straight to Polo Sport across the street.
Other location *Ralph Lauren Boutique, 380 Bleecker
St between Charles and Perry Sts (1-212-645-5513);
Polo Sport, 381 Bleecker St between Charles and Perry
Sts (1-646-638-0684).*

Stella McCartney

*429 W 14th St between Ninth and Tenth Aves (1-212-
255-1556/www.stellamccartney.com). Subway: A, C, E
to 14th St; L to Eighth Ave.* **Open** *Mon–Sat 11am–
7pm; Sun 12:30–6pm.* **Credit** *AmEx, DC, Disc,
MC, V.*

Conceptually yours

Feel like your clothes, your home, heck, even your dog could all use a revamp? Fret not: With a single swipe of your credit card, you can achieve an instant lifestyle upgrade at one of NYC's concept stores.

The seven-year-old Parisian shop Colette is widely regarded as having sparked worldwide enthusiasm for these stylish one-stop shops that mix the fashion savvy (and chic) of small boutiques with the broad sandals-to-sofas range of department stores. The difference is in the curating: Instead of offering a grand sprawl of 20 lipstick brands or 30 different towels, a concept store offers only the items that suit its particular aesthetic vision.

Despite their popularity in Europe, concept stores haven't exactly taken the States by storm, though Americans have gotten comfortable with the, er, concept, thanks to mall-friendly chains like Anthropologie and Urban Outfitters. But in recent years, a handful of New York retailers have put their spin on the idea of selling a unified style to the whole consumer.

One of the first was **Kirna Zabête** (96 Greene St between Prince and Spring Sts, 1-212-941-9656), which opened in 1999. The Nick Dine–designed space stocks avant-garde-yet-wearable women's clothing and shoes from haute designers like Jean Paul Gaultier and Balenciaga, along with jewelry, home accessories, cosmetics, coffee-table books, and outfits for stylish urban kids—and dogs. On the lower level, shoppers can take a break to check their e-mail on bubble-gum pink iMacs or help themselves to the candy in enticing glass jars.

The New York outpost of London's **Terence Conran Shop** (407 E 59th St between First and York Aves, 1-212-888-3008) has been peddling its brand of "hip classicism" since 2000, in an atriumlike shop under the Queensborough Bridge. The store sells no clothing, but offers "ideas for living" in the form of quirky office supplies (think animal-shaped rubber bands), furniture, handbags, flowers and Nigella Lawson's sexy kitchenware.

Of course, space-deprived Manhattan means some stores deliver their lifestyle prescriptions on a smaller scale. The Soho shop **Lunettes et Chocolat** (25 Prince St between Elizabeth and Mott Sts, 1-212-334-8484), for instance, serves up rich hot cocoa, luscious chocolates and hard candy beside a selection of uberhip eyewear from the likes of Chloé, Gucci and Selima. Chocolates and spectacles? *Mais bien sûr*—both are seductive and stylishly presented.

However, it wasn't until last year that a true concept store—that is, after the European model—finally appeared on our shores. From the moment **Utowa** (17 W 18th St between Fifth and Sixth Aves, 1-866-929-4800) opened in April 2004, it began to draw comparisons with Colette. The store's monastic white walls are punctuated with large, embedded LED screens, flickering with nature-inspired graphics for a Zen-modern effect. Like the French pioneer, which hawks cell phones and digital cameras next to beauty products and clothing, Utowa offers a seasonally changing selection of cosmetics, CDs, art, and floral arrangements alongside minimalist duds for men and women from such lines as Philippe Dubuc and [un]designed by Carol Young. Leave it to a Japanese company to finally bring a European trend to the shores of America.

There's room for for all the elements of your lifestyle at concept stores like **Utowa**.

Opening Ceremony. *See p223.*

Celeb designer McCartney, who won acclaim for her rock-star collections for Chloé, now showcases pricey lines of glam-sprite womenswear, shoes and accessories at her first-ever store.

Boutiques

Bond 07

7 Bond St between Broadway and Lafayette St (1-212-677-8487). Subway: B, D, F, V to Broadway–Lafayette St; 6 to Bleecker St. **Open** *Mon–Sat 11am–7pm; Sun noon–7pm.* **Credit** *AmEx, MC, V.*
Selima Salaun, of the famed Le Corset (*see p227*) and Selima Optique (*see p231*), has branched out from undies and eyewear to embrace an eclectic mix of clothing (Alice Roi, Colette Dinnigan), accessories and French furniture. Vintage eyewear and bags are also available.

Calypso Christiane Celle

654 Hudson St between Gansevoort and W 13th Sts (1-646-638-3000/www.calypso-celle.com). Subway: A, C, E to 14th St; L to Eighth Ave. **Open** *Mon–Sat 11am–7pm; Sun noon–7pm.* **Credit** *AmEx, DC, MC, V.*
Christiane Celle has created a Calypso empire, of which the recently opened outpost in the Meatpacking District is the crown jewel. Stop by

any of the shops for gorgeous slip dresses, suits, sweaters and scarves, many from little-known French designers.
Other locations *throughout the city.*

Cantaloup

1036 Lexington Ave at 74th St (1-212-249-3566). Subway: 6 to 77th St. **Open** *Mon–Sat 11am–7pm; Sun noon–6pm.* **Credit** *AmEx, MC, V.*
Finally, a boutique that gives UES girls a reason to skip the trip down to Nolita. Cantaloup is chock-full of emerging labels such as James Coviello and Chanpaul, and it's less picked-over than the below-Houston boutiques.

Comme des Garçons

520 W 22nd St between Tenth and Eleventh Aves (1-212-604-9200). Subway: C, E to 23rd St. **Open** *Tue–Sat 11am–7pm; Sun noon–6pm.* **Credit** *AmEx, DC, Disc, MC, V.*
In this austere store devoted to Rei Kawakubo's architecturally constructed designs for men and women, clothing is hung like art in an innovative space that feels like a gallery—well placed in Chelsea.

Elizabeth Charles

639½ Hudson St between Gansevoort and Horatio Sts (1-212-243-3201/www.elizabeth-charles.com). Subway: A, C, E to 14th St; L to Eighth Ave.

Open *Tue–Sat noon–7:30pm; Sun noon–6:30pm.*
Credit *AmEx, MC, V.*
Oz native Elizabeth Charles transferred her eponymous shop from the West Village to the Meatpacking
District last year, allowing for an even greater selection of flirty clothes from Down Under designers.
Most labels are exclusive to the store, so chances are
you won't see your outfit on anyone else—unless you
go to Australia.

Hotel Venus by Patricia Field
*382 West Broadway between Broome and Spring
Sts (1-212-966-4066/www.patriciafield.com). Subway:
C, E to Spring St.* **Open** *Sun–Fri 11am–8pm; Sat
11am–9pm.* **Credit** *AmEx, Disc, MC, V.*
Patricia Field is a virtuoso at blending eclectic club
and street styles (she assembled the costumes for *Sex
and the City*). Her idiosyncratic mix of jewelry, makeup and cool clothing proves it.

ISA
*88 North 6th St between Berry St and Wythe Ave,
Williamsburg, Brooklyn (1-718-387-3363). Subway:
L to Bedford St.* **Open** *Mon–Fri 1–9pm; Sat
noon–10pm; Sun 1–7pm.* **Credit** *AmEx, MC, V.*
A sleek glass-and-concrete motif sets this warehouse-
style shop apart from the rest of the street's grunge.
The rolling racks—full of A.P.C., Marc Jacobs and
Pleasure Principle—say Manhattan, but the young
sales-clerk/DJ reminds you that you're in Billyburg.

Martin
*206 E 6th St between Bowery and Second Ave (1-212-
358-0011). Subway: L to First Ave; 6 to Astor Pl.*
Open *Tue–Sun 1–7pm.* **Credit** *AmEx, Disc, MC, V.*
Welcome to the androgynous zone. Anne Johnston
Albert's spartan boutique may be girls only, but it's
far from girly (it's named for her husband, after all).
Low-slung denims and corduroys, drapey tops and
fitted army-style jackets are Johnston's signatures.

Opening Ceremony
*35 Howard St between Broadway and Lafayette St
(1-212-219-2688). Subway: J, M, Z, N, Q, R,
W, 6 to Canal St.* **Open** *Mon–Sat 11am–8pm;
Sun noon–7pm.* **Credit** *AmEx, MC, V.*
Opening Ceremony offers a stylish trip around the
world, in a warehouse-size space gussied up with
grape-colored walls and crystal chandeliers. The boutique presents fashions by country (2005 kicked off
with Germany, and the U.K. will swoop in next).
Buyers cull from couture labels, independent designers, mass-market brands and open-air markets.

Pieces
*671 Vanderbilt Ave at Park Pl, Prospect Heights,
Brooklyn (1-718-857-7211/www.piecesofbklyn.com).
Subway: 2, 3 to Grand Army Plaza.* **Open** *Tue–Thu
11am–7pm; Fri, Sat 11am–8pm; Sun 11am–6pm.*
Credit *AmEx, MC, V.*
At this husband-and-wife-owned store, whitewashed
brick walls are the backdrop for vibrant coed clothing and accessories—Pretty Punk miniskirts, Ant
pin-striped dress shirts and Anja Flint clutches.

Other location *Pieces of Harlem, 228 W 135th St
between Adam Clayton Powell Jr. Blvd (Seventh Ave)
and Frederick Douglass Blvd (Eighth Ave) (1-212-
234-1725).*

Rebecca Taylor
*260 Mott St between Houston and Prince Sts (1-212-
966-0406/www.rebeccataylor.com). Subway: B, D, F,
V to Broadway–Lafayette St; N, R, W to Prince St; 6
to Bleecker St.* **Open** *Mon–Thu, Sat, Sun 11am–7pm;
Fri 11am–8:30pm.* **Credit** *AmEx, MC, V.*
This New Zealand designer's shop is adorned with
murals of fairy worlds and butterflies—arguably the
source of inspiration for her whimsical, kittenish
dresses and jackets.

Scoop
*861 Washington St between 13th and 14th Sts
(1-212-691-1905/www.scoopnyc.com). Subway: A,
C, E to 14th St; L to Eighth Ave.* **Open** *Mon–Fri
11am–8pm; Sat 11am–7pm; Sun noon–6pm.*
Credit *AmEx, DC, Disc, MC, V.*
Scoop is the ultimate fashion editor's closet.
Clothing from Juicy Couture, Diane von Furstenberg,
Philosophy and others is arranged by hue, not label.

**The
best Shops…**

…for vintage "I do" diamonds
Doyle & Doyle. *See p233.*

…for up-and-coming labels
30 Vandam. *See p224.*

…for a big, fat stogie
Nat Sherman. *See p251.*

**…for bellying up to the
Genius Bar**
The Apple Store. *See p251.*

**…for the finest custom-filled
cream puff you'll ever eat**
Beard Papa. *See p238.*

…for I'm-just-looking luxe
Bottega Veneta. *See p216.*

**…for the best Aussie imports
since Kidman and Crowe**
Elizabeth Charles. *See p222.*

…for whips and buttless chaps
Leather Man. *See p251.*

**…for the friendliest piercers
and tattoo artists**
New York Adorned. *See p252.*

…for the trip home
Flight 001. *See p252.*

Eat, Drink, Shop

The newest outposts, in the Meatpacking District, have fab finds for both genders at neighboring stores; hit the Soho shop for women only, uptown for a more classic look for guys and gals. **Other locations** *532 Broadway between Prince and Spring Sts (1-212-925-2886); 1275 Third Ave between 73rd and 74th Sts (1-212-535-5577).*

Steven Alan

103 Franklin St between Church St and West Broadway (1-212-343-0692/www.stevenalan.com). Subway: 1, 9 to Franklin St. **Open** *Mon–Wed, Fri, Sat 11:30am–7pm; Thu 11:30am–8pm.* **Credit** *AmEx, MC, V.*

Decorated like an old-school general store, this roomy shop leans slightly in favor of the ladies—the front section is earmarked for hot-chick labels such as Botkier, Christopher Deane and, of course, Steven Alan. The back area does right by the gents, though, with Rogan jeans and items from Filson, an outdoorsmen's line. Don't skip the jewelry and apothecary tables up front.

Other location *475 Amsterdam Ave between 82nd and 83rd Sts (1-212-595-8451).*

TG-170

170 Ludlow St between Houston and Stanton Sts (1-212-995-8660/www.tg170.com). Subway: F to Delancey St; J, M, Z to Delancey–Essex Sts. **Open** *noon–8pm daily.* **Credit** *AmEx, MC, V.*

Terri Gillis has an eye for emerging designers: She was the first to carry Built by Wendy and Pixie Yates. Nowadays, you'll find Jared Gold and Liz Collins pieces hanging in her newly expanded store.

30 Vandam

30 Vandam St between Sixth Ave and Varick St (1-212-929-5224/www.30vandam.com). Subway: C, E to Spring St. **Open** *Mon–Sat 11am–7pm; Sun noon–6pm.* **Credit** *AmEx, MC, V.*

A glossy market showing 50 *Vogue*-worthy designers at a time (Cinderloop and NatureVsFuture are chiefs among the chosen tribe), 30 Vandam is a pit

The next blue thing

Denim lines go in and out of vogue faster than a Hollywood ingenue, but some places always seem to stock the newest labels promising the most staying power. Get your butt into the right baby blues at these stores.

Barneys Co-op

2151 Broadway at 75th St (1-212-450-8624). Subway: 1, 2, 3, 9 to 72nd St.
The third Co-op from luxe department store Barneys New York recently settled on the Upper West Side, which means uptown girls and guys can now score their fair share of hot-label jeans from G-Star, Loomstate, Paper Denim & Cloth, Salt, Slab and Yanuk. Be sure to check out the special-edition cut from Citizens for Humanity made just for Barneys.

Bird

430 Seventh Ave between 14th and 15th Sts, Park Slope, Brooklyn (1-718-768-4940). Subway: F to 15th St–Prospect Park.
Park Slope's Bird has always been a favorite of neighborhood girls, but new owner Jennifer Mankins recently made it *the* spot in brownstone Brooklyn for jeans. The store stocks dozens of styles from lines including Chip & Pepper, Citizens for Humanity, Habitual, James Jeans, Levi's and Wrangler.

Diesel

1 Union Sq West at 14th St (1-646-336-8552/www.diesel.com). Subway: L, N, Q, R, W, 4, 5, 6 to 14th St–Union Sq.

This 14,000-square-foot emporium will satisfy any denim craving you have. The 55 DSL line is carried exclusively at the Union Square flagship, while Soho's Diesel StyleLab sells even more upmarket, experimental designs.
Other locations *770 Lexington Ave at 60th St (1-212-308-0055); Diesel StyleLab Store, 416 West Broadway between Prince and Spring Sts (1-212-343-3863).*

Earl Jean

160 Mercer St between Houston and Prince Sts (1-212-226-8709). Subway: B, D, F, V to Broadway–Lafayette St; N, R, W to Prince St; 6 to Bleecker St.
Industrial design meets rockabilly romp at this Soho shop. Earl's low-slung, formfitting jeans bring it all together: Whether you like yours dark, light, stretchy or tight, you've got a good shot at finding a new favorite pair.

Jean Shop

435 W 14th St between Ninth and Tenth Aves (1-212-366-5326). Subway: A, C, E to 14th St; L to Eighth Ave.
Stationed on the Meatpacking District's northern border, this rugged denim boutique's Marlboro Man—handsome salespeople peddle Jean Shop—label leather bomber jackets (from $900 to $13,000) and high-end customized jeans ($240 and up) to guys and girls.

stop for many local design darlings on their way to Bendel's and Barneys. If you snag some of their one-of-a-kinds here, you'll be able to say you knew these up-and-comers way back when.

Bargains

Century 21

22 Cortlandt St between Broadway and Church St (1-212-227-9092/www.c21stores.com). Subway: R, W to Cortlandt St. **Open** *Mon–Wed, Fri 7:45am–8pm; Thu 7:45am–8:30pm; Sat 10am–8pm; Sun 11am–7pm.* **Credit** *AmEx, MC, V.*
A white Gucci men's suit for $300? A Marc Jacobs cashmere sweater for less than $200? Roberto Cavalli sunglasses for a scant $30? You're not dreaming—you're shopping at Century 21. The score is rare but intoxicating; savings are usually between 25 and 75 percent off regular retail.
Other location *472 86th St between Fourth and Fifth Aves, Bay Ridge, Brooklyn (1-718-748-3266).*

Find Outlet

229 Mott St between Prince and Spring Sts (1-212-226-5167). Subway: N, R, W to Prince St; 6 to Spring St. **Open** *noon–7pm daily.* **Credit** *MC, V.*
Skip the sample sales and head to Find Outlet instead. High-fashion samples and overstock are at drastically reduced prices (50 percent off, on average) so you can you dress like a fashion editor on an editorial assistant's budget.
Other location *261 W 17th St between Eighth and Ninth Aves (1-212-243-3177).*

The Market NYC

268 Mulberry St between Houston and Prince Sts (1-212-580-8995/www.themarketnyc.com). Subway: B, D, F, V to Broadway–Lafayette St; N, R, W to Prince St; 6 to Bleecker St. **Open** *Sat 11am–7pm.* **Credit** *Cash only.*
Yes, it's housed in the gymnasium of a church's youth center, but it's no small shakes. Every Saturday, contemporary fashion and accessory designers hawk their (usually unique) wares here.

Nom de Guerre

640 Broadway at Bleecker St (1-212-253-2891). Subway: B, D, F, V to Broadway–Lafayette St; 6 to Bleecker St.
Beneath the Swatch store, accessed via an unmarked staircase, a hidden two-level gem rewards treasure hunters with a collection of (expensive) rare, imported and discontinued men's and women's threads and shoes, along with exclusive APC and Rogan cuts.

Selvedge

250 Mulberry St between Prince and Spring Sts (1-212-219-0994). Subway: N, R, W to Prince St; 6 to Spring St.
Did you know that because of wartime rationing in 1944, the double-seam "stitching" on Levi's 501 blue jeans was screen-painted on rather than sewn in? At Selvedge, a boutique fittingly named after a stitched-fabric edge, you can score a pair of these old denims, plus the highly coveted Levi's Red and Vintage collections.

Union

172 Spring St between Thompson St and West Broadway (1-212-226-8493). Subway: C, E to Spring St.
As the exclusive New York dealer for famed British streetwear label the Duffer of St. George, this tiny closet-size shop is a haven for T-shirt freaks. Also available are jeans from Rogan, Levi's, PRPS and 5EP, and offerings from the Union label.

Jonesing for jeans? **Diesel** satisfies.

London's calling at British designer **Paul Smith**'s handsome Chelsea boutique. *See p228.*

Children's clothing

Babybird
428 Seventh Ave between 14th and 15th Sts, Park Slope, Brooklyn (1-718-788-4506). Subway: F to Seventh Ave. Open Mon–Fri 10:30am–6:30pm; Sat, Sun noon–6pm. Credit AmEx, MC, V.
An offshoot of the neighboring Bird (an ultracool store for grown-up girls; *see p224* **The next blue thing**), Babybird is filled with comfy basics in stylish colors. Lilliputians will love the fish tank built into the register counter.

Calypso Enfants
426 Broome St between Crosby and Lafayette Sts (1-212-966-3234/www.calypso-celle.com). Subway: 6 to Spring St. Open Mon–Sat 11am–7pm; Sun noon–7pm. Credit AmEx, MC, V.
Fans of Calypso (*see p222*) adore this Francophile children's boutique: The tiny wool coats look as if they were lifted from the pages of the Madeline books.

Sam & Seb
208 Bedford Ave between North 5th and 6th Sts, Williamsburg, Brooklyn (1-718-486-8300/ www.samandseb.com). Subway: L to Bedford Ave. Open Mon–Fri noon–7pm; Sat, Sun 11am–8pm. Credit AmEx, DC, Disc, MC, V.
For style-conscious procreators who won't settle for generic baby clothes, Sam & Seb delivers groovy '60s-

and '70s-inspired play clothes and funky consignment pieces by local designers along with silk-screened Jimi Hendrix and Bob Marley tees.

Yoya
636 Hudson St between Horatio and Jane Sts (1-646-336-6844/www.yoyashop.com). Subway: A, C, E to 14th St; L to Eighth Ave. Open Mon–Sat 11am–7pm. Credit AmEx, Disc, MC, V.
Various Village sensibilities—European, bohemian, and hip—come together in this store aimed at infants to six-year-olds. Labels like Erica Tanov, Temperley for Little People, and Imps & Elves are available, as well as tiny-size (but not tiny-priced) Diesel tees.

Lingerie & swimwear

Most department stores have comprehensive lingerie and swimwear sections, and Victoria's Secret shops abound, but these spots are special places to go for extra-beautiful bedroom and beachside wear.

Agent Provocateur
133 Mercer St between Prince and Spring Sts (1-212-965-0229/www.agentprovocateur.com). Subway: B, D, F, V to Broadway–Lafayette St; N, R, W to Prince St; 6 to Spring St. Open Mon–Sat 11am–7pm; Sun noon–6pm. Credit AmEx, MC, V.

If you're looking for something to rev up your sweetie's heartbeat, then check out this patron saint of provocative panties. Va-va-voomy bras, garters and bustiers are dubbed with Bond-girl names.

Eres

621 Madison Ave between 58th and 59th Sts (1-212-223-3550/www.eres.fr). Subway: N, R, W to Fifth Ave–59th St. **Open** *Mon–Sat 10am–6pm.* **Credit** *AmEx, DC, Disc, MC, V.*
Paris's reigning queen of sophisticated bathing togs fits in swimmingly on New York's toniest avenue. Sunny white walls and serene blond-wood floors and counters give the merchandise the pedestal treatment. Precious intimates and colorful bathing suits are displayed on custom-made hangers, fabric busts and mannequins.
Other location *98 Wooster St between Prince and Spring Sts (1-212-431-7300).*

Le Corset by Selima

80 Thompson St between Broome and Spring Sts (1-212-334-4936). Subway: C, E to Spring St. **Open** *Mon–Fri 11am–7pm; Sat 11am–8pm; Sun noon–7pm.* **Credit** *AmEx, DC, Disc, MC, V.*
In addition to Selima Salaun's slinky designs, this boudoirlike boutique stocks antique camisoles, vintage silk kimonos, comely lingerie and Victorian- and Edwardian-inspired corsets.

Malia Mills

199 Mulberry St between Kenmare and Spring Sts (1-212-625-2311/www.maliamills.com). Subway: 6 to Spring St. **Open** *Mon–Sat noon–7pm; Sun noon–6pm.* **Credit** *AmEx, MC, V.*
Ever since one of her designs made the cover of *Sports Illustrated*'s swimsuit issue a dozen years ago, Malia Mills's swimwear has been a staple for St. Bart's bathing beauties. Flip-flops and long, luxurious terry-cloth robes are provided for ladies trying on bikini separates.
Other location *Malia Mills Outlet, 263 W 38th St between Seventh and Eighth Aves, 16th floor (1-212-354-4200, ext 214).*

Mixona

262 Mott St between Houston and Prince Sts (1-646-613-0100/www.mixona.com). Subway: B, D, F, V to Broadway–Lafayette St; N, R, W to Prince St; 6 to Bleecker St. **Open** *Sun–Fri 11am–7:30pm; Sat 11am–8pm.* **Credit** *AmEx, MC, V.*
Luxurious under-things by 30 designers are found here, including Christina Stott's leather-trimmed mesh bras and Passion Bait's lace knickers.

Vilebrequin

1070 Madison Ave at 81st St (1-212-650-0353/www.vilebrequin.com). Subway: 6 to 77th St. **Open** *10am–7pm daily.* **Credit** *AmEx, DC, MC, V.*
Boxer-style swim shorts (men's only) in five adult styles (plus one for boys) are the mainstay of this Saint-Tropez-based company's shop. Styles and patterns include sea horses and demure stripes.
Other location *436 West Broadway at Prince St (1-212-431-0673).*

Maternity wear

Cadeau

254 Elizabeth St between Houston and Prince Sts (1-212-994-1801/www.cadeaumaternity.com). Subway: F, V to Lower East Side–Second Ave. **Open** *Mon–Sat 11am–7pm; Sun noon–6pm.* **Credit** *AmEx, MC, V.*
Meant to celebrate rather than camouflage the pregnant belly, Cadeau ("gift" in French) offers sleek, sophisticated maternity wear. Armoires and free-standing mirrors lend the shop a residential feel.

Liz Lange Maternity

958 Madison Ave between 75th and 76th Sts (1-212-879-2191/www.lizlange.com). Subway: 6 to 77th St. **Open** *Mon–Fri 10am–7pm; Sat 10am–6pm; Sun noon–5pm.* **Credit** *AmEx, MC, V.*
Former *Vogue* editor Liz Lange is the mother of hip maternity wear, and high-profile moms like Catherine Zeta-Jones and Iman are among her many customers.

Veronique

1321 Madison Ave at 93rd St (1-212-831-7800/www.veroniquematernity.com). Subway: 6 to 96th St. **Open** *Mon–Thu 10am–7pm; Fri, Sat 10am–6pm; Sun noon–5pm.* **Credit** *AmEx, MC, V.*
Veronique is dedicated to providing maternity clothes just as cool as your regular duds. Try a pair of sexy, low-cut Seven jeans, plus styles by Nicol Caramel, Amy Zoller and Cadeau.

Menswear

A.

125 Crosby St between Houston and Prince Sts (1-212-941-8435). Subway: N, R, W to Prince St. **Open** *Mon–Fri 11am–7pm; Sat noon–7pm; Sun noon–6pm.* **Credit** *AmEx, DC, MC, V.*
When A. Atelier dropped women's clothes from its racks last year, it also dropped *atelier* from its name. Now a sophisticated men's-only store, A. distinguishes itself from the high-fashion Soho pack with rarefied labels such as Balenciaga, Cloak and Les Hommes. Score one for the boys.

agnès b. homme

79 Greene St between Broome and Spring Sts (1-212-431-4339/www.agnesb.com). Subway: N, R, W to Prince St; 6 to Spring St. **Open** *11am–7pm daily.* **Credit** *AmEx, DC, Disc, MC, V.*
French New Wave cinema from the 1960s is clearly an inspiration for agnès b.'s designs. Men's basics include her classic snap-button cardigan sweater and striped, long-sleeved T-shirts.

Comme des Garçons

See *p222* for listing.

Duncan Quinn

8 Spring St between Bowery and Elizabeth St (1-212-226-7030/www.duncanquinn.com). Subway: J, M, Z to Bowery. **Open** *Tue–Sun noon–8pm.* **Credit** *AmEx, DC, Disc, MC, V.*
Young Brit Duncan Quinn aims to clean up scruffy

Eat, Drink, Shop

boys with old-fashioned tailored suits and shirts in eye-popping colors and prints. His namesake shop stocks slim-fitting button-downs in windowpane checks and candy-colored stripes, along with narrow-cut suits and flamboyant silk ties.

Foley & Corinna Men
For listing, see p231 **Foley & Corinna**.

INA Men
262 Mott St between Houston and Prince Sts (1-212-334-2210). Subway: B, D, F, V to Broadway–Lafayette St; N, R, W to Prince St. **Open** *Sun–Thu noon–7pm; Fri, Sat noon–8pm.* **Credit** *AmEx, MC, V.*
For review, *see p231* **INA**.

Jack Spade
For listing, see p232 **Kate Spade**.

Original Penguin
1077 Sixth Ave at 41st St (1-646-443-3520/www.penguinclothing.com). Subway: B, D, F, V to 42nd St–Bryant Park; 7 to Fifth Ave. **Open** *Mon–Sat 10am–7:30pm; Sun 12:30–6pm.* **Credit** *AmEx, Disc, MC, V.*
Forget the alligator: Penguin's logo graced the lapels of Arnold Palmer and Bob Hope in the '70s, then drifted into dormancy for two decades. But when revived in spring 2003, the retro-chic signature polos and men's plaid trousers were as au courant as ever—as is the new midtown boutique.

Paul Smith
108 Fifth Ave between 15th and 16th Sts (1-212-627-9770/www.paulsmith.co.uk). Subway: L, N, Q, R, W, 4, 5, 6 to 14th St–Union Sq. **Open** *Mon–Wed, Fri, Sat 11am–7pm; Thu 11am–8pm; Sun noon–6pm.* **Credit** *AmEx, Disc, MC, V.*
Paul Smith devotees love this store's raffish English-gentleman look. They're even more partial to the designs and accessories that combine elegance, quality and wit (and some serious price tags).

Scoop Men
873 Washington St between 13th and 14th Sts (1-212-929-1244). Subway: A, C, E to 14th St; L to Eighth Ave. **Open** *Mon–Fri 11am–8pm; Sat 11am–7pm; Sun noon–6pm.* **Credit** *AmEx, DC, Disc, MC, V.*
For review, *see p223* **Scoop**.

Seize sur Vingt
243 Elizabeth St between Houston and Prince Sts (1-212-343-0476/www.16sur20.com). Subway: B, D, F, V to Broadway–Lafayette St; N, R, W to Prince St; 6 to Bleecker St. **Open** *Mon–Sat 11am–7pm; Sun noon–6pm.* **Credit** *AmEx, Disc, MC, V.*
Ready-to-wear men's shirts are available, but the real draws for the highly discriminating man are the bespoke suits and custom-cut button-downs. Shirts come in Wall Street pinstripes and preppy gingham, with mother-of-pearl buttons and short, square collars. Check out the selection of fine handkerchiefs.

Steven Alan
See p224 for listing.

Thomas Pink
520 Madison Ave at 53rd St (1-212-838-1928/www.thomaspink.co.uk). Subway: E, V to Fifth Ave–53rd St. **Open** *Mon–Wed, Fri 10am–7pm; Thu 10am–8pm; Sat 10am–6pm; Sun noon–6pm.* **Credit** *AmEx, DC, MC, V.*
Thomas Pink's shirts are made in bold, dynamic colors that animate conservative suits. But the shop is no longer strictly for men: The women's department includes accessories, jewelry and—of course—shirts.
Other location *1155 Sixth Ave at 44th St (1-212-840-9663).*

Streetwear

Autumn
436 E 9th St between First Ave and Ave A (1-212-677-6220/www.autumnskateboarding.com). Subway: L to First Ave; 6 to Astor Pl. **Open** *noon–8pm daily.* **Credit** *AmEx, Disc, MC, V.*
Proprietor and amateur skateboarder David Mimms and his wife, Kristen Yaccarino, stock DVS, Emerica, Etnies, iPath, Lakai and Vans for your half-pipe pleasure. Tees and jeans, not to mention scores of boards, are available, too.

Brooklyn Industries
162 Bedford Ave at North 8th St, Williamsburg, Brooklyn (1-718-486-6464/www.brooklynindustries.com). Subway: L to Bedford Ave. **Open** *Mon–Sat 11am–9pm; Sun noon–8pm.* **Credit** *AmEx, Disc, MC, V.*
Bags sporting the skyline label and zippered sweatshirt hoodies with BROOKLYN emblazoned across the chest are just the tip of the iceberg at Brooklyn Industries' borough-loving space.
Other locations *286 Lafayette St between Prince and Spring Sts (1-212-219-0862); 206 Fifth Ave at Union St, Park Slope, Brooklyn (1-718-789-2764).*

Dave's Quality Meat
7 E 3rd St between Bowery and Second Ave (1-212-505-7551/www.davesqualitymeat.com). Subway: F, V to Lower East Side–Second Ave. **Open** *Mon–Sat noon–7pm; Sun noon–6pm.* **Credit** *AmEx, Disc, MC, V.*
Dave Ortiz—formerly of urban-threads label Zoo York—and professional skateboarder Chris Keefe stock top-shelf streetwear in their wittily designed shop, complete with meat hooks and mannequins in butcher's aprons. House-made graphic-print tees are wrapped in plastic and displayed in a deli case.

Phat Farm
129 Prince St between West Broadway and Wooster St (1-212-533-7428/www.phatfarmstore.com). Subway: C, E to Spring St; N, R, W to Prince St. **Open** *Mon–Sat 11am–7pm; Sun noon–6pm.* **Credit** *AmEx, Disc, MC, V.*
Find Def Jam impresario Russell Simmons's classy, conservative take on hip-hop couture: phunky-phresh baggy clothing, and for gals, the curvy Baby Phat line.

Get your kicks (not your chops) at super sneaker shop **Dave's Quality Meat**. *See p228.*

Eat, Drink, Shop

Prohibit NYC

269 Elizabeth St between Houston and Prince Sts (1-212-219-1469/www.prohibitnyc.com). Subway: F, V to Lower East Side–Second Ave. **Open** *noon–8pm daily.* **Credit** *AmEx, MC, V.*
City guys can get all the necessities at this spare, polished upscale streetwear boutique, from well-made threads and special-edition sneakers to haircuts (with hot-towel treatment, $30) while seated in an apple-red vintage barber's chair.

Recon

237 Eldridge St between Houston and Stanton Sts (1-212-614-8502). Subway: F, V to Lower East Side–Second Ave. **Open** *Mon–Sat noon–7pm; Sun noon–6pm.* **Credit** *AmEx, MC, V.*
The joint venture of onetime graffiti artists Stash and Futura, Recon offers graf junkies a chance to wear the work on clothing and accessories.

Stüssy

140 Wooster St between Houston and Prince Sts (1-212-274-8855). Subway: N, R, W to Prince St. **Open** *Mon–Thu noon–7pm; Fri, Sat 11am–7pm; Sun noon–6pm.* **Credit** *AmEx, MC, V.*
Tricky isn't the only one who wants to be dressed up in Stüssy. Come here for all the skate and surf wear that made Sean Stüssy famous, as well as offerings from utilitarian Japanese bag company Headporter.

Supreme

274 Lafayette St between Jersey and Prince Sts (1-212-966-7799). Subway: B, D, F, V to Broadway–Lafayette St; N, R, W to Prince St; 6 to Spring St. **Open** *Mon–Sat 11:30am–7pm; Sun noon–6pm.* **Credit** *AmEx, MC, V.*
Filled mostly with East Coast brands such as Chocolate, Independent and Zoo York, this skate-wear store also stocks its own line. Look for pieces by Burton and DC Shoe—favorites of skaters like Colin McKay and Danny Way.

Triple Five Soul

290 Lafayette St between Houston and Prince Sts (1-212-431-2404/www.triple5soul.com). Subway: B, D, F, V to Broadway–Lafayette St; N, R, W to Prince St; 6 to Bleecker St. **Open** *Sun–Thu 11am–7pm; Fri, Sat 11am–7:30pm.* **Credit** *AmEx, Disc, MC, V.*
Although the label is no longer exclusive to New York, the city can still boast the brand's sole stores. Find the very necessary hooded sweatshirts and tees stamped with the Triple Five logo at this Soho spot. **Other location** *145 Bedford Ave at North 9th St, Williamsburg, Brooklyn (1-718-599-5971).*

Unis

226 Elizabeth St between Houston and Prince Sts (1-212-431-5533). Subway: B, D, F, V to Broadway–Lafayette St; N, R, W to Prince St; 6 to

Time Out New York **229**

Brooches bloom at **Alexis Bittar**. *See p232.*

Bleecker St. **Open** *Sun–Wed noon–7pm; Thu–Sat noon–7:30pm.* **Credit** *AmEx, Disc, MC, V.*
Korean-American designer Eunice Lee's structured streetwear used to be for boys only, but she let the girls in on the fun in 2003. Both collections are featured in her sleek Nolita boutique, along with Botkier bags and other accessories.

VICE
252 Lafayette St between Prince and Spring Sts (1-212-219-7788/www.viceland.com). Subway: N, R, W to Prince St; 6 to Spring St. **Open** *Mon–Sat noon–8pm; Sun noon–7pm.* **Credit** *AmEx, MC, V.*
Magazine and clothier extraordinaire VICE dictates downtown fashion. Peruse racks of Brooklyn Industries, Ben Sherman, Crypto, Religion and (of course) VICE, among other style superstars.

Sneakers

Alife Rivington Club
158 Rivington St between Clinton and Suffolk Sts (1-212-375-8128). Subway: F to Delancey St; J, M, Z

to *Delancey–Essex Sts.* **Open** *noon–6:30pm daily.* **Credit** *AmEx, MC, V.*
"Sneakers" equal "religion" in this tiny, out-of-the-way shop, which is arguably the city's main hub for hard-to-get shoes. The store, like its wares, has an exclusive vibe: There's no sign, no street number, no indication the joint even exists from the outside. Look closely and ring the bell to check out the rotating selection of 60 or so styles.

Classic Kicks
298 Elizabeth St between Houston and E 1st Sts (1-212-979-9514). Subway: B, D, F, V to Broadway–Lafayette; 6 to Bleecker St. **Open** *Mon–Sat noon–7pm; Sun noon–6pm.* **Credit** *AmEx, MC, V.*
One of the more female-friendly sneaker shops, Classic Kicks stocks mainstream and rare styles of Converse, Lacoste, Puma and Vans, to name a few, for both boys and girls, along with a decent selection of clothes.

Clientele
267 Lafayette St at Prince St (1-212-219-0531). Subway: N, R, W to Prince St; 6 to Spring St. **Open** *Sun–Thu noon–7pm; Fri, Sat noon–8pm.* **Credit** *AmEx, MC, V.*
Set up like an art-gallery display, the kicks line one wall of the minimalist store, and patrons sit on a long wooden bench to better admire the goods.

Puma
521 Broadway between Broome and Spring Sts (1-212-334-7861/www.puma.com). Subway: N, R, W to Prince St; 6 to Spring St. **Open** *Mon–Sat 10am–8pm; Sun 11am–7pm.* **Credit** *AmEx, Disc, MC, V.*
Head to the basement level of the futuristic space to check out Pumas in all colors and styles for men and women.

Vintage & thrift

Goodwill and the Salvation Army are great for vintage finds, but it can take hours of digging to discover a single gem. Enter thrift boutiques, where the digging has been done for you. We've listed a wide range here, from the more extravagant shops that cherry-pick vintage YSL and Fiorucci for their racks to your general T-shirt havens, as well as a few that fall in between.

Allan & Suzi
416 Amsterdam Ave at 80th St (1-212-724-7445/ www.allanandsuzi.net). Subway: 1, 9 to 79th St. **Open** *Mon–Sat 12:30–7pm; Sun noon–6pm.* **Credit** *AmEx, Disc, MC, V.*
Models and celebs drop off worn-once Gaultiers, Muglers, Pradas and Manolos here. The platform-shoe collection is flashback-inducing and incomparable, as is the selection of vintage jewelry.

Beacon's Closet
88 North 11th St between Berry St and Wythe Ave, Williamsburg, Brooklyn (1-718-486-0816/

www.beaconscloset.com). Subway: *L to Bedford Ave.*
Open *Mon–Fri noon–9pm; Sat, Sun 11am–8pm.*
Credit *AmEx, Disc, MC, V.*
At this Brooklyn fave, the prices are great, and so is the Williamsburg-appropriate clothing selection.
Other location *220 Fifth Ave between President and Union Sts, Park Slope, Brooklyn (1-718-230-1630).*

D/L Cerney
13 E 7th St between Second and Third Aves (1-212-673-7033). Subway: N, R, W to 8th St–NYU; 6 to Astor Pl. **Open** *noon–7:30pm daily.* **Credit** *AmEx, MC, V.*
Specializing in timeless, original designs for stylish fellows, the store also carries menswear from the 1940s to the '60s. Mint-condition must-haves include hats (some pristine fedoras), ties and shoes. An adjacent shop carries D/L Cerney's new women's line.

Edith & Daha
104 Rivington St between Essex and Ludlow Sts (1-212-979-9992). Subway: F to Delancey St; J, M, Z to Delancey–Essex Sts. **Open** *Mon–Fri 1–8pm; Sat, Sun noon–8pm.* **Credit** *AmEx, MC, V.*
Check out one of the city's best collections of (mostly) fine leather bags, not to mention an army of shoes, at this slightly below-street-level shop. There's no trash here—only the cream of the vintage crop. The front rack displays Edith & Daha's own line of clothing.

Foley & Corinna
108 Stanton St between Essex and Ludlow Sts (1-212-529-2338/www.foleyandcorinna.com). Subway: F to Delancey St; J, M, Z to Delancey–Essex Sts. **Open** *Mon–Fri 1–8pm; Sat, Sun noon–8pm.* **Credit** *AmEx, MC, V.*
Vintage-clothing fiends like Liv Tyler and Donna Karan know they can have it both ways: Shoppers freely mix old (Anna Corinna's vintage finds) with new (Dana Foley's original creations, including lace tops, leather-belted pants and sheer wool knits) to compose a truly one-of-a-kind look. Spiff up the boy in your life at the men's store, around the corner.
Other location *Foley & Corinna Men, 143 Ludlow St between Rivington and Stanton Sts (1-212-529-5043).*

INA
101 Thompson St between Prince and Spring Sts (1-212-941-4757). Subway: C, E to Spring St. **Open** *Sun–Thu noon–7pm; Fri, Sat noon–8pm.* **Credit** *AmEx, MC, V.*
For the past 11 years, INA on Thompson Street has reigned over the downtown consignment scene. The Soho location features drastically reduced couture pieces, while the Nolita shop, on Prince Street, carries trendier clothing. Be sure to visit the men's store (for listing, *see p228* **INA Men**).
Other locations *21 Prince St between Elizabeth and Mott Sts (1-212-334-9048); 208 E 73rd St between Second and Third Aves (1-212-249-0014).*

Marmalade
172 Ludlow St between Houston and Stanton Sts (1-212-473-8070). Subway: F, V to Lower East Side–
Second Ave. **Open** *Sun–Thu noon–9pm; Fri, Sat noon–10pm.* **Credit** *AmEx, MC, V.*
Marmalade, one of the cutest vintage-clothing stores on the Lower East Side, has some of the hottest '70s and '80s threads to be found below Houston Street. That slinky cocktail dress or ruffled blouse is tucked amid a selection of well-priced, well-cared-for items. Accessories, vintage shoes and a small selection of men's clothing are also available.

Fashion accessories

Eyewear

Fabulous Fanny's
335 E 9th St between First and Second Aves (1-212-533-0637/www.fabulousfannys.com). Subway: L to First Ave; 6 to Astor Pl. **Open** *noon–8pm daily.* **Credit** *AmEx, MC, V.*
The city's premier source of period eyeglasses for more than 17 years, this former booth at the 26th Street flea market now calls the East Village home. You'll find more than 10,000 pairs of spectacles, everything from WWII-era aviator goggles to '70s rhinestone-encrusted Versace shades.

Selima Optique
59 Wooster St at Broome St (1-212-343-9490/www.selimaoptique.com). Subway: C, E to Spring St. **Open** *Mon–Sat 11am–8pm; Sun noon–7pm.* **Credit** *AmEx, Disc, MC, V.*
Selima Salaun's wear-if-you-dare frames are popular with such famous four-eyes as Lenny Kravitz and Sean Lennon (both of whom have glasses named for them). At Lunettes et Chocolat (*see p221* **Conceptually yours**), you can stock up on fancy chocolates while you browse through Selima's specs.
Other locations *throughout the city.*

Sol Moscot Opticians
118 Orchard St at Delancey St (1-212-477-3796/www.moscots.com). Subway: F to Delancey St; J, M, Z to Delancey–Essex Sts. **Open** *Mon–Sat 10am–6pm; Sun 9am–5pm.* **Credit** *AmEx, DC, Disc, MC, V.*
This 84-year-old family-run emporium offers the same big names you'll find uptown—for about 20 percent less. It also carries vintage frames, Chanel and Gucci sunglasses, and bifocal contacts.
Other locations *69 W 14th St at Sixth Ave (1-212-647-1550); 107-20 Continental Ave (71st Ave) between Austin St and Queens Blvd, Forest Hills, Queens (1-718-544-2200).*

Handbags

Destination
32–36 Little W 12th St between Ninth Ave and Washington St (1-212-727-2031). Subway: A, C, E to 14th St; L to Eighth Ave. **Open** *Mon–Sat 11am–8pm; Sun noon–7pm.* **Credit** *AmEx, MC, V.*
Manhattan's largest accessories boutique is in the Meatpacking District. The bags, shoes, hats and jewelry, created by more than 30 designers, include

Vegas-worthy baubles and handbags crafted from Vietnamese filmstrips.

Kate Spade

454 Broome St at Mercer St (1-212-274-1991/ www.katespade.com). Subway: N, R, W to Prince St; 6 to Spring St. **Open** *Mon–Sat 11am–7pm; Sun noon–6pm.* **Credit** *AmEx, Disc, MC, V.*

Popular handbag designer Kate Spade sells her classic boxy tote, as well as other smart numbers, in this bright store. Spade also stocks shoes, pajamas and rain slickers. Accessories for men are sold at Jack Spade.

Other location *Jack Spade, 56 Greene St between Broome and Spring Sts (1-212-625-1820).*

Ro

150 W 28th St between Sixth and Seventh Aves (1-212-477-1595/www.gotoro.com). Subway: 1, 9 to 28th St. **Open** *By appointment only.* **Credit** *AmEx, Disc, MC, V.*

Gene Miao and Yvonne Roe's signature travel accoutrements, such as sleek suitcase-shaped wallets, hang on pegs in the foyer-size store. In an era of overly fussy accessories, Ro's streamlined satchels are appealing indeed.

Jewelry

Agatha

611 Madison Ave at 58th St (1-212-758-4301/ www.agatha.fr). Subway: N, R, W to Fifth Ave–59th St; 4, 5, 6 to 59th St. **Open** *Mon–Sat 10am–7pm; Sun noon–6pm.* **Credit** *AmEx, Disc, MC, V.*

The queen of the costume-jewelry joints, Agatha stocks low-priced trinkets that look like a million bucks. Jumbo pearls, chunky rings and graphic, modern designs abound.

Other location *159A Columbus Ave between 67th and 68th Sts (1-212-362-0959).*

Alexis Bittar

465 Broome St between Greene and Mercer Sts (1-212-625-8340). Subway: N, R, W to Prince St; 6 to Spring St. **Open** *Mon–Sat 11am–7pm; Sun 11am–6pm.* **Credit** *AmEx, MC, V.*

A Brooklyn-based designer known for his chunky

Man*hat*tan

Trucker hat, RIP. These days, New York's fashion-forward men are sporting more sophisticated headgear, from bowlers to berets, and turning to the city's millinery specialists to find them.

"I'm seeing more men buying and wearing hats now than in the eight years I've been in business," says **Kelly Christy** (235 Elizabeth St between Houston and Prince Sts, 1-212-965-0686). At her eponymous shop, men can choose a hat off the rack or have one custom made. Christy focuses on classics, like fedoras with grosgrain ribbon details, and is also known for her vintage-inspired bridal collection, which includes hats and veils.

Ellen Christine (255 W 18th St between Seventh and Eighth Aves, 1-212-242-2457), offers a wide range of new and vintage hats for men, including turn-of-the-century top hats, jazz-age porkpies and Russian fur *chapkas* (plus romantic Victorian offerings for the ladies). Christine says fedoras are especially popular at the moment, noting that men seem to be learning that a little attention to accessories can create a quirky personal style.

Established in 1911, **J.J. Hat Center** (310 Fifth Ave at 32nd St, 1-212-239-4368) is New York's oldest hat shop, with potted palms and chandeliers harking back to the

One of **Ellen Christine**'s natty toppers.

day when every Bogart wanna-be topped off his suit with a fedora. Kevin Gerber, a sales associate at J.J. Hat Center, points to modern role models such as Kid Rock and Bruce Willis: "Hats are on TV and on celebrities," he says. "It's hard to ignore."

For Harlem-based milliner Bunn—yes, just Bunn—the question isn't why hats are back, but why they ever fell out of favor. "You don't want to get dressed in a nice suit and put on a baseball cap—it's a contradiction," he says. First-time visitors to **Hats. By Bunn.** (2283 Adam Clayton Powell Jr. Blvd [Seventh Ave] between 134th and 135th Sts, 1-212-694-3590) may be shy at first: "Men come in like they're going to the dentist," Bunn says. "But then once they get their first hat, I can't keep them out of here!"

Lucite and semiprecious-stone accessories, Bittar adorned his recently opened boutique with vintage wallpaper and a Victorian lion's-paw table.

Borealis

229 Elizabeth St between Houston and Prince Sts (1-917-237-0152). Subway: B, D, F, V to Broadway–Lafayette; N, R, W to Prince St; 6 to Bleecker St. **Open** *Mon–Sat noon–7pm; Sun 1–6pm.* **Credit** *AmEx, MC, V.*
The brainchild of style guru Steven Alan and jewelry designer Aurora Lopez, this minuscule Nolita boutique showcases contemporary bijoux from more than 40 designers.

Doyle & Doyle

189 Orchard St between Houston and Stanton Sts (1-212-677-9991/www.doyledoyle.com). Subway: F, V to Lower East Side–Second Ave. **Open** *Tue, Wed, Fri, Sat 1–7pm; Thu 1–8pm; Sun noon–7pm.* **Credit** *AmEx, Disc, MC, V.*
Whether your taste is Art Deco or Nouveau, Victorian or Edwardian, gemologist sisters Pam and Elizabeth Doyle (who specialize in estate and antique jewelry) will have that intimate, one-of-a-kind piece you're looking for, including engagement rings and eternity bands.

Fragments

116 Prince St between Greene and Wooster Sts (1-212-334-9588/www.fragments.com). Subway: B, D, F, V to Broadway–Lafayette St; N, R, W to Prince St. **Open** *Mon–Sat 11am–7pm; Sun noon–6pm.* **Credit** *AmEx, DC, Disc, MC, V.*
Over two decades, Fragments owner Janet Goldman has assembled a stable of more than 100 pet jewelry designers, who offer their creations to her before selling them to department stores such as Barneys.

Tiffany & Co.

727 Fifth Ave at 57th St (1-212-755-8000/ www.tiffany.com). Subway: E, V to Fifth Ave–53rd St; F to 57th St; N, R, W to Fifth Ave–59th St. **Open** *Mon–Fri 10am–7pm; Sat 10am–6pm; Sun noon–5pm.* **Credit** *AmEx, DC, Disc, MC, V.*
The heyday of Tiffany's was at the turn of the 20th century, when Louis Comfort Tiffany, son of founder Charles Lewis Tiffany, took the reins and created sensational Art Nouveau jewelry. Today, the design stars are Paloma Picasso and Elsa Peretti. Three floors are stacked with precious jewels, silver, watches, porcelain and the classic Tiffany engagement rings. FYI: Breakfast is not served.

Shoes

Camper

125 Prince St at Wooster St (1-212-358-1842/ www.camper.es). Subway: N, R, W to Prince St. **Open** *Mon–Sat 11am–8pm; Sun noon–6pm.* **Credit** *AmEx, DC, MC, V.*
Dozens of styles from the line of Spanish-made casual shoes are stocked in this large corner store.

Christian Louboutin

941 Madison Ave between 74th and 75th Sts (1-212-396-1884). Subway: 6 to 77th St. **Open** *Mon–Sat 10am–6pm.* **Credit** *AmEx, MC, V.*
Serious shoe hounds should plan to drop several C-notes on a pair of Christian Louboutin's irresistibly sexy shoes, distinguished by their vertiginous heels and signature scarlet sole. The racy footwear could easily convince you to walk on water (or glide over slush puddles, at the very least). Don't try it—and don't try hobbling more than a block or two in these fierce spikes, either.

Chuckies

1073 Third Ave between 63rd and 64th Sts (1-212-593-9898). Subway: F to Lexington Ave–63rd St. **Open** *Mon–Fri 10:45am–7:45pm; Sat 10:45am–7:30pm; Sun 12:30–7pm.* **Credit** *AmEx, DC, Disc, MC, V.*
An alternative to department stores, Chuckies carries high-profile labels for men and women. Its stock ranges from old-school Calvin Klein and Jimmy Choo to up-and-coming Ernesto Esposito.

Constança Basto

573 Hudson St between Bank and W 11th Sts (1-212-645-3233/www.constancabasto.com). Subway: A, C, E to 14th St; L to Eighth Ave. **Open** *Tue–Sat 11am–7pm; Sun noon–6pm.* **Credit** *AmEx, MC, V.*
Even chicks who don't have a thing for shoes are drawn to this circuslike, orange-and-white-striped West Village boutique. Classic pumps, rendered in supple calfskin, suede, alligator or snakeskin, have sexy but wearable three-inch stiletto heels.

Jimmy Choo

645 Fifth Ave at 51st St (1-212-593-0800/ www.jimmychoo.com). Subway: E, V to Fifth Ave–53rd St. **Open** *Mon–Wed, Fri 10am–6pm; Thu 10am–7pm; Sun noon–5pm.* **Credit** *AmEx, MC, V.*
Jimmy Choo, famed for conceiving Princess Diana's custom-shoe collection, has conquered America with his six-year-old emporium, which features chic boots, sexy stilettos, curvaceous pumps and kittenish flats. Prices start at $450.

Manolo Blahnik

31 W 54th St between Fifth and Sixth Aves (1-212-582-3007). Subway: E, V to Fifth Ave–53rd St. **Open** *Mon–Fri 10:30am–6pm; Sat 10:30am–5:30pm.* **Credit** *AmEx, MC, V.*
The high priest of timelessly glamorous shoes will put high style in your step—and a deep, deep dent in your wallet.

Otto Tootsi Plohound

137 Fifth Ave between 20th and 21st Sts (1-212-460-8650). Subway: N, R, W to 23rd St. **Open** *Mon–Fri 11:30am–8pm; Sat 11am–8pm; Sun noon–7pm.* **Credit** *AmEx, DC, Disc, MC, V.*
One of the best places for the latest shoe styles, Tootsi has a big selection of trendy (and slightly overpriced) imports for women and men. **Other locations** *throughout the city.*

Health & Beauty

Beauty & cosmetics

Alcone

235 W 19th St between Seventh and Eighth Aves (1-212-633-0551/www.alconeco.com). Subway: 1, 9 to 18th St. **Open** *Mon–Sat 11am–6pm.* **Credit** *AmEx, MC, V.*

Frequented by makeup artists on the prowl for the German brand Kryolan and for kits of fake blood and bruises, this shop also attracts mere mortals looking to score its own line of sponges and pre-made palettes—trays of a dozen or more eye, lip and cheek colors.

Other location *5-49 49th Ave between Vernon Blvd and 5th St, Long Island City, Queens (1-718-361-8373).*

Face Stockholm

110 Prince St at Greene St (1-212-966-9110/www. facestockholm.com). Subway: N, R, W to Prince St. **Open** *Mon–Sat 11am–7pm; Sun noon–6pm.* **Credit** *AmEx, MC, V.*

In addition to a full line of eye shadows, lipsticks, blushes and tools, Face offers makeup application and lessons to help improve your own technique.

Other locations *226 Columbus Ave between 70th and 71st Sts (1-212-769-1420); 1263 Madison Ave between 90th and 91st Sts (1-212-987-1411).*

Fresh

57 Spring St between Lafayette and Mulberry Sts (1-212-925-0099/www.fresh.com). Subway: N, R, W to Prince St; 6 to Bleecker St. **Open** *Mon–Sat 10am–8pm; Sun noon–6pm.* **Credit** *AmEx, MC, V.*

Fresh is a Boston company that bases its soaps, lotions, candles and other products on natural ingredients such as honey, milk, soy and sugar. Stores are sleekly modern; goodies like the Brown Sugar Body Polish smell divine.

Other locations *throughout the city.*

John Masters Organics

77 Sullivan St between Spring and Broome Sts (1-212-343-9590/www.johnmasters.com). Subway: N, R, W to Prince St; C, E to Spring St. **Open** *Mon–Sat 11am–7pm.* **Credit** *AmEx, MC, V.*

Organic doesn't get more orgasmic than John Masters' chic apothecary line. Blood orange and vanilla body wash and lavender and avocado intensive conditioner are just two of the good-enough-to-eat products that you can get to go.

Kiehl's

109 Third Ave between 13th and 14th Sts (1-212-677-3171/www.kiehls.com). Subway: L to Third Ave; N, Q, R, W, 4, 5, 6 to 14th St–Union Sq. **Open** *Mon–Sat 10am–7pm; Sun noon–6pm.* **Credit** *AmEx, DC, MC, V.*

Although it is 154 years old and has recently expanded, this New York institution is *still* a mob scene. Check out the Motorcycle Room, full of vin-

tage Harleys (the owner's obsession). Try one dab of Kiehl's moisturizer, lip balm or body lotion from the plentiful free samples, and you'll be hooked.

Other location *150 Columbus Ave between 66th and 67th Sts (1-212-799-3438).*

Lush

1293 Broadway between 33rd and 34th Sts (1-212-564-9120/www.lush.com). Subway: B, D, F, V, N, Q, R, W to 34th St–Herald Sq. **Open** *Mon–Sat 10am–8pm; Sun 11am–7pm.* **Credit** *AmEx, Disc, MC, V.*

This wildly popular U.K. "beauty deli" has finally come west with a 500-square-foot Herald Square flagship. The sweet-smelling store is stuffed with fresh handmade products such as fruity soaps cut from giant cheeselike wheels, shampoos in bar form and fizzing Gobstopperesque Bath Bombs.

M•A•C

113 Spring St between Greene and Mercer Sts (1-212-334-4641/www.maccosmetics.com). Subway: C, E to Spring St. **Open** *Mon–Wed 11am–7pm; Thu–Sat 11am–8pm; Sun noon–7pm.* **Credit** *AmEx, DC, Disc, MC, V.*

Makeup Art Cosmetics is famous for lipsticks and eye shadows in must-have colors and for offbeat celebrity spokesmodels like RuPaul and k.d. lang.

Other locations *throughout the city.*

Make Up Forever

409 West Broadway between Prince and Spring Sts (1-212-941-9337/www.makeupforever.com). Subway: C, E to Spring St; N, R, W to Prince St. **Open** *Mon–Sat 11am–7pm; Sun noon–6pm.* **Credit** *AmEx, MC, V.*

MUF's line of French cosmetics is popular with glam women and drag queens. Colors range from bold purples and fuchsias to muted browns and soft pinks. The mascara is essential.

Ricky's

509 Fifth Ave between 42nd and 43rd Sts (1-212-949-7230/www.rickys-nyc.com). Subway: B, D, F, V to 42nd St–Bryant Park; 7 to Fifth Ave. **Open** *Mon–Fri 8am–9pm; Sat 10am–8pm; Sun 10am–7pm.* **Credit** *AmEx, Disc, MC, V.*

Stock up on tweezers, cheap travel containers and makeup cases that look like souped-up tackle boxes. Ricky's in-house makeup line, Mattése, includes fake lashes and glitter nail polish.

Other locations *throughout the city.*

Santa Maria Novella

285 Lafayette St between Jersey and Prince Sts (1-212-925-0001/www.lafcony.com). Subway: B, D, F, V to Broadway–Lafayette St; N, R, W to Prince St; 6 to Bleecker St. **Open** *Mon–Wed, Fri, Sat 11am–7pm; Thu 11am–8pm; Sun noon–6pm.* **Credit** *AmEx, MC, V.*

The 470 skin creams and fragrances at this retail outlet for the hard-to-find Florentine toiletries are produced at the Italian monastery where they were conceived in the year 1210.

Find peace of mind at New York's only organic salon, **John Masters Organics**. *See p234.*

Three Custom Color Specialists

54 W 22nd St at Sixth Ave, third floor (1-888-262-7714/www.threecustom.com). Subway: F, V to 23rd St. **Open** *By appointment only.* **Credit** *AmEx, MC, V.*
Beauty-industry veterans Trae Bodge, Scott Catto and Chad Hayduk have been blending custom lipsticks, cream blushes and eye shadows since 1997. They offer a ready-to-wear line at their new minimalist white-and-silver studio.

Perfumeries

Bond No. 9

9 Bond St between Broadway and Lafayette St (1-212-228-1940). Subway: B, D, F, V to Broadway–Lafayette St; 6 to Bleecker St. **Open** *Mon–Sat 11am–8pm; Sun noon–6pm.* **Credit** *AmEx, MC, V.*
Custom-blended bottles of bliss and scents that pay olfactory homage to New York City—Wall Street, Nouveau Bowery, New Harlem—are available here. Don't worry, there's no Chinatown Sidewalk.
Other locations *680 Madison Ave at 61st St (1-212-838-2780); 897 Madison Ave at 73rd St (1-212-794-4480).*

Jo Malone

949 Broadway at 22nd St (1-212-673-2220/ www.jomalone.com). Subway: N, R, W to 23rd St.
Open *Mon–Sat 10am–8pm; Sun noon–6pm.*
Credit *AmEx, DC, Disc, MC, V.*
British perfumer Jo Malone champions the "layering" of scents as a way of creating a personalized aroma. Along with perfumes and colognes, her Flatiron District boutique offers candles, skin-care products and superpampering facials.
Other location *946 Madison Ave between 74th and 75th Sts (1-212-472-0074).*

Pharmacists

For 24-hour pharmacies, *see p371.*

C.O. Bigelow Chemists

414 Sixth Ave between 8th and 9th Sts (1-212-533-2700/www.bigelowchemists.com). Subway: A, C, E, B, D, F, V to W 4th St. **Open** *Mon–Fri 7:30am–9pm; Sat 8:30am–7pm; Sun 8:30am–5:30pm.*
Credit *AmEx, Disc, MC, V.*
A Greenwich Village institution, Bigelow is the complete apothecary—pretty and comprehensive.

Zitomer

969 Madison Ave between 75th and 76th Sts (1-212-737-4480/www.zitomer.com). Subway: 6 to 77th St. **Open** *9am–8pm daily.* **Credit** *AmEx, DC, Disc, MC, V.*
Zitomer seems to stock every beauty and health product under the sun.

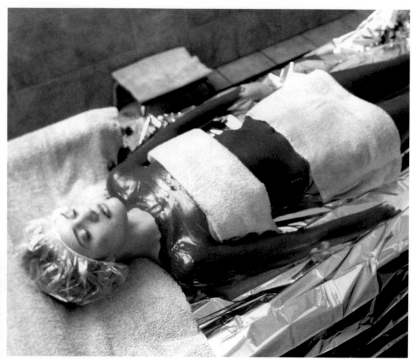

The **Oasis Day Spa** will put you flat on your back with a detoxifying body wrap. *See p237.*

Salons & spas

Salons

New York is the city of fresh starts; what better way to begin anew than with your hair? Whether you want a full-out makeover, a rock & roll do, or just a trim, we have the salon for you. The stylin' superstars at **Frédéric Fekkai Beauté de Provence** (1-212-753-9500) and **Louis Licari** (1-212-758-2090) are top-notch, but they charge hair-raising prices. The following salons offer specialized services—budget, rocker, ethno-friendly—and unique settings for your special NYC cut.

Astor Place Hair Stylists

2 Astor Pl at Broadway (1-212-475-9854). Subway: N, R, W to 8th St–NYU; 6 to Astor Pl. **Open** *Mon–Sat 8am–8pm; Sun 9am–6pm.* **Credit** *Cash only.*
An army of barbers does everything from neat trims to shaved designs. You can't make an appointment; just take a number and wait outside with the crowd. Sunday mornings are quiet. Cuts start at $12; blow-drys, $20; dreads, $75.

Ebony 2000

831 Third Ave between 50th and 51st Sts, third floor (1-212-750-8950). Subway: E, V to Lexington–53rd St; 6 to 51st St. **Open** *Tue–Fri 10am–6pm; Sat 8am–3pm.* **Credit** *AmEx, MC, V.*
Specializing in African-American hair, Ebony 2000 will color, press-and-curl, relax or weave the way to a new you. Coloring starts at $75.

John Masters Organics

See p234 for listing.
It's like visiting an intoxicating botanical garden: The organic scalp treatment will send you into relaxed oblivion, and ammonia-free, herbal-based color treatments will appeal to your inner purist. Cuts or coloring start at $90.

Laicale

129 Grand St between Broadway and Crosby St (1-212-219-2424). Subway: J, M, Z, N, Q, R, W, 6 to Canal St. **Open** *Tue, Wed, Fri 11am–8pm; Thu 11am–10pm; Sat 9am–6pm.* **Credit** *AmEx, MC, V (gratuities accepted in cash only).*
Get your locks chopped at this industrial chrome-and-glass hair mecca while the shop's own DJ spins tunes. Most of the stylists here also work for magazines and runway shows. Cuts start at $75; highlights, $125.

Miwa/Alex Salon
*24 E 22nd St between Broadway and Park Ave South
(1-212-228-4422/www.miwaalex.com). Subway:
N, R, W, 6 to 23rd St.* **Open** *Mon 8:30am–5:30pm;
Tue–Sat 8:30am–7pm.* **Credit** *MC, V.*
Tucked inside a posh, friendly space in the Flatiron
District, Miwa/Alex delivers the sort of cut you expect
in New York: smart, unique and perfectly coordinated
with color. Cuts start at $65 for women; $50 for men.

Mudhoney
*148 Sullivan St between Houston and Prince Sts
(1-212-533-1160). Subway: C, E to Spring St.*
Open *Tue–Fri noon–8pm; Sat, Sun noon–6pm.*
Credit *Cash only.*
Don't be surprised if the stylist never removes his
orange-tinted sunglasses; you're in the city's premier
rock & roll salon. The decor alone—a torture chair,
lascivious stained-glass—will make the time in this
tiny, attitude-packed salon fly by. Cuts start at $75.
Other locations *7 Bond St between Broadway and
Lafayette St (1-212-228-8128); 888 Broadway at 19th
St (1-212-473-7407).*

Ouidad
*846 Seventh Ave between 54th and 55th Sts, fifth floor
(1-212-888-3288/www.ouidad.com). Subway: B, D, E
to Seventh Ave.* **Open** *Tue, Wed, Fri 9:30am–6:30pm;
Thu 10am–7pm; Sat 9am–5pm.* **Credit** *MC, V.*
Lebanese-born Ouidad founded the first curlcentric
salon (and product line) 20 years ago. She is still the
gold standard, and even maintains a private room for
veiled clients. Cuts start at $115.

Spas

Amore Pacific
*114 Spring St between Greene and Mercer Sts (1-212-
966-0400). Subway: N, R, W to Prince St; 6 to Spring
St.* **Open** *Tue–Sat 11am–7pm; Sun noon–6pm.*
Credit *AmEx, DC, Disc, MC, V.*
This is the only U.S. outlet for the superswanky product line AP, a Korean company. The skin-care system uses botanicals (red ginseng, bamboo sap) in
conjunction with a high-tech process so that treatments quickly penetrate and revitalize the skin.
Reflexology and massage are also available.

Cornelia
*663 Fifth Ave between 52nd and 53rd Sts, eighth and
ninth floors (1-212-759-9375). Subway: E, V to
Fifth Ave–53rd St.* **Open** *Mon–Fri 9am–8pm; Sat
10am–6pm.* **Credit** *AmEx, MC, V.*
Aesthetician Cornelia Zicu's luxury spa features
20,000 square feet of visage- and body-doting
space, including a rooftop garden and sundeck, an
open-air massage area and an outdoor café. A basic
facial is $140.

Juvenex
*25 W 32nd St between Broadway and Fifth Ave,
fifth floor (1-646-733-1330/www.juvenexspa.com).
Subway: B, D, F, V, N, Q, R, W to 34th St–Herald Sq.*
Open *24 hrs daily.* **Credit** *AmEx, Disc, MC, V.*

This formerly girls-only 24-hour spa gained a cult
following among postpartyers seeking communal
detox in its jade igloo sauna. But boys can finally join
the fun every night after 9pm. Treatments (unlike the
sauna) are private; facials include the Oxygen ($130
for 75 minutes) and the Energizing Ginseng ($105 for
60 minutes). Massages start at $95.

Nickel
*77 Eighth Ave at 14th St (1-212-242-3202/ www.
nickelformen.com). Subway: A, C, E to 14th St; L to
Eighth Ave.* **Open** *Sun, Mon 1–9pm; Tue–Fri 11am–
9pm; Sat 10am–9pm.* **Credit** *AmEx, Disc, MC, V.*
New York's official temple of male grooming offers
facials, waxing, massages, manicures and pedicures.
The product line includes Washing Machine shower
gel and Fire Insurance aftershave, as well as Self-
Absorbed suntan oil—for the Narcissus in all of us.

Oasis Day Spa
*108 E 16th St, between Union Sq East and
Irving Pl, second floor (1-212-254-7722/www.oasis
dayspanyc.com). Subway: L, N, Q, R, W, 4, 5, 6 to
14th St–Union Sq.* **Open** *Mon–Fri 10am–10pm;
Sat, Sun 9am–9pm.* **Credit** *AmEx, Disc, MC, V.*
The flagship location of this posh wellness sanctuary
features everything from hair styling and detoxifying mud wraps to acupuncture. Stressed-out travelers can stop at the airport branch (JFK International
Airport Jet Blue Terminal 6, 1-212-254-7722) for manicures, hot shaves or even full-body massages.
Other locations *throughout the city.*

The Spa at Chelsea Piers
*The Sports Center at Chelsea Piers, Pier 60, 23rd St at
Twelfth Ave (1-212-336-6780/www.chelseapiers.com).
Subway: C, E to 23rd St.* **Open** *Mon–Fri 10am–9pm;
Sat, Sun 10am–7pm.* **Credit** *AmEx, Disc, MC, V.*
Treat yourself to a massage ($85 and up), facial ($80
and up) and more at this intimate, full-service spa
inside the mammoth Chelsea Piers Sports Center,
and get a free day pass to the exercise club, where
you can try yoga or rock-climbing, have a dip in the
pool or grab a smoothie. Then head to the riverfront
deck for a well-deserved nap in the sun.

Spa at Mandarin Oriental New York Hotel
*Time Warner Center, 80 Columbus Circle at 60th St,
35th floor (1-212-805-8880/www.mandarin
oriental.com). Subway: A, C, B, D, 1, 9 to 59th
St–Columbus Circle.* **Open** *Mon–Fri 9am–8pm; Sat,
Sun 9am–7pm.* **Credit** *AmEx, Disc, MC, V.*
If you have deep pockets or are just in the mood to
splurge, then this luxe 14,500-square-foot oasis is definitely worth the dough. Exotic pampering treatments
include the Lomi Lomi, a deep tissue massage (80
minutes, $285), and the Purva Karma Influence,
a half-day program that combines a salt-and-oil scrub,
a four-handed massage and a facial with eye-lift treatment (three hours, $855). Access to the gorgeous spa
facilities (including a vitality pool and amethyst-
crystal steam room) is gratis with all treatments.

Eat, Drink, Shop

Nails

Jin Soon Natural Hand & Foot Spa

56 E 4th St between Bowery and Second Ave (1-212-473-2047). Subway: F, V to Lower East Side–Second Ave; 6 to Bleecker St. **Open** *11am–8pm daily.* **Credit** *MC, V.*

Most mani and pedi salons feel more like factory assembly lines than places to be pampered. Not Jin Soon, which has private rooms and a tranquil Zen vibe. Basic manicures ($15) and pedicures ($30) are refreshingly affordable. Nail treatments are meticulously administered, and the floating foot-tub specials include season-specific ingredients like spring flowers or spiced orange.
Other location *23 Jones St between Bleecker and W 4th Sts (1-212-229-1070).*

Rescue Beauty Lounge

34 Gansevoort St between Greenwich and Hudson Sts, second floor (1-212-206-6409/www.rescuebeauty.com). Subway: A, C, E to 14th St; L to Eighth Ave. **Open** *Tue–Fri 11am–8pm; Sat, Sun 10am–6pm.* **Credit** *AmEx, MC, V.*

Rescue doesn't look overly posh, but it doesn't skimp on luxury: Manicures start at $23 and pedicures, $43. The stylishly minimalist salon is also well stocked with high-end beauty products—tony moisturizers from La Mer, Go Smile tooth whitener, and Dr. Hauschka lotions and oils.
Other location *8 Centre Market Pl at Grand St (1-212-431-0449).*

Sweet Lily

222 West Broadway between Franklin and North Moore Sts (1-212-925-5441/www.sweetlilyspa.com). Subway: A, C, E to Canal St; 1, 9 to Franklin St. **Open** *Mon–Fri 11am–8pm; Sat 10am–6pm.* **Credit** *AmEx, MC, V (gratuities accepted in cash only).*

Although it's in the middle of trendy Tribeca, this spa's comforting shabby-chic decor gives it the feel of a country cottage. Sweet Lily further sweetens the deal by replacing generic salon chairs with giant, overstuffed floral armchairs. Seasonal pedis include grapefruit and mint in summer, and apple, brown sugar and cinnamon in the fall.

Food & Drink

Farm-fresh, high-quality produce, meats, cheeses and grains are expected—no, demanded—by city dwellers. Listed below are a few locally beloved city markets and sweets spots.

Bakeries & cupcakes

Thanks to Magnolia bakery, cupcakes have become a portable obsession among New Yorkers in recent years; here's where to grab your sugar fix.

Amy's Bread

672 Ninth Ave between 46th and 47th Sts (1-212-977-2670/www.amysbread.com). Subway: N, R, W to 49th St; C, E to 50th St. **Open** *Mon–Fri 7:30am–11pm; Sat 8am–11pm; Sun 9am–6pm.* **Credit** *Cash only.*

Whether you want sweet (chocolate-chubbie cookies) or savory (semolina-fennel bread or hefty French sourdough *boules*), Amy's never disappoints.
Other locations *Chelsea Market, 75 Ninth Ave between 15th and 16th Sts (1-212-462-4338); 972 Lexington Ave between 70th and 71st Sts (1-212-537-0270).*

Beard Papa

2167 Broadway between 76th and 77th Sts (1-212-799-3770). Subway: 1, 2, 3, 9 to 72nd St. **Open** *10am–8pm daily.* **Credit** *MC, V.*

The oversize cream puffs sold by this Japanese chain are filled to order (using a snazzy custard-squirting machine), so you'll never get a soggy puff.
Other location *740 Broadway at 8th St (1-212-353-8888).*

Billy's Bakery

184 Ninth Ave between 21st and 22nd Sts (1-212-647-9956/www.billysbakerynyc.com). Subway: C, E to 23rd St. **Open** *Sun–Thu 9am–11pm; Fri, Sat 9am–12:30am.* **Credit** *AmEx, DC, Disc, MC, V.*

Amid super-sweet retro delights such as coconut cream pie, Hello Dollies and Famous Refrigerator Cake, you'll find friendly service in a setting that will remind you of Grandma's kitchen—if your grandmother was Betty Crocker.

The Magnolia Bakery

401 Bleecker St at 11th St (1-212-462-2572). Subway: 1, 9 to Christopher St. **Open** *Mon noon–11:30pm; Tue–Thu 9am–11:30pm; Fri 9am–12:30am; Sat 10am–12:30am; Sun 9am–11:30pm.* **Credit** *AmEx, Disc, MC, V.*

Part sweet market, part meet market, Magnolia skyrocketed to fame thanks to *Sex and the City*. The pastel-iced cupcakes are much vaunted, but you can also pick up a cup of custardy, Southern-style banana pudding or get a scoop from the summertime ice-cream cart. Then, join the other happy eaters clogging nearby apartment stoops.

Chocolatiers

Jacques Torres Chocolate Haven

350 Hudson St between Charlton and King Sts, entrance on King St (1-212-414-2462/www.jacquestorres.com). Subway: 1, 9 to Houston St. **Open** *Mon, Wed–Fri 9am–7pm; Sat 10am–8pm; Sun 11am–7pm.* **Credit** *AmEx, MC, V.*

Walk into Jacques Torres's new glass-walled shop and café, and you'll be surrounded by a Willy Wonka–esque chocolate factory that turns raw cocoa beans into luscious goodies before your very eyes. Sweets for sale range from the sublime (deliciously rich hot chocolate, steamed to order) to the ridiculous (chocolate-covered fortune cookies).

Between heaven and well

"I want to be taking vitamins when I get older, not prescription pills," says Donna Turro, director of the women's day spa **Soho Sanctuary** (119 Mercer St between Prince and Spring Sts, third floor, 1-212-334-5550). Turro isn't alone in her aspiration. Spa-goers who prefer toning their thighs with yoga rather than liposuction have driven a trend toward more holistic pampering. Recently, several spas that focus exclusively on wellness have opened throughout the city, offering a natural alternative to extreme medical-spa procedures such as laser resurfacing and Botox injections.

"The body is a smart machine; it has everything it needs to change," Turro says. "We provide women with a soothing, supportive environment in which they can commit to being healthier." To that end, Soho Sanctuary uses only natural products in all its skin and body treatments, including the detoxifying mud wrap ($170) and an herbal massage with Thai ginger, turmeric and tamarind ($175) to energize the mind and body. Clients can also use the eucalyptus steam room, free with all treatments.

Sea Change Healing Center (31 W 26th St between Broadway and Sixth Ave, 1-212-889-7300) also focuses on the body's innate power to heal itself. The center offers acupuncture, herbal medicine, massage, yoga, tai chi and meditation classes. Not that Sea Change neglects beauty treatments—after all, the skin *is* the largest organ. Facial and body treatments here are designed to clean, balance and hydrate the skin and to improve circulation and cell renewal. Holistic cosmetic procedures are also available, including a lymphatic massage to reduce cellulite ($95 for one hour) and an acupuncture face-lift ($305), which lasts about as long as Botox, says Sea Change's founder and director, Deborah Musso, D.C.

If your definition of wellness involves toned arms and washboard abs, then you'll want to check out one of the growing number of mind-body spas that dish out beauty and fitness in equal measure, like **Exhale** (980 Madison Ave between 76th and 77th Sts, 1-212-249-3000). Designed by the architects behind Zen-cool store Takashimaya (*see p216*), the space is a stunning fusion of luxury spa, fitness club and Buddhist temple, aptly reflecting the spa's offerings.

Exhale: a body- and mind-bending encounter.

"We wanted to create a destination-spa concept and put it in the heart of the city," says Exhale founder, Annbeth Eschbach. "We want to offer a place where people can make change happen on a daily basis and do it in a way that is meaningful and therapeutic."

In addition to a healing menu that includes acupuncture, energy therapies and guided relaxation, Exhale specializes in indulgent treatments like Thai-massage pedicures ($48) as well as Core Fusion exercise classes, which combine Pilates, yoga and core conditioning to tone and stretch the body—so you'll emerge feeling just as fine as you look.

Eat, Drink, Shop

Kitschy cakes at **Billy's Bakery**. See p238.

Other location *Jacques Torres Chocolate, 66 Water St between Dock and Main Sts, Dumbo, Brooklyn (1-718-875-9772).*

La Maison du Chocolat

1018 Madison Ave between 78th and 79th Sts (1-212-744-7117/www.lamaisonduchocolat.com). Subway: 6 to 77th St. **Open** *Mon–Sat 10am–7pm; Sun noon–6pm.* **Credit** *AmEx, MC, V.*
This suave cocoa-brown boutique, the creation of Robert Linxe, packages refined (and pricey) examples of edible Parisian perfection like fine jewelry. A small café serves hot and cold chocolate drinks and a selection of sweets.
Other location *30 Rockefeller Plaza, 49th St between Fifth and Sixth Aves (1-212-265-9404).*

Richart

7 E 55th St between Madison and Fifth Aves (1-888-742-4278/www.richart-chocolates.com). Subway: E, V to Fifth Ave–53rd St. **Open** *Mon–Fri 10am–7pm; Sat 10am–6pm.* **Credit** *AmEx, MC, V.*
French master-chocolatier Michel Richart is an intellectual sensualist, one who's as likely to fill a bonbon with green-tea essence or basil ganache as with the more expected coffee or hazelnuts. His precisely geometric squares are topped with cool graphic patterns—swirls, bubbles, even leopard prints—to indicate the fillings within.

Scharffen Berger

473 Amsterdam Ave at 83rd St (1-212-362-9734/www.scharffenberger.com). Subway: 1, 9 to 86th St. **Open** *Mon–Thu 10am–8pm; Fri, Sat 10am–9pm; Sun 11am–7pm.* **Credit** *AmEx, Disc, MC, V.*
The Berkeley, California, artisanal chocolate maker opened its first East Coast boutique last year. Along with gift boxes of its remarkable dark-chocolate (adored by professional pastry chefs), the bite-size shop also sells ganache-filled treats (in flavors like fresh lemon and sea-salt caramel), jars of dreamy chocolate sauce and chocolate-mint lip balm.

Vosges Haut Chocolat

132 Spring St between Greene and Wooster Sts (1-212-625-2929/www.vosgeschocolate.com). Subway: C, E to Spring St; N, R, W to Prince St. **Open** *11am–8pm daily.* **Credit** *AmEx, MC, V.*
This stylish, oh-so-Soho sweetshop isn't for the spice-shy; exotic essences like wasabi, ginger and even curry are blended in many of the chocolates, and their notorious "Rooster" truffle is a layered extravaganza of bittersweet chocolate, Taleggio cheese, walnuts and vanilla.

Liquor stores

Most supermarkets and corner delis sell beer; for wine or spirits, you need to go to a liquor store. For the first time since before Prohibition, some of them are now open seven days a week.

Astor Wines & Spirits

12 Astor Pl at Lafayette St (1-212-674-7500/www.astoruncorked.com). Subway: N, R, W to 8th St–NYU; 6 to Astor Pl. **Open** *Mon–Sat 9am–9pm; Sun noon–6pm.* **Credit** *AmEx, Disc, MC, V.*
This modern wine supermarket could serve as the perfect blueprint for a chain, but legal obstacles prevent liquor stores from branching out.

Sherry-Lehmann

679 Madison Ave at 61st St (1-212-838-7500/www.sherry-lehmann.com). Subway: F to Lexington Ave–63rd St; N, R, W to Fifth Ave–59th St; 4, 5, 6 to 59th St. **Open** *Mon–Sat 9am–7pm.* **Credit** *AmEx, MC, V.*
Perhaps the most famous of New York's numerous upscale liquor stores, Sherry-Lehmann has a vast selection of liquors as well as a superb assortment of American, French and Italian wines.

Vintage New York

482 Broome St at Wooster St (1-212-226-9463/www.vintagenewyork.com). Subway: C, E to Spring St; N, R, W to Prince St. **Open** *Mon–Sat 11am–9pm; Sun noon–9pm.* **Credit** *AmEx, Disc, MC, V.*
An outpost of an upstate winery, Vintage focuses on the bounty of New York State's vines, from Long Island to the Finger Lakes. The shop's liberal tastings make it a lovely spot to pick up an unusual souvenir.
Other location *2492 Broadway at 93rd St (1-212-721-9999).*

Markets

There are more than 20 open-air Greenmarkets, sponsored by city authorities, in various locations on different days. The largest and best-known is at **Union Square** (*see p97*), where small producers of cheese, flowers, herbs, fruits and vegetables hawk their goods. Arrive early, before the prime stuff sells out. For other venues, check with the **Council on the Environment of NYC** (1-212-477-3220, www.cenyc.org).

Dean & DeLuca

560 Broadway at Prince St (1-212-431-1691/www.deananddeluca.com). Subway: N, R, W to Prince St. **Open** *Mon–Sat 10am–8pm; Sun 10am–7pm.* **Credit** *AmEx, Disc, MC, V.*
Dean & DeLuca's flagship store (one of only two that offer more than just a fancy coffeebar) provides the most sophisticated (and pricey) selection of specialty food items in the city.
Other locations *throughout the city.*

Myers of Keswick

634 Hudson St between Horatio and Jane Sts (1-212-691-4194/www.myersofkeswick.com). Subway: A, C, E to 14th St; L to Eighth Ave. **Open** *Mon–Fri*

10am–7pm; Sat 10am–6pm; Sun noon–5pm. **Credit** *AmEx, MC, V.*
This charming English market is a frequent stop for Brits and local Anglophiles. While some come looking for a hint of home or a jolly good meet-and-greet, others flock to the store for prepared foods like Cornish pasties, homemade sausages, baked beans, steak-and-kidney pies, and assorted British candies and tea biscuits.

Whole Foods

Time Warner Center, 10 Columbus Circle at Broadway, concourse level (1-212-823-9600/www.wholefoods.com). Subway: A, C, B, D, 1, 9 to 59th St–Columbus Circle. **Open** *8am–10pm daily.* **Credit** *AmEx, Disc, MC, V.*
You'll feel healthier just walking around this veritable cornucopia of fresh food. Gorgeous as well as good for you, Whole Foods is the city's best bet for organic offerings. Take advantage of the well-stocked wine store seven days a week.
Other locations *4 Union Sq South between Broadway and University Pl (slated to open in spring 2005); 250 Seventh Ave at 24th St (1-212-924-5969).*

Zabar's

2245 Broadway at 80th St (1-212-787-2000/www.zabars.com). Subway: 1, 9 to 79th St. **Open** *Mon–Fri*

A shop in the dark

That old saw about New York being the "city that never sleeps" usually conjures images of clubs, swank bars and restaurants packed to the gills till the wee hours. But natives are a famously around-the-clock bunch in every sort of way: They work late, they dine late, and thanks to the extended hours of a growing number of stores, they now also shop well into the evening. Most places stay open a bit later on Thursdays; if you crave a retail fix any other night of the week, then the East Village and the Lower East Side are your best bets.

One East Village favorite open till 9pm is **Alphabets** (115 Ave A between 7th and 8th Sts, 1-212-475-7250), a gift shop hawking hipster staples like Fred Perry and ironic T-shirts (IS JESUS YOUR HOMEBOY?). You'll also find surefire gifts like Umbra photo frames, Votivo candles, funky greeting cards and knickknacks. Home store **Las Venus** (163 Ludlow St between Houston and Stanton Sts, 1-212-982-0608) is another great gift spot, with iconic '50s, '60s and '70s vintage furniture and accessories for sale until midnight on Saturdays, and 9pm on other days.

Ladies can maintain their style without elbowing through the weekend crowds at boutiques like **3 Turtle Doves** (201 E 2nd St between Aves A and B, 1-212-529-3288), which makes its girlish vintage clothing and delicate, modern accessories available until 10pm Tuesdays through Sundays. For basics, guys and girls head to **American Apparel** (183 Houston St at Orchard St, 1-212-598-4600). Open until 10pm Monday through Thursday, and midnight on Fridays and Saturdays, this L.A.-based company (which eschews sweatshop labor) supplies colorful cotton tees and sweats to comfort-seeking minimalists. Between beers at the historic, sawdust-floored McSorley's Ale House, boys can hit the neighboring **Village Scandal** (19 E 7th St between Second and Third Aves, 1-212-677-0124) until midnight and try on a chic fedora (there are retro cloches for women, too).

Finally, swing by **Toys in Babeland** (*see p251*), open until 10pm nightly, and 7pm on Sundays, where you can browse the impressive variety of sex toys or simply pick up some bedtime reading. Titles include *Sex Toys 101* and *The Seductive Art of Japanese Bondage*. Think of it as the end of a great night out—or the beginning of a great one in.

Eat, Drink, Shop

8am–7:30pm; Sat 8am–8pm; Sun 9am–6pm.
Credit *AmEx, MC, V.*
Zabar's is more than just a market—it's a New York City landmark. You might leave the place feeling a little light in the wallet, but you can't beat the topflight prepared foods. Besides the famous smoked fish and rafts of Jewish delicacies, Zabar's has fabulous selections of bread, cheese and coffee—and an entire floor of decently priced gadgets and housewares.

Sundries

Guss' Pickles
85–87 Orchard St between Broome and Grand Sts (1-917-805-4702). Subway: F to Delancey St; J, M, Z to Delancey–Essex Sts. **Open** *Mon–Thu 9:30am–6:30pm; Fri 9:30am–4pm; Sun 10am–6pm.* **Credit** *AmEx, MC, V.*
Its wandering days are over. After moving twice in recent years, the Pickle King has settled down, and the complete line of sours and half sours, pickled peppers, watermelon rinds and sauerkraut is available once again.

Russ & Daughters
179 E Houston St between Allen and Orchard Sts (1-212-475-4880/www.russanddaughters.com). Subway: F, V to Lower East Side–Second Ave. **Open** *Mon–Sat 9am–7pm; Sun 8am–5:30pm.* **Credit** *AmEx, Disc, MC, V.*
Russ & Daughters, open since 1914, sells eight kinds of smoked salmon and many Jewish-inflected Eastern European delectables, along with dried fruits, chocolates, and Russian and Iranian caviar.

Home & Gifts

Children's toys

Gepetto's Toy Box
10 Christopher St between Greenwich Ave and Gay St (1-212-620-7511). Subway: 1, 9 to Christopher St. **Open** *Mon–Sat 11:30am–7pm; Sun 12:30–5:30pm.* **Credit** *AmEx, Disc, MC, V.*
Like all good toys-for-tots stores, Gepetto's focuses on constructive, nonconfrontational diversions like a wooden make-your-own Empire State Building kit.

Kidding Around
60 W 15th St between Fifth and Sixth Aves (1-212-645-6337). Subway: F, V to 14th St; L to Sixth Ave. **Open** *Mon–Wed 10am–7pm; Thu, Fri 10am–9pm; Sun 11am–6pm.* **Credit** *AmEx, Disc, MC, V.*
Loyal customers frequent this quaint shop for clothing and learning toys for the brainy baby. The play area in the back will keep your little one occupied while you shop.

The Scholastic Store
557 Broadway between Prince and Spring Sts (1-212-343-6166). Subway: B, D, F, V to

Broadway–Lafayette St; N, R, W to Prince St; 6 to Bleecker St. **Open** *Mon–Sat 10am–7pm; Sun noon–6pm.* **Credit** *AmEx, Disc, MC, V.*
After checking out the huge selection of Scholastic books, move along to the toy section. This is the city's Harry Potter headquarters.

Toys "R" Us
Times Square
1514 Broadway between 44th and 45th Sts (1-800-869-7787). Subway: N, Q, R, W, 42nd St S, 1, 2, 3, 9, 7 to 42nd St–Times Sq. **Open** *Mon–Sat 9am–10pm; Sun 11am–6pm.* **Credit** *AmEx, Disc, MC, V.*
The chain's flagship location is the world's largest toy store—big enough for a 60-foot-high Ferris wheel inside and an animatronic tyrannosaur to greet you at the door. Brands rule here: a two-story Barbie dollhouse and a café with its very own sweetshop, Candy Land, which is designed to look like the board game.
Other locations *throughout the city.*

West Side Kids
498 Amsterdam Ave between 83rd and 84th Sts (1-212-496-7282). Subway: 1, 9 to 86th St. **Open** *Mon–Sat 10am–7pm; Sun 10am–6pm.* **Credit** *AmEx, Disc, MC, V.*
Owner Alice Bergman fills her shelves with cute items such as primary-colored stoves and multicultural dolls.

Flea markets

Among bargain-hungry New Yorkers, flea-market rummaging is pursued with religious devotion. What better way to walk off that overstuffed omelette and Bloody Mary from brunch than to explore aisles of old vinyl records, 8-track tapes, vintage nightgowns and funky furniture?

Annex Antiques Fair
& Flea Market
Sixth Ave between 24th and 26th Sts (1-212-243-5343). Subway: F, V to 23rd St. **Open** *Sat, Sun sunrise–sunset.* **Credit** *Cash only.*
Designers and the occasional dolled-down celebrity hunt regularly—and early—at the Annex. Divided into scattered sections (one of which charges $1 admission), the market has heaps of secondhand and antique clothing, old bicycles, birdcages, household items and various accessories. The nearby indoor Garage, especially welcoming on cold days, always carries unusual items.
Other location *The Garage, 112 W 25th St between Sixth and Seventh Aves (1-212-647-0707).*

Greenflea
Intermediate School 44, Columbus Ave at 76th St (1-212-721-0900). Subway: B, C to 72nd St; 1, 9 to 79th St. **Open** *Sun 10am–5:30pm.* **Credit** *Cash only.*
Greenflea is an extensive market that offers rare books, African art, handmade jewelry and eatables like vegetables and spiced cider (hot or cold, depend-

Toys take a back seat to the real attractions at **Toys "R" Us Times Square.** *See p242.*

ing on the season). Visit both the labyrinthine interior and the schoolyard.
Other location *Greenwich Ave at Charles St (1-212-721-0900).*

Gift shops

Auto
805 Washington St between Gansevoort and Horatio Sts (1-212-229-2292). Subway: A, C, E to 14th St; L to Eighth Ave. **Open** *Tue–Sat noon–7pm; Sun noon–6pm.* **Credit** *AmEx, MC, V.*
A cool gallery vibe makes this white-walled shop inviting. The owners buy from gifted artisans who produce everything from handblown-glass pieces and personalized ceramic Shrinky Dink necklaces to paintings and bedding.

Love Saves the Day
119 Second Ave at 7th St (1-212-228-3802). Subway: 6 to Astor Pl. **Open** *noon–9pm daily.* **Credit** *AmEx, MC, V.*
Yoda dolls, Elvis lamps, ant farms, lurid machine-made tapestries of Madonna, glow-in-the-dark crucifixes, collectible toys and Mexican Day of the Dead statues: Kitsch reigns. Vintage clothing is peppered throughout the store.

Metropolitan Opera Shop
136 W 65th St at Broadway (1-212-580-4090/ www.metguild.org/shop). Subway: 1, 9 to 66th St–Lincoln Ctr. **Open** *Mon–Sat 10am–10pm; Sun noon–6pm.* **Credit** *AmEx, Disc, MC, V.*
This shop in the Metropolitan Opera House at Lincoln

Center sells CDs and cassettes, opera books, memorabilia and DVDs. Kids aren't forgotten, either: There are plenty of educational CDs.

Move Lab
803 Washington St between Gansevoort and Horatio Sts (1-212-741-5520). Subway: A, C, E to 14th St; L to Eighth Ave. **Open** *Tue–Sat noon–7pm; Sun noon–6pm.* **Credit** *AmEx, MC, V.*
Quirky, modern-looking objects bear visible marks of craftsmanship and a sense of history. Move Lab boasts an exciting blend of furniture, jewelry (including Braille-inscribed rings) and other baubles.

Mxyplyzyk
125 Greenwich Ave at 13th St (1-212-989-4300/ www.mxyplyzk.com). Subway: A, C, E to 14th St; L to Eighth Ave. **Open** *Mon–Sat 11am–7pm; Sun noon–5pm.* **Credit** *AmEx, MC, V.*
The moniker doesn't mean anything, though it's reminiscent of a character in the Superman comics. Mxyplyzyk offers cool gifts, lighting, furniture, housewares, stationery, toys, pet gear and lots of novelty books—on important topics such as taxi drivers' words of wisdom.

Pearl River Mart
477 Broadway between Broome and Grand Sts (1-212-431-4770/www.pearlriver.com). Subway: J, M, Z, N, Q, R, W to Canal St; 6 to Spring St. **Open** *10am–7:20pm daily.* **Credit** *AmEx, Disc, MC, V.*
This browse-worthy downtown emporium is crammed with all things Chinese: slippers, clothing,

Catch the midcentury wave, at the **MoMA Design Store**. See p245.

gongs, groceries, medicinal herbs, stationery, teapots and all sorts of fun trinkets and gift items.
Other location *200 Grand St between Mott and Mulberry Sts (1-212-966-1010).*

Home design

ABC Carpet & Home

888 Broadway at 19th St (1-212-473-3000/ www.abchome.com). Subway: L, N, Q, R, W, 4, 5, 6 to 14th St–Union Square. **Open** *Mon–Thu 10am–8pm; Fri, Sat 10am–6:30pm; Sun noon–6pm.*
Credit *AmEx, Disc, MC, V.*
At this shopping landmark, the selection of accessories, linens, rugs, and reproduction and antique furniture (Western and Asian) is unbelievable; so are the mostly steep prices. For bargains, head to ABC's warehouse outlet in the Bronx.
Other locations *20 Jay St at Plymouth St, Dumbo, Brooklyn (1-718-643-7400); ABC Carpet & Home Warehouse, 1055 Bronx River Ave between Bruckner Blvd and Westchester Ave, Bronx (1-718-842-8772).*

Area I.D. Moderne

262 Elizabeth St between Houston and Prince Sts (1-212-219-9903). Subway: B, D, F, V to Broadway–Lafayette St; 6 to Bleecker St.
Open *Mon–Fri noon–7pm; Sat, Sun noon–6pm.*
Credit *AmEx, MC, V.*
Home accessories and furniture from the 1950s, '60s

and '70s, both vintage and reproduction, are this shop's métier, but the furniture has been reupholstered in luxurious fabrics. You'll find a wide selection of fur throws and rugs.

Bodum Café and Home Store

413–415 W 14th St between Ninth and Tenth Aves (1-212-367-9125/www.bodum.com). Subway: A, C to 14th St; L to Eighth Ave. **Open** *Mon–Sat 10am–7pm; Sun noon–6pm.* **Credit** *AmEx, MC, V.*
Bodum isn't just about coffee presses: The smartly designed Meatpacking District store has lots of gadgets for the kitchen, as well as office, dining-room and bathroom supplies. If the sheer number of items overwhelms you, take a break at the coffee bar and regain your strength.

Butter & Eggs

83 West Broadway at Warren St (1-212-676-0235/ www.butterandeggs.com). Subway: A, C, E, 1, 2, 3, 9 to Chambers St. **Open** *Mon–Wed, Fri, Sat noon–7pm; Thu noon–8pm; Sun noon–5pm.*
Credit *AmEx, MC, V.*
Warren Street was the hub of NYC's butter-and-egg business in the 1800s. Nowadays, eclectic home emporium Butter & Eggs sells sake sets and handmade pillows.

Design Within Reach

142 Wooster St between Houston and Prince Sts (1-212-475-0001/www.dwr.com). Subway: B, D, F, V

to Broadway–Lafayette St; N, R, W to Prince St.
Open Mon–Sat 11am–7pm; Sun noon–6pm.
Credit AmEx, MC, V.
All the greats can be found at this 3-D version
of the California-based company's catalog (the
aesthete's equivalent of the King James Bible):
George Nelson, Philippe Starck and the Eameses,
among others.
Other locations throughout the city.

FuturePerfect

115 North 6th St at Berry St, Williamsburg, Brooklyn
(1-718-599-6278). Subway: L to Bedford Ave.
Open Tue–Fri 2–9pm; Sat noon–10pm; Sun
noon–6pm. **Credit** AmEx, MC, V.
Most of these hip, yet arguably unnecessary home
accessories are locally made and eco-friendly.

MoMA Design Store

44 W 53rd St between Fifth and Sixth Aves
(1-212-767-1050/www.momastore.org). Subway: E, V
to Fifth Ave–53rd St. **Open** Sun–Thu, Sat 10am–
6:30pm; Fri 10am–8pm. **Credit** AmEx, MC, V.
The store is as wide-ranging as the museum's collection. State-of-the-art home items on display
include casseroles, coffee tables, high-design chairs,
lighting, office workstations, kids' furniture, jewelry, calendars and lots of Christmas ornaments.
Other location 81 Spring St at Crosby St (1-646-
613-1367).

Moss

146 Greene St between Houston and Prince Sts
(1-212-204-7100). Subway: B, D, F, V to Broadway–
Lafayette St; N, R, W to Prince St; 6 to Bleecker St.
Open Mon–Sat 11am–7pm; Sun noon–6pm.
Credit AmEx, Disc, MC, V.
Many of the streamlined clocks, curvy sofas and
funky saltshakers are kept under glass at this muse-
umlike temple of contemporary home design.

Urban Archaeology

143 Franklin St between Hudson and Varick Sts,
second floor (1-212-431-4646/www.urbanarchaeology.
com). Subway: 1, 9 to Franklin St. **Open** Mon–Fri
8am–6pm. **Credit** AmEx, Disc, MC, V.
Old building parts are salvaged, refurbished and
sold here as architectural artifacts, from Corinthian
columns and lobby-size chandeliers to bathtubs
and doorknobs. Reproductions are also available.
Other location 239 E 58th St between Second and
Third Aves (1-212-371-4646).

West Elm

112 W 18th St between Sixth and Seventh Aves
(1-866-937-8356/www.westelm.com). Subway: F,
V to 14th St; L to Sixth Ave; 1, 9 to 18th St.
Open Mon–Sat 10am–9pm; Sun 11am–7pm.
Credit AmEx, Disc, MC, V.
The 10,000-square-foot flagship store for this mini-
malist Pottery Barn sibling showcases the line's
stark geometric sofas, sturdy tables and graphic-
print floor cushions.
Other location 75 Front St at Main St, Dumbo,
Brooklyn (1-718-875-7757).

Leisure

Bookstores

Chain stores

Barnes & Noble has a number of
megastores and several feature readings by
visiting authors. The smaller **Borders** chain
also provides under-one-roof browsing. Check
the phone book for the location nearest you,
and pick up Time Out New York for weekly
listings of readings at bookstores and other
venues. (See also pp272–274.)

General interest

Coliseum Books

11 W 42nd St between Fifth and Sixth Aves (1-212-
803-5890/www.coliseumbooks.com). Subway: B, D,
F, V to 42nd St–Bryant Park; 7 to Fifth Ave.
Open Mon–Fri 8am–8:30pm; Sat 11am–8:30pm;
Sun noon–7pm. **Credit** AmEx, DC, Disc, MC, V.
Coliseum is something of a miracle: In 2002, the
beloved haunt of bibliophiles was forced out of its
57th Street location by a rent hike. A year later, it
magically resurfaced 15 blocks south, with many of
the same staffers and fixtures.

192 Books

192 Tenth Ave between 21st and 22nd Sts (1-212-
255-4022/www.192books.com). Subway: C, E to 23rd
St. **Open** Sun, Mon noon–6pm; Tue–Sat 11am–7pm.
Credit AmEx, MC, V.
In an era when many an indie bookshop has closed
its doors, this youngster, opened in 2003, is proving
that quirky boutique-booksellers can make it after
all. Owned and "curated" by art dealer Paula Cooper
and her husband, editor Jack Macrae, 192 offers a
strong selection of art books and literature, as well
as sections on gardening, history, politics, design,
music and memoirs.

St. Mark's Bookshop

31 Third Ave between 8th and 9th Sts (1-212-260-
7853/www.stmarksbookshop.com). Subway: N, R, W to
8th St–NYU; 6 to Astor Pl. **Open** Mon–Sat 10am–
midnight; Sun 11am–midnight. **Credit** AmEx, Disc,
MC, V.
Students, academics and art professionals gravitate
to this East Village bookseller, which maintains
strong inventories on cultural theory, graphic
design, poetry and film studies, as well as numerous
avant-garde journals and zines.

Used books

Housing Works Used Book Cafe

126 Crosby St between Houston and Prince Sts
(1-212-334-3324/www.housingworksubc.com).
Subway: B, D, F, V to Broadway–Lafayette St; N, R,

Eat, Drink, Shop

W to Prince St; 6 to Bleecker St. **Open** *Mon–Fri 10am–9pm; Sat noon–9pm; Sun noon–7pm.* **Credit** *AmEx, MC, V.*

Housing Works bookstore is extraordinarily endearing. The two-level Soho space—which stocks literary fiction, nonfiction and collectibles—is a peaceful spot for solo relaxation or for meeting friends over coffee or wine. All proceeds go to support services for homeless people living with HIV/AIDS.

Labyrinth Books
536 W 112th St between Amsterdam Ave and Broadway (1-212-865-1588/www.labyrinthbooks.com). Subway: 1, 9 to 110th St–Cathedral Pkwy. **Open** *Mon–Fri 9am–10pm; Sat 10am–8pm; Sun 11am–7pm.* **Credit** *AmEx, Disc, MC, V.*

The academic crowd thrives in Labyrinth's rarefied air. You may find remaindered copies of *Heidegger, Coping, and Cognitive Science* or a coffee-table book entitled *Black Panthers 1968.*

Skyline Books and Records
13 W 18th St between Fifth and Sixth Aves (1-212-675-4773/1-212-759-5463/www.skylinebooksnyc.com). Subway: F, V to 14th St; L to Sixth Ave; 1, 9 to 18th St. **Open** *Mon–Sat 10am–8pm; Sun 11am–7pm.* **Credit** *AmEx, Disc, MC, V.*

Skyline's two rooms are well stocked (but not crammed) with beautiful first editions of modern fiction classics, healthy supplies of poetry and drama, and a growing list of photography and art titles.

Strand Book Store
828 Broadway at 12th St (1-212-473-1452/www.strandbooks.com). Subway: L, N, Q, R, W, 4, 5, 6 to 14th St–Union Sq. **Open** *Mon–Sat 9:30am–10:30pm; Sun 11am–10:30pm.* **Credit** *AmEx, DC, Disc, MC, V.*

Owned by the Bass family since 1927, the legendary Strand—with its "18 miles of books"—offers incredible deals on new releases, loads of used books and the city's largest rare-book collection. **Other locations** *Strand Annex, 95 Fulton St between Gold and William Sts (1-212-732-6070); Strand Kiosk, Central Park, Fifth Ave at 60th St (1-646-284-5506).*

Specialty stores

Books of Wonder
18 W 18th St between Fifth and Sixth Aves (1-212-989-3270/www.booksofwonder.net). Subway: F, V to 14th St; L to Sixth Ave; 1, 9 to 18th St. **Open** *Mon–Sat 10am–7pm; Sun noon–6pm.* **Credit** *AmEx, Disc, MC, V.*

It recently moved two doors down and combined forces with the Cupcake Café in late 2004, but the city's only independent children's bookstore still features both the very new (the staff hosted a midnight-madness party to celebrate the release of the last Harry Potter) and the very old (rare and out-of-print editions), plus foreign-language and reference titles, and a special collection of Oz books.

East West
78 Fifth Ave between 13th and 14th Sts (1-212-243-5994/www.eastwest.com). Subway: L, N, Q, R, W, 4, 5, 6 to 14th St–Union Sq. **Open** *Mon–Sat 10am–7:30pm; Sun 11am–6:30pm.* **Credit** *AmEx, Disc, MC, V.*

Helping harried urbanites follow their bliss for 27 years and counting, this spiritual titleholder devotes equal space to Eastern and Western traditions, from alternative health and yoga to philosophy.

Forbidden Planet
840 Broadway at 13th St (1-212-475-6161/www.fpnyc.com). Subway: L, N, Q, R, W, 4, 5, 6 to 14th St–Union Sq. **Open** *Sun, Mon 11am–8pm; Tue–Sat 10am–10pm.* **Credit** *AmEx, Disc, MC, V.*

Embracing both the pop-culture mainstream and the cult underground, the Planet takes all comics seriously. You'll find graphic novels (Neil Gaiman's *Sandman*, Craig Thompson's *Blankets*), serials (*Asterix, Batman*), and film and TV tie-ins (*The Simpsons, Star Wars, The X-Files*).

Hue-man Bookstore and Cafe
2319 Frederick Douglass Blvd (Eighth Ave) between 124th and 125th Sts (1-212-665-7400/www.hueman bookstore.com). Subway: A, C, B, D to 125th St. **Open** *Mon–Sat 10am–8pm; Sun 11am–7pm.* **Credit** *AmEx, Disc, MC, V.*

Focusing on African-American fiction and nonfiction, this superstore-size Harlem indie also stocks best-sellers and general-interest books.

The Mysterious Bookshop
129 W 56th St between Sixth and Seventh Aves (1-212-765-0900/www.mysteriousbookshop.com). Subway: F, N, Q, R, W to 57th St. **Open** *Mon–Sat 11am–7pm.* **Credit** *AmEx, DC, Disc, MC, V.*

Devotees of mystery, crime and spy genres will know owner Otto Penzler, both as an editor and from his book recommendations on Amazon.com. His shop holds a wealth of paperbacks, hardcovers and autographed first editions.

Spoonbill & Sugartown
218 Bedford Ave between North 4th and 5th Sts, Williamsburg, Brooklyn (1-718-387-7322/www.spoonbillbooks.com). Subway: L to Bedford Ave. **Open** *11am–9pm daily.* **Credit** *AmEx, Disc, MC, V.*

Located in Williamsburg's minimall, this hipster haven specializes in new and used books on contemporary art, art history, architecture and design. It also carries an eclectic array of fiction and nonfiction.

Cameras & electronics

When buying expensive electronic gear, check newspaper ads for price guidelines (start with the inserts in Sunday's *New York Times*). It pays to go to a well-known store, where you'll get reliable advice about a device's compatibility with systems in the country in which you plan to use it. For specialized photo processing, we recommend **Duggal** (*see p376*).

Eighteen miles of books await you at the **Strand Book Store**. *See p246.*

B&H

420 Ninth Ave at 34th St (1-212-444-5040/www.bh photovideo.com). Subway: A, C, E to 34th St–Penn Station. **Open** *Mon–Thu 9am–7pm; Fri 9am–1pm; Sun 10am–5pm.* **Credit** *AmEx, Disc, MC, V.*
B&H is the ultimate one-stop shop for all your photographic, video and audio needs (including professional audio equipment and discounted Bang & Olufsen products). Note that B&H is closed Friday afternoon, all day Saturday and on Jewish holidays.

Harvey

2 W 45th St between Fifth and Sixth Aves (1-212-575-5000). Subway: B, D, F, V to 42nd St–Bryant Park; 7 to Fifth Ave. **Open** *Mon–Wed, Fri 10am–7pm; Thu 10am–8pm; Sat 10am–6pm; Sun noon–5pm.* **Credit** *AmEx, MC, V.*
Although Harvey is known mainly for its huge selection of high-end electronics, it stocks plenty of realistically priced items and stereo furniture, too. **Other location** *ABC Carpet & Home, 888 Broadway at 19th St, mezzanine level (1-212-228-5354).*

J&R Music and Computer World

23 Park Row between Ann and Beekman Sts (1-212-238-9000/1-800-221-8180/www.jr.com). Subway: A, C to Broadway–Nassau St; J, M, Z, 4, 5 to Fulton St; 2, 3 to Park Pl. **Open** *Mon–Sat 9am–7:30pm; Sun 10:30am–6:30pm.* **Credit** *AmEx, Disc, MC, V.*

Every electronic device you'll ever need (PCs, TVs, CD players…and battery-powered nose-hair trimmers) can be found at this block-long shop.

Gadget repairs

Computer Solutions Provider

See p368 for listing.

Photo-Tech Repair Service

110 E 13th St between Third and Fourth Aves (1-212-673-8400/www.phototech.com). Subway: L, N, Q, R, W, 4, 5, 6 to 14th St–Union Sq. **Open** *Mon, Tue, Thu, Fri 8am–4:45pm; Wed 8am–6pm; Sat 10am–3pm.* **Credit** *AmEx, Disc, MC, V.*
Open since 1959, this shop has 18 on-site technicians and guarantees that it can fix your camera regardless of the brand. Rush service is available.

Tekserve

119 W 23rd St between Sixth and Seventh Aves (1-212-929-3645/www.tekserve.com). Subway: F, V to 23rd St. **Open** *Mon–Fri 9am–7pm; Sat 10am–5pm; Sun noon–5pm.* **Credit** *AmEx, DC, MC, V.*
Tekserve is the city's resident Apple specialist. Lines are long, but take a ticket and check out the new products while you're waiting for your number to be called.

Music

Superstores

J&R Music and Computer World
See p247 for listing.

Tower Records
692 Broadway at 4th St (1-212-505-1500/1-800-648-4844/www.towerrecords.com). Subway: N, R, W to 8th St–NYU; 6 to Astor Pl. **Open** *9am–midnight daily.* **Credit** *AmEx, Disc, MC, V.*
Tower has all the current sounds on CD and tape. Visit the clearance store down the block (22 E 4th St at Lafayette St, 1-212-228-5100) for markdowns in all formats, including vinyl (especially classical). **Other locations** *throughout the city.*

Virgin Megastore
52 E 14th St at Broadway (1-212-598-4666/www.virginmega.com). Subway: L, N, Q, R, W, 4, 5, 6 to 14th St–Union Sq. **Open** *Mon–Sat 9am–1am; Sun 10am–midnight.* **Credit** *AmEx, Disc, MC, V.*

Besides a huge selection of every genre of music, Virgin Megastore has in-store performances and a great selection of CDs from the U.K. Books, DVDs and videos are also available.
Other location *1540 Broadway between 45th and 46th Sts (1-212-921-1020).*

Multigenre

Bleecker Bob's
118 W 3rd St between MacDougal St and Sixth Ave (1-212-475-9677/www.bleeckerbobs.com). Subway: A, C, E, B, D, F, V to W 4th St. **Open** *Sun–Thu 11am–1am; Fri, Sat 11am–3am.* **Credit** *AmEx, MC, V.*
Come for hard-to-find new and used music, especially on vinyl.

Etherea
66 Ave A between 4th and 5th Sts (1-212-358-1126/www.ethereaonline.com). Subway: F, V to Lower East Side–Second Ave. **Open** *Sun–Thu noon–10pm; Fri, Sat noon–11pm.* **Credit** *AmEx, Disc, MC, V.*

On the record

Indie rock has sparked a revival in the popularity of vinyl records, but for many New Yorkers, the format never faded, thanks to the city's thriving club culture. While CDs—and later, downloads—took over the music industry, celebrity DJs kept vinyl on the radar. In the early and mid-'80s, club kids would leave hot spots like Paradise Garage in the morning and immediately make the short trek to **Vinylmania** (60 Carmine St between Bleecker St and Seventh Ave South, 1-212-924-7223, www.vinylmania.com) to pick up copies of whatever the DJ had spun the night before. Today, the city even boasts its own trade school for all things vinyl: **Scratch DJ Academy** (434 Sixth Ave between 9th and 10th Sts, 1-212-529-1599, www.scratch.com), where wanna-be turntablists can take private lessons in mixing, beat-matching and scratching.

The high demand for vinyl means that good records are hard to find, especially at old-school prices. One solution: Lose the crowd. An hour north of midtown Manhattan, **Mooncurser Records** (229 City Island Ave between Centre and Schofield Sts, City Island, Bronx, 1-718-885-0302) is a terrific repository of 100,000 LPs, 45s and 78s. Encompassing nearly every genre—Latin, big band, children's music, bluegrass and more—the stacks of records

fill hundreds of bins and even hang on the walls. Sadly, Roger Roberge, who owned and ran the vinyl-only oddity for 30 years, died last summer. As his children would like to sell the store, its future was uncertain at press time; be sure to call before making the trip.

Less out of the way, **Halcyon** (57 Pearl St between Plymouth and Water Sts, Dumbo, Brooklyn, 1-718-260-9299, www.halcyonline.com) has been a club-scene fixture since 1999. At its new Dumbo digs, the shop serves up vinyl and DJ gear—plus clothes, books and art—to the audiophile hipsters who scour the bins for new and used underground electronica and hip-hop. Also in Brooklyn, at Williamsburg newbie **Sound Fix** (110 Bedford Ave at North 11th St, Williamsburg, Brooklyn, 1-718-388-8090), picky locals choose from indie, krautrock and psych-folk, among other nuggets. You can weigh your options—Caetano Veloso or the Fall?—over coffee at the mellow Fix Café, in the back of the store.

Back in Manhattan, **A-1 Records** (439 E 6th St between First Ave and Ave A, 1-212-473-2870) carries some of the most obscure hip-hop and funk records in the city. Want proof? Check out the Polaroids of big-name DJs and producers, from Fatboy Slim to Kurtis Blow, who trawl the small

Etherea stocks mostly electronic, experimental, house, indie and rock CDs.

Mondo Kim's

6 St. Marks Pl between Second and Third Aves (1-212-598-9985/www.kimsvideo.com). Subway: 6 to Astor Pl. **Open** *9am–midnight daily.* **Credit** *AmEx, MC, V.*
Each branch of this movie-and-music minichain has a slightly different name (see the website for locations) but all offer a great selection for collector geeks: electronic, indie, krautrock, prog, reggae, soul, soundtracks and used CDs.
Other locations *throughout the city.*

Other Music

15 E 4th St between Broadway and Lafayette St (1-212-477-8150/www.othermusic.com). Subway: N, R, W to 8th St–NYU; 6 to Astor Pl. **Open** *Mon–Fri noon–9pm; Sat noon–8pm; Sun noon–7pm.* **Credit** *AmEx, MC, V.*
This wee audio temple is dedicated to small-label, often imported new and used CDs and LPs. It organizes music by arcane categories (for instance,

"La Decadanse" includes lounge, Moog and slow-core soundtracks) and sends out a free weekly e-mail with staffers' reviews of their favorite new releases.

St. Marks Sounds

16–20 St. Marks Pl between Second and Third Aves (1-212-677-2727/1-212-677-3444). Subway: 6 to Astor Pl. **Open** *Sun–Thu noon–8pm; Fri, Sat noon–9pm.* **Credit** *Cash only.*
Housed in two neighboring storefronts, Sounds is the best bargain on the block for new and used music. The shop at 20 St. Marks Place specializes in jazz and international recordings.

Subterranean Records

5 Cornelia St between Bleecker and W 4th Sts (1-212-463-8900). Subway: A, C, E, B, D, F, V to W 4th St. **Open** *Mon–Wed noon–8pm; Thu–Sat noon–10pm; Sun noon–7pm.* **Credit** *MC, V.*
Just off Bleecker Street, this shop carries new, used and live recordings, as well as a large selection of imports. Vinyl LPs and 45s fill the basement.

Harmonious times are at hand in **Halcyon**, where the vibe is always hip.

space for Grade-A beats. Four turntables allow you to test-drive a 12-inch before buying. A few blocks away, **Dance Tracks** (*see p250*) specializes in house and garage imports and also carries a thorough selection of New York dance singles from the late '80s. If you think your vinyl collection needs more theatrical flair, then **Footlight Records** (113 E 12th St between Third and Fourth Aves, 1-212-533-1572) is your source. French divas share shelf space with obscure Broadway relics and Fellini soundtracks. Just hum a few bars of that Edith Piaf tune stuck in your head, and

the expert staff will point you in the right direction.

If you love records enough to plan a trip around them, then keep June and December open: **The ARChive of Contemporary Music** (54 White St between Broadway and Church St, 1-212-226-6967, www.arcmusic.org), a vast music library and research center, unloads more than 10,000 extras from its encyclopedic collection of 20th-century popular music in twice-yearly sales. Gems old and new go for next to nothing. Blow your savings here—it's a small price to pay to keep vinyl from going the way of the dodo bird.

Let your fingers have a field day in "try me" heaven: the **Apple Store**. *See p251.*

Classical

Gryphon Record Shop

*233 W 72nd St between Broadway and West End Ave
(1-212-874-1588). Subway: 1, 2, 3, 9 to 72nd St.
Open Mon–Fri 9:30am–8pm; Sat 11am–8:30pm;
Sun noon–6pm.* **Credit** *MC, V.*
This solidly classical store has traditionally stocked
vinyl only, but the 21st century has swept in a wave
of CDs. Gryphon also carries a sprinkling of jazz
records and drama and film books.

Electronica

Dance Tracks

*91 E 3rd St at First Ave (1-212-260-8729/www.
dancetracks.com). Subway: F, V to Lower East
Side–Second Ave. Open Mon–Fri noon–9pm;
Sat noon–8pm; Sun noon–7pm.* **Credit** *AmEx,
Disc, MC, V.*
European imports hot off the plane are what make
this store a must. But it also has racks of domestic
house, enticing bins of Loft/Paradise Garage classics
and private decks on which to sample.

Hip-hop & R&B

Beat Street Records

*494 Fulton St between Bond St and Elm Pl, Downtown
Brooklyn (1-718-624-6400/www.beatst.com). Subway:
A, C, G to Hoyt–Schermerhorn; 2, 3, 4, 5 to Nevins St.
Open Mon–Wed 10am–7pm; Thu–Sat 10am–
7:30pm; Sun 10am–6pm.* **Credit** *AmEx, Disc, MC, V.*
In a block-long basement with two DJ booths, Beat
Street proffers the latest vinyl. CDs run from dance-
hall to gospel, but the 12-inch singles and new hip-

hop albums make this the first stop for local DJs
seeking killer breakbeats and samples.

Fat Beats

*406 Sixth Ave between 8th and 9th Sts, second floor
(1-212-673-3883/www.fatbeats.com). Subway: A, C,
E, B, D, F, V to W 4th St. Open Mon–Sat noon–9pm;
Sun noon–6pm.* **Credit** *MC, V.*
Everyone—Beck, DJ Evil Dee, DJ Premier, Mike D,
Q-Tip—shops at this tiny Greenwich Village shrine
to vinyl for treasured hip-hop, jazz, funk and reggae releases; underground magazines (*Wax Poetics*);
and cult flicks (*Wild Style*).

Jazz

Jazz Record Center

*236 W 26th St between Seventh and Eighth Aves,
room 804 (1-212-675-4480/www.jazzrecordcenter.
com). Subway: C, E to 23rd St; 1, 9 to 28th St.
Open Mon–Sat 10am–6pm.* **Credit** *Disc, MC, V.*
The city's best jazz store stocks current and out-of-
print records, books, videos and other jazz-related
merchandise. Worldwide shipping is available.

World music

World Music Institute

*49 W 27th St between Broadway and Sixth Ave, suite
930 (1-212-545-7536/www.worldmusicinstitute.org).
Subway: N, R, W to 28th St. Open Mon–Fri
10am–6pm.* **Credit** *AmEx, MC, V.*
The shop is small, but if you can't find what you're
looking for, then WMI's expert, helpful employees
can order sounds from the remotest corners of the
planet and have them shipped to you, usually within two to four weeks.

Sex shops

Leather Man

*111 Christopher St between Bleecker and Hudson Sts
(1-212-243-5339/www.theleatherman.com). Subway:
1, 9 to Christopher St.* **Open** *Mon–Sat noon–10pm;
Sun noon–8pm.* **Credit** *AmEx, Disc, MC, V.*

Cock rings, padlocks and sturdy handcuffs beckon
from wall-mounted cabinets on the first floor, while
the basement (of course) is where serious bondage
apparel is hung. There are also fake penises of every
imaginable (and unimaginable) description.

Toys in Babeland

*94 Rivington St between Ludlow and Orchard Sts
(1-212-375-1701/www.babeland.com). Subway: F, V
to Lower East Side–Second Ave.* **Open** *Mon–Sat
noon–10pm; Sun noon–7pm.* **Credit** *AmEx, MC, V.*

At this friendly sex-toy boutique—run by women
and skewed toward women, although everyone is
welcome—engrossed browsers are encouraged to
handle all manner of buzzing, wriggling and bendable playthings. The ladies at Babeland also host
frank sex-ed classes (open to all genders and sexual-
ities), such as "Strap-On Seductions."
Other location *43 Mercer St between Broome and
Grand Sts (1-212-966-2120).*

Specialties & eccentricities

The Apple Store

*103 Prince St at Greene St (1-212-226-3126/
store.apple.com). Subway: N, R, W to Prince St.*
Open *Mon–Sat 10am–8pm; Sun 11am–7pm.*
Credit *AmEx, DC, Disc, MC, V.*

Maybe it's the bright-white high-design interior, or
maybe it's the chance to try out just about every
shiny, nifty innovation. Perhaps it's the free seminars
or the friendly troubleshooters behind the Genius Bar.
Whatever the reason, buying or repairing high-tech
gear here—or just gawking—is *fun.*

Arthur Brown & Brothers

*2 W 46th St between Fifth and Sixth Aves (1-212-575-
5555). Subway: B, D, F, V to 47–50th Sts–Rockefeller
Ctr; 7 to Fifth Ave.* **Open** *Mon–Fri 9am–6:30pm;
Sat 10am–6pm.* **Credit** *AmEx, DC, Disc, MC, V.*

The staggering selection of pens includes high-end
brands like Cartier, Dupont, Montblanc, Porsche
and Schaeffer.

Big City Kites

*1210 Lexington Ave at 82nd St (1-212-472-2623/
www.bigcitykites.com). Subway: 4, 5, 6 to 86th St.*
Open *Mon–Wed, Fri 11am–6:30pm; Thu 11am–
7:30pm; Sat 10am–6pm. Call for summer hours.*
Credit *AmEx, Disc, MC, V.*

Act like a kid again and go fly a kite. Choose from
more than 150 styles.

Jerry Ohlinger's
Movie Material Store

*242 W 14th St between Seventh and Eighth Aves
(1-212-989-0869/www.moviematerials.com).*

Subway: A, C, E, 1, 2, 3, 9 to 14th St; L to Eighth Ave.
Open *1–7:45pm daily.* **Credit** *AmEx, Disc, MC, V.*

On the premises: the city's most extensive stock of
"paper material" from movies past and present,
including photos, posters, programs and fascinating celebrity curios.

Kate's Paperie

*561 Broadway between Prince and Spring Sts
(1-212-941-9816/www.katespaperie.com). Subway:
N, R, W to Prince St; 6 to Spring St.* **Open** *10am–
7:30pm daily.* **Credit** *AmEx, Disc, MC, V.*

Kate's is the ultimate paper mill. Choose from more
than 5,000 kinds of paper by mining the rich vein
of stationery, custom-printing services, journals,
photo albums and creative, amazingly beautiful
gift wrap.
Other locations *throughout the city.*

Nat Sherman

*500 Fifth Ave at 42nd St (1-212-764-5000/www.
natsherman.com). Subway: B, D, F, V to 42nd
St–Bryant Park; 7 to Fifth Ave.* **Open** *Mon–Fri
10am–8pm; Sat 10am–7pm; Sun 11am–5pm.*
Credit *AmEx, DC, MC, V.*

Just across the street from the New York Public
Library, Nat Sherman offers its own brand of slow-
burning cigarettes, as well as cigars and related
accoutrements. Flick your Bic in the upstairs
smoking room.

Pearl Paint

*308 Canal St between Broadway and Church St
(1-212-431-7932/www.pearlpaint.com). Subway: J,
M, Z, N, Q, R, W, 6 to Canal St.* **Open** *Mon–Fri
9am–7pm; Sat 10am–6:30pm; Sun 10am–6pm.*
Credit *AmEx, Disc, MC, V.*

This huge art- and drafting-supply commissary
sells everything you could possibly need to create
your own masterpiece.
Other location *207 E 23rd St between Second and
Third Aves (1-212-592-2179).*

Quark International

*537 Third Ave between 35th and 36th Sts (1-212-
889-1808). Subway: 6 to 33rd St.* **Open** *Mon–Fri
10am–6:30pm; Sat noon–5pm.* **Credit** *AmEx, DC,
Disc, MC, V.*

Spy wanna-bes and budding paranoids can buy
body armor or high-powered bugs here. The store
will also custom-bulletproof your favorite jacket.

Sam Ash Music

*160 W 48th St between Sixth and Seventh Aves
(1-212-719-2299/www.samashmusic.com). Subway: B,
D, F, V to 47–50th Sts–Rockefeller Ctr; N, R, W to
49th St.* **Open** *Mon–Sat 10am–8pm; Sun noon–6pm.*
Credit *AmEx, MC, V.*

This octogenarian musical-instrument emporium
dominates its midtown block with four contiguous
shops. New, vintage and custom guitars are available, along with amps, DJ equipment, drums, key-
boards, recording equipment, turntables and an
array of sheet music.
Other locations *throughout the city.*

Eat, Drink, Shop

Spot

*78 Seventh Ave between 15th and 16th Sts
(1-212-604-0331). Subway: 1, 2, 3, 9 to 14th St.*
Open *Mon–Sat 11am–8pm; Sun noon–6pm.*
Credit *AmEx, Disc, MC, V.*
Do doggy duds get you panting? The compact lime-green space is stocked with clothes (hoodies with BITCH or STUD stitched across the back), beds, toys and tons of treats for your four-legged friends. Merchandise changes seasonally, so your pooch or puss will never be out of fashion.

Stack's Coin Company

*123 W 57th St between Sixth and Seventh Aves
(1-212-582-2580). Subway: F, N, Q, R, W to 57th St.*
Open *Mon–Fri 10am–5pm.* **Credit** *Cash only.*
The oldest, largest coin dealer in the U.S. trades in rarities from all over the world.

West Marine

*12 W 37th St between Fifth and Sixth Aves
(1-212-477-6065/www.westmarine.com). Subway:
B, D, F, V, N, Q, R, W to 34th St–Herald Sq.*
Open *Mon–Fri 10am–6pm; Sat, Sun 10am–3pm.*
Credit *AmEx, Disc, MC, V.*
Basic seafaring supplies, deck shoes and fishing gear are for sale. Or perhaps you need a $2,000 global positioning system?

Sports

Blades, Board and Skate

*659 Broadway between Bleecker and Bond Sts
(1-212-477-7350/www.blades.com). Subway: B, D,
F, V to Broadway–Lafayette St; 6 to Bleecker St.*
Open *Mon–Sat 10am–9pm; Sun 11am–7pm.*
Credit *MC, V.*
The requisite clothing and gear is sold alongside in-line skates, skateboards and snowboards.
Other locations *throughout the city.*

Gerry Cosby & Co.

*3 Pennsylvania Plaza, Madison Square Garden,
Seventh Ave at 32nd St (1-212-563-6464/1-877-563-
6464/www.cosbysports.com). Subway: A, C, E, 1, 2, 3,
9 to 34th St–Penn Station.* **Open** *9:30am–7:30pm
daily.* **Credit** *AmEx, Disc, MC, V.*
Cosby has a huge selection of official team wear and other sporting necessities. The store is open during—and until 30 minutes after—evening Knicks and Rangers games, in case you feel like celebrating.

Niketown

*6 E 57th St between Fifth and Madison Aves (1-212-
891-6453/1-800-671-6453/www.niketown.com).
Subway: N, R, W to Fifth Ave–59th St.*
Open *Mon–Sat 10am–8pm; Sun 11am–7pm.*
Credit *AmEx, Disc, MC, V.*
Don't despair if you have difficulty choosing from among the 1,200 models of footwear: A huge screen drops down every 23 minutes and plays a Nike ad, to focus your desires. Look also for sports attire to outfit men, women and kids for all kinds of play.

Paragon Sporting Goods

*867 Broadway at 18th St (1-212-255-8036/www.
paragonsports.com). Subway: L, N, Q, R, W, 4, 5, 6 to
14th St–Union Sq.* **Open** *Mon–Sat 10am–8pm; Sun
11:30am–7pm.* **Credit** *AmEx, DC, Disc, MC, V.*
Three floors of equipment and clothing for almost every activity (at every level of expertise) make this the New York sports-gear mecca.

Tattoos & piercing

Tattooing was made legal in New York in 1998; piercing, however, remains relatively unregulated, so mind your nipples.

New York Adorned

*47 Second Ave between 2nd and 3rd Sts (1-212-473-
0007/www.newyorkadorned.com). Subway: F, V to
Lower East Side–Second Ave.* **Open** *Sun–Thu
1–9pm; Fri, Sat 1–10pm.* **Credit** *AmEx, MC, V (cash
only for tattoos).*
Proprietor Lori Leven recruits world-class tattoo artists to wield the needles at her eight-year-old gothic-elegant establishment. Those with low pain thresholds can go for gentler body decorations such as henna tattoos, and finery like ethereal white-gold cluster earrings, crafted by Leven, or pieces by a group of emerging body-jewelry designers.

Venus Modern Body Arts

*199 E 4th St between Aves A and B (1-212-473-
1954). Subway: F, V to Lower East Side–Second Ave.*
Open *Sun–Thu 1–9pm; Fri, Sat 1–10pm.*
Credit *AmEx, Disc, MC, V.*
Venus has tattooed and pierced New Yorkers since 1992—before body art became de rigueur. It also offers an enormous selection of jewelry, so you can put diamonds in your navel and platinum in your tongue.

Travel & luggage

Coach

*595 Madison Ave at 57th St (1-212-754-0041/www.
coach.com). Subway: N, R, W to Fifth Ave–59th St.*
Open *Mon–Sat 10am–8pm; Sun 11am–6pm.*
Credit *AmEx, DC, Disc, MC, V.*
Coach's butter-soft leather briefcases, wallets and handbags have always been exceptional, but the Manhattan Coach stores also stock the label's luxurious outerwear collection.
Other locations *throughout the city.*

Flight 001

*96 Greenwich Ave between Jane and W 12th Sts
(1-212-691-1001/www.flight001.com). Subway: A, C,
E to 14th St; L to Eighth Ave.* **Open** *Mon–Fri
11am–8:30pm; Sat 11am–8pm; Sun noon–6pm.*
Credit *AmEx, DC, Disc, MC, V.*
Forget something? This one-stop West Village shop carries guidebooks and chic luggage, along with fun travel products such as pocket-size aromatherapy kits. Flight 001's "essentials" wall features packets of Woolite, mini-dominoes and everything in between.

Arts & Entertainment

Features

Festivals & Events

Perennial, annual, seasonal, occasional—the time is always right.

New Yorkers have plenty to complain about—sky-high rents, sweltering summers, constant noise—but hey, at least we're never, ever bored. Every day, the city is alive with parades, fairs, festivals, and assorted free shows and performances (for more events, check out the other chapters in the **Arts & Entertainment** section). The following is but a sampling of the biggest and best seasonal delights the city has to offer. Keep in mind that before you set out or plan a trip around an event, it's always wise to call and make sure the fling is still set to swing.

Spring

Whitney Biennial
For listing, see p151 **Whitney Museum of American Art**. Dates *Mar–May.*
A captivating and often provocative showcase of contemporary works by both established and emerging artists is mounted in even-numbered years. The next show will be held in spring 2006.

The Armory Show
Piers 90 and 92, Twelfth Ave between 50th and 52nd Sts (1-212-645-6440/www.thearmoryshow.com). Subway: C, E to 50th St. Dates *Mar 11–14.*
The show that, in 1913, heralded the arrival of modern art in America has morphed into a huge contemporary-art mart.

St. Patrick's Day Parade
Fifth Ave from 44th to 86th Sts (www.saintpatricksdayparade.com). Date *Mar 17.*
This massive march is one of the city's longest-running annual traditions—it dates from 1762. If you feel like braving huge crowds and potentially nasty weather, you'll see thousands of green-clad merrymakers strutting to the sounds of pipe bands. Celebrations continue late into the night as the city's Irish bars teem with suds-swigging revelers.

Ringling Bros. and Barnum & Bailey Circus Animal Parade
34th St from the Queens Midtown Tunnel to Madison Square Garden, Seventh Ave between 31st and 33rd Sts (1-212-307-7171/www.ringling.com). Dates *Mar 24, Apr 10.*
Elephants, horses, camels and zebras march through the tunnel and onto the streets of Manhattan in this unmissable spectacle. Stay up late to witness the free midnight parade, which opens (and closes) the circus's run in Manhattan.

New York International Auto Show
Jacob K. Javits Convention Center, Eleventh Ave between 34th and 39th Sts (1-800-282-3336/www.autoshowny.com). Subway: A, C, E to 34th St–Penn Station. Dates *Mar 25–Apr 3.*
This gearheads' paradise has more than a thousand autos and futuristic concept cars on display.

Easter Parade
Fifth Ave from 49th to 57th Sts (1-212-484-1222). Subway: E, V to Fifth Ave–53rd St. Date *Mar 27.*
Parade is a misnomer for this little festival of creative hat-making. Starting at 11am on Easter Sunday, Fifth Avenue becomes a car-free promenade of gussied-up crowds milling and showing off extravagant bonnets. Arrive early to secure a prime viewing spot near St. Patrick's Cathedral, at 50th Street.

Tribeca Film Festival
Various Tribeca locations (1-212-941-2400/www.tribecafilmfestival.org). Subway: A, C, 1, 2, 3, 9 to Chambers St. Dates *Apr 21–May 1.*
Organized by neighborhood resident Robert De Niro, this festival is packed with hundreds of screenings of independent and animated films; it's attended by more than 300,000 film fans.

New York Antiquarian Book Fair
Park Avenue Armory, Park Ave between 66th and 67th Sts (1-212-777-5218/www.sanfordsmith.com). Subway: 6 to 68th St–Hunter College. Dates *Apr 29–May 1.*
Book dealers from around the globe showcase first editions, illuminated manuscripts, and all manner of rare and antique tomes; you'll even find original screenplays and shooting scripts.

Cherry Blossom Festival
For listing, see p124 **Brooklyn Botanic Garden**. Dates *Apr 30, May 1.*
Nature's springtime blooms adorn the garden's 200-plus cherry trees at this annual festival. Performances, demonstrations and workshops are all part of the fun.

You Gotta Have Park
Various locations throughout the city (1-212-360-3456). Dates *May.*
Created to launch the summer season of outdoor events, this celebration of public greenery includes concerts, markets, kids' events and cleanup days in NYC's major parks.

Bike New York: The Great Five Boro Bike Tour
Battery Park to Staten Island (1-212-932-2453/www.bikenewyork.org). Subway: A, C, J, M, Z, 1, 2,

Hats off to the dancing ladies of Brooklyn's annual **Cherry Blossom Festival**. *See p254.*

See p254.

3, 9 to Chambers St; R, W to City Hall; 4, 5, 6 to Brooklyn Bridge–City Hall. Then bike to Battery Park. **Date** *May 1.*
Thousands of cyclists take over the city for a 42-mile (68-kilometer) Tour de New York. (Pedestrians and motorists should plan on extra getting-around time.) Advance registration is required. Event organizers suggest the trains listed above, as some subway exits below Chambers Street may be closed to bike-toting cyclists for safety reasons, and bikes are not allowed at the South Ferry (1, 9 trains), Whitehall Street (R, W) and Bowling Green (4, 5) stations.

Red Hook Waterfront Arts Festival
Various locations in Red Hook, Brooklyn (1-718-287-2224/www.dancetheatreetcetera.org/www.bwac.org). Travel: A, C, F to Jay St–Borough Hall, then take the B61 bus to Van Brunt St; F, G to Smith–9th Sts, then take the B77 bus to Van Brunt St. **Date** *Third Saturday in May.*
A rapidly evolving neighborhood cultural bash includes dance and music performances, along with the Brooklyn Waterfront Artists' Pier Show.

Fleet Week
For listing, see p162 **Intrepid** Sea-Air-Space **Museum. Dates** *Last week in May.*
New York's streets swell with good-looking sailors—and all varieties of military personnel—during this weeklong event honoring the armed forces. Head to the *Intrepid* to catch tugs-of-war, eating contests, arm wrestling and other entertainments.

Lower East Side Festival of the Arts
Theater for the New City, 155 First Ave at 10th St (1-212-254-1109/www.theaterforthenewcity.net). Subway: L to First Ave; 6 to Astor Pl. **Dates** *May 28–30.*
This celebration of artistic diversity features performances by dozens of theatrical troupes and appearances by local celebrities.

Washington Square Outdoor Art Exhibit
Various streets surrounding Washington Square Park (1-212-982-6255). Subway: A, C, E, B, D, F, V to W 4th St; N, R, W to 8th St–NYU. **Dates** *May 28–30, Jun 4, 5.*
Since 1931, this outdoor exhibit has lined the streets of central Greenwich Village with photography, sculpture, paintings and one-of-a-kind crafts. It's a great way for browsers and buyers to spend an afternoon.

Summer

Met in the Parks
Various locations (1-212-362-6000/www.metopera.org). **Dates** *June.*
The Metropolitan Opera stages free opera performances in Central Park and other NYC parks. Grab a blanket, pack a picnic (no alcohol or glass bottles), and show up in the afternoon to nab a good spot.

Arts & Entertainment

Monday night at the movies in **Bryant Park**.

Bryant Park Free Summer Season
*Bryant Park, Sixth Ave at 42nd St
(1-212-768-4242/www.bryantpark.org).
Subway: B, D, F, V to 42nd St–Bryant Park;
7 to Fifth Ave.* **Dates** *Jun–Aug.*
One of the highlights of the park's free-entertainment season is the ever popular Monday-night alfresco movie series, but there's plenty of fun in the daylight hours as well. You can catch Broadway-musical numbers as part of the Broadway in Bryant Park series; *Good Morning America* miniconcerts featuring big-name acts; and a variety of readings, classes and public-art projects.

Central Park SummerStage
*Rumsey Playfield, Central Park, entrance on Fifth Ave at 72nd St (1-212-360-2777/www.summerstage.org).
Subway: 6 to 68th St–Hunter College.* **Dates** *Jun–Aug.*
Rockers, symphonies, authors and dance companies take over the stage at this superpopular, mostly free annual series. Show up early or plan to listen from a spot outside the gates (not such a bad option, if you bring a blanket—and some snacks!). Admission is charged for benefit shows.

Shakespeare in Central Park at the Delacorte Theater
See p347 for listing. **Dates** *Jun–Aug.*
One of Manhattan's best summertime events gets boldface stars to pull on their tights for a whack at the Bard.

River to River Festival
Various venues along the West Side and southern waterfronts of Manhattan (www.rivertorivernyc.org). **Dates** *Jun–Sept.*

Lower Manhattan organizations present more than 500 free summer shows in some of the city's coolest waterfront locations. Performers last year ranged from Curtis Stigers to Aimee Mann. The Hudson River Festival (1-212-528-2733, www.hudsonriverfestival.com) augments the affair with visual-arts shows, walking tours, theater, dance and family events.

SOFA New York
*Seventh Regiment Armory, 643 Park Ave at 67th St
(1-800-563-7632/www.sofaexpo.com). Subway: 6 to 68th St–Hunter College.* **Dates** *Jun 1–5.*
Browse this giant show of Sculptural Objects and Functional Art, and you might find that perfect conversation piece for your home.

Museum Mile Festival
*Fifth Ave from 82nd to 105th Sts (1-212-606-2296/
www.museummilefestival.org).* **Date** *Jun 6.*
For one day each year, nine of the city's major museums open their doors free of charge to the public. You can also catch live music, street performers and other arty happenings along Fifth Avenue.

National Puerto Rican Day Parade
Fifth Ave from 44th to 86th Sts (1-718-401-0404).
Date *Second Sunday in June.*
Salsa music blares, and scantily clad revelers dance along the route and ride colorful floats at this freewheeling party celebrating the city's largest Hispanic community.

Broadway Bares
Roseland Ballroom, 239 W 52nd St between Broadway and Eighth Ave (1-212-840-0770/www.broadway cares.org). Subway: 1, 9 to 50th St. **Dates** *Mid-June.*

The new annual fund-raiser for Broadway Cares/ Equity Fights AIDS is your chance to see some of the Great White Way's hottest bodies sans costumes—and it's for a great cause!

JVC Jazz Festival

Various locations (1-212-501-1390/ www.festivalproductions.net). **Dates** *Mid-June.*
A direct descendant of the Newport Jazz Festival, this jazz bash is an NYC institution. The fest not only fills Carnegie and Avery Fisher Halls with big draws, but also sponsors gigs in Harlem and downtown clubs.

Mermaid Parade

Coney Island, Brooklyn (1-718-372-5159/ www.coneyisland.com). **Subway:** *D, F, Q to Coney Island–Stillwell Ave.* **Date** *Jun 25.*
Decked-out mermaids and mermen of all shapes and sizes share the parade route with elaborate, kitschy floats, come rain or shine. It's the wackiest summer-solstice event ever. Check the website for details, as the parade location varies from year to year.

Gay and Lesbian Pride March

From Fifth Ave at 52nd St to Christopher St (1-212-807-7433/www.hopinc.org). **Date** *Jun 26.*
Downtown Manhattan becomes a sea of rainbow flags as gays and lesbians from the city and beyond parade down Fifth Avenue in commemoration of the 1969 Stonewall riots. After the march, there's a massive street fair and a dance on the West Side piers, which often features a surprise guest (last year, Janet Jackson popped by).

Summer Restaurant Week

Various locations (www.restaurantweek.com). **Dates** *Late June, early July.*
Twice a year, for two weeks at a stretch, some of the city's finest restaurants dish out three-course prix-fixe lunches for $20.05; some places also offer dinner for $30.05. (The lunch price reflects the year.) For the full list of participating restaurants, visit the website. You are advised to make reservations well in advance.

Midsummer Night Swing

Lincoln Center Plaza, Columbus Ave between 64th and 65th Sts (1-212-875-5766/www.lincolncenter. org). **Subway:** *1, 9 to 66th St–Lincoln Ctr.* **Dates** *Late Jun–mid-Jul.*
Lincoln Center's plaza is transformed into a giant outdoor dance floor as bands play salsa, Cajun, swing and other music. Each night is devoted to a different style of dance, and performances are preceded by free lessons.

Celebrate Brooklyn! Performing Arts Festival

Prospect Park Bandshell, Prospect Park West at 9th St, Park Slope, Brooklyn (1-718-855-7882/ www.celebratebrooklyn.org). **Subway:** *F to Seventh Ave.* **Dates** *Late Jun–late Aug.*
Outdoor events include music, dance, film and spoken-word performances. Huge crowds flock to the park's bandshell to hear major artists such as They Might Be Giants and Los Lobos. A $3 donation is requested, and admission is charged for a few benefit shows.

Macy's Fireworks Display

East River, exact location varies (1-212-494-4495). **Date** *Jul 4 at approximately 9pm.*
This world-famous annual fireworks display is the city's star attraction on Independence Day. The pyrotechnics are launched from barges in the East River, so look for outdoor vantage points along the lower FDR Drive (closed to traffic), the Brooklyn and Long Island City waterfronts, or on Roosevelt Island. Keep in mind, however, that spectators are packed like sardines at the prime public spots.

New York Philharmonic Concerts in the Parks

Various locations (1-212-875-5709/ www.newyorkphilharmonic.org). **Dates** *Jul–Aug.*
The New York Philharmonic has presented a varied classical-music program in many of New York's larger parks for more than 40 years.

Seaside Summer and Martin Luther King Jr. Concert Series

Various locations (1-718-469-1912/ www.brooklynconcerts.com). **Dates** *Jul–Aug.*
Grab a lawn chair and listen to free pop, funk, soul and gospel at these outdoor concerts in Brooklyn.

The best Places to...

...eat a deep-fried Oreo

At the **Feast of San Gennaro**, greasy street food and carnival games draw huge crowds to Little Italy. *See p258.*

...see a Broadway star in the buff

Get a real backstage view at the new **Broadway Bares** fund-raiser. *See p256.*

...cruise hipsters in Queens

Drink, dance and check out the eye candy at P.S. 1's summer-afternoon **Warm Up**. *See p258.*

...watch movies while reclining outside

Catch classic crowd-pleasers after dark, courtesy of the **Bryant Park Free Summer Season**. *See p256.*

...frolic with chicks of the sea

Rain or shine, kooky mermaids and mermen strut their stuff at Coney Island's **Mermaid Parade**. *See p257.*

Arts & Entertainment

P.S. 1 Warm Up

See p293 for listing. **Dates** *Jul–Sept Sat 2–9pm.*
For years, this weekly Saturday-afternoon bash in the museum's courtyard has drawn hipsters from all over the city to dance, drink beer and relax in a beachlike environment. Local and international DJs provide the soundtrack for your summer amusement.

Mostly Mozart

Lincoln Center, Columbus Ave between 64th and 65th Sts (1-212-875-5766/www.lincolncenter.org). Subway: 1, 9 to 66th St–Lincoln Ctr. **Dates** *Late Jul–Aug.*
For more than 35 years, this four-week-long festival has been mounting a packed schedule of works by Mozart and his contemporaries.

Lincoln Center Out of Doors Festival

See p326 for listing. **Dates** *August.*
Dance, music, theater, opera and more make up this ambitious festival of classic and contemporary works.

New York International Fringe Festival

Various locations (1-212-279-4488/www.fringe nyc.org). **Dates** *August.*
Wacky, weird and sometimes great, downtown's Fringe Festival shoehorns hundreds of performances into 16 theater-crammed days.

Central Park Zoo Chill Out Weekend

Central Park, entrance on Fifth Ave at 65th St (1-212-439-6500). Subway: N, R, W to Fifth Ave–59th St. **Dates** *Early August.*
If you're roaming the city's streets during the dog days of August, this two-day party offers the perfect chilly treat. The weekend freeze-fest features penguin and polar-bear talent shows, games, zookeeper challenges and other frosty fun.

Harlem Week

Various Harlem locations (1-212-862-8477/ www.harlemdiscover.com). Subway: B, C, 2, 3 to 135th St. **Dates** *Third week in August.*
Get into the groove at this massive street fair, which serves up live music, art and food along 135th Street. Concerts, film, dance, fashion and sports events are on tap all week.

Howl!

Various East Village locations (1-212-505-2225/ www.howlfestival.com). **Dates** *Third week in August.*
Taking its name from the seminal poem by longtime

▶ **NYC & Company** (www.nycvisit.com), the convention and visitors' bureau, has additional info on year-round events.
▶ For more seasonal events, see the Around Town section of *Time Out New York*.
▶ Go to **www.timeoutny.com** and click on This Week's Picks for *TONY* critics' picks for each day of the week.
▶ For film festivals, *see p297*.

---

neighborhood resident Allen Ginsberg, this all-things–East Village fest is a grab bag of art events, films, performance art, readings and much more.

West Indian–American Day Carnival

Eastern Pkwy from Utica Ave to Grand Army Plaza, Brooklyn (1-718-625-1515/www.wiadca.org). Subway: 3, 4 to Crown Hts–Utica Ave. **Date** *Sept 5.*
The streets come alive with the jubilant clangor of steel-drum bands and the steady throb of calypso and soca music. *Mas* bands—elaborately costumed marchers—dance along the parade route, thousands move to the beat on sidewalks, and vendors sell Caribbean crafts, clothing, souvenirs and food.

Broadway on Broadway

43rd St at Broadway (1-212-768-1560/ www. broadwayonbroadway.com). Subway: N, Q, R, W, 42nd St S, 1, 2, 3, 9, 7 to 42nd St–Times Sq. **Date** *Early September.*
Broadway's biggest stars convene in the middle of Times Square to belt out showstopping numbers. The season's new productions mount sneak previews, and it's all free.

Fall

Atlantic Antic

Atlantic Ave from Fourth Ave to Hicks St, Brooklyn (1-718-875-8993/www.atlanticave.org). Subway: B, Q, 2, 3, 4, 5 to Atlantic Ave; D, M, N, R to Pacific St. **Dates** *Mid-September.*
Entertainment, ethnic foods, kids' activities and the World Cheesecake-Eating Contest fill the avenue at this monumental Brooklyn festival.

Feast of San Gennaro

Mulberry St from Canal to Houston Sts (1-212-768-9320/www.sangennaro.org). Subway: J, M, Z, N, Q, R, W, 6 to Canal St. **Dates** *Mid-September.*
This massive street fair stretches along the main drag of what's left of Little Italy. Come on opening and closing days to see the marching band of old-timers, or after dark, when sparkling lights arch over Mulberry Street and the smells of frying *zeppole* and sausages hang in the sultry air.

New York Is Book Country

Various locations (www.nyisbookcountry.com). **Dates** *Late September or early October.*
After years of operating on Fifth Avenue, this literary blowout moved to the confines of Washington Square Park in 2004. The two-day event offers panel discussions and author chats, plus dozens of vendors to satisfy your shopping needs.

New York Film Festival

Alice Tully Hall, Avery Fisher Hall and Walter Reade Theater at Lincoln Center, Broadway at 65th St (1-212-875-5050/www.filmlinc.com). Subway: 1, 9 to 66th St–Lincoln Ctr. **Dates** *Early to mid-October.*
This uptown institution, founded in 1962, is still a worthy cinematic showcase, packed with premieres, features and short flicks from around the

Fireworks follow a **New York Philharmonic** concert in Central Park.

Sesame Street's Grover does a flyby at the **Macy's Thanksgiving Day Parade**. *See p261.*

globe, plus a stellar list of celebrities for the red-carpet events.

Next Wave Festival
For listing, see p325 **Brooklyn Academy of Music**. **Dates** *Oct–Dec.*
The best of the best in the city's avant-garde music, dance, theater and opera scenes are performed at this lengthy annual affair.

Open House New York
Various locations (1-917-583-2398/www.ohny.org). **Dates** *Early to mid-October.*
Get an insider's view—literally—of the city that even most locals haven't seen. More than 100 sites of architectural interest normally off-limits to visitors throw open their doors and welcome the curious during a weekend of urban exploration.

d.u.m.b.o. art under the bridge
Various locations in Dumbo, Brooklyn (1-718-694-0831/www.dumboartscenter.org). Subway: A, C to High St; F to York St. **Dates** *Mid-October.*
Dumbo (Down Under the Manhattan Bridge Overpass) has become a Brooklyn art destination, and this weekend of art appreciation, featuring concerts, forums, a short-film series and in-studio visits, is a popular event.

CMJ Music Marathon, MusicFest and FilmFest
Various locations (1-917-606-1908/www.cmj.com). **Dates** *Mid- to late October.*
The annual *College Music Journal* schmooze fest draws thousands of young fans and music-industry types to one of the best showcases for new rock, indie-rock, hip-hop and electronica acts.

Village Halloween Parade
Sixth Ave from Spring to 22nd Sts (www.halloween-nyc.com). **Date** *Oct 31 at 8pm.*
The sidewalks at this iconic Village shindig are always packed beyond belief. Our advice for the best vantage point: Strap on a costume and watch from *inside* the parade (lineup starts at 6:30pm on Sixth Avenue at Spring Street).

New York City Marathon
Staten Island side of the Verrazano-Narrows Bridge to Tavern on the Green, in Central Park (1-212-423-2249/www.nycmarathon.org). **Date** *Early November.*
The sight of 35,000 marathoners hotfooting it through all five boroughs over a 26.2-mile (42-kilometer) course is an impressive one. Scope out a spot somewhere in the middle (the starting and finish lines are mobbed) to get a good view of the herd.

Macy's Thanksgiving Day Parade and Eve Balloon Blowup

Central Park West at 77th St to Macy's, Broadway at 34th St (1-212-494-4495/www.macysparade.com). **Date** *Nov 24 at 9am.*
The stars of this nationally televised parade are the gigantic, inflated balloons, the elaborate floats and good ol' Santa Claus. New Yorkers brave the cold night air to watch the rubbery colossi take shape at the inflation area on the night before Thanksgiving (from 77th to 81st Sts, between Central Park West and Columbus Ave).

Winter

The Nutcracker

New York State Theater, Lincoln Center, Columbus Ave at 63rd St (1-212-870-5570/www.nycballet.com). Subway: 1, 9 to 66th St–Lincoln Ctr. **Dates** *Nov 25– first week in Jan.*
Performed by the New York City Ballet, George Balanchine's fantasy world of fairies, princes and toy soldiers is a family-friendly holiday diversion.

Radio City Christmas Spectacular

For listing, see p318 **Radio City Music Hall.** **Dates** *Nov–early Jan.*
The high-kicking Rockettes and an onstage nativity scene with live animals are the attractions at this (pricey) annual homage to the yuletide season.

Christmas Tree–Lighting Ceremony

Rockefeller Center, Fifth Ave between 49th and 50th Sts (1-212-332-6868/www.rockefellercenter.com). Subway: B, D, F, V to 47–50th Sts–Rockefeller Ctr. **Date** *First week in December.*
Be very wary of attending the actual lighting ceremony: Even those who show up early will be forced to contend with crushing crowds (though they will be treated to celebrity appearances and pop-star performances). There's plenty of time during the holiday season to marvel at the giant evergreen.

The National Chorale
Messiah Sing-In

Avery Fisher Hall, Lincoln Center, Columbus Ave at 65th St (1-212-333-5333/www.lincolncenter.org/ www.nationalchorale.org). Subway: 1, 9 to 66th St– Lincoln Ctr. **Dates** *Mid-December.*
Hallelujah! Chase those holiday blues by joining with the National Chorale and hundreds of your fellow shower-singing audience members in a rehearsal and performance of Handel's *Messiah.* No experience is necessary, and you can buy the score on-site.

New Year's Eve Ball Drop

Times Square (1-212-768-1560/www.timessquare bid.org). Subway: N, Q, R, W, 42nd St S, 1, 2, 3, 9, 7 to 42nd St–Times Sq. **Date** *Dec 31.*
Meet up with half a million of your closest friends and watch the giant illuminated ball descend amid a blizzard of confetti and cheering. Expect freezing temperatures, densely packed crowds, absolutely no bathrooms—and very tight security.

New Year's Eve Fireworks

Naumburg Bandshell, middle of Central Park at 72nd St (1-212-423-2284/www.centralparknyc.org). Subway: B, C to 72nd St; 6 to 68th St–Hunter College. **Date** *Dec 31.*
The fireworks explode at midnight, and you can participate in a variety of evening festivities, including dancing and a costume contest. The best views are from Tavern on the Green (at 67th Street), Central Park West at 72nd Street, and Fifth Avenue at 90th Street.

New Year's Eve Midnight Run

Naumburg Bandshell, middle of Central Park at 72nd St (1-212-423-2284/www.nyrrc.org). Subway: B, C to 72nd St; 6 to 68th St–Hunter College. **Date** *Dec 31.*
Start the new year with a four-mile jog through the park. There's also a masquerade parade, fireworks, prizes and a booze-free toast at the halfway mark.

New Year's Day Marathon Poetry Reading

For listing, see p274 **The Poetry Project.** **Date** *Jan 1.*
Big-name bohemians (Patti Smith, Richard Hell, Jim Carroll) step up to the mike during this free, all-day spoken-word spectacle.

Winter Antiques Show

Seventh Regiment Armory, 643 Park Ave between 66th and 67th Sts (1-718-292-7392/ www.winter antiquesshow.com). Subway: 6 to 68th St–Hunter College. **Dates** *Mid- to late January.*
One of the world's most prestigious antiques shows brings together more than 70 American and international dealers.

Winter Restaurant Week

See p257 **Summer Restaurant Week.** **Dates** *Late January, early February.*

Chinese New Year

Around Mott St, Chinatown (1-212-966-0100). Subway: J, M, Z, N, Q, R, W, 6 to Canal St. **Dates** *Early February.*
Gung hay fat choy! Chinatown bustles with energy during the two weeks of the Lunar New Year. Festivities include a staged fireworks display, a dragon parade (which snakes in and out of several restaurants), various performances and delicious food.

The Art Show

Seventh Regiment Armory, 643 Park Ave between 66th and 67th Sts (1-212-940-8590/ www.artdealers.org). Subway: 6 to 68th St–Hunter College. **Dates** *Mid- to late February.*
Whether you're a serious collector or just a casual art fan, this vast fair is a great chance to peruse some of the world's most impressive for-sale pieces dating from the 17th century to the present.

Arts & Entertainment

Art Galleries

Warhol, Judd, Barney, Stella, Arbus… Just another day in New York.

New York is a mecca for visual art. Thousands of artists and hundreds of galleries thrive here. Contemporary art dominates the ever-expanding West Chelsea and Meatpacking districts, and you'll find everything from museum-quality shows by blue-chip artists to offbeat closet-size exhibits by young art-school dropouts. You could easily devote an entire day to exploring galleries, with a pit stop for lunch, cocktails or dinner at a fashionable restaurant or bar, or a shopping spree around these now designer-drenched neighborhoods.

For art lovers craving visual comfort food, the uptown emporiums off Museum Mile are filled with works by the old masters; you can also drop by any of 57th Street's prestigious galleries for a host of haute options. While Soho's once booming art scene has dwindled considerably, it still boasts an impressive collection of nonprofit spaces. Similarly, new venues in Harlem and the Lower East Side won't disappoint. A quick jaunt over (or under) the East River will definitely be worth the trip: Williamsburg, now home to some 40 galleries, has become a true art-lover's destination in Brooklyn; and a number of exhibition spaces have popped up in Long Island City, in Queens—many near **MoMA** affiliate **P.S. 1 Contemporary Art Center** (*see p151*)—and even along the banks of the Brooklyn waterfront in Dumbo. Basically, if an area feels revitalized, fresh and fun, chances are it's because pioneering artists (and real estate–canny gallerists) are calling it home.

The most reliable gallery listings and reviews can be found in *Time Out New York* magazine and in the Friday and Sunday editions of the *New York Times*. Always consult them before heading out. For uncritical (but extensive) listings, pick up the monthly Gallery Guide (www.galleryguide.org). It's generally available for free in galleries, or for around $3 at newsstands and bookstores.

Visitors should note that from May or June to early September, most galleries are open only on weekdays, and some close for the entire month of August. Most spaces also close on major U.S. holidays (*see p372* **Holidays**). Summer hours are listed for some galleries that have set their calendar, but it's always best to call before visiting.

Lower East Side

The Lower East Side, once a land of pushcarts and pickles, is experiencing a major renaissance. For an overview of the evolving scene (which includes artist-run spaces too numerous to mention), your best bet is to take the **ELS-LES** self-guided walking tour (*see below*).
Subway: F to East Broadway or Delancey St; F, V to Lower East Side–Second Ave; J, M, Z to Delancey–Essex Sts.

ELS-LES (Every Last Sunday on the Lower East Side) Open Studios
Various studios and galleries (1-646-602-2338/ www.lowereastsideny.com/artwalkparticipant.htm). **Open** *1–7pm daily.* **Admission** *free, though a donation is suggested.*
On the last Sunday of every month, a number of artist- and artisan-run studios on the Lower East Side open their doors to the public. (Download a map from the website to find the venues.) Participants vary, but ABC No Rio (*see p274* **Our Unorganicized Reading**), Metalstone Gallery (175 Stanton St at Clinton St, 1-212-253-8308) and Zito Studio Gallery (122 Ludlow St between Delancey and Rivington Sts, 1-646-602-2338) are likely to be among them.

Maccarone Inc.
45 Canal St between Ludlow and Orchard Sts (1-212-431-4977). **Open** *Sept–May Wed–Sun noon–6pm. Jun, Jul Tue–Fri noon–6pm.*
Run by former Luhring Augustine director Michele Maccarone, the four-floor gallery, which was once a hardware store, focuses on emerging European and local talent.

Participant Inc.
95 Rivington St between Ludlow and Orchard Sts (1-212-254-4334). **Open** *Wed–Sun noon–7pm.*
Overseen by savvy curator Lia Gangitano, this glass-fronted gallery is a Lower East Side hot spot. Expect entertaining, intelligent exhibitions that crossbreed visual and performing arts with literature and new media.

Rivington Arms
102 Rivington St between Essex and Ludlow Sts (1-646-654-3213). **Open** *Sept–Jul Wed–Fri 11am–6pm; Sat, Sun noon–6pm.*
This intimate storefront space, run by Melissa Bent and Mirabelle Marden (painter Brice Marden's daughter), has attracted both a fashionable crowd of followers and critical kudos.

There's plenty of room to flaunt Richard Serra's curves at **Gagosian Gallery**. *See p265*.

Soho

The main concentration of Manhattan galleries may have shifted to the western blocks of Chelsea, but a few notables still reside here, and a number of the city's most important nonprofit venues (*see p270*) continue to make the area a vital stop on the art map.
Subway: A, C, E, J, M, Z, N, Q, R, W, 1, 9, 6 to Canal St; B, D, F, V to Broadway–Lafayette St; N, R, W to Prince St; 6 to Spring St.

Peter Blum

99 Wooster St between Prince and Spring Sts (1-212-343-0441/www.peterblumgallery.com).
Open *Tue–Fri 10am–6pm; Sat 11am–6pm.*
This elegant space is manned by a dealer with an impeccable eye and wide-ranging tastes. Past exhibitions have run the gamut from drawings by art stars Robert Ryman and Alex Katz to terra-cotta funerary figures from West Africa and colorful quilts by African-American folk artist Rosie Lee Tompkins.

Deitch Projects

18 Wooster St between Canal and Grand Sts (1-212-343-7300). **Open** *Tue–Sat noon–6pm.*
Jeffrey Deitch is an art-world impresario whose gallery features live spectacles as well as large-scale—and sometimes overly ambitious—efforts by artists who work in virtually all media. (By comparison, Deitch's original Grand Street site seems small and sedate, but it's the one of his three Soho spaces that we most confidently recommend.) Solo shows here, by the likes of Yoko Ono, aim to be both complex and accessible.
Other locations *26 Wooster St between Canal and Grand Sts (1-212-343-7300); 76 Grand St between Greene and Wooster Sts (1-212-343-7300).*

Ronald Feldman Fine Arts

31 Mercer St between Canal and Grand Sts (1-212-226-3232/www.feldmangallery.com).
Open *Sept–Jun Monday by appointment only; Tue–Sat 10am–6pm. Jul, Aug Mon–Thu 10am–6pm; Fri 10am–3pm.*
This Soho pioneer has brought us landmark shows of such legendary avant-gardists as Eleanor Antin, Leon Golub and Hannah Wilke. Feldman also regularly takes chances on newer talents like British photographer Keith Cottingham—all to good effect.

Leo Koenig Inc.

249 Centre St between Broome and Grand Sts (1-212-334-9255). **Open** *Tue–Sat 10am–6pm.*
Leo Koenig's father is Kasper Koenig, the internationally known curator and museum director, but Leo has been making a name for himself by show-

casing cutting-edge American and German talents—Meg Cranston, Torben Giehler and Lisa Ruyter among them.

Satellite (a division of Roebling Hall)
94 Prince St at Mercer St, second floor (1-212-966-9043). **Open** *Sept–Jul Tue–Sat noon–6pm. August by appointment only.*
This Soho space is run by dealers Christian Viveros-Fauné and Joel Beck of Williamsburg's Roebling Hall (*see p270*); it presents work by Sebastiaan Bremer, Bjørn Melhus and Guy Richards Smit.

Chelsea

Chelsea has the city's highest concentration of galleries; just be advised that it can be hard to see even half the neighborhood in one day. The subway takes you only as far as Eighth Avenue, so you'll have to walk at least one long block westward to get to the galleries. You can also take the M23 crosstown bus.
Subway: A, C, E to 14th St; C, E to 23rd St; L to Eighth Ave.

Alexander and Bonin
132 Tenth Ave between 18th and 19th Sts (1-212-367-7474/www.alexanderandbonin.com). **Open** *Sept–May Tue–Sat 10am–6pm. Jun–Aug Tue–Fri 10am–6pm.*
This long, cool drink of an exhibition space features

contemporary painting, sculpture and photography by artists such as Willie Doherty, Mona Hatoum, Rita McBride, Doris Salcedo and Paul Thek.

Bellwether
134 Tenth Ave between 18th and 19th Sts (1-212-929-5959/www.bellwethergallery.com). **Open** *Sept–Jul Tue–Sat 11am–6pm.*
The hot-pink neon sign in the window heralds the arrival of this former Brooklyn stalwart to new street-level digs in Chelsea. Setting trends since 1999, Bellwether represents such promising talents as Ellen Altfest, Sarah Bedford and Adam Cvijanovic.

Mary Boone Gallery
541 W 24th St between Tenth and Eleventh Aves (1-212-752-2929/www.maryboonegallery.com). **Open** *Tue–Sat 10am–6pm (closed last three weeks in August).*
Mary Boone made her name representing Julian Schnabel, Jean-Michel Basquiat and Francesco Clemente at her Soho gallery in the '80s. She later moved to midtown (*see p268*) and, in 2000, added this sweeping space in Chelsea, showing established artists like David Salle, Barbara Kruger and Eric Fischl alongside the work of young up-and-comers like Kevin Zucker and Hilary Harkness.

John Connelly Presents
526 W 26th St between Tenth and Eleventh Aves, suite 1003 (1-212-337-9563). **Open** *Sept–Jun Tue–Sat 11am–6pm. Jul, Aug Mon–Fri 11am–6pm.*

Two wrongs make a right

For those who love art but find Chelsea's scene a bit wearying, the Wrong Gallery has the perfect solution: You don't have to go inside. In fact, that's not an option. Behind its locked glass door, which is next to the Andrew Kreps Gallery (*see p267*) on West 20th Street, lies just one square foot of exhibition space (on view when the Kreps security gate is open). Yet this tiny vestibule gallery has managed to present some of the biggest names in contemporary art since it was launched in 2003.

The Wrong Gallery is the pet project of Ali Subotnick, who is a former editor of the big-deal art journal *Parkett,* independent curator Massimiliano Gioni and contemporary artist Maurizio Cattelan. The trio has run the nonprofit space on less than a shoestring.

"We wanted to do something with zero resources," Subotnick explains, as a reaction to the overdesigned mega galleries in the neighborhood. The inaugural exhibit

in the diminutive space (which is actually an entrance to the building's boiler room) was a sound installation by Turner Prize winner Martin Creed. The gallery has since featured works by such art-world luminaries as Lawrence Weiner, Elizabeth Peyton, Sam Durant, Isa Genzken, and Jason Rhoades and Paul McCarthy. The gallery's name, Subotnick explains, came from an offhand remark that art dealer Jeffrey Deitch made to Cattelan. "He was talking about an artist and said, 'Good artist, wrong gallery.'"

The three are no strangers to art pranks and provocation. Together, they have launched *Charley,* an irregularly published conceptual magazine, and twice curated anti-sales booths (nothing's for sale!) at London's annual Frieze Art Fair. These antics have garnered them attention and art-world appreciation. Their next project? Curating the Berlin Biennial in 2006.

But Wrong is their most visible New York success. In fact, in *Artforum* magazine,

Connelly, longtime director of Andrea Rosen Gallery (*see p267*), recently struck out on his own and quickly earned a reputation as one of the most exciting young dealers around. Expect provocative, rambunctious works by emerging young artists, with an emphasis on installation.

Paula Cooper Gallery

534 W 21st St between Tenth and Eleventh Aves (1-212-255-1105). **Open** *Sept–May Tue–Sat 10am–6pm. Jun–Aug Mon–Fri 9:30am–5pm.*

First in Soho and early to Chelsea, Cooper has built an impressive art temple. (She has also opened a second space, across the street.) The gallery is best known for Minimalist and Conceptualist work, including that by photographers Zoe Leonard and Andres Serrano and sculptors Carl Andre, Donald Judd, Sherrie Levine and Tony Smith. You'll also see younger artists who are just starting to make a name for themselves, like Kelley Walker and John Tremblay.
Other location *521 W 21st St between Tenth and Eleventh Aves (1-212-255-5247).*

Gagosian Gallery

555 W 24th St between Tenth and Eleventh Aves (1-212-741-1111/www.gagosian.com). **Open** *Sept–May Tue–Sat 10am–6pm. Jun–Aug Mon–Fri 10am–6pm.*

Larry Gagosian's mammoth (20,000-square-foot) contribution to 24th Street's top-level galleries was launched in 1999 with an exhilarating show of Richard Serra sculptures. Follow-up exhibitions have featured works by Douglas Gordon, Ellen Gallagher, Damien Hirst, Ed Ruscha, Julian Schnabel and Andy Warhol.

Barbara Gladstone

515 W 24th St between Tenth and Eleventh Aves (1-212-206-9300). **Open** *Sept–mid-Jun Tue–Sat 10am–6pm. Mid-Jun–Labor Day Mon–Fri 10am–6pm.*

Gladstone is strictly blue-chip, with an emphasis on the Conceptualist, the philosophical and the daring. Matthew Barney, Anish Kapoor, Richard Prince and Rosemary Trockel show here.

Gorney Bravin + Lee

534 W 26th St between Tenth and Eleventh Aves (1-212-352-8372/www.gblgallery.com). **Open** *Sept–Jun Tue–Sat 10am–6pm. Jul Tue–Fri 10am–6pm. August by appointment only.*

This refreshingly friendly gallery is especially strong in photography and sculpture. It has an attention-getting stable of contemporary artists, including Sarah Charlesworth, Justine Kurland, Catherine Opie and Alexis Rockman.

Greene Naftali Gallery

526 W 26th St between Tenth and Eleventh Aves, eighth floor (1-212-463-7770). **Open** *Sept–Jun Tue–Sat 10am–6pm. Jul Mon–Fri 10am–6pm.*

Although this gallery is worth a visit just for its wonderful light and spectacular bird's-eye view, the keen vision of gallerist Carol Greene is what's most

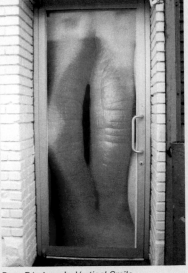

Whitney Museum curator Chrissie Illes named the gallery as one of 2003's top venues, and the Public Art Fund recently gave the gallerists a grant that has allowed them to open a second gallery just down the street. At two feet deep, it's twice as large, which lets invited artists present twice as much stuff. "One of the things we have always wanted to do is present an artist locked inside for the month," says Subotnick. While they wouldn't tell the artists how to use the gallery, "This second space is just large enough that that could happen."

Shows slated for 2005 include a project by Andreas Slominski, an installation of works by On Kawara, and a collaboration between Richard Prince and Christopher Wool. Stop by either space. It's worth the nonprice of nonadmission.

The Wrong Gallery

516A½ and 520A½ W 20th St between Tenth and Eleventh Aves. Subway: C, E to 23rd St. **On display** *Tue–Sat 10am–6pm.*

Dara Friedman's *Vertical Smile.*

Claes Oldenburg and Coosje van
Bruggen's *Balzac Pétanque*
at **PaceWildenstein**. *See p267.*

impressive here. Mavericks like sculptor Rachel Harrison, painter Jaqueline Humphries and video artist Lucy Gunning draw rave reviews from critics and collectors alike.

Anton Kern Gallery

532 W 20th St between Tenth and Eleventh Aves (1-212-367-9663/www.antonkerngallery.com). **Open** *Sept–Jul Tue–Sat 10am–6pm. August by appointment only.*
The son of artist Georg Baselitz, Kern presents young American and European artists whose installations have provided the New York art scene with some of its most visionary shows. The likes of Kai Althoff, Sarah Jones, Michael Joo, Jim Lambie and scary Monica Bonvicini show here.

Andrew Kreps Gallery

516A W 20th St between Tenth and Eleventh Aves (1-212-741-8849). **Open** *Sept–Jul Tue–Sat 10am–6pm. Aug 1–14 Mon–Fri 10am–6pm.*
The radicals in Kreps's adventurous stable include Ricci Albenda, Roe Ethridge, Robert Melee and Ruth Root.

Lehmann Maupin

540 W 26th St between Tenth and Eleventh Aves (1-212-255-2923/www.lehmannmaupin.com). **Open** *Sept–Jun Tue–Sat 10am–6pm. Jul–Labor Day Tue–Fri 10am–6pm. August by appointment only.*
This gallery left its Rem Koolhaas–designed loft in Soho for new Koolhaas-styled digs in a former garage. Epic exhibitions feature hip international artists, including Teresita Fernandez, Do-Ho Suh, Kutlug Ataman and Tracy Emin.

Luhring Augustine Gallery

531 W 24th St between Tenth and Eleventh Aves (1-212-206-9100/www.luhringaugustine.com). **Open** *Sept–May Tue–Sat 10am–6pm. Jun–Aug Mon–Fri 10am–5:30pm.*
Designed by Richard Gluckman, the area's architect of choice, this cool gallery features work from an impressive index of artists such as British sculptor Rachel Whiteread, Swiss video star Pipilotti Rist, Japanese photo artist Yasumasa Morimura, and Americans Janine Antoni, Larry Clark, Jenny Gage, Paul McCarthy and Christopher Wool.

Matthew Marks Gallery

522 W 22nd St between Tenth and Eleventh Aves (1-212-243-1650/www.matthewmarks.com). **Open** *Sept–Jun Tue–Sat 11am–6pm. Jul, Aug Mon–Fri 11am–6pm.*
The Matthew Marks Gallery was a driving force behind Chelsea's transformation into an art destination, and with three outposts to its name, it remains one of the neighborhood's powerhouses. Marks showcases such international talent as Lucian Freud, Nan Goldin, Andreas Gursky, Ellsworth Kelly, Brice Marden and Ugo Rondinone. **Other locations** *521 W 21st St between Tenth and Eleventh Aves (212-243-0200); 523 W 24th St between Tenth and Eleventh Aves (1-212-243-0200).*

Metro Pictures

519 W 24th St between Tenth and Eleventh Aves (1-212-206-7100). **Open** *Sept–mid-Jun Tue–Sat 10am–6pm. Mid-Jun–Labor Day Mon–Fri 10am–6pm.*
The gallery is best known for representing art-world superstar Cindy Sherman, along with such big contemporary names as Mike Kelley, Robert Longo and the late German artist Martin Kippenberger.

Robert Miller Gallery

524 W 26th St between Tenth and Eleventh Aves (1-212-366-4774/www.robertmillergallery.com). **Open** *Sept–Jun Tue–Sat 10am–6pm. Call for summer hours.*
This former 57th Street stalwart often shows works by well-established artists you might expect to see at a museum: painters Lee Krasner, Joan Mitchell, and Alice Neel, and photographers Bruce Weber and Diane Arbus.

PaceWildenstein Gallery

534 W 25th St between Tenth and Eleventh Aves (1-212-929-7000/www.pacewildenstein.com). **Open** *Sept–May Tue–Sat 10am–6pm. Jun–Aug Mon–Thu 10am–6pm; Fri 10am–4pm.*
In a space designed by artist Robert Irwin, this welcoming branch of the famous 57th Street gallery (*see p269*) houses grand-scale shows by major contemporaries such as Chuck Close, Alex Katz, Sol LeWitt, Elizabeth Murray and Kiki Smith.

Friedrich Petzel Gallery

535 W 22nd St between Tenth and Eleventh Aves (1-212-680-9467). **Open** *Sept–Jun Tue–Sat 10am–6pm; Jul, Aug Mon–Fri 10am–6pm.*
The gallery represents some of the brightest young stars on the international scene, so you can count on intriguing shows. Sculptor Keith Edmier, photographer Dana Hoey, painter and filmmaker Sarah Morris, and installation artists Jorge Pardo and Philippe Parenno show here.

Postmasters Gallery

459 W 19th St between Ninth and Tenth Aves (1-212-727-3323/www.postmastersart.com). **Open** *Sept–Jul Tue–Sat 11am–6pm.*
Postmasters, run by the savvy Magdalena Sawon and Tamas Banovich, emphasizes technologically inflected art (most of which leans toward the Conceptualist) in the form of sculpture, painting, new media, and installations from the likes of Diana Cooper, Christian Schumann and Wolfgang Staehle.

Andrea Rosen Gallery

525 W 24th St between Tenth and Eleventh Aves (1-212-627-6000/www.andrearosengallery.com). **Open** *Sept–Jun Tue–Sat 10am–6pm. Jul, Aug Mon–Fri 10am–6pm.*
During the past 15 years, Andrea Rosen has established several major careers: The late Felix Gonzalez-Torres got his start here (the gallery handles the estate), as did Wolfgang Tillmans, Andrea Zittel and John Currin (who left for Gagosian in 2003).

Arts & Entertainment

You can go from pillar to post at **David Zwirner**'s Chelsea gallery.

Recent additions to the roster, such as highly touted young sculptor David Altmejd, promise more of the same high quality to come.

Sonnabend
536 W 22nd St between Tenth and Eleventh Aves (1-212-627-1018). **Open** *Sept–Jul Tue–Sat 10am–6pm. August by appointment only.*
A well-established standby in a museumlike space shows new work by Ashley Bickerton, Gilbert & George, Candida Höfer, Jeff Koons, Haim Steinbach and Matthew Weinstein.

303 Gallery
525 W 22nd St between Tenth and Eleventh Aves (1-212-255-1121/www.303gallery.com). **Open** *Sept–Jun Tue–Sat 10am–6pm. Jul, Aug Mon–Fri 10am–6pm.*
Expect to see critically acclaimed artists who work in a variety of media—among them filmmaker Doug Aitken, photographers Thomas Demand and Collier Schorr, and painters Inka Essenhigh, Karen Kilimnik and Sue Williams.

David Zwirner
525 W 19th St between Tenth and Eleventh Aves (1-212-727-2070/www.davidzwirner.com). **Open** *Sept–Jun Tue–Sat 10am–6pm. Jul, Aug Mon–Fri 10am–6pm.*
This German expatriate has a head-turning roster of international contemporary artists that includes Stan Douglas, Marcel Dzama, Toba Khedoori, Neo Rauch and Diana Thater. (*See also p269* **Zwirner & Wirth**.)

57th Street

The home of Carnegie Hall, Tiffany & Co., Bergdorf Goodman and a number of art galleries, the area surrounding 57th Street is a beehive of commercial activity that's lively, cultivated, chic—and expensive.
Subway: E, V to Fifth Ave–53rd St; F to 57th St; N, R, W to Fifth Ave–59th St.

Mary Boone Gallery
745 Fifth Ave between 57th and 58th Sts, fourth floor (1-212-752-2929/www.maryboonegallery.com). **Open** *Sept–Jun Tue–Sat 10am–6pm.*
Here, onetime Soho celeb Boone continues to produce hit shows featuring young artists, but her most prized venue is her newer gallery in Chelsea (*see p264*). The star attractions at both locations are established players such as Ross Bleckner, Peter Halley and hip provocateur Damian Loeb.

Marian Goodman Gallery
24 W 57th St between Fifth and Sixth Aves, fourth floor (1-212-977-7160/www.mariangoodman.com). **Open** *Sept–Jun Mon–Sat 10am–6pm. Jul, Aug Mon–Fri 10am–6pm.*

This well-known space offers a host of renowned names. Look for artists John Baldessari, Christian Boltanski, Maurizio Cattelan, Gabriel Orozco, Gerhard Richter, Thomas Struth and Jeff Wall.

Greenberg Van Doren Gallery

730 Fifth Ave at 57th St, seventh floor (1-212-445-0444/www.agvdgallery.com). Open Sept–May Tue–Sat 10am–6pm. Jun–Aug Mon–Fri 10am–5:30pm.
This elegant gallery represents established artists Jennifer Bartlett and Richard Diebenkorn, as well as younger talent like painters Benjamin Edwards and Cameron Martin, video artist Alix Pearlstein, and photographers Jessica Craig-Martin, Katy Grannan and Malerie Marder.

PaceWildenstein Gallery

32 E 57th St between Madison and Park Aves, second floor (1-212-421-3292/www.pacewildenstein. com). Open Sept–May Tue–Fri 9:30am–6pm. Jun–Aug Mon–Fri 10am–6pm.
To view shows by a few of the 20th century's most significant artists, head to this institution. You'll find pieces by Chuck Close, Agnes Martin, Pablo Picasso, Ad Reinhardt, Mark Rothko, Lucas Samaras, Elizabeth Murray or Kiki Smith. The Pace Prints division at this location exhibits works on paper by everyone from old masters to notable contemporaries. The gallery also deals in fine ethnic and world art. (*See also p267.*)

The Project

37 W 57th St between Fifth and Sixth Aves, third floor (1-212-688-4673). Open Sept–Jun Tue–Sat noon–6pm. Call for summer hours.
This gallery has been the darling of European critics and curators since it opened in 1998, and its recent move from Harlem to midtown has only increased its following. Expect work by acclaimed young artists including Julie Mehretu, Peter Rostovsky and Stephen Vitiello.

Upper East Side

Many galleries on the Upper East Side sell masterpieces to billionaires. Still, anyone can look for free, and some pieces are treasures that will vanish from public view for years, if sold.
Subway: 6 to 68th St–Hunter College or 77th St.

C&M Arts

45 E 78th St at Madison Ave (1-212-861-0020/www.c-m-arts.com). Open Sept–May Tue–Sat 10am–5:30pm. Jun–Aug Mon–Fri 10am–5:30pm.
If you'd like to view or study the works of historic figures like Louise Bourgeois, Joseph Cornell, Franz Kline, Mark Rothko or Cy Twombly, then check out this major player in the secondary art market.

Gagosian Gallery

980 Madison Ave at 76th St (1-212-744-2313/www.gagosian.com). Open Sept–May Tue–Sat 10am–6pm. Jun–Aug Mon–Fri 10am–6pm.
Long a force to be reckoned with in the world of contemporary art, Larry Gagosian commands pristine temples uptown and in Chelsea (*see p265*). Regularly featured artists include Francesco Clemente and Richard Serra, as well as younger stars like Cecily Brown and Damien Hirst.

Knoedler & Co.

19 E 70th St between Fifth and Madison Aves (1-212-794-0550). Open Sept–May Tue–Fri 9:30am–5:30pm. Jun–Aug Mon–Fri 9:30am–5pm.
Opened in 1846, the oldest gallery in New York represents museum-quality postwar and contemporary artists such as Lee Bontecou, Helen Frankenthaler, Nancy Graves and John Walker.

Mitchell-Innes & Nash

1018 Madison Ave between 78th and 79th Sts, fifth floor (1-212-744-7400/www.miandn.com). Open Sept–May Tue–Sat 10am–5pm. Jul Mon–Fri 10am–5pm. Call for August hours.
This 11-year-old gallery is run by two former Sotheby's specialists who have an ambitious program that ranges from modern masters like Willem de Kooning to contemporary up-and-comers like Kojo Griffin.

Zwirner & Wirth

32 E 69th St between Madison and Park Aves (1-212-517-8677/www.zwirnerandwirth.com). Open Sept–Jun Tue–Sat 10am–6pm. Jul–Labor Day Mon–Fri 10am–6pm.
Z&W, in a recently renovated townhouse space, exhibits modern and contemporary masters like Dan Flavin, Martin Kippenberger and Bruce Nauman. (*See also p268* **David Zwirner.**)

Harlem

Triple Candie

461 W 126th St between Morningside and Amsterdam Aves (1-212-865-0783/www.triple candie.org). Subway: A, C, B, D, 1, 9 to 125th St. Open Thu–Sun noon–5pm.
This multicultural contemporary-arts center brings exhibitions and educational programs to Harlem's west side.

Brooklyn

Presently, there are about 60 galleries in Brooklyn, and that number is growing. Most are open on Sundays and Mondays, when the majority of Manhattan galleries are closed. Artists who live and work in Brooklyn have created a thriving art scene, with Williamsburg as its uncontested hub. (For a printable map of the area's show spaces, visit www.williamsburggalleryassociation.com.)

▶ For weekly reviews and gallery listings, pick up a copy of *Time Out New York*.

Arts & Entertainment

Pierogi 2000

177 North 9th St between Bedford and Driggs Aves,
Williamsburg, Brooklyn (1-718-599-2144/
www.pierogi2000.com). Subway: L to Bedford Ave.
Open *Sept–Jul Thu–Mon noon–6pm and by*
appointment.
Pierogi, one of Williamsburg's established galleries,
presents the *Flat Files,* a series of drawers containing works on paper by some 800 artists. Don't
pass up the chance to don those special white
gloves and handle the archived artwork yourself.

Plus Ultra Gallery

235 South 1st St at Roebling St, Williamsburg,
Brooklyn (1-718-387-3844/www.plusultragallery.
com). Subway: J, M, Z to Marcy Ave; L to Bedford
Ave. **Open** *Sept–Jul Mon, Fri–Sun noon–6pm.*
Artist Joshua Stern and art entrepreneur Ed
Winkleman run the newly expanded Plus Ultra
Gallery, lending it an ambience of serious fun. Shows
by Leslie Brack, Joe Fig and Andy Yoder have been
mounted here.

Roebling Hall

390 Wythe Ave at South 4th St, Williamsburg,
Brooklyn (1-718-599-5352/www.brooklynart.com).
Subway: J, M, Z to Marcy Ave; L to Bedford Ave.
Open *Mon, Fri–Sun noon–6pm.*
Directors Joel Beck and Christian Viveros-Fauné cook
up provocative shows featuring emerging local
and international talent.

Nonprofit spaces

apexart

291 Church St between Walker and White Sts
(1-212-431-5270/www.apexart.org). Subway: J, M,
Z, N, Q, R, W, 6 to Canal St; 1, 9 to Franklin St.
Open *Sept–Jul Tue–Sat 11am–6pm.*
At this unconventional space, inspiration comes
from the independent critics, curators and artists
selected for apexart's curatorial program. The work
rarely follows prevailing fashions; more often, it
anticipates them.

Art in General

79 Walker St between Broadway and Lafayette St
(1-212-219-0473/www.artingeneral.org). Subway: J,
M, Z, N, Q, R, W, 6 to Canal St. **Open** *Sept–Jun*
Tue–Sat noon–6pm.
Now celebrating its 24th year, this Chinatown oddball has a vigorous resident-artist program that introduces newcomers—from New York, Europe, and
Cuba and elsewhere in Latin America—in a homey,
almost familial atmosphere.

The Drawing Center

35 Wooster St between Broome and Grand Sts
(1-212-219-2166/www.drawingcenter.org). Subway:
A, C, E, J, M, Z, N, Q, R, W, 6 to Canal St.
Open *Sept–Jul Tue–Fri 10am–6pm; Sat 11am–6pm.*
This 28-year-old Soho standout, a stronghold of
works on paper, assembles critically acclaimed programs that feature not only soon-to-be art stars but

also museum-caliber legends such as James Ensor,
Ellsworth Kelly and even Rembrandt.

Grey Art Gallery
at New York University

100 Washington Sq East between Washington
and Waverly Pls (1-212-998-6780/www.nyu.edu/
greyart). Subway: A, C, E, B, D, F, V to W 4th St;
N, R, W to 8th St–NYU. **Open** *Mid-Sept–mid-Jul*
Tue, Thu, Fri 11am–6pm; Wed 11am–8pm; Sat
11am–5pm. **Admission** *suggested donation $3.*
NYU's museum-laboratory has a multimedia collection of nearly 6,000 works covering the entire
range of visual art. The emphasis is on the late 19th
and the 20th centuries.

Momenta Art

72 Berry St between North 9th and 10th Sts,
Williamsburg, Brooklyn (1-718-218-8058/
www.momentaart.org). Subway: L to Bedford Ave.
Open *Sept–Jun Mon–Fri noon–6pm.*
Momenta is housed in a tiny Brooklyn space, yet
it conveys the importance of a serious Chelsea
gallery. You'll find solo and group exhibitions from
a cross section of emerging artists, most of whom
display a Conceptualist bent.

SculptureCenter

44-19 Purves St at Jackson Ave, Long Island City,
Queens (1-718-361-1750/www.sculpture-center.org).
Subway: E, V to 23rd St–Ely Ave; G to Long Island
City–Court Sq; 7 to 45th Rd–Court House Sq.
Open *Mon, Thu–Sun 11am–6pm.*
One of the best places to see work by blossoming
and midcareer artists, this gallery is known for its
very broad definition of sculpture. The impressive
steel-and-brick digs, designed by architect Maya
Lin, opened in late 2002.

Smack Mellon Gallery

56 Water St between Dock and Main Sts, Dumbo,
Brooklyn (1-718-834-8761/www.smackmellon.org).
Subway: A, C to High St; F to York St. **Open** *Wed–*
Sun noon–6pm.
Avant-garde group shows fill this multidisciplinary
gallery's drafty but accommodating quarters.
Originally a foundry, the 6,000-square-foot structure
dates from before the Civil War. Call before visiting;
a move to 92 Plymouth Street at Washington Street,
one block away, is planned in late 2005.

Photography

New York is photo country, no doubt about
it. For a comprehensive overview of local
shows, look for the bimonthly directory
Photograph ($5).

Edwynn Houk Gallery

745 Fifth Ave between 57th and 58th Sts, fourth
floor (1-212-750-7070/www.houkgallery.com).
Subway: N, R, W to Fifth Ave–59th St.
Open *Sept–Jul Tue–Sat 11am–6pm. Call*
for summer hours.

Galleries like **Pierogi 2000** will have you trucking out to Williamsburg. *See p270.*

This respected specialist in vintage and contemporary photography exhibits works by Brassaï, Lynn Davis, Dorothea Lange, Annie Leibovitz, Man Ray and Alfred Stieglitz, each commanding top dollar.

International Center of Photography

1133 Sixth Ave at 43rd St (1-212-857-0000/ www.icp.org). Subway: B, D, F, V to 42nd St–Bryant Park; 7 to Fifth Ave. **Open** *Tue–Thu 10am–5pm; Fri 10am–8pm; Sat, Sun 10am–6pm.* **Admission** *$10, seniors and students $7, children under 12 free. Voluntary donation Fri 5–8pm.*

In 2001, ICP's galleries, once split between midtown and uptown locations, were consolidated in a redesigned building that also accommodates a school and a library (a major archive of photography magazines and thousands of biographical and photographic files). Begun in the 1960s as the International Fund for Concerned Photography, ICP houses work by photojournalists Werner Bischof, Robert Capa, David Seymour and Dan Weiner, who were tragically killed on assignment. News and documentary photography remains an important part of the center's program, which also includes contemporary photos and video (in 2003, the first-ever ICP Photo Triennial further solidified ICP's position in the contemporary photo scene). Two floors of exhibition space often showcase retrospectives devoted to a single artist; recent shows have focused on the work of Mary Ellen Mark, Weegee and Garry Winogrand.

Klotz/Sirmon Gallery

511 W 25th St between Tenth and Eleventh Aves, suite 701 (1-212-741-4764/www.klotzsirmon.com). Subway: C, E to 23rd St. **Open** *Sept–Jun Tue, Wed by appointment only; Thu–Sat 11am–6pm. Jul–Aug Wed–Fri 11am–6pm.*

In addition to its stock of high-quality vintage and contemporary works, this gallery also functions as the NYC agent for the *New York Times*' photo archives, which comprises some 5 million prints. If you're in New York in December, then don't miss the gallery's annual holiday sale. Curators and collectors rub elbows with just plain folks, and they're all looking for bargains.

Pace/MacGill

32 E 57th St between Madison and Park Aves, ninth floor (1-212-759-7999). Subway: N, R, W to Lexington Ave–59th St; 4, 5, 6 to 59th St. **Open** *Sept–late Jun Tue–Fri 9:30am–5:30pm; Sat 10am–6pm. Late Jun–Aug Mon–Thu 9:30am–5:30pm; Fri 9am–4pm.*

This established gallery frequently shows work by such well-known names as Walker Evans, Robert Frank, Irving Penn and Alfred Stieglitz, in addition to groundbreaking contemporaries like Guy Bourdin, Chuck Close, Philip-Lorca DiCorcia and Kiki Smith.

Books & Poetry

Live readings and spoken-word slams are a *def* sentence.

We know your kind: You're quite proud of your blog and wonder if you could parlay it into a writing career. Or you've been toiling on your groundbreaking novel for a year and you're desperate for feedback. Well, come on down! Unleash your literary visions on discriminating audiences while sizing up the competition at dozens of spoken-word venues across the city. If you're lucky, you may meet your future agent/editor/mentor/writing partner in the process. At the very least, you'll get a taste of the agony and ecstasy that are the writing life.

Still searching for inspiration? Sit in on a reading by an author you admire. On any given night, a variety of writers—from best-selling novelists to little-known poets and cult favorites—grace the stages of bookstores and bars. Most are happy to chat about the source of their ideas or sign copies of their work. You might even persuade a sympathetic soul to glance at your manuscript.

For a current schedule of who's reading where and when, call or visit each venue's website, or pick up *Time Out New York* magazine.

Author appearances

Asian-American Writers' Workshop

16 W 32nd St between Fifth Ave and Broadway, tenth floor (1-212-494-0061/www.aaww.org). Subway: B, D, F, V, N, Q, R, W to 34th St–Herald Sq. **Admission** *suggested donation $5.*
Acclaimed writers of Asian heritage—including Maxine Hong Kingston and Jessica Hagedorn—and up-and-comers lecture on the publishing biz or share their work at this respected organization.

Barbès

376 9th St at Sixth Ave, Park Slope, Brooklyn (1-718-965-9177/www.barbesbrooklyn.com). Subway: F to Seventh Ave; M, R to Fourth Ave–9th St. **Admission** *free–$8.*
Too many cafés host a few readings and suddenly declare themselves "community centers." Barbès, a bar and performance space owned by two French musicians, is one of the few places that really earns the appellation. At press time, Wednesday evenings were devoted to local authors of varying renown, while Thursdays belonged to writers from the lit journal *McSweeney's.*

At **KGB**, literary comrades gather for readings from noted writers like Nani Power. *See p273.*

Barnes & Noble

33 E 17th St between Broadway and Park Ave South (1-212-253-0810/www.barnesandnoble.com). Subway: L, N, Q, R, W, 4, 5, 6 to 14th St–Union Sq. **Admission** *free.*
Nearly every author tour touches down at a Barnes & Noble. This Union Square location offers an especially varied schedule. Recent marquee names include Joyce Carol Oates, T.C. Boyle and Tom Wolfe.

Bluestockings

172 Allen St between Rivington and Stanton Sts (1-212-777-6028/www.bluestockings.com). Subway: F, V to Lower East Side–Second Ave. **Admission** *suggested donation free–$10.*
This self-proclaimed progressive bookstore and café hosts frequent readings and discussions, often on feminist and lesbian themes.

Books of Wonder

18 W 18th St between Fifth and Sixth Aves (1-212-989-3270/www.booksofwonder.net). Subway: F, V to 14th St; L to Sixth Ave. **Admission** *free.*
Given the many successful authors trying their hands at children's books, you're just as likely to see Michael Chabon as Maurice Sendak reading at this kiddie shop.

Coliseum Books

See p245 for listing. **Admission** *free.*
The new and improved Coliseum draws some big guns: Recent readings have included Dave Eggers and Gish Jen.

Galapagos Art and Performance Space

See p315 for listing. **Admission** *free–$5.*
Books and beer—what could be better? This quirky Brooklyn bar hosts regular readings and literary variety shows.

The Half King

505 W 23rd St between Tenth and Eleventh Aves (1-212-462-4300/www.thehalfking.com). Subway: C, E to 23rd St. Mon 7pm. **Admission** *free.*
Co-owned by *Perfect Storm* author Sebastian Junger, this Chelsea pub features mostly journalists and novelists at its Monday night readings.

Housing Works Used Book Cafe

See p245 for listing. **Admission** *free, book donations encouraged.*
The emerging and the illustrious mingle at the mike and in the audience at this Soho bookstore and café. Profits go to provide shelter and support services to homeless people living with HIV and AIDS.

Hue-Man Bookstore

2319 Frederick Douglass Blvd (Eighth Ave) at 125th St (1-212-665-7400/www.huemanbookstore.com). Subway: A, C, B, D to 125th St. **Admission** *free.*
This spacious Harlem bookstore features frequent readings and in-store appearances by authors (Bill Clinton, whose office is nearby, held a signing of

Jon Stewart hustles at **Barnes & Noble**.

his memoir here), with an emphasis on African-American writers and topics.

Humanities and Social Sciences Library

See p162 for listing. **Admission** *$10.*
The Celeste Bartos Forum at the main research library presents excellent live interviews with influential authors such as J.M. Coetzee and Maya Angelou, as well as literary lectures and readings.

KGB

85 E 4th St between Second and Third Aves, second floor (1-212-505-3360/www.kgbbar.com). Subway: F, V to Lower East Side–Second Ave; 6 to Astor Pl. **Admission** *free.*
This dark and formerly smoky East Village hangout with an old-school Communist theme runs several top-notch weekly series, featuring NYC writers, poets, fantasy authors and so on.

The National Arts Club

15 Gramercy Park South between Park Ave South and Irving Pl (1-212-475-3424/www.national artsclub.org). Subway: 6 to 23rd St. **Admission** *free, except for benefits.*
A posh Gramercy Park address and grand Victorian

> ▶ For more on bookstores, see **Shops & Services** and **Gay & Lesbian** (*pp299–309* and *pp214–252*).

Arts & Entertainment

interiors make this a suitably dramatic setting for gazing upon your literary idol. Lectures and readings are open to the public as space permits; check the website for upcoming events. And leave that hoodie and trucker cap at home—business attire is required.

New School University

66 W 12th St between Fifth and Sixth Aves (1-212-229-5353/tickets 1-212-229-5488/ www.newschool.edu). Subway: F, V to 14th St; L to Sixth Ave. Admission *free–$15; students free.*

Grace Paley, Rita Dove and Jonathan Franzen are a few of the notable writers to participate in the university's wide-ranging readings and literary forums. Look also for political discussions and poetry nights.

92nd Street Y

1395 Lexington Ave at 92nd St (1-212-415-5500/ www.92y.org). Subway: 6 to 96th St. Admission *$16–$35.*

Canonical novelists, journalists and poets preside over grand intellectual feasts. A recent schedule previewed talks by poet Adrienne Rich and critic James Wood, as well as novelists John Irving, Umberto Eco and—in a double bill—Jonathan Safran Foer and William T. Vollman.

Soft Skull Shortwave

71 Bond St at State St, Boerum Hill, Brooklyn (1-718-643-1599/www.softskull.com/shortwave.php). Subway: A, C, G to Hoyt–Schermerhorn; F, G to Bergen St. Admission *free.*

Discover gritty, experimental poets and edgy new fiction writers at this avant-garde bookstore in Boerum Hill.

Sunny's Bar

253 Conover St between Beard and Reed Sts, Red Hook, Brooklyn (1-718-625-8211). Travel: F, G to Smith–9th Sts, then take the B77 bus to Conover St. Admission *$3 donation.*

If you're feeling adventurous, make the trip out to this old waterfront joint to hear an eclectic lineup of local literati such as Jonathan Ames, S.J. Rozan and poet Vijay Seshadri. Scheduling varies, so be sure to call ahead.

Spoken word

Most spoken-word events begin with a featured poet or two before moving on to an open mike. If you'd like to participate, show up a little early and ask for the sign-up sheet. Remember to adhere to poetry-slam etiquette: Feel free to express your approval out loud, but keep criticism to yourself (silence speaks louder than words). For an up-to-date schedule of events throughout the city, check out the **Ultimate NYC Poetry Calendar** (www.poetz.com/calendar).

Bowery Poetry Club

308 Bowery between Bleecker and Houston Sts (1-212-614-0505/www.bowerypoetry.com). Subway: B, D, F, V to Broadway–Lafayette St; 6 to Bleecker St. Admission *free–$15.*

Celebrating the grand oral traditions and cyberific future of poetry, the funky BPC features high-energy spoken-word events every night, with readings and performance workshops in the afternoon. The Urbana National Slam team leads an open mike on Thursdays.

Cornelia Street Café

29 Cornelia St between Bleecker and W 4th Sts (1-212-989-9319/www.corneliastreetcafe.com). Subway: A, C, E, B, D, F, V to W 4th St. Admission *free–$6, one-drink minimum.*

This charming West Village restaurant is home to several long-running series of spoken-word events, along with live music and theater. At press time, the café's basement performance space was devoting various nights to Arab-, Greek- and Italian-American writers. The popular open-mike Pink Pony series continues on Fridays (arrive before 6pm to sign up for a slot).

The Moth StorySLAM

www.themoth.org.

Better at talking than at writing? The Moth, known for its big-name monthly storytelling shows, also sponsors open slams in various venues. Ten raconteurs get five minutes each to tell a favorite story (no notes allowed!) to a panel of judges.

Nuyorican Poets Cafe

236 E 3rd St between Aves B and C (1-212-505-8183/ www.nuyorican.org). Subway: F, V to Lower East Side–Second Ave. Admission *$5–$15.*

This 30-plus-year-old community arts center, deep in the heart of the East Village, is known for its long history of raucous poetry slams, jam sessions and anything-goes open mikes.

Our Unorganicized Reading

ABC No Rio, 156 Rivington St between Clinton and Suffolk Sts (1-212-254-3697/www.abcnorio.org). Subway: F to Delancey St; J, M, Z to Delancey–Essex Sts. Sun 3pm. Admission *$2.*

ABC No Rio's long-running Sunday-afternoon open mike promises a welcoming vibe, no time limits and, best of all, "no B.S." Just remember, brevity is still the soul of wit.

The Poetry Project

St. Mark's Church in-the-Bowery, 131 E 10th St at Second Ave (1-212-674-0910/www.poetryproject. com). Subway: L to First Ave; 6 to Astor Pl. Admission *$8, seniors and students $7.*

The Project, housed in a beautiful old church, has hosted an amazing roster of poets since its inception in 1966, including Allen Ginsberg, Patti Smith, John Ashbery and Adrienne Rich. It also offers workshops, lectures, book parties and an open poetry reading on the first Monday of each month.

Cabaret & Comedy

So, a chanteuse and a stand-up comic walk into a bar...

Cabaret

In these days of arena rock, pumping dance beats and megaconcerts on pay-per-view, cabaret is sometimes dismissed as a relic or, more kindly, a throwback—a safe haven for almost-corny standards crooned without irony in front of a blue-blazered audience. But while the golden age of cabaret in New York waned with the advent of rock & roll, plenty of singers and fans have found fresh ways to honor the classic sound.

Performed in relatively small venues, usually with spare accompaniment, cabaret music draws from what's known as the Great American Songbook: a vast repertoire of tunes derived from vintage musical theater—Cole Porter, George Gershwin, Rodgers and Hart—and supplemented with songs by contemporary composers. (Randy Newman and Joni Mitchell are especially popular.) You can hear some of the same material at jazz clubs, but with a different emphasis; jazz singers focus on music, whereas cabaretists emphasize storytelling and lyrical interpretation. The top performers can make each person in the audience feel as if he or she is being personally serenaded. More than anything else, cabaret is an act of intimacy, making it an excellent option for a retro-romantic evening.

Today's cabaret venues fall into two groups. Shows at **Cafe Carlyle**, **Feinstein's at the Regency**, and the **Oak Room** offer old-school New York style and sophistication; you'll feel like you've stepped into one of the better Woody Allen movies. Neighborhood clubs such as **Danny's Skylight Room** and the **Duplex** are less formal and less pricey. After a rash of closings a few years back, new venues for cabaret are now popping up all over town. Mid-October brings the Cabaret Convention, a showcase of the genre at **Town Hall** (*see p319*) that attracts topflight performers.

At its best, cabaret can summon a world of nostalgia—for a Nick-and-Nora New York, where men wore hats and women wore gloves—while maintaining its emotional relevance in the present moment. The Great American Songbook may be old-fashioned, but until people stop falling in and out of love, it will never be out of date.

The Hideaway Room at Helen's. *See p277.*

Classic nightspots

Cafe Carlyle

The Carlyle, 35 E 76th St at Madison Ave (1-212-744-1600/reservations 1-800-227-5737/ www.thecarlyle.com). Subway: 6 to 77th St. **Shows** *Mon–Thu 8:45pm; Fri, Sat 8:45, 10:45pm.* **Cover** *$75.* **Credit** *AmEx, DC, Disc, MC, V.*
This elegant boîte in the Carlyle hotel (*see p62*), with its airy murals by Marcel Vertes, is the epitome of New York chic, especially when the great Bobby Short performs. Woody Allen sometimes sits in as clarinetist with Eddie Davis and his New Orleans

Jazz Band on Monday nights (call ahead to confirm). Don't dress casually—embrace the high life. To drink in some atmosphere without spending quite so much, try Bemelmans Bar across the hall, which always features an excellent pianist (Mon–Sat 5:30pm–12:30am; $20–$25 cover).

Feinstein's at the Regency

Regency Hotel, 540 Park Ave at 61st St (1-212-339-4095/www.feinsteinsattheregency.com). Subway: N, R, W to Lexington Ave–59th St; 4, 5, 6 to 59th St. Shows Tue–Thu 8:30pm; Fri, Sat 8:30, 11pm. Cover $60, $30–$40 food-and-drink minimum. Credit AmEx, DC, Disc, MC, V.
Cabaret's crown prince, Michael Feinstein, draws A-list talent to this swank room in the Regency Hotel. It's megapricey, but you get what you pay for. Recent performers have included some of the very top names in the business: Patti LuPone, Rita Moreno, Keely Smith and the late Cy Coleman, to name just a few.

The Oak Room

Algonquin Hotel, 59 W 44th St between Fifth and Sixth Aves (1-212-840-6800/reservations 1-212-419-9331/www.algonquinhotel.com). Subway: B, D, F, V to 42nd St–Bryant Park; 7 to Fifth Ave. Shows Tue–Thu 9pm; Fri, Sat 9, 11:30pm. Cover $50, $20 drink minimum; dinner compulsory at first Friday and Saturday shows. Credit AmEx, DC, Disc, MC, V.
This resonant, banquette-lined room is the place to enjoy such cabaret luminaries as Karen Akers and Andrea Marcovicci, plus rising young stars of the jazz world (including the great Paula West). And yes, all you Dorothy Parker fans, it's *that* Algonquin (*see p50*).

Standards

Danny's Skylight Room

Grand Sea Palace, 346 W 46th St between Eighth and Ninth Aves (1-212-265-8130/1-212-265-8133/www.dannysgsp.com). Subway: A, C, E to 42nd St–Port Authority. Shows Times vary. Piano bar 8–11pm daily. Cover $10–$25, $10–$15 food-and-drink minimum. No cover for piano bar. Credit AmEx, DC, Disc, MC, V.
A pastel-hued nook within the Grand Sea Palace on Restaurant Row, Danny's features up-and-comers (including last year's discovery Maude Maggart) as well as a few mature cabaret and jazz standbys, such as the ageless Blossom Dearie.

Don't Tell Mama

343 W 46th St between Eighth and Ninth Aves (1-212-757-0788/www.donttellmama.com). Subway: A, C, E to 42nd St–Port Authority. Shows Times vary, 2–3 shows per night. Piano bar 9pm–4am daily. Cover free–$20, two-drink minimum. No cover for piano bar, two-drink minimum. Credit AmEx, DC, Disc, MC, V.
Showbiz pros and piano-bar buffs adore this dank but homey Theater District stalwart, where acts range from strictly amateur to potential stars of tomorrow. The nightly lineup may include pop, jazz or Broadway singers, as well as female impersonators, magicians, comedians or musical revues.

The Duplex

61 Christopher St at Seventh Ave South (1-212-255-5438/www.theduplex.com). Subway: 1, 9 to Christopher St–Sheridan Sq. Shows 7, 9pm daily. Piano bar 9pm–4am daily. Cover $5–$25, two-drink minimum. Credit AmEx, Disc, MC, V.
The Duplex may not have classic glamour, but it's the city's oldest cabaret. Going strong for 50-plus years, the place is known for campy, good-natured fun, and has become a home away from home for such local favorites as Lisa Asher and Jeanne MacDonald.

The Hideaway Room at Helen's

168 Eighth Ave between 18th and 19th Sts (1-212-206-0609). Subway: A, C, E to 14th St; 1, 9 to 18th St. Shows Times vary, 2–3 shows per night. Piano bar times vary. Open mike 10pm–4am daily. Cover $15–$25, $15 food-and-drink minimum. No cover for piano bar. Credit AmEx, MC, V.
The latest addition to the scene is a fresh, friendly boîte that has risen, phoenixlike, on the site of the late Judi's Chelsea. With a bustling piano bar and a promising lineup—led last year by the legendary Julie Wilson—this newcomer is poised to emerge as the midpriced cabaret space of choice.

Mama Rose's

219 Second Ave between 13th and 14th Sts (1-212-533-0558/www.mamaroses.net). Subway: L to Third Ave; N, Q, R, W, 4, 5, 6 to 14th St–Union Sq. Shows Times vary. Cover Prices vary; two-drink minimum. Credit AmEx, MC, V.
Sing out, Louise! This newish club, named after *Gypsy*'s stage mother from hell, is designed specifically for cabaret performances; the sound is especially crisp and clear. The decor is on the cheesy side—white piano, silver balls hanging from the ceiling—but happily, the performers are not.

Opia

Habitat Hotel, 130 E 57th St at Lexington Ave (1-212-688-3939/www.liveatopia.com). Subway: N, R, W to Lexington Ave–59th St; 4, 5, 6 to 59th St. Shows Times vary. Cover $15–$45, $15 food-and-drink minimum. Credit AmEx, DC, MC, V.
Christened in spring 2003, this roomy and comfy Euro-flavored lounge is still finding its voice, but the results have been encouraging so far. Soul and world-music acts alternate with more traditional cabaret.

Alternative venues

Joe's Pub

See p316 for listing. Shows Times vary, 2 shows per night. Cover $10–$30.
This plush club and restaurant in the Public Theater is both hip and elegant, and boasts an extraordinarily eclectic mix of performers (usually booked for a single night). Among the rock, jazz and world-music acts, you'll occasionally find a Broadway performer reaching into cabaret.

Comedy

New York City's comedy scene is as large as the skyline, and just as diverse. While **Carolines on Broadway**, one of the best known of the mainstream clubs, still has a lock on headliners (with prices to match), the **New York Improv**, a stand-up institution, reopened in 2004, and several new venues have joined the mix as well.

As comedy-oriented theaters train more students and breed more competition, the quality of shows continues to rise at the city's improv houses, incidentally the best places to look for sketch comedy. Walk into the **Upright Citizens Brigade Theatre** and you're bound to find something amazing on any day of the week.

The edgier underground stand-up scene is alive and well, too. Many rising stars who've appeared on Comedy Central, and dazzled David Letterman's and Conan O'Brien's audiences now host their own shows in local bars, inviting their contemporaries to share the stage. Thanks to a flurry of new television shows in production here, comics are sticking around rather than fleeing to L.A., meaning New York is once again reclaiming its title as the comedy capital of the country. Lucky you!

Boston Comedy Club

82 W 3rd St between Sullivan and Thompson Sts (1-212-477-1000/www.bostoncomedyclub.com). Subway: A, C, E, B, D, F, V to W 4th St. **Shows** *Sun–Thu 9:30pm; Fri, Sat 8, 10pm, 12:15am.* **Cover** *$8–$12, students $5; Mon–Thu one-drink minimum; Fri, Sat two-drink minimum.* **Credit** *AmEx, MC, V (food and drink only).*
This club reflects its Village environs: casual and a little seedy, which is why you can expect younger, edgier rising stars (most of the time, at least).

Carolines on Broadway

1626 Broadway between 49th and 50th Sts (1-212-757-4100/www.carolines.com). Subway: N, R, W to 49th St; 1, 9 to 50th St. **Shows** *Mon, Tue 7, 9:30pm; Wed 7:30, 9:30pm; Thu, Sun 8, 10pm; Fri, Sat 8, 10:30pm, 12:30am.* **Cover** *$10–$40, two-drink minimum.* **Credit** *AmEx, MC, V.*
You can occasionally catch guys like Gilbert Gottfried here doing schtick that matches the '80s decor, but you'll also find current stars such as Greg Fitzsimmons, Dane Cook and *Last Comic Standing* contestants. Be warned: The bigger the star, the bigger the cover charge.

Comedy Cellar

117 MacDougal St between Bleecker and W 3rd Sts (1-212-254-3480/www.comedycellar.com). Subway: A, C, E, B, D, F, V to W 4th St. **Shows** *Sun–Thu 9, 11pm; Fri 9, 10:45pm, 12:30am; Sat 7:30, 9:15,*

The sketch comedy at the **Upright Citizens Brigade Theatre** is a class act. *See p279.*

11pm, 12:45am. **Cover** *$10–$15, two-item minimum.* **Credit** *AmEx, MC, V.*
This club is a good bet since *SNL* and *Tough Crowd* star, Colin Quinn, is almost always around, with his big-name friends (including Patrice O'Neal, Greg Giraldo, Jim Norton and Nick DiPaolo) in tow.

Dangerfield's

1118 First Ave between 61st and 62nd Sts (1-212-593-1650/www.dangerfields.com). Subway: N, R, W to Lexington Ave–59th St; 4, 5, 6 to 59th St. **Shows** *Sun–Thu 8:45pm; Fri 8:30, 10:30pm; Sat 8, 10:30pm, 12:30am.* **Cover** *$13–$20.* **Credit** *AmEx, MC, V.*
Opened by the late Rodney Dangerfield in 1969, this old-school lounge predates not only its competitors, but also many of its performers. The club offers good food and cheap parking—and no drink minimum, which alone makes a visit here worthwhile…even if it gets no respect.

Eating It

Luna Lounge, 171 Ludlow St between Houston and Stanton Sts (1-212-260-2323/www.eatingit.net). Subway: F to Delancey St; J, M, Z to Delancey–Essex Sts. **Shows** *Sept–Jun Mon 8pm.* **Cover** *$8, includes one drink ticket.* **Credit** *Cash only.*
While this is the place to see comics on the brink of fame, you'll also see well-known performers who've been on *Conan, Letterman* and *SNL*. A must-see show for comedy fans and industry insiders alike.

Gotham Comedy Club

34 W 22nd St between Fifth and Sixth Aves (1-212-367-9000/www.gothamcomedyclub.com). Subway: F, V, N, R, W to 23rd St. **Shows** *Sun–Thu 8:30pm; Fri 8:30, 10:30pm; Sat 8:30, 10:30pm, 12:30am.* **Cover** *$10–$16, two-drink minimum.* **Credit** *AmEx, DC, MC, V.*
You may not know their names, but if you follow stand-up, you'll recognize many of the faces that appear at this relatively upscale club. Regulars have included Judy Gold, Ted Alexandro and Lewis Black.

The Laugh Factory

303 W 42nd St at Eighth Ave (1-212-586-7829/www.laughfactory.com). Subway: A, C, E to 42nd St–Port Authority. **Shows** *Tue, Sun 8pm; Wed, Thu 8:30pm; Fri, Sat 8:30, 10:30pm, 12:30am.* **Cover** *$15–$30, two-drink minimum.* **Credit** *AmEx, DC, Disc, MC, V.*
The long-running L.A. club with the same moniker opened a satellite near Times Square where you can catch comics like Jim David, Ross Bennett and even Andrew "Dice" Clay, if you're into that.

Laugh Lounge nyc

151 Essex St between Rivington and Stanton Sts (1-212-614-2500/www.laughloungenyc.com). Subway: F to Delancey St; J, M, Z to Delancey–Essex Sts. **Shows** *Tue–Thu 8:30pm; Fri, Sat 8:30, 10:30pm.* **Cover** *$8–$15, two-drink minimum.* **Credit** *AmEx, Disc, MC, V.*
A proper stand-up club on the LES may seem strange, but features like the *Cringe Humor*

Comedy Show—which regularly showcases some of the scene's fiercer performers—pay homage to the neighborhood's edgy vibe. Of course, you may also see established names here, like Dean Edwards and Judah Freidlander.

New York Improv

318 W 53rd St between Eighth and Ninth Aves (1-212-757-2323/www.newyorkimprov.com). Subway: C, E to 50th St. **Shows** *Sun–Thu 9pm; Fri 9, 11:30pm; Sat 9, 11pm, 12:45am.* **Cover** *$10–$15.* **Credit** *AmEx, DC, MC, V.*
Originally opened in 1963, the legendary Improv's stage was graced with such greats as Richard Pryor, Robin Williams and George Carlin. This recent reincarnation trots out some of today's rising stars, many of whom are already working the TV circuit.

The People's Improv Theater

154 W 29th St between Sixth and Seventh Aves (1-212-563-7488/www.thepit-nyc.com). Subway: 1, 9 to 28th St. **Shows** *Times vary.* **Cover** *$5–$10.* **Credit** *Cash only.*
The PIT specializes in the same kind of innovative improv and sketch comedy that its predecessor, Improv Olympic, imported from Chicago in the late '90s. In particular, look for performances by Neutrino, Ms. Jackson and the theater's long-running *Faculty* show. The PIT also offers excellent classes.

Stand-Up New York

236 W 78th St at Broadway (1-212-595-0850/www.standupny.com). Subway: 1, 9 to 79th St. **Shows** *Mon 8:30pm; Tue, Wed 6, 9pm; Thu 6, 9, 11:30pm; Fri, Sat 8, 10pm, 12:30am; Sun 7, 9:15pm.* **Cover** *$5–$15, two-drink minimum.* **Credit** *AmEx, MC, V.*
The Upper West Side's only club features a mix of circuit regulars (Laurie Kilmartin, Jim Gaffigan and Dean Obeidallah), along with fresh new talents.

The Tank

432 W 42nd St between Ninth and Tenth Aves (1-212-563-6269/www.thetanknyc.org). Subway: A, C, E to 42nd St–Port Authority. **Shows** *Times vary.* **Cover** *$5–$10.* **Credit** *Cash only.*
Although this new venue showcases theater and music, its comedy programs are far from neglected and include stand-up and variety, as well as more experimental shows.

Upright Citizens Brigade Theatre

307 W 26th St between Eighth and Ninth Aves (1-212-366-9176/www.ucbtheatre.com). Subway: C, E to 23rd St. **Shows** *Times vary.* **Cover** *$5–$8.* **Credit** *Cash only.*
The UCBT presents some of the most adventurous comedy in NYC, and always at budget prices. You'll often see performers from *Conan, Saturday Night Live* and *The Daily Show* parading the sketch and improv talents that put them there. (Sunday is the typical night for celebrity drop-ins.) Take a class, if you're feeling frisky.

Children

Toddlers, kids, tweens or teens—New York is a city for the ages.

To kids, New York is a playground for the senses. Daily thrills number in the hundreds, from hearing subterranean trumpet players blast over the squeal of the subway to seeing how the blazing lights of Times Square turn nighttime into fantastically garish day. No surprise, then, that the city generates undeniable excitement in young visitors, including really cool tweens and teens. Remember, it takes *years* for even a homegrown New York City kid to get blasé about this place. But be forewarned: All of this stimulation can overload the circuits of smaller children.

So take in the standard sights but, in between the Empire State Building and the Statue of Liberty, put away the map and wander. You never know what you'll see—a street performer in head-to-toe glitter, a parade full of clamoring bagpipes or the Olsen twins on their way to class at NYU.

Of course, you'll want to take in some of New York's more tried-and-true offerings, too. We've listed spots that cater to the city's little hipsters, as well as some traditional fare that has entertained generations of NYC children. To keep up with the kid-friendly events happening during your stay, pick up a copy of *Time Out New York Kids*.

Where to stay

Most hotels, especially the big chains, will move a crib or an extra bed into your room to accommodate your tot. Ask if this service is available when you book, and check on the size of the room; sometimes, the hipper the hotel, the smaller the rooms, since most of the trendy places assume their guests will be out on the town all night. The relatively few hotels that offer kid-specific services (unfortunately, they tend to be among the more expensive places in town)—like a milk-and-cookie turndown or access to an outdoor pool—are listed below. For more on hotels, see **Where to Stay** (*pp39–67*).

The Carlyle
35 E 76th St between Madison and Park Aves (1-212-744-1600/1-800-227-5737/www.thecarlyle.com). For review, *see p62*.

> ▶ Need a babysitter? *See p367.*

The Holiday Inn Midtown
440 W 57th St between Ninth and Tenth Aves (1-800-465-4329/www.hi57.com). See *p57* **Chain gang**.

Le Parker Meridien
118 W 57th St between Sixth and Seventh Aves (1-212-245-5000/1-800-543-4300/www.parker meridien.com). For review, *see p54*.

The Plaza Hotel
768 Fifth Ave at Central Park South (1-212-759-3000/1-800-759-3000/www.fairmont.com). For review, *see p65*.

The Roger Smith
501 Lexington Ave between 47th and 48th Sts (1-212-755-1400/1-800-445-0277/www.rogersmith.com). For review, *see p56*.

Classic kids' New York

Astroland Amusement Park
1000 Surf Ave at West 10th St, Coney Island, Brooklyn (1-718-372-0275/www.astroland.com). Subway: D, F, Q to Coney Island–Stillwell Ave. **Open** *Mid-Apr–mid-Jun Sat, Sun noon–6pm, weather permitting. Mid-Jun–Labor Day noon–midnight. Early Sept–early Oct Sat, Sun open at noon; closing time depends on weather.* **Admission** *$2–$5 per ride; $17.99–$22.99 per six-hour session.* **Credit** *MC, V.*
This well-aged Coney Island amusement park has an appealing grunginess that makes it a welcome alternative to certain slick, mouse-themed parks. Kids over 54 inches in height can ride the world-famous Cyclone roller coaster ($5); the young ones will prefer the Tilt-A-Whirl or the carousel.

Dinosaurs at the Museum of Natural History
For listing, see p146 **American Museum of Natural History**.
Children of all ages request repeat visits to this old-fashioned, exhibit-based museum—especially to see the dinosaur skeletons, the enormous blue whale and, in the colder months, the free-flying butterflies. During the holiday season, look for the Christmas tree decorated with masterfully folded origami ornaments (they include dinosaur shapes, of course). Paper-folders are on hand to help visitors make their own.

The Nutcracker
See p261 for listing.

Kids get a jump on the fun in the gymnastics center at **Chelsea Piers**. *See p286.*

Generations of New York kids have counted on the New York City Ballet to provide this Balanchine holiday treat. The pretty two-act production features an onstage snowstorm, a flying sleigh, a one-ton Christmas tree and child dancers.

Storytelling at the Hans Christian Andersen Statue

Central Park, entrance on Fifth Ave at 72nd St (www.hcastorycenter.org). Subway: 6 to 68th St–Hunter College. **Dates** *Jun–Sept Sat 11am–noon.* **Admission** *free.*
Children five and older have gathered for decades at the foot of this climbable statue to hear master storytellers from all over the country tell folk and fairy tales. This will be an especially festive year, as the storytelling institution celebrates its 50th anniversary as well as Andersen's 200th birthday in April.

Temple of Dendur at the Met

For listing, see p148 **Metropolitan Museum of Art**.
The Met can be overwhelming unless you make a beeline for one or two galleries. The impressive Temple of Dendur, a real multiroomed, ancient temple with carvings and reliefs (and graffiti), was brought here from Egypt, stone by stone, and it's a perennial hit. Also check out the mummies in the Egyptian room and the medieval arms and armor collection.

Winnie the Pooh and Friends

For listing, see p162 **Donnell Library Center**. Open *Mon, Wed, Fri noon–6pm; Tue 10am–6pm;*

Thu noon–8pm; Sat noon–5pm; Sun 1–5pm. Call for summer hours. **Admission** *free.*
The toys that belonged to Christopher Robin Milne are still ensconced in a glass case in this library's Central Children's Room, despite a 1998 diplomatic crisis in which the U.K. demanded their return.

Arts festivals

Some of the city's annual arts festivals incorporate interesting kids' programming. Of particular note is the **Lincoln Center Out of Doors Festival** (*see p258*), which offers pared-down performances for children. Downtown's **River to River Festival** (*see p256*) also provides family fun.

Circuses

Each spring, **Ringling Bros. and Barnum & Bailey**'s three-ring circus (*see p254*) comes to Madison Square Garden, and so do animal-rights picketers. You can't beat the world-famous circus for spectacle, but the smaller alternatives are more fun.

Big Apple Circus

Damrosch Park, Lincoln Center, 62nd St between Columbus and Amsterdam Aves (1-212-268-2500/ www.bigapplecircus.org). Subway: 1, 9 to 66th St–Lincoln Ctr. **Dates** *Oct–Jan. Call or visit website for schedule and prices.* **Credit** *AmEx, Disc, MC, V.*
New York's traveling circus was founded 28 years

ago as an intimate answer to the Ringling Bros. extravaganza. The clowns in this nonprofit show are among the most creative in the country.

UniverSoul Big Top Circus

1-800-316-7439/www.universoulcircus.com. **Dates** *Early Apr–late May. Call or visit website for venue, schedule and prices.* **Credit** *AmEx, DC, Disc, MC, V.*
This one-ring African-American circus has the requisite clowns and animals with a twist: Instead of familiar circus music, you get hip-hop, R&B, salsa—and a great ringmaster. The group usually appears in Brooklyn's Prospect Park in the spring.

Film

New York International Children's Film Festival

Various venues (1-212-349-0330/www.gkids.com). **Dates** *Feb–Mar. Call or visit website for schedule and prices.* **Credit** *AmEx, MC, V.*
This three-week fest is a hot ticket. An exciting mix of shorts and full-length features is presented to everyone from tots through teens. Many of the films are by international indie filmmakers—and not just those who make kids' flicks. Children determine the festival's winners, which are then screened at an awards ceremony.

Tribeca Film Festival

Various Tribeca venues (www.tribecafilmfestival.org). **Dates** *Late April or early May. Visit the website for schedule and prices.*
Robert De Niro's affair includes two weekends of screenings for kids, both commercial premieres and shorts programs, plus an outdoor street festival.

Museums & exhibitions

Museums usually offer weekend and school-break workshops as well as interactive exhibitions. Even the very young love exploring the **American Museum of Natural History**; its **Rose Center for Earth and Space** (*see p146*) features exhibits and a multimedia space show within the largest suspended-glass cube in the U.S. Children of

Here's to the babies who brunch

On weekends, New Yorkers do brunch. And that includes very young New Yorkers, who no longer have to whine and fidget as their parents dawdle over that third cup of coffee. Instead of just tossing a handful of crayons on the table, many restaurants now offer creative distractions for the juice-box set. Movies, live music and separate playrooms leave grown-ups free to scan the Sunday papers, sip Bloody Marys and luxuriate in a couple of almost-like-the-old-days hours. There's no reason why you shouldn't join the locals—with tots in tow—in this popular culinary ritual.

Big City Bar and Grill

1600 Third Ave at 90th St (1-212-369-0808). Subway: 4, 5, 6 to 86th St. Sat, Sun noon–4pm.
This huge, noisy all-American joint offers PlayDine, an in-house play area supervised by child-care professionals, during its brunch service. (PlayDine is available during lunch and dinner, too.) For a charge of $10 per child (the price decreases for additional children), kids play out of earshot while parents indulge in a leisurely meal of fancy frittatas, eggs Benedict or apple pancakes. A quick-order kids' menu lets the wee ones scarf down some French toast before heading to the playroom.

Bubby's

1 Main St between Plymouth and Water Sts, Dumbo, Brooklyn (1-718-222-0666/ www.bubbys.com). Subway: A, C to High St; F to York Ave. Sat, Sun 10am–4pm.
Want to skip the subway for once? From the South Street Seaport, take a five-minute New York Water Taxi ride across the river to the Fulton Ferry Landing. At the Brooklyn outpost of this famously family-friendly Tribeca restaurant, a well-stocked play area (plus crayons and balloons at the table) keeps little hands occupied while adults chow down on spicy huevos rancheros. Bonus: Across the street, there's a scenic waterfront playground. Don't forget to grab cones at the Brooklyn Ice Cream Factory nearby. **Other location** *120 Hudson St at North Moore St (1-212-219-0666).*

Church Lounge

Tribeca Grand Hotel, 2 Sixth Ave between Church and White Sts (1-212-519-6677/ www.tribecagrand.com). Subway: A, C, E to Canal St. Sun 10am–3pm.
For $25, adults can linger over the fabulous all-you-can-eat smorgasbord while kids gobble their $10 brunch and then watch seasonal movies. Toddlers can snack for free on whatever looks tasty, be

all ages will be fascinated by the amazing scale model *Panorama of the City of New York* at the **Queens Museum of Art** (*see p154*) and with the toy collection, which includes teddy bears, games, dolls and dollhouses, at the **Museum of the City of New York** (*see p156*). Hands-on fun can be had inside the pitch-black Touch Tunnel at the **Liberty Science Center** (*see p163*). At the **American Museum of the Moving Image** (*see p161*), kids mess with *Jurassic Park* sound effects and play with moving-image technology. The ***Intrepid* Sea-Air-Space Museum** (*see p162*) houses interactive battle-related exhibits on an aircraft carrier. Many art museums offer family tours and workshops that may include sketching in the galleries. To find out what's available, visit the websites of the **Brooklyn Museum**, the **Metropolitan Museum of Art** and the **Whitney Museum of American Art** (*see p151*). The **Museum of Modern Art**,

too, is now catering to families in its newly expanded midtown home (*see p153* **Thoroughly Modern Manhattan**).

Brooklyn Children's Museum

145 Brooklyn Ave at St. Marks Ave, Crown Heights, Brooklyn (1-718-735-4400/www.bchildmus.org). Travel: A to Nostrand Ave; C to Kingston–Throop Ave; 3 to Kingston Ave. **Open** *Sept–Jun Wed–Fri 1–6pm; Sat, Sun 11am–6pm. Jul, Aug Tue–Fri 1–6pm; Sat, Sun 11am–6pm. Call or visit website for holiday hours.* **Admission** *$4, children under 1 free. Families free first Thursday of the month all day, and Sat, Sun 11am–noon.* **Credit** *AmEx, Disc, MC, V.*

Founded in 1899, BCM is the world's first museum designed for kids. It has more than 27,000 artifacts in its Collection Central gallery, including prehistoric fossils and present-day toys from around the world. Hands-on exhibits and live small animals rule the Animal Outpost, and the People Tube, a huge sewer pipe, connects four exhibit floors. On weekends, a free shuttle bus makes a circuit from the Grand Army Plaza subway station to the Brooklyn Museum and this museum.

La Belle Epoque.

it sushi, mac and cheese, or a Mickey Mouse–shaped waffle.

Iridium Jazz Club

1650 Broadway at 51st St (1-212-582-2121). B, D, E to Seventh Ave; N, R, W to 49th St; 1, 9 to 50th St. Sun 11am, 1pm seatings.
Many folks remember Bob Dorough as the host of TV's *Schoolhouse Rock*. But Dorough, now 81, was a disciple of Charlie Parker and contributed to a '60s Miles Davis album. So the ponytailed hepcat puts a little bit of everything on the menu—including "Conjunction Junction"—when he and his trio play the weekly jazz brunch at Iridium. Guests, some of them kids, often join him onstage, and the all-you-can-eat buffet ($22) is a treat. Older kids should have a great time here.

La Belle Epoque

827 Broadway between 12th and 13th Sts (1-212-254-6436/www.belleepoquenyc.com). Subway: L, N, Q, R, W, 4, 5, 6 to 14th St–Union Sq. Noon–3pm one Saturday a month. Call for exact date.
At this New Orleans–style club and restaurant, the monthly baby brunch keeps little ones busy with blocks, Pack 'n Plays, Exersaucers and doll strollers. Adults can enjoy made-to-order omelettes, French toast and mimosas with live jazz in the background.

The **Swedish Cottage Marionette Theater.**

gy while they play on slides and giant seesaws. Other standouts include the first interactive exhibit devoted to math (designed by Charles and Ray Eames) and a large preschool science area.

Sony Wonder Technology Lab

Sony Plaza, 56th St between Fifth and Madison Aves (1-212-833-8100/www.sonywondertechlab.com). Subway: E, V to Fifth Ave–53rd St; N, R, W to Fifth Ave–59th St. **Open** *Tue, Wed, Fri, Sat 10am–6pm; Thu 10am–8pm; Sun noon–6pm; reservations recommended.* **Admission** *free.*
Recently refurbished, this digital wonderland lets visitors use state-of-the-art communication technology to play at designing video games, assisting in surgery, editing a TV show and operating robots. Kids eight and older get the most out of this place.

Outdoor places

Nelson A. Rockefeller Park

Battery Park City, Hudson River at Chambers St (1-212-267-9700/www.bpcparks.org). Subway: A, C, 1, 2, 3, 9 to Chambers St. **Open** *6am–1am daily.* **Admission** *free.*
Besides watching the boats along the Hudson, kids can enjoy one of New York's best playgrounds, which has balls, board games and other toys for the borrowing. Events for children are held May through October (visit the website for a schedule).

Piers 25 and 26

Hudson River Park, Hudson River at North Moore St (1-212-627-2020). Subway: 1, 9 to Franklin St. **Open** *1am–1am daily.* **Admission** *free.*
Pier 25 has the ramshackle feel of a seaside town, with volleyball, mini golf (May through October; $2), a snack shack, a water-and-sand play area, and easels for budding artists. On Pier 26, the Downtown Boathouse (1-646-613-0740, www.downtownboathouse.org) provides kayaks for free paddles between piers (summer weekends and holidays 9am to 6pm; weekdays 5 to 7pm).

Riverbank State Park

Hudson River at 145th St (1-212-694-3600). Subway: 1, 9 to 145th St. **Open** *6am–11pm daily. Ice-skating Nov–Jan; call for hours.* **Admission** *free. Rink $1, skate rental $4.*
Besides the skating rink and other athletic facilities, the main draw at this unusual 28-acre park is the Totally Kid Carousel (open June through August), designed by children.

Central Park

Most New Yorkers don't have yards—they have parks. The most popular is Central Park (*see p106* **Central Park**), with places and programs just for kids. (Visit www.centralparknyc.org for a calendar.) Don't miss the beautiful antique carousel ($1.25 per ride). The **Heckscher Playground**

Children's Museum of the Arts

182 Lafayette St between Broome and Grand Sts (1-212-274-0986/www.cmany.org). Subway: 6 to Spring St. **Open** *Wed, Fri–Sun noon–5pm; Thu noon–6pm.* **Admission** *$6. Voluntary donation Thu 4–6pm.* **Credit** *AmEx, MC, V ($35 minimum).*
Kids under seven love this low-key museum and its floor-to-ceiling chalkboards, art computers and vast store of art supplies.

Children's Museum of Manhattan

212 W 83rd St between Amsterdam Ave and Broadway (1-212-721-1234/www.cmom.org). Subway: 1, 9 to 86th St. **Open** *Wed–Sun 10am–5pm. Call for summer and holiday hours.* **Admission** *$7, seniors $4.* **Credit** *AmEx, MC, V.*
This children's museum promotes several types of literacy through playful interactive exhibitions; a big hit is the *Seuss!* show (through September 2005). In the Inventor Center, computer-savvy kids can take any idea they dream up—a flying bike, a talking robot—and design it onscreen using digital imaging.

New York Hall of Science

See p163 for listing.
Inside a former 1964 World's Fair pavilion and flanked by rockets from the U.S. space program, this museum is worth a trek for its discovery-based exhibits. From March through December, the 30,000-square-foot outdoor Science Playground teaches children the principles of balance, gravity and ener-

(one of 20), will soon boast an up-to-date adventure area.

Central Park Zoo
See p107 for listing.
The stars of this refurbished wildlife center are the polar bears and penguins, which live in glass habitats so you can watch their underwater antics. They're celebrated each summer during the Chill Out festival (*see p258*).

Conservatory Water
Central Park, entrance on Fifth Ave at 72nd St. Subway: 6 to 68th St–Hunter College. Open Jul, Aug Sun–Fri 11am–7pm; Sat 2–7pm, weather permitting. Admission free.
Stuart Little Pond, named after E.B. White's storybook mouse, is a mecca for model-yacht racers. When the boat master is around, rent a remote-controlled vessel ($10 per hour).

Henry Luce Nature Observatory
See p109 for listing.
Inside the Gothic Belvedere Castle, telescopes, microscopes and hands-on exhibits teach kids about the plants and animals living in the park. With ID, you can borrow a Discovery Kit: binoculars, a bird-watching guide and other cool tools.

North Meadow Recreation Center
Central Park, midpark at 97th St (1-212-348-4867/ www.centralparknyc.org). Subway: B, C, 6 to 96th St. Open Check website for hours.
Park visitors with photo ID can check out the Field Day Kit, which includes a Frisbee, hula hoop, jump rope, kickball, and Wiffle ball and bat.

Victorian Gardens
Central Park, Wollman Rink (1-212-982-2229/ www.victoriangardensnyc.com). Subway: N, R, W to Fifth Ave–59th St. Open Mid-May–mid-Sept Mon–Fri 11am–7pm; Sat, Sun 10am–8pm. Admission $9, children $14, children under 3 ft (1 meter) tall free.
Central Park's first Disneyesque feature is this new nostalgia-themed amusement park geared to young children. The mini teacup carousel and Rio Grande train are bound to be hits with little kids.

Wollman Rink
See 336 for listing.
Skating in Central Park amid snowy trees, with grand apartment buildings towering in the distance, is a New York City tradition. This popular rink offers lessons and skate rentals, plus a snack bar where you can warm up with hot chocolate.

Gardens

Brooklyn Botanic Garden
See p124 for listing.
In the 13,000-square-foot Discovery Garden, children can play botanist, make toys out of natural materials, weave a wall, and generally get their hands dirty.

New York Botanical Garden
See p139 for listing.
The Everett Children's Adventure Garden is a whimsical museum of the natural world. In the Family Garden (early spring through late October), kids can run under a giant caterpillar topiary, poke around in a touch-tank, and plant or harvest vegetables.

Performing arts

The Adventures of Maya the Bee
45 Bleecker Theater, 45 Bleecker St at Lafayette St (1-212-253-9983/www.45bleecker.com/maya.html). Subway: F, V, D, F, V to Broadway–Lafayette St; 6 to Bleecker St. Shows Oct–Jun Sat 11am. Tickets $15. Credit AmEx, MC, V.
The star of the Culture Project's long-running jazz puppet play is the sweetest little bee that kids are likely to meet. But some of the creatures Maya encounters are not so nice—this is the insect world, after all. Recommended for children ages five to nine.

Carnegie Hall Family Concerts
See p325 for listing. Admission $8.
Even kids who profess to hate classical music are impressed by a visit to Carnegie Hall. The Family Concert series features first-rate world music and jazz performers, plus pre-concert workshops and storytelling. Concerts run fall through spring and are recommended for ages 5 to 12.

Family Matters
For listing, see p351 Dance Theater Workshop. Tickets $20, children $10.
Curated by a pair of choreographer parents and geared for children ages three and up, Family Matters is a quirky variety show blending art, dance, music and theater. Call or check the website for schedule.

Jazz for Young People
For listing, see p323 The house that jazz built.
These participatory concerts, held at Jazz at Lincoln Center's sparkling new digs and modeled on the New York Philharmonic Young People's Concerts, are led by trumpeter and jazz great Wynton Marsalis.

Kids 'n Comedy
Gotham Comedy Club, 34 W 22nd St between Fifth and Sixth Aves (1-212-877-6115/www. kidsncomedy.com). Subway: F, V, N, R, W to 23rd St. Shows Call or visit website for schedule; reservations required. Tickets $15 plus one-drink minimum. Credit AmEx, MC, V.
Kids 'n Comedy has developed a stable of funny kids, ages 9 to 17, who deliver their own stand-up material, much of it in the homework-sucks vein.

Little Orchestra Society
Various venues (1-212-971-9500/www.little orchestra.org). Tickets $10–$50.
Since 1947, this orchestra has presented classical concerts for kids, including the popular interactive *Peter and the Wolf* for preschoolers and December's

Arts & Entertainment

spectacular *Amahl and the Night Visitors*, complete with live sheep. Call or visit the website for a schedule.

The New Victory Theater

See p345 for listing. **Tickets** *$10–$50.*
As New York's only full-scale young people's theater, the New Victory presents international theater and dance companies at junior prices. Shows often sell out well in advance, so reserve seats early.

New York Theatre Ballet

Florence Gould Hall, 55 E 59th St between Madison and Park Aves (1-212-355-6160/www.nytb.org).
Subway: N, R, W to Lexington Ave–59th St; 4, 5, 6 to 59th St. **Tickets** *$30, children under 12 $25.*
Tickets also available through Ticketmaster.
Credit *AmEx, MC, V.*
Enjoy one-hour adaptations of classic ballets such as the holiday chestnut *The Nutcracker*. The interactive *Carnival of the Animals* teaches the audience basic dance moves, and *Alice in Wonderland* is a lively, kooky vaudeville-style romp.

Swedish Cottage Marionette Theater

Central Park West at 81st St (1-212-988-9093).
Subway: B, C to 81st St–Museum of Natural History.
Shows *Oct–Jun Tue–Fri 10:30am, noon; Sat 1pm.*
Jul, Aug Mon–Fri 10:30am, noon. **Tickets** *$6, children $5.* **Credit** *Cash only.*
Reservations are essential at this intimate theater in an old Swedish schoolhouse run by the City Parks Foundation.

Urban Word NYC

Various venues (1-212-691-6590/
www.urbanwordnyc.org).
A DJ hosts poetry slams and open mikes for "the next generation." Teens bring their own (uncensored) poems and freestyle rhymes or give props to other kids performing theirs.

Sports & activities

For kayaking, *see p337*. For bicycling, horseback riding and ice-skating, *see pp334–336*.

Chelsea Piers

See p334 for listing.
A roller rink, gymnasium, pool, toddler gym and extreme-skating park help kids burn energy. You'll also find ice-skating rinks, batting cages and rock-climbing walls in this vast complex. Day passes are available. The Flip 'n Flick program (7 to 11pm) allows parents to get a night off while the kids enjoy athletic activities and a movie.

Sydney's Playground

66 White St between Broadway and Church St
(1-212-431-9125/www.sydneysplayground.com).
Subway: J, M, Z, N, Q, R, W, 6 to Canal St.
Open *10am–6pm daily.* **Admission** *$8.50.*
Credit *AmEx, Disc, MC, V.*

This huge, architecturally striking indoor play space has been designed to resemble a streetscape, complete with a multilevel "climbing city," a "roadway" for ride-on toys and a café.

Trapeze School New York

See p338 for listing.
Kids over age six can fly through the air with the greatest of ease. (You can also just stop along the esplanade and watch.) Children under 12 must be accompanied by an adult.

Tours

ARTime

1-718-797-1573. **Open** *Oct–Jun first Saturday of the month 11am–12:30pm.* **Admission** *$25 per parent-child pair, each additional child $5.*
Credit *Cash only.*
Since 1994, art historians with education backgrounds have led contemporary-art tours of Soho and Chelsea galleries for kids ages five to ten.

Confino Family Apartment Tour

For listing, see p155 **Lower East Side Tenement Museum**.
A weekly interactive tour teaches children ages 5 to 14 about immigrant life in the early 20th century. Kids participate in games, try on period costumes and handle knickknacks from that era.

Wildman Ecology Walks

Various city parks (1-914-835-2153/www.wildman stevebrill.com). **Open** *weekends, some holidays 11:45am–3:45pm; reservations required 24hrs in advance.* **Admission** *suggested donation $10, children under 12 $5.* **Credit** *Cash only.*
Steve Brill, an urban forager and wild-food expert, gives kids a chance to dig, gather and taste all kinds of wild foods growing right in the city.

Zoos

Bronx Zoo

See p139 for listing.
Inside the Bronx Zoo is the Bronx Children's Zoo, with lots of domesticated critters to pet, plus exhibits that show the world from an animal's point of view. Beyond the Children's Zoo, camel rides (April through October) and sea lion feedings (11am and 3pm) are other can't-miss attractions for visitors with kids.

New York Aquarium

Surf Ave at West 8th St, Coney Island, Brooklyn
(1-718-265-3474/www.nyaquarium.com). Subway:
D to Coney Island–Stillwell Ave; F, Q to W 8th St–
NY Aquarium. **Open** *Visit website for hours.*
Admission *$11, seniors and children 2–12 $7.*
Credit *AmEx, Disc, MC, V.*
Like the rest of Coney Island, this aquarium is just a little shabby, but kids enjoy seeing the famous beluga whale family, the scary sharks and the entertaining sea lion show.

Arts & Entertainment

Clubs

The newest clubs are packed—but don't despair. We'll help you get down tonight.

To the casual observer, it might appear as though the New York City nightlife scene—which was once exalted as the world's greatest but fell on hard times during the 1990s—has undergone something of a renaissance. Three new superclubs (**Avalon**, **Crobar** and **Spirit**) and a bevy of smaller venues have opened in recent years, and they can get jam-packed, at least on weekends. Whether your taste in clubs is elegant or down 'n' dirty, whether your dance music of choice is house, hip-hop, rock or Latin, the after-dark horizons appear limitless.

That's the rose-tinted version, at least; the real picture is a little murkier. To underground clubbers, those superclubs aren't so super, since they come from the commercial end of the nightlife spectrum. In a sign of the times, all three are part of chains that are headquartered elsewhere: Spirit hails from Dublin, Crobar is based in Chicago, and Avalon comes out of Boston. But hey, if your idea of fun is bumping and grinding in a packed-to-the-rafters mega dance club with like-minded souls then, by all means, join the swaying fray.

The city's attitude toward nightlife hasn't helped. A bizarre cabaret law (*see p291* **The old song and dance**) continues to put a huge damper on the scene, and enforcement of noise ordinances—with *noise* denoting any louder-than-a-whisper dance beat—is one of the city's top quality-of-life priorities. Many thought that with famous club-hater Mayor Rudy Giuliani gone, the situation would improve, but it has actually slightly declined under the Bloomberg regime.

Enough kvetching: The city still has a plethora of possibilities for the determined insomniac. Smaller clubs like **APT**, **Cielo** and

Crobar. *See p289.*

Spirit. *See p290.*

Lotus. *See p289.*

Table 50 are scoring some of the world's top spinners to pack their lilliputian (or in the case of APT, nonexistent) dance floors. And one-shot parties of dubious legality are available to those whose ears are attuned to nightlife scuttlebutt.

So much is going on, in fact, that it's sometimes hard to know what's what in the ever-changing swirl. Luckily, there is a network of folks who are fighting to keep NYC's scene vibrant and are determined to let you know the score. Various websites list worthy events; **Rhythmism** (www.rhythmism.com) is one of the best. You can also get on one of the many update lists: **DJ Spinoza's Beyond Events Calendar** (subscribe by e-mailing nyc_electronic_events_calendar-subscribe@ yahoogroups.com) is great for lovers of underground electronic music. And you should, of course, pick up the latest copy of *Time Out New York*. Party on!

Clubs

Avalon
660 Sixth Ave between 20th and 21st Sts (1-212-807-7780). Subway: F, V to 23rd St. **Open** *Thu 10pm–5am; Fri–Sun 10pm–7am.* **Cover** *$15–$30.* **Average drink** *$8.*
Limelight got a new lease on life when the folks behind Boston superclub Avalon took over the space and reopened the landmark-church–cum–dance-hall. Avalon may not pack the punch of its club-kid-populated predecessor, but there's still something about partying in a church (even a deconsecrated one) that can make you feel slightly wicked. Expect house and techno in the stunning main room, and hip-hop and R&B elsewhere in the mazelike venue. Sundays are given over to one of the city's biggest gay dance affairs.

Cielo
18 Little W 12th St between Ninth Ave and Washington St (1-212-645-5700/www.cieloclub.com). Subway: A, C, E to 14th St; L to Eighth Ave. **Open** *10pm–4am daily.* **Cover** *$5–$20.* **Average drink** *$10.*
You'd never guess from the red carpet and the Euro-dude manning the door that the attitude inside this boîte is zero, at least on weeknights. It's a wonderful little joint—the urban-ski-lodge decor looks terrific, the sunken dance floor is a nice touch, and the place boasts one of the city's clearest sound systems. On weekends, Cielo features top-shelf house from world-class DJs (including the fabled Frankie Knuckles). On Mondays, the club is treated to DJ deity François K.'s dub-heavy Deep Space sessions. If you're not dressed to the nines, though, or if your group is particularly testosterone-heavy, then you'll have to talk a good game to gain entry. And if you *do* get in, be prepared to part with some serious cash to secure one of the booths—they're largely reserved for bottle-service patrons only.

Club Shelter

20 W 39th St between Fifth and Sixth Aves (1-212-719-4479/www.clubshelter.com). Subway: B, D, F, V to 42nd St–Bryant Park; 7 to Fifth Ave. **Open** *Sat 10pm–noon.* **Cover** *$15–$20.* **Average drink** *$6.*

There's really only one thing you need to know about Club Shelter: It's the home of the world-famous Shelter party. DJ Timmy "the Maestro" Regisford is the ringmaster of this long-running Saturday-night affair, spinning soulful house and classics to an enthusiastic (and sexually and racially mixed) crowd that doesn't leave until long after the sun rises on Sunday. Club Shelter also hosts the occasional Dance Ritual bash (www.danceritualnyc.com), with Master at Work Louis Vega on the wheels of steel.

Copacabana

560 W 34th St at Eleventh Ave (1-212-239-2672/www.copacabanany.com). Subway: A, C, E to 34th St–Penn Station. **Open** *Tue, Thu 6pm–3am; Fri, Sat 10pm–5am.* **Cover** *$5–$30.* **Average drink** *$9.*

Miami meets Las Vegas in the Copa's pink-palm-tree-lined lobby. Women throw curves in skintight pants and peekaboo blouses; gentlemen bump it up a notch with suits and ties. Some 3,000 Latinos—and those who love them—pack the Copa's 48,000 square feet to dance the night away. Upstairs, live bands play salsa and merengue as synchronized showgirls shake the large dance floor; for house music, head downstairs.

Coral Room

512 W 29th St between Tenth and Eleventh Aves (1-212-244-1965/www.coralroomnyc.com). Subway: A, C, E to 34th St–Penn Station; 1, 9 to 28th St. **Open** *10pm–4am daily.* **Cover** *$10–$20.* **Average drink** *$10.*

After a promising start in early 2003, the club has devolved largely into just another NYC meet market, attracting a crowd that looks chic but acts cheap. Still, the Coral Room does have one of the best gimmicks going: a kitschy live mermaid gallivanting in a giant fish-filled aquarium. And on rare occasions, the club will feature a great DJ or band.

Crobar

530 W 28th St between Tenth and Eleventh Aves (1-212-629-9000/www.crobar.com). Subway: C, E to 23rd St. **Open** *Mon, Thu 11pm–4am; Fri–Sun 10pm–6am.* **Cover** *$20–$30.* **Average drink** *$9.*

The splendiferous Crobar is as close to a full-on superclub as NYC has to offer: It can squeeze 2,750 revelers into its amazing main room and two smaller party dens, it has a great sound system, and it flashes the many varieties of disco lights that modern science has produced. As with most huge ventures, though, the beats lean toward the lowest-common-denominator end of the dance-music spectrum. Regardless, the club has to be commended for taking an occasional chance, such as the DJ residencies of nightlife kooks Larry Tee and Johnny Dynell, and it's a must-see on the city's after-dark circuit.

Lightship *Frying Pan*

Pier 63, Twelfth Ave at 23rd St (1-212-989-6363/www.fryingpan.com). Subway: C, E to 23rd St. **Open** *Dates and times vary.* **Cover** *$5–$10.* **Average drink** *$6.*

A onetime floating lighthouse salvaged from the briny deep, this lightship has found new life as one of the city's more eccentric spots to toss a party. The stationary vessel is basically a lovable floating scrap heap, with ferric oxide as the design element of choice. It's hard to believe that the *Frying Pan* is legal for revelry. Apparently, the city has trouble believing it as well: The boat and its adjacent pier have been shut down numerous times by the city elders. When she's open for business, though, the *Pan* is a blast—there's something about being on the water that brings out the drunken sailor in every clubber. The best night is Friday, when the dub-funky Turntables on the Hudson crew (*see p293*) mans the decks.

Lotus

409 W 14th St between Ninth Ave and Washington St (1-212-243-4420/www.lotusnewyork.com). Subway: A, C, E to 14th St; L to Eighth Ave. **Open** *10pm–4am daily.* **Cover** *$10–$20.* **Average drink** *$8.*

Lotus was one of the first upscale clubs to invade the once-scuzzy Meatpacking District, so it immediately attracted legions of celebs, models and gawkers. Happily, the venue's trendy patina has faded and now Lotus can be appreciated as a well-furnished restaurant, lounge and dance club whose DJs spin a mainstream mix of sounds to an affluent bridge-and-tunnel crowd. Getting past the doorman is still a task, so dress to impress.

The best Clubs

These are the perfect nightspots to...

...meet a mermaid

Scantily clad beauties grace the 10,000-gallon aquarium at **Coral Room** (*see p289*).

...dance without going deaf

Cielo (*see p288*) features such a crystal-clear sound system that cranking up the volume isn't necessary for sonic bliss.

...find the perfect beat

APT (*see p292*) books the city's hottest underground DJs.

...dance the summer nights away

Art center P.S. 1's Saturday **Warm Up** (*see p293*) is one of the best parties around.

Lunatarium

10 Jay St at John St, Dumbo, Brooklyn (1-718-852-6515/www.dumboluna.com). Subway: A, C to High St; F to York St. **Open** *Fri, Sat 10pm–4am.* **Cover** *free–$25.* **Average drink** *$6.*

If *Mad Max 2: The Road Warrior* had included a club scene, then it would have been set in Dumbo's postapocalyptic Lunatarium. The immense (20,000-square-foot) venue has the look of a bombed-out concrete bunker, though its most recent preclub function was as a wine cellar. Lunatarium is *so* big that it overwhelms small events, but when the joint is packed, it absolutely rocks. Parties—usually featuring huge rosters of DJs spinning underground house, drum 'n' bass or techno—are held on an irregular basis; it's best to check the website for the lowdown on upcoming events.

Marquee

289 Tenth Ave between 26th and 27th Sts (1-646-473-0202). Subway: C, E to 23rd St. **Open** *Tue–Sat 10pm–4am.* **Cover** *$20.* **Average drink** *$9.*

The centerpiece of Marquee, which is located in a former garage, is a spectacular double-sided staircase that leads to the mezzanine, where a glass wall overlooks the action below. Although not quite as searingly red-hot as it was when it opened in '03, the 600-person space remains very popular—in other words, you're likely to have trouble getting past the velvet rope. The deejayed music tends toward radio-friendly, none-too-thought-provoking hip-hop, pop and rock.

Pyramid

101 Ave A between 6th and 7th Sts (1-212-228-4888). Subway: F, V to Lower East Side–Second Ave; L to First Ave; 6 to Astor Pl. **Open** *10pm–4am daily.* **Cover** *free–$15.* **Average drink** *$7.*

Back in the '80s and early '90s, this little dive was one of the epicenters of downtown's performance-art and drag scenes. Since then, the joint has been lying somewhat fallow; Monday night's Konkrete Jungle drum 'n' bass bash and Friday's gay-leaning 1984 pop fest are the only real shindigs of note.

Rare

416 W 14th St between Ninth Ave and Washington St (1-212-675-2220). Subway: A, C, E to 14th St; L to Eighth Ave. **Open** *10pm–4am daily.* **Cover** *varies.* **Average drink** *$7.*

The former Cooler and onetime abattoir is among the least la-di-da hangouts in the ultratrendy Meatpacking District. All sorts of wingdings—from glitchy electronica to mainstream hip-hop affairs—go down in the low-ceilinged space, but our favorite night is the drum 'n' bass–heavy Direct Drive blast,

▶ For more on queer nightlife, *see pp304–309*.

▶ For comprehensive listings, pick up the *Time Out New York Nightlife* guide.

which coaxes major stars of the scene (Doc Scott and Bryan Gee, for example) to rinse it out on the decks.

Roxy

515 W 18th St between Tenth and Eleventh Aves (1-212-645-5156/www.roxynyc.com). Subway: A, C, E to 14th St; L to Eighth Ave. **Open** *Wed 8pm–2am (roller-skating only); Fri 11pm–4am; Sat 11pm–6am.* **Cover** *$15–$30.* **Average drink** *$8.*

Roxy began its life as a humongous roller-skating rink (the immense main room can squeeze 2,200 revelers onto its dance floor), but in the early '80s, it became a great cross-cultural hangout, with B-boys poppin' and lockin' as downtown arty types looked on. Nowadays, it's known for Saturday night's massive boy bash, with thousands of hedonists (including a smattering of women and straight men) dancing to house beats all night long. Fridays showcase mixed sounds that range from hip-hop fests to events featuring superstar DJs like Paul Van Dyke. On Wednesdays, Roxy stays true to its roots with a roller-skating jam.

Sapphire

249 Eldridge St between Houston and Stanton Sts (1-212-777-5153/www.sapphirenyc.com). Subway: F, V to Lower East Side–Second Ave. **Open** *7pm–4am daily.* **Cover** *$5.* **Average drink** *$5.*

Itty-bitty Sapphire was one of the first Lower East Side bars to feature DJs, and its management had the foresight to secure a cabaret license before the city clamped down. Mondays through Wednesdays, the music falls somewhere along the techno-house-disco continuum, and local heroes E-man and Adam Goldstone are joined by the occasional slumming-it big name. Thursdays through Saturdays, hip-hop and funk rule, with beloved veteran DJ Jazzy Nice often running things. Warning: Weekends can be brutally crowded; dress to sweat.

Spirit

530 W 27th St between Tenth and Eleventh Aves (1-212-268-9477/www.spiritnewyork.com). Subway: C, E to 23rd St. **Open** *Thu–Sat 10pm–5am.* **Cover** *free–$30.* **Average drink** *$8.*

The sister club to one of Dublin's top niteries had to battle the ghosts of the address's former tenant, the much-missed Twilo. So far, it's been a losing battle. When Spirit first opened in '04, it tried using Twilo-style forward-thinking house and techno; crowds were sparse. Nowadays, the beats are usually pedestrian in nature, resulting in a few more paying customers but far less of a vibe. Spirit's macrobiotic restaurant and New Agey spa may draw some folks.

Subtonic Lounge at Tonic

107 Norfolk St between Delancey and Rivington Sts (1-212-358-7501/www.tonicnyc.com). Subway: F to Delancey St; J, M, Z to Delancey–Essex Sts. **Open** *Thu–Sat 7:30pm–2am.* **Cover** *free–$12.* **Average drink** *$6.*

Subtonic Lounge, the unadorned basement of the Lower East Side's avant-bohemian Tonic performance space, features DJs spinning myriad

The old song and dance

Of all the troubles that afflict New York City's nightlife, the most insidious—and the weirdest—have to be the citywide cabaret laws. The regulations determine which establishments can let people dance with abandon and which must restrict folks to tapping their tootsies. And unfortunately, the latter venues are far more common, since it's tough to procure the license that allows would-be froogers to work the floor. How did such a freakish ordinance come to be, and why is the seeming anachronism still enforced?

The laws were created in 1926, in the midst of Prohibition, when boozing it up with assorted showgirls didn't stop then Mayor Jimmy Walker and his Tammany Hall cretins from doing their job: regulating the hell out of anything they didn't like. Claiming that citizens were "running wild" at Harlem jazz clubs (lore has it that the real intention was to deter whites and blacks from mingling), they passed cabaret laws mandating that clubs needed licenses to allow dancing by groups of three or more people. One particularly nutty passage required musicians to "be of good moral character."

Some genius erased that last clause in 1967 (no doubt after witnessing a Velvet Underground gig), and by then, the largely forgotten rules were cited only in zoning issues. But the '90s brought Big Rudy Giuliani, who, as part of his quality-of-life craze, created the Nightclub Enforcement Task Force, in 1996. Many nightlife hangouts were shuttered, but others employed sneaky gambits to foil the

NO DANCING ALLOWED

violation-hunting goon squad; at the Cooler (now known as Rare; *see p290*), in the Meatpacking District, the doorman would flip a hidden switch, signaling the DJ to swap the drum 'n' bass for lite country hits.

New Yorkers have rebelled: The artist-activists of the Dance Liberation Front have staged a number of quirky protests over the years, including a Million Mambo March. Similarly, Jak Karako, a dance instructor and chair of Manhattan's Libertarian Party, has targeted the laws in his many bids for public office, even staging a demonstration in which he rallied against injustice by performing flashy Argentine tango steps.

Unfortunately, such actions have been to no avail—so far. The laws still stand and, if anything, enforcement has been stepped up under the current regime. But at least the Bloomberg administration is a little more polite about it: During the Giuliani years, Rudy Washington, deputy mayor at the time, famously referred to nightclubs as "little buckets of blood."

Arts & Entertainment

underground beats from challenging IDM (intelligent dance music) to dirty disco. The sound system might not be all that, but the party throwers and the patrons (who rest on banquettes inside giant, ancient wine casks) make up for it with sheer exuberance.

Table 50
643 Broadway at Bleecker St (1-212-253-2560/ www.table50.com). Subway: B, D, F, V to Broadway–Lafayette St; 6 to Bleecker St. **Open** *10pm–4am daily.* **Cover** *free–$10.* **Average drink** *$10.*
Table 50, along with Cielo (*see p288*), belongs to a breed of club that NYC had been sorely lacking: It's small, intimate, and manages to be both classy and raunchy. The grit factor is supplied by the dance club's music policy, which touts such great

local spinners as the funk archivist Qool DJ Marv, the world-beat-on-dope DJs from Turntables on the Hudson (*see p293*) and the minimal-housers of the Wednesday-night Robots party. The swank spot's speakeasy aura—it's located in a windowless basement of a restaurant—adds to the appeal.

Webster Hall
125 E 11th St between Third and Fourth Aves (1-212-353-1600/www.webster-hall.com). Subway: L, N, Q, R, W, 4, 5, 6 to 14th St–Union Sq. **Open** *Thu–Sat 10pm–5am.* **Cover** *free–$30.* **Average drink** *$6.*
Should you crave the sight of big hair, muscle shirts and gold chains, Webster Hall offers all that and, well, not much more. The grand four-level space, built in the 1800s as a dance hall, is nice enough, and the DJs aren't bad (choose from disco,

hip-hop, soul, Latin, progressive house or pop hits), but it's hard to forget who you're sharing the dance floor with. Wet-T-shirt and striptease contests ratchet up the get-me-out-of-here ambience.

Lounges & DJ bars

APT
419 W 13th St between Ninth Ave and Washington St (1-212-414-4245/www.aptwebsite.com). Subway: A, C, E to 14th St; L to Eighth Ave. **Open** *6pm–4am daily.* **Cover** *varies.* **Average drink** *$9.*
Labeled "snootissimo" when it opened, this bi-level boîte is now the city's prime place for hearing cool underground beats. Everyone from techno deity Carl Craig to Zulu Nation founder Afrika Bambaataa has played the platters here, in either the sleek basement bar or the cozy, well-appointed street-level room. The resident spinners—no slouches themselves—include lounge-kitsch slinger Ursula 1000, the electrofunky Negroclash crew, and soulful-house guru Neil Aline. APT gets sardine-packed on weekends and on headliner guest nights, but at least you're squeezed in with one of the best-looking crowds in town.

Church Lounge
Tribeca Grand Hotel, 2 Sixth Ave between Walker and White Sts (1-212-519-6677/www.tribecagrand.com). Subway: A, C, E to Canal St; 1, 9 to Franklin St. **Open** *7am–2am daily.* **Average drink** *$10.*
When the Tribeca Grand first started showcasing

DJs and live music in its posh pub, it unexpectedly became one of the city's top spots for underground beats—thanks mostly to its totally-of-the-moment electroclash and nu-rock. Things have calmed down a lot since then, but the place still rocks when a big-time act takes over the joint.

Opaline
85 Ave A between 5th and 6th Sts (1-212-995-8684). Subway: F, V to Lower East Side–Second Ave; 6 to Astor Pl. **Open** *Tue–Sat 5pm–4am.* **Average drink** *$7.*
At first glance, Opaline doesn't have much going for it—it's basically a square room with a crappy sound system. But it hosts a couple of the city's most fun soirees: the gay-leaning Friday-night blast, Area 10009, and the slightly straighter Saturday party, Rated X. Both of these club-kid-studded affairs are utterly trashy, with DJs playing pop and rock to a how-fast-can-we-drink crowd. And Rated X has an interesting side premise: Folks who remove their pants at the door receive half-priced cocktails throughout the night.

Openair
121 St. Marks Pl between First Ave and Ave A (1-212-979-1459/www.openairbar.com). Subway: L to First Ave; 6 to Astor Pl. **Open** *Thu–Sat 8pm–4am; Sun 5pm–3am.* **Average drink** *$6.*
Nearly invisible from the street, this semisecret lounge is one of the grooviest high-tech venues in the city. House, hip-hop, techno, drum 'n' bass and ambient music pump through an ace sound system.

Club rules

Clubbing in NYC can be a little intimidating. Keep this simple advice in mind to avoid the most common pitfalls.

Avoid run-ins with the law
Know that you may be searched—so leave weapons at home (duh). Also, the city's nightlife crackdown has made clubs *very* paranoid about drug use. Be smart.

Dress the part
If you're going to a trendy spot, look sharp—those dirty Cons and XXL-size tees ain't gonna cut it. But if you're heading to a grunge pit, leave the Armani at home.

Guys, don't travel in packs
In order to maintain a gender balance, straight-oriented venues often refuse entry to large groups of men. But if you're heading to a gay-leaning spot, the more the merrier!

Make nice at the door
Screaming "I'm on the list!" (even if you are) won't get you anywhere with seen-it-all doormen. However, a smile and a bit of patience might. And don't forget ID!

Phone ahead
Parties can change lineup or location at a moment's notice. Before you leave, call the club, visit its website or check a current issue of *Time Out New York*.

Pick your night wisely
If possible, hit the clubs any night except Friday or Saturday; going out on weekdays ensures you'll be hanging with the cool kids.

Play it safe
The subway is a lot safer than it used to be, but if you're out late, we recommend that you take a cab or a car service home (*see p366*).

The Slipper Room

*167 Orchard St at Stanton St (1-212-253-7246/
www.slipperroom.com). Subway: F, V to Lower
East Side–Second Ave.* **Open** *Tue–Sat 8pm–4am.*
Average drink *$8.*

New York City has a healthy neoburlesque scene,
and the petite Slipper Room is, if not at that scene's
nexus, pretty darn near it. Many of the Victorian-
looking venue's happenings, notably Friday's Hot
Box hoedown, feature plenty of bump-and-grind
action, with DJs spinning the appropriate beats; the
occasional live band completes the picture.

Roving & seasonal parties

New York has a number of peripatetic and
season-specific shindigs. Nights, locations and
prices vary, so telephone, e-mail or hit the
websites for the latest updates.

Cooper-Hewitt Summer Sessions: Design + DJs + Dancing

For listing, see p147 **Cooper-Hewitt, National
Design Museum.** **Open** *Jul, Aug Fri 6–9pm.*
Cover *$10 (includes museum admission).* **Average
drink** *$8.*

In the warmer months, the city's premier design
museum hosts after-work revelry, but these aren't
garden parties in the traditional sense. DJs ranging
from local funksters to international superstars
work the crowd with all manner of underground
beats. Still, the vibe is a lot more genteel than the
similar P.S. 1 Warm Up party (*see below*).

Giant Step

www.giantstep.net.

Giant Step parties have been among the best of the
nu-soul scene since the early '90s—back before
there *was* a nu-soul scene. Sadly, the gang doesn't
throw nearly as many fetes at once did, now pre-
ferring to concentrate on live shows and record
promotions. But on the rare occasion that Giant
Step does decide to pack a dance floor, don't miss
it: The music is always great, and the multiculti
crowd is gorgeous.

Motherfucker

www.motherfuckernyc.com.

The Motherfucker gang celebrates messy omnisex-
ual rock & roll hanky-panky, long the favored form
of entertainment in New York. Michael T. and Justine
D. spin power-pop, glam, new wave and disco, usually on those designated drunken eves of the big
national holidays. Many nightlife veterans consider this the best party going in town right now, and
they ought to know.

P.S. 1 Warm Up

*P.S. 1 Contemporary Art Center, 22-25 Jackson
Ave at 45th Rd, Jackson Heights, Queens
(1-718-784-2084/www.ps1.org). Subway: E, V to
23rd St–Ely Ave; G to 21st St–Jackson Ave;
7 to 45th Rd–Court House Sq.* **Open** *Jul–Sept Sat*

APT. *See p292.*

2–9pm. **Cover** *$8 (includes museum admission).*
Average drink *$5.*

Back in '97, who could have guessed that the courtyard of the Museum of Modern Art–affiliated P.S. 1
Contemporary Art Center would play host to some
of the most anticipated clubbing events in the city?
Since the Warm Up series kicked off, summer
Saturdays truly haven't been the same. Thousands
of dance-music fanatics pack the space, swigging
beer, dancing and generally making a mockery of
the soiree's arty setting. The sounds range from spir-
itually inclined soul to full-bore techno, spun by local
stars and international DJ deities.

Turntables on the Hudson

1-212-560-5593/www.turntablesonthehudson.com.

This ultrafunky affair has a permanent Friday
home at the Lightship *Frying Pan* (*see p289*), but
it pops up all over the place on other nights
of the week. DJs Nickodemus, Mariano and guests
do the dub-funky, world-beat thing, and live
percussionists add to the flavor. If you like to
shake it, this is as good as it gets: Wherever the
Turntables party happens, the dance floor is
packed all night long.

Film & TV

There are plenty of lights, cameras and action in the naked city.

Walking through New York City feels a lot like starring in a movie or TV show. Every block and corner is distinguished, from the Empire State Building (*King Kong*) to Trump Tower ("You're fired!") and the 59th Street Bridge (*Manhattan*). The New York County Courthouse not only frequently pops up in *Law & Order,* but it's where Barzini is gunned down in *The Godfather.* Welcome to the constant show that is New York City.

Film

New York has no peer when it comes to the comprehensive presentation of current cinema. Splashy multiplexes, many built during the cash-rich '90s, carry all the latest Hollywood releases. But New York's real cinematic treasures are its dozens of revival, art and foreign-film houses that offer everything from African documentaries to Korean horror flicks. Films unspool at boutique art houses, elegant historic theaters or intimate museum screening rooms. And film festivals, director retrospectives, theme nights and cult-classic revivals are all over town.

For current listings, check the daily newspapers or pick up *Time Out New York.*

Art & revival houses

Angelika Film Center
18 W Houston St at Mercer St (1-212-995-2000/ www.angelikafilmcenter.com). Subway: B, D, F, V to Broadway–Lafayette St; N, R, W to Prince St; 6 to Bleecker St. **Tickets** *$10.25, seniors and children under 12 $6.50.* **Credit** *AmEx, MC, V.*
A Soho mainstay since 1989, the six-screen Angelika emphasizes independent fare, both American and foreign. The complex is a zoo on weekends, so come extra early or visit the website to buy tickets in advance.

> ► Purchase tickets in advance through **www.moviefone.com**, or by calling 1-212-777-FILM or 1-800-535-TELL.
> ► Museums often host special film series and experimental films. *See pp143–163.*

BAM Rose Cinemas
For listing, see p325 **Brooklyn Academy of Music**. **Tickets** *$10; seniors, students and children under 12 $7 (Mon–Thu).* **Credit** *AmEx, MC, V.*
You can't go wrong at Brooklyn's premier art-film venue, which does double duty as a repertory house for well-programmed classics and a first-run multiplex for independent films.

Cinema Village
22 E 12th St between Fifth Ave and University Pl (1-212-924-3363/www.cinemavillage.com). Subway: L, N, Q, R, W, 4, 5, 6 to 14th St–Union Sq. **Tickets** *$9, seniors and children under 13 $5.50, students $7.* **Credit** *MC, V.*
Three-screen Cinema Village specializes in American indie flicks and foreign movies. The theater was a turn-of-the-century firehouse; check out the subway turnstile that admits ticket-holders into the lobby.

Film Forum
209 W Houston St between Sixth Ave and Varick St (1-212-727-8110/www.filmforum.com). Subway: 1, 9 to Houston St. **Tickets** *$10, seniors and children under 12 $5 (senior discount Mon–Fri before 5pm).* **Credit** *Cash only at box office; AmEx, MC, V on website.*
Even though the seats and sight lines leave something to be desired, this three-screen art theater presents great documentaries, new and repertory films, and a cute crowd of budding NYU auteurs and film geeks in horn-rimmed glasses.

The ImaginAsian
239 E 59th St between Second and Third Aves (1-212-371-6682/www.theimaginasian.com). Subway: N, R, W to Lexington Ave–59th St; 4, 5, 6 to 59th St. **Tickets** *$10, seniors and children under 12 $8.* **Credit** *MC, V.*
We have high hopes for this newly rechristened 300-seat movie palace, once named for D.W. Griffith and now devoted to all things Asian or Asian-American. Early offerings included a fun retrospective of J-horror bad boy Takashi Miike, as well as the New York Korean Film Festival.

Landmark's Sunshine Cinema
143 E Houston St between First and Second Aves (1-212-330-8182/1-212-777-3456). Subway: F, V to Lower East Side–Second Ave. **Tickets** *$10.25, seniors over 63 $6.75.* **Credit** *AmEx, Disc, MC, V.*
A beautifully restored 1898 Yiddish theater has become one of New York's snazziest art houses, presenting some of the finest new independent cinema in stadium-seated, air-conditioned luxury.

Landmark's Sunshine Cinema.

Leonard Nimoy Thalia

Symphony Space, 2537 Broadway at 95th St, entrance on 95th St (1-212-864-5400). Subway: 1, 2, 3, 9 to 96th St. **Tickets** *$10, seniors and students $8.* **Credit** *AmEx, MC, V.*

The famed Thalia art house—featured in *Annie Hall*—was recently rebuilt. It's much more comfortable now, and it continues to offer retrospectives of foreign classics, but with more cutting-edge stuff sometimes thrown into the mix.

Paris Theatre

4 W 58th St between Fifth and Sixth Aves (1-212-688-3800/1-212-777-3456). Subway: F to 57th St; N, R, W to Fifth Ave–59th St. **Tickets** *$10, seniors and children $6.* **Credit** *Cash only at box office; AmEx, MC, V on website.*

Located near the Plaza Hotel, this posh theater is de rigueur for cinéastes who love foreign-language films.

Quad Cinema

34 W 13th St between Fifth and Sixth Aves (1-212-255-8800/www.quadcinema.com). Subway: F, V to 14th St; L to Sixth Ave. **Tickets** *$9.50, seniors and children 5–12 $6.50.* **Credit** *Cash only at box office; AmEx, MC, V on website.*

Four small screens (in downtown's first multiple-screen theater) show a broad selection of foreign and American independent films, as well as documentaries; many deal with politics and sexuality. Children under five are not admitted.

Two Boots Pioneer Theater

155 E 3rd St between Aves A and B (1-212-254-3300/ www.twoboots.com). Subway: F, V to Lower East Side–Second Ave. **Tickets** *$9; seniors, students and children $6.50.* **Credit** *AmEx, Disc, MC, V.*

Phil Hartman, founder of the Two Boots pizza chain, also runs this East Village alternative film center,

which shows an assortment of newish indies, revivals and themed festivals.

Museums & societies

American Museum of the Moving Image

See p161 for listing.

Moving Image, the first American museum devoted solely to the art of motion pictures, puts on an impressive schedule of more than 700 films a year, many of which are organized into some of the most creatively curated series in the city.

Anthology Film Archives

32 Second Ave at 2nd St (1-212-505-5181/www. anthologyfilmarchives.org). Subway: F, V to Lower East Side–Second Ave. **Tickets** *$8, seniors and students $5.* **Credit** *Cash only.*

Housed in a crumbling landmark building, Anthology is a fiercely independent cinema showcasing foreign and experimental film and video (upon opening in 1970, its first offering was a typewritten manifesto).

Brooklyn Museum

See p147 for listing.

The eclectic roster at Brooklyn's stately palace of fine arts concentrates on offbeat foreign films and smart documentaries.

Film Society of Lincoln Center

Walter Reade Theater, Lincoln Center, 165 W 65th St between Broadway and Amsterdam Ave, plaza level above Alice Tully Hall (1-212-875-5601/www.filmlinc.com). Subway: 1, 9 to 66th St–Lincoln Ctr. **Tickets** *$10, seniors $5 (Mon–Fri before 6pm), students $7.* **Credit** *Cash only at box office; MC, V on website.*

Ain't nothin' like the real thing

New York is well aware of its iconic status on the big screen—from classic location shoots like *On the Waterfront* and *Serpico* to last summer's *Spider-Man 2*—and the city boasts one of the most experienced and well-established film commissions in the world: the **Mayor's Office of Film, Theatre & Broadcasting**. The office is responsible for issuing permits, providing police and traffic stewards to movie crews, and otherwise helping to manage all the details that go with creating a fictional universe in an around-the-clock city of 8 million people.

There's a promotional aspect to getting the city on film, but it's also big business: Film and television shoots contribute an estimated $5 billion a year in revenue through hotels, restaurants, taxi travel and local crew labor.

"You just can't fake New York," says Katherine Oliver, commissioner of the office since August 2002. "Even the average person can see the difference. There's just an energy, a richness that you feel when you walk around the city, and that's reflected onscreen." "Faking it" is exactly what many films have tried to do in recent years, shooting on the side streets of Pittsburgh and Toronto. But Oliver knows better and has the numbers to prove it: Overall production has risen an impressive 30 percent on her watch, with TV shoots up a whopping 47 percent.

Much of this can be attributed to Oliver's confident, let's-make-it-happen attitude, which led her to modernize the agency's technology and fast-track the permit process. "We are the one-stop shop," she says, pointing out that the services of a specially dedicated NYPD unit come gratis with every permit. "We did the math—we're saving production about $19,000 a week with the free police," Oliver explains. "In other places around the world, you pay. But our view has always been: Let's make it as easy as possible."

Free and *easy* are terms that would make any production manager smile. Does this bode well for student auteurs hoping to shut down Times Square for their own corrective versions of *Vanilla Sky*? "We're not going to do that for everyone," Oliver advises. "But if you're going to spend your entire budget in our city, and employ lots of people and showcase our great assets, we'll give you the Brooklyn Bridge," she says, referring to the recent production of the 2005 suicide-thriller *Stay,* starring Ewan McGregor and Naomi Watts, which diverted Manhattan-bound bridge traffic for ten days. "That was amazing, watching what they were doing at 2 o'clock in the morning *and* having an incredible view of the city."

Another coup for Oliver was securing the use of the U.N. for Sydney Pollack's *The Interpreter* (also a 2005 film, starring Nicole Kidman)—a location denied Alfred Hitchcock, among others. "We are going to go above and beyond for those shows," she says. "We're going to take care of the people who are making an investment here. We want the Spike Lees and Martin Scorseses of tomorrow, to teach them how to use the city effectively. And hopefully, they'll never want to go and make movies anywhere else."

We'd say that's a pretty safe bet.

Visit www.nyc.gov/film to get your own production rolling or to find out what's currently in the works.

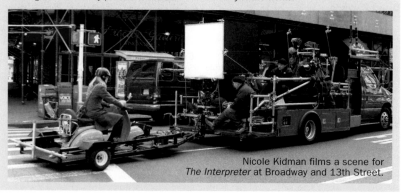

Nicole Kidman films a scene for *The Interpreter* at Broadway and 13th Street.

The FSLC was founded in 1969 to support film-makers and promote contemporary film and video. The Society operates the Walter Reade Theater, a state-of-the-art venue in Lincoln Center that features the city's most comfortable cinema seats and best sight lines. Programs are usually thematic and have an international perspective. Every autumn, the Society hosts the New York Film Festival (*see p258*) at Alice Tully Hall.

IMAX Theater
For listing, see p146 **American Museum of Natural History**.
The IMAX screen is an eye-popping four stories high; the kid-friendly movies explore the myriad wonders of the natural world.

Metropolitan Museum of Art
See p148 for listing.
The Met offers a program of documentaries on art—many relating to current museum exhibitions—that are screened in the Uris Center Auditorium (near the 81st Street entrance).

The Museum of Modern Art
See p151 for listing.
Freshly renovated and reopened in November 2004, MoMA resumes its superb programming of significant art films and experimental work, drawing from a vast vault that's second to none.

The Museum of Television & Radio
See p161 for listing.
The museum's collection includes thousands of TV programs that can be viewed at private consoles.

Foreign-language films

Many of the institutions listed above screen films in languages other than English, but the following organizations show foreign-language flicks exclusively.

Asia Society and Museum
See p158 for listing.
See works from China, India and other Asian countries, as well as Asian-American productions.

French Institute Alliance Française
For listing, see p326 **Florence Gould Hall**.
FIAF shows French and francophone movies.

Goethe-Institut New York
See p159 for listing.
The Goethe-Institut screens German films in various locations around the city, and in its own opulent auditorium.

Japan Society
See p159 for listing.
The Japan Society Film Center organizes a carefully chosen schedule of current and classic Japanese fare.

The café at the **Angelika**. *See page 294.*

Film festivals

Each spring, MoMA and the Film Society of Lincoln Center (*see p295*) sponsor the highly regarded **New Directors/New Films** series, presenting works by on-the-cusp filmmakers from around the world. The FSLC, together with Lincoln Center's *Film Comment* magazine, also puts on the popular *Film Comment* **Selects** series, which allows the magazine's editors to showcase their favorite movies that have yet to be distributed in the U.S. Plus, every September and October since 1963, the FSLC has hosted the prestigious **New York Film Festival**. (For more information on any of these three festivals, visit www.filmlinc.com.) **The New York Independent Film and Video Festival** (1-212-777-7100, www.nyfilmvideo.com) lures cinéastes twice yearly, in April and November. Every May, Robert De Niro rolls out his relatively new but increasingly well-regarded **Tribeca Film Festival** (*see p254*). The popular **New York Lesbian & Gay Film Festival** screens in early June (1-212-571-2170, www.newfestival.org). January brings the annual **New York Jewish Film Festival** (1-212-875-5600) to Lincoln Center's Walter Reade Theater.

Arts & Entertainment

Television

Studio tapings

Tickets are available to several popular TV shows taped in New York City.

The Daily Show with Jon Stewart

513 W 54th St between Tenth and Eleventh Aves (1-212-586-2477/www.comedycentral.com/ dailyshow). Subway: C, E to 50th St. **Tapings** *Mon–Thu 5:30pm.*
Reserve tickets at least three months ahead by phone, or call at 11:30am on the Friday before you'd like to attend and see if you can take advantage of someone else's last-minute cancellation. You must be at least 18 and have a photo ID.

Last Call with Carson Daly

30 Rockefeller Plaza, Sixth Ave between 49th and 50th Sts (1-888-452-8499/www.1iota.com). Subway: B, D, F, V to 47–50th Sts–Rockefeller Ctr. **Tapings** *Call or visit website for schedule.*
A couple of weeks in advance, make a reservation online or by phone. For standby tickets, get in line at NBC's 49th Street entrance no later than 11am on weekdays. After that, leftover tickets might be available in the lobby's NBC Experience Store. Daly fans take note: Unlike at *Total Request Live*, you must be at least 16 to attend this show.

Late Night with Conan O'Brien

30 Rockefeller Plaza, Sixth Ave between 49th and 50th Sts (1-212-664-3056/www.nbc.com/conan). Subway: B, D, F, V to 47–50th Sts–Rockefeller Ctr. **Tapings** *Tue–Fri 5:30pm.*
Call at least three months in advance for tickets (four-ticket limit). A small number of same-day standby tickets are distributed at 9am (49th Street entrance); one ticket per person. You must be at least 16 and have a photo ID.

Late Show with David Letterman

1697 Broadway between 53rd and 54th Sts (1-212-975-1003/www.lateshowaudience.com). Subway: B, D, E to Seventh Ave. **Tapings** *Mon–Wed 5:30pm; Thu 5:30, 8pm.*
Seats can be hard to come by. Try requesting tickets for a specific date by filling out a form on the show's website. You may also be able to get a standby ticket by calling 1-212-247-6497 at 11am on the day of taping. You must be at least 18 and have a photo ID.

Saturday Night Live

30 Rockefeller Plaza, Sixth Ave between 49th and 50th Sts (1-212-664-3056/www.nbc.com/snl). Subway: B, D, F, V to 47–50th Sts–Rockefeller Ctr. **Tapings** *Dress rehearsal at 8pm; live show at 11:30pm.*
Tickets are notoriously difficult to snag, so don't get your hopes up. The season is assigned by lottery every fall. Send an e-mail to sntickets@nbc.com, anytime during August, or try the standby-ticket lottery on the day of the show. Line up by 7am under

Get in line for Letterman.

the NBC Studio marquee (50th St between Fifth and Sixth Aves). You must be at least 16.

Tours

These tours sell out, so reserve in advance.

Kramer's Reality Tour

The Producers Club, 358 W 44th St between Eighth and Ninth Aves (1-800-572-6377/www. kennykramer.com). Subway: A, C, E to 42nd St–Port Authority. **Tours** *Sat, Sun (holiday weekends only) 11:45am; reservations required.* **Fee** *$40.* **Credit** *AmEx, Disc, MC, V.*
Kenny Kramer (yes, the guy who inspired that *Seinfeld* character) takes you to many of the show's locations on his tour bus.

Sex and the City Tour

Meet at Pulitzer Fountain near the Plaza Hotel, Fifth Ave between 58th and 59th Sts (1-212-209-3370/ www.sceneontv.com). **Tours** *Mon, Fri 11am; Sat, 10, 11am, 3pm; Sun 10am, 3pm. Subway: N, R, W to Fifth Ave–59th St.* **Fee** *$35.* **Credit** *MC, V.*
The show has long since wrapped, but it manages to live on in syndication and, apparently, in this tour. Visit more than 35 sites where Carrie & Co. once ate, drank, hooked up, gossiped and shopped.

The Sopranos Tour

Meet at the giant button sculpture, Seventh Ave at 39th St. (1-212-209-3370/www.sceneontv.com). Subway: N, Q, R, W, 42nd St S, 1, 2, 3, 9, 7 to 42nd St–Times Sq. **Tours** *Sat, Sun 2pm.* **Fee** *$40.* **Credit** *MC, V.*
A bus takes you to New Jersey to check out Tony's haunts, from the Bada-Bing to Pizzaland.

Gay & Lesbian

We're here; we're queer. And we like it that way.

Picture this: lesbian mommies with Asian babies in tow, hip-hop homo-thugs cruising "on the down-low," old-school drag queens lip-synching "The Trolley Song," tattooed go-go boys shaking it in East Village clubs, fresh-faced trannies holding court in downtown dyke bars. Now come and see it, live. NYC's got 'em all—none are in short supply. There's a scene for everyone, every day of the week, whether at a bar, club, theater, park, restaurant or bookstore. The city's **Lesbian, Gay, Bisexual & Transgender Community Center** (*see p300*) is a great first stop for the queer out-of-towner. More than 300 groups use the facility, from the Lesbian Sex Mafia to the New York Bears. And then there's the annual **Gay Pride Week** in June, when LGBT folks flock here from around the world to revel in their orientation and to whoop it up at the week's high point, the **Gay and Lesbian March** (*see p257*), which draws a whopping half-million spectators and participants. Other summer events include the popular **NewFest** gay film festival, held in mid-June, and the new **QueerFest NYC**, a monthlong extravaganza of LGBT theater in July.

There's a multitude of reasons why New York is such a homo haven. For starters, it was the site of the 1969 Stonewall riots (in Manhattan's West Village), which jump-started the American gay-rights movement. Plus, the city is rife with queer role models, including openly gay politicians, artists, performers, writers and activists. There's no shortage of places to hang out, from gaycentric bars to gay-oriented neighborhoods. Even the laws here foster a healthy queer existence: They criminalize antigay violence, forbid discrimination in the workplace and afford same-sex couples comprehensive domestic-partnership rights. It's up to you whether you want to seek out queer spots or grab your lover's hand and jump right into any ol' integrated neighborhood. Either way, you'll feel right at home.

Books & media

Because of the mainstreaming of gay culture (and the rise of Internet shopping), gay bookstores aren't faring as well as they have in years past. But these three rock-solid establishments are still great places to browse, buy or catch a reading.

Bluestockings

172 Allen St between Rivington and Stanton Sts (1-212-777-6028/www.bluestockings.com). Subway: F, V to Lower East Side–Second Ave. **Open** *1–10pm daily.* **Credit** *AmEx, MC, V.*
This former feminist bookseller, founded in 1999, now bills itself more broadly as a radical bookstore, fair-trade café and activist resource center. It also continues to stock plenty of LGBT writings and erotica, and it hosts regular events such as Dyke Knitting Circle gatherings and monthly women's open-mike nights.

Creative Visions

548 Hudson St between Charles and Perry Sts (1-212-645-7573/www.creativevisionsbooks.com). Subway: 1, 9 to Christopher St–Sheridan Sq. **Open** *Sun–Fri 1–10pm; Sat noon–10pm.* **Credit** *AmEx, Disc, MC, V.*
Housed in the original location of A Different Light's now defunct New York outpost, this gay emporium

Fly to the **Gay Pride March**. *See p257.*

offers an impressive collection of new and vintage gay books and magazines, including rare and out-of-print erotica, plus frequent readings from local queer novelists.

Oscar Wilde Bookshop

15 Christopher St between Sixth and Seventh Aves (1-212-255-8097/www.oscarwildebooks.com). Subway: 1, 9 to Christopher St–Sheridan Sq. **Open** *11am–7pm daily.* **Credit** *AmEx, Disc, MC, V.*
The world's first gay bookstore (it opened in 1967) is small but loaded with atmosphere. Come for the history, the picturesque neighborhood, and the store's collection of new and used books. Keep an eye out for first-edition classics.

Publications

Time Out New York's Gay & Lesbian section offers a lively weekly guide to city happenings. Both of New York's weekly gay entertainment magazines—*HX* and *Next*—include extensive boycentric information on bars, clubs, restaurants, events and group meetings. *HX*'s Getting Off section lists loads of private sex parties. The monthly *Go NYC*, "a cultural road map for the city girl," gives the lowdown on the local lesbian scene. The newspaper *Gay City News* provides feisty political coverage with an activist slant; its archrival, the *New York Blade,* focuses on queer politics and news. All five are free and widely available in street boxes or at gay and lesbian bars and bookstores. *MetroSource* ($4.95) is a bimonthly glossy with a guppie slant and tons of listings. Martin Quinn's *Queer New York City 2004–2005* (On Your Own Publications, $11.95), is the most up-to-date guidebook of its kind.

Television & radio

These days, New York's biggest contribution to TV is the surprise mainstream hit *Queer Eye for the Straight Guy,* which is shot locally. It stars the Fab Five, a group of style-obsessed lads who can often be seen cavorting around town at various A-list events. You'll also find a hodgepodge of lesser-known gay-related broadcast programs, though much of it appears only on public-access cable channels. (Programming varies by cable company, so you may not be able to watch these shows on a hotel TV.) *HX* and *Next* provide the most current TV listings. On the radio, NYC's community-activist station, WBAI-FM 99.5, features the progressive gay talk show *Out-FM* on Mondays at 11am. And online, Sirius satellite radio offers the show *OutQ* 24/7, with programming from such New York personalities as Michelangelo Signorile, Frank DeCaro and Larry Flick.

Centers & help lines

Gay & Lesbian Switchboard of New York Project

1-212-989-0999/www.glnh.org. **Open** *Mon–Fri 4pm–midnight; Sat noon–5pm.*
This phone service offers excellent peer counseling, legal referrals, details on gay and lesbian organizations, and information on bars, hotels and restaurants. Outside New York (but within the U.S.), callers can use the toll-free Gay & Lesbian National Hotline (1-888-THE-GLNH).

Gay Men's Health Crisis

119 W 24th St between Sixth and Seventh Aves (1-212-367-1000/AIDS advice hotline 1-212-807-6655/www.gmhc.org). Subway: F, V, 1, 9 to 23rd St. **Open** *Hotline Mon–Fri 10am–9pm; Sat 11am–3pm; recorded information in English and Spanish at other times. Office Mon–Fri 10am–6pm.*
GMHC was the world's first organization dedicated to helping people with AIDS. Its threefold mission is to push for better public policies; to educate the public to prevent the further spread of HIV; and to provide services and counseling to people living with HIV. Support groups usually meet in the evening.

Lesbian, Gay, Bisexual & Transgender Community Center

208 W 13th St between Seventh and Eighth Aves (1-212-620-7310/www.gaycenter.org). Subway: A, C, E, 1, 2, 3, 9 to 14th St; L to Eighth Ave. **Open** *9am–11pm daily.*
This is where ACT UP and GLAAD got their starts. The center provides info for gay tourists; political, cultural, spiritual and emotional support; and meeting space to 300-odd groups. Both the National Museum and Archive of Lesbian and Gay History and the Pat Parker/Vito Russo Library are housed here.

Lesbian Herstory Archives

484 14th St between Eighth Ave and Prospect Park West, Park Slope, Brooklyn (1-718-768-3953/ www.lesbianherstoryarchives.org). Subway: F to 15th St–Prospect Park. **Open** *Wed 7–9pm; other times vary. Call or visit website for more information.*
Located in Brooklyn's Park Slope neighborhood, the Herstory Archives contain more than 20,000 books (cultural theory, fiction, poetry, plays), 1,600 periodicals, and assorted memorabilia. The cozy space also hosts occasional film screenings, readings and social gatherings.

Michael Callen–Audre Lorde Community Health Center

356 W 18th St between Eighth and Ninth Aves (1-212-271-7200/www.callen-lorde.org). Subway: A, C, E to 14th St; L to Eighth Ave; 1, 9 to 18th St. **Open** *Mon, Tue 8:30am–8pm; Wed 12:30–8pm; Thu, Fri 9am–4:30pm.*
This is the country's largest health center serving primarily the gay, lesbian, bisexual and transgender community. It offers comprehensive medical

If you're born to read Wilde, then head over to the **Oscar Wilde Bookshop**. *See p300.*

care, HIV treatment, STD screening and treatment, mental-health services, peer counseling and free adolescent services (including the youth hotline HOTT, 1-212-271-7212).

NYC Gay & Lesbian Anti-Violence Project

240 W 35th St between Seventh and Eighth Aves, suite 200 (24-hour hotline 1-212-714-1141/ 1-212-714-1184/www.avp.org). Subway: A, C, E, 1, 2, 3, 9 to 34th St–Penn Station. **Open** *Mon–Thu 10am–8pm; Fri 10am–6pm.*
The Project provides support to victims of antigay and antilesbian crimes. Working with the police department, volunteers offer advice on seeking police help. Long- and short-term counseling are available.

Queer perspective

Which neighborhood is the gayest? That's a tough call these days. The most *visibly* queer area is bustling **Chelsea** (*see p94*), where hot, upwardly mobile men cruise one another along the "runway"—Eighth Avenue between 16th and 23rd Streets. The strip is bulging with boutiques hawking club clothing and sleek home designs, as well as lounges and eateries offering froufy cocktails and a range of gastronomic goodies. But even this high concentration of queerness has spread out during the past year, creeping northward to **Hell's Kitchen** (*see p101*), which gay men, always on the lookout for the next frontier, have decided is the next 'hood to haunt. The neighborhood, also known as Clinton, is home to a growing number of gay-owned eateries, bars and housewares boutiques.

Plenty of other queer nabes exist, though— and they're far more ethnically and stylistically diverse than Chelsea and Hell's Kitchen. Christopher Street, in the **West Village** (NYC's renowned gay ghetto; *see p93*), draws crowds of young African-American and Latino men and women, especially along the recently remodeled Christopher Street Pier. Dykes of all types gather at several popular lesbian bars here. And of course, the Village is home to such historic gay sites as the **Stonewall** (*see p305*), as well as friendly show-tune piano cabarets and stores full of rainbow knickknacks and I'M NOT A LESBIAN BUT MY GIRLFRIEND IS T-shirts.

An edgier crowd thrives in the **East Village**'s (*see p89*) network of small, divey bars where skinny go-go boys work their boyish, junkie-chic charms. In addition to the heavy bohemian contingent here—artists, drag queens, punk-rock baby dykes—you'll also find the yuppies and college students who've given the neighborhood a more gentrified feel.

Outside Manhattan, Brooklyn's tree-lined **Park Slope** (*see p123*) is a major lesbian enclave, especially for couples with kids. Plenty of mellow gay men have joined them in recent years, seeking refuge from the big-city scene. During the first weekend in June, the Slope hosts the annual **Brooklyn Pride March**, a scaled-down version of Manhattan's parade. The Brooklyn event is much like the **Queens Pride**

March, which is held in mid-June in the Latino and South Asian neighborhood of **Jackson Heights** (*see p129*), home to several South American queer bars, including **Atlantis 2010** (76-19 Roosevelt Ave between 76th and 77th Sts, 1-718-457-3939) and **Chueca** (69-04 Woodside Ave at 69th St, 1-718-424-1171), a popular spot for salsa-dancing lesbian couples.

Men of all ages, shapes and sizes frequent fetish bars and clubs, like the **Eagle** (*see p305*) in Chelsea. For open-air cruising, try the **Ramble** in Central Park, between the 79th Street transverse and the lake (but beware of police entrapment for drugs). And despite the city's efforts to clean up Times Square and turn it into a neon-flashing, family-oriented Disney World, you can still find nude male burlesque at the **Gaiety Theatre** (201 W 46th St between Broadway and Eighth Ave, 1-212-221-8868). The **West Side Club** bathhouse (27 W 20th St between Fifth and Sixth Aves, 1-212-691-2700), in Chelsea, and its brother establishment, the **East Side Club** (227 E 56th St at Second Ave, 1-212-888-1884), provide old-school, towel-draped shenanigans. Libidinous lesbians should head to one of the friendly, dyke-owned **Toys in Babeland** (*see p251*) boutiques, which hold occasional workshops on topics from female ejaculation to anal pleasure, or to the wild women's sex party **Submit** (1-718-789-4053), where a den of slings, shower rooms and handcuffs awaits you monthly.

Where to stay

Chelsea Mews Guest House

344 W 15th St between Eighth and Ninth Aves (1-212-255-9174). Subway: A, C, E to 14th St; L to Eighth Ave. **Rates** *$100–$200 single/double.* **Credit** *Cash only.*
Built in 1840, this guest house caters to gay men. Rooms are comfortable and well furnished and, in most cases, have semiprivate bathrooms. Laundry service and bicycles are complimentary.

Chelsea Pines Inn

317 W 14th St between Eighth and Ninth Aves (1-212-929-1023/1-888-546-2700/www.chelseapines inn.com). Subway: A, C, E to 14th St; L to Eighth Ave. **Rates** *$100–$140; Continental breakfast included.* **Credit** *AmEx, DC, Disc, MC, V.*
On the border of Chelsea and the West Village, this inn welcomes gay guests, male and female. The 25 rooms are clean and comfortable; most have private bathrooms, and all include a radio, TV and refrigerator.

A (queer) place in the sun

The gay beach at **Jacob Riis Park** in the Rockaways, Queens, is fine for an easy warm-weather escape. But when you want to go farther than your MetroCard can take you, check out our primer on queer summer enclaves. After all, you'd hate to be a fish out of water—or a beer-drinkin' lesbian stuck in the Fire Island Pines.

Cherry Grove, Fire Island, NY

www.fireislandqnews.com.
Travel time Just under 2 hours by car and ferry or Long Island Rail Road and ferry.
Who goes there Oft-naked gym-averse boys and ethnically diverse dykes with two things in common: tiny budgets and a big thirst for alcohol.
Main activities Drinking, beachgoing, drinking, eating in, drinking.
Key events Drag queens raise money for abandoned pets at the annual Cherry Grove P.A.W.S. Benefit at the Ice Palace in late June. The Invasion, another drag blowout, is July 4. (See website for info on both events.)

East Hampton, NY

www.hamptonstravelguide.com.

Travel time 2½ hours by car, Long Island Rail Road (1-718-217-5477) or Hampton Jitney (1-800-936-0440).
Who goes there Wealthy power dykes who are into golf; rich uptown fags.
Main activities Fund-raiser-hopping, seeing and being seen.
Key events Don white linen shorts and frolic on the lush grounds of a private estate to raise money for the gay political lobbyist group Empire State Pride Agenda (www.pride agenda.org), which holds its Annual Hamptons Tea Dance benefit in early July. July's also the time for the Dancing on the Beach fund-raiser for the city's LGBT Community Center (www.gaycenter.org).

The Pines, Fire Island, NY

www.fireislandqnews.com.
Travel time Same as Cherry Grove, left.
Who goes there Chelsea boys and other well-heeled, well-sculpted men who prefer snorting to sipping.
Main activities Beach cruising, toasting at grandiose dinner parties.
Key events The Fire Island Dance Festival, a fund-raiser for Dancers Responding to AIDS, is

Colonial House Inn

*318 W 22nd St between Eighth and Ninth Aves
(1-212-243-9669/1-800-689-3779/
www.colonialhouseinn.com). Subway: C, E to
23rd St. Rates $80–$125 single/double with
shared bath; $125–$140 single/double with private
bath (higher on weekends); Continental breakfast
included. Credit MC, V.*
This beautifully renovated 1850s townhouse sits
on a quiet street in the heart of Chelsea. Run by
and primarily for gay men, Colonial House is a
great place to stay, even if some of the less expensive rooms are a bit snug. Bonuses: a fireplace in
three of the deluxe rooms and a rooftop deck for
all (nude sunbathing allowed!).

East Village B&B

*244 E 7th St between Aves C and D (1-212-260-
1865). Subway: F, V to Lower East Side–Second
Ave. Rates $75 single; $100 double; $275
apartment; breakfast included. Credit Cash only.*
This lesbian-owned gem is tucked into a turn-of-
the-century apartment building on a quiet East
Village block. The recently remodeled space has
gleaming wood floors and exposed brick, plus an
eclectic art collection. The bedrooms are done up
in bold colors, one of the bathrooms has a small
tub, and the living room has a TV and CD player.

Incentra Village House

*32 Eighth Ave between Jane and W 12th Sts
(1-212-206-0007). Subway: A, C, E to 14th St; L to
Eighth Ave. Rates $119–$169 single/double;
$149–$199 suite. Credit AmEx, MC, V.*
Two cute 1841 townhouses in the West Village
make up this recently renovated guest house run
by gay men. The spacious rooms come with private bathrooms and kitchenettes; some have working fireplaces. A 1939 Steinway baby-grand piano
is in the parlor for show-tune enthusiasts.

Ivy Terrace

*230 E 58th St between Second and Third Aves
(1-516-662-6862/www.ivyterrace.com). Subway: N,
R, W to Lexington Ave–59th St; 4, 5, 6 to 59th St.
Rates $175–$209 single/double; $1,100–$1,400
weekly; breakfast included. Credit AmEx, MC, V.*
This lovely lesbian-run B&B sits on the same block
as boy haunts O.W. Bar and the Townhouse (*see
p306 and p309*). The three cozy rooms feature
wood floors and lacy bedspreads on old-fashioned
sleigh beds. Owner Vinessa Milando (who runs the
inn with partner and lesbian-party promoter Sue
Martino) delivers breakfast to your room each
morning. You're also free to create your own meals:
Each room is equipped with a gas stove and a full-
size fridge.

in mid-July (www.dradance.org); the annual
Pines Party fund-raiser for Gay Men's Health
Crisis (www.gmhc.org) is in early August;
Empire State Pride Agenda (www.pride
agenda.org) throws its annual benefit, Rites of
Summer—a magnet for party-circuit boys—in
mid-August.

Cape May, NJ

www.capemay.com.
Travel time 2½ hours by car or NJ Transit bus
(1-973-762-5100).
Who goes there Monogamous boy couples
(and plenty of hetero pairs) seeking pricey
Victorian B&Bs and refined cuisine.
Main activities Beach romping, bird-watching,
dining out.
Key events In early August, check out the
Queen Maysea Coronation ceremony, a local
favorite. Talk about *camp!*

New Hope, PA

www.newhopepa.com.
Travel time About 2 hours by car or Trans-
Bridge bus (1-610-868-6001).
Who goes there Middle-American lesbians
and gay men (and plenty of straight people,
too) who drink Bud with lunch, prefer the
country to the beach and go to bed early.

Beach boys bust out at **Fire Island Pines**.

Main activities Bicycling and tchotchke
shopping.
Key events The Performing Arts Festival,
featuring theater, music and art exhibitions all
over town, runs from mid-July through late
August. For berry picking and pie eating—
especially if you have kids—hit the annual
Blueberry Festival in mid-July. (See the
website, above, for info on both events.)

Bars

Most gay bars in New York offer drink specials, happy hours and colorful theme nights; some have go-go contests, kiss-offs, amateur drag nights and slutty game shows. Go with a sense of adventure—and perhaps even a willingness to take it all off for the chance of winning some big bucks! Unfortunately for the ladies, the East Village's much loved Meow Mix closed in 2004. At press time, owner Brooke Webster was still securing a new location. For updates, check *Time Out New York*'s Gay & Lesbian listings.

Lower East Side & East Village

Boysroom

9 Ave A between 1st and 2nd Sts (1-212-358-1440/ www.tripwithus.com). Subway: F, V to Lower East Side–Second Ave. **Open** *9pm–4am daily.* **Cover** *$5–$10.* **Average drink** *$7.* **Credit** *Cash only.*
The newest addition to the East Village scene is a dark, two-level lounge from downtown creature-of-the-night Misstress Formika—DJ, drag queen and hostess with the mostest. Pile in for the young crowds, amateur go-go contests and porn, which is piped in on mounted TV screens.

Girls Room

210 Rivington St between Pitt and Ridge Sts (1-212-995-8684/www.girlsroomnyc.com). Subway: F to Delancey St; J, M, Z to Delancey–Essex Sts. **Open** *9pm–4am daily.* **Cover** *free–$3.* **Average drink** *$6.* **Credit** *Cash only.*
Quickly swooping into the Lower East Side to fill the gap left by Meow Mix's closing, this new seven-night-a-week lesbian bar offers '80s karaoke on Wednesdays and the popular Sex for the City Girl soiree on Saturdays, with martini specials and CD giveaways. Visit the website for a schedule of events.

Nowhere

322 E 14th St at First Ave (1-212-477-4744). Subway: L to First Ave. **Open** *3pm–4am daily.* **Average drink** *$5.* **Credit** *Cash only.*
A friendly, spacious watering hole—from the same folks who brought you the nearby Phoenix (447 E 13th St between First Ave and Ave A, 1-212-477-9979)—Nowhere attracts attitude-free crowds, from dykes (Mondays) to bears (Tuesdays), with its lineup of fun theme nights.

The Slide

356 Bowery between Great Jones and E 4th Sts (1-212-420-8885). Subway: B, D, F, V to Broadway–Lafayette St; 6 to Bleecker St. **Open** *5pm–4am daily.* **Average drink** *$5.* **Credit** *Cash only.*
Located in a space that housed one of Manhattan's first openly gay bars in the 1800s, the Slide—with its party-hearty promoter Daniel Nardicio—came on the scene in 2003 to restore some pre-Giuliani sleaze to the East Village. Prepare yourself for dirty drag queens, naked go-go boys and underwear parties.

Starlight Bar and Lounge

167 Ave A between 10th and 11th Sts (1-212-475-2172/www.starlightbarlounge.com). Subway: L to First Ave; N, Q, R, W, 4, 5, 6 to 14th St–Union Sq. **Open** *Sun–Thu 6pm–3am; Fri, Sat 6pm–4am.* **Average drink** *$6.* **Credit** *AmEx.*
On weekends, this bar is almost too popular for its own good. During the week, the scene is more manageable, and a nice bonus is that top-notch local entertainers often perform free shows in the comfy back lounge (usually around 10pm). Sunday nights, the popular lesbian party Starlette is in full swing, bringing in a mix of glamour gals, tomboys and college students.

West Village

Chi Chiz

135 Christopher St at Hudson St (1-212-462-0027). Subway: 1, 9 to Christopher St–Sheridan Sq. **Open** *10pm–4am daily.* **Average drink** *$5.* **Credit** *Cash only.*
This hot spot for men of color, just steps from the Christopher Street Pier, is a cruisy, sultry kind of place. Swarms form at Monday night's karaoke, Tuesday's "She-Chiz Ladies' Night" and Thursday-evening pool tournaments.

Cubbyhole

281 W 12th St at 4th St (1-212-243-9041). Subway: A, C, E to 14th St; L to Eighth Ave. **Open** *Mon–Wed 4pm–2am; Thu, Fri 4pm–4am; Sat, Sun 2pm–4am.* **Average drink** *$6.* **Credit** *Cash only.*
The legendary lesbian spot is always chock-full of girls tying one on, with the standard set of Melissa Etheridge or k.d. lang blaring in the background.

Arts & Entertainment

Chinese paper lanterns, tissue-paper fish and old holiday decorations add to the homemade charm.

Henrietta Hudson

438 Hudson St at Morton St (1-212-924-3347/ www.henriettahudson.com). Subway: 1, 9 to Christopher St–Sheridan Sq. **Open** *Mon–Fri 4pm–4am; Sat, Sun 1pm–4am.* **Average drink** *$6.* **Credit** *Cash only.*
A casual lesbian watering hole, HH is a magnet for young hottie girls from all over the New York area, especially the New Jersey and Long Island burbs. You'll see everything from long-nailed J. Lo types and cute baby butches to old-school gym teachers and their wives. Various DJs mix it up on weekends, and the pool table provides endless entertainment.

The Monster

80 Grove St at Sheridan Sq (1-212-924-3558). Subway: 1, 9 to Christopher St–Sheridan Sq. **Open** *Mon–Fri 4pm–4am; Sat, Sun 2pm–4am.* **Average drink** *$5.* **Credit** *Cash only.*
Upstairs, locals gather to sing show tunes in the piano lounge. (And, honey, you haven't lived till you've witnessed a bunch of tipsy queers belting out the best of Broadway.) The downstairs disco caters to a young outer-borough crowd just itchin' for fun.

The Stonewall

53 Christopher St between Seventh Ave South and Waverly Pl (1-212-463-0950). Subway: 1, 9 to Christopher St–Sheridan Sq. **Open** *4pm–4am daily.* **Average drink** *$6.* **Credit** *Cash only.*
This is *the* gay landmark, next door to the actual location of the 1969 gay rebellion against police harassment. For years, the joint was a snore, but lately, it's gotten an infusion of sexy shenanigans such as go-go boys, strip contests and nights reserved for college boys. Yum.

Chelsea

Barracuda

275 W 22nd St between Seventh and Eighth Aves (1-212-645-8613). Subway: C, E to 23rd St. **Open** *4pm–4am daily.* **Average drink** *$6.* **Credit** *Cash only.*
Hordes of boys are drawn to this bar, maybe because it's friendlier and more comfortable than the neighborhood competition. A traditional bar is up front; a frequently redecorated lounge is in the back. Drag-queen celebrities perform throughout the week, and there's never a cover.

The Eagle

554 W 28th St between Tenth and Eleventh Aves (1-646-473-1866/www.eaglenyc.com). Subway: C, E to 23rd St. **Open** *Mon–Sat 10pm–4am; Sun 5pm–4am.* **Average drink** *$5.* **Credit** *Cash only.*
The Meatpacking District was once home to NYC's outpost of kink, the Lure. Now the action has moved to this classic Levi's-and-leather fetish bar. Look for beer blasts, foot-worship fetes and nights dedicated to the hunky stylings of Tom of Finland.

Therapy is absolutely cathartic. *See p306.*

Arts & Entertainment

You sexy **Motherfucker**. *See p307.*

G

*225 W 19th St between Seventh and Eighth Aves
(1-212-929-1085). Subway: 1, 9 to 18th St.*
Open *4pm–4am daily.* **Average drink** *$7.*
Credit *Cash only.*
One of the area's most popular destinations, especially for the well-scrubbed, fresh-faced set. The lounge is often filled to capacity later in the evening, so go early to stake your place.

XES Lounge

*157 W 24th St between Sixth and Seventh Aves
(1-212-604-0212/www.xesnyc.com). Subway: F, V, 1,
9 to 23rd St.* **Open** *4pm–4am daily.* **Average
drink** *$7.* **Credit** *AmEx, MC, V.*
The newest gay bar in the city is also one of the slickest. It's got exposed brick walls, metal coffee tables and Eames chairs. But the pièce de résistance is the backyard patio, with Japanese maples, Philippe Starck furniture and a much appreciated smoking-allowed policy.

xl

*357 W 16th St between Eighth and Ninth Aves
(1-646-336-5574/www.xlnewyork.com). Subway: A,
C, E to 14th St; L to Eighth Ave.* **Open** *4pm–4am
daily.* **Average drink** *$8.* **Credit** *Cash only.*
This sleek trilevel bar is a study in style: Witness the 30-foot aquarium in the unisex bathroom. Fashion divas, musclemen, fag hags and a few drag queens run amok under one roof. Sunday and Monday nights feature free shows starring top-notch Broadway and cabaret performers.

Midtown

O.W. Bar

*221 E 58th St at Second Ave (1-212-355-3395).
Subway: N, R, W to Lexington Ave–59th St; 4, 5, 6 to
59th St.* **Open** *Mon–Sat 4pm–4am; Sun 2pm–4am.*
Average drink *$6.* **Credit** *AmEx, Disc, MC, V.*

Oscar Wilde's initials adorn this East Side watering hole. In addition to the tony lounge area, jam-packed digital jukebox and lovely patio, there are frequent drag and cabaret performances.

Posh

*405 W 51st St between Ninth and Tenth Aves
(1-212-957-2222). Subway: C, E to 50th St.*
Open *4pm–4am daily.* **Average drink** *$6.*
Credit *AmEx, MC, V.*
Okay, so it's not exactly the poshest place in town, but the small, homey lounge is sweet. Delish drinks and specialty evenings, such as the delovely Who's on Top? game show on Wednesdays, mean this neighborhood spot may become a destination yet.

Therapy

*348 W 52nd St between Eighth and Ninth Aves
(1-212-397-1700/www.therapy-nyc.com). Subway: C, E
to 50th St.* **Open** *Sun–Wed 5pm–2am; Thu–Sat 5pm–
4am.* **Average drink** *$7.* **Credit** *AmEx, MC, V.*
Therapy is the main event in Hell's Kitchen, and with good reason: the minimalist yet dramatic two-level design; performances by bona fide Broadway stars; a clever cocktail menu that includes the Oral Fixation and the Freudian Sip; and the beautiful crowd of boys. You'll even find good grub here.

Uptown

Candle Bar

*309 Amsterdam Ave at 74th St (1-212-874-9155).
Subway: 1, 2, 3, 9 to 72nd St.* **Open** *2pm–4am daily.*
Average drink *$5.* **Credit** *Cash only.*
After closing for renovation, the Upper West Side's mainstay is back and better than ever. The small watering hole is still a cruisy, neighborhood kind of place, but new ownership has rekindled the joint's spark. Catch nightly drink specials for $2.50, from ice-cold Bud to cloying appletinis.

Eight of Clubs

230 W 75th St between Broadway and West End Ave (1-212-874-9155). Subway: 1, 2, 3, 9 to 72nd St. **Open** *7pm–4am daily.* **Average drink** *$5.* **Credit** *Cash only.*

This tiny, old-school watering hole offers a pool table, video games and a backyard patio that hosts a variety of happenings when the weather is warm. It's not trendy, hot or particularly popular, but it's down to earth and nonjudgmental indeed.

Brooklyn

Excelsior

390 Fifth Ave between 6th and 7th Sts, Park Slope (1-718-832-1599). Subway: M, R to Union St. **Open** *Mon–Fri 6pm–4am; Sat, Sun 2pm–4am.* **Average drink** *$7.* **Credit** *Cash only.*

Refined Excelsior, bathed in red, black and chrome, has a spacious deck out back, a beautiful garden, an eclectic jukebox and an excellent selection of beers on tap. And the boys are mighty fine.

Ginger's Bar

363 Fifth Ave between 5th and 6th Sts, Park Slope (1-718-788-0924). Subway: M, R to Union St. **Open** *Mon–Fri 5pm–4am; Sat, Sun 2pm–4am.* **Average drink** *$6.* **Credit** *Cash only.*

The front room, with its dark-wood bar, looks out onto a bustling street scene. The back, with an always busy pool table, has a rec-room feel. Come summertime, the outdoor patio feels like a friend's yard. This congenial local hang (and Excelsior neighbor) is full of all sorts of dykes, many with their dogs—or favorite gay boys—in tow.

Metropolitan

559 Lorimer St at Metropolitan Ave, Williamsburg (1-718-599-4444). Subway: L to Lorimer St; G to Metropolitan Ave. **Open** *3pm–4am daily.* **Average drink** *$5.* **Credit** *Cash only.*

The hipster enclave Williamsburg has its fair share of queers, and this is its sole gay standby. Stop in for an icy brew while you're tooling around the neighborhood; you'll find a mellow crowd (with lots of beards—of the facial-hair variety), video games, an outdoor patio and drink specials galore.

Clubs

A number of New York clubs have gay parties or gay nights. For more clubs, plus additional information about some of those listed below, *see pp287–293.*

Dance clubs & parties

Avalon Sunday

660 Sixth Ave between 20th and 21st Sts (1-212-807-7780). Subway: F, V, to 23rd St. **Open** *Sun 10pm–7am.* **Cover** *$15–$20.* **Average drink** *$8.* **Credit** *MC, V.*

John Blair, the legendary gay-party promoter, is throwing his latest massive boy bash at the club that was once the Limelight. Expect throngs of young studs writhing to the pounding beats of rotating big-name DJs.

Crobar

530 W 28th St between Tenth and Eleventh Aves (1-212-629-9000/www.crobar.com). Subway: C, E to 23rd St. **Open** *Mon, Thu–Sun 10pm–4am.* **Cover** *$25.* **Average drink** *$9.* **Credit** *AmEx, DC, Disc, MC, V.*

This incarnation of the nightclub Playland—which also has outposts in Miami and Chicago—is a massive, flashy spot with a roster of wild offerings. Among the queerest are Disgraceland, on Thursdays, brought to you by Larry Tee and Jon Jon Battles, and Johnny Dynell's Utopia Parkway on Saturdays. The roving circuit party Alegria also blows through every couple of months or so.

Heaven

579 Sixth Ave at 16th St (1-212-539-3982/ www.juliesnewyork.com). Subway: F, V to 14th St; L to Sixth Ave. **Open** *Wed 5pm–4am; Thu 8pm–4am; Fri 6pm–5am; Sat, Sun 9pm–4am.* **Cover** *free–$15.* **Average drink** *$7.* **Credit** *Cash only.*

A slew of lesbian and gay-boy bashes, offered by Girl Club Events, are held at this Chelsea club. Wednesday is Noche Latina, with merengue and salsa beats. Kaleidoscope Fridays promise such treats as thong contests and hot go-go dancers. And Sexy Sundays have DJ Tanco spinning reggae, hip-hop and more.

Lovergirl

Club Shelter, 20 W 39th St between Fifth and Sixth Aves (1-212-252-3397). Subway: B, D, F, V to 42nd St–Bryant Park; 7 to Fifth Ave. **Open** *Sat 10pm–5am.* **Cover** *$10–$12.* **Average drink** *$6.* **Credit** *Cash only.*

Lovergirl, a popular women's party, takes advantage of Club Shelter's dynamite sound system and state-of-the-art lighting. The multiracial crowd, which doesn't start flowing in until after midnight, enthusiastically shakes it to hip-hop, R&B, funk, reggae and Latin music, while ultrasexy go-go gals sport the latest in fashionable G-strings.

Motherfucker

www.motherfuckernyc.com.

If rock & roll is your style, you'll want to check out Motherfucker, the wildly popular polysexual dance party that takes place about seven times a year, rarely at the same venue. (*See also p293.*)

Roxy

515 W 18th St between Tenth and Eleventh Aves (1-212-645-5156). Subway: A, C, E to 14th St; L to

---

► For more nightlife, see **Bars** and **Clubs** (*see pp203–213* and *pp287–293*).

Arts & Entertainment

Eighth Ave. **Open** *Sat 11pm–4am.* **Cover** *$15–$25.*
Average drink *$8.* **Credit** *MC, V.*
Promoter John Blair still packs this megaclub with
a tasty range of muscle-bound boys who jump to
house and techno spun by some of the biggest
names on the DJ circuit. A classic-rock lounge is
upstairs, for old-schoolers who prefer beers to
bumps. The famous roller-skating party still happens every Wednesday.

Saint at Large
1-212-674-8541/www.saintatlarge.com.
The now mythical Saint was one of the first venues
where New York's gay men could enjoy dance-floor
freedom. The club closed, but the clientele keeps
the memory alive with four huge parties each year
(the fetishy Black Party, the White Party, and the
Halloween and New Year's Eve fetes), which attract
body-conscious men from around the U.S.

SBNY
*50 W 17th St between Fifth and Sixth Aves (1-212-
691-0073/www.splashbar.com). Subway: F, V to 14th
St; L to Sixth Ave.* **Open** *Sun–Thu 4pm–4am; Fri,
Sat 4pm–5am.* **Cover** *$5–$20.* **Average drink** *$7.*
Credit *Cash only.*
This Chelsea institution offers a large dance space
as well as the famous onstage showers, where
hunky go-go boys get wet and wild. And—can it
be?—the supermuscular bartenders seem bigger
than ever. Nationally known DJs rock the house,
local drag celebs give good face, and in-house
VJs flash eclectic snippets of classic musicals
and videos.

Restaurants & cafés

Few New York restaurateurs would bat an
eyelash at a same-sex couple enjoying an
intimate dinner. But if you're concerned about
being in the minority where you dine, then
check out the following gayest eateries in town.

Better Burger NYC
*178 Eighth Ave at 19th St (1-212-989-6688).
Subway: C, E to 23rd St; 1, 9 to 18th St.*
Open *Sun–Thu 11am–midnight; Fri, Sat 11am–
1am.* **Average burger** *$6.* **Credit** *AmEx, MC, V.*
Gayest burger joint ever! It's also the healthiest. But
don't worry, the menu—which includes lean patties
of beef, turkey, soy or veal—is as delicious as the
hunky clientele. And although it is a fast-food joint,
it's a classy one, listing organic beers and wines to
go with your burger and air-baked fries.

Big Cup
*228 Eighth Ave between 21st and 22nd Sts
(1-212-206-0059). Subway: C, E to 23rd St.*
Open *Mon–Fri 7am–12:30am; Sat, Sun 8am–1am.*
Average sandwich *$5.75.* **Credit** *Cash only.*
Big Cup is as unmistakably Chelsea Boy as a pair
of shiny Lycra bikini briefs. The coffee is fine, as
are the snacks—brownies and Rice Krispies Treats,
plus sandwiches and soups. Not much attention is

paid to those, though, because Big Cup is one of
New York's classic gay meet markets. After all,
you don't hang a disco ball in a Chelsea coffeebar
and expect the patrons to lose themselves in Kafka
or Kierkegaard.

Cafeteria
*119 Seventh Ave at 17th St (1-212-414-1717).
Subway: 1, 9 to 18th St.* **Open** *24 hrs daily.* **Average
main course** *$15.* **Credit** *AmEx, DC, MC, V.*
This is the fresh-faced version of Foodbar (*see
below*), where throngs of neighborhood boys gather
for updated comfort food (savory meat loaf, mac and
cheese), lean cuisine (salads, granola with fruit) and
juicy cocktails. It's open round-the-clock (need a
postclub pick-me-up?) and even has a dark lounge
of its own, down in the sexy basement.

Counter
*105 First Ave between 6th and 7th Sts (1-212-982-
5870). Subway: F, V to Lower East Side–Second
Ave.* **Open** *Tue–Thu, Sun 11am–midnight; Fri, Sat
11am–1am.* **Average main course** *$15.*
Credit *AmEx, MC, V.*
This hip, lesbian-owned East Village spot takes vegetarian cuisine to a whole new level, adding a wine
bar with a dozen organic offerings. Pair a glass or
two with one of the lip-smackin' vegan tapas, or try
bigger eats, such as portobello au poivre or curried
plantain dumplings drizzled in coconut sauce.

Elmo
*156 Seventh Ave between 19th and 20th Sts
(1-212-337-8000). Subway: 1, 9 to 18th St.*
Open *Mon–Thu 11am–midnight; Fri, Sat
11am–2am; Sun 10am–2am.* **Average main
course** *$14.* **Credit** *AmEx, Disc, MC, V.*
This spacious, brightly decorated eatery has good,
reasonably priced food and a bar that offers a view
of the dining room, which is jammed with guys in
clingy tank tops—regardless of the weather.

Foodbar
*149 Eighth Ave between 17th and 18th Sts
(1-212-243-2020). Subway: 1, 9 to 18th St.*
Open *11am–4pm, 5pm–midnight daily.* **Average
main course** *$15.* **Credit** *AmEx, Disc, MC, V.*
Foodbar's globally influenced American menu
will get your mouth watering, if the customers
haven't already. Balsamic-glazed roasted chicken, a
Moroccan salad and steak au poivre are each entirely
satisfying. Servers are efficient and coquettish—a
combination we happen to treasure.

44 & X Hell's Kitchen
*622 Tenth Ave at 44th St (1-212-977-1170).
Subway: A, C, E to 42nd St–Port Authority.*
Open *Mon–Wed 5:30pm–midnight; Thu, Fri
5:30pm–12:30am; Sat, Sun 11:30am–12:30am.*
Average main course *$15.* **Credit** *AmEx, MC, V.*
Fabulous queens pack the sleek dining space of the
one bright spot on a bleak strip of Tenth Avenue.
It's situated alongside the Theater District and the
Manhattan Plaza high-rises, home to thousands of
artistes. Oh, and the food's great, too—classics

Arts & Entertainment

Go for the gold (and the lovely ladies) at **Rubyfruit Bar & Grill**.

like creamy mac and cheese, buttermilk-flour-and-pecan–battered fried chicken, portobello-and-polenta stew and turkey meat loaf. It's the perfect post-theater or preclub pit stop.

Lips

2 Bank St at Greenwich Ave (1-212-675-7710). Subway: 1, 2, 3, 9 to 14th St. **Open** *Mon–Thu 5:30pm–midnight; Fri, Sat 5:30pm–1am; Sun 11:30am–4pm, 5:30–11pm.* **Average main course** *$17.* **Credit** *AmEx, DC, MC, V.*
This festive restaurant certainly does provide a jovial atmosphere: The drag-queen waitstaff serves tasty meals *and* performs for very enthusiastic patrons. Midweek events (like Wednesday's Bitchy Bingo), tend to be a lot gayer than the weekends, when scores of shrieking straight chicks descend on the place for their bachelorette parties.

Rubyfruit Bar & Grill

531 Hudson St between Charles and Washington Sts (1-212-929-3343). Subway: 1, 9 to Christopher St–Sheridan Sq. **Open** *Mon–Thu 2pm–4am;*

Fri, Sat 3pm–4am; Sun 11:30am–2am. **Average main course** *$20.* **Credit** *AmEx, DC, Disc, MC, V.*
The food is good, but it's not the main selling point at this dedicated lesbian restaurant and bar. An eclectic mix of music and congenial customers make for a great place for fun-loving, old-school dykes.

The Townhouse

206 E 58th St at Third Ave (1-212-826-6241). Subway: N, R, W to Lexington Ave–59th St; 4, 5, 6 to 59th St. **Open** *Mon–Thu noon–3:30pm, 5–11pm; Fri, Sat noon–3:30pm, 5pm–midnight; Sun noon–4pm, 5–11pm.* **Average main course** *$20.* **Credit** *AmEx, DC, MC, V.*
If you're a reasonably attractive man under 40, you're likely to be greeted—or at least ogled—by one of the soused middle-aged regulars at this "gentlemen's" restaurant. In the dining room beyond the bar, couples are in various stages of courtship; flirty service makes this a good place for solo diners, too.

Music

Listen to this.

Popular Music

Buddhists are fond of saying that the only constant in the universe is change, and that rule certainly applies to the ever mutable New York music scene. In fact, the unending bounty of opportunity is what draws many young musicians to the city in the first place. And of course, once they get here, they instigate even more change. (Those Buddhists are really onto something.)

This may explain why the recent New York rock explosion that began with the Strokes is no longer grabbing headlines. In fact, so rarely do the Strokes appear on NYC stages that they hardly seem like a local band anymore. But Interpol, which released its sophomore album in fall 2004, looks headed for a global-fame breakthrough, with contenders such as the Secret Machines waiting in the wings. The one thing that hasn't changed is the Lower East Side's status as hipster-rock epicenter—though new space **Rothko** has grabbed the hot-club crown from **Pianos**.

And if you don't count yourself among the rock & roll set, you'll still find plenty to listen to—world-class jazz, hip-hop, soul, folk and pretty much every international flavor and fusion, made by legends and rising stars, across the five boroughs.

To help you navigate the scene, we've organized the city's most active and notable venues by genre. Note to the anal: These categories are loose. Many spots can throb with a techno beat one night and rock out the next, or skip from hip-hop to Brazilian music in a single evening. A relaxed attitude helps, as does a willingness to hang around and do some people-watching: If a listing says your favorite band is going on at 11pm, you might wait till midnight or later.

A valid photo ID proving that you're 21 or over is essential, not only to drink but often, just to get in (a passport or a driver's license are best). NYC bouncers have heard it all, and they're notoriously impervious to excuses.

Tickets are usually available from clubs in advance and at the door. A few small and medium-size venues also sell advance tickets through local record stores. For larger events, it's wise to buy through **Ticketmaster** (*see p380*)

on the Web, over the phone or at one of the outlets located throughout the city. Tickets for some events are available through **Ticket Web** (www.ticketweb.com). You can also purchase them online from websites of specific venues (URLs are included in venue listings where available). For more ticket details, *see pp380–381*. And remember to call ahead for info and show times, which may change without notice.

Arenas

Continental Airlines Arena
For listing, see p331 **Meadowlands Sports Complex**.
North Jersey's answer to Madison Square Garden recently played host to U2, Eminem, Britney Spears and Van Halen. Oldies showcases and radio-sponsored pop and hip-hop extravaganzas also happen here.

Madison Square Garden
See p331 for listing.
Madison Square Garden, one of the world's most famous arenas, is where the biggest acts—Prince, Madonna, Bob Dylan—come out to play. Whether you can see them well depends a lot on your seat, or your binoculars.

Nassau Veterans Memorial Coliseum
See p332 for listing.
Long Island's arena hosts mainstream acts like Rush, Incubus and Sarah McLachlan, punctuated by occasional teen-pop sock hops (*American Idol Live,* Hilary Duff) and garish Bollywood showcases.

Rock, pop & soul

Apollo Theater
253 W 125th St between Adam Clayton Powell Jr. Blvd (Seventh Ave) and Frederick Douglass Blvd

---

▶ For a calendar of annual events, see **Festivals & Events** (*pp254–261*).
▶ For more live-music venues, see **Bars**, **Cabaret & Comedy**, **Clubs** and **Gay & Lesbian** (*pp203–213*, *pp275–279*, *pp287–293* and *pp299–309*).
▶ For specific shows and previews of upcoming concerts, pick up the latest *Time Out New York*.

(Eighth Ave) (1-212-531-5305/www.apollo theater.com). Subway: A, C, B, D, 1, 9 to 125th St. **Box office** *Mon, Tue, Thu, Fri 10am–6pm; Wed 10am–8:30pm; Sat noon–6pm.* **Tickets** *$16–$100.* **Credit** *AmEx, DC, Disc, MC, V.*

Harlem's venerable Apollo still acts as the city's home of R&B and soul music. After all, it helped launch the careers of Ella Fitzgerald, Michael Jackson and D'Angelo, to name just a few. While the elegant yet lived-in theater continues to host the revamped *Showtime at the Apollo* TV program, it has also been welcoming rock and pop stars of late—when Morrissey booked his first NYC shows in years, he did so here.

Arlene's Grocery

95 Stanton St between Ludlow and Orchard Sts (1-212-995-1652/www.arlene-grocery.com). Subway: F to Delancey St; J, M, Z to Delancey– Essex Sts. **Cover** *free–$7; Doors open Mon–Thu 7pm; Fri–Sun noon.* **Credit** *Cash only.*

The best **Scenes**

Here's where you'll find...

...artsy East Village types
The Bowery Poetry Club (*see p313*) hosts hip-hop, folk and rock as well as poetry readings, theater acts and madcap open mikes, all with that do-it-yourself downtown charm.

...up-to-the-minute trends
Rothko (*see p318*) has become the go-to Lower East Side hangout, where the young and the hip choose between the live-music room upstairs and the DJ lounge below.

...musicians at ease
Tonic (*see p319*) is so laid-back and unclublike that the artists—many of whom are of the avant-garde stripe—get loose and go deep.

...the love
At the **Living Room** (*see p317*), the singer-songwriter spot that helped launch Norah Jones's career, the vibe is so welcoming that some in the audience can't wait for the hat to be passed their way.

...the world
Satalla (*see p323*) has established itself as the city's most wide-ranging global-music spot, and it also reaches out to local ethnic communities.

Rock bands are as packed in here as the cans of Goya beans were on the shelves of the bodega this club replaced. As many as six midlevel rock acts are booked a night, and Arlene's often schedules shows on Saturday afternoons. Monday-night heavy-metal karaoke is an LES don't-miss.

BAMcafé at Brooklyn Academy of Music

For listing, see p325 **Brooklyn Academy of Music**.

Like Brooklyn itself, the Brooklyn Academy of Music offers a winning mix of genres. On weekend nights, the BAMcafé above the lobby features folk, spoken word, hip-hop, world music and more by performers such as Zemog El Gallo Bueno, Rha Goddess and the JC Hopkins Biggish Band. The Next*Next* series, which began in 2002, focuses on performers in their twenties.

B.B. King Blues Club & Grill

237 W 42nd St between Seventh and Eighth Aves (1-212-997-4144/www.bbkingblues.com). Subway: A, C, E to 42nd St–Port Authority; N, Q, R, W, 42nd St S, 1, 2, 3, 9, 7 to 42nd St–Times Sq. **Box office** *10:30am–midnight daily.* **Tickets** *$12–$150.* **Credit** *AmEx, DC, Disc, MC, V.*

B.B.'s joint in Times Square plays host to a wide variety of music: Cover bands and soul tributes fill the gaps between big-name bookings such as Aretha Franklin, Merle Haggard, and Blood, Sweat and Tears. Lately, the club has also proved a viable space for extreme metal bands (Napalm Death, Meshuggah, Nile) and neosoul and hip-hop acts (such as Angie Stone and various Wu-Tangers). For many shows, the best seats are at the dinner tables up front, but menu prices are steep. The Harlem Gospel Choir buffet brunch, on Sundays, raises the roof, while live classic-rock, jazz and blues groups play for free most nights at Lucille's Bar & Grill the cozy restaurant named for King's cherished guitar.

Beacon Theatre

2124 Broadway at 74th St (1-212-496-7070). Subway: 1, 2, 3, 9 to 72nd St. **Box office** *Mon–Fri 11am–7pm; Sat noon–6pm.* **Tickets** *$15–$175.* **Credit** *Cash only.*

This sizable Upper West Side theater hosts a variety of popular acts, from Dido to Yo La Tengo—and once a year, the Allman Brothers take over the place for a lengthy residency. Complaints have been raised about the theater's sound and vastness, but there's something nicely old-timey about its gilded interior and uptown location.

The Bowery Ballroom

6 Delancey St between Bowery and Chrystie St (1-212-533-2111/www.boweryballroom.com). Subway: J, M, Z to Bowery; 6 to Spring St. **Box office** *at the Mercury Lounge, see p317.* **Tickets** *$13–$40.* **Credit** *AmEx, MC, V (bar only).*

Quite simply one of the best venues in the city to see indie bands either on the way up or holding

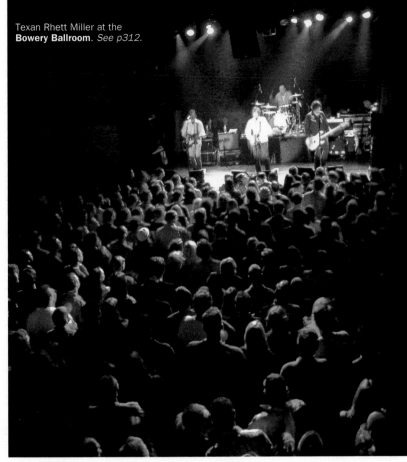

Texan Rhett Miller at the
Bowery Ballroom. *See p312.*

their own; excellent bookings over the past year include locals Blonde Redhead, Scissor Sisters and Secret Machines, and out-of-towners Muse and Neko Case. The spacious downstairs lounge is a great place to relax and socialize between (or during) sets.

The Bowery Poetry Club

308 Bowery at Bleecker St (1-212-614-0505/ www.bowerypoetry.com). Subway: B, D, F, V to Broadway–Lafayette St; 6 to Bleecker St. **Cover** *$3–$10; check website for schedule.* **Credit** *AmEx, MC, V (bar only).*
This colorful shoebox-size joint on the Bowery has its roots in the poetry-slam scene, but it's also a haven for the East Village's current generation of creative types: All kinds of jazz, folk, hip-hop and improv theater can be found here routinely. And the BPC offers a range of sandwiches and hot and cold drinks.

CBGB

315 Bowery at Bleecker St (1-212-982-4052/ www.cbgb.com). Subway: B, D, F, V to Broadway– Lafayette St; 6 to Bleecker St. **Cover** *$3–$12, two-drink minimum; check website for schedule.* **Credit** *Cash only.*
The tarnished mecca of punk rock has seen better days. But even if the club—which helped launch Blondie, the Ramones and the Talking Heads—is a shell of its former self, with dull local metal and hardcore bands mainly ruling the stage, you can still feel the history. You can smell it, too: Brace yourself for your first trip to the notoriously skanky bathroom.

CB's Lounge/CB's 313 Gallery

313 Bowery at Bleecker St (1-212-677-0455/www.cbgb. com). Subway: B, D, F, V to Broadway– Lafayette St; 6 to Bleecker St. **Cover** *$5–$10; shows start around 7pm.* **Credit** *AmEx, MC, V (bar only, $20 minimum).*
The main space of CBGB has arguably become a

front for a lavish T-shirt operation, but its smaller next-door neighbors (the Lounge is downstairs from the Gallery) are more cultivated. CB's 313 Gallery displays art (not band stickers) on its walls up-and-coming singer-songwriters on its stage. The lower level has the feeling of a suburban rec room and hosts a great weekly jazz show on Sundays.

Continental

25 Third Ave at St. Marks Pl (1-212-529-6924/www.continentalnyc.com). Subway: N, R, W to 8th St–NYU; 6 to Astor Pl. **Cover** *free–$6; doors open at 4pm.* **Credit** *Cash only.*
The Continental may book a lot of soundalike thrashers, but it remains the best rock club in the city for drinking: A thrilling sign above the bar reads FIVE SHOTS OF ANYTHING—$10. Most of the bands here are at least competent, and some are true legends—punk forefather Cheetah Chrome, Boston's the Real Kids, rockabilly fixture Robert Gordon—prefer the Continental to any other NYC venue. The sound is of weapons-grade quality, so bring earplugs, if you're so inclined.

Don Hill's

511 Greenwich St at Spring St (1-212-219-2850/www.donhills.com). Subway: C, E to Spring St; 1, 9 to Canal St. **Cover** *free–$10; doors open at 7:30pm.* **Credit** *AmEx, DC, Disc, MC, V.*
The favorite of ambisexual downtown types for more than a decade, this, unassuming, boxy space isn't much for new live bands these days. But Saturday night's Britpoppy Tiswas party often features strong locals, and Thursday's '80s dance party

Show and tell (all)

Local musicians sound off on the best and worst clubs—even down to the nastiest bathroom sightings.

What's your favorite (or least favorite) place to play?

Carlos D., Interpol: Bowery Ballroom, hands down. The world would be a better place if all venues emulated this one: great onstage sound, superior sound in the audience.
KT Sullivan, cabaret singer: I love the Algonquin (*see p277* The Oak Room) because of the history and the location. People who don't already know you actually come in.
El-P, rapper: My least favorite is Northsix. Backstage is like a kiddie-porn dungeon made of asbestos, there are dolphins living in the stage monitors, and the crowd is just a little too fucking cool for a live hip-hop show.

Ethan Iverson.

Alley Deheza, On!Air!Library!: Sin-é puts together good bills that make sense. My absolute least favorite place to play is Pianos, because of the sound. I don't ask for much—just to be able to distinguish a few instruments from a garage full of vacuum cleaners.

Favorite place to catch a show?

Ethan Iverson, the Bad Plus: The Village Vanguard is just about the only real jazz club left. No food, no frills—just music and history.
Aaron Warren, Black Dice: Tommy's Tavern (1041 Manhattan Ave at Freeman St, Greenpoint, Brooklyn, 1-718-383-9699, www.tommystavern.com) is the best. The room capacity must be, like, 20 people, so

El-P.

BeavHer and Wednesday's glam-punk bonanza Röck Cändy are always solid bets.

Fez
Under Time Cafe, 380 Lafayette St at Great Jones St (1-212-533-2680/www.feznyc.com). Subway: B, D, F, V to Broadway–Lafayette St; 6 to Bleecker St. **Cover** *$10–$25, two-drink minimum; doors open one hour before show.* **Credit** *AmEx, MC, V (food and drink only).*
A dinner-theater-style basement space, Fez hosts singer-songwriters, odd underground pop acts, drag queens, jazz bands, comedians and even Joan Rivers. Local cult stars like Kiki & Herb and the Trachtenburg Family Slideshow Players have played runs here; just be prepared for a strictly enforced two-drink minimum.

Galapagos Art and Performance Space
70 North 6th St between Kent and Wythe Aves, Williamsburg, Brooklyn (1-718-782-5188/www.galapagosartspace.com). Subway: L to Bedford Ave. **Cover** *free–$7; show times vary.* **Credit** *Cash only.*
This airy Williamsburg venue, famed for the dark pool at its entrance, has suffered since closing its back room, where most of the live acts appeared. But shows continue in the front room, with readings and film screenings thrown in for good measure. Burlesque and vaudeville nights are weekly staples.

Hammerstein Ballroom
Manhattan Center, 311 W 34th St between Eighth and Ninth Aves (1-212-279-7740/www.mcstudios.com). Subway: A, C, E to 34th St–Penn Station.

Jean Grae.

it's always packed, and the room is megaloud. Plus, the beer is $2!

Best place to find new talent?
Paddy Boom, Scissor Sisters: Karaoke at Arlene's Grocery, Monday nights. I saw the bass player from the Buzzcocks sing a Sex Pistols song there once.
John Flansburgh, They Might Be Giants: The Loser's Lounge show at Fez. Without it, I wouldn't be aware of a lot of New York's best artists: Mike Viola, Jenifer Jackson, Kiki & Herb, John Cameron Mitchell and a lot of others.

Worst thing you've seen in a club bathroom?
Aesop Rock, rapper: A dude passed out in his own puke with pants around his ankles in the bathroom at CBGB's once.

Aesop Rock.

Sara Shaw, the Occasion: I saw a cockroach on a roll of toilet paper. I'm not mentioning the name of the club, but it rhymes with *heebie-jeebies*.

What makes or breaks a show for you?
Jean Grae, rapper: The energy from the crowd, especially in New York— when you get love from your hometown, it always feels good. New York rap fans are also notoriously very "So what, I can do that, too" kind of people. So when they give it up for you, you know it's genuine.
Marlon Sporer, the Occasion: If I go backstage and I see towels, I'm psyched. Irving Plaza is good with the towels.

The Living Room. *See p317.*

Box office *Mon–Sat noon–5pm.* **Tickets** *$10–$50.* **Credit** *AmEx, MC, V.*
No one sets out for this cavernous hall simply to check out some music—you're here only if a band you like is booked. And despite the many drawbacks—insane drink prices, brusque staff, a stage that's a quarter mile away—Hammerstein does bring in the artists you've just got to see, such as Modest Mouse, PJ Harvey and the reunited Pixies.

The Hook
18 Commerce St between Dwight and Richards Sts, Red Hook, Brooklyn (1-718-797-3007/www.the hookmusic.com). Subway: F, G to Carroll St. **Open** *Show days 8:30pm–4am.* **Cover** *$8–$15.* **Credit** *Cash only.*
Despite being located in a remote corner of Brooklyn, the Hook has quickly become a live-music oasis. The spacious club has a long bar, a wide-open floor, and a huge area out back for smokers. On show nights (usually Mondays and Thursdays through Saturdays), you can catch a

variety of locals and bigger names. (ESG and even a poststardom Norah Jones have gigged here.) Just don't expect to include the Hook in your clubhopping plans; once you're here, you're here—which is nowhere near any other venue. Bring the phone number for a car service (*see p367*) to get home.

Irving Plaza
17 Irving Pl at 15th St (1-212-777-6800/www. irvingplaza.com). Subway: L, N, Q, R, W, 4, 5, 6 to 14th St–Union Sq. **Box office** *Mon–Fri noon–6:30pm; Sat 1–4pm.* **Tickets** *$10–$60.* **Credit** *AmEx.*
An NYC fixture, the midsize Irving Plaza looms large in the city's music history and has hosted local and international acts of all kinds over the years. The lived-in ballroom routinely features established artists such as Los Lobos, Blonde Redhead and Richard Thompson, but it's known more for being the go-to venue for younger rising stars—Le Tigre, Auf der Maur, the Walkmen and Dizzee Rascal have each packed the room recently. Show up early for a good view of the stage.

Joe's Pub
The Public Theater, 425 Lafayette St between Astor Pl and E 4th St (1-212-539-8770/www.joespub.com). Subway: N, R, W to 8th St–NYU; 6 to Astor Pl. **Box office** *1–7:30pm daily.* **Tickets** *$12–$30.* **Credit** *AmEx, MC, V.*
Tiny, tony Joe's Pub is one of the most satisfying places in town for eclectic, adult-oriented fare. Recent bookings have included acerbic singer-songwriter Sam Phillips, Senegalese superstar Youssou N'Dour and eclectic Brazilian troubadour Vinicius Cantuária, as well as an extended run by larger-than-life cabaret personality Jackie Hoffman.

Knitting Factory
74 Leonard St between Broadway and Church St (1-212-219-3132/www.knittingfactory.com). Subway: A, C, E to Canal St; 1, 9 to Franklin St. **Box office** *Mon–Sat 10am–11pm; Sun 2–11pm.* **Tickets** *$5–$20.* **Credit** *AmEx, MC, V.*
It was once the city's home for avant-garde jazz, then a space for arty rock. Now the Knitting Factory is a pretty standard rock club, with indie bands (the Good Life, Camera Obscura), metal (Dillinger Escape Plan), frat music (the Dan Band, Blues Traveler) and more. The smaller Tap Bar and Old Office, both under the main room, still host the occasional jazz show.

Lakeside Lounge
162 Ave B between 10th and 11th Sts (1-212-529-8463/www.lakesidelounge.com). Subway: L to First Ave; N, Q, R, W, 4, 5, 6 to 14th St–Union Sq. **Cover** *free; shows start at 9:30 or 10pm.* **Credit** *AmEx, MC, V (bar only).*
The large windows here mean that bands and patrons get plenty of gawkers, but the Lakeside's vibe is so casual that no one seems to mind. This endearingly scruffy city roadhouse is the place to find country-rock and all its variants, provided mainly by locals.

But occasional bigger names—from Beat Rodeo to co-owner (and Steve Earle's guitarist) Eric Ambel—frequent the well-liked spot.

Lit Lounge

93 Second Ave between 5th and 6th Sts (1-212-777-7987/www.litloungenyc.com). Subway: F, V to Lower East Side–Second Ave; 6 to Astor Pl. **Cover** *free–$8; shows start at 9pm.* **Credit** *AmEx, MC, V (bar only, $20 minimum).*

Although many of the bands that crowd Lit's dank, low-ceilinged basement are deservedly unknown, the room, which holds only a hundred and change, has played host to some excellent grimy, gutsy rock. Rub elbows on weeknights with too-cool-for-school types and see some great under-the-radar acts, but expect an onslaught of NYU students on weekends.

The Living Room

154 Ludlow St between Rivington and Stanton Sts (1-212-533-7235/www.livingroomny.com). Subway: F to Delancey St; J, M, Z to Delancey–Essex Sts. **Open** *Mon, Tue 6pm–4am; Wed–Sat 2pm–4am; Sun 6pm–2am.* **Cover** *free, one-drink minimum.* **Credit** *Cash only.*

Playing host to regular singer-songwriter talent like Teddy Thompson and Chiara Civello is nothing new for this intimate, unassuming club. Just ask Norah Jones, who donated a piano to the room as a thank-you for her early gigs here.

Luna Lounge

171 Ludlow St between Houston and Stanton Sts (1-212-260-2323/www.lunalounge.com). Subway: F to Delancey St; J, M, Z to Delancey–Essex Sts. **Cover** *free; shows start around 8pm.* **Credit** *Cash only.*

At this laid-back LES hangout, nightly no-cover showcases by local indie bands are at best a great way to catch up-and-coming bands. Even on weakly booked nights, the front barroom is cozy, and at least you won't have blown cash on a cover.

Makor

35 W 67th St between Central Park West and Columbus Ave (1-212-601-1000/www.makor.org). Subway: 1, 9 to 66th St–Lincoln Ctr. **Box office** *Mon–Thu 9am–9pm; Fri 9am–5pm; Sat 7–10pm; Sun 9am–10pm.* **Tickets** *$9–$30.* **Credit** *AmEx, MC, V.*

This unassuming Upper West Side Jewish cultural center offers a diverse mix of folk, blues, roots, world music, and local singer-songwriters in its welcoming if nondescript basement space. Jewish musicians, such as klezmer star David Krakauer and Israeli singer-songwriter David Broza, routinely rub shoulders with legends of folk (John Renbourn and Jacqui McShee), jazz (Andrew Cyrille), and even salsa and bossa nova artists.

Maxwell's

1039 Washington St at 11th St, Hoboken, NJ (1-201-798-0406/www.maxwellsnj.com). Travel: PATH train to Hoboken, then take a cab, the Red Apple bus or NJ Transit #126 bus to 11th St. **Box office** *Visit website for hours.* **Tickets** *$6–$20.* **Credit** *AmEx, Disc, MC, V.*

Hoboken's flagship rock club for more than 20 years is also a bit of a drag to get to, but plenty worth it—and sometimes, a band won't come any closer to NYC than here. The restaurant in front is big and friendly, and for dessert, you can feast on indie-rock fare from popular artists like Kristin Hersh, the Decemberists, the Ponys or any number of new local rockers. Hometown heroes Yo La Tengo stage their more or less annual Hanukkah shows here.

The Mercury Lounge

217 E Houston St between Essex and Ludlow Sts (1-212-260-4700/www.mercuryloungenyc.com). Subway: F, V to Lower East Side–Second Ave. **Box office** *Mon–Sat noon–7pm.* **Cover** *$8–$15; some shows require advance tickets.* **Credit** *AmEx, DC, Disc, MC, V (bar only).*

The Mercury Lounge doesn't look like much: It's a modest, boxy brick-walled room stuffed behind a crowded narrow bar. But the Lower East Side club is a veritable institution for rock bands, both local and touring. The White Stripes, Franz Ferdinand and many more have played here in recent years; mostly, however, the Lounge hosts smaller acts—some on their way up, some content to stay right where they are.

New Jersey Performing Arts Center

1 Center St at the waterfront, Newark, NJ (1-888-466-5722/www.njpac.org). Travel: PATH train to Newark, then take the Loop shuttle bus to NJPAC. **Box office** *Mon–Sat noon–6pm; Sun 10am–3pm.* **Tickets** *$12–$100.* **Credit** *AmEx, Disc, MC, V.*

Surprisingly close to midtown Manhattan, thanks to a remarkably effective transit system, Newark's gorgeous performing-arts center increasingly presents topflight talent, including bookings that don't come to New York. Recent visitors have included Bob Weir's Ratdog, Shirley Horn, Sister Carol and Larry Harlow's Legends of Fania. A free summer series on the plaza emphasizes Newark's multicultural mix.

92nd Street Y

See p274 for listing.

The Y's popular-music schedule extends to gospel, mainstream jazz and indigenous folk. The small, handsome theater provides a fine setting for mature music shows, be it Jazz in July or the hall's Summer Lyrics & Lyricists series, which celebrates the American Songbook.

Northsix

66 North 6th St between Kent and Wythe Aves, Williamsburg, Brooklyn (1-718-599-5103/ www.northsix.com). Subway: L to Bedford Ave. **Box office** *4–11pm daily (advance online purchase recommended).* **Tickets** *$6–$18.* **Credit** *AmEx, Disc, MC, V (advance purchases only).*

Easily accessible via the L train, this warehouselike space consistently brings in solid local and touring

Arts & Entertainment

indie acts, like Grant-Lee Phillips, Deerhoof, Mary Timony and the Blood Brothers, and even a pre-supernova Franz Ferdinand last year. The viewing bleachers, front-room pool table and cheap Pabst Blue Ribbon help it to feel more like a cool club-house than an impersonal rock space.

Pete's Candy Store

709 Lorimer St between Frost and Richardson Sts, Williamsburg, Brooklyn (1-718-302-3770/www.petes candystore.com). Subway: G to Metropolitan Ave; L to Lorimer St. **Open** *Sun–Wed 5pm–2am; Thu–Sat 5pm–4am.* **Cover** *free.* **Credit** *AmEx, DC, Disc, MC, V (bar only).*

The performance space at Pete's Candy Store is, in New York apartment parlance, "cozy." It's a bit of a walk from the subway—and under a highway over-pass, no less—but the club is generally worth the trip. Acoustic performers, such as the young Russian folk singer Julia Vorontsova, sound especially nice in these lovely, intimate confines; bands that plug in also dot the schedule.

Pianos

158 Ludlow St between Rivington and Stanton Sts (1-212-505-3733). Subway: F to Delancey St; J, M, Z to Delancey–Essex Sts. **Box office** *5pm–4am daily.* **Cover** *free–$12; shows start around 8pm.* **Credit** *AmEx, DC, MC, V.*

It's not quite the supermodel-spotting haven it was when it opened, but this style-conscious bar-cum-club retains a fairly high quotient of the see-and-be-seen crowd. Some bookings are low-on-the-radar locals, but the occasional live stunner—like an intimate set by PJ Harvey or Joseph Arthur—does creep into the mix. A steadier bet is the emerging talent booked in the often charming, always free upstairs lounge.

Radio City Music Hall

1260 Sixth Ave at 50th St (1-212-247-4777/ www.radiocity.com). Subway: B, D, F, V to 47–50th Sts–Rockefeller Ctr. **Box office** *Mon–Sat 10am–8pm; Sun 11am–8pm.* **Tickets** *$25–$125.* **Credit** *AmEx, MC, V.*

Neil Young, Elton John and Jessica Simpson are just three of the stars who have headlined Radio City recently. Of course, the greatest challenge for any performer playing here is not to get upstaged by the awe-inspiring Art Deco hall.

Roseland

239 W 52nd St between Broadway and Eighth Ave (1-212-247-0200/www.roselandballroom.com). Subway: B, D, E to Seventh Ave; C to 50th St. **Box office** *at Irving Plaza, see p316.* **Tickets** *$17–$75.* **Credit** *Cash only.*

As the city's midsize venues go, Roseland is far better than Hammerstein Ballroom, and a recent face-lift has wiped away much of the old grime. Still, long lines at the door and the bar can be a pain—but you're here for the music, which ranges from A-list stars like Ghostface and Youssou N'Dour to hot young bands like Jet and Franz Ferdinand.

Rothko

116 Suffolk St between Delancey and Rivington Sts (www.rothkonyc.com). Subway: F to Delancey St; J, M, Z to Delancey–Essex Sts. **Cover** *free–$8; shows start around 8pm.* **Credit** *Cash only.*

The booking at this hot new spot revolves mainly around quality locals such as Tight Fit, Dälek and Asobi Seksu but also includes electronic artists such as Richard Devine and international bands like Colder. Among its many recent buzzworthy events, Rothko hosted two completely mobbed shows with Vincent Gallo and his musical co-conspirator Sean Lennon.

Sidewalk

94 Ave A at 6th St (1-212-473-7373). Subway: F, V to Lower East Side–Second Ave; 6 to Astor Pl. **Cover** *free, two-drink minimum; shows start around 7:30pm.* **Credit** *AmEx, MC, V (bar only).*

A small space with poor sight lines that's located in the back of an East Village bar and restaurant, the Sidewalk café has become the focal point of the city's antifolk scene—though that category means just about anything from piano pop to wry folk. Nellie McKay, Regina Spektor and the Moldy Peaches all got started here.

Sin-é

150 Attorney St between Houston and Stanton Sts (1-212-388-0077/www.sin-e.com). Subway: F to Delancey St; J, M, Z to Delancey–Essex Sts. **Open** *7:30pm–1am daily.* **Cover** *$7–$15.* **Credit** *Cash only.*

This unassuming little LES space is now in its third incarnation, having most recently hopped back from Brooklyn. The roster still steadily features solid, if not often spectacular, local bands, plus a few touring standouts. Liquor up beforehand, though; this is strictly a beer-and-wine establishment.

S.O.B.'s

204 Varick St at Houston St (1-212-243-4940/ www.sobs.com). Subway: 1, 9 to Houston St. **Box office** *Mon–Sat 11am–6pm.* **Tickets** *$10–$25.* **Credit** *AmEx, DC, Disc, MC, V (food and bar only).*

S.O.B. stands for Sounds of Brazil, but Brazilian music is just one of the myriad global genres that are this club's bread and butter. Reggae and salsa have always figured prominently into the mix, but now the club has also become one of the city's prime venues for neosoul, urban rock and hip-hop acts: Within the past year, Jill Scott, Cee-Lo, Raphael Saadiq, Dead Prez and Talib Kweli have rocked its stage.

Southpaw

125 Fifth Ave between Sterling and St. Johns Pls, Park Slope, Brooklyn (1-718-230-0236/www.spsounds.com). Subway: B, Q, 2, 3, 4, 5 to Atlantic Ave; D, M, N, R to Pacific St. **Open** *Show times vary.* **Tickets** *$7–$20.* **Credit** *Cash only.*

A diverse, impressive mix of performers (Neko Case, the Trachtenburg Family Slideshow Players, Eek-a-Mouse, Vic Chesnutt), a low-key crowd and plenty of elbow room make this Park Slope club a great

Cat Power at **Tonic**.

alternative to hipster-filled Williamsburg haunts. Top-notch sound and great views of the stage sweeten the deal.

The Theater at Madison Square Garden

Seventh Ave between 31st and 33rd Sts (1-212-465-6741/www.thegarden.com). Subway: A, C, E, 1, 2, 3, 9 to 34th St–Penn Station. **Box office** *Mon–Sat noon–6pm.* **Tickets** *vary.* **Credit** *AmEx, DC, Disc, MC, V.*

This smaller, classier extension of Madison Square Garden has better sound than the arena. The Theater has hosted world-music celebrations, mainstream hip-hop shows, R&B extravaganzas, and medium-size rock shows with the Strokes, James Taylor and Bonnie Raitt.

Tonic

107 Norfolk St between Delancey and Rivington Sts (1-212-358-7503/www.tonicnyc.com). Subway: F to Delancey St; J, M, Z to Delancey–Essex Sts. **Cover** *$5–$40; doors open at 7:30pm.* **Credit** *Cash only.*

Tonic, in a former kosher winery on the Lower East Side, remains the focal point of New York's avant-garde, creative and experimental music scenes; improvising folkies alternate with avant-jazzers and laptop abstractionists. Downtown icon John Zorn treats Tonic as his home away from home,

and trumpeters Dave Douglas and Roy Campbell mount a brassy annual festival here. In Subtonic (*see p290*), the basement DJ lounge, guests can loll around on banquettes built into giant (but alas, empty) wine casks.

Town Hall

123 W 43rd St between Sixth and Seventh Aves (1-212-997-1003/www.the-townhall-nyc.org). Subway: B, D, F, V to 42nd St–Bryant Park; N, Q, R, W, 42nd St S, 1, 2, 3, 9, 7 to 42nd St–Times Sq. **Box office** *Mon–Sat noon–6pm.* **Tickets** *$15–$85.* **Credit** *AmEx, MC, V ($1 surcharge).*

Town Hall was conceived decades ago as the "people's auditorium." Its excellent acoustics are ideal for folk—Dylan and Baez played here in the '60s—and softer rock: Rufus Wainwright, the Magnetic Fields and Ben Folds have taken the stage in recent years.

Warsaw at the Polish National Home

261 Driggs Ave at Eckford St, Greenpoint, Brooklyn (1-718-387-0505/www.warsawconcerts.com). Subway: G to Nassau Ave. **Box office** *Tue–Sun 5pm–midnight (advance online purchase recommended).* **Tickets** *$10–$25.* **Credit** *Cash only.*

A mammoth, old-fashioned space positioned just at the edge of Greenpoint's most densely Polish area,

Jazz Standard. *See p321.*

Warsaw's gigs—few and far between as they may be—are generally worth catching and are well attended by carefully scruffy cool kids from nearby Williamsburg. The last year welcomed the Yeah Yeah Yeahs and a three-night stand with Patti Smith; a newly improved sound system is the cherry on top of the space's high-school-prom vibe.

Webster Hall

125 E 11th St between Third and Fourth Aves (1-212-353-1600/www.websterhall.com). Subway: L to Third Ave; N, Q, R, W, 4, 5, 6 to 14th St–Union Sq. **Open** *Visit website for hours.* **Tickets** *free–$30.* **Credit** *AmEx, DC, MC, V.*

Although Webster Hall is still best known for its bridge-and-tunnel-crowd weekend parties (Penthouse Pets, anyone?), the ballroomlike space recently boosted its live-music cred by getting select big shows—Sonic Youth, the Melvins, the Libertines—booked here by the indie-savvy folks from Bowery Ballroom. The sound system has been pumped up

and now rates among the best in town, making Webster Hall a worthy alternative to the Clear Channel–operated Irving Plaza.

Jazz & experimental

Barbès

376 9th St at Sixth Ave, Park Slope, Brooklyn (1-718-965-9177/www.barbesbrooklyn.com). Subway: F to Seventh Ave. **Tickets** *free–$8.* **Credit** *Disc, MC, V (bar only).*

The two-year-old Barbès, run by two musically inclined French expats, has quickly become Brooklyn's most adventurous home for jazz of the traditional swing and outward-bound varieties, plus a steady steam of delicious folk- and world-music-derived hybrids.

Birdland

315 W 44th St between Eighth and Ninth Aves (1-212-581-3080/www.birdlandjazz.com). Subway: A, C, E to 42nd St–Port Authority. **Box office** *Reservations required; call club.* **Tickets** *$20–$50, $10 food-and-drink minimum.* **Credit** *AmEx, DC, Disc, MC, V.*

Birdland brought jazz back to the Theater District in grand fashion a decade ago, and some of the area's Broadway glitz has now worked its way into the club's gestalt. In addition to showcasing great jazz musicians (Joe Lovano, Marian McPartland) and bands in residence (the Chico O'Farrill Afro-Cuban Jazz Orchestra owns Sundays), the club has begun to draw musical-theater mavens by booking cabaret (Jim Caruso's Cast Party).

Blue Note

131 W 3rd St between MacDougal St and Sixth Ave (1-212-475-8592/www.bluenote.net). Subway: A, C, E, B, D, F, V to W 4th St. **Box office** *Call or visit website for reservations.* **Tickets** *$10–$65, $5 food-and-drink minimum.* **Credit** *AmEx, DC, MC, V.*

The Blue Note prides itself on being "the jazz capital of the world," a place where the biggest names in jazz (Herbie Hancock), blues (Taj Mahal) and adult pop (Cassandra Wilson, Eartha Kitt) play in a setting so intimate that patrons are forced to get to know their neighbors. The Late Night Groove series and the Sunday brunches are the best bargain bets.

Carnegie Hall

See p325 for listing.

Carnegie Hall remains synonymous with hitting the big time, and in recent years, the welcome mat has been laid out for an ever expanding roster of the world's greatest artists. Although the acoustics of the venerable Isaac Stern Auditorium were designed for classical music, the space has proven amenable to performers such as Ornette Coleman, Caetano Veloso and David Byrne. Zankel Hall, a state-of-the-art 599-seat subterranean theater, has significantly expanded Carnegie's pop, jazz and world-music offerings, including artist-curated series that culminate in big-hall finales.

Cornelia Street Café
29 Cornelia St between Bleecker and W 4th Sts
(1-212-989-9319/corneliastreetcafe.com).
Subway: A, C, E, B, D, F, V to W 4th St.
Cover *$8–$12, $6 drink minimum; doors open at*
9pm. **Credit** *AmEx, DC, MC, V.*
Cornelia Street Cafe seems like a mellow Greenwich
Village eatery on the surface, but anyone who
walks downstairs will encounter a music room that
hosts everything from adventurous jazz, poetry
and world music to folk newcomers and rookie
singer-songwriters.

Fat Cat
75 Christopher St between Seventh Ave South and
Bleecker St (1-212-675-7369/www.fatcatjazz.com).
Subway: 1, 9 to Christopher St–Sheridan Sq.
Cover *$10–$15; show times vary.* **Credit** *Cash only.*
While looking for Fat Cat, you will happen upon a
standard-looking billiard hall. Don't turn away—the
veritable jazz oasis is just behind the door to the right
of the concession booth. Inside, the comfy couches
and tables encourage you to settle in for sets played
by musicians Jason Lindner and Sam Yahel, who tour
with the stars.

55 Bar
55 Christopher St between Seventh Ave South and
Waverly Pl (1-212-929-9883/www.55bar.com).
Subway: 1, 9 to Christopher St–Sheridan Sq.
Cover *free–$15; doors open Fri, Sat 5:30pm; Sun*
9:30pm. **Credit** *Cash only.*
This Prohibition-era dive has become one of New
York's most artist-friendly rooms, thanks to its
knowledgeable, appreciative audience. You can catch
emerging talent almost every night of the week at the
free-of-charge early shows, while late sets regularly
feature established artists including Mike Stern,
Wayne Krantz, Leni Stern and Michael Blake.

Iridium Jazz Club
1650 Broadway at 51st St (1-212-582-2121/
www.iridiumjazzclub.com). Subway: 1, 9 to 50th St.
Box office *Reservations recommended; call venue.*
Tickets *$25–$35, $10 food-and-drink minimum.*
Credit *AmEx, DC, Disc, MC, V.*
Located smack in the middle of Broadway's bright
lights, Iridium keeps the crowds satisfied with
shows split between household names and those
known only to the jazz-savvy. Recent guests include
Jackie McLean, Kenny Garrett and Hank Jones.
Monday nights belong to guitar hero Les Paul, while
the Sunday-brunch crowd is entertained by
Schoolhouse Rock composer Bob Dorough.

Jazz at Lincoln Center
See p323 **The house that jazz built.**

Jazz Gallery
290 Hudson St between Dominick and Spring Sts
(1-212-242-1063/www.jazzgallery.org). Subway: C,
E to Spring St. **Box office** *Reservations strongly*
recommended; call club. **Tickets** *$12–$15; shows at*
9, 10:30pm. **Credit** *Cash only.*

The Jazz Gallery is a place to witness true works
of art, from the obscure but always interesting
jazzers who play the club (Tia Fuller, Miguel
Zenón, Gretchen Parlato) to the museum-quality,
jazz-themed photos and artifacts displayed on the
walls. The tiny room's acoustics are sublime.

Jazz Standard
116 E 27th St between Park Ave South and Lexington
Ave (1-212-576-2232/www.jazzstandard.com).
Subway: 6 to 28th St. **Box office** *Call for reservations.*
Tickets *$15–$30.* **Credit** *AmEx, DC, Disc, MC, V.*
Restaurateur Danny Meyer's Blue Smoke barbecue
joint has a classy jazz operation beneath it. The room's
marvelous sound matches its splendid sight lines, and
in keeping with the rib-sticking chow, the jazz is often
of the groovy, hard-swinging variety, with musicians
such as pianist Cedar Walton and guitarists James
Blood Ulmer and Peter Bernstein.

Lenox Lounge
See p212 for review.

Merkin Concert Hall
See p326 for listing.
Just north of Lincoln Center, Merkin's polished digs
provide an intimate setting for chamber music and
jazz, folk and experimental performers. This season,
Thomas Buckner's Interpretations series celebrates
15 years of presenting eclectic creators. A newly
invigorated jazz series has paired Brad Mehldau with
Fred Hersch, and Jason Moran with Andrew Hill,
among others, while the New York Guitar Festival
mounts elaborate multiartist tribute concerts that feature the cream of the six-string crop.

Smoke
2751 Broadway between 105th and 106th Sts
(1-212-864-6662/www.smokejazz.com). Subway: 1, 9
to 103rd St. **Shows** *Mon–Sat 9, 11pm, 12:30am;*
Sun 6pm. **Cover** *Sun–Thu free, $10 drink*
minimum; Fri, Sat $15–$25. **Credit** *Disc, MC, V.*
Smoke is a classy little room that has figured out how
to lure patrons from both uptown and downtown.
Early in the week, evenings are themed: On Sunday,
it's Latin jazz; Tuesday, organ jazz; and Wednesday,
funk. On weekends, internationally renowned jazz
locals (George Coleman, Eddie Henderson, Cedar
Walton) hit the stage, relishing the opportunity to
play informal gigs in their own backyard.

Sweet Rhythm
88 Seventh Ave South between Bleecker and Grove Sts
(1-212-255-3626/www.sweetrhythmny.com). Subway:
1, 9 to Christopher St–Sheridan Sq. **Shows** *Sun–*
Thu 8, 10pm; Fri, Sat 8, 10pm, midnight.
Cover *$10–$25, $10 minimum per person per set.*
Credit *AmEx, DC, MC, V.*
Once a blue-chip jazz club called Sweet Basil, the new
Sweet Rhythm is inhabited by ghosts of jazz past.
Fine swing and bop remain on the menu (the Frank
and Joe Show, Gary Bartz), though it's no longer the
only course: Blues, world-music and even comedy
acts are on hand.

Arts & Entertainment

Swing 46

*349 W 46th St between Eighth and Ninth Aves
(1-212-262-9554/www.swing46.com). Subway: A, C, E
to 42nd St–Port Authority.* **Cover** *Sun–Thu $10;
Fri, Sat $12; shows start at 9:30pm.* **Credit** *AmEx,
DC, Disc, MC, V.*

You don't have to throw on a zoot suit to make the
scene at this midtown bastion of retro, but it could
help you fit in. Bands that jump, jive and wail await
you, so be sure to wear your dancin' shoes.

Tonic

See p319 for review.

Upover Jazz Café

*351 Flatbush Ave at Seventh Ave, Park Slope,
Brooklyn (1-718-398-5413/www.upoverjazz.com).
Subway: B, Q to Seventh Ave; 2, 3 to Grand
Army Plaza.* **Shows** *Mon, Tue 9:30pm; Wed
10:30pm, midnight; Thu 9:30, 11pm; Fri, Sat 9,
11pm, 12:30am.* **Cover** *$10–$18, $5 minimum.*
Credit *Cash only.*

The Upover Jazz Café booking policy isn't quite
as rigid as its claim of being "Brooklyn's nothin'
but jazz" club would make you think. Bop rules
the roost much of the time, but some of the club's
rising-star talents (Bilal Oliver, Robert Glasper)
make no secret of their affinity for R&B and hip-
hop. No matter what's on, you're guaranteed a
funky good time.

Village Vanguard

*178 Seventh Ave South at Perry St (1-212-255-4037/
www.villagevanguard.com). Subway: A, C, E, 1, 2, 3, 9
to 14th St; L to Eighth Ave.* **Shows** *Sun–Thu 9,
11pm; Fri, Sat 9, 11pm, 12:30am.* **Tickets** *$20,
$10 drink minimum; call or visit website for
reservations.* **Credit** *AmEx, MC, V (online
purchases only).*

Septuagenarian Village Vanguard is still going
strong, offering patrons the chance to take bop's
current temperature and to shake hands with history: John Coltrane, Miles Davis and Bill Evans
have all grooved in this hallowed hall. The 16-piece
Vanguard Jazz Orchestra has been the Monday-
night regular for almost 40 years. Reservations are
strongly recommended, and the Vanguard takes
only cash or traveler's checks at the door.

Blues, country & folk

B.B. King Blues Club & Grill

See p312 for review.

Paddy Reilly's Music Bar

*519 Second Ave at 29th St (1-212-686-1210/
www.paddyreillys.com). Subway: 6 to 28th St.*
Shows *Mon–Fri 9:30pm; Fri, Sat 10, 11pm; Sun
4pm.* **Cover** *$5–$7.* **Credit** *AmEx, Disc, MC, V.*
Patrons flock to this Gramercy institution for the
silky Guinness, the house's only draft; but they
stay for the lively Irish folk and rock acts that bring
the room to life. Once a Friday-night staple, popular pub-rockers the Prodigals have become as spo-
radic as their name suggests, so check listings
before you make the trek to see them.

Arts & Entertainment

The house that jazz built

"We don't just play jazz," trumpeter Wynton
Marsalis, artistic director of Jazz at Lincoln
Center, is fond of saying about the
organization's mission. The list of other
responsibilities that JALC has taken on in its
13-year history seems both exhausting and
awe-inspiring. "We teach [jazz], write it, dance
it, sing it, present it, film it, photograph it,
archive it, record it, broadcast it and
celebrate it," Marsalis said at a 2002 press
conference to unveil plans for the Frederick P.
Rose Hall, JALC's new 100,000-square-foot,
$128 million headquarters nestled in the Time
Warner Center, at 10 Columbus Circle. "Now,"
he concluded, "we have a home for it."

The facility's fall 2004 grand opening made
clear, however, that the primary goal is
performance. The new hall has been outfitted
with a classroom, a rehearsal space and a
recording studio in order to continue JALC's
extensive educational outreach programs, but
the real standouts are its three venues—the
1,231-person-capacity Rose Theater, the 550-
seat Allen Room and the cozy nightspot
Dizzy's Club Coca-Cola—from which the
musicians "come out swinging," as Marsalis
likes to say.

Lincoln Center took a big step a decade ago
by adding jazz to its high-culture blend of
opera, ballet and classical music, but one
obstacle still had to be overcome. "This is the
first facility designed for the sound, function
and feeling of jazz," Marsalis states. "Most of
the time, the halls we play in were not built
with the needs of swing- and blues-based
music in mind," he continues. "There's a lot
of echo, which can muddy the mix. We also
have drums playing all the time, which is not
the case with symphonic music. Jazz needs a
space where the frequencies are evenly
distributed, not just split between the highs of
a drum cymbal and the lows of a bass."

It turns out that what's good for jazz is great
for the other performing arts as well.

Rodeo Bar & Grill
375 Third Ave at 27th St (1-212-683-6500/
www.rodeobar.com). Subway: 6 to 28th St.
Cover *free; shows start at 10pm.* **Credit** *AmEx,*
DC, Disc, MC, V (bar only).
The city's best roots club lassoes top-shelf acts, both
touring (Dale Watson, rockabilly filly Rosie Flores)
and local (the Moonlighters, Fort Bragg). The unpre-
tentious crowd and roadhouse atmosphere make this
a great spot to kick up your boots.

Latin, reggae & world

Copacabana
560 W 34th St between Tenth and Eleventh Aves
(1-212-239-2672/www.copacabanany.com). Subway:
A, C, E to 34th St–Penn Station. Cover $10–$40,
$30 at tables; doors open Tue 6pm; Fri, Sat 10pm.
Credit *AmEx, Disc, MC, V.*
The city's most iconic destination for Latin music
has now become a full-fledged party palace. It's still
a prime stop for salsa, *cumbia* and merengue, but
in addition to booking world-renowned stars
(Ruben Blades, El Gran Combo, and Tito Nieves
with Conjunto Clasico), the Copa now has an alternative nook called the House Room, where dancers
can spin to disco, house and Latin freestyle.

Satalla
37 W 26th St between Broadway and Sixth Ave
(1-212-576-1155/www.satalla.com). Subway: N, R, W
to 28th St. Cover $10–$25; shows start at 8 or 10pm.
Credit *AmEx, Disc, MC, V.*

Every evening at Satalla transports you to another part of the world. It's a lounge dedicated to the
globalist flavor of New York, which means that you
might happen upon a Celtic band tonight, and then
come back tomorrow to find African drummers or
a Greek singing troupe. The decor is a tad psyche-
delic, but the couches are so comfy that it's easy to
settle into the trip.

S.O.B.'s
See p318 for review.

Zinc Bar
90 W Houston St between La Guardia Pl and
Thompson St (1-212-477-8337/www.zincbar.com).
Subway: A, C, E, B, D, F, V to W 4th St. **Open** *6pm–*
3:30am daily. **Cover** *$5.* **Credit** *AmEx, DC, Disc,*
MC, V (bar only).
Located where Greenwich Village meets Soho, Zinc
Bar is the place to hoot and holler with die-hard
night owls. The after-hours atmosphere is enhanced
by the cool mix of African, flamenco, jazz and
samba bands.

Summer venues

Castle Clinton
Battery Park, Battery Pl at State St (1-212-835-2789).
Subway: R, W to Rector St; 1, 9 to South Ferry; 4, 5 to
Bowling Green. **Tickets** *free.*
At the very bottom of Manhattan, in the heart of
Battery Park, this historic fort welcomes a hand-
ful of established stars every season, from rockers

Dizzy's Club Coca-Cola.

Designed by Rafael Viñoly Architects, both
the Rose Theater and the Allen Room are
multipurpose entities, created to suit the
needs of a number of art forms. The Rose
Theater's configuration easily adjusts from
standard proscenium to theater-in-the-round,
which gives maximum flexibility for a wide
range of theater and dance pieces. (Marsalis
has been readying a collaboration with
Elizabeth Streb, who choreographs highly
acrobatic dances.) Though smaller, the Allen
Room resembles a Greek amphitheater and
offers a spectacular view of Central Park.

When Marsalis talks about the project, his
conversation is peppered with references to
swing, but musicians from many different
genres will be playing here. It's almost as if
the spirits of jazz past, from Louis Armstrong,
Billie Holiday and Duke Ellington up to Miles
Davis and John Coltrane, will be smiling down
on musicians and audiences of every stripe
for decades to come.

Jazz at Lincoln Center's Frederick P. Rose Hall
Broadway at 60th St, Columbus Circle
(1-212-258-9800/www.jazzatlincolncenter.com).
Subway: A, B, C, D, 1, 9 to 59th St–Columbus
Circle. **Box office** *Mon–Sat 10am–8:30pm;*
Sun 11am–8:30pm. **Tickets** *$30–$150.*
Credit *AmEx, MC, V.*

the Stills and Soundtrack of Our Lives to jazz and gospel legends such as Cecil Taylor and Mavis Staples. Tickets are always free but have to be picked up in person on the day of a show, and they always go fast.

Central Park SummerStage

See p256 for listing.
The catholic booking policy of the folks at the City Parks Foundation means that summers in the park are filled with every sound under the sun (Devo, Nas, the Strokes, Lucinda Williams). A number of Middle Eastern traditional musicians dropped by in 2004. The sound can be dodgy but improves every year, and the setting can't be beat.

Giants Stadium

For listing, see p331 **Meadowlands Sports Complex.**
At New Jersey's Giants Stadium, you can catch biggies like the Rolling Stones and Bruce Springsteen—though band members look like ants, and you'll wait a long, long time for beer.

Lincoln Center Plaza

For listing, see p326 **Lincoln Center.**
Lincoln Center's multitiered floor plan allows for several outdoor stages in one sprawling facility, but the most popular venues are the North Plaza, which houses the well-loved Midsummer Night Swing (*see p257*) dance concerts, and the Damrosch Park Bandshell, which rolls out the red carpet for the likes of sax icon Sonny Rollins. When the

weather's hot, a wide variety of music from around the world creates a rich global feast.

Prospect Park Bandshell

For listing, see p257 **Celebrate Brooklyn! Performing Arts Festival.**
Prospect Park Bandshell is to Brooklynites what Central Park SummerStage is to Manhattan residents: the place to hear great music in the great outdoors. Programming for the summer festival Celebrate Brooklyn! mirrors the borough's diversity. The music runs from pop (Rufus Wainwright, Los Lobos) and salsa (the Spanish Harlem Orchestra) to Afropop (Rokia Traore) and hip-hop (Talib Kweli). Prospect Park also books indie-pop touring bands and excellent modern-dance troupes.

Tommy Hilfiger at Jones Beach Theatre

Jones Beach, Long Island (1-516-221-1000/www. tommyhilfigerjonesbeach.com). Travel: LIRR from Penn Station, Seventh Ave at 32nd St, to Freeport, then take the Jones Beach bus. **Box office** *Monday show days 10am–9pm; Tue–Sat 10am–6pm; Sun noon–6pm; open till 9pm show days.* **Tickets** *$30–$135.* **Credit** *AmEx, MC, V.*
It's a long haul, especially if you don't have your own wheels, and the sound is generally indifferent. Still, you can't beat the open-air setting at this beachside amphitheater. From July to September, the biggest tours stop here, including package shows like Ozzfest and Projekt Revolution, as well as veterans such as David Bowie, Fleetwood Mac and Yes.

Copacabana. *See p323.*

Classical

The classical-music community in New York City has seldom been in such a state of flux as it is right now. Having recently weathered an abortive attempt to merge the **New York Philharmonic** and **Carnegie Hall**, as well as a failed effort by **New York City Opera** to move downtown, **Lincoln Center** continues to reaffirm its plan for extensive renovation. The impending retirement of powerful **Metropolitan Opera** general manager Joseph Volpe at the end of the 2005–06 season augurs major change at that august institution, and the unexpected death of Carnegie Hall general director Robert Harth, in early 2004, rocked an organization that had already struggled through some turbulent years. Despite these difficulties, however, New York's classical-music presenters and performers continue to thrive artistically. Columbia University's **Miller Theatre** and a newly resurgent **Merkin Concert Hall** continue to raise the bar for innovative programming, while Carnegie's **Zankel Hall** and—surprisingly enough—Lincoln Center's formerly hoary **Mostly Mozart** festival offer proof that even tradition-bound Goliaths can rise to the challenge of facing the world's most demanding audiences.

Tickets

You can buy tickets directly from most venues, whether by phone, online, or at the box office. However, a surcharge is generally added to tickets not bought in person. For more ticket information, *see p380.*

CarnegieCharge
1-212-247-7800/www.carnegiehall.org. **Box office** *By phone 8am–8pm daily.* **Fee** *$5.50 surcharge per ticket.* **Credit** *AmEx, DC, Disc, MC, V.*

Centercharge
1-212-721-6500. **Box office** *By phone Mon–Sat 10am–8pm; Sun noon–8pm.* **Fee** *$5.50 surcharge per ticket.* **Credit** *AmEx, Disc, MC, V.*
Centercharge sells tickets for events at Alice Tully Hall, Avery Fisher Hall and the Juilliard School, as well as for the Lincoln Center Out of Doors Festival.

Metropolitan Opera
1-212-362-6000/www.metopera.org. **Box office** *By phone Mon–Sat 10am–8pm.* **Fee** *$5.50 surcharge per ticket.* **Credit** *AmEx, Disc, MC, V.*
The Met sells tickets for performances held in its opera house, including those of the resident American Ballet Theatre.

Backstage passes

Curious music lovers can go behind the scenes at several of the city's major concert venues. **Backstage at the Met** (1-212-769-7020, www.metguild.org/education) shows you around the famous house during opera season, which runs from September to May; **Lincoln Center Tours** (1-212-875-5350) escorts you inside Avery Fisher and Alice Tully Halls, as well as the New York State Theater; **Carnegie Hall** (1-212-247-7800) guides you through what is perhaps the world's most famous concert hall. For a small fee, you may also sit in on rehearsals of the **New York Philharmonic** (1-212-875-5656), usually held on the Thursday before a concert.

Concert halls

Brooklyn Academy of Music
30 Lafayette Ave between Ashland Pl and St. Felix St, Fort Greene, Brooklyn (1-718-636-4100/ www.bam.org). Subway: B, Q, 2, 3, 4, 5 to Atlantic Ave; C to Lafayette Ave; D, M, N, R to Pacific St; G to Fulton St. **Box office** *Mon–Sat noon–6pm; Sunday show days noon–4pm.* **Admission** *varies.* **Credit** *AmEx, MC, V.*
America's oldest academy for the performing arts continues to present some of the freshest and most adventurous programming in the city. Every fall and winter, the Next Wave Festival provides an overview of avant-garde music, dance and theater, while spring brings lauded European opera productions to town. The BAM Harvey Theater, located nearby, offers a smaller, more atmospheric setting for new creations by composers such as Tan Dun and Meredith Monk, as well as innovative stagings of Baroque opera. Meanwhile, the resident Brooklyn Philharmonic Orchestra has reached new heights of creative excellence under the direction of soon-to-depart conductor Robert Spano.

Carnegie Hall
154 W 57th St at Seventh Ave (1-212-247-7800/ www.carnegiehall.org). Subway: N, Q, R, W to 57th St. **Box office** *Mon–Sat 11am–6pm; Sun noon–6pm.* **Admission** *varies.* **Credit** *AmEx, DC, Disc, MC, V.*
The stars—both soloists and orchestras—in the classical-music firmament continue to shine most brightly in the venerable Isaac Stern Auditorium, inside the renowned concert hall. Still, it's the

▶ For information on concerts, show times and venues, see *Time Out New York* magazine's Classical & Opera listings.
▶ The **Theatre Development Fund** (*see p339*) provides information on all music events via its NYC/Onstage service.

Arts & Entertainment

spunky upstart Zankel Hall that has generated the most buzz; the below-street-level space offers an eclectic mix of classical, contemporary, jazz, pop and world music. Next door, Weill Recital Hall hosts intimate concerts and chamber-music programs.

Florence Gould Hall
French Institute Alliance Française, 55 E 59th St between Madison and Park Aves (1-212-355-6160/ www.fiaf.org). Subway: N, R, W to Fifth Ave–59th St; 4, 5, 6 to 59th St. **Box office** *Tue–Fri 11am–7pm; Sat 11am–3pm.* **Admission** *$10–$35.* **Credit** *AmEx, MC, V.*
Programming in this small, comfortable hall has a decidedly French tone, in artists and repertoire.

Merkin Concert Hall
Kaufman Center, 129 W 67th St between Broadway and Amsterdam Ave (1-212-501-3330/ www.kaufman-center.org). Subway: 1, 9 to 66th St–Lincoln Ctr. **Box office** *Sun–Thu noon–7pm; Fri noon–4pm.* **Admission** *$10–$25.* **Credit** *AmEx, MC, V (advance purchases only).*
Tucked away on a side street in the shadow of Lincoln Center, this unimposing gem of a hall offers a robust mix of early music and avant-garde programming, as well as an increasing amount of jazz, folk and more eclectic fare. Here, the New York Festival of Song has finally found a comfortable home, while regular performances sponsored by WNYC-FM afford opportunities for casual interaction with composers and performers.

New Jersey Performing Arts Center
See p317 for listing.
It takes only 15 or 20 minutes to reach Newark's sumptuous performing-arts complex from midtown, and the rewards are well worth the trip. Tickets for big-name acts that may be sold out at Manhattan venues can often be found here, and performances may be slightly different from those in concurrent Gotham gigs.

92nd Street Y
See p274 for listing.
The Y has always stood for solidly traditional orchestral, solo and chamber masterpieces. But it also fosters the careers of young musicians, and explores European and Jewish-American music traditions with innovative, far-reaching results.

Lincoln Center

Built in the 1960s, this massive complex is the nexus of Manhattan's performing-arts scene. Lincoln Center hosts lectures and symposia in the Rose Building, in addition to events in the main halls: **Alice Tully Hall**, **Avery Fisher Hall**, **Metropolitan Opera House**, **New York State Theater**, and the **Vivian Beaumont** and **Mitzi E. Newhouse Theaters**. Also on the premises are the **Juilliard School** (*see p330*) and the **Fiorello H. La Guardia High School**

of Music and Art and Performing Arts (108 Amsterdam Ave between 64th and 65th Sts, www.laguardiahs.org), which frequently hosts professional performances. Big stars like Itzhak Perlman, András Schiff and Richard Goode are Lincoln Center's meat and potatoes, but lately, the great divide between the flagship Great Performers season and the relatively audacious, multidisciplinary **Lincoln Center Out of Doors Festival** (*see p258*) has begun to narrow, thanks to fresher programming. Even the **Mostly Mozart** festival (*see p258*), a longtime summer staple, has begun drawing a younger, hipper crowd with its progressive bookings and innovative artistic juxtapositions.

Lincoln Center
Columbus Ave at 65th St (1-212-546-2656/www. lincolncenter.org). Subway: 1, 9 to 66th St–Lincoln Ctr.
This is the main entry point for Lincoln Center, but the venues that follow are spread out across the square of blocks from 62nd to 66th Streets, between Amsterdam and Columbus Avenues.

Alice Tully Hall
1-212-875-5050. **Box office** *Mon–Sat 11am–6pm; Sun noon–6pm.* **Admission** *free–$75.* **Credit** *AmEx, Disc, MC, V.*
Built to house the Chamber Music Society of Lincoln Center (1-212-875-5788, www.chambermusicsociety. org), Alice Tully Hall somehow makes its 1,096 seats feel cozy. It has no center aisle, and the seating offers decent legroom. Its Art of the Song recital series is one of the most extensive in town.

Avery Fisher Hall
1-212-875-5030. **Box office** *Mon–Sat 10am– 6pm; Sun noon–6pm.* **Admission** *$20–$114.* **Credit** *AmEx, Disc, MC, V.*
This handsome, comfortable 2,700-seat hall is the headquarters of the New York Philharmonic (1-212-875-5656, www.nyphilharmonic.org), the country's oldest symphony orchestra (founded in 1842) and one of its finest. The sound, which ranges from good to atrocious, depending on who you ask, stands to be improved in the years to come. Inexpensive, early-evening "rush hour" concerts and open rehearsals are presented on a regular basis. The Great Performers series features top international soloists and ensembles.

Metropolitan Opera House
1-212-362-6000/www.metopera.org. **Box office** *Mon–Sat 10am–8pm; Sun noon–6pm.* **Admission** *$12–$295.* **Credit** *AmEx, Disc, MC, V.*
The Met is the grandest of the Lincoln Center buildings, so it's a spectacular place to see and hear opera. It hosts the Metropolitan Opera from September to May, and major visiting companies during the summer. Opera's biggest stars (think Domingo, Fleming and Mattila) appear here regularly, and artistic director James Levine has turned the orchestra into a true symphonic force. Audiences are knowledgeable and

The Kronos Quartet in a searing performance at **Brooklyn Academy of Music**. *See p325.*

See p325.

fiercely partisan, with subscriptions remaining in families for generations. Still, the Met has tried to be more inclusive; digital English-language subtitles, which appear on screens affixed to railings in front of each seat, are convenient for the novice and unobtrusive to his more seasoned neighbor. Tickets are expensive, and unless you can afford good seats, the view won't be great; standing-room-only tickets start at $12, and you'll have to wait in line on Saturday morning to buy them. At least you'll be able to see the eye-popping, gasp-inducing sets (by directors like Zeffirelli) that remain the gold standard here.

New York State Theater

1-212-870-5570. **Box office** *Mon 10am–7:15pm; Tue–Sat 10am–8:15pm; Sun 11:30am–7:15pm.* **Admission** *$25–$110.* **Credit** *AmEx, DC, Disc, MC, V.*
NYST houses the New York City Ballet (www.nycballet.com) as well as the New York City Opera (www.nycopera.com). The opera company has tried to overcome its second-best reputation by being both ambitious and defiantly populist. Rising young American singers often take their first bows at City Opera (many of them eventually make the trek across the plaza to the Met), where casts and productions tend to be younger and sexier than those of its more patrician counterpart. Known for its fierce commitment to the unconventional—from modern American works and musical-theater productions to intriguing Handel stagings and forgotten bel canto gems—City Opera is considerably cooler than its neighbor, and about half the price. But truly splashy grand spectacle remains the province of the Met.

Walter Reade Theater

1-212-875-5600. **Box office** *2–6pm daily.* **Admission** *$12–$15.* **Credit** *Cash only.*
The Walter Reade Theater's acoustics are less than fabulous; still, the Chamber Music Society uses the space regularly, and the Great Performers series offers Sunday-morning events fueled by pastries and hot beverages sold in the lobby.

Opera

The Metropolitan Opera and the New York City Opera may be the leaders of the pack, but they're hardly the only game in town. Feisty upstarts and long-standing grassroots companies insure that Manhattan's operaphiles are among the best-served in the world. Call the organizations or visit their websites for

ticket prices, schedules and venue details. The music schools (*see p330*) have opera programs, too.

Amato Opera Theater
319 Bowery at 2nd St (1-212-228-8200/www.amato. org). Subway: B, D, F, V to Broadway–Lafayette St; 6 to Bleecker St. **Admission** *$30; seniors, students and children $25.* **Credit** *AmEx, Disc, MC, V.*
New York's beloved mom-and-pop opera shop offers charming, fully staged productions in a theater only 20 feet wide—it's almost like watching opera in your living room. Casting can be inconsistent, but many well-known singers have performed here.

American Opera Projects
South Oxford Space, 138 South Oxford St between Atlantic Ave and Hanson Pl, Fort Greene, Brooklyn (1-718-398-4024/www.operaprojects.org). Subway: B, Q, 2, 3, 4, 5 to Atlantic Ave; C to Lafayette Ave; D, M, N, R to Pacific St; G to Fulton St. **Admission** *varies.* **Credit** *Cash only.*
AOP is not so much an opera company as a living, breathing workshop that allows you the opportunity to follow a new work from gestation to completion.

Dicapo Opera Theatre
184 E 76th St between Lexington and Third Aves (1-212-288-9438/www.dicapo.com). Subway: 6 to 77th St. **Admission** *$47.50.* **Credit** *MC, V.*
This top-notch chamber-opera troupe benefits from City Opera–quality singers performing in an intimate setting in the basement of St. Jean Baptiste Church.

New York Gilbert & Sullivan Players
For listing, see p329 **Symphony Space**.
Is Victorian camp your vice? This troupe presents a rotating schedule of the Big Three (*H.M.S. Pinafore, The Mikado* and *The Pirates of Penzance*), plus lesser-known G&S works.

Other venues

Bargemusic
Fulton Ferry Landing between Old Fulton and Water Sts, Dumbo, Brooklyn (1-718-624-2083/www.barge music.org). Subway: A, C to High St; F to York St. **Admission** *$25–$40.* **Credit** *MC, V.*
This former coffee-bean barge presents four chamber concerts a week—and a great view of the Manhattan skyline. It's a magical experience, but bundle up in winter. When the weather warms, you can enjoy a drink on the upper deck during intermission.

The Frick Collection
See p148 for listing.
Concerts in the museum's elegantly appointed concert hall are a rare treat, featuring lesser-known but world-class performers. Tickets are free, but acquiring them can be a chore: You must submit a written request in advance, and seats are often snatched up weeks or months ahead of time. A line for returned tickets forms

Puccini's *Madama Butterfly* at the **Metropolitan Opera House. See p326.**

Metropolitan Museum of Art
See p148 for listing.
When it comes to established virtuosos and revered chamber ensembles, the Metropolitan Museum's programming is consistently rich and full (and ticket prices are correspondingly high). The museum has also established a youthful resident ensemble, Metropolitan Museum Artists in Concert. Seasonally inspired early-music concerts are held uptown in the stunning Fuentidueña Chapel at the Cloisters (*see p147*).

Miller Theatre at Columbia University
Broadway at 116th St (1-212-854-7799/www.miller theatre.com). Subway: 1, 9 to 116th St–Columbia Univ. **Box office** *Mon–Fri noon–6pm. Show days open 2 hours before performance.* **Admission** *$20, students $12.* **Credit** *AmEx, MC, V.*
Columbia's Miller Theatre has single-handedly made contemporary classical music sexy in New York City. The credit belongs to executive director George Steel, who proved that presenting challenging fare by composers such as Birtwistle, Carter and Babbitt in a casual, unaffected setting could attract a young audience—and hang onto it. Miller's early-music offerings, many of which are conducted by Steel, are also exemplary.

The New York Public Library for the Performing Arts
See p162 for listing.
The library's Bruno Walter Auditorium regularly hosts free recitals, solo performances and lectures.

one hour before each event, but if you miss out, take heart; the concerts are also broadcast live into the Garden Court, where tickets are not required.

The Kaye Playhouse
Hunter College, 68th St between Park and Lexington Aves (1-212-772-4448/www.kayeplayhouse.hunter. cuny.edu). Subway: 6 to 68th St–Hunter College. **Box office** *Mon–Sat noon–6pm.* **Admission** *$10–$70.* **Credit** *AmEx, MC, V.*
Named for its benefactors—comedian Danny Kaye and his wife, Sylvia—this refurbished theater offers an eclectic program of professional music and dance.

The Kitchen
See p347 for listing.
Occupying a 19th-century icehouse, the Kitchen has been a meeting place for the avant-garde in music, dance and theater for more than 30 years. Show prices range from free to $25.

The Kosciuszko Foundation
15 E 65th St at Fifth Ave (1-212-734-2130/ www.thekf.org). Subway: F to Lexington Ave– 63rd St; 6 to 68th St–Hunter College. **Admission** *$15–$30.* **Credit** *MC, V.*
This East Side townhouse hosts a chamber-music series with a mission: Each program must feature at least one work by a Polish composer. You're less likely to choke on Chopin than to hear something novel by Bacewicz, Paderewski or Szymanowski.

Symphony Space
2537 Broadway at 95th St (1-212-864-5400/ www.symphonyspace.org). Subway: 1, 2, 3, 9 to 96th St. **Box office** *Tue–Sun noon–7pm.* **Admission** *varies ($2 surcharge per order).* **Credit** *AmEx, MC, V.*
Despite its name, Symphony Space provides programming that is anything but symphony-centric: a recent season was packed with new music by Steve Reich, Japanese drumming, children's concerts, and performances of Purcell's opera *Dido and Aeneas.* The Annual Wall to Wall marathons serve up a full day of music—free of charge—focusing on a particular composer, from Johann Sebastian Bach to Miles Davis.

Tishman Auditorium
New School University, 66 W 12th St at Sixth Ave (1-212-243-9937). Subway: F, V to 14th St; L to Sixth Ave. **Admission** *free–$15.* **Credit** *Cash only.*
The New School's modestly priced Schneider Concerts chamber-music series features up-and-coming musicians. Established artists also play here; for a fraction of the prices charged elsewhere.

Churches

From sacred to secular, a thrilling variety of music is performed in New York's churches.

Arts & Entertainment

Superb acoustics, out-of-this-world choirs and serene surroundings make these houses of worship particularly attractive venues. Bonus: Some concerts are free or very cheap.

The Cathedral Church of St. John the Divine

1047 Amsterdam Ave at 112th St (1-212-316-7540/ www.stjohndivine.org). Subway: B, C, 1, 9 to 110th St–Cathedral Pkwy. **Box office** *Mon–Fri 2–6pm; Sat, Sun 10am–6pm.* **Admission** *varies.* **Credit** *AmEx, Disc, MC, V.*

The stunning neo-Gothic, 3,000-seat sanctuary provides a heavenly atmosphere for the church's own choir and visiting ensembles, though the acoustics are murky.

Christ and St. Stephen's Church

120 W 69th St between Columbus Ave and Broadway (1-212-787-2755/www.csschurch.org). Subway: 1, 2, 3, 9 to 72nd St. **Admission** *varies.* **Credit** *Cash only.*

This small, pleasant West Side church offers one of the most diverse concert rosters in the city, including an annual presentation of Bach's choral *Christmas Oratorio.*

Church of the Ascension

12 W 11th St between Fifth and Sixth Aves (1-212-358-1469/www.voicesofascension.org). Subway: N, R, W to 8th St–NYU. **Admission** *$10–$50.* **Credit** *MC, V (advance purchases only).*

There's a first-rate professional choir, the Voices of Ascension, at this little Village church. You can catch the choir at Lincoln Center on occasion, but home turf is the best place to hear it.

Church of St. Ignatius Loyola

980 Park Ave at 84th St (1-212-288-2520/ www.saintignatiusloyola.org). Subway: 4, 5, 6 to 86th St. **Admission** *$10–$40.* **Credit** *AmEx, Disc, MC, V.*

The Sacred Music in a Sacred Space series is a high point of Upper East Side music culture. Lincoln Center also holds concerts here, capitalizing on the church's fine acoustics and prime location.

Corpus Christi Church

529 W 121st St between Amsterdam Ave and Broadway (1-212-666-9266/www.mb1800.org). Subway: 1, 9 to 116th St–Columbia Univ. **Admission** *varies.* **Credit** *MC, V.*

Early-music fans can get their fix from Music Before 1800, a series that regularly imports the world's leading antiquarian artists and ensembles.

St. Bartholomew's Church

109 E 50th St between Park and Lexington Aves (1-212-378-0248/www.stbarts.org). Subway: E, V to Lexington Ave–53rd St; 6 to 51st St. **Admission** *varies.* **Credit** *AmEx, MC, V.*

This magnificent church hosts the Summer Festival of Sacred Music, one of the city's most ambitious choral-music series, and fills the rest of the year with performances by resident ensembles and guests.

St. Thomas Church Fifth Avenue

1 W 53rd St at Fifth Ave (1-212-757-7013/www. saintthomaschurch.org). Subway: E, V to Fifth Ave–53rd St. **Admission** *$15–$70.* **Credit** *AmEx, MC, V.*

The country's only fully accredited choir school for boys keeps the great Anglican choral tradition alive and well in New York. St. Thomas's annual performance of Handel's *Messiah* is a must-hear that's well worth the rather steep ticket price.

Trinity Church/ St. Paul's Chapel

Trinity Church, Broadway at Wall St; St. Paul's Chapel, Broadway at Fulton St (1-212-602-0747/ www.trinitywallstreet.org). Subway: R, W to Rector St; 4, 5 to Wall St. **Admission** *Concerts at One series $2 donation.* **Credit** *Cash only.*

Historic Trinity, in the heart of the Financial District, plays host to the inexpensive Concerts at One series. Performances are held at 1pm on Mondays at St. Paul's Chapel, and Thursdays at Trinity Church.

Schools

The Juilliard School and the Manhattan School of Music are renowned for their talented students, faculty and artists-in-residence, all of whom regularly perform for free or at low cost. Lately, Mannes College of Music has made great strides to rise to the same level. Noteworthy music and innovative programming can also be found at several other colleges and schools in the city.

The Juilliard School

60 Lincoln Center Plaza, Broadway at 65th St (1-212-769-7406/www.juilliard.edu). Subway: 1, 9 to 66th St–Lincoln Ctr. **Admission** *usually free.*

New York's premier conservatory stages weekly concerts by student soloists, orchestras and chamber ensembles, as well as elaborate opera productions that rival many professional presentations.

Manhattan School of Music

120 Claremont Ave at 122nd St (1-212-749-2802, ext 4428/www.msmnyc.edu). Subway: 1, 9 to 125th St. **Admission** *usually free.*

MSM offers master classes, recitals and off-site concerts by its students, faculty and visiting pros. The American String Quartet, in residence since 1984, gives concerts regularly, and the Augustine Guitar Series includes recitals by top soloists.

Mannes College of Music

150 W 85th St between Columbus and Amsterdam Aves (1-212-580-0210/www.mannes.edu). Subway: B, C, 1, 9 to 86th St. **Admission** *usually free.*

In addition to student concerts and faculty recitals, Mannes also mounts ambitious, historically themed concert series; the summer is given over to festivals and workshops for instrumentalists, most of which provide affordable performances by some of the world's leading musicians.

Sports & Fitness

Let the games begin.

Scream. Sweat. Stomp. Buy a hot dog. Scream again. In this city, a game is much more than just a spectator sport. Two pro football teams, three pro hockey teams, three pro basketball teams and two major-league and two minor-league baseball teams call the area home. And if raucous cheering doesn't get your blood pumping fast enough, then you can kayak in the Hudson, go ice-skating at Rockefeller Center, swing a golf club at Chelsea Piers, ride a horse in Central Park, or pedal a bike along well-maintained park trails in any of the five boroughs—and even over the George Washington Bridge to New Jersey. Or intone your "om" at one of the city's many yoga centers.

Spectator sports

Major venues

All advance tickets for events at these venues are sold through **Ticketmaster** (*see p380*).

Madison Square Garden

Seventh Ave between 31st and 33rd Sts (1-212-465-6741/www.thegarden.com). Subway: A, C, E, 1, 2, 3, 9 to 34th St–Penn Station. **Box office** *Mon–Fri 9am–6pm; Sat 10am–6pm; Sun noon–1 hour after event begins.* **Tickets** *$25–$350.* **Credit** *AmEx, DC, Disc, MC, V.*

Meadowlands Sports Complex

East Rutherford, NJ (1-201-935-3900/ www.meadowlands.com). Travel: NJ Transit Meadowlands Sports Complex bus from Port Authority Bus Terminal (1-212-564-8484), Eighth Ave at 42nd St; one way $3.50. **Box office** *Mon–Sat 11am–6pm; Sundays 2 hours prior to an event.* **Tickets** *from $25.* **Credit** *Cash only for Giants and Jets games and Meadowlands Racetrack. All other events: AmEx, DC, Disc, MC, V.*
Continental Airlines Arena, Giants Stadium and the Meadowlands Racetrack are part of this massive multivenue complex across the river, and all are serviced by the same bus.

You could be a contender: Go a few rounds at the renowned **Gleason's Gym**. *See p333.*

Jockeys jockey at **Belmont Park**. *See p334.*

Nassau Veterans Memorial Coliseum

1255 Hempstead Tpke, Uniondale, Long Island (1-516-794-9303/www.nassaucoliseum.com). Travel: From Penn Station, Seventh Ave at 32nd St, take LIRR (www.lirr.org) to Hempstead, then take the N70, N71 or N72 bus to the coliseum. **Tickets** *from $25.* **Credit** *AmEx, Disc, MC, V.*

Baseball

Talk of the national pastime dominates the papers, airwaves and watercoolers through the summer and into early fall. New York is home to two teams—the **Mets** and the **Yankees**—and each one (along with its fan base) has a distinct personality. The American League's Yankees are the team with the rich history (Babe Ruth, Mickey Mantle), the long list of championships and a payroll that would bankrupt a small country. The National League's Mets are the relatively new kids on the block: They came along in 1961 to fill the gap created when the working-class favorite Brooklyn Dodgers decamped for Los Angeles in 1958. The club's scruffy underdog personality keeps many baseball fans pulling for them (fruitlessly, on the whole) year after year. Minor-league excitement returned in 2001, when the **Staten Island Yankees** and the **Brooklyn Cyclones** (the Mets' minor-league team) opened new ballparks in wonderful cityscape settings.

Brooklyn Cyclones

KeySpan Park, 1904 Surf Ave between West 17th and 19th Sts, Coney Island, Brooklyn (1-718-449-8497/www.brooklyncyclones.com). Subway: D, F, Q to Coney Island–Stillwell Ave. **Box office** *Mon–Sat 10am–4pm.* **Tickets** *$5–$12.* **Credit** *AmEx, Disc, MC, V.*

New York Mets

Shea Stadium, 123-01 Roosevelt Ave at 126th St, Flushing, Queens (1-718-507-8499/www.mets.com). Subway: 7 to Willets Point–Shea Stadium. **Box office** *Mon–Fri 9am–5:30pm; Sat, Sun 9am–2pm.* **Tickets** *$5–$53.* **Credit** *AmEx, Disc, MC, V.*

New York Yankees

Yankee Stadium, River Ave at 161st St, Bronx (1-718-293-6000/www.yankees.com). Subway: B, D, 4 to 161st St–Yankee Stadium. **Box office** *Mon–Sat 9am–5pm; Sun 10am–4pm; and during games.* **Tickets** *$8–$95.* **Credit** *AmEx, Disc, MC, V.*

Staten Island Yankees

Richmond County Bank Ballpark, 75 Richmond Terr at Bay St, Staten Island (1-718-720-9200/www.siyanks. com). Travel: Staten Island Ferry to St. George Terminal. **Box office** *Mon–Fri 9am–6pm; Sat 10am–6pm; and during games.* **Tickets** *$8, $10.* **Credit** *AmEx, Disc, MC, V.*

Basketball

Both of the area's NBA teams—the **New York Knicks** and the **New Jersey Nets**—are in what could tactfully be described as a "rebuilding phase." After a few years near the top of the Eastern Conference, the Nets are hoping to make the finals again by pairing younger players with star guard Jason Kidd. The Knicks, the true New York home team, have stumbled, but recent trades may help. Watching either squad in its home arena can be an exciting way to spend a night, and tickets are easier to come by these days. The Knicks play at Madison Square Garden; many seats are filled with basketball diehards (like Spike Lee), while Nets games (at the Continental Airlines Arena in New Jersey) are more family-friendly. The ladies of the WNBA's **New York Liberty** hold court at MSG in the summer.

New Jersey Nets

Continental Airlines Arena (for listing, see p331 **Meadowlands Sports Complex***). 1-800-765-6387/www.njnets.com.* **Tickets** *$15–$150.*

New York Knicks

Madison Square Garden (see p331 for listing). www.nyknicks.com. **Tickets** *$34–$115.*

New York Liberty

Madison Square Garden (see p331 for listing). www.nyliberty.com. **Tickets** *$10–$65.*

Boxing

Church Street Boxing Gym

*25 Park Pl between Broadway and Church St
(1-212-571-1333/www.nyboxinggym.com). Subway:
2, 3 to Park Pl; 4, 5, 6 to Brooklyn Bridge–
City Hall.* **Open** *Call or visit website for schedule.*
Tickets *$20–$30.* **Credit** *Cash only.*
Church Street is a workout gym and amateur-boxing
venue housed in an atmospheric cellar. Evander
Holyfield, Mike Tyson and other heavy hitters have
trained here before Garden matches. About ten times
a year, on Fridays, the gym hosts white-collar bouts
that draw a young, single, energetic crowd.

Gleason's Gym

*83 Front St between Main and Washington Sts,
Dumbo, Brooklyn (1-718-797-2872/www.gleasons
gym.net). Subway: F to York St.* **Open** *Call or
visit website for schedule.* **Tickets** *$15.*
Credit *DC, Disc, MC, V.*
Although it occupies an undistinguished second-floor
warehouse space in a now-groovy neighborhood,
Gleason's is *the* professional boxer's address in New
York. The "sweet scientists" who have trained at the
city's most storied gym include Muhammad Ali and
Jake (*Raging Bull*) La Motta. Monthly white-collar
fights draw doctors, lawyers and stockbrokers—in
and out of the ring.

Madison Square Garden

See p331 for listing. **Tickets** *$30–$305.*
Once the country's premier boxing venue, the Garden
still hosts some pro fights and the city's annual Golden
Gloves amateur championships.

Dog show

Westminster Kennel Club Dog Show

*Madison Square Garden (see p331 for listing).
www.westminsterkennelclub.org.* **Tickets** *$40–$95.*
Dates *February.*
America's most prestigious dog show prances into
Madison Square Garden each February. One of the
oldest sporting events in the country, it's your chance
to see some of the most beautiful, well-trained pooches
on the planet compete for the coveted Best in Show—
and a Snausage.

Football

Every Sunday from September through January,
New Yorkers get religious…about football. New
York, uniquely, lays claim to two NFL teams, and
the **Giants** and the **Jets** have followings that are
equally rabid—so rabid that every home game
for both squads is officially sold out. But the
teams sometimes release a few seats (generally,
those that weren't claimed by the visiting team)
on the day of the game. Call for availability on the
Friday before kickoff. You can also try your luck

on eBay or with a scalper (risky; tickets may be
counterfeit). Fans of the fast-paced, high-scoring
arena-football league can head out to Nassau
Coliseum to see the **New York Dragons**, who
play from February to May.

New York Dragons

*Nassau Veterans Memorial Coliseum (see p332 for
listing). 1-866-235-8499/www.newyorkdragons.
com.* **Tickets** *$15–$110.*

New York Giants

*Giants Stadium (for listing, see p331)
Meadowlands Sports Complex). 1-201-
935-8222/www.giants.com.* **Tickets** *$65–$85.*

New York Jets

*Giants Stadium (for listing, see p331)
Meadowlands Sports Complex). 1-516-
560-8100/www.newyorkjets.com.* **Tickets** *$60–$80.*

Hockey

The National Hockey League's 2005 season
was thrown into limbo by labor strife. Check
newspapers to see if play is on. The formerly
powerful **New York Rangers** have failed to
make the playoffs for an uncomfortable number of
seasons. The upstart **New Jersey Devils** have
captured three Stanley Cups in the last ten years
and always play an exciting, hard-nosed brand
of hockey. The **New York Islanders** skate at
the suburban Nassau Coliseum on Long Island.
Tickets for all three teams are on sale throughout
the season, which runs from October to April.

New Jersey Devils

*Continental Airlines Arena (for listing, see p331)
Meadowlands Sports Complex).
www.newjerseydevils.com.* **Tickets** *$20–$90.*

New York Islanders

*Nassau Veterans Memorial Coliseum
(see p332 for listing). www.newyorkislanders.com.*
Tickets *$25–$175.*

New York Rangers

*Madison Square Garden (see p331 for listing).
www.newyorkrangers.com.* **Tickets** *$23–$630.*

Horse racing

There are three major racetracks near
Manhattan: Thoroughbreds run at **Aqueduct**,
Belmont and the **Meadowlands**. If you don't
want to trek to Long Island or New Jersey, then
catch the action (and the seedy atmosphere)
at any Off-Track Betting (OTB) parlor (check
the yellow pages for locations).

▶ For up-to-the-minute local sports
listings, pick up *Time Out New York*.

Aqueduct Racetrack

110-00 Rockaway Blvd at 110th St, Jamaica, Queens (1-718-641-4700/www.nyra.com/aqueduct). Subway: A to Aqueduct Racetrack. **Races** *Thoroughbred Oct–May Wed–Sun.* **Admission** *clubhouse $2, grandstand $1. Free Jan 2–Mar 7.* **Credit** *Cash only.*
The Wood Memorial, a test run for promising three-year-olds, is held each spring (April 16, in 2005). Aqueduct typically posts a nine-race card. Betting is, of course, legal at all New York tracks.

Belmont Park

2150 Hempstead Tpke, Elmont, Long Island (1-516-488-6000/www.nyra.com/belmont). Travel: From Penn Station, Seventh Ave at 32nd St, take LIRR (www.lirr .org) to Belmont Park. **Races** *Thoroughbred May–Jul, Sept, Oct Wed–Sun.* **Admission** *clubhouse $5, grandstand $2.* **Credit** *Cash only.*
This big beauty of an oval is home to the third and longest leg of horse racing's Triple Crown, the mile-and-a-half Belmont Stakes (June 11, in 2005).

Meadowlands Racetrack

For listing, see p331 **Meadowlands Sports Complex***. 1-201-843-2446/www.thebigm.com.* **Races** *Thoroughbred Oct, Nov; harness Nov–Aug; check website for schedule.* **Admission** *clubhouse $3, grandstand $1.* **Credit** *Cash only.*
The Meadowlands offers both harness (trotting) and Thoroughbred racing. Top harness racers compete for more than $1 million in the prestigious Hambletonian, held the first Saturday in August.

Soccer

The Brits call it football; many Americans call it boring. Still, in a city that's home to such a large immigrant population, footy commands a huge number of fans. You'll find pickup games in many city parks, and the pro **MetroStars** play across the river at Giants Stadium, which also occasionally hosts top European teams (including Manchester United) for exhibition games in front of tens of thousands of crazed hooligans. Check www.meadowlands.com for the schedule.

MetroStars

Giants Stadium (for listing, see p331 **Meadowlands Sports Complex***). 1-888-463-8768/www. metrostars.com.* **Tickets** *$18–$38.*

Tennis

U.S. Open

USTA National Tennis Center, Flushing Meadows–Corona Park, Queens (1-866-673-6849/www. usopen.org). Subway: 7 to Willets Point–Shea Stadium. **Tickets** *$22–$120.* **Credit** *AmEx, MC, V.*
Tickets go on sale late in the spring for this grand-slam thriller, which the USTA says is the highest-attended annual sporting event in the world. Check the website for match schedules.

Active sports

A visit to New York means a lot of watching—watching plays, watching concerts, watching that weird cowboy guy who plays guitar in his underwear in Times Square. But if you get a hankering to do something yourself, the city won't let you down.

All-in-one sports center

Chelsea Piers

Piers 59–62, W 17th through 23rd Sts at Eleventh Ave (1-212-336-6666/www.chelseapiers.com). Subway: C, E to 23rd St.
This massive sports complex, which occupies a six-block stretch of riverfront real estate, offers just about every popular recreational activity in a bright, clean, well-maintained facility. Would-be Tigers can practice their swings at the **Golf Club** (Pier 59, 1-212-336-6400); bowlers can set up their pins at the **AMF Lanes** (between Piers 59 and 60, 1-212-835-2695). Ice-skaters spin and glide at the **Sky Rink** (Pier 61, 1-212-336-6100). Rather skate on wheels? Hit the **Roller Rink and Skate Park** (Pier 62, 1-212-336-6200). The **Field House** (Pier 62, 1-212-336-6500) has a Toddler Adventure Center, a rock-climbing wall, a gymnastics training center, batting cages, basketball courts, indoor playing fields and more. Just looking for a spinning class or yoga session? At the **Sports Center** (Pier 60, 1-212-336-6000) gym, you'll find classes in every-thing from triathlon training to hip-hop dance. Hours and fees vary; call or consult the website for more information.

Bicycling

Hundreds of miles of paths make it easy for the recreational biker to get pretty much anywhere in New York. Construction continues on the paths that run alongside the East and Hudson Rivers, and it will soon be possible for riders to completely circumnavigate Manhattan island. Visitors can either take a DIY trip using rental bikes and path maps or go on organized rides. A word of caution: Cycling in the city is serious business. Riders must stay alert and abide by traffic laws, especially because drivers and pedestrians often don't. If you keep your ears and eyes open—and wear a helmet—you'll enjoy an adrenaline-pumping ride. Or forget the traffic and just take a spin through one of the city's many parks, including Central and Prospect Parks.

Bike-path maps

Department of City Planning Bookstore
22 Reade St between Broadway and Elk St (1-212-720-3667). Subway: J, M, Z to Chambers St; R, W to City Hall; 4, 5, 6 to Brooklyn Bridge–City Hall. **Open** *Mon–Fri 10am–4pm. The city's Bicycle Master*

Get acquainted with the city while rubber meets road during **Bike the Big Apple**.

Plan includes nearly 1,000 miles of cycling lanes. Free annual updates are available at this shop or at www.nyc.gov.

Transportation Alternatives *115 W 30th St between Sixth and Seventh Aves, suite 1207 (1-212-629-8080/www.transalt.org). Subway: B, D, F, V, N, Q, R, W to 34th St–Herald Sq; 1, 2, 3, 9 to 34th St–Penn Station.* **Open** *Mon–Fri 9:30am–6pm.* TA is a nonprofit citizens' group that lobbies for more bike-friendly streets. You can pop into the office to get free maps or download them from the website.

Bike rentals

Gotham Bike Shop *112 West Broadway between Duane and Reade Sts (1-212-732-2453/www.gothambikes.com). Subway: A, C, 1, 2, 3, 9 to Chambers St.* **Open** *Mon–Wed, Fri, Sat 10am–6:30pm; Thu 10am–7:30pm; Sun 10:30am–5pm.* **Fees** *$30 for 24hrs, plus $5 helmet rental.* **Credit** *AmEx, MC, V.* Rent a sturdy set of wheels from this shop and ride the short distance to the Hudson River esplanade.

Loeb Boathouse *Central Park, entrance on Fifth Ave at 72nd St (1-212-517-2233/www.centralparknyc.org). Subway: 6 to 68th St–Hunter College.* **Open** *10am–5pm daily, weather permitting.* **Fees** *$6–$20 per hour (includes helmet).* **Credit** *AmEx, MC, V (credit card and ID required for rental).* If you want to cruise through Central Park, this place has more than 100 bikes available.

Metro Bicycles *133 Lexington Ave at 88th St (1-212-427-4450/www.metrobicycles.com). Subway 4, 5, 6 to 86th St.* **Open** *9:30am–6pm daily.* **Fees** *$7 per hour; $35 per day.* **Credit** *AmEx, Disc, MC, V.* Trek and Fisher bikes are available by the day; check Metro's website or call for additional locations in Manhattan.

Organized bike rides

Bike the Big Apple *1-201-837-1133/www.bikethebigapple.com.* Tag along with a tour company that combines biking with sightseeing. Trips include a Lower East Side and Brooklyn ride that makes stops at chocolate and beer factories.

Fast and Fabulous *1-212-567-7160/www.fastnfab.org.* This "queer and queer-friendly" riding group leads tours throughout the year, usually meeting in Central Park and heading out of the city.

Five Borough Bicycle Club *1-212-932-2300, ext 115/www.5bbc.org.* This local club always offers a full slate of leisurely rides around the city, as well as jaunts that head farther afield for more experienced riders. Best of all, most trips are free.

Time's Up! *1-212-802-8222/www.times-up.org.* An alternative-transportation advocacy group, Time's Up! sponsors rides year-round, including Critical Mass, in which hundreds of cyclists and skaters meet at Union Square Park (7pm on the last Friday of every month) and go tearing through the city, often ending up in Greenwich Village.

Bowling

Bowlmor Lanes

110 University Pl between 12th and 13th Sts (1-212-255-8188/www.bowlmor.com). Subway: L, N, Q, R, W, 4, 5, 6 to 14th St–Union Sq. **Open** *Mon 11am–3am; Tue, Wed, Sun 11am–1am; Thu 11am–2am; Fri, Sat 11am–4am.* **Fees** *$6.45 per person per game weekdays before 5pm; $7.95 weekdays after 5pm, and weekends and holidays; $5 shoe rental. Under 21 not admitted Tue–Sun after 5pm.* **Credit** *AmEx, MC, V.*
Renovation turned a seedy but historic Greenwich

Village alley (Richard Nixon bowled here!) into a hip downtown nightclub. Monday evening's Night Strike features glow-in-the-dark pins and a techno-spinning DJ in addition to unlimited bowling from 10pm to 3am ($20 per scenester includes shoes).

Gyms

Many gyms offer single-day memberships. If you can schedule a workout during nonrush hours (instead of just before or after the workday), then you'll be better off. Call for class details.

Crunch

623 Broadway between Bleecker and Houston Sts (1-212-420-0507/1-888-227-8624/www.crunch .com). Subway: B, D, F, V to Broadway–Lafayette St; 6 to Bleecker St. **Open** *Mon–Fri 6am–10pm; Sat, Sun 9am–7pm.* **Fee** *day pass $24.* **Credit** *AmEx, DC, Disc, MC, V.*
For a downtown feel without the attitude, Crunch wins hands down. Most of the ten New York locations feature NetPulse cardio equipment, which lets you surf the Web or watch a personal TV while you exercise. Visit Crunch's website for other locations.

New York Sports Club

151 E 86th St between Lexington and Third Aves (1-800-301-1231/www.nysc.com). Subway: 4, 5, 6 to 86th St. **Open** *Mon–Fri 5:30am–10pm; Fri 5:30am–10pm; Sat, Sun 8am–9pm.* **Fee** *day pass $25.* **Credit** *AmEx, MC, V.*
A day membership at New York Sports Club includes aerobics classes and access to the weight room, cardio machines, steam room and sauna. The 62nd and 86th Street branches feature squash courts. Visit the website for other gym locations.

Horseback riding

Claremont Riding Academy

175 W 89th St between Columbus and Amsterdam Aves (1-212-724-5100). Subway: 1, 9 to 86th St. **Open** *Mon–Fri 6:30am–8pm; Sat, Sun 8am–5pm.* **Fees** *rental $50 per hour; lessons $60 per half hour or 3 lessons for $165.* **Credit** *MC, V.*
Beginners use an indoor arena; experienced riders can take a leisurely canter along on six miles of trails in Central Park. Be prepared to prove your English-saddle-mounted mettle: Claremont interviews all riders to determine their level of experience.

Kensington Stables

51 Caton Pl at East 8th St, Kensington, Brooklyn (1-718-972-4588/www.kensingtonstables.com). Subway: F to Fort Hamilton Pkwy. **Open** *10am–sunset.* **Fees** *guided trail ride $25 per hour; private lessons $45 per hour.* **Credit** *AmEx, Disc, MC, V.*
The paddock is small, but miles of lovely trails wind through Prospect Park (*see p123*), particularly in the Ravine, which was designed to be seen from horseback.

Ice-skating

Lasker Rink

Central Park, midpark between 106th and 108th Sts (1-212-534-7639/www.centralparknyc.org). Subway: B, C to 110th St. **Open** *Nov–Mar Mon, Wed, Thu 10am–3:45pm; Tue, Fri 10am–10pm; Sat 12:30–10pm; Sun 12:30–4:30pm.* **Fees** *$4.50, children $2.25; skate rental $4.75.* **Credit** *MC, V.*
This neighborhood rink has two skate areas: one for high-school hockey teams and one for the average joe.

Rockefeller Center Ice Rink

1 Rockefeller Plaza, from 49th to 50th St, between Fifth and Sixth Aves (1-212-332-7654/www.therinkat rockcenter.com). Subway: B, D, F, V to 47–50th Sts–Rockefeller Ctr. **Open** *Oct–Apr; call or visit website for hours.* **Fees** *$9–$17; children under 12 $7–$12; skate rental $7–$8.* **Credit** *AmEx, Disc, MC, V.*
Easily among the city's most recognizable tourist attractions, Rockefeller Center's rink, under the giant statue of Prometheus, is perfect for atmosphere—but bad for elbow room. The rink opens with an energetic ice show in mid-October but attracts the most visitors when the towering Christmas tree is lit.

Wollman Rink

Central Park, midpark at 62nd St (1-212-439-6900/ www.wollmanskatingrink.com). Subway: N, R, W to Fifth Ave–59th St. **Open** *Late Oct–Mar Mon, Tue 10am–2:30pm; Wed, Thu, Sun 10am–9pm; Fri, Sat 10am–11pm.* **Fees** *Mon–Thu $8.50, children $4.25; Fri–Sun $11, children $4.50; skate rental $4.75.* **Credit** *Cash only.*
Less crowded—especially after the holidays—than Rock Center, the rink offers a lovely setting beneath the trees of Central Park.

In-line skating

In-line skating is extremely popular in New York: The choking traffic makes it practical, and the landscape makes it pleasurable (a beautiful paved loop circumnavigates Central Park; bike paths run along the Hudson River). Join a group skate, or go it alone. The gear shop **Blades, Board and Skate** (120 W 72nd St between Columbus and Amsterdam Aves, 1-212-787-3911) rents by the day ($20).

Empire Skate Club of New York

P.O. Box 20070, London Terrace Station, New York, NY 10011 (1-212-774-1774/www. empireskate.org).
This club organizes in-line and roller-skating events throughout the city, including island-hopping tours and nighttime rides such as the Thursday Evening Roll: Skaters meet May through October at Columbus Circle (Broadway at 59th St, southwest corner of Central Park) at 6:45pm.

Kayaking

Kayaking is a great way to explore New York Harbor and the Hudson River. Given the tricky currents, the tidal shifts and the hairy river traffic, it's best to go on an organized excursion.

Downtown Boathouse
Pier 26 between Hubert and North Moore Sts (1-646-613-0740/www.downtownboathouse.org). Subway: 1, 9 to Franklin St. **Open** *May 15–Oct 15.* **Fee** *free.*
From May to October, weather permitting, this volunteer-run organization offers free kayaking (no appointment necessary) in front of the boathouses at both locations. They also offer free Wednesday-evening classes and three-hour guided kayak trips on weekend mornings. All trips are offered on a first-come, first-served basis, and you must know how to swim.
Other location *Pier 66A, Twelfth Ave at 26th St (1-646-613-0740).*

Manhattan Kayak Company
Pier 63 Maritime, Twelfth Ave at 23rd St (1-212-924-1788/www.manhattankayak.com). Subway: C, E to 23rd St. **Open** *Call or visit website for schedule and prices.* **Credit** *AmEx, Disc, MC, V.*
Run by veteran kayaker Eric Stiller, who once paddled halfway around Australia, Manhattan Kayak offers beginner to advanced classes and tours. Adventures include the Sushi Tour ($100 per person), in which the group paddles to Edgewater, New Jersey, to dine at a sushi restaurant.

Running

The path ringing the Central Park reservoir is probably the most popular jogging trail in the entire city, but dozens of parks and paths are waiting to be explored. Just tie on a cushy pair of sneakers and go where your feet lead you.

New York Road Runners
9 E 89th St between Fifth and Madison Aves (1-212-860-4455/www.nyrrc.org). Subway: 4, 5, 6 to 86th St. **Open** *Mon–Fri 10am–8pm; Sat 10am–5pm; Sun 10am–3pm.* **Fees** *Call or visit website.* **Credit** *AmEx, MC, V.*
Hardly a weekend passes without some sort of run or race sponsored by the NYRR, which is responsible for the New York City Marathon. Most races take place in Central Park and are open to the public. The club also offers classes and clinics.

NYC Hash House Harriers
1-212-427-4692/www.hashnyc.com. $15 covers food and beer after the run.
This energetic, slightly wacky group has been running in the Big Apple for more than 20 years and always welcomes newcomers. A "hash" is part training run, part scavenger hunt, part keg party. The participants follow a three- to five-mile trail that a member (called "the Hare") marks with chalk or other visual clues. After the exercise, the group retires to a local watering hole for drinks and grub.

NYC Speed Zones
Fifth Ave at 90th St (1-917-574-5771/www.geocities.com/dresdalek/runners). Subway: 4, 5, 6 to 86th St. **Open** *Tue 9pm.*
This running club was founded specifically for younger runners, generally under 30. During the weekly four-mile runs, the emphasis is on sociability rather than competition.

Swimming

The **Harlem, Vanderbilt** and **West Side YMCAs** (www.ymcanyc.org) have decent-size pools (and day passes), as do some private gyms. Many hotel pools provide day-pass access as well. The city of New York maintains several Olympic-size (and smaller) facilities. Its outdoor pools are free of charge and open from late June to Labor Day: **Hamilton Fish** (Pitt St between Houston and Stanton Sts, 1-212-

Arts & Entertainment

Show the city what you've got at the **Trapeze School New York**.

387-7687); **Asser Levy Pool** (23rd St between First Ave and FDR Drive, 1-212-447-2020); **Tony Dapolito Recreation Center** (Clarkson St at Seventh Ave South, 1-212-242-5228). **Recreation Center 54** (348 54th St between First and Second Aves, 1-212-754-5411) has an indoor pool. For more information, call **New York Parks & Recreation** (1-212-639-9675, www.nycgovparks.org).

Tennis

From April through November, the city maintains excellent municipal courts throughout the five boroughs. Single-play (one-hour) tickets cost $7. For a list of city courts, visit www.nycgovparks.org.

Trapeze

Trapeze School New York

Hudson River Park between Canal and Vestry Sts (1-917-797-1872/www.trapezeschool.com). **Open** *May–Nov, weather permitting.* **Fees** *two-hour class $47–$65, plus $22 application fee.* **Credit** *AmEx, Disc, MC, V.*
Sarah Jessica Parker did it on an episode of *Sex and the City* a couple years ago, so it *must* be cool. Set in a large, cagelike construction on the bank of the Hudson River (a tent is in the works at Pier 40, for year-round operation), the school will teach those ages six and up to fly through the air with the greatest of ease. You can also watch while a loved one has a fling.

Yoga

Laughing Lotus Yoga Center

59 W 19th St between Fifth and Sixth Aves, third floor (1-212-414-2903/www.laughinglotus.com). Subway: F, V, N, R, W to 23rd St. **Open** *Call or check website for schedule.* **Fees** *single class $10–$15.* **Credit** *AmEx, Disc, MC, V.*
Roomy (4,000-square-foot) new Chelsea digs accommodate a kind of yogic community center that has weekly holistic workshops, classes and an in-house tarot reader and astrologist. Among the regular offerings: midnight yoga, reflexology and Absolute Beginner classes.

Levitate Yoga

780 Eighth Ave between 47th and 48th Sts (1-212-974-2288/www.levitateyoga.com). Subway: C, E, to 50th St. **Open** *Call or check website for schedule.* **Fees** *single class $18, students $12.* **Credit** *AmEx, MC, V.*
This modern-looking studio caters to beginners, tourists from area hotels, and casts and crews performing at nearby theaters. In the warm months, special classes are held on the 2,000-square-foot rooftop terrace.

Om Yoga Center

826 Broadway between 12th and 13th Sts, sixth floor (1-212-254-9642/www.omyoga.com). Subway: L, N, Q, R, W, 4, 5, 6 to 14th St–Union Sq. **Open** *Call or check website for schedule.* **Fee** *single class $16.* **Credit** *AmEx, Disc, MC, V.*
Cyndi Lee's famed yoga spot offers all-level, flowing-style vinyasa yoga classes with a focus on alignment. Weekly workshops target specific areas of the body.

Arts & Entertainment

Theater & Dance

Ribald puppets, blue body paint, sinister insects: So many shows, so little time.

Theater

Perhaps you've heard the theater referred to as the "fabulous invalid." The joke underscores the conundrum in the industry today: It's always thriving, yet always ailing. Although New York is still the theater capital of the world, with hundreds of shows opening year-round—and **Broadway** at the top of the food chain—the economic logistics of sustaining a show are ever more daunting. Broadway flops routinely lose millions; artistic **Off Broadway** successes sometimes shutter after a two-month run for lack of a big producer. And goodness knows how many brilliant works go unnoticed in the cash-poor precincts of **Off-Off Broadway**. Despite all that, New York theater survives. And if diversity is any indication, some might even say it flourishes. There are perennial family-friendly draws like *The Lion King* and *Beauty and the Beast,* cheery revivals like *Wonderful Town* and top-drawer drama such as Michael Frayn's *Democracy.* But you can also catch terrific examples of pop-driven musicals, such as the ABBA-inspired *Mamma Mia!* and Tony Award winner *Avenue Q,* an irreverent show best described as *Rent* meets *Sesame Street.*

From midtown's landmark palaces and slightly more intimate venues to downtown's offbeat Off Broadway and Off-Off Broadway spaces, there's a place—and a show—to suit every taste.

BUYING TICKETS

If you have a major credit card, then buying Broadway tickets is as easy as picking up a phone. Nearly all Broadway and Off Broadway shows are served by one of the city's 24-hour ticketing agencies, which are listed in the shows' print advertisements or in the capsule reviews that run each week in *Time Out New York.* The venues' information lines can also refer you to ticket agents sometimes by merely transferring your call (for additional ticketing info, *see p380*). Theater box offices usually charge a small fee for phone orders.

Some of the cheapest tickets on Broadway are "rush" tickets (purchased the day of a show at the theater's box office), which cost an average of $25—but not all theaters offer

these, and some reserve them for students. A few theaters distribute rush tickets through a lottery, usually held two hours before the performance. If a show is sold out, it's worth waiting for standby tickets just before curtain time. Tickets are slightly cheaper for matinees (typically on Wednesdays, Saturdays and Sundays) and previews, and for students or groups of 20 or more. For discount seats, your best bet is **TKTS** (*see p380*), where you can get tickets on the day of the performance for as much as 75 percent off the face value. Arrive early to beat—or at least get a jump on—the long lines. TKTS also sells matinee tickets the day before a show. (Beware of scam artists trying to sell tickets to those waiting in line: Their tickets are often fake.) Consider purchasing a set of vouchers from the **Theatre Development Fund** if you're interested in seeing more than one Off-Off Broadway show or dance event.

Theatre Development Fund

1501 Broadway between 43rd and 44th Sts (1-212-221-0013/www.tdf.org). Subway: N, Q, R, W, 42nd St S, 1, 2, 3, 9, 7 to 42nd St–Times Sq. **Open** *Mon–Fri 10am–6pm.* **Credit** *Check or money order only.*
TDF offers a book of four vouchers for $28, which can be purchased only at its office by visitors who bring their passport or out-of-state driver's license, or by students and residents on the TDF mailing list. Each voucher is good for one admission to an Off-Off Broadway theater, dance or music event at venues such as the Atlantic Theater Company, the Joyce, the Kitchen, Performance Space 122 and many more. TDF's NYC/Onstage service (1-212-768-1818) provides information by phone on all events in town.

Broadway

Technically speaking, "Broadway" is the Theater District that surrounds Times Square on either side of Broadway (the avenue), mainly between 41st and 53rd Streets. This is where you'll find the grand theaters that were built

---

▶ For current listings, pick up **Time Out New York**, available on newsstands.
▶ For a specific show, call the **Broadway Line** (1-212-302-4111, outside New York 1-888-276-2392; www.ilovenytheater.com) for tickets.

largely between 1900 and 1930. Officially, 38 are designated as being part of Broadway—full-price tickets at one of them can cost more than $100. The big shows are hard to ignore; high-profile revivals and new blockbusters announce themselves from giant billboards and drench the airwaves with radio advertisements. Still, there's more to Broadway than splashy musicals and flashy pop spectacles. In recent years, provocative dramas like *Take Me Out* and madcap comedies such as *Urinetown* have had remarkable success, as have revivals of American classics such as Lorraine Hansberry's *A Raisin in the Sun* and Eugene O'Neill's *Long Day's Journey into Night*.

The **Roundabout Theatre Company** (American Airlines Theatre, 227 W 42nd St between Seventh and Eighth Aves, 1-212-719-1300; Studio 54, 254 W 54th St between Broadway and Eighth Ave) is critically acclaimed for putting on classics that feature all-star casts; it was also the force behind the brilliant revival of *Assassins* by Stephen Sondheim and John Weidman in 2004. You can subscribe to the Roundabout's full season or buy single tickets, if they're available.

Broadway (Theater District)
Subway: C, E, 1, 9 to 50th St; N, Q, R, W, 42nd St S, 2, 3, 7 to 42nd St–Times Sq.

She, the people

It's not just alliteration that makes you want to call **Sarah Jones**, a darling of downtown drama, a diva. Since the lithe, fresh-faced poet, playwright and performer got her start slamming at the famed Nuyorican Poets Cafe in the mid-'90s, her star has risen with several successful one-woman shows, most notably, 2004's huge Off Broadway hit *bridge & tunnel,* which moved to Broadway in March 2005. "Diva," however, is one title that Jones doesn't aspire to.

"Women only get called divas because we don't have anything dangling between our legs," Jones says. "If we were men, we would just be called assertive, or driven, or powerful or ambitious."

Jones's rejection of divadom goes deeper. Unlike Margaret Cho, John Leguizamo or Eric Bogosian—other popular solo performers who dig through the details of their personal lives onstage—Jones doesn't go the me-myself-and-I route. In *bridge & tunnel,* which is set at an immigrants' poetry slam in Queens, Jones shifts shapes, voices, accents and outlooks to portray 14 unique, deeply felt and utterly engaging characters, from a wheelchair-bound Mexican union organizer to a Chinese matron grappling with her daughter's sexuality.

Meryl Streep, another legendary chameleon (and the show's coproducer), says, "Her compassionate, tough and hilarious take on what makes us different as human beings, and the commonality we can't deny, is unique." As Streep suggests, it's not just Jones's skill that sets her apart—it's her profound connection with her characters.

The audience Jones draws is as varied as her cast of characters. During the show's original downtown run, young outer-borough black and Latino kids filled the seats, next to typically older white theatergoers. Getting the show on Broadway is a chance, Jones says, "to turn new audiences on to theater and get traditional audiences accustomed to thinking of theater as belonging to everybody, not just one Great White Way. We can afford to color it up a little bit."

Four friends. One road trip...
And the summer that changes their lives.

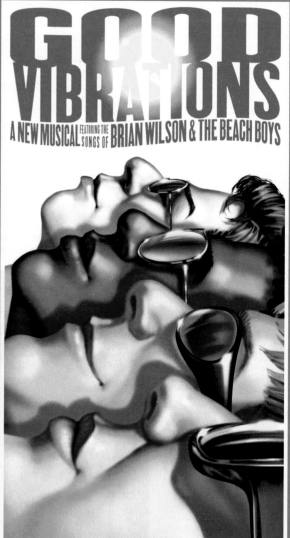

GOOD VIBRATIONS

A NEW MUSICAL FEATURING THE SONGS OF BRIAN WILSON & THE BEACH BOYS

Illustration: Shawn McKelvey

Telecharge.com (212)239-6200
Outside Metro NY (800)432-7250 • Groups (877)5 DODGER

♪ Eugene O'Neill Theatre, 230 West 49th St.
www.GoodVibrationsOnBroadway.com

Long-running shows

Straight (nonmusical) plays can provide some of Broadway's most stirring experiences, but they're less likely than musicals to enjoy long runs. If you aren't in search of song, check *Time Out New York* for current listings and reviews of new or revived dramatic plays.

Avenue Q
Golden Theater, 252 W 45th St between Broadway and Eighth Ave (1-212-239-6200/www.avenueq.com). Subway: A, C, E to 42nd St–Port Authority. **Box office** *Mon–Sat 10am–8pm; Sun noon–7pm.* **Tickets** *$46, $96.* **Credit** *AmEx, DC, Disc, MC, V.*
Mixing puppets and live actors with irreverent jokes and snappy songs, this clever, good-hearted musical comedy has been a surprise hit. It garnered several 2004 Tony Awards, including Best Musical.

Hairspray
Neil Simon Theatre, 250 W 52nd St between Broadway and Eighth Ave (1-212-307-4100/ www.hairsprayonbroadway.com). Subway: C, E, 1, 9 to 50th St. **Box office** *Mon–Sat 10am–8pm; Sun noon–6pm.* **Tickets** *$65–$100.* **Credit** *AmEx, DC, Disc, MC, V.*
John Waters's classic kitsch film has become an eye-popping song-and-dance extravaganza that's bigger, brighter, more satirical and much funnier than the original.

The Producers
St. James Theatre, 246 W 44th St between Seventh and Eighth Aves (1-212-239-6200/www.producers onbroadway.com). Subway: N, Q, R, W, 42nd St S, 1, 2, 3, 9, 7 to 42nd St–Times Sq. **Box office** *Mon–Sat 10am–8pm; Sun noon–6pm.* **Tickets** *$36–$100.* **Credit** *AmEx, DC, Disc, MC, V.*
Mel Brooks's ode to tastelessness mixes Broadway razzamatazz with Borscht Belt humor. Original stars Nathan Lane and Matthew Broderick left the cast, but the show still delivers plenty of laughs.

Wicked
Gershwin Theatre, 222 W 51st St between Broadway and Eighth Ave (1-212-307-4100). Subway: C, E, 1, 9 to 50th St. **Box office** *Mon–Sat 10am–8pm; Sun noon–6pm.* **Tickets** *$50–$100.* **Credit** *AmEx, DC, Disc, MC, V.*
Based on novelist Gregory Maguire's 1995 riff on the *Wizard of Oz* mythology, *Wicked* provides a witty prequel to the classic children's book and movie. At press time, Joe Mantello's sumptuous production starred Jennifer Laura Thompson (*Urinetown*) and Idina Menzel (winner of the 2004 Tony for Best Leading Actress) as young versions of Glinda the Good Witch and the Wicked Witch of the West.

Off Broadway

As the cost of mounting a show on Broadway continues to soar, many serious playwrights are opening their shows in the more adventurous (and less financially demanding) Off Broadway houses. Off Broadway theaters have between 200 and 500 seats, and tickets usually run from $20 to $70. Below are some of our favorite long-running shows, followed by a few of the best theaters and repertory companies.

Long-running shows

Blue Man Group
Astor Place Theater, 434 Lafayette St between Astor Pl and E 4th St (1-212-254-4370/www.blueman.com). Subway: N, R, W to 8th St–NYU; 6 to Astor Pl. **Box office** *noon–7:45pm daily.* **Tickets** *$55–$65.* **Credit** *AmEx, DC, Disc, MC, V.*
Three men with extraterrestrial imaginations (and head-to-toe blue body paint) carry this longtime favorite—a show that's as smart as it is ridiculous.

BUG
Barrow Street Theatre, 27 Barrow St at Seventh Ave South (1-212-239-6200/www.bugtheplay.com). Subway: 1, 9 to Christopher St–Sheridan Sq. **Box office** *Tue–Sat noon–8pm; Sun noon–7:30pm.* **Tickets** *$55–$60.* **Credit** *AmEx, DC, Disc, MC, V.*
Tracy Lett's engrossing white-trash noir drama pits a paranoid drifter and a lonely waitress against mysterious insectoid forces. *BUG* was last season's scariest thrill ride, and it should have (numerous) legs.

The Donkey Show
Club El Flamingo, 547 W 21st St between Tenth and Eleventh Aves (1-212-477-2477/www.thedonkey show.com). Subway: C, E to 23rd St. **Box office** *Wed, Thu 6:30–8:45pm; Fri, Sat 6:30–10:45pm.* **Tickets** *$40–$75.* **Credit** *AmEx, DC, Disc, MC, V.*
Bring your dancing shoes to this *Midsummer Night's Dream* disco, where Shakespearean comedy shakes it to '70s hits like "Car Wash" and "You Sexy Thing."

Stomp
Orpheum Theater, 126 Second Ave between St. Marks Pl and E 7th St (1-212-477-2477). Subway: N, R, W to 8th St–NYU; 6 to Astor Pl. **Box office** *Tue–Fri 1–7pm.* **Tickets** *$35–$60.* **Credit** *AmEx, MC, V.*
This show is billed as a "percussion sensation" because there's no other way to describe it. Using garbage-can lids, buckets, brooms, sticks and just about anything they can get their hands on, these aerobicized dancer-musicians make a lovely racket.

Repertory companies & venues

Atlantic Theater Company
336 W 20th St between Eighth and Ninth Aves (Telecharge 1-212-239-6200/www.atlantic theater.org). Subway: C, E to 23rd St. **Box office** *Tue–Fri 6–8pm; Sat noon–2pm, 6–8pm; Sun 3–8pm.* **Credit** *AmEx, DC, Disc, MC, V.*
Created in 1985 as an offshoot of acting workshops taught by playwright David Mamet and film star William H. Macy, this dynamic theater has presented

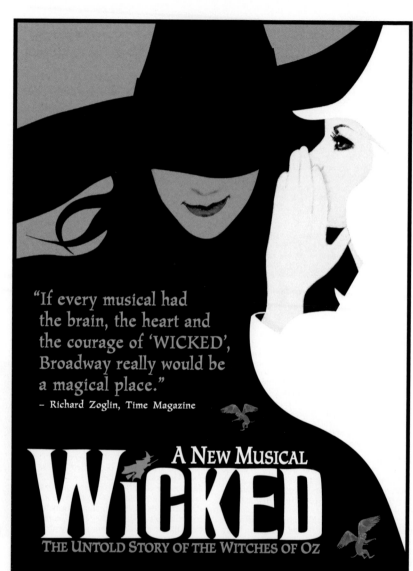

nearly 100 plays, including Mamet's *American Buffalo* and Woody Allen's *Writer's Block*.

Brooklyn Academy of Music

See p325 for listing.
Brooklyn's grand old opera house—along with the Harvey Theater, two blocks away on Fulton Street—stages the famous multidisciplinary Next Wave Festival every October through December. The 2004 festival included avant-garde director Robert Wilson's *The Temptation of St. Anthony* and the U.K.'s Cheek by Jowl production of *Othello*.

Classic Stage Company

136 E 13th St between Third and Fourth Aves (Ticket Central 1-212-279-4200/www.classic stage.org). Subway: L, N, Q, R, W, 4, 5, 6 to 14th St–Union Sq. **Box office** *Mon–Fri noon–5pm.* **Credit** *AmEx, MC, V.*
From Greek tragedies to medieval mystery plays, the Classic Stage Company (under the tutelage of artistic director Brian Kulick) makes the old new again. The 2005 schedule includes open rehearsals, staged readings and productions such as Samuel Beckett's *Happy Days*.

Dodger Stages

340 W 50th St between Eighth and Ninth Aves (1-646-871-1730/www.dodgerstages.com). Subway: C, E, 1, 9 to 50th St. **Box office** *Sun, Mon 1–6pm; Tue–Sat 1–7:30pm.* **Credit** *AmEx, MC, V.*
Formerly a movie multiplex, this new center boasts a shiny, space-age interior and five gorgeous, fully renovated theaters presenting everything from the underwater puppet spectacle *Symphonie Fantastique* to world premieres of new musicals. Dodger Theatrical, an organization that produces Broadway shows, is behind this $20 million undertaking, one of the biggest in recent theater history.

59E59

59 E 59th St between Madison and Park Aves (1-212-279-4200/www.59e59.org). Subway: N, R, W to Lexington Ave–59th St; 4, 5, 6 to 59th St. **Box office** *noon–7pm daily.* **Credit** *AmEx, MC, V.*
This chic new East Side venue, which comprises an Off Broadway space and two smaller theaters, made a splash in its first year with the Brits Off Broadway festival. Theater company Primary Stages now makes its home at 59E59.

Irish Repertory Theatre

132 W 22nd St between Sixth and Seventh Aves (1-212-727-2737/www.irishrepertorytheatre.com). Subway: F, V, 1, 9 to 23rd St. **Box office** *Mon–Fri 10am–6pm; Sat, Sun 11am–6pm.* **Credit** *AmEx, MC, V.*
This Chelsea company puts on compelling shows by Irish playwrights. Past productions include Frank McCourt's *The Irish and How They Got That Way* and Enda Walsh's *Bedbound*.

Lincoln Center

See p326 for listing.
The majestic Lincoln Center complex includes two amphitheater-style drama venues: the 1,138-seat Vivian Beaumont Theater (the Broadway house) and the 338-seat Mitzi E. Newhouse Theater (Off Broadway). Expect polished, often star-studded productions of classic plays (such as *Henry IV* featuring Kevin Kline and Ethan Hawke) and new plays (A.R. Gurney's *Big Bill*).

Manhattan Theatre Club

City Center, 131 W 55th St between Sixth and Seventh Aves (1-212-581-1212/Telecharge 1-212-239-6200/www.mtc-nyc.org). Subway: B, D, E to Seventh Ave. **Box office** *Sun, Mon 11am–5pm; Tue–Sat noon–7pm.* **Credit** *AmEx, DC, Disc, MC, V.*
Manhattan Theatre Club has a history of sending young playwrights to Broadway, as seen with such successes as David Auburn's *Proof.* The club's two theaters are located in the basement of City Center. The 275-seat Stage I Theater features four plays a year; the Stage II Theater offers works-in-progress, workshops and staged readings, as well as full-length productions. MTC also has a Broadway home in the renovated Biltmore Theatre (261 W 47th St between Broadway and Eighth Ave; Telecharge 1-212-239-6200).

The New Victory Theater

209 W 42nd St between Seventh and Eighth Aves (1-646-223-3020/Telecharge 1-212-239-6200/www.newvictory.org). Subway: N, Q, R, W, 42nd St S, 1, 2, 3, 9, 7 to 42nd St–Times Sq. **Box office** *Sun, Mon 11am–5pm; Tue–Sat noon–7pm.* **Credit** *AmEx, MC, V.*
The New Victory is a perfect symbol for the transformation of Times Square. Built in 1900 by Oscar Hammerstein II, Manhattan's oldest theater became a strip club and adult cinema in the '70s and '80s. Renovated by the city in 1995, the building now features a full season of family-friendly plays.

New York Theatre Workshop

79 E 4th St between Bowery and Second Ave (1-212-460-5475/www.nytw.org). Subway: F, V to Lower East Side–Second Ave; 6 to Astor Pl. **Box office** *Tue–Sun 1–6pm.* **Credit** *AmEx, MC, V.*
Founded in 1979, the New York Theatre Workshop works with emerging directors who are eager to take on challenging pieces. Besides plays by the likes of Caryl Churchill (*Far Away, A Number*) and Tony Kushner (*Homebody/Kabul*), this company also premiered *Rent*, Jonathan Larson's Pulitzer Prize–winning musical, which still packs 'em in on Broadway.

Playwrights Horizons

416 W 42nd St between Ninth and Tenth Aves (Ticket Central 1-212-279-4200/www.playwrights horizons.org). Subway: A, C, E to 42nd St–Port Authority. **Box office** *noon–8pm daily.* **Credit** *AmEx, MC, V.*
More than 300 important contemporary plays have premiered here, including dramas such as *Driving Miss Daisy* and *The Heidi Chronicles*. Recent sea-

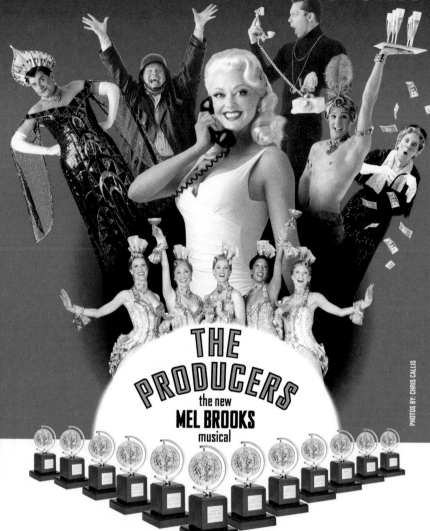

MORE TONY AWARDS TH█N ANY SHOW IN BROADWAY HISTORY!

PHOTOS BY: CHRIS CALLIS

THE PRODUCERS
the new
MEL BROOKS
musical

sons have included works by Doug Wright (*I Am My Own Wife*) and Theresa Rebeck (*Bad Dates*).

Public Theater

425 Lafayette St between Astor Pl and E 4th St (1-212-539-8500/Telecharge 1-212-239-6200/ www.publictheater.org). Subway: N, R, W to 8th St–NYU; 6 to Astor Pl. **Box office** *Sun, Mon 1–6pm; Tue–Sat 1–7:30pm.* **Credit** *AmEx, MC, V.*
Founded by the late Joseph Papp and dedicated to the work of new American playwrights and performers, this Astor Place landmark is also known for its Shakespeare productions (*see below* Shakespeare in Central Park). The building houses five stages and the cabaret space Joe's Pub (*see p316*). The Public recently hired Oskar Eustis (formerly of the Trinity Repertory Company in Providence, R.I.) to serve as the new artistic director.

Second Stage Theatre

307 W 43rd St at Eighth Ave (1-212-246-4422/ www.secondstagetheatre.com). Subway: A, C, E to 42nd St–Port Authority. **Box office** *Tue–Sun noon–6pm.* **Credit** *AmEx, MC, V.*
Now located in a beautiful Rem Koolhaas–designed space near Times Square, Second Stage produces the works of new American playwrights, including the New York premieres of Mary Zimmerman's *Metamorphoses* and Lisa Loomer's *Living Out*.

Shakespeare in Central Park at the Delacorte Theater

Park entrance on Central Park West at 81st St, then follow the signs (1-212-539-8750/www.public theater.org). Subway: B, C to 81st St–Museum of Natural History.
The Delacorte Theater in Central Park is the fair-weather sister of the Public Theater (*see above*). When not producing Shakespeare in the East Village, the Public offers the best of the Bard out-doors during the New York Shakespeare Festival (Jun–Sept). Tickets are free (two per person); they're distributed at both theaters at 1pm on the day of the performance. Normally, 9am is a good time to begin waiting, though the line can start as early as 6am when big-name stars are on the bill.

The Vineyard Theatre

108 E 15th St at Union Sq East (1-212-353-0303/ box office 1-212-353-0303/www.vineyardtheatre. org). Subway: L, N, Q, R, W, 4, 5, 6 to 14th St–Union Sq. **Box office** *Mon–Fri 10am–6pm.* **Credit** *AmEx, MC, V.*
This theater near Union Square produces excellent new plays and musicals including Pulitzer Prize winner Paula Vogel's *The Long Christmas Ride Home* and the Tony Award–winning Broadway hit *Avenue Q* (*see p343*).

Off-Off Broadway

Technically, "Off-Off Broadway" denotes a show that is presented at a theater with fewer than 100 seats and created by artists who aren't necessarily card-carrying union pros. It's where some of the most daring writers and performers create their edgiest work. The **New York International Fringe Festival** (1-212-279-4488, www.fringenyc.org), held every August, is a great way to catch the wacky side of theater. The cheekily named **National Theater of the United States of America** (www.ntusa.org) and the **Civilians** (www.thecivilians.org) are two companies that consistently offer inspired experimental work. But Off-Off Broadway—where tickets run $10 to $25—is not restricted to experimental or solo shows. You can also see classical works and more traditional plays staged by companies such as the **Mint Theater** (311 W 43rd St between Eighth and Ninth Aves, fifth floor, 1-212-315-0231, www.minttheater.org) and at venues like **HERE** and **Performance Space 122**.

Repertory companies & venues

The Brick

575 Metropolitan Ave between Lorimer St and Union Ave, Williamsburg, Brooklyn (1-718-907-3457/ www.bricktheater.com). Subway: G to Metropolitan Ave; L to Lorimer St. **Box office** *Open 15 minutes prior to curtain.* **Credit** *Cash only.*
This chic, brick-lined venue in Williamsburg presents a variety of experimental work. Last summer, it made a joyful noise with the Hell Festival.

HERE

145 Sixth Ave at Broome St (1-212-647-0202/ Smart-tix 1-212-868-4444/www.here.org). Subway: C, E to Spring St. **Box office** *4–10pm daily.* **Credit** *AmEx, MC, V.*
Containing three intimate performance spaces, an art gallery and a chic café, this lovely Tribeca arts complex has hosted a number of exciting companies. It was the launching pad for such well-known shows as Eve Ensler's *The Vagina Monologues*.

The Kitchen

512 W 19th St between Tenth and Eleventh Aves (1-212-255-5793, ext 11/www.thekitchen.org). Subway: A, C, E to 14th St; L to Eighth Ave. **Box office** *Tue–Sat 2–6pm.* Show days open one hour before performance. **Credit** *AmEx, MC, V.*
Founded in Soho in 1971, this cutting-edge perform-ance space still cooks up thought-provoking avant-garde work.

Performance Space 122

150 First Ave at 9th St (1-212-477-5288/ www.ps122.org). Subway: L to First Ave; 6 to Astor Pl. **Box office** *11am–6pm daily.* **Credit** *AmEx, MC, V.*
One of New York's most interesting venues, this non-profit arts center presents experimental dance, per-formance art, music, film and video. Eric Bogosian, Whoopi Goldberg, John Leguizamo and others have developed projects here.

Arts & Entertainment

The most FANTASMAGORICAL musical in the history of everything!

IAN FLEMING'S

"CHITTY CHITTY BANG BANG"

Call Ticketmaster: 212-307-4100

Visit ChittytheMusical.com

Hilton Ⓗ Theatre

213 West 42nd Street

Dance

The rich heritage of New York dance is astounding. In the '30s, Martha Graham, the mother of modern dance, transformed the art form with her powerful, daring movement. In the '40s, classical ballet was given a face-lift by the revolutionary choreographer George Balanchine and his New York City Ballet. Twenty years later, dance was redefined by groundbreaking choreographers like Yvonne Rainer, David Gordon, Steve Paxton and Trisha Brown. The postmodern Judson Dance Theater collective turned the world upside down, proving that dance needn't be held hostage to antiquated rules.

Experimentation remains alive in New York and is on display at an abundance of venues that showcase exceptional modern-day artists, including John Jasperse, Sarah Michelson, David Neumann and Yasuko Yokoshi. The World Music Institute presents a variety of ethnic dance at **Symphony Space** and **City Center**, and the Japan Society is a goldmine for discovering both experimental voices and the purity of traditional dance.

Despite the absence of substantial government funding, classical and contemporary dance in all their forms continue to thrive in New York City. There are two major dance seasons—March to June, and October to December. The spring season is particularly busy: Not only does Paul Taylor present his marvelous troupe each March, but the American Ballet Theatre and the New York City Ballet also present their programs. And the offerings don't end in June; both the open-air **Central Park SummerStage** (*see p256*) and the **Lincoln Center Out of Doors Festival** (*see p258*) schedule performances throughout the summer.

If watching all those beautiful bodies inspires you, there are dozens of dance schools that offer classes (some are affiliated with established companies). Information about workshops is listed in *Time Out New York*. You can call ahead for a schedule, but walk-ins are welcome at most spaces. The **Mark Morris Dance Center** (3 Lafayette Ave between Ashland Pl and Flatbush Ave, Fort Greene, Brooklyn, 1-718-624-8400, www.mmdg.org) offers classes in ballet, modern, West African and Afro-Caribbean dance. Modern-dance classes are taught by current and former company members; when Morris is in town, he often teaches a class himself.

Traditional venues

Brooklyn Academy of Music

See p325 for listing.

BAM, which showcases superb local and out-of-town companies, is one of New York's most prominent cultural institutions. The Howard Gilman Opera House, with its Federal-style columns and carved marble, is a stunning dance venue. (The Mark Morris Dance Group generally performs here in the spring.) The 1904 Harvey Theater (651 Fulton St between Ashland and Rockwell Pls, Fort Greene, Brooklyn), formerly the Majestic, has hosted choreographers John Jasperse and Ralph Lemon; in 2005, Wally Cardona will present his work here, followed by Sarah Michelson in 2006. Each fall, BAM's Next Wave Festival highlights established and experimental dance groups; in spring, an assortment of ballet, hip-hop and modern dance are on the bill.

Burlesque babe Julie Atlas Muz.

City Center

*131 W 55th St between Sixth and Seventh Aves
(1-212-581-7907/www.citycenter.org). Subway:
B, D, E to Seventh Ave; F, N, Q, R, W to 57th St.*
Tickets *$15–$180.* **Credit** *AmEx, MC, V ($4.75
per-ticket surcharge).*
Before the creation of Lincoln Center changed
the cultural geography of New York, this was the
home of American Ballet Theatre, the Joffrey Ballet
and the New York City Ballet (originally known
as the Ballet Society). City Center's lavish decor is
golden—as are the companies that pass through.
You can count on superb performances by ABT in the
fall, the Alvin Ailey American Dance Theater in
December, the Paul Taylor Dance Company in the
spring and others throughout the year.

The Joyce Theater

*175 Eighth Ave at 19th St (1-212-242-0800/
www.joyce.org). Subway: A, C, E to 14th St; 1, 9 to
18th St; L to Eighth Ave.* **Tickets** *$28–$45.*
Credit *AmEx, DC, Disc, MC, V.*
The intimate space, formerly a cinema, is one of the
finest theaters in town. Of the 472 seats at the Joyce,
there's not a single bad one. Companies and choreographers who present work here, including Ballet
Hispanico, David Parsons and Doug Varone, tend to
be more traditional than experimental. The Joyce also
hosts out-of-town crowd-pleasers like Pilobolus
Dance Theatre (June). During the summer, when
many theaters are dark, the Joyce continues its programming. At Joyce Soho, emerging companies present work nearly every weekend.
Other location *Joyce Soho, 155 Mercer St between
Houston and Prince Sts (1-212-431-9233).*

Metropolitan Opera House

See p326 for listing.
A range of international companies, from the Paris
Opera Ballet to the Kirov Ballet, perform at the Met.
In spring, this majestic space is home to American
Ballet Theatre, which presents full-length tradition-
al story ballets, as well as contemporary classics by
Frederick Ashton and Antony Tudor. The acoustics
are wonderful, but the theater is immense, so get as
close to the stage as you can afford.

New York State Theater

*Lincoln Center, 64th St at Columbus Ave
(1-212-870-5570/www.nycballet.com). Subway:
1, 9 to 66th St–Lincoln Ctr.* **Tickets** *$32–$96.*
Credit *AmEx, DC, Disc, MC, V.*
The neoclassical New York City Ballet headlines at
this opulent theater, which Philip Johnson designed
to resemble a jewel box. NYCB has two seasons:

Monday-night fever

New York's best-kept dance secret is
Movement Research. Having celebrated its
25th anniversary in 2004, the community-
based, artist-centered organization has
become a prime training ground for
experimental dance—and a required stop
for out-of-town dancers. But classes and
workshops are only part of Movement
Research's mission. Every Monday evening
for nearly nine months of the year, the
organization also presents **Movement
Research at the Judson Church** (*see p352*),
a free performance showcase. If you want to
see the up-and-coming dance community
of New York City, then a visit to this church
gymnasium should be on your agenda.

Inaugurated in 1991 in a historic church
near Washington Square Park, the Judson
performance programs are mostly artist-
curated. This is an important distinction
from more commercial dance venues,
says executive director Carla Peterson:
"Movement Research is not in the business
of curating; it's in the business of
supporting research and development for
artists at all stages of their careers. We
support emerging ideas within this dance
ecology—and how that translates into the
work that artists are doing is determined
best by them."

Judson programs are special for many
reasons. "Dance has been alive in that
space since the early '60s—there's
45 years of some of the most profound
movement investigation that's ever
taken place," Peterson says. "And those
investigations have really informed the work
that the general populace ends up seeing on
more conventional dance stages." For those
who are not well versed in contemporary
dance, Peterson acknowledges that the
experiments may not automatically make
sense: "Whether the audience understands
it or not, or it seems like the artist is falling
flat, what comes out of it ends up informing
the evolution of the art form." You may
not like everything you see, but you aren't
likely to be bored.

Throughout its history, Movement
Research has nurtured experimentation in
movement-based art forms and pushed
to create dialogues between dance and
other performance genres. Among its many
respected programs are the annual
Improvisation Festival, held each December,
and the biennial *Movement Research*

Winter begins just before Thanksgiving and features more than a month of performances of George Balanchine's magical *The Nutcracker;* the season continues through February with repertory performances. The nine-week spring season usually begins in April. The best seats are in the first ring, where the music comes through loud and clear and—even better—you can enjoy the dazzling patterns of the dancers. The works are by Balanchine (the 89-by-58-foot stage was built to his specifications); Jerome Robbins; Peter Martins, the company's ballet master in chief; and resident choreographer Christopher Wheeldon, whose innovative work has injected the troupe with new life. Weekly cast lists are available online or at the theater.

Alternative venues

Aaron Davis Hall
City College, Convent Ave at 135th St (1-212-650-7100/www.aarondavishall.org). Subway: 1, 9 to 137th St–City College. **Tickets** *$15–$35.* **Credit** *AmEx, MC, V.*
Performances here celebrate African-American life and culture. Companies that have graced the modern, spacious theater include the Bill T. Jones/Arnie Zane Dance Company and the Ailey II repertory.

Brooklyn Arts Exchange
421 Fifth Ave at 8th St, Park Slope, Brooklyn (1-718-832-0018/www.bax.org). Subway: F, M, R to Fourth Ave–9th St. **Tickets** *$8–$15.* **Credit** *Disc, MC, V.*
Brooklyn Arts Exchange, a multi-arts nonprofit organization, presents a variety of dance concerts by emerging choreographers. There are also performances just for children.

Central Park SummerStage
See p256 for listing.
This outdoor dance series runs during the heat of summer. Temperatures can get steamy, but at least you're outside. Count on seeing traditional and contemporary dance; arrive early to secure a spot close to the stage.

Dance Theater Workshop
Bessie Schönberg Theater, 219 W 19th St between Seventh and Eighth Aves (1-212-691-6500/ tickets 1-212-924-0077/www.dtw.org). Subway: 1, 9 to 18th St. **Tickets** *$20–$25.* **Credit** *AmEx, MC, V.*
DTW, led by Cathy Edwards, hosts work by contemporary choreographers, both local and foreign. This space features a 194-seat theater, two dance studios and an artists' media lab.

Alejandra Martorell and Noemi Segarra perform a Kathy Westwater piece at **Judson Church**.

Performance Journal, a printed forum that is focused on current issues in dance. In a way, the Judson shows put all that talk into action. And Peterson assures us the performances will always be free.

"The mission of the church is to provide space free of charge to a variety of different social and political organizations," she says. "Dance artists are at the bottom of the art hierarchy in terms of the economy." So Judson keeps it democratic: No matter what their background, viewers "can always come to see dance on Monday nights," Peterson says.

American Ballet Theatre dancers perform William Forsythe's *workwithinwork*.

Danspace Project

St. Mark's Church in-the-Bowery, 131 E 10th St at Second Ave (1-212-674-8112/tickets 1-212-674-8194/ www.danspaceproject.org). Subway: L to Third Ave; 6 to Astor Pl. **Tickets** *$12–$20.* **Credit** *Cash only.*
Director Laurie Uprichard selects choreographers who lean toward pure movement rather than technological experimentation. The gorgeous, high-ceilinged sanctuary for downtown dance is at its most sublime when the music is live.

Galapagos Art and Performance Space

See p315 for listing.
This casual Brooklyn club, which plays host to all sorts of creative types, often showcases movement-based performances, including burlesque on Mondays.

The Kitchen

512 W 19th St between Tenth and Eleventh Aves (1-212-255-5793). Subway: A, C, E to 14th St; L to Eighth Ave. **Credit** *AmEx, MC, V.*
Although best known as an avant-garde theater space, the Kitchen also offers experimental dance by inventive, often provocative artists. Choreographers Sarah Michelson and Dean Moss have created work here. Debra Singer, formerly a curator at the Whitney Museum of Contemporary Art, runs the show.

Merce Cunningham Studio

55 Bethune St between Washington and West Sts, 11th floor (1-212-691-9751/www.merce.org). Subway: A, C, E to 14th St; L to Eighth Ave. **Tickets** *$10–$30.* **Credit** *Cash only.*
Located in the Westbeth complex on the edge of the West Village, the Cunningham Studio is rented to independent choreographers. As a result, performance quality varies, but some shows are wonderful. The

stage and seating area are in a large dance studio; be prepared to take off your shoes. Arrive early, too, or you'll have to sit on the floor.

Movement Research

Judson Church, 55 Washington Sq South at Thompson St (1-212-598-0551/www.movementresearch.org). Subway: A, C, E, B, D, F, V to W 4th St. **Tickets** *free.*
Director Carla Peterson carries on the tradition of free Monday-night performances at the Judson Church (*see also p350* **Monday-night fever**). At least two choreographers' works are shown each night, and the series runs from September to May.

New Jersey Performing Arts Center

See p317 for listing.
The New Jersey Performing Arts Center is the home of the New Jersey Symphony Orchestra. It has also hosted the Alvin Ailey American Dance Theater, the Miami City Ballet and Suzanne Farrell Ballet. Large, open theaters make NJPAC a choice venue for dance. And it's not *that* far away.

The New Victory Theater

See p345 for listing.
Since reopening in 1995, this intimate, brilliantly renovated venue has offered exceptional dance programming. Much of it is geared toward children.

Performance Space 122

See p347 for listing.
An appealing range of up-and-coming choreographers like DD Dorvillier, Yasuko Yokoshi and Sarah Michelson present unconventional new works.

Symphony Space

See p329 for listing.
The World Music Institute hosts many international dance troupes here, and the regular season features contemporary choreographers.

Arts & Entertainment

Trips Out of Town

Trips Out of Town

Beat a speedy retreat to the mountains, valleys, sand or shore.

Sometimes, New Yorkers need a break from the frenetic pace of the city—and so might you. Whether you prefer to sun and swim in the Hamptons or to hike through the Catskill Mountains, you'll easily find bucolic peace and quiet just a few hours (or less) from the concrete jungle. Many getaway spots are accessible by public transportation; save yourself the high car-rental rates (and hellish summer-weekend traffic in and out of town) by hopping on a bus or train. If you *must* drive, try leaving town midweek. You'll probably score better hotel rates then, too.

GENERAL INFORMATION

NYC & Company, the New York visitors and convention bureau (*see p384* **Websites**), has many brochures on upstate excursions. Look for special packages if you're planning to spend a few days away. *The New York Times* publishes a travel section every Sunday that carries advertised deals for transportation and lodging. *Time Out New York*'s annual Summer Getaways issue will also point you in the right direction.

TRANSPORTATION

We've included information on how to reach all listed destinations from New York City. **Metro-North** and the **Long Island Rail Road**, or **LIRR** (*see p364*), are the two main commuter-rail systems. Both offer theme tours in the summer. Call the **Port Authority Bus Terminal** (*see p363*) for information on all bus transportation from the city. For a more scenic route, travel by water: **NY Waterway** (*see p72*) offers service to areas outside Manhattan. If you want to drive, be forewarned that New York's car-rental rates are exorbitant. For more information on airports, buses, car rentals and trains, *see pp365–367*.

Beaches

Those seeking a quick, sun-kissed day trip can catch the subway to the boardwalk of Coney Island or Brighton Beach. However, serious swimmers will prefer Long Island's more scenic beaches. From Memorial Day (late May) to Labor Day weekend (early September), New Yorkers flock to summer rentals or day-trip destinations on Fire Island and in the Hamptons.

Nearby

When the city heats up, shore relief is only 45 minutes from Manhattan. Visitors head to **Jones Beach** (1-516-785-1600, www.jonesbeach.org) for picnicking and sunbathing. It's also the site of big-name-headliner summer music concerts. Closer still is **Long Beach** (1-516-431-1000, www.longbeachny.org), easily accessible by the LIRR. At the tip of the Rockaways peninsula is **Jacob Riis Park** (1-718-318-4300). Riis is a family-friendly beach at the western end and a gay nude beach at the eastern end, which almost touches Fire Island.

Getting there

Jacob Riis Park

Take the A train or the Rockaway S shuttle train to the last stop, Beach 116th St–Rockaway Park. (Note: The A train has three separate final destinations. Before you board, make sure your train terminates at Beach 116th St–Rockaway Park, not Far Rockaway–Mott Ave or Ozone Park–Lefferts Blvd.) Then walk one block to Rockaway Park Boulevard and take the Q22 bus to Jacob Riis Park.

Jones Beach

From late May through Labor Day, the **LIRR** offers a $14 package from Penn Station that covers round-trip train and bus fare, plus entry to the beach. Take the Babylon line of the LIRR to Freeport (change at Jamaica Station), then board a bus to the beach. Check the LIRR website for a schedule.

Long Beach

As with Jones Beach, the **LIRR** has a $15 deal from Penn Station that includes round-trip train fare and entry to the beach. Take the Long Beach line of the LIRR to its terminus; the beach is two blocks south of the station. Check the LIRR website for a schedule.

Fire Island

Long known as a summer hangout for the city's gay population, this narrow island is actually home to at least 15 different communities, each with its own name, identity and ferry stop. Why so many ferries? Because this skinny slip of land, a barrier beach between the Atlantic Ocean and the Great South Bay, is almost completely car-free; residents and visitors get around on foot or by bicycle, giving the island a mellow, laid-back vacation vibe. **Cherry**

Summertime, and the livin' is easy on the beach at **Robert Moses State Park**.

Grove and **Fire Island Pines** (commonly known as the Pines), at the eastern end of the island, are predominantly gay. Farther west are **Ocean Bay Park**, **Seaview** and **Ocean Beach**, the chosen playgrounds of college kids, young postgrads and many families. Ocean Beach has the most of what passes for nightlife on the island, plus a cute (if tiny) shopping district and bizarrely draconian laws governing public behavior: no picnicking, dogs or ball-playing on beaches. **Robert Moses State Park** (1-631-669-0449), located on the western tip, is a popular destination for day-trippers, thanks to its long stretch of white sand fronted by grassy dunes. Head east along the shore toward the lighthouse, and let it all hang out at the friendly nude beach. The island is almost exclusively a summer resort; most of the restaurants, bars, shops and hotels are open only from May to October.

Where to stay, eat & drink

The **Out Restaurant** (Bay Walk, Kismet, 1-631-583-7400, www.theoutrestaurant.com) offers a standard seafood menu. **Flynn's** (1 Cayuga St at Bayview Ave, Ocean Bay Park, 1-631-583-5000) is a partygoer's dream: cheap margaritas; DJs; live bands; a young,

boisterous crowd—and oh, yeah, decent seafood. Take an outside seat overlooking the water at **Maguire's** (1 Bay Walk, Ocean Beach, 1-631-583-8800) and enjoy the gussied-up pub grub. **Rachel's Bakery** (325 Bay Walk between Bungalow Walk and Ocean Rd, Ocean Beach, 1-631-583-9340, www.rachels fireisland.com) offers coffee, tasty breakfast pastries, cookies and brownies. If you don't know anyone with a summer rental, book a room at **Clegg's Hotel** (478 Bayberry Walk, Ocean Beach, NY 11770; 1-631-583-5399) or **Jerry's Accommodations** (168 Cottage Walk, Ocean Beach, NY 11770; 1-631-583-8870). In the Pines, guest rooms are available at **The Botel** (Harbor Walk, Fire Island Pines, NY 11782; 1-631-597-6500) or **Pines Place** (P.O. Box 5309, Fire Island Pines, NY 11782; 1-631-597-6162, www.pinesplace.com).

Getting there

Ocean Beach

By train Take the Montauk line of the **LIRR** (one way $8.25–$12.25) to Bay Shore, then take a van service ($3.50) to the ferry dock. *By van* **Tommy's Taxi** (1-631-665-4800) runs regular van service from various Manhattan locations (Mon–Sat round-trip $18, Sundays and holidays $21); reservations are required. *By ferry* From Bay Shore, take the **Fire**

Island Ferry (99 Maple Ave near Aldrich Ct, Bay Shore, 1-631-665-3600, www.fireislandferries.com; round-trip $12.50, children $6).

The Pines

By train Take the Montauk line of the **LIRR** (round-trip $15) to Sayville, then take a van ($3.50) to the ferry dock. *By bus* From May to October, **Islanders Horizon Coach & Buses** (1-212-228-7100, 1-631-654-2622, 1-888-839-0550, www.islanderstravel.com; one way $25) runs between Manhattan and the Sayville ferry station. *By ferry* From Sayville, take the **Sayville Ferry** (41 River Rd at Willow St, 1-631-589-0810, www.sayvilleferry.com; round-trip $12, children under 12 $6).

Robert Moses State Park

By train Take the Babylon line of the **LIRR** to Babylon and board a bus to the park. Buses run approximately every half hour on weekend days and hourly on weekdays.

The Hamptons

The south fork of Long Island was once home to sleepy fishing and farming towns far removed from the city rat race. Now the Hamptons are overrun every summer with the see-and-be-seen Manhattan crowd, and multimillion-dollar mansions sprawl where potatoes once grew. Fancy restaurants and nightclubs, posh shops and sunny beaches have become playgrounds for media moguls, socialites, artists and celebrity-gawkers. For an up-to-date social calendar, pick up the free local rags *Dan's Paper* or *The Independent,* available at area stores. The glossy *Hamptons Magazine* displays plenty of red-carpet pics from parties past. The *East Hampton Star* and the *Southhampton Press* carry local news. For more information, check the website for

The great indoors

Forgot to pack your favorite sunglasses or sparkly sandals? Need to refresh your beachside wardrobe? The Hamptons' trendy East End shops offer all the summer threads needed for a day by the shore or a night of partying. And once you've started shopping, you might have too much fun to make it to the beach.

Antony Todd Nina Griscom

28 Jobs Ln, Southampton (1-631-204-1100).
This swanky boutique is the joint venture of boldface names: party-circuit fixture Nina Griscom and floral designer Antony Todd. Inside the spare yet homey shop are antiques and dishware from around the world, as well as fresh blossoms.

Blue & Cream

60 The Circle, East Hampton (1-631-329-1392).
Proprietors Jeff Goldstein, a club promoter, and his ex-girlfriend Kira Cohen furnished their loungey store with couches and flat-screen TVs broadcasting favorite films like *Heathers* and *Breakfast at Tiffany's.* The shop is filled with girls' and guys' threads from such under-the-radar lines as Ulla Johnson, Twinkle and Ssurplus.

Catherine Malandrino

25 Newtown Ln, East Hampton (1-631-329-6990).
This Parisian clothier's East Hampton outpost—a Saint-Tropez-chic space with citrus-yellow shelving and a mirrored bed strewn with cushions—has a large selection of soiree-ready getups. Conscious of her constituency, Malandrino stocks the 1,000-square-foot shop with loads of beach-appropriate accessories.

East Coast Cowboy

47 Newtown Ln, East Hampton (1-631-329-7676).
Sick of pink and pretty? Head to this Western-biker-themed shop, opened by local leather experts Sarah VonFrank and Robert Curtis. The narrow storefront, outfitted with tan Ultrasuede walls and a cowhide rug, offers a collection of chunky boots, cowboy hats and rockabilly threads. The motocross-rodeo wares are perhaps best kept away from the sand, but VonFrank's wide-brimmed straw hats are beach-party perfect.

Elegant Setting

27 Main St, Southampton (1-631-283-4747).
Want to get invited back next weekend? Butter up your host with Elegant Setting's refined housewares. Longtime Hamptons weekender Stephanie Finkelstein adorned her quaint home shop with wainscoting, restored cabinets and alabaster-colored tin ceilings. She curates a collection of high-end new and vintage home beautifiers, including Hermès and Anna Weatherly china and William Yeoward glassware.

the Hamptons Visitors Council,
www.hamptonstravelguide.com.

During the summer, **Two Mile Hollow
Beach** (Two Mile Hollow Rd, East Hampton) is
a popular gay beach, while **Gibson Beach** and
Sagg Beach (both in Sagaponack) are packed
with post-collegiate, share-house types. Of
course, there are plenty of spas around to help
you get your body beachworthy. **Style Bar**
(1 Bay St at Marine Park Dr, Sag Harbor,
1-631-725-6730, www.stylebarspa.com) offers
Endermologie, a mechanical massage technique
that claims to be a cellulite reducer. Also
available are airbrushed faux tanning, the
Tutti-Frutti pedicure and more. Those looking
for mind-body relaxation should visit
Samadhi House Yoga Studio and Spa
(83 South Elmwood Ave at South Edison Ave,
second floor, Montauk, 1-631-668-5555,

www.samadhihouse.com). You can get your
pranayama on before or after your mani-pedi;
other indulgences include custom herbal
facials and Thai massage.

Montauk, a seaside village that's technically
part of East Hampton, has little in common with
its neighbors; the locals like to keep their ruffian
rep intact. The **Montauk Point Lighthouse**
(Montauk Pt at end of Rte 27, Montauk, 1-888-
685-7646, www.montauklighthouse.com) is the
oldest (built in 1796) in New York State, and
historic memorabilia are displayed inside.

Where to eat & drink

Dining out is a prime spectator sport in the
Hamptons, so be sure to book ahead if you want
to score a Friday- or Saturday-night table.
Named for its hotshot chef, **Starr Boggs**

Jackie Rogers

*3 Newtown Ln, East Hampton
(1-631-329-6923).*
If you're going to be hobnobbing with the
Botox-and-bling set, drop in here to get your
fancy duds. Park Avenue princesses swear
by Rogers, who comes here on weekends
to perform custom fittings and make last-
minute adjustments to her pricey black-tie-
worthy garments.

Scoop Beach for Men

*51 Newtown Ln, East Hampton
(1-631-329-6800).*
Superpopular Manhattan boutique Scoop
opened a second beachside property this
spring. Founder Stefani Greenfield planted
her new guys-only store two doors down
from the mobbed ladies' boutique, Scoop
Beach, which opened in 1999. The men's
shop, a shiny white space punctuated with
bright-yellow leather benches and a collage
of retro-style slogan tees displayed on one
wall, caters to vacationing guys too young to
be stuffy prepsters but too old to pull off the
surfer-stoner look.

Theory

*46 Newtown Ln, East Hampton
(1-631-324-3285).*
This sleek basics label rounds out the crop
of boutiques transplanted from Manhattan's
chic Soho neighborhood. What used to be
the Barefoot Contessa, a gourmet-food
emporium, is now a 3,000-square-foot store

Elegant Setting.

with sea-green hardwood floors and 1940s
sofas (perfect for parking that bored
boyfriend while you shop). Theory is well
stocked with polished summer threads as
well as stylish sunglasses, beauty products
and other beach-centered accoutrements
you won't find at the store's urban locations.

(6 Parlato Dr, West Hampton, 1-631-288-3500) is the latest must-go spot, with a seasonal seafood-focused menu. Heavy hitters head for the chef's table on the outdoor patio, where they can order the special tasting menu and be tended to by Boggs himself. **JLX Bistro** (16 Main St, Sag Harbor, 1-631-725-9100), wears a French-bistro uniform with a maritime twist. Executive chef Julio Quisbert goes from surf to turf with freshly shucked oysters, a soft-shell-crab sandwich and steak frites. **Fresno** (8 Fresno Pl, East Hampton, 1-631-324-8700) draws locals and weekenders alike with its outdoor garden and a menu featuring local delicacies like Montauk lobster, Long Island duck breast and North Fork wines. During dinner hours, popular new trattoria **Acqua Terre** (17 South Edison St, Montauk, 1-631-668-6828) is a bar and Northern Italian restaurant with live jazz; later, it becomes a full-fledged jazz and blues club.

Getting there

By train Take the Montauk line of the **LIRR** (one way $10.25–$15.25) to Southampton, East Hampton or Montauk. *By bus* The **Hampton Jitney** (1-800-936-0440, ww.hamptonjitney.com; one way $23–$27) runs regular service from four locations in Manhattan to stops in every town in the Hamptons.

Mountains

Urban dwellers longing for gorgeous valley views, quaint towns and lush foliage make year-round excursions to the glacier-formed mountainous region just north of Manhattan. Although a trip there and back can be made in a day, plan on at least two to enjoy all that the area affords.

Catskill Mountains

Established in 1904, **Catskill Park** is composed of both forest reserves and private land and spans more than 700,000 acres. Visit the area around the town of **Woodstock**, in northern Ulster county, where a new generation of artists, musicians and writers have taken up residence. The **Woodstock Film Festival** (www.woodstockfilmfestival.com) remains a top draw—screenings are

> ▶ **Time Out New York** publishes an annual Summer Getaways issue with info on places to go near the city. Find past years' articles at **www.timeoutny.com/archives**.

accompanied by celebrity panels and concerts. Near the town of **Saugerties**, ski enthusiasts can hit the slopes of **Hunter Mountain** (1-800-486-8376, www.huntermtn.com) and **Windham Mountain** (1-800-754-9463, www.skiwindham.com).

Where to stay, eat & drink

Satisfy your sweet tooth by grabbing breakfast at **Sweet Sue's** (Main St, Phoenicia, 1-845-688-7852), which boasts 22 kinds of pancakes. A creative American menu and outdoor patio draw weekend crowds to **Bear Café** (Rural Route 212, 295A Tinker St off Old Forge Rd, Bearsville, 1-845-679-5555), a short drive from the center of Woodstock. Stay at the **Woodstock Country Inn** (P.O. Box 704, Cooper Lake Rd, Woodstock, NY 12498; 1-845-679-9380, www.woodstockcountryinn.com), surrounded by rolling meadows, and hike to nearby **Cooper Lake**. The inn's staff will even provide transportation to and from the Trailways bus stop in town.

Getting there

By bus A two-and-a-half-hour ride from Port Authority lands you in the center of Woodstock. Check **Trailways** (1-800-858-8555; round-trip $44.10) for information and reservations. *By car* Take the New York State Thruway (I-87) to Exit 19, then Rte 375 to Woodstock (two hours). To get to Saugerties, take Exit 20. From there, you can take Route 32 north into town, or continue up and take the lovely winding Route 23A to Hunter and Windham Mountains.

Hudson Valley

Magnificent historic homes (and their sprawling estates) dot the hills overlooking the Hudson River. The **Historic Hudson Valley** (1-914-631-8200, www.hudsonvalley.org) maintains most of these sites, which are open to the public throughout much of the year.

Kykuit

Pocantico Hills, Tarrytown, NY 10591 (1-914-631-9491/www.hudsonvalley.org). **Open** *Late Apr–early Nov Mon, Wed–Sun 9am–3pm.* **Admission** *$22, seniors $20, children 10–17 $18; not recommended for children under 10.* **Credit** *AmEx, MC, V.*
John D. Rockefeller Jr.'s Kykuit, pronounced "KYE-kut," is located on the banks above the Hudson. In addition to the house and gardens, there are carefully maintained antique carriages and automobiles in the coach barn. Tickets are sold on a first-come, first-served basis at the Philipsburg Manor visitors' center (see website for directions), so arrive early.

Lyndhurst Castle

635 South Broadway, Tarrytown, NY 10591 (1-914-631-4481/www.lyndhurst.org). **Open** *Mid-Apr–Oct Tue–Sun, Mon holidays 10am–4:15pm. Nov–mid-Apr Sat, Sun, Mon holidays 10am–3:30pm.* **Admission** *$10, seniors $9, students 12–17 $4, children under 12 free; grounds only $4.* **Credit** *AmEx, MC, V.*
Several notable figures have called this Gothic Revival mansion home, including former New York City Mayor William Paulding and robber baron Jay Gould. The interior is sumptuously decorated and excellently maintained. From Grand Central, the estate is a scenic 40-minute trip by Metro-North (Hudson line) to Tarrytown and a five-minute taxi ride from the train station.

Olana

5720 Rte 9G, Hudson, NY 12534 (1-518-828-0135/ www.olana.org). **Open** *Apr–Nov Tue–Sun 10am–5pm, Jan–Mar Sat, Sun 10am–4pm. Dec Sat, Sun, holidays 10am–4pm.* **Admission** *$7, seniors $5, children 5–12 $2, children under 5 free.* **Credit** *MC, V.*
Hudson River School artist Frederic Church built his home here after seeing the views from the site. The richly colored design incorporates many Moorish touches. Reservations are strongly recommended.

Springwood

4097 Albany Post Rd off Rte 9, Hyde Park, NY 12538 (1-845-229-9115/www.nps.gov/hofr). **Open** *buildings 9am–5pm; grounds 7am–dusk; closed major holidays.* **Admission** *buildings $14, children under 16 free; grounds free.* **Credit** *AmEx, Disc, MC, V.*
Springwood, Franklin D. Roosevelt's boyhood home, is filled with family photos and the former President's artifacts. In the nearby library and museum, you can examine presidential documents and FDR's pony cart. Reservations are a good idea, since the house is accessible only by guided tour. You can call or make reservations online at reservations.nps.gov.

Sunnyside

West Sunnyside Ln off Rte 9, Tarrytown, NY 10591 (1-914-591-8763/1-914-631-8200/ www.hudsonvalley.org). **Open** *Mar Sat, Sun 10am–3pm. Apr–Oct Mon, Wed–Sun 10am–4pm. Nov, Dec Mon, Wed–Sun 10am–3pm.* **Admission** *$9, seniors $8, children 5–17 $5, children under 5 free.* **Credit** *AmEx, Disc, MC, V.*
Author Washington Irving renovated and expanded his little 18th-century Dutch Colonial cottage in Tarrytown, adding a stepped-gable entrance and a Spanish-style tower. To visit the cemetery of Sleepy Hollow, the village Irving immortalized in print, call for a taxi.

The headless horseman beckons you to Washington Irving's **Sunnyside** in Tarrytown.

Luck *is* a lady...in **Atlantic City**.

Vanderbilt Mansion

4097 Albany Post Rd, Hyde Park, NY 12538 (1-845-229-9115/www.nps.gov/vama). **Open** *9am–5pm daily; closed holidays.* **Admission** *$8, children under 16 free.* **Credit** *AmEx, Disc, MC, V.*
Compared with his siblings' opulent homes, Frederick Vanderbilt's estate is modest. Built on a bluff high above the river, the Greek Revival structure and its grounds offer sweeping views.

Where to stay, eat & drink

At the prestigious **Culinary Institute of America** (1946 Campus Dr, Hyde Park, 1-845-471-6608, www.ciachef.edu), young chefs-in-training prepare French, Italian, American contemporary and American regional cuisine in four different dining rooms. The CIA's **Apple Pie Bakery Café** is stocked with treats made by pastry majors. Rhinebeck's **Beekman Arms Inn** (6387 Mill St, Rhinebeck, NY 12572; 1-845-876-7077, 1-800-361-6517, www.beekmandelamaterinn.com) is the nation's oldest continuously operating hotel (more than 300 years), but the kitchen is au courant: Celeb chef (and CIA grad) Larry Forgione runs the Inn's **Traphagen Restaurant** (1-845-876-1766). Show up in the town of New Paltz with an appetite: **The Bakery** (13A North Front St off Rte 32, New Paltz 1-845-255-8840, www.ilovethebakery.com) offers excellent house-made sandwiches, salads and baked

goods. In Putnam County, the 1832 **Hudson House** (2 Main St, Cold Spring, NY 10516; 1-845-265-9355, www.hudsonhouseinn.com) is a peaceful, convenient inn with a notable contemporary American restaurant. Named after FDR's Scottish terrier, **Fala Bed and Breakfast** (38 E Market St, Hyde Park, NY 12538; 1-845-229-5937) is a private one-bedroom guest house with a swimming pool.

Getting there

By train Ask about special package rates from **NY Waterway**. **Metro-North** runs trains daily along the Hudson Valley; the Hudson line ends at Poughkeepsie, a 20-minute taxi ride from Rhinebeck. Alternatively, you can take **Amtrak** (*see p364*), but that's more expensive. *By bus* **Short Line Buses** (1-212-736-4700, 1-800-631-8405, www.shortline bus.com; round-trip $28.35) offers regular service to Hyde Park and Rhinebeck. Connecting service is available for some destinations. Check website for more info.

Casinos

These gambling resorts—only a short bus ride away—are your best, er, bets.

Atlantic City

Convention and Visitors Bureau, Atlantic City, NJ (1-888-228-4748/1-800-262-7392/www.atlantic citynj.com). Travel: Greyhound from Port Authority Bus Terminal (round-trip $27). Call 1-800-231-2222 for schedule.
Less fabulous than Las Vegas, this seaside resort in New Jersey still tries hard, with 13 casinos, headline entertainment, boxing matches, a famed boardwalk and the Miss America pageant.

Foxwoods

39 Norwich Westerly Rd, Mashantucket, CT 06338 (1-800-369-9663/www.foxwoods.com). Travel: Greyhound from Port Authority Bus Terminal (round-trip $26; includes $10 match-play coupon and $5 keno coupon). Call 1-800-231-2222 for schedule.
Opened in 1986 as a high-stakes bingo hall (purport-edly the world's largest), this enormous Connecticut casino now boasts 6,400 slots and 350 tables.

Mohegan Sun

1 Mohegan Sun Blvd, Uncasville, CT 06382 (1-888-226-7711/www.mohegansun.com). Travel: Academy Bus Tours from Port Authority Bus Terminal (round-trip $26; includes $10 food coupon and free match-play coupon). Call 1-800-442-7272 for schedule.
This massive (5.6-million-square-foot) casino has something for everyone: shopping, dining, cabaret, comedy and more than 6,000 slot machines.

Directory

Features

Directory

Getting to & from NYC

By air

Three major airports service the New York City area (there's also a smaller one on Long Island); for details, *see right* **Airports**. Here are a few sources for purchasing airline tickets.

Airlines

Air Canada 1-800-361-5373
Air France 1-800-237-2747
Alitalia 1-800-223-5730
American Airlines 1-800-433-7300
British Airways 1-800-247-9297
Delta Air Lines 1-800-221-1212
JetBlue Airways 1-800-538-2583
KLM 1-800-374-7747
Lufthansa 1-800-645-3880
Swissair 1-877-359-7947
United Airlines 1-800-241-6522
US Airways 1-800-428-4322
Virgin Atlantic 1-800-862-8621

Newspapers

If the travel section of your local paper is no help, get a Sunday *New York Times*. It will have plenty of advertisements for discounted fares.

Satellite Airlines Terminal

125 Park Ave between 41st and 42nd Sts (1-212-986-0888). Subway: 42nd St S, 4, 5, 6, 7 to 42nd St–Grand Central. Mon–Fri 8am–7pm; Sat 9am–5pm. This one-stop shop has ticket counters for major international airlines. You can redeem frequent-flier mileage; process passports, birth certificates and driver's licenses; and arrange for transportation and city tours. Call the information line above or individual carriers. **Other location** *Satellite Airlines Center, 1843 Broadway between 60th and 61st Sts.*

Travel agents

Agents are specialized, so find one who suits your needs. Do you want luxury? Are you traveling around the world? Are you a student? (*See p379* **Students**.) Find an agent through word of mouth, newspapers, the yellow pages phone directory or the Internet. Knowledgeable travel agents can help with far more than air tickets, and a good relationship with an agent can be invaluable, especially if you travel often and prefer not to deal with the details.

Websites

Sites to investigate for low fares:
www.airfare.com
www.cheaptickets.com
www.expedia.com
www.orbitz.com
www.priceline.com
www.travelocity.com
www.travelzoo.com

To & from the airport

For a list of transportation services between New York City and its major airports, call 1-800-247-7433. Public transport is the cheapest method, but it can be frustrating and time-consuming. Private bus or van services are usually the best bargains (*see p363* **Bus services**). Medallion (city-licensed) yellow cabs, which can be flagged on the street or at designated locations around the airports, are more expensive but offer convenient curb-to-door service. You may also reserve a car service in advance to pick you up or drop you off (*see p366* **Taxis & car services**). Although it is illegal, many car-service drivers and unlicensed "gypsy cabs" solicit riders around the baggage-claim areas. Avoid them.

Airports

John F. Kennedy International Airport

1-718-244-4444/www.panynj.gov.

At $2, the bus-and-subway link from JFK is dirt cheap, but it can take up to two hours to get to Manhattan. At the airport, look for the yellow shuttle bus to the Howard Beach station (free), then take the A train to Manhattan. In late 2003, JFK's AirTrain began offering service between all eight airport terminals and the A, E, J and Z subway lines, as well as the Long Island Rail Road, for $5. Visit www.airtrainjfk.com for more information. Private bus and van services are a good compromise between value and convenience (*see p363* **Bus services**). A medallion yellow cab from JFK to Manhattan will charge a flat $45 fare, plus toll (varies by route, but usually $4) and tip (if service is fine, give at least $5). Although metered (not a flat fee), the fare to JFK from Manhattan will be about the same cost. Check out www.nyc.gov/taxi for the latest rates.

La Guardia Airport

1-718-244-4444/www.panynj.gov.

Seasoned New Yorkers take the M60 bus ($2), which runs between the airport and 106th Street at Broadway. The ride takes 40 minutes to an hour (depending on traffic) and runs from 4:30am to 1:30am daily. The route crosses Manhattan at 125th Street in Harlem. Get off at Lexington Avenue for the 4, 5 and 6 trains; at Malcolm X Boulevard (Lenox Avenue) for the 2 and 3; or at St. Nicholas Avenue for the A, C, B and D trains. You can also disembark on Broadway at 116th or 110th Street for the 1 and 9 trains. Less time-consuming options: Private bus services cost around $14 (*see p363* **Bus services**); taxis and car services charge about $25, plus toll and tip.

Newark Liberty International Airport

1-973-961-6000/www.newark airport.com.

Although it's in next-door New Jersey, Newark has good mass-transit access to NYC. The best bet is a 40-minute, $11.55 trip by the New Jersey Transit to or from Penn Station. The airport's monorail, AirTrain Newark (www.airtrain newark.com), is now linked to the NJ Transit and Amtrak train systems. For inexpensive buses, *see below* **Bus services**. A car service will run about $40 and a taxi around $45, plus toll and tip.

MacArthur Airport

1-631-467-3210/www.macarthur airport.com.
Some flights into this airport in Islip, Long Island, may be cheaper than flights into those above. Getting to Manhattan, of course, will take longer and be more expensive. Colonial Transportation (1-631-589-3500) will take up to four people to Manhattan for $143, including tolls and tip. Visit the airport's website for other alternatives.

Bus services

New York Airport Service

1-212-875-8200/www.nyairport service.com. Call or visit website for schedule.
Buses operate frequently between Manhattan and both JFK (one way $15, round-trip $27) and La Guardia (one way $12, round-trip $21), from early morning to late at night, with stops near Grand Central Terminal (Park Ave between 41st and 42nd Sts), near Penn Station (33rd St at Seventh Ave), inside the Port Authority Bus Terminal (*see right* **By bus**) and outside a number of midtown hotels (for an extra charge). There are also buses that operate from JFK to La Guardia (one way $13).

Olympia Trails

1-212-964-6233/1-877-894-9155/ www.olympiabus.com. Call or visit website for schedule.
Olympia operates between Newark Airport and Manhattan, stopping outside Penn Station (34th St at Eighth Ave) and Grand Central (41st St between Park and Lexington Aves), and inside Port Authority (*see right* **By bus**). The fare is $12 one way (round-trip $19); buses leave every 15 to 20 minutes, all day and night.

SuperShuttle

1-212-209-7000/www.supershuttle. com. 24hrs daily.
Blue SuperShuttle vans offer door-to-door service between NYC and the three major airports. Allow extra time when catching a flight, as vans will be picking up other passengers. The fare varies from $13 to $22, depending on pickup location and destination. Always call to confirm.

By bus

Buses are an inexpensive means of getting to and from New York City, though the ride takes longer and is sometimes uncomfortable. Buses are particularly useful if you want to leave in a hurry; many don't require reservations. Most out-of-town buses come and go from the **Port Authority Bus Terminal**.

Bus stations

George Washington Bridge Bus Station

4211 Broadway between 178th and 179th Sts (1-800-221-9903/ www.panynj.gov). Subway: A, 1, 9 to 181st St. 5am–1am daily.
A few bus lines that serve New Jersey and Rockland County, New York, use this station.

Port Authority Bus Terminal

625 Eighth Ave between 40th and 42nd Sts (1-212-564-8484/ www.panynj.gov). Subway: A, C, E to 42nd St–Port Authority.
This is the hub for many transportation companies offering commuter and long-distance bus service to and from New York City. Call for additional information.

Long-distance lines

Greyhound Trailways

1-800-229-9424/www.greyhound. com. 24hrs daily. AmEx, DC, Disc, MC, V.
Greyhound offers long-distance bus travel to destinations across North America.

New Jersey Transit

1-973-762-5100/1-800-772-2222/ www.njtransit.com. Call or visit website for schedules. MC, V.
NJT provides bus service to nearly everywhere in the Garden State and some destinations in New York State; most buses run around the clock.

Peter Pan

1-800-343-9999/www.peterpanbus. com. 24hrs daily. MC, V.
Peter Pan runs extensive service to cities across the Northeast; its tickets are also valid on Greyhound.

By car

If you drive to the city, you may encounter delays at bridge and tunnel crossings (check **www.nyc.gov** and **www.panynj.gov** before driving in). Tune your car radio to **WINS** (1010 on the AM dial) for up-to-the-minute traffic reports. Delays can run anywhere from 15 inutes to 2 hours—plenty of time to get your money out for the toll ($4 is average). Note that street parking in the city is very restricted, especially in summer, so be prepared to shell out for a space in a parking garage (*see p364* **Parking**).

Car rental

For those interested in heading out of town by car, rentals are much cheaper in the city's outskirts and in New Jersey and Connecticut than in Manhattan; reserve ahead for weekends. Another way to save money is to rent from an independent agency, such as **Aamcar**. Log on to www.carrentalexpress.com for more independent companies.

New York State honors valid foreign-issued driver's licenses. All car-rental companies listed below add sales tax (8.625 percent). Companies located outside New York State offer a "loss damage waiver" (LDW). This is expensive, but without it, you are responsible for the cost of repairing even the slightest scratch. If you rent with a credit card, the LDW may be partially covered by your credit-card company; the LDW may also be covered by a reciprocal agreement with an automotive organization such as AAA. Personal-liability insurance is optional—and recommended (but see if your travel insurance or home policy already covers it).

Directory

Rental companies in New York are required by law to insure their own cars, so the LDW is not available. Instead, the renter pays for the first $100 in damage to the rental vehicle, and the company is responsible for anything beyond that. You will need a credit card (or a large cash deposit) to rent a car, and you usually have to be at least 25 years old. If you know you want to rent a car before you travel, ask your travel agent or airline to check for special deals and discounts.

Aamcar
315 W 96th St between West End Ave and Riverside Dr (1-800-722-6923/1-212-222-8500/ www.aamcar.com). Compact rates from $49.95 per day, unlimited mileage; $39.95 with 100 free miles. Mon–Fri 7:30am–7:30pm; Sat 9am–midnight; Sun 9am–5pm. AmEx, DC, Disc, MC, V.

Avis
1-800-230-4898/www.avis.com. 24hrs daily, most locations. Rates from $60 a day, unlimited mileage. AmEx, DC, Disc, MC, V.

Budget Rent-a-Car
1-800-527-0700/www.budget.com. In the city, call for hours; airport counters 5am–2am daily. Rates from $35 per weekday, $70 per day on weekends; unlimited mileage. AmEx, DC, Disc, MC, V.

Enterprise
1-800-325-8007/www.enterprise.com. Mon–Fri 7:30am–6pm; Sat 9am–noon. Rates from $30 per day outside New York City; around $50 per day in New York City; unlimited mileage restricted to New York, New Jersey and Connecticut. AmEx, DC, Disc, MC, V.
This inexpensive, reliable company has easily accessible branches outside Manhattan. Try the Greenwich, Connecticut, location (take Metro-North from Grand Central). Rental agents will pick you up at the station. Call or visit the website for locations within the five boroughs.

Parking
If you drive to NYC, then find a garage, park your car, and leave it there. Parking on the street is subject to byzantine

rules (for information on restrictions, call **311**); ticketing is rampant (if you can't decipher the parking signs, find another spot); and car theft is common. Garages are plentiful but expensive. If you want to park for less than $15 a day, try a garage outside Manhattan and take public transportation into the city. Listed below are Manhattan's better deals. For other options—there are many—try the yellow pages. (*See also p365* **Driving**.)

Central Kinney System
www.centralparking.com. 24hrs daily, most locations. AmEx, MC, V.
One of the city's largest parking companies, Kinney is accessible and reliable, though not the cheapest in town. Rates vary, so call for prices.

GMC Park Plaza
1-212-888-7400. 24hrs daily, most locations. AmEx, MC, V.
GMC has more than 70 locations in the city. At $23 overnight, including tax, the one at 407 E 61st Street between First and York Avenues (1-212-838-4158) is the least expensive.

Icon Parking
1-877-727-5464/www.icon parking.com. 24hrs daily, most locations. AmEx, MC, V.
Choose from more than 160 locations via the website to guarantee a spot and price ahead of time.

Mayor Parking
Pier 40, West St at W Houston St (1-800-494-7007). 24hrs daily. $16 for 12 hours. AmEx, MC, V.
Mayor Parking, another of the city's large chains, offers indoor and outdoor parking. Call for information and other locations.

By train

Thanks to America's love affair with the automobile, passenger trains are not as common here as in other parts of the world. American rails are used primarily for cargo, and passenger trains from New York are used mostly by commuters. For longer hauls, call **Amtrak**. (*See also pp353–360* **Trips Out of Town**.)

Train service

Amtrak
1-800-872-7245/www.amtrak.com. Amtrak provides all long-distance train service in North America. Traveling by Amtrak is more comfortable than by bus, but it's also less flexible and more expensive (a sleeper will likely cost more than flying). All trains depart from Penn Station.

Long Island Rail Road
1-718-217-5477/www.lirr.org. LIRR provides rail service from Penn Station, Brooklyn and Queens.

Metro-North
1-212-532-4900/1-800-638-7646/ www.mnr.org. Commuter trains service towns north of Manhattan and leave from Grand Central Terminal.

New Jersey Transit
1-973-762-5100/1-800-772-2222/ www.njtransit.com. Service from Penn Station reaches most of New Jersey, some points in New York State and Philadelphia.

PATH Trains
1-800-234-7284/www.pathrail.com. PATH (Port Authority Trans-Hudson) trains run from six stations in Manhattan to various places across the Hudson River in New Jersey, including Hoboken, Jersey City and Newark. The system is fully automated, and entry costs $1.50. You need change or crisp bills for the ticket machines, and trains run 24 hours a day. Manhattan PATH stations are marked on the subway map (*see p412*).

Train stations

Grand Central Terminal
From 42nd to 44th Sts, between Vanderbilt and Lexington Aves. Subway: 42nd St S, 4, 5, 6, 7 to 42nd St–Grand Central. Grand Central is home to Metro-North, which runs trains to more than 100 stations throughout New York State and Connecticut. Schedules are available at the terminal.

Penn Station
From 31st to 33rd Sts, between Seventh and Eighth Aves. Subway: A, C, E, 1, 2, 3, 9 to 34th St–Penn Station. Amtrak, Long Island Rail Road and New Jersey Transit trains depart from this terminal, which has printed schedules available.

Getting Around

Under normal circumstances, New York City is easy to navigate. However, subway and bus changes can occur at the last minute, so pay attention to the posters on subway station walls and listen carefully to any announcements you may hear in trains and on subway platforms.

Metropolitan Transportation Authority (MTA)
Travel info 1-718-330-1234/ hourly updates 1-718-243-7777/ www.mta.info.
The MTA runs the subway and bus lines, as well as a number of alternative commuter services to points outside Manhattan. You can get news of service interruptions and download the most current MTA maps from the website.

City buses

MTA buses are fine…if you're not in a hurry. They are white and blue and display a digital destination sign on the front along with a route number (in Manhattan, look for those that begin with an *M*). If your feet hurt from walking around, a bus is a good way to continue sightseeing. The $2 fare is payable with a **MetroCard** (*see right* **Subways**) or exact change (coins only; no pennies). The MTA's express buses usually head to the outer boroughs; these cost $4.

MetroCards allow automatic transfers from bus to bus and between buses and subways. If you use coins, and you're traveling uptown or downtown and want to go crosstown (or vice versa), ask the driver for a transfer when you get on—you'll be given a ticket for use on the second leg of your journey. Maps are posted on most buses and at all subway stations; they're

also available from **NYC & Company** (*see p384* **Websites**). The Manhattan Bus Map is reprinted in this guide (*see p411*). All buses are equipped with wheelchair lifts. Contact the MTA for further information.

Driving

Manhattan drivers (especially cabbies) are fearless; taking to the streets is not for the faint of heart. For details on the layout of Manhattan's streets, see *p367* **Walking**, and keep in mind that almost all even-numbered streets run east, while odd streets run west (major crosstown streets, such as 42nd, are two-way). Avenues run north-south. Try to restrict your driving to evening hours, when traffic is lighter and there's more street parking available. Even then, keep your eyes on the road and stay alert.

Street parking

Make sure you read the parking signs and never park within 15 feet (5 meters) of a fire hydrant (to avoid a $115 ticket and/or having your car towed). Parking is off-limits on most streets for at least a few hours each day. Even where meters exist, daytime parking can be restricted. The **Department of Transportation** (dial 311) provides information on daily changes to parking regulations. If precautions fail, call 1-718-935-0096 for NYC towing and impoundment information. (*See also p364* **Parking**.)

Emergency towing

Citywide Towing
514 W 39th St between Tenth and Eleventh Aves (1-212-244-4420).

24hrs daily; repairs 9am–5pm daily. MC, V.
All types of repairs are made on domestic and foreign autos.

24-hour gas stations

Exxon
24 Second Ave at 1st St (1-212-979-7000). AmEx, MC, V.
Repairs.

Hess
502 W 45th St at Tenth Ave (1-212-245-6594). AmEx, DC, Disc, MC, V.
No repairs.

Subways

The subway is the fastest way to get around town during the day, and it's far cleaner and safer than it was 20 years ago. The city's system is one of the world's largest and cheapest—$2 will get you from the depths of Brooklyn to the northernmost reaches of the Bronx and anywhere in between (though the subway doesn't service Staten Island). Trains run around the clock, but with sparse service and fewer riders at night, it's advisable (and usually quicker) to take a cab after 10pm.

Ongoing improvements have resulted in several changes. This guide provides the most current subway map at press time (*see pp412–414*), but you can also ask MTA workers in service booths for a free map.

To ensure safety, don't stand near the edge of the platform. Late nights and early mornings, board the train from the designated off-peak waiting area, usually near the middle of the platform; this area is more secure than the ends of the platforms or the outermost cars, which are often less populated at night. Standard urban advisory: Hold your bag with the opening facing you or keep your wallet in a front pocket, and don't wear flashy jewelry. Remember, petty crime increases during the holidays.

MetroCards

To enter the subway system, you need a **MetroCard** (it also works on buses), which you can buy from a booth inside the station entrance or from one of the brightly colored MetroCard vending machines that accept cash, debit cards and credit cards (AmEx, Disc, MC, V). Free transfers between buses and subways are only available with a MetroCard.

There are two types of cards: **pay-per-use** and **unlimited-ride**. Any number of passengers can use a pay-per-use card, which is sold in denominations from $4 (two trips) to $80. A $20 card offers 12 trips for the price of 10. If you're planning to use the subway or buses often, the unlimited-ride MetroCard is a great value (although at press time, the MTA was planning to raise rates on unlimited-ride cards in 2005). These cards are offered in three amounts: a 1-day **Fun Pass** ($7, available at station vending machines but not at booths), a **7-day pass** ($21) and a **30-day pass** ($70). These are good for unlimited rides, but you can't share a card with your travel companions, since you can only swipe it once every 18 minutes at a given subway station or on a bus.

Subway lines

Trains are identified by letters or numbers and are color-coded according to the line on which they run. Stations are most often named for the street at which they're located. Entrances are marked with a green globe (open 24 hours) or a red globe (limited hours). Many stations have separate entrances for the uptown and downtown platforms—look before you pay.

Local trains stop at every station on the line; express trains make major-station stops only. Check a subway map (posted in all stations and trains and available for free at service booths; *see also pp412–414*) before you board. Keep an eye out for posted notices indicating temporary changes along a particular line.

Taxis & car services

Taxicabs

Yellow cabs are hardly ever in short supply—except, of course, at rush hour and in nasty weather. Use only yellow medallion (licensed) cabs; avoid unregulated gypsy cabs. If the center light on top of the taxi is lit, that means the cab is available and it should stop if you flag it down. Jump in and *then* tell the driver where you're going. (New Yorkers generally give cross streets rather than addresses—for an explanation of the city's streets, *see p367* **Walking**.)

Taxis carry up to four people for the same price: $2.50 plus 40¢ per fifth of a mile, with an extra 50¢ charge from 8pm to 6am and a $1 surcharge during rush hour (weekdays from 4 to 8pm). The average fare for a three-mile (4.5 kilometer) ride is $9 to $11, depending on the time of day and on traffic (the meter adds another 20¢ per minute while the car is idling). Cabbies rarely allow more than four passengers in a cab (it's illegal, unless the fifth person is a child under age seven), though it may be worth asking.

Not all drivers know their way around the city, so it helps if you know where you're going—and speak up. By law, taxis cannot refuse to take you anywhere inside the five boroughs or to New York airports, so don't be duped by a reluctant cabbie. They may still refuse; to avoid an argument, get out and try another cab. If you have a problem, take down the medallion and driver's numbers, posted on the partition. Always ask for a receipt—there's a meter number on it. To complain or to trace lost property, call the **Taxi & Limousine Commission** (1-212-227-0700, Mon–Fri 8am–4pm) or visit the website, www.nyc.gov/taxi. In general, tip 15 percent, as you would at a restaurant, or 20 percent if the service is great.

Late at night, cabs stick to fast-flowing routes. Try the avenues and key streets (Canal, Houston, 14th, 23rd, 34th, 42nd, 57th, 72nd and 86th). Bridge and tunnel exits are also good for a steady flow of taxis returning from airports, and available cabbies will usually head for nightclubs and big hotels. Otherwise, try the following:

Chinatown
Chatham Square, where Mott Street meets the Bowery, is an unofficial taxi stand. You can also try hailing a cab exiting the Manhattan Bridge at Bowery and Canal Street.

Lincoln Center
The crowd heads toward Columbus Circle for a cab; those in the know go west to Amsterdam Avenue.

Lower East Side
Katz's Deli (Houston St at Ludlow St) is a cabbies' hangout; also try Delancey Street, where cabs come in over the Williamsburg Bridge.

Midtown
Penn Station, Grand Central Terminal and the Port Authority Bus Terminal attract cabs all night.

Soho
If you're on the west side, try Sixth Avenue; east side, the intersection of Houston Street and Broadway.

Times Square
This busy area has 30 taxi stands—look for the yellow globes atop nine-foot poles.

Tribeca

Cabs head up Hudson Street. The Tribeca Grand (2 Sixth Ave between Walker and White Sts) is also a good bet.

Car services

Car services, too, are regulated by the Taxi & Limousine Commission (*see p366*). Unlike cabs, the cars aren't yellow and drivers can make only prearranged pickups. If you see a black Lincoln Town Car, it most likely belongs to a car service. Don't try to hail one, and be wary of those that offer you a ride; they may not be licensed or insured, and you could get ripped off.

The following companies will pick you up anywhere in the city, at any time of day or night, for a set fare.

Carmel

1-212-666-6666.

Dial 7

1-212-777-7777.

Tri-State Limousine

1-212-777-7171/1-212-410-7600.

Walking

One of the best ways to take in NYC is on foot. Most of the streets are laid out in a grid pattern and are relatively easy to navigate. Our maps (*see pp400–410*) make it even easier. Manhattan is divided into three major sections: **downtown**, which includes all neighborhoods south of 14th Street; **midtown**, roughly the area between 14th and 59th Streets; and **uptown**, north of 59th Street.

Generally, avenues run north-south along the length of Manhattan. They are parallel to one another and are logically numbered, with a few exceptions, such as Broadway, Columbus and Lexington Avenues. Manhattan's center is Fifth Avenue, so all buildings located east of it will have "East" addresses, with numbers getting higher toward the East River, and those west of it will have "West" numbers that get higher toward the Hudson River. Streets are also parallel to one another, but they run east to west, or **crosstown**, and are numbered, from 1st Street up to 220th Street.

The neighborhoods of lower Manhattan—including the **Financial District**, **Tribeca**, **Chinatown** and **Greenwich Village**— were settled prior to urban planning and can be confusing to walk through. Their charming lack of logic makes the use of a map essential.

Resources A to Z

Age restrictions

In most cases, you must be at least 25 years old to rent a car in the U.S. In NYC, you must be 18 to buy tobacco products and 21 to buy or to be served alcohol. Some bars and clubs will admit patrons who are between 18 and 21, but you will be removed from the establishment if you are caught drinking alcohol (carry a picture ID at all times). The age of sexual consent in New York is 17. You must be 18 to purchase pornography and other adult material, to play the lottery or to gamble (where the law allows).

Babysitting

The Baby Sitters' Guild

1-212-682-0227/www.babysitters guild.com. Bookings: 9am–9pm daily. Cash only.
Long- or short-term multilingual sitters cost $20 and up per hour (four-hour minimum), plus cab fare (around $10). Babysitters are available around the clock.

Pinch Sitters

1-212-260-6005. Bookings: Mon–Fri 8am–5pm. Cash only.
Charges are $16 per hour (four-hour minimum), plus cab fare after 9pm ($10 maximum).

Business

Consumer information

Better Business Bureau

1-212-533-6200/ www.newyork.bbb.org.
The BBB offers advice on consumer-related complaints (shopping, services, etc.). Each phone inquiry costs $5 (plus New York City tax) and must be charged to a credit card; the online service is free.

New York City Department of Consumer Affairs

42 Broadway between Beaver St and Exchange Pl (311/1-212-487-4110). Subway: 4, 5 to Bowling Green. Mon–Fri 9am–5pm.
File complaints on consumer-related matters here.

Messenger services

A to Z Couriers

106 Ridge St between Rivington and Stanton Sts (1-212-253-6500/ www.atozcouriers.com). Subway: F to Delancey St; J, M, Z to Delancey–Essex Sts. Mon–Fri 8am–8pm. AmEx, MC, V.
These cheerful couriers will deliver in the city (and on Long Island).

Breakaway

335 W 35th St between Eighth and Ninth Aves (1-212-947-4455/www. breakawaycourier.com). Subway: A, C, E to 34th St–Penn Station. Mon–Fri 7am–9pm; Sat 9am–5pm; Sun noon–5pm. AmEx, MC, V.
Breakaway is a highly recommended local delivery service that promises to pick up and deliver within 90 minutes.

Jefron Messenger Service

55 Walker St between Church St and West Broadway (1-212-431-6610/ www.jefron.com). Subway: 1, 2, 3, 9 to Chambers St. Mon–Fri 4am–8pm. Cash only.
Jefron specializes in transporting import and export documents.

Photocopying & printing

Dependable Printing
10 E 22nd St at Broadway (1-212-533-7560). Subway: N, R, W to 23rd St. Mon–Fri 8:30am–7pm; Sat 10am–4pm. AmEx, MC, V.
Dependable provides offset, laser and color printing; fax service; large-format photocopies; binding; and more.
Other location *71 W 23rd St between Fifth and Sixth Aves (1-646-336-6999).*

FedEx Kinko's
See right **Computers.**

Fitch Graphics
See right **Computers.**

Servco
1150 Sixth Ave between 44th and 45th Sts (1-212-575-0991). Subway: B, D, F, V to 47–50th Sts–Rockefeller Ctr; 7 to Fifth Ave. Mon–Fri 8:30am–8pm.
Photocopying, offset printing, blueprints and binding services are available.

City information

Citizen Service Center
311. 24hrs daily.
The city's nonemergency help line. Questions (on, say, parking rules or parade hours, changes to subway service) and complaints (blocked driveway, noisy revelers) can be handled in 171 different languages.

Computers

There are hundreds of computer dealers in Manhattan. However, many out-of-state dealers advertise in New York papers and magazines, so you might consider buying from them to avoid the hefty sales tax (8.625 percent). A few reliable places for rentals or repairs are listed below:

Computer Solutions Provider
45 W 21st St between Fifth and Sixth Aves, second floor (1-212-463-
9744/www.cspny.com). Subway: F, V, N, R, W to 23rd St. Mon–Fri 9am–6pm. AmEx, MC, V.
Specialists in Macs, PCs and related peripherals, CSP staffers can recover lost data and help you through other computer disasters; they even make house calls.

FedEx Kinko's
240 Central Park South at Broadway (1-212-258-3750/1-800-254-6567/ www.fedexkinkos.com). Subway: A, C, B, D, 1, 9 to 59th St–Columbus Circle. 24hrs daily. AmEx, DC, Disc, MC, V.
This is a very efficient computer and copy center. Most branches have Windows and Macintosh workstations and design stations, plus Internet connection and all the major software ($18 per hour). Printing is available (color, 89¢ per page; black-and-white, 50¢), as are laptop hookups ($6 per hour). Check the phone book for other locations.

Fitch Graphics
229 W 28th St between Seventh and Eighth Aves (1-800-332-1237/ www.fitchgroup.com). Subway: 1, 9 to 28th St. Mon–Fri 9am–5pm. AmEx, MC, V.
Fitch is a full-service desktop-publishing outfit with color laser output and prepress facilities. Fitch works on Mac and Windows platforms and has an electronic bulletin board so customers can reach the shop online.

USRental.com
1-800-877-3672/www.usrental.com. Mon–Fri 9am–5pm. AmEx, MC, V.
Rent by the day, week, month or year. Rush delivery service (within three hours) is also available.

Consulates

Check the phone book for a complete list of consulates and embassies. *See also p382* **Travel advice.**

Australia
1-212-351-6500.

Canada
1-212-596-1628.

Great Britain
1-212-745-0200.

Ireland
1-212-319-2555.

New Zealand
1-212-832-4038.

Directory

Customs & immigration

When planning your trip, check with a U.S. embassy or consulate to see whether you need a visa to enter the country (*see p377* **Passport alert**). Standard immigration regulations apply to all visitors arriving from outside the United States, which means you may have to wait at least an hour in customs upon arrival. Owing to tightened security at American airports, you can expect even slower-moving lines. During your flight, you will be handed immigration and customs-declaration forms to be presented to an official when you land.

You may be expected to explain your visit, so be polite and prepared. You will usually be granted an entry permit to cover the length of your stay. Work permits are hard to get, and you are not allowed to work without one (*see right* **Student immigration**).

U.S. Customs allows foreigners to bring in $100 worth of gifts (the limit is $800 for Americans) without paying duty. One carton of 200 cigarettes (or 50 cigars) and one liter of liquor (spirits) are allowed. Plants, meat and fresh produce cannot be brought into the country. You will have to fill out a form if you carry more than $10,000 in currency.

If you must bring prescription drugs into the U.S., make sure the container is clearly marked, and bring your doctor's statement or a prescription. Marijuana, cocaine and most opiate derivatives, along with a number of other drugs and chemicals, are not permitted: Possession of them is punishable by a stiff fine and/or imprisonment. Check with the **U.S. Customs Service** (www.customs.gov) before you arrive if you have any questions

about what you can bring. If you lose or need to renew your passport once inside the U.S., contact your country's embassy (*see p368* **Consulates**).

Student immigration

Upon entering the U.S. as a student, you will need to show a passport, a special visa and proof of your plans to leave (such as a return airline ticket).

Before applying for a visa, nonnationals who want to study in the U.S. must obtain an I-20 Certificate of Eligibility from the school or university they plan to attend. If you are enrolling in an authorized visitor-exchange program, including summer courses, wait until you have been accepted before worrying about immigration. The school will guide you through the process.

You are admitted as a student for the length of your course. Requests for any extension or change must be submitted 30 days before your completion date. Approval is granted jointly between your school and the U.S. Citizenship and Immigration Services (*see below*). You may be allowed to stay in the country for an additional 12 months after completing your course work, to pursue practical training. At the completion of your studies or training, you will be given 60 days to prepare to leave the country, unless you are granted a change to, or an extension of, your immigration status. The rules are strict, and you risk deportation if you break them.

Information on these and all other immigration matters is available from the **U.S. Citizenship and Immigration Services** (USCIS). The agency's 24-hour hotline (1-800-375-5283) has a vast menu of recorded information in English and Spanish; advisers are available from 8am to 6pm, Monday through Friday.

You can visit the USCIS at its New York office, located in the Jacob Javits Federal Building (26 Federal Plaza, Broadway between Duane and Worth Sts, third floor). The office is open 7:30am to 3:30pm, Monday through Friday, and cannot be reached directly by telephone.

The **U.S. Embassy** also offers guidance on obtaining student visas (*see p382* **Visas**). Or in the U.K., you can write to the Visa Branch of the Embassy of the United States of America (Attn: Nonimmigrant visa section; 24 Grosvenor Sq, London W19 19E).

When you apply for a student visa, you'll be expected to prove your means of financial support (including the payment of school fees) without working for at least the first full academic year of your studies. After those nine months, you may be eligible to hold a part-time job, but you must have specific permission (again from both your school and the USCIS) to do so.

If you are a student from the U.K. who wants to spend a summer vacation working in the States, then contact the **British Universities North America Club** (BUNAC) for help in arranging a temporary job and the requisite visa (16 Bowling Green Ln, London EC1R 0QH; 020-7251-3472, www.bunac.org/uk).

Disabled access

Under New York City law, all facilities constructed after 1987 must provide complete access for the disabled—restrooms, entrances and exits included. In 1990, the Americans with Disabilities Act made the same requirement federal law. In the wake of this legislation, many older buildings have added disabled-access features. There has been widespread (though imperfect) compliance with the

Directory

law, so it's always a good idea to call ahead and check.

New York can be challenging for a disabled visitor. One useful resource is *Access for All*, a guide to New York's cultural institutions published by **Hospital Audiences Inc.** (1-212-575-7660, www.hospaud. org). The online guide tells how accessible each location really is and includes information on the height of telephones and water fountains; hearing and visual aids; and passenger-loading zones and alternative entrances. HAI's service for the visually impaired provides descriptions of theater performances on audiocassettes.

All Broadway theaters are equipped with devices for the hearing impaired; call **Sound Associates** (1-212-582-7678, 1-888-772-7686) for more information. There are a number of other stage-related resources for the disabled. Call **Telecharge** (1-212-239-6200) to reserve tickets for wheelchair seating in Broadway and Off Broadway venues. **Theatre Development Fund's Theater Access Project** (1-212-221-1103, www.tdf.org) arranges sign-language interpretation and captioning in American Sign Language for Broadway and Off Broadway shows. **Hands On** (1-212-740-3087, www.handson.org) does the same.

Lighthouse International
111 E 59th St between Park and Lexington Aves (1-800-829-0500/ www.lighthouse.org). Subway: N, R, W to Lexington Ave–59th St; 4, 5, 6 to 59th St. Mon–Fri 10am–6pm; Sat 10am–5pm.
In addition to running a store that sells handy items for the vision-impaired, this organization provides helpful information for blind residents of and visitors to New York City.

Mayor's Office for People with Disabilities
100 Gold St between Frankfort and Spruce Sts, second floor (1-212-788-2830). Subway: J, M, Z to Chambers

St; 4, 5, 6 to Brooklyn Bridge–City Hall. Mon–Fri 9am–5pm.
This city office provides a broad range of services for the disabled.

New York Society for the Deaf
161 William St between Ann and Beekman Sts (1-212-777-3900/ www.nysd.org). Subway: A, C to Broadway–Nassau St; J, M, Z, 2, 3, 4, 5 to Fulton St. Mon–Thu 9am–5pm; Fri 9am–4:30pm.
The deaf and hearing-impaired come here for information and services.

The Society for Accessible Travel and Hospitality
347 Fifth Ave between 33rd and 34th Sts, suite 610 (1-212-447-7284/www.sath.org). Subway: B, D, F, V, N, Q, R, W to 34th St–Herald Sq.
This nonprofit group was founded in 1976 to educate the public about travel facilities for people with disabilities and to promote travel for the disabled worldwide. Membership is $45 a year ($30 for seniors and students) and includes access to an information service and a quarterly travel magazine. No drop-ins; membership by mail only.

Electricity

The U.S. uses 110–120V, 60-cycle alternating current rather than the 220–240V, 50-cycle AC used in Europe and elsewhere. The transformers that power or recharge many newer electronic devices such as laptop computers are designed to handle either current and may need nothing more than an adapter for the wall outlet. However, most electrical appliances, including hairdryers, will require a power converter as well. Adapters and converters of various sorts are available at airport shops, at several pharmacies and department stores, and at **Radio Shack** branches around the city (consult the phone book for store locations).

Emergencies

Ambulance
In an emergency only, dial **911** for an ambulance or call the operator (dial **0**). To complain about slow emergency

service or poor treatment, call the **Fire Department Complaint Hotline** (1-718-999-2646).

Fire
In an emergency only, dial **911**.

Police
In an emergency only, dial **911**. For the location of the nearest police precinct or for general information about police services, call 1-646-610-5000.

Health & medical facilities

The public health-care system is virtually nonexistent in the United States, and private health care is prohibitively expensive. If possible, make sure you have comprehensive medical insurance when you travel to New York.

Clinics

Walk-in clinics offer treatment for minor ailments. Most require immediate payment, though some will send their bill directly to your insurance company if you're a U.S. resident. You will have to file a claim to recover the cost of prescription medication.

D•O•C•S
55 E 34th St between Madison and Park Aves (1-212-252-6000). Subway: 6 to 33rd St. Walk-in Mon–Thu 8am–8pm; Fri 8am–7pm; Sat 9am–3pm; Sun 9am–2pm. Extended hours by appointment. Base fee $135–$300. AmEx, Disc, MC, V.
These excellent primary-care facilities, affiliated with Beth Israel Medical Center, offer by-appointment and walk-in services. If you need X-rays or lab tests, go as early as possible—no later than 6pm—Monday through Friday.
Other locations *202 W 23rd St at Seventh Ave (1-212-352-2600); 1555 Third Ave at 88th St (1-212-828-2300).*

Dentists

NYU College of Dentistry
345 E 24th St between First and Second Aves (1-212-998-9872/off-hours emergency care 1-212-998-

9828). *Subway: 6 to 23rd St.*
Mon–Thu 8:30am–7pm; Fri
8:30am–3pm. Base fee $90. Disc,
MC, V.
If you need your teeth fixed on a
budget, the final-year students here
are slow but proficient, and an
experienced dentist is always on
hand to supervise. Go before 2pm to
ensure a same-day visit.

Emergency rooms

You will be billed for
emergency treatment. Call
your travel-insurance
company's emergency number
before seeking treatment to
find out which hospitals accept
your insurance. Emergency
rooms are always open at:

Cabrini Medical Center

227 E 19th St between Second and
Third Aves (1-212-995-6000).
Subway: L to Third Ave; N, Q, R, W,
4, 5, 6 to 14th St–Union Sq.

Mount Sinai Hospital

Madison Ave at 100th St (1-212-
241-7171). Subway: 6 to 103rd St.

New York–Presbyterian Hospital/Weill Cornell Medical Center

525 E 68th St at York Ave (1-212-
746-5454). Subway: 6 to 68th St.

St. Luke's–Roosevelt Hospital

1000 Tenth Ave at 59th St
(1-212-523-6800). Subway:
A, C, B, D, 1, 9 to 59th St–
Columbus Circle.

St. Vincent's Hospital

153 W 11th St at Seventh Ave
(1-212-604-7998). Subway:
F, V, 1, 2, 3, 9 to 14th St;
L to Sixth Ave.

Gay & lesbian health

See p300 **Centers &
help lines**.

House calls

NY Hotel Urgent Medical Services

952 Fifth Ave between 76th and 77th
Sts, suite 1D (1-212-737-1212/www.

travelmd.com). Subway: 6 to 77th St.
24 hrs daily; appointments required.
Weekday hotel-visit fee $175–$450;
weekday office-visit fee $55–$165
(higher for nights and weekends).
AmEx, MC, V.
Dr. Ronald Primas and his partners
provide medical attention right
in your Manhattan hotel room or
private residence. Whether you
need a simple prescription, urgent
medical care or a thorough
examination, this service can
provide a specialist.

Pharmacies

See also p235 **Pharmacists**.
Be aware that pharmacies
will not refill foreign
prescriptions.

Duane Reade

224 W 57th St at Broadway (1-212-
541-9708/www.duanereade.com).
Subway: N, Q, R, W to 57th St.
24hrs daily. AmEx, MC, V.
This chain operates all over the
city, and some stores are open
24 hours. Check the website for
additional branches.
Other 24-hour locations
24 E 14th St at University Pl (1-212-
989-3632); 155 E 34th St at Third
Ave (1-212-683-3042); 1279 Third
Ave at 74th St (1-212-744-2668);
2465 Broadway at 91st St (1-212-
799-3172).

Rite Aid

303 W 50th St at Eighth Ave
(1-212-247-8736/www.riteaid.com).
Subway: C, E to 50th St. 24hrs daily.
AmEx, Disc, MC, V.
Select stores have 24-hour
pharmacies. Call 1-800-748-3243
or check the website for a listing of
all branches.
Other 24-hour locations
408 Grand St at Clinton St (1-212-
529-7115); 301 W 50th St at
Eighth Ave (1-212-247-8384);
146 E 86th St between Lexington
and Third Aves (1-212-876-0600);
2833 Broadway at 110th St
(1-212-663-3135).

STDs, HIV & AIDS

Chelsea Clinic

303 Ninth Ave at 28th St (1-212-
239-1718/1-212-239-0843).
Subway: C, E to 23rd St. Mon–Fri
8:30am–4:30pm; Sat 9am–2pm.
Since the hours of walk-in clinics
may change, you should call ahead
before visiting. Arrive early, because
testing is offered on a first-come,
first-served basis. (Check the phone
book or see www.nyc.gov for other
free clinics.)

Women's health

Liberty Women's Health Care of Queens

37-01 Main St at 37th Ave,
Flushing, Queens (1-718-888-0018/
www.libertywomenshealth.com).
Subway: 7 to Flushing–Main St. By
appointment only. MC, V.
This facility provides surgical
and nonsurgical abortions until the
24th week of pregnancy. Unlike
many other clinics, Liberty uses
abdominal ultrasound before,
during and after the abortion to
ensure safety.

Parkmed Eastern Women's Center

44 E 30th St between Madison Ave
and Park Ave South, fifth floor
(1-212-686-6066/www.eastern
womenscenter.com). Subway: 6 to
28th St. By appointment only.
AmEx, Disc, MC, V.
Urine pregnancy tests are free.
Counseling, contraception services
and nonsurgical abortions are
also available.

Planned Parenthood of New York City

Margaret Sanger Center, 26
Bleecker St at Mott St (1-212-965-
7000/1-800-230-7526/www.
ppnyc.org). Subway: B, D, F, V to
Broadway–Lafayette St; N, R, W to
Prince St; 6 to Bleecker St. Mon,
Tue 8am–4:30pm; Wed–Fri
8am–6:30pm; Sat 7:30am–4:30pm.
AmEx, MC, V.
This is the best-known, most
reasonably priced network of family-
planning clinics in the U.S. Counseling and treatment are available for a
full range of needs, including
abortion, contraception, HIV testing
and treatment of STDs. Call for more
information on other services
or to make an appointment at any
of the centers. Walk-ins are welcome
for emergency contraception and free
pregnancy tests.
Other locations *44 Court St*
between Joralemon and Remsen
Sts, Brooklyn Heights, Brooklyn;
349 E 149th St at Courtlandt
Ave, Bronx.

Help lines

Alcohol & drug abuse

Alcoholics Anonymous

1-212-647-1680. 9am–10pm daily.

Cocaine Anonymous

24-hour recorded info
1-212-262-2463.

Directory

Drug Abuse Information Line

1-800-522-5353. 8am–10pm daily.
This hotline refers callers to recovery programs around the state as well as to similar programs in the rest of the U.S.

Pills Anonymous

24-hour recorded info 1-212-874-0700.
You'll find information on drug-recovery programs for users of marijuana, cocaine, alcohol and other addictive substances, as well as referrals to Narcotics Anonymous meetings. You can also leave a message so that a counselor can call you back.

Child abuse

Childhelp USA's National Child Abuse Hotline

1-800-422-4453. 24hrs daily.
Counselors provide general crisis consultation and can help in an emergency. Callers include abused children, runaways and parents having problems with children.

Gay & lesbian

See p300 **Centers & help lines**.

Health

Visit the **Centers for Disease Control and Prevention** (CDC) website (www.cdc.gov) for up-to-date national health information, or call one of the toll-free hotlines below.

National STD & AIDS Hotline

1-800-342-2437. 24hrs daily.

Travelers' Health

1-877-394-8747 or visit CDC website. 24hrs daily.
Provides alerts on disease outbreaks and other information via a recording.

Psychological services

The Samaritans

1-212-673-3000. 24hrs daily.
People thinking of committing suicide or suffering from depression, grief, sexual anxiety or alcoholism can call this organization for advice.

Rape & sex crimes

Safe Horizon Crisis Hotline

1-212-577-7777/www.safe horizon.org. 24hrs daily.
SH offers telephone and in-person counseling for any victim of domestic violence, rape or other crime, as well as practical help with court procedures, compensation and legal aid.

Special Victims Liaison Unit of the New York Police Department

Rape hotline 1-212-267-7273. 24hrs daily.
Reports of sex crimes are fielded by a female detective from the Special Victims Liaison Unit. She will inform the appropriate precinct, send an ambulance if requested, and provide counseling and medical referrals. Other issues handled: violence against gays and lesbians, child victimization, and referrals for the families and friends of crime victims.

St. Luke's–Roosevelt Hospital Crime Victims Treatment Center

1-212-523-4728. Mon–Fri 9am–5pm.
The Rape Crisis Center provides a trained volunteer who will accompany you through all aspects of reporting a rape and getting emergency treatment.

Holidays

See left **Holidays**.

Insurance

If you are not an American, it's advisable to take out comprehensive insurance before arriving here; insurance for foreigners is almost impossible to arrange in the U.S. Make sure you have adequate health coverage; medical costs are high. For a list of New York urgent-care facilities, *see p371* **Emergency rooms**.

Internet

Internet access

Cyber Café

250 W 49th St between Broadway and Eighth Ave (1-212-333-4109). Subway: C, E, 1, 9 to 50th St; N, R, W to 49th St. Mon–Fri 8am–11pm; Sat, Sun 11am–11pm. $6.40 per half hour; 50¢ per printed page. AmEx, MC, V.
This is a standard Internet-access café that serves great coffee.

Holidays

Most banks and government offices close on major U.S. holidays, but stores, restaurants and some museums are usually open. If you will be in New York during or around a holiday, be sure to call the venues you plan to visit to check for special hours.

New Year's Day
January 1

Martin Luther King Day
third Monday in January

Presidents' Day
third Monday in February

Memorial Day
last Monday in May

Independence Day
July 4

Labor Day
first Monday in September

Columbus Day
second Monday in October

Veterans Day
November 11

Thanksgiving Day
fourth Thursday in November

Christmas Day
December 25

FedEx Kinko's
See p368 **Computers**.

New York Public Library
See p162 for listing.
The branch libraries throughout the five boroughs are great places to e-mail and surf the Web for free. However, the scarcity of computer stations may make for a long wait, and user time is limited. The Science, Industry and Business Library, 188 Madison Avenue at 34th Street, has more than 40 workstations that you can use for up to an hour per day.

Wi-Fi

NYC Wireless
www.nycwireless.net.
This group has established 113 nodes in the city for free wireless access. (For example, most parks below 59th Street are covered.) Visit the website for more information.

Starbucks
www.starbucks.com. AmEx, MC, V.
Many branches offer wireless access through T-Mobile (10¢ per minute).

Laundry

See also p382 **Wardrobe services**.

Dry cleaners

Madame Paulette Custom Couture Cleaners
1255 Second Ave between 65th and 66th Sts (1-212-838-6827). Subway: 6 to 68th St–Hunter College. Mon–Fri 7:30am–7pm; Sat 8am–5pm. AmEx, MC, V.
After more than 50 years in business, this luxury dry cleaner knows how to treat delicate garments. Take advantage of free pickup and delivery throughout Manhattan; there's also a worldwide shipping service.

Meurice Garment Care
31 University Pl between 8th and 9th Sts (1-212-475-2778). Subway: N, R, W to 8th St–NYU. Mon, Tue, Thu, Fri 7:30am–7pm; Wed 7:30am–7pm; Sat 9am–6pm; Sun 9:30am–3pm. AmEx, MC, V.
Laundry is serious business here. High-profile clients include Armani and Prada, and the company handles tricky stain removal and repair jobs.
Other location *245 E 57th St between Second and Third Aves (1-212-759-9057).*

Midnight Express Cleaners
1-212-921-0111. Mon–Fri 5am–5pm. AmEx, MC, V.
Midnight Express will pick up your dry cleaning anywhere below 141st Street ($50 minimum may apply), at a mutually convenient time, and return it to you the next day (that goes for bulk laundry, too).

Self-service laundry
Most neighborhoods have self-service laundries with coin-operated machines, but in New York, it doesn't cost much more to drop off your wash and let someone else do the work. Check the phone book for more establishments.

Ecowash
72 W 69th St between Central Park West and Columbus Ave (1-212-787-3890). Subway: B, C to 72nd St; 1, 9 to 66th St–Lincoln Ctr. Mon–Fri 7:30am–10pm; Sat, Sun 8am–7pm. Cash only.
For the green-minded, Ecowash uses only natural, nontoxic detergent. Wash your own duds, starting at $2.25 per load, or leave up to seven pounds for $7.50 (each additional pound is 75¢).

Legal assistance
If you're arrested for a minor violation (disorderly conduct, harassment, loitering, rowdy partying, etc.) and you are very polite to the officer during the arrest (and carry proper ID), then you'll probably get fingerprinted and photographed at the station and be given a desk-appearance ticket with a date to show up at criminal court. Then, you'll most likely get to go home.

Arguing with a police officer or engaging in more serious criminal activity (possession of a weapon, drunken driving, illegal gambling or prostitution, for example) might get you "processed," which means a 24- to 30-hour journey through the system. If the courts are backed up (and they usually are), you'll be held temporarily at a precinct pen. You can make a phone call after you've been fingerprinted. When you get through central booking, you'll arrive at 100 Centre Street for arraignment. A judge will decide whether you should be released on bail and will set a court date. If you can't post bail, then you'll be held at Rikers Island. The bottom line: Try not to get arrested, and if you are, don't act foolishly.

Legal Aid Society
1-212-577-3300/www.legal-aid.org. Mon–Fri 9am–5pm.
Legal Aid gives general information and referrals on legal matters.

Sandback, Birnbaum & Michelen Criminal Law
1-800-640-2000/1-212-517-3200. 24hrs daily.
You might want to carry these numbers with you, in case you find the cops reading you your rights in the middle of the night. If no one at this firm can help you, then you'll be directed to lawyers who can.

Libraries
See p162 **New York Public Library**.

Locksmiths
The emergency locksmiths listed below are open 24 hours. Both require ID and proof of car ownership or residency (license, registration, utility bill).

Champion Locksmiths
30 locations in Manhattan (1-212-362-7000). $15 service charge, $39 minimum to replace the lock they have to break. AmEx, Disc, MC, V.

Elite Locksmiths
470 Third Ave between 32nd and 33rd Sts (1-212-685-1472). Subway: 6 to 33rd St. $55 during the day; $85 at night. Cash only.

Lost property
For property lost in the street, contact the police. For lost credit cards or traveler's checks, *see p375* **Money**.

Buses & subways

New York City Metropolitan Transit Authority, 34th St–Penn Station, near the A-train platform (1-212-712-4500). Mon–Wed, Fri 8am–noon; Thu 11am–6:30pm. Call if you've left something on a subway train or a bus.

Grand Central Terminal

1-212-340-2555. Mon–Fri 7am–6pm; Sat 8:45am–5pm. Call if you've left something on a Metro-North train.

JFK Airport

1-718-244-4444, or contact your airline.

La Guardia Airport

1-718-533-3400, or contact your airline.

Newark Liberty International Airport

1-973-961-6230, or contact your airline.

Penn Station

1-212-630-7389. Mon–Fri 7:30am–4pm. Call for items left on Amtrak, New Jersey Transit or the Long Island Rail Road.

Taxis

1-212-692-8294/www.nyc.gov/taxi. Call for items left in a cab.

Media

Daily newspapers

Daily News

The *News* has drifted politically from the Neanderthal right to a more moderate but tough-minded stance under the ownership of real-estate mogul Mort Zuckerman.

New York Post

Founded in 1801 by Alexander Hamilton, the *Post* is the nation's oldest continuously published daily newspaper. It has swerved sharply to the right under current owner Rupert Murdoch. The *Post* includes more gossip than any other local paper, and its headlines are often sassy and sensational.

The New York Times

As Olympian as ever after more than 150 years, the *Times* remains the city's, and the nation's, paper of record. It has the broadest and deepest coverage of world and national events and, as the masthead proclaims, it delivers "All the News That's Fit to Print." The mammoth Sunday *Times* can weigh a full five pounds and typically contains hundreds of pages, including a well-regarded magazine as well as book-review, travel, real-estate and other sections.

Other dailies

The *Amsterdam News*, one of the nation's oldest black newspapers, offers a trenchant African-American viewpoint. New York also supports three Spanish-language dailies: *El Diario, Hoy* and *Noticias del Mundo. Newsday* is the Long Island–based daily with a tabloid format but a sober tone (it also has a city edition). *USA Today* keeps weary travelers abreast of national news. You may even find your own local paper at a Universal News shop (check the phone book for locations).

Weekly newspapers

Downtown journalism is a battlefield, pitting the *New York Press* against the *Village Voice.* The *Press* consists largely of opinion columns; it's full of youthful energy and irreverence as well as cynicism and self-absorption. The *Voice* is sometimes passionate and ironic but just as often strident and predictable. Both papers are free. In contrast, the *New York Observer* focuses on the doings of the upper echelons of business, finance, media and politics. *Our Town, Chelsea Clinton News,* the *West Sider* and *Manhattan Spirit* are on the sidelines; these free sister publications feature neighborhood news and local political gossip, and they can be found in street-corner dispensers around town. In a class all its own is the hilarious, satirical national weekly the *Onion.*

Magazines

New York

This magazine is part newsweekly, part lifestyle reporting and part listings.

The New Yorker

Since the 1920s, the *New Yorker* has been known for its fine wit, elegant prose and sophisticated cartoons. Today, it's a forum for serious long-form journalism. It usually makes for a lively, intelligent read.

Time Out New York

Of course, the best place to discover what's going on in town is *Time Out New York,* launched in 1995. Based on the tried-and-trusted format of its London parent, *TONY* is an indispensable guide to the life of the city (if we do say so ourselves).

Other magazines

Since its launch in 1996, the bimonthly *Black Book Magazine* has covered New York high fashion and culture with intelligent bravado. *Gotham,* a monthly from the publisher of the glossy gab-rags *Hamptons* and *Aspen Peak,* unveiled its larger-than-life celeb-filled pages in 2001. And for two decades now, *Paper* has reported monthly on the city's trend-conscious, offering plenty of insider buzz on bars, clubs, downtown boutiques—and the people you'll find in them.

Radio

Nearly 100 stations serve the New York area. On the AM dial, you can find talk radio and phone-in shows that attract everyone from priests to sports nuts. Flip to FM for free jazz, the latest Franz Ferdinand single or any other auditory craving. Radio highlights are printed weekly in *Time Out New York,* and daily in the *Daily News.*

College radio

College radio is innovative and free of commercials. However, smaller transmitters mean that reception is often compromised by Manhattan's high-rise topography.
  WNYU-FM 89.1 and **WKCR-FM 89.9** (*see also p375* **Jazz**) are, respectively, the stations of New York University and Columbia; programming spans the musical spectrum.
  WFUV-FM 90.7, Fordham University's station, plays mostly folk and Irish music but also airs a variety of shows, including *Beale Street Caravan,* the most widely distributed blues program in the world.

Dance & pop

American commercial radio is rigidly formatted, which makes most pop stations extremely tedious and repetitive during the day. Tune in on evenings and weekends for more interesting programming.

WQHT-FM 97.1, "Hot 97," is a commercial hip-hop station with all-day rap and R&B.

WKTU-FM 103.5 is the premier dance-music station.

WWPR-FM 105.1, "Power 105," plays top hip-hop, and a few old-school hits.

WBLS-FM 107.5 showcases classic and new funk, soul and R&B.

Jazz

WBGO-FM 88.3 is strictly jazz. Dee Dee Bridgewater's weekly *JazzSet* program features many legendary artists.

WKCR-FM 89.9, the student-run radio station of Columbia University, is where you'll hear legendary jazz DJ Phil Schaap.

Rock

WSOU-FM 89.5, the station of Seton Hall University, a Catholic college, focuses primarily on hard rock and heavy metal.

WAXQ-FM 104.3 offers classic rock.

WXRK-FM 92.3's alternative music format attracts morning listeners with Howard Stern's 6 to 10am weekday sleazefest.

Other music

WQEW-AM 1560, "Radio Disney," has kids' programming.

WNYC-FM 93.9 (*see also below* News & talk) and **WQXR-FM 96.3** serve up a range of classical music; WNYC tends toward the progressive end of the classical spectrum.

WCAA-FM 105.9/WZAA-FM 92.7 spin Spanish and Latin.

News & talk

WABC-AM 770, WCBS-AM 880 (*see also right* **Sports**), **WINS-AM 1010** and **WBBR-AM 1130** (*see also right* **Sports**) offer news throughout the day, plus traffic and weather reports. WABC hosts a morning show featuring the street-accented demagoguery of Guardian Angels founder Curtis Sliwa along with civil rights attorney Ron Kuby (weekdays 5 to 10am). Right-winger Rush Limbaugh also airs his views here (noon till 3pm).

WNYC-AM 820/FM 93.9, a commercial-free, public radio station, provides news and current-affairs commentary, and programming from NPR.

WBAI-FM 99.5 is a left-leaning community radio station.

WLIB-AM 1190 is the flagship station of Air America, a liberal answer to right-wing talk radio.

Sports

WFAN-AM 660 airs Giants, Nets, Mets and Devils games. Talk-radio fixture Don Imus offers his opinion on…everything (Mon–Fri 5:30–10am).

WCBS-AM 880 covers the Yankees, New York's pride and joy.

WEPN-AM 1050 is devoted to news and sports talk and is the home of the Jets, Knicks and Rangers.

WBBR-AM 1130 broadcasts Islanders games.

WADO-AM 1280 provides Spanish-language coverage of many sports events.

Television

A visit to New York often includes some TV time, which can cause culture shock, particularly for British and European visitors.

Time Out New York offers a rundown of TV highlights. For full schedules, save the Sunday *New York Times* TV section or buy a daily paper.

Networks

Six major networks broadcast nationwide. All offer ratings-driven variations on a theme.

CBS (Channel 2 in NYC) has the top investigative show, *60 Minutes*, on Sundays at 7pm; overall programming is geared to a middle-aged demographic.

NBC (4) is the home of *Law & Order*, the long-running sketch-comedy series *Saturday Night Live* (Saturdays at 11:30pm), and popular sitcoms such as *Will & Grace*.

Fox-WNYW (5) is popular with twentysomethings and teens for shows like *The Simpsons* and *The O.C.*

ABC (7) is the king of daytime soaps and family-friendly sitcoms (*My Wife and Kids*).

WXTV (41) and **WNJU** (47) are Spanish-language channels that offer game shows and racy Mexican dramas. They're also your best noncable bets for soccer.

Public TV

Public TV is on channels 13, 21 and 25. Documentaries, arts shows and science series alternate with *Masterpiece Theatre* and reruns of British shows like *Inspector Morse*. Channel 21 broadcasts *BBC World News* daily at 6am and at 7 and 11pm.

Cable

All channel numbers listed are for Time Warner Cable in Manhattan. In other locations, or for other cable systems, such as Cablevision or RCN, check a local paper's TV listings.

NY1 (1) focuses on local news.

Nickelodeon (6) presents programming suitable for kids and adults nostalgic for shows like *The Brady Bunch* and *Happy Days*.

The History Channel (17), **Sci Fi** (44) and **The Weather Channel** (72) are self-explanatory. **Discovery Channel** (18) and **The Learning Channel** (52) feature educational nature and science programs.

VH1 (19), MTV's mature sibling, airs the popular *Behind the Music* series, which delves into the lives of artists like Vanilla Ice and the Partridge Family.

MTV (20) increasingly offers fewer music videos and more of its original programming (*The Osbournes, Newlyweds* and *The Real World*).

FUSE (132), a new music-video channel, aims for early MTV style.

FSN (Fox Sports Network, 26), **MSG** (Madison Square Garden, 27), **ESPN** (28) and **ESPN2** (29) are all-sports stations.

Bravo (64) shows arts programming such as *Inside the Actors Studio*, art-house films and *Queer Eye for the Straight Guy*.

Comedy Central (45) is all comedy, airing the raunchy cartoon *South Park* (Wed 10pm), and *The Daily Show with Jon Stewart* (Mon–Thu 7, 11pm).

Cinemax, Disney Channel, HBO, The Movie Channel and **Showtime** are premium channels often available in hotels. They show uninterrupted feature films, exclusive specials and acclaimed original series such as *The Sopranos* and *Six Feet Under*.

Money

Over the past few years, much of American currency has undergone a subtle face-lift—partly to deter increasingly adept counterfeiters. However, "old" money is still in circulation. All denominations except for the $1 bill have recently been updated by the U.S. Treasury. One dollar ($) equals 100 cents (¢). Coins include copper pennies (1¢) and

Directory

silver-colored nickels (5¢), dimes (10¢) and quarters (25¢). Half-dollar coins (50¢) and the gold-colored dollar coins are less commonly seen, except as change from vending machines.

All paper money is the same size, so make sure you fork over the right bill. It comes in denominations of $1, $2, $5, $10, $20, $50 and $100 (and higher, but you'll never see those bills). The $2 bills are quite rare and make a smart souvenir. Small shops will seldom break a $50 or $100 bill, and cab drivers aren't required to change bills larger than $20, so it's best to carry smaller denominations.

ATMs

The city is full of automated teller machines (ATMs), located in bank branches, delis and many small shops. Most accept American Express, MasterCard, Visa and major bank cards, if they have been registered with a personal identification number (PIN). Commonly, there's a usage fee of $1 to $2, though the superior exchange rate often makes ATMs worth the extra charge.

If you've lost your PIN or your card becomes damaged, most banks will give cash to cardholders who have proper ID.

Banks & currency exchange

Banks are generally open from 9am to 3pm Monday through Friday, though some stay open longer. You need a photo ID, such as a passport, to cash traveler's checks. Many banks will not exchange foreign currency, and the *bureaux de change,* limited to tourist-trap areas, close between 6 and 7pm.

It's best to arrive with a few dollars in cash and to pay mostly with credit cards or traveler's checks (accepted in most restaurants and larger stores—but ask first, and be prepared to show ID). In emergencies, most large hotels offer 24-hour exchange facilities; the catch is that they charge high commissions and don't give good rates.

Chase Bank
1-888-242-7324/www.chase.com. Chase's website gives information on foreign currency exchange, banking locations and credit cards. For foreign currency delivered in a hurry, call the number listed above.

Commerce Bank
1-888-751-9000/www.commerce online.com. All of Commerce's 17 Manhattan locations are open seven days a week.

People's Foreign Exchange
575 Fifth Ave at 47th St, third floor (1-212-883-0550). Subway: E, V to Fifth Ave–53rd St; 7 to Fifth Ave. Mon–Fri 9am–6pm; Sat, Sun 10am–3pm. People's provides foreign exchange on bank notes and traveler's checks of any denomination for a $2 fee.

Travelex
29 Broadway at Morris St (1-212-363-6206). Subway: 4, 5 to Bowling Green. Mon–Fri 9am–5pm. A complete range of foreign-exchange services is offered. **Other location** *510 Madison Ave at 53rd St (1-212-753-0117).*

Credit cards

Bring plastic if you have it, or be prepared for a logistical nightmare. Credit cards are essential for renting cars and booking hotels, and handy for buying tickets over the phone and the Internet. The five major cards accepted in the U.S. are American Express, Diners Club, Discover, MasterCard and Visa. If cards are lost or stolen, contact:

American Express
1-800-528-2122.

Diners Club
1-800-234-6377.

Discover
1-800-347-2683.

MasterCard
1-800-826-2181.

Visa
1-800-336-8472.

Traveler's checks

Like credit cards, traveler's checks are also routinely accepted at banks, stores and restaurants throughout the city. Bring your driver's license or passport for identification. If checks are lost or stolen, contact:

American Express
1-800-221-7282.

Thomas Cook
1-800-223-7373.

Visa
1-800-336-8472.

Wire services

If you run out of cash, don't expect the folks at your consulate to lend you money— they won't, though they may repatriate you. In case of an emergency, you can have money wired to you from your home.

MoneyGram
1-800-926-9400/ www.moneygram.com.

Western Union
1-800-325-6000/ www.westernunion.com.

Photo processing

Photo-developing services are offered by most drugstores (CVS and Rite Aid, for example) and megastores such as Kmart, but the best results can be expected from labs that develop on the premises.

Duggal
29 W 23rd St between Fifth and Sixth Aves (1-212-924-8100). Subway: F, V, N, R, W to 23rd St. Mon–Fri 7am–midnight; Sat, Sun 8am–6pm. AmEx, Disc, MC, V. Duggal has amassed a dedicated following that includes artists like David LaChapelle. Started by

Baldev Duggal more than 40 years ago, this shop develops any type of film, flawlessly. Prices reflect that mastery.

Postal services

Stamps are available at all U.S. post offices and from drugstore vending machines. It costs 37¢ to send a one-ounce (28g) letter within the U.S. Each additional ounce costs 23¢. Postcards mailed within the U.S. cost 23¢; for international postcards, it's 70¢. Airmailed letters to anywhere overseas cost 80¢ for the first ounce and 75¢ for each additional ounce.

For faster Express Mail, you must fill out a form, either at a post office or by arranging a pickup. Twenty-four-hour delivery to major U.S. cities is guaranteed. International delivery takes two to three days, with no guarantee. Call 1-800-275-8777 for more information.

General Post Office
421 Eighth Ave between 31st and 33rd Sts (24-hour information 1-800-275-8777/www.usps.com). Subway: A, C, E to 34th St–Penn Station. 24hrs daily.
This is the city's main post office; call for the branch nearest you. Lines are long, but stamps are available from self-service vending machines. Branches are usually open Monday through Friday, 9am to 5pm; Saturday hours vary from office to office.

General Delivery
390 Ninth Ave between 31st and 33rd Sts (1-212-330-3099). Subway: A, C, E to 34th St–Penn Station. Mon–Sat 10am–1pm.
U.S. residents without local addresses can receive their mail here; it should be addressed to the recipient, General Delivery, 390 Ninth Ave, New York, NY 10001. You will need to show identification—a passport or ID card—when picking up letters.

Poste Restante
421 Eighth Ave between 31st and 33rd Sts, window 29 (1-212-330-2912). Subway: A, C, E to 34th St–Penn Station. Mon–Sat 8am–6pm.
Foreign visitors without U.S. addresses can receive mail here; mail should be addressed to recipient's name, General Post Office, Poste Restante, 421 Eighth Avenue, attn: Window 29, New York, NY 10001. Be sure to bring some form of identification to claim your letters.

Couriers & private mail services

DHL Worldwide Express
Various locations throughout the city; call to find the office nearest you or to arrange a pickup at your door (1-800-225-5345/www.dhl.com). AmEx, DC, Disc, MC, V.
DHL will send a courier to pick up packages at any address in New York City, or you can deliver packages in person to one of its offices or drop-off points. Cash is not accepted.

FedEx
Various locations throughout the city; call to find the office nearest you
or to arrange a pickup at your door (1-800-247-4747/www.fedex.com). AmEx, DC, Disc, MC, V.
FedEx's rates (like those of its main competitor, UPS) are based on the distance shipped, the weight of the package and the service chosen. A FedEx envelope to Los Angeles costs about $17; one to London, $30. Packages headed overseas should be dropped off by 6pm for International Priority delivery (depending on destination), and by 9pm for packages to most destinations in the U.S. (some locations have a later cutoff time; call to check).

UPS
Various locations throughout the city; free pickup at your door (1-800-742-5877/www.ups.com). Hours vary by office; call for locations and times. AmEx, MC, V.
Like DHL and FedEx, UPS will send a courier to pick up parcels at any address in the five boroughs. The city's 30 retail locations (formerly known as Mail Boxes Etc.) also offer mailbox rental, mail forwarding, packaging, phone-message service, photocopying and faxing. UPS provides domestic and international service.

Religion

Here are just a few of New York's many religious organizations and places of worship. Check the phone book for more listings.

Baptist

The Abyssinian Baptist Church
See p119 for listing.

Passport alert: Do you need a visa?

In October 2004, passport regulations for visitors entering the U.S. on the Visa Waiver Program changed. Now *all* visitors must carry machine-readable passports, or MRPs. If you are traveling with an old passport, then you must get a visa, which can easily take two to three months and costs $100. Another program, called U.S. Visit, was put into effect in 2004, requiring all foreign visitors to be photographed and fingerprinted. Regulations are expected to change again on October 26, 2006, when passports will have to contain microchips with biometric data, such as fingerprints. (Many countries, the U.K. included, don't yet have the technology to produce such information.) If you travel without the correct passport, and you don't have a visa, you risk refusal when you try to enter the country. The best advice is to renew your passport, even if it's not about to expire. Well in advance of your trip, call the nearest U.S. Embassy or visit www.travel.state.gov/visa. Children need their own passports, and business travelers who have been going without visas had better apply now.

Buddhist

New York Buddhist Church

331–332 Riverside Dr between 105th and 106th Sts (1-212-678-0305/www.newyorkbuddhistchurch. org). Subway: 1, 9 to 103rd St.

Catholic

St. Patrick's Cathedral

See p105 for listing.

Episcopal

The Cathedral Church of St. John the Divine

See p116 for listing.

Jewish

UJA–Federation of New York Resource Line

1-212-753-2288/www.young leadership.org. Mon–Thu 9am–5pm; Fri 9am–4pm.
This hotline provides referrals to other organizations, groups, temples, philanthropic activities and synagogues, as well as advice on kosher food and restaurants in the city.

Methodist

Church of St. Paul and St. Andrew, United Methodist

263 W 86th St between Broadway and West End Ave (1-212-362-3179/www.spsanyc.org). Subway: 1, 9 to 86th St.

Muslim

Islamic Cultural Center of New York

1711 Third Ave between 96th and 97th Sts (1-212-722-5234). Subway: 6 to 96th St.

Presbyterian

Madison Avenue Presbyterian Church

921 Madison Ave at 73rd St (1-212-288-8920/www.mapc.com). Subway: 6 to 72nd St.

Restrooms

See p381 **Toilet talk**.

Safety

New York's crime rate, particularly for violent crime, has waned during the past decade. Most crime occurs late at night in low-income neighborhoods. Don't arrive thinking your safety is at risk wherever you go; it is unlikely that you will ever be bothered.

Still, a bit of common sense won't hurt. If you look comfortable rather than lost, you should deter troublemakers. Do not flaunt your money and valuables. Avoid desolate and poorly lit streets; if necessary, walk facing oncoming traffic so no one can drive up alongside you undetected. On deserted sidewalks, walk close to the street—or even on it. Muggers prefer to hang back in doorways and shadows. If you do find yourself threatened, hand over your wallet or other valuables at once (your attacker will likely be as anxious to get it over with as you), then dial **911** as soon as you can (it's a free call).

Be extra alert to pickpockets and street hustlers—especially in crowded tourist areas like Times Square—and don't be seduced by scam artists you may encounter. That shrink-wrapped camcorder you bought out of a car trunk for 50 bucks could turn out to be a couple of bricks when you open the box.

New York women are used to the brazenness with which they are stared at by men, and they usually develop a dismissive attitude toward the ogling. Should unwelcome admirers ever get verbal or start following you, ignoring them is better than responding. Walking into the nearest shop is the best way to get rid of a persistent offender. If you've been seriously victimized, *see p370* **Emergencies** or *p372* **Rape & sex crimes** for assistance.

Smoking

New Yorkers live under some of the strictest antismoking laws on the planet. The 1995 NYC Smoke-Free Air Act makes it illegal to smoke in

Size charts

Women's clothing

U.K.	France	U.S.
4	32	2
6	34	4
8	36	6
10	38	8
12	40	10
14	42	12
16	44	14

Women's shoes

U.K.	France	U.S.
3	36	5
4	37	6
5	38	7
6	39	8
7	40	9
8	41	10
9	42	11

Men's suits

U.K.	France	U.S.
34	44	34
36	46	36
38	48	38
40	50	40
42	52	42
44	54	44
46	56	46

Men's shoes

U.K.	France	U.S.
6	39	7
7½	40	7½
8	41	8
8	42	8½
9	43	9½
10	44	10½
11	45	11

Directory

virtually all indoor public places, including the subway and movie theaters. Recent legislation went even further, banning smoking in nearly all restaurants *and* bars. Be sure to ask before you light up.

Students

Student life in NYC is unlike that of anywhere else in the world. An endless extracurricular education exists right outside the dorm room—the city is both teacher and playground. For further guidance, check the *Time Out New York Student Guide*, available in August for free on campuses, and $2.95 at Hudson News outlets (consult the phone book for locations).

Student identification

Foreign students should get an **International Student Identity Card** (ISIC) as proof of student status and to secure discounts. These can be bought from your local student-travel agent (ask at your student union). If you buy the card in New York, then you will also get basic accident insurance—a bargain. The New York branch of the **Council on International Educational Exchange** (205 E 42nd St between Second and Third Aves, 1-212-822-2700, www.ciee.org), can supply one on the spot. Note that a student identity card may not always be accepted as proof of age for drinking (you must be 21).

Student travel

Most agents offer discount fares for those under 26; specialists in student deals include:

STA Travel
205 E 42nd St between Second and Third Aves (1-212-822-2700/for other locations 1-800-777-0112/www. statravel.com). Subway: 42nd St S, 4, 5, 6, 7 to 42nd St–Grand Central. Mon–Sat 10am–6pm.

Tax & tipping

In restaurants, it is customary to tip at least 15 percent, and since NYC tax is 8.625 percent, a quick method for calculating the tip is to double the tax. In many restaurants, when you are with a group of six or more, the tip will be included in the bill. For tipping on taxi fares, *see p366.*

Telephones

New York, like most of the world's busy cities, is overrun with telephones, cellular phones, pagers and faxes. (Check with your carrier to be sure that service will be available here.) This increasing dependence on a dial tone accounts for the city's abundance of area codes. As a rule, **you must dial 1 + the area code** before a number, even if the place you are calling is in the same area code. The area codes for Manhattan are 212 and 646; Brooklyn, Queens, Staten Island and the Bronx are 718 and 347; 917 is reserved mostly for cellular phones and pagers. Long Island area codes are 516 and 631; codes for New Jersey are 201, 551, 848, 862, 609, 732, 856, 908 and 973. Numbers preceded by 800, 877 and 888 are free of charge when dialed from anywhere in the United States. When numbers are listed as letters (e.g., 1-800-AIR-RIDE) for easy recall, dial the corresponding numbers on the telephone keypad.

Remember, if you carry a cellular phone, make sure you turn it off on trains and buses and at restaurants, plays, movies, concerts and museums. New Yorkers are quick to show their annoyance at an ill-timed ring. Some establishments even post signs designating "cellular-free zones."

General information

The yellow pages and the white pages phone books contain a wealth of useful information in the front, including theater-seating diagrams and maps; the blue pages in the center of the white pages directory list all government numbers and addresses. Hotels will have copies; otherwise, try libraries or Verizon (the local phone company) payment centers.

Collect calls & credit-card calls
Collect calls are also known as reverse-charge calls. Dial 0 followed by the area code and number, or dial AT&T's 1-800-CALL-ATT, MCI's 1-800-COLLECT or Sprint's 1-800-ONE-DIME.

Directory assistance
Dial 411 or 1 + area code + 555-1212. Doing so may be free, depending on the pay phone you use; carrier fees may apply. Long-distance directory assistance may also incur long-distance charges. For a directory of toll-free numbers, dial 1-800-555-1212.

Emergency
Dial **911**. All calls are free (including those from pay and cell phones).

International calls
Dial 011 + country code (Australia 61; New Zealand 64; U.K. 44), then the number.

Operator assistance
Dial 0.

Pagers & cell phones

InTouch USA
1-800-872-7626. Mon–Fri 8am–5:30pm. AmEx, DC, Disc, MC, V.
InTouch, the city's largest cellular-phone rental company, leases equipment by the day, week or month.

Public pay phones & phone cards

Public pay phones are easy to find. Some of them even work (non-Verizon phones tend to be poorly maintained). Phones take any combination of silver coins: Local calls usually cost 25¢ for three minutes; a few pay phones require 50¢ but allow unlimited time on the call. If you're not used to American phones, then note that the ringing tone is long; the "engaged" tone, or busy signal, is short and higher pitched.

To call long-distance or to make an international call from a pay phone, you need to go through one of the long-distance companies. Most pay phones in New York automatically use AT&T, but phones in and around transportation hubs usually contract other long-distance carriers, whose charges can be outrageous. Look in the phone book under Telephone Companies. MCI and Sprint are respected brand names (*see p379* **Collect calls & credit-card calls**). Make the call by either dialing 0 for an operator or dialing direct, which is cheaper. To find out how much a call will cost, dial the number, and a computerized voice will tell you how much money to deposit. You can pay for calls with your credit card.

The best way to make long-distance calls is with a **phone card**, available from any post office branch or from chain stores like Duane Reade or Rite Aid (*see p371* **Pharmacies**). Delis and newspaper kiosks sell phone cards, including the New York Exclusive, which has favorable international rates. Dialing instructions are on the card.

Telephone answering service

Messages Plus Inc.
1317 Third Ave between 75th and 76th Sts (1-212-879-4144). Subway: 6 to 77th St. 24hrs daily. AmEx, DC, Disc, MC, V.
Messages Plus provides an answering service with specialized (medical, bilingual, etc.) receptionists, if required, and plenty of ways to deliver your messages. It also offers telemarketing, voice mail and interactive website services.

Tickets

It's always show time somewhere in New York. And depending on what you're after—music, sports, theater—scoring tickets can be a real hassle. Smaller venues often have their own box offices that sell tickets. Large arenas like Madison Square Garden have ticket agencies—and many devoted spectators. You may have to try more than one tactic to get into a popular show.

Box-office tickets

Fandango
1-800-326-3264/www.fandango.com. 24hrs daily. Surcharge $1.50 per ticket. AmEx, Disc, MC, V.
Fandango is one of the newer services to offer advance credit-card purchase of movie tickets online or over the phone. Tickets can be picked up at an automated kiosk in the theater lobby (not available in all theaters).

Moviefone
1-212-777-FILM/www.moviefone. com. 24hrs daily. Surcharge $1.50 ($1 if purchased online) per ticket. AmEx, Disc, MC, V.
Purchase advance movie tickets by credit card over the phone or online; pick them up at an automated kiosk in the theater lobby. This service is not available for every theater.

Telecharge
1-212-239-6200/www.telecharge.com. 24hrs daily. Average surcharge $6 per ticket. AmEx, DC, Disc, MC, V.
Broadway and Off Broadway shows are on offer here.

Ticket Central
416 W 42nd St between Ninth and Tenth Aves (1-212-279-4200/ www.ticketcentral.org). Subway: N, Q, R, W, 42nd St S, 1, 2, 3, 9, 7 to 42nd St–Times Sq. Box office and phone orders noon–8pm. Surcharge varies depending on ticket price. AmEx, MC, V.
Off and Off-Off Broadway tickets are available at the office or by phone.

Ticketmaster
1-212-307-4100/www.ticketmaster. com. Surcharge $3–$10 per ticket. AmEx, DC, Disc, MC, V.
This reliable service sells tickets to rock concerts, Broadway shows,

sports events and more. You can buy tickets by phone, online or at outlets throughout the city— Tower Records, J&R Music and Computer World, and Filene's Basement, to name a few.

TKTS
Duffy Square, 47th St at Broadway (1-212-221-0013/www.tdf.org). Subway: N, Q, R, W, 42nd St S, 1, 2, 3, 9, 7 to 42nd St–Times Sq. Mon–Sat 3–8pm; Sun 11am–7pm. Matinee tickets Wed, Sat 10am–2pm; Sun 11am–2pm. Surcharge $3 per ticket. Cash only.
TKTS has become a New York tradition. Broadway and Off Broadway tickets are sold at discounts of 25, 35 and 50 percent for same-day performances; tickets to other highbrow events are also offered. The line can be long, but it's often worth the wait.
Other location 199 Water St; booth is at the corner of Front and John Sts.

Scalpers & standby tickets

When a show sells out, there's always the illegal scalper option, though the risk that you might end up with a forged ticket does exist. Before you part with any cash, make sure the ticket has the correct details, and be warned: The police have been cracking down on such trade.

Some venues also offer standby tickets right before show time, while others give reduced rates for tickets purchased on the same day as the performance.

Ticket brokers

Ticket brokers function like scalpers but are legal because they operate from out of state. They can almost guarantee tickets, however costly, for sold-out events and tend to deal only in better seats. For brokers, look under Ticket Sales in the yellow pages. Listed below are three of the more established outfits.

Apex Tours
1-800-248-9849/www.tixx.com. Mon–Fri 9am–5pm. AmEx, Disc, MC, V.

Prestige Entertainment
1-800-243-8849/www.prestige entertainment.com. Mon–Fri 8am–6pm; Sat 8am–noon. AmEx, MC, V.

TicketCity
1-800-765-3688/www.ticketcity.com. Mon–Fri 8:30am–8pm; Sat 10am–6pm; Sun 11am–4pm. AmEx, Disc, MC, V.

Time & date

New York is on Eastern Standard Time, which extends from the Atlantic coast to the eastern shore of Lake Michigan and south to the Gulf of Mexico. This is five hours behind Greenwich Mean Time. Clocks are set forward one hour in early April for Daylight Savings Time and back one hour at the end of October. Going from east to west, Eastern Time is one hour ahead of Central Time, two hours ahead of Mountain Time and three hours ahead of Pacific Time. In the U.S., the date is written as month, day and year; so 2/8/05 is February 8, 2005.

Toilets

See below **Toilet talk**.

Tourist information

Hotels are usually full of maps, brochures and free tourist magazines that include paid listings (so the recommendations cannot be viewed as objective). Many local magazines, including *Time Out New York,* offer opinionated, reliable info.

NYC & Company
810 Seventh Ave between 52nd and 53rd Sts (1-800-NYC-VISIT/ www.nycvisit.com). Subway: B, D, E to Seventh Ave. Mon–Fri 8:30am–6pm; Sat, Sun 9am–5pm.
The city's official visitors' and information center gives out leaflets, coupons, free maps and advice.
Other location *33–34 Carnaby St, London, U.K., W1V 1CA (020-7437-8300).*

Times Square Visitors Center
1560 Broadway between 46th and 47th Sts (1-212-869-1890). Subway: N, Q, R, W, 42nd St S, 1, 2, 3, 9, 7 to 42nd St–Times Sq. 8am–8pm daily.

Toilet talk

When nature calls, here's where to answer.

Visitors to New York are always on the go. But in between all that go, go, go, sometimes you've really got to *go.* Contrary to what your nose may sometimes lead you to believe, the streets and alleys are no place to find relief. The real challenge lies in finding a legal public place to take care of your business. Although they don't exactly have an open-door policy, the numerous **McDonald's** restaurants, **Starbucks** coffee shops and **Barnes & Noble** bookstores contain (usually clean) restrooms.

If the door to the loo is locked, you may have to ask a cashier for the key. Don't announce that you're not a paying customer and you should be all right. The same applies to most other fast-food joints (**Au Bon Pain**, **Wendy's**, etc.), major stores (**Barneys**, **Macy's**, **Toys "R" Us**; *see p214, p215 and p242*) and hotels and bars that don't have a host at the door. Here are a few other options that can offer sweet relief (though you may have to hold your breath and forgo soap).

Downtown

Battery Park
Castle Clinton. Subway: 1, 9 to South Ferry; 4, 5 to Bowling Green.

Tompkins Square Park
Ave A at 9th St. Subway: L to First Ave; 6 to Astor Pl.

Washington Square Park
Thompson St at Washington Sq South. Subway: A, C, E, B, D, F, V to W 4th St.

Midtown

Bryant Park
42nd St between Fifth and Sixth Aves. Subway: B, D, F, V to 42nd St–Bryant Park; 7 to Fifth Ave.

Grand Central Terminal
42nd St at Park Ave, Lower Concourse. Subway: 42nd St S, 4, 5, 6, 7 to 42nd St–Grand Central.

Penn Station
Seventh Ave between 31st and 33rd Sts. Subway: A, C, E, 1, 2, 3, 9 to 34th St–Penn Station.

Uptown

Avery Fisher Hall at Lincoln Center
Broadway at 65th St. Subway: 1, 9 to 66th St–Lincoln Ctr.

Charles A. Dana Discovery Center
Central Park, north side of Harlem Meer, 110th St at Malcolm X Blvd (Lenox Ave). Subway: 2, 3 to 110th St–Central Park North.

Delacorte Theater
Central Park, midpark at 81st St. Subway: B, C to 81st St–Museum of Natural History.

This center offers discount coupons for Broadway tickets, Internet access, MetroCards, and other useful goods and services.

Translation & language services

All Language Services
77 W 55th St between Fifth and Sixth Aves (1-212-986-1688/fax 1-212-265-1662). Subway: 42nd St S, 4, 5, 6, 7 to 42nd St–Grand Central. 24hrs daily. AmEx, MC, V.
ALS will type or translate documents in any of 59 languages and provide interpreters.

Visas

Some 27 countries participate in the **Visa Waiver Program**. Citizens of Andorra, Australia, Austria, Belgium, Brunei, Denmark, Finland, France, Germany, Iceland, Ireland, Italy, Japan, Liechtenstein, Luxembourg, Monaco, the Netherlands, New Zealand, Norway, Portugal, San Marino, Singapore, Slovenia, Spain, Sweden, Switzerland and the United Kingdom do not need a visa for stays in the U.S. shorter than 90 days (business or pleasure), as long as they have a machine-readable passport that is valid for the full 90-day period and a return ticket (the exemption includes children). An open standby ticket is acceptable. Anyone without a machine-readable passport will need a visa. If you are in any doubt as to whether your passport is machine-readable, check with the passport-issuing authority of your country.

Canadians and Mexicans don't need visas but must have legal proof of residency. All other travelers must apply for visas. You can obtain information and application forms from your nearest U.S. embassy or consulate. In general, submit an application at least three weeks before you plan to travel. To apply for a visa on shorter notice, contact your travel agent.

For information on student visas, *see p369*.

U.S. Embassy Visa Information
In the U.S., 1-202-663-1225/in the U.K., 09055-444546, 60p per minute/ www.travel.state.gov/visa/index.html.

Wardrobe services

See also p373 **Laundry**.

Clothing rental

Zeller Tuxedos
1010 Third Ave at 60th St (1-212-355-0707). Subway: N, R, W to Lexington Ave–59th St; 4, 5, 6 to 59th St. Mon–Fri 9am–6:30pm; Sat 10am–5:30pm; Sun 11am–4:30pm. AmEx, Disc, MC, V.
Calvin Klein and other tuxes are available. Check the phone book for other locations.

At press time, no similar services for women existed.

Clothing repair

Ramon's Tailor Shop
306 Mott St between Bleecker and Houston Sts (1-212-226-0747). Subway: F, V to Broadway–Lafayette St; 6 to Bleecker St. Mon–Fri 7:30am–8pm; Sat 8am–7:30pm; Sun 11am–4pm. By appointment only. Cash only.
Ramon's can alter or repair "anything that can be worn on the body." There's also an emergency service, and pickup and delivery is free in much of Manhattan.

Jewelry & watch repair

Zig Zag Jewelers
1336A Third Ave between 76th and 77th Sts (1-212-794-3559). Subway: 6 to 77th St. Mon–Fri 11am–7pm; Sat 10am–6:30pm. AmEx, DC, Disc, MC, V.
These experts don't do costume jewelry, but they'll restring and reclasp your broken Bulgaris and Harry Winstons. Watch repairs are trustworthy, and estimates are free. **Other location** *963 Madison Ave between 75th and 76th Sts (1-212-472-6373).*

Shoe repair

Andrade Shoe Repair
103 University Pl between 12th and 13th Sts (1-212-529-3541). Subway: L, N, Q, R, W, 4, 5, 6 to 14th St–Union Sq. Mon–Fri 7:30am–7pm; Sat 9am–6:30pm. Cash only.
Andrade is a basic but reliable shoe-repair chain. Check the phone book for other locations.

Weather

See p368 **Climate**.

Work permits

For more information on working during the summer, get in touch with the **Council on International Educational Exchange** (*see p379*), Work Exchanges Department, 205 East 42nd Street, New York, NY 10017, USA.

Travel advice

For current information on travel to a specific country— including the latest news on health issues, safety and security, local laws and customs—contact your home country's government department of foreign affairs. Most have websites with useful advice for would-be travelers.

Australia
www.dfat.gov.au/travel

Canada
www.voyage.gc.ca

Ireland
www.irlgov.ie/iveagh

New Zealand
www.mft.govt.nz/travel

United Kingdom
www.fco.gov.uk/travel

USA
www.state.gov/travel

Directory

Further Reference

In-depth guides

Edward F. Bergman *The Spiritual Traveler: New York City* This is a guide to sacred and peaceful spaces in the city.

Eleanor Berman *Away for the Weekend: New York* Trips within a 200-mile radius of New York City.

Eleanor Berman *New York Neighborhoods* This foodie's guide focuses on ethnic enclaves.

William Corbett *New York Literary Lights* A compendium of info about NYC's literary past.

Dave Frattini *The Underground Guide to New York City Subways*

Gerri Gallagher and Jill Fairchild *Where to Wear* A staple for shopaholics.

Suzanne Gerber *Vegetarian New York City* Includes restaurants, markets and lodging for veg heads.

Alfred Gingold and Helen Rogan *Cool Parent's Guide to All of New York* A smartly written book useful for in-depth exploration of the city with kids.

Hagstrom *New York City 5 Borough Pocket Atlas* You won't get lost when you carry this thorough street map.

Colleen Kane (ed.) *Sexy New York City* Discover erotica in the Naked City.

Chuck Katz *Manhattan on Film 2* A must for movie buffs who want to scope out the city on foot.

Lyn Skreczko and Virginia Bell *The Manhattan Health Pages* Everything from aerobics to Zen.

Earl Steinbicker (ed.) *Daytrips New York*

Linda Tarrant-Reid *Discovering Black New York* This guide focuses on African-American museums, landmarks and more.

Time Out New York Eating & Drinking 2005 The annual comprehensive critics' guide to thousands of places to eat and drink in the five boroughs.

Zagat Survey *New York City Restaurants* The popular opinion survey.

Architecture

Richard Berenholtz *New York, New York Mini* Panoramic images of the city through the seasons.

Stanley Greenberg *Invisible New York* Photographic account of hidden architectural triumphs.

Landmarks Preservation Commission *New York City Landmarks Preservation Guide*

Karl Sabbagh *Skyscraper* How the tall ones are built.

Robert A.M. Stern et al. *New York 1930* A massive coffee-table slab with stunning pictures.

Norval White and Elliot Willensky *AIA Guide to New York City* A comprehensive directory of important buildings.

Gerard R. Wolfe *New York: A Guide to the Metropolis* Historical and architectural walking tours.

Culture & recollections

Irving Lewis Allen *The City in Slang* How New York has spawned new words and phrases.

Candace Bushnell *Sex and the City* Smart women, superficial New York.

George Chauncey *Gay New York* The evolution of New York gay culture from 1890 to 1940.

William Cole (ed.) *Quotable New York*

Martha Cooper and Henry Chalfant *Subway Art*

Josh Alan Friedman *Tales of Times Square* Sleaze and decay in the old Times Square.

Nelson George *Hip Hop America* The history of hip-hop, from Grandmaster Flash to Puff Daddy.

Robert Hendrickson *New Yawk Tawk* Dictionary of NYC slang.

Jane Jacobs *The Death and Life of Great American Cities*

A.J. Liebling *Back Where I Came From* Personal recollections from the *New Yorker* columnist.

Gillian McCain and Legs McNeil *Please Kill Me* Oral history of the city's 1970s punk scene.

Frank O'Hara *The Collected Poems of Frank O'Hara* The great NYC poet found inspiration in his hometown.

Alice Leccese Powers et al. *The Brooklyn Reader: 30 Writers Celebrate America's Favorite Borough*

Andrés Torres *Between Melting Pot and Mosaic* African-American and Puerto Rican life in the city.

Heather Holland Wheaton *Eight Million Stories in a New York Minute*

E.B. White *Here Is New York* A clear-eyed love letter to Gotham.

History

Herbert Asbury *The Gangs of New York: An Informal History of the Underworld* A racy journalistic portrait of the city at the turn of the 20th century.

Robert A. Caro *The Power Broker* A biography of Robert Moses, New York's mid-20th-century master builder, and his checkered legacy.

Federal Writers' Project *The WPA Guide to New York City* A wonderful snapshot of the 1930s by writers employed under FDR's New Deal.

Sanna Feirstein *Naming New York* How Manhattan places got their names.

Mitchell Fink and Lois Mathias *Never Forget: An Oral History of September 11, 2001* A collection of first-person accounts.

Alice Rose George (ed.) *Here Is New York* A collection of nearly 900 powerful amateur photos that document the aftermath of September 11, 2001.

Clifton Hood *722 Miles: The Building of the Subways and How They Transformed New York*

Kenneth T. Jackson (ed.) *The Encyclopedia of New York City* An ambitious and useful reference guide.

David Levering Lewis *When Harlem Was in Vogue* A study of the Harlem Renaissance.

Shaun O'Connell *Remarkable, Unspeakable New York* The history of New York as literary inspiration.

Mitchell Pacelle *Empire* The story of the fight to build the Empire State Building.

Jacob A. Riis *How the Other Half Lives* A pioneering photojournalistic record of squalid tenement life.

Marie Salerno and Arthur Gelb *The New York Pop-up Book* An interactive historical account of NYC.

Luc Sante *Low Life* Opium dens and brothels in New York from the 1840s to the 1920s.

Mike Wallace and Edwin G. Burrows *Gotham: A History of*

New York City to 1898 The first volume in a planned mammoth history of NYC.

Fiction

Kurt Andersen *Turn of the Century* Millennial Manhattan seen through the eyes of media players.

Paul Auster *The New York Trilogy: City of Glass, Ghosts, the Locked Room* A search for the madness behind the method of Manhattan's grid.

Kevin Baker *Dreamland* A poetic novel about Coney Island's glory days.

James A. Baldwin *Another Country* Racism under the bohemian veneer of the 1960s.

Michael Chabon *The Amazing Adventures of Kavalier and Clay* Pulitzer Prize–winning account of Jewish comic-book artists in the 1940s.

Bret Easton Ellis *Glamorama* A satirical view of dazzling New York City nightlife.

Jack Finney *Time and Again* An illustrator travels back to 19th-century New York.

Larry Kramer *Faggots* Devastating satire of gay New York.

Jonathan Lethem *The Fortress of Solitude* Growing up in a gentrifying 1970s Brooklyn.

Phillip Lopate (ed.) *Writing New York* An excellent anthology of short stories, essays and poems set in New York.

Tim McLoughlin (ed.) *Brooklyn Noir* An anthology of crime tales set in Brooklyn.

Toni Morrison *Jazz* The glamour and grit of 1920s Harlem.

David Schickler *Kissing in Manhattan* Explores the lives of quirky tenants in a Manhattan apartment building.

Hubert Selby Jr. *Last Exit to Brooklyn* Dockland degradation, circa 1950s.

Time Out Book of New York Short Stories Naturally, we like these original short stories by 23 American and British authors.

Edith Wharton *Old New York* Four novellas of 19th-century New York by the author of *The Age of Innocence.*

Colson Whitehead *The Colossus of New York: A City in 13 Parts* A lyrical tribute to city life.

Tom Wolfe *The Bonfire of the Vanities* Rich/poor, black/white. An unmatched slice of 1980s New York.

Films

See also pp32–34 **Cinema City**.

Annie Hall (1977) Woody Allen costars with Diane Keaton in this appealingly neurotic valentine to living and loving in Manhattan.

Breakfast at Tiffany's (1961) Blake Edwards gave Audrey Hepburn her signature role as the cash-poor socialite Holly Golightly.

Do the Right Thing (1989) The hottest day of the summer leads to racial strife in Bedford-Stuyvesant in Spike Lee's incisive drama.

The French Connection (1971) As detective Jimmy "Popeye" Doyle, Gene Hackman ignores all traffic lights to chase down drug traffickers in William Friedkin's thriller.

The Godfather (1972) and ***The Godfather: Part II*** (1974) Francis Ford Coppola's brilliant commentary about capitalism in America is told through the violent saga of Italian gangsters.

Midnight Cowboy (1969) Street creatures "Ratso" Rizzo and Joe Buck face an unforgiving Times Square in John Schlesinger's dark classic.

Taxi Driver (1976) Robert De Niro is a crazed cabbie who sees all of New York as a den of iniquity in Martin Scorsese's bold drama.

Music

Beastie Boys "No Sleep Till Brooklyn" These now middle-aged hip-hoppers began showing their love for their favorite borough two decades ago.

Leonard Cohen "Chelsea Hotel #2" Of all the songs inspired by the Chelsea, this bleak vision of doomed love is on a level of its own.

George Gershwin *Rhapsody in Blue* Gershwin's composition was inspired by the rhythmic cacophony of a train.

Billy Joel "New York State of Mind" This heartfelt ballad exemplifies the city's effect on the souls of its visitors and residents.

Charles Mingus *Mingus Ah Um* Mingus brought the gospel to jazz and created a N.Y. masterpiece.

Public Enemy *It Takes a Nation of Millions to Hold Us Back* A ferociously political tour de force from the Long Island hip-hop group whose own Chuck D once called rap "the CNN for black America."

Ramones *Ramones* Four Queens roughnecks, a few buzzsaw chords, and clipped musings on turning tricks and sniffing glue—it transformed rock and roll.

Frank Sinatra "Theme song from *New York, New York*" Trite and true, Frank's bombastic love letter melts those little-town blues.

Bruce Springsteen "My City of Ruins" The Boss praises the city's resilience post–September 11 with this track from *The Rising.*

The Strokes *Is This It* The effortlessly hip debut of this hometown band garnered praise and worldwide attention.

The Velvet Underground *The Velvet Underground & Nico* Lou Reed and company's first album is still the gold standard of downtown cool.

Websites

www.timeoutny.com
The *Time Out New York* website covers all the city has to offer. When planning your trip, check out the New York City Guide section for a variety of itineraries that you can use in conjunction with this guide.

eatdrink.timeoutny.com
Subscribe to the TONY Eating & Drinking online guide and instantly search thousands of reviews written by our critics.

www.nycvisit.com
The site of NYC & Company, the local convention and visitors' bureau.

www.mta.info
Subway and bus service changes are always posted here.

www.nyc.gov
City Hall's official New York City website has lots of links.

www.nytimes.com
"All the News That's Fit to Print" online from the *New York Times.*

www.centralpark.org
Discover the nitty-gritty of the city's favorite park.

www.clubplanet.com
Follow the city's nocturnal scene and buy advance tickets to big events.

www.livebroadway.com
"The Official Website of Broadway" is the source for theaters, tickets and tours.

www.hipguide.com
A short 'n' sweet site for those looking for what's considered hip.

www.forgotten-ny.com
Remember old New York here.

www.newyorkfirst.com
Gotham-inspired gifts, from cheesecake to T-shirts.

www.manhattanusersguide.com
An insiders' guide to what's going on around town.

Directory

Index

Index

Index

Index

Advertisers' Index

Maps

Street Index

Calyer St: W5
Cambridge Pl: V8
Carlton Ave: V8
Carroll St: T8–U8, U8–9, U9–X9
Caton Ave: V10
Central Ave: X7
Centre St: T9–U9
Chauncey St: X8
Cherry St: X5–6
Chester Ave: U10
Church Ave: V10–X10
Clarendon Rd: W10–X10
Clark St: U7
Clarkson Ave: W10–X10
Classon Ave: V7–W7, W7–8
Claver Pl: W8
Clay St: W5
Clermont Ave: V7–8
Clifton Pl: V8–W8
Clinton Ave: V7–8
Clinton St: T9–U9, U9–8, V8–7
Clymer St: V7
Coffey St: T8–9
Columbia St: T9–8, T8–U8
Commerce St: T8
Commercial St: W5
Concord St: U7–V7
Congress St: U8–V8
Conover St: T8–9
Conselyea St: W6
Cook St: X7
Cortelyou Rd: W10–X10
Court St: U8–9
Cranberry St: U7
Creamer St: U9
Crooke Ave: V10–W10
Crown St: W9–X9
Cumberland St: V7–8

Dahill Rd: V10
Dean St: V8–X8
Decatur St: W8–X8
DeGraw St: T8–V8
DeKalb Ave: V8–W8, W8–7, W7–X7
Delavan St: T8
Devoe St: W6–X6
Diamond St: W5–6
Dikeman St: T8–9
Division Ave: V7
Division Pl: X6
Dobbin St: W5–6
Douglass St: U8–V8
Downing St: W8
Driggs Ave: V7–6, V6–X6
Duffield St: U7–8
Dupont St: W5
Dwight St: T8–9

E 2nd St: V10
E 3rd St: V10
E 4th St: V10
E 5th St: V10
E 7th St: V10
E 8th St: V10
E 19th St: W10
E 21st St: W10
E 22nd St: W10
E 28th St: W10
E 29th St: W10
E 31st St: W10
E 32nd St: W10
E 34th St: W10
E 35th St: W10
E 37th St: W10
E 38th St: W10

E 39th St: W10–X10
E 40th St: X10
E 42nd St: X10
E 43rd St: X10
E 45th St: X9–10
E 46th St: X9–10
E 48th St: X10
E 49th St: X9–10
E 51st St: X9–10
E 52nd St: X9–10
E 53rd St: X9–10
E 54th St: X10
E 55th St: X10
E 56th St: X10
E 57th St: X10
E 58th St: X10
E 59th St: X10
E 91st St: X9–10
E 93rd St: X9–10
E 95th St: X9
E 96th St: X9
E 98th St: X9
Eagle St: W5
East New York Ave: W9–X9
Eastern Pkwy: V9–X9
Eckford St: W5–6
Ellery St: W7
Empire Blvd: W9–X9
Engert Ave: W6
Erasmus St: W10
Evergreen Ave: X7

Fairview Pl: W10
Fenimore St: W10
Ferris St: T8
Flatbush Ave: V8–9, V9–W9, W9–10
Flushing Ave: W7–X7, X7–6
Ford St: X9
Fort Greene Pl: V8
Fort Hamilton Pkwy: U10–V10
Franklin Ave: W7–9
Franklin St: W7
Freeman St: W5
Frost St: W6
Fulton St: U8–X8
Furman St: U7

Gardner Ave: X5–6
Garfield Pl: U9–V9
Garnet St: T9–10
Gates Ave: W8–X8
George St: X7
Gerry St: W7
Gold St: U7
Gowanus Expwy: U9
Graham Ave: W7–8
Grand Ave: V7–8, V8–W8
Grand St: X6
Grand St Ext: W6–X6
Grattan St: X7
Green St: W5
Greene Ave: V8–X8, X8–7
Greenpoint Ave: W5–X5
Greenwood Ave: V10
Guernsey St: W5–6

Hall St: V7–8
Halleck St: T9–U9
Halsey St: W8–X8
Hamilton Ave: T8–U8, U8–9
Hancock St: W8–X8
Hanson Pl: V8
Harrison Ave: W7
Harrison Pl: X7

Hart St: W7–X7
Hausman St: X5–6
Havemeyer St: W6
Hawthorne St: W10
Henry St: T9–8, T8–U8
Herkimer St: W8–X8
Hewes St: W7
Heyward St: W7
Hicks St: T8–U8, U8–7
Hooper St: V7–W7, W7–6
Hopkins St: W7
Howard Ave: X8
Hoyt St: U8
Hudson Ave: V8
Humboldt St: W5–7, W7–X7
Huntington St: U8–9
Huron St: W5

Imlay St: T8
India St: W5
Ingraham St: X7
Irving Pl: W8
Irving St: T8–U8

Jackson St: W6
Java St: W5
Jay St: U7
Jefferson Ave: W8–X8
Jefferson St: X7
Jewel St: W5
John St: U7–V7
Johnson Ave: X6–7
Johnson St: U7

Kane St: T8–U8
Keap St: W6–7
Kent Ave: V7–W7, W7–8
Kent St: W5
King St: T8
Kings Hwy: X9–10
Kingsland Ave: W5–7, W6–7
Kingston Ave: W8–10
Knickerbocker Ave: X7
Kosciusko St: W8–X8, X8–7
Kosciuszko Bridge: X5
Kossuth Pl: X7

Lafayette Ave: V8–X8, X8–7
Lawrence St: U7–8
Lee Ave: W7
Lefferts Ave: W9–X9
Lefferts Pl: V8–W8
Lenox Rd: W10–X10
Leonard St: W6–7
Lewis Ave: X7–8
Lexington Ave: V8–X8
Lincoln Pl: V8–9, V9–X9
Lincoln Rd: W9
Linden Blvd: W10–X10
Livingston St: U8–V8
Lombardy St: W6
Lorimer St: W6–7
Lorraine St: T9–U9
Lott St: W10
Luquer St: U8
Lynch St: W7

Macdonough St: W8–X8
Macon St: W8–X8
Madison St: W8–X8
Malcolm X St: X7–8
Manhattan Ave: W5
Manhattan Bridge: U7
Maple St: W9–X9
Marcy Ave: W6–8

Marginal St East: T9–10
Marion St: X8
Marlborough Rd: V10
Marshall St: V7
Martense St: W10
Maspeth Ave: X6
Maujer St: W6–X6
McGuinness Blvd: W5–6
McKeever Pl: W9
McKibbin St: W7–X7
Meadow St: X6
Melrose St: X7
Meserole Ave: W5
Meserole St: W7–X7, X7–X6
Metropolitan Ave: V6–X6
Middagh St: U7
Middleton St: W7
Midwood St: W9–X9
Milton St: W5
Minna St: U10–V10
Monitor St: W5–6
Monroe St: W8–X8
Montague St: U7
Montgomery St: W9–X9
Montrose Ave: W7–X7
Moore St: W7–X7
Morgan Ave: X6
Moultrie St: W5
Myrtle Ave: U7–X7

Nassau Ave: W6–5, W5–X5
Nassau St: U7–V7
Navy St: V7–8
Nelson St: U8–9
Nevins St: U8–V8
New York Ave: W9–10
Newell St: W5–6
Noble St: W5
Noll St: X7
Norman Ave: W6–5, W5–X5
North 1st St: V6–W6
North 3rd St: V6–W6
North 4th St: V6–W6
North 5th St: V6–W6
North 6th St: V6–W6
North 7th St: W6
North 8th St: W6
North 9th St: W6
North 10th St: W6
North 11th St: W6
North 12th St: W6
North 13th St: W6
North 14th St: W6
North 15th St: W6
North Oxford St: V7
North Portland Ave: V7
Nostrand Ave: W7–10

Oak St: W5
Ocean Pkwy: V10
Onderdonk Ave: X6
Orange St: U7
Orient Ave: X6
Otsego St: T9

Pacific St: U8–X8
Paidge Ave: W5
Parade Pl: V10
Park Ave: V7–W7
Park Pl: V8–9, V9–X9
Parkside Ave: V10–W10
Patchen Ave: X8
Pearl St: U7
Penn St: W7
Pierrepont St: U7
Pineapple St: U7

Pioneer St: T8
Plymouth St: U7–V7
Poplar St: U7
Porter Ave: X6
Powers St: W6–X6
President St: T8–V8, V8–9, V9–X9
Prince St: U7–8
Prospect Ave: U9–10, U10–V10
Prospect Expwy: U9–10, U10–V10
Prospect Park SW: V10
Prospect Park W: V9–10
Prospect Pl: V8–W8, W8–9, W9–X9
Provost St: W5
Pulaski Bridge: W5
Pulaski St: W7–X7
Putnam Ave: W8–X8

Quincy St: W8–X8

Raleigh Pl: W10
Ralph Ave: X8–9
Randolph St: X6
Reed St: T9
Remsen Ave: X9–10
Remsen St: U7
Rewe St: X6
Richards St: T8–9
Richardson St: W6
River St: V6
Rochester Ave: X8–9
Rock St: X7
Rockaway Pkwy: X9
Rockwell Pl: V8
Rodney St: W6–7
Roebling St: W6
Rogers Ave: W8–10
Ross St: V7–W7
Rugby Rd: V10
Russell St: W5–6
Rutland Rd: W10–9, W9–X9
Rutledge St: W7
Ryerson St: V7

Sackett St: T8–V8
Sandford St: W7
Sands St: U7–V7
Schenectady St: X8–10
Schermerhorn St: U8–V8
Scholes St: W7–6, W6–X6
Scott Ave: X5–6
Seabring St: T8
Sedgwick St: T8–U8
Seeley St: V10
Seigel St: W7–X7
Sharon St: X6
Sherman St: V10
Skillman Ave: W6
Skillman St: W7–8
Smith St: U8–9
Snyder Ave: W10–X10
South 1st St: V6–W6
South 2nd St: V6–W6
South 3rd St: V6–W6
South 4th St: V6–W6
South 5th St: V6–W6, W6–7
South 6th St: V6
South 8th St: V6–W6
South 9th St: V6–7, V7–W7
South 10th St: V7
South 11th St: V7
South Elliott Pl: V8

398 Time Out New York

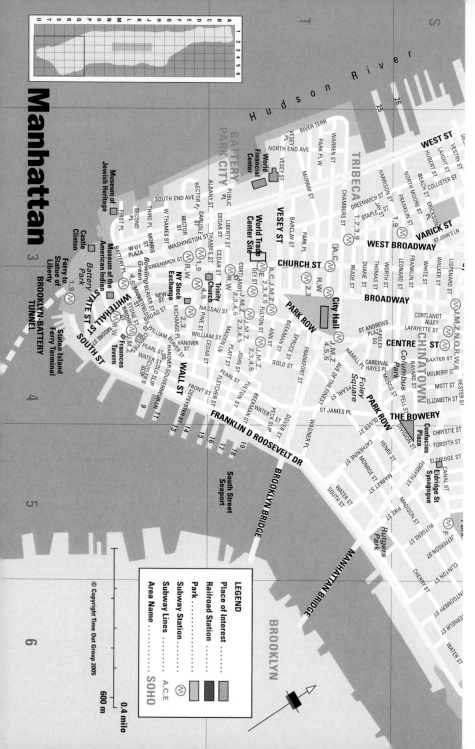

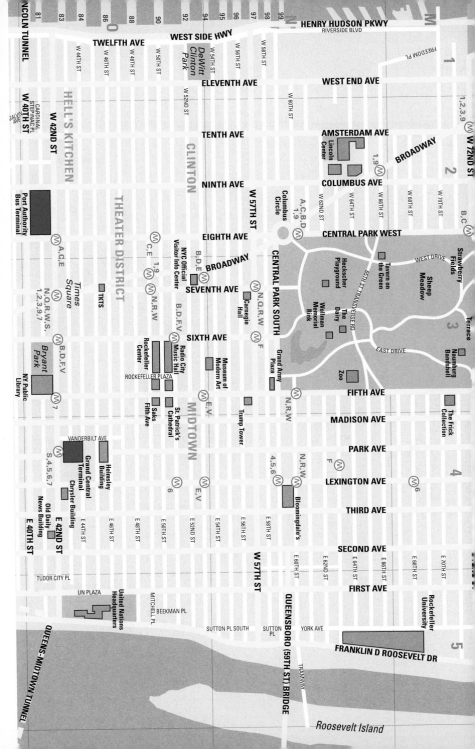